THE
OPEN
LEARNING
FOUNDATION

An Active Learning Approach

Operations Management

THE OPEN LEARNING FOUNDATION

An Active Learning Approach

OPERATIONS MANAGEMENT

John Bicheno and
Brian B. R. Elliott

Blackwell
Publishing

Copyright © Open Learning Foundation Enterprises Ltd, 1997

First published 1997
Transferred to digital print 2002

Blackwell Publishers Ltd
108 Cowley Road
Oxford OX4 1JF
UK

Blackwell Publishers Inc.
350 Main Street
Malden, Massachusetts 02148
USA

British Library Cataloging in Publication Data

A CIP catalogue record for this book is available from
the British Library

Library of Congress Cataloging-in-Publication Data

Library of Congress data has been applied for.

The ISBN for this title is 0–631–20180–7

Typeset in 10 on 12pt Times New Roman

Printed in Great Britain by
Marston Lindsay Ross International Ltd, Oxford

Acknowledgments

For the Open Learning Foundation

Martin Gibson, *Series Editor*

David Royle, *Copy and Open Learning Editor*

David Bryde, *Reviewer*

Leslie Mapp, *Director of Programmes*

Stephen Moulds, (DSM Partnership), *Production Manager*

Tim Gutteridge, *Publishing Manager*

Rachel Spungin, *Programmes Assistant*

The Foundation would also like to thank Kathleen Farren and Lynda Kerley for their assistance in producing this text.

Copyright acknowledgments

Unit 9: page 462, Figure 1, 'The Five Zeros', extensive simplification to the figure *Enterprise Requirements Planning and Execution* with permission of APICS, *The Performance Advantage*, 1995, from an article by Richard Brown.

Unit 9: page 501, Figure 15, 'Value added assessment'. from Dr H. J. Harrington, *Value Added Assessment, Business Process Improvement*, 1991, McGraw Hill Inc. Material is reproduced with the permission of McGraw Hill Inc.

Unit 9: page 518, Figure 19, 'The Evolution of Logistics', adapted with permission of APICS, the Educational Society for Resource Management, Falls Church, Virginia, USA, from an article by Roger T. Miles in the 37th International Conference Proceedings, October 1994, p.438.

Unit 9: page 522, Figure 20, 'Purchasing's New Role', adapted with permission of APICS, the Educational Society for Resource Management, Virginia, USA, from the Just-in -Time Certification Review Course, 1992. Original material appeared in The *Implementation of Zero Inventory/Just-in-Time*, by Robert W. Hall, APICS, 1986.

Unit 9: pages 524–525, Table 1and 2, reproduced from *Beyond Partnership* by Richard Lamming, 1993, by permission of the publisher of McGraw Hill Inc.

Resource Item 2.1: page 540,'Strategic Innovation' from the *Journal of Strategic Change* by Dr Jan Eppink. Copyright John Wiley & Sons, Ltd. Reprinted by permission of John Wiley & Sons, Ltd.

Resource Item 6.2: page 575, 'Getting the Numbers Right',© 1996 European Quality Publications Limited. All rights reserved. *European Quality* is a high level management journal focused on Quality.

Contents

Resources section   531

Glossary   607

GUIDE FOR STUDENTS

Course Introduction

Welcome to *Operations Management*. This book is part of a major new national programme of interactive texts which covers the curriculum of an undergraduate Business Studies degree.

The objectives of this guide are:

- to give you an outline of the subject of operations management
- to explain the importance of studying operations management as part of your Business Studies course
- to describe the nature of the material on which this workbook is based
- to outline the programme which you will be following
- to offer practical hints and advice on how to study operations management using the open learning approach
- to point out some of the advantages to you of studying operations management by the method used in this book.

What is operations management?

Operations management is a comparatively new discipline and may not even feature in all Business Studies degree programmes. However, operations management techniques have been practised for centuries. Operations management is concerned with the ways of achieving the most effective and efficient use of an organisation's resources, such as its financial and human resources, its capital resources and its raw materials. It is concerned with making a better product or service and with making it more efficiently or at lower cost. Operations management is therefore centrally concerned with the achievement of organisational objectives and ultimately with the achievement of business success. As you will see, the study of operations management is not just about the manufacturing of products in assembly line environments – it concerns every business, large or small. And it is not just about the use of mathematical techniques or information technology, as useful as these may be. Fundamentally it is about doing things better, however simple or complicated that may be. Although the module presents operations management as a specialist business function, it will become clear that many of the ideas and techniques are relevant to many other management specialists.

In your other Business Studies courses you may have come across ideas such as project management, scheduling, stock control and method study as well as relatively recent developments such as lean production, just-in-time manufacturing, total quality management and so on. As you will see, these are all part of the discipline of operations management and are likely to be of value to any manager in any business. A companion text to this one, *Business Functions*, contains a useful overview to the whole subject.

What is in this workbook?

The core of the workbook is nine study units. These were written specifically for undergraduate business students by authors who are experienced in teaching such courses. The content has been revised as a result of comments from experienced Business Studies tutors who have worked through the material.

The units are particularly useful to students who may be following a course where an open learning approach is being adopted. The features which make it particularly suitable for open learning include:

- very careful sequencing of the materials so that there is a clear and logical progression
- a step-by-step approach so that you will be able to understand each new point thoroughly before proceeding to the next one
- very clear layout with relatively short sections and paragraphs
- numerous short examples which help to illustrate the ideas
- many worked examples with an emphasis on understand the methods and techniques
- lots of opportunities for you to check that you understand what you have just read
- review activities for each unit which enable you to extend and apply your knowledge as well as to test your understanding
- plenty of opportunities for you to test your progress through end-of-unit exercises.

The combination of all these factors should make it possible to develop your understanding of operations management with only limited support from tutors and traditional means such as lectures and seminars. Students on more conventional courses will also find that the workbook provides a useful supplement to other text books which they may have been recommended.

At the back of the book there is a resource section which consists of a collection of journal articles and other materials. This allows you the opportunity of wider reading but in a way which ensures that it is highly relevant to and closely integrated with the material covered in the units. Many of the activities in the workbook relate to these readings. Particular features of the resources section are:

- a significant number of journal articles and extracts, each dealing with a key issue in operations management
- up-to-date material, much of which deals with topical issues
- short articles and extracts written in clear, non-technical language
- material particularly relevant to undergraduate Business Studies students
- other resources such as forms and sheets for analysis.

Although the workbook is designed to be complete in itself, your understanding of operations management will be improved by wider reading. Each unit therefore has a list of recommended reading to guide you towards some of the more important and useful literature.

The workbook also contains a helpful glossary which defines many of the key terms which you will encounter in the units.

Unit structure

Unit 1 introduces you to the theory, practice and techniques of operations management and places the development of operations management in an historical context. We examine the crucial role of operations management in satisfying consumer needs and achieving business objectives. Unit 2 introduces the concepts of product planning and positioning and explores the relationship between operations management and other key management functions such as finance and marketing. Unit 3 examines the development of operational and facilities strategies and considers how locations are selected and integrated manufacturing or servicing systems are constructed. We also discuss the layout of production facilities together with the advantages of different approaches for different kinds of business.

We then go on to consider, in Unit 4, the theory and practice of the management of consumer demand, paying particular attention to the issues concerned with forecasting demand and ensuring that sufficient inventory is available to ensure product (or service) availability. Operations management often involves the management of discrete projects and this is the focus of Unit 5, which considers a number of key techniques for the effective planning and control of resources.

Unit 6 addresses the vital issue of quality together with a variety of approaches to improving and controlling the quality of goods and service provision. Unit 7 considers a variety of approaches to the improvement of productivity, in particular the use of work study techniques as part of operations management. Unit 8 explores the ways in which operations managers can improve business efficiency and effectiveness through proper production scheduling and the management of production capacity.

Unit 9 concludes the module with a detailed consideration of some of the newer developments in operations management such as lean production systems, just-in-time techniques, business process re-engineering and supply chain management.

Using the workbook

You will probably find it most effective to work through the units in sequence. You should begin by noting the points which the unit outlines identify as the crucial aspects of the material. This will put the contents of the units into context and guide you through them.

Each unit is interspersed with a number of activities and review activities. All of these are intended to be attempted by you as they arise and completed before you move on. The suggested solutions to each activity are given immediately following the activity. The solutions to the review activities are given at the end of the relevant unit.

The activities are intended to be a combination of a check that you are following and understanding the unit and a way of helping to make your learning a more active experience for you. By working through the activities, you can effectively divide your study time between that which is necessary for taking on new ideas and that which is necessary to reinforce those ideas. Avoid the temptation to skip through the activities quickly. They are there to assist you in developing your understanding of the material.

Typically, the activities will only take you a few minutes to deal with. By contrast, the review activities may take considerably longer to complete and may involve reading an article from the resource section and thinking about the issues raised. It is important that you discipline yourself to complete each activity, self-assessment question or exercise before you refer to the answer provided.

You should read the items in the resource section when recommended. They have been carefully chosen to aid or broaden your understanding of the subject.

There are frequent cross checks in the text to refer you back to where underpinning ideas or techniques have been presented. Do take the time to refer back to these points in order to refresh your memory and test your understanding.

Avoid rote learning

You should avoid any attempt at rote learning the material in this workbook. You should aim to understand the underlying logic in the ideas being presented by working through all the activities. Simply trying to learn the theories or remember the techniques is inappropriate and insufficient. Rather, you should attempt to understand the principles behind the theoretical ideas and models and understand the thinking behind the particular operations management techniques presented. Wherever possible look for connections between the theories and ideas explored here and those covered elsewhere in your Business Studies course.

Set aside time for your studies

At the start of the study period you will not know how long it will take to do the necessary work. It is sensible, therefore, to make a start on the work at an early stage in the study period. Try to discipline yourself to set aside particular times in the week to study, though not necessarily the same times each week. Experiment with different ways of studying the material to find the one which suits you. Try skimming each unit to get a grasp of the ideas covered before you go through it in detail. Alternatively, try reading the unit objectives and the summaries before you settle down to study the unit in depth. Try to find the most suitable time to study when your concentration is at its highest and interruptions are at a minimum. And do set aside sufficient time to complete all the activities – they are a crucial part of the learning process.

INTRODUCTION TO THE MODULE

Welcome to the study of operations management. This discipline is a comparatively new addition to business studies degrees, yet operations management has been practised for centuries. It concerns the most effective and efficient use of resources such as materials, labour, money, and machinery, for the purpose of making something or the providing of a service. Operations management is relevant to all organisations from whatever sector, as every organisation is producing something whether it is a product or a service. Operations management is concerned with transferring the 'whats' of an organisation's objectives into the 'hows' of execution and success. It is not just about manufacturing a product on an assembly line which you may have initially thought, it concerns any and every business. And, it is not just about mathematics, logistics and computers, it is about doing things better however simple or complicated that might be.

In your other business studies, you may have already met the expressions objectives, strategy, productivity, project management, quality control, total quality management, time management, scheduling, budgeting, feasibility study, just-in-time manufacturing, inventories, stock control, change, flat hierarchy, restructuring outsourcing, and many others. In this module, you will see that they are all part of the discipline of operations management and of value to any manager in any business. In today's fast changing world, organisations have to be efficient and effective and adaptable to the changing environment to succeed. The operations manager can be the key to this success.

This module consists of nine units which start by laying the foundations of the discipline and then look at some major issues in detail. They cover the broad spectrum of operations management theory, technique and practice. The Resource section provides additional articles that we refer to within the units. The Glossary provides further definitions and descriptions for some key terms. We will now look at the content of each unit in detail

Unit 1   Introduction to Operations Management

In this unit, we look at what operations management actually is and how it has developed over the years. We use marketing, as a function, to link and framework some fundamental concepts and practices of operations management. The marketing approach, rather than the product approach, to business involves a commitment to satisfying the customers' needs for the organisation's product or service. Operations management is crucial to the success of service as well as manufacturing industries, and we identify some specific roles for the operations manager within any organisation.

Unit 2   Product Planning and Positioning

In Unit 2 we will look at an organisation's product (or service) strategies which form part of this overall strategy. We particularly emphasise the role of Research and Development. The concept of product planning and positioning will be examined showing the interaction between functional areas such as marketing and finance with operations management.

The product life cycle will be considered from an operations management perspective. Various creative thinking approaches in common usage will be described and the stages of value engineering and analysis procedures outlined.

Unit 3 Process Design

Various types of focus will be described, together with the development of operational and facilities strategies. We will consider how locations are decided and integrated manufacturing or servicing systems are constructed. The layout of facilities will be examined, with a comparison of the advantages of each option for different kinds of business.

Unit 4 Managing Demand and Supply of Materials

Unit 4 is about managing one of the most important inputs and one of the most important outputs, that is inventories or materials, with reference to the transformation model of operations. To allow for variation in customer demand and for processing economies, very often inventory (stock) has to be held. Although operations managers and financial managers would generally prefer not to hold inventories, since they represent money tied up, without such inventories there would be considerable disruption to operations and inconvenience to customers.

We tend to take for granted that when we go to a shop we will find what we require. We are sometimes annoyed when the shoe shop does not have our size in stock, but we would be angry if milk and bread were not available at the supermarket. The fact that so many goods are so easily available is as much due to operations managers as it is to economic system.

Unit 4, goes 'behind the scenes' to look at the theories that make such availability possible. Forecasting is clearly needed, and, so-called 'independent demand' inventory theory (where items are bought independently from one another) aims at selecting the correct order quantities, as well as looking at the decision of when to buy and how much to hold to insure against fluctuations in demand.

In this unit we will also look at the management of 'dependent' materials, that is where an end item such as a car generates demand for the components to make the car.

Unit 5 Project Management

In Unit 5 we will examine the logic principles which underpin the techniques used in project management. We shall consider critical path methods, PERT, precedence diagrams and line of balance technique.

The use of network planning for effective control of resources during the planning and execution phases of projects will be emphasised. The roles played by operations managers and the importance of operational management will be examined. Techniques within projects will be discussed in relation to the cost/time aspects of a project. Software packages can provide help in designing and controlling a project.

Unit 6 Quality Management

Unit 6 will explore what is meant by 'quality', how we translate the ideas of customers into product or service designs, how quality is controlled, how it is assured, and very importantly for quality and productivity, how it is improved.

In the transformation model, quality management, at least in its modern sense, is about understanding customers, controlling the transformation processes to ensure consistency, and working with suppliers to ensure that defect-free materials are delivered to the transformation process.

In Unit 2 we saw a little of the importance of 'quality' of goods and services. We discussed both design quality and product conformance quality, and we know from our own experience to what extent 'quality' has become an expectation, particularly in products although less so in services. We noted that quality has emerged as being one of the great unifying themes of operations management, if not management in general.

Unit 7 Productivity, Methods and Measurements

Unit 7 will concentrate upon productivity issues. After defining productivity, we will examine how it is measured and which techniques can be used to improve it.

We will concentrate our studies upon common productivity-raising techniques used under the umbrella title of 'work study' or 'management services', their methodologies, practices and objectives. You will learn how to analyse and measure work, and how existing work methods can be redesigned to raise productivity levels.

Unit 8 Scheduling and Capacity

Different scheduling techniques are applicable to different processes. Capacity issues also follow the volume variety matrix, with higher volume processes generally requiring larger units of capacity to be installed at any time, and requiring longer times to install. These are the issues dealt with in this unit.

In the transformation model, scheduling and capacity is relevant to the transformation process itself. Any transformation, whether in manufacturing or service, needs to consider which work to process first in order to meet customer requirements, and the ability or capacity of the transformation process to undertake the work. For example, a travel agent continually has to decide which bookings to do next, and management has to decide on staffing levels. Too much capacity is generally uneconomic, but too little leads to delays or loss of custom. Capacity is inextricably linked with scheduling; the greater the capacity the easier the scheduling.

Unit 9 Time Based Operations

In this 'leading edge' unit we consider some of the exciting developments that are taking place, which are changing both operations and marketing. This includes just-in-time (JIT) operations, supply chain logistics, and business process reengineering. This unit overlaps with several other units such as Unit 4, *Managing Demand and Materials,* Unit 6, *Quality Management*, and Unit 8, *Scheduling and Capacity,* but serves as a capstone unit to bring these areas together and relate them to current practice.

In the transformation model, time is of course involved in transforming inputs into outputs. There are significant issues here: the time that it takes to bring a new product to market, and the time to produce and distribute a product. In recent years, pressure has built up on all operations managers, both in manufacturing and service, to reduce both these times. Reducing time often also has the effect of improving customer service, improving quality (through, for example, being able to solve problems earlier, and fresher often means better), reducing inventories ('don't store, ship'), and higher productivity (through squeezing out the waste in processes).

UNIT 1
INTRODUCTION TO OPERATIONS MANAGEMENT

Introduction

In this unit, we define operations management, identify the stages in its historical development and identify where the operations manager can help in today's organisation. Although operations management is concerned with all functional areas, we look at marketing as it provides us with some frameworks on which to base our concepts and techniques. Also marketing and operations are inextricably linked through the product itself. Specifically we look at Porter's idea of a value chain for every business; the notion of the operations system and its transformation of inputs to outputs; and the operations mix, which we can compare with the marketing mix; the product life cycle; links with particular product processes; and operations management as a means of competitive advantage. Operations management is not just appropriate in manufacturing industries but also service industries; we look at its varying roles.

Throughout this unit and some of the other earlier units you will encounter some concepts and terms that we return to later in the module. Don't be worried by this, we are trying to give you an overall view of operations management and the extent of its far-reaching implications in organisations. You do not need to understand the details of every concept at this stage, just bear in mind where they fit in the wider picture, when you meet them later in your studies. Many of the concepts and practices are also interrelated so you will meet them in different contexts as we discuss each major aspect of operations management in turn. The Glossary provides some descriptions and definitions of key words and phrases which will help you as you progress through your studies.

Objectives

By the end of this unit, you should be able to:

- define operations management and identify its application in the manufacturing and service industries.
- explain the significance of, and relationship between the inputs, transformation process and the outputs of a system
- provide an insight into the origins of modern operations management showing how current practice has developed
- explain why an understanding of operations management is essential for the business studies student and the serving business manager

SECTION 1

What is Operations Management?

Introduction

In this section, we define operations management and look at its origins, tracing the historical events which have contributed to its development. Finally, we consider the continuing and new challenges that operations managers face.

1.1 Definitions of operations management

We can define operations management as the planning, scheduling, and control of the activities that transform inputs into finished goods and services. We can also define it as 'a field of study that focuses on the effective planning, scheduling, use, and control of a manufacturing or service organisation through the study of concepts from design engineering, industrial engineering, management information systems, quality management, production management, accounting, and other functions as they affect the operation.'(*APICS Dictionary*, 1995)

Let's look at some other definitions.

'...is concerned with the efficient conversion of an organisation's resources into the goods or services that it has been set up to provide.'(Barnett, 1996)

'...is concerned with creating, operating and controlling a transformation system which takes inputs of a variety of resources and produces outputs of goods and services which are needed by customers.'(Naylor, 1996)

'...is concerned with all activities involved in making a product or providing a service: it is responsible for the transformation of various kinds of inputs to useful outputs.'(Waters, 1991)

'...is the management of systems or processes that create goods and/or provide services.'(Stevenson, 1993)

ACTIVITY 1

Define operations management in your own words.

Operations management concerns making the most efficient use of whatever resources an organisation has, so as to provide the finished goods or services that its customers need in a timely and cost-effective manner (Barnett, 1996). Operations management is linked to the organisation's aims and objectives. It concerns all the organisation's resources: people, equipment, materials, money and time. This means that it is involved in all functional areas within the organisation, as all areas within each organisation are concerned with producing some product or service from their resources. This may be an 'internal' product or service to elsewhere in the organisation or to the outside world. The **operations system** covers this process of 'transforming' resources or inputs into the finished outputs. As you can see, regardless of which functional area you consider there is a transformation process which needs managing to achieve effective and efficient outcomes. A knowledge of operations management concepts and techniques is important to achieve this.

Operations management is as necessary and appropriate in a manufacturing organisation as it is in a service organisation. It is not just to do with producing a 'product' more effectively and efficiently, it is to do with producing any output. Although obviously a key area that operations management can contribute to is the 'operations' or production function itself.

1.2 Origins of modern operations management

Although we can see operations management in action over the centuries, whether it was in coordinating manpower to build an ancient temple or an igloo, or to hunt for food or firewood, or to defend a castle from attackers or a ship from pirates, or to pack food and water for the duration of a ship's voyage, it has only relatively recently been formalised into a body of theory and practice. It has its real roots in the scientific management principles put forward by Frederick Taylor in the nineteenth century who provided the basis for many production lines of the early twentieth century. Since then many ideas and concepts of effective working have been developed as we have discovered more about the human mind and body and what it is capable of achieving and in parallel, technology has changed the way that we can achieve things both through automation of production and the development of information technology.

Operations management is as old as industry itself. The first person who simplified a job which needed doing by use of reason, can be considered the unconscious founder of the discipline. Until comparatively recently, it was part of the unformulated wisdom of craft, gained by a lifetime of experience. It was practised, not as a formal feature of business, but as an unconscious art. Skilled people, whether engaged in manual, service or administrative roles tended to work in very traditional ways. The development in the last 300 years of many new ways of looking at work and the resources used in its performance inevitably affected the discipline of operations management. The process of innovation and speed of change in the last 50 years has accelerated the growth of the range of approaches and techniques available to the operations manager.

THE HISTORICAL CONTEXT

Table 1 identifies some major events over the past three centuries that have contributed to the development of operations management. You may recognise a variety of technological and management developments that you may have met in your other business studies. These range from those of the Industrial Revolution in the eighteenth century to modern-day management concepts. We haven't included the vast number of achievements that computers have achieved this century from not only revolutionising the way we manufacture products, but also to how we conduct almost everything in business, whether its the accounting system, the database for customers, marketing information, computerised payroll, or whatever. Again you can see the role that effective use of resources and operations management has across an entire business.

Table 1 is based largely on Frank Sperotto's *In the Footsteps of Homo Industrialis* (1994).

1700 Sweden:	Christopher Polhelm set up a business which recognised the advantages of mechanisation and the division of labour. He recorded that 'nothing increases demand so much as low prices. Therefore there is a great need of machines and appliances which will diminish the amount or intensity of heavy work'.
1705 UK:	Thomas Newcomen patented the first piston-operated steam engine.
1709 UK:	Abraham Darby pioneered the process of iron smelting.
1725 France:	Basile Bouchon and Jacques Vaucausson devised a system using perforated cards to control loom mechanisms.
1733 UK:	John Kay invented the 'flying shuttle', which improved the speed and potential of the weaving process.
1952 USA:	Peter Drucker identified the principles underlying 'management by objectives' (MBO).
1956 USA:	Armand Feigenbaum coined the term 'total quality control' (TQC).

1760 France:	Jean Perronet undertook calculations to determine the number of man-hours required for each stage of pin manufacturing.
1764 UK:	James Hargreaves invented the 'spinning jenny', which was able to spin more than one yarn at a time.
1769 UK:	Richard Arkwright invented the 'water frame', which was a water-powered spinning machine. In his factory, Arkwright began to use managerial control systems to regulate production levels.
1776 UK:	James Watt built the first successful steam engine.
1776 USA:	Adam Smith wrote on the division of labour.
1776 France:	Jean Baptiste Gribeauval advocated the standardisation of parts in a manufacturing process aimed at mass production.
1797 UK:	Robert Owen began to institute new and progressive personnel management procedures in his textile factory.
1801 France:	Joseph Jacquard designed an automatic control system for weaving looms based upon numerical control principles.
1814 UK:	George Stephenson built the first steam locomotive.
1821 UK:	Michael Faraday demonstrated the principles of the electric motor.
1829 UK:	Charles Babbage, a professor of mathematics, devised the principles which were to underpin digital computing. He later advocated the use of an analytical approach using precise times and costs to improve manufacturing operations. Babbage later designed a mechanical calculator which he called 'a difference engine'.
1835 USA:	Samuel Morse invented the telegraph to improve communications.
1881 USA:	Frederick Winslow Taylor began developing time study and 'scientific management' concepts.
1885 USA:	Frank Gilbreth, the founder of 'motion study', began investigating work methods on repetitive tasks. He was increasingly assisted by his wife, Dr Lilian Gilbreth, a qualified psychologist. They began to use photography in their research, and developed techniques which they termed chronocyclegraphs and micromotion analysis.
1896 Italy:	Vilfredo Pareto produced the 'Pareto curve' to explain income distribution across a population.

1903 USA:	Henry Gantt designed the 'Gantt chart' to facilitate planning and control procedures.
1913 USA:	Henry Ford established a car assembly plant in Michigan which was based upon principles laid down by F W Taylor. This used mechanised production lines, and standardised parts.
1916 France:	Henri Fayol identified the major features of the managerial process.
1927 USA:	Elton Mayo conducted research into worker motivation at the Hawthorne company.
1930 Canada:	Charles Bedaux developed the technique of 'rating' to assess worker speed and effectiveness, thereby greatly reducing the amount of work necessary to time-study a job.
1934 USA:	Joseph Quick developed the work factor system, which gave times to jobs using tables of predetermined values which were generated from film analysis.
1943 USA:	Abraham Maslow set out his theory on the hierarchy of human motivational needs.
1946 USA:	The first electronic digital computer was built at Pennsylvania State University.
1947 USA:	Laurence Miles developed 'value analysis' at General Electric Co.
1947 USA:	The American Society of Mechanical Engineers (ASME) defined the five process charting symbols now in universal use.
1948 Japan:	W Edwards Deming, Joseph Juran and Armand Feigenbaum were sent from the USA to create quality awareness in Japanese industry. In the UK, the Operational Research Club is formed and in the USA, the Institute of Industrial Engineers is founded.
1950 UK:	Professor K F H Murrell coined the word 'ergonomics' to describe the body of knowledge resulting from research into the effects of working conditions upon worker performance.
1958 UK:	Russell Currie of ICI Ltd began to use the term 'work study' to describe the growing discipline of 'time and motion study'.

1958 USA:	The network planning technique known as PERT, (program evaluation and review technique), was developed by consultants Booz, Allen and Hamilton to handle project uncertainty in the development of Polaris weapons.
1959 USA:	Frederick Herzberg set out his motivation-hygiene theory of work.
1961 Japan:	Kaoru Ishikawa proposed the setting up of 'quality circles' in the workplace for problem solving and quality awareness.
1965 USA:	IBM produced the 'floppy disk' to store computer files.
1967 USA:	Automated flexible manufacturing systems (FMS) introduced.
1968 USA:	Jay W Forrester set out the principles of 'systems dynamics' which gave new insights into information feedback and resource control.
1971 Japan:	Taiichi Ohno developed the first 'just-in-time' system at Toyota.
1972 Japan:	Quality function deployment, based on the work of Dr Yogi Akao, was used at Mitsubishi Shipyards.
1973 USA:	J Harrington published ideas on computer integrated manufacturing (CIM).
1974 Sweden:	Volvo Cars began to set up small groups of workers, each capable of fully assembling a vehicle.
1975 USA:	Joseph Orlicky set out his ideas on material requirements planning (MRP).
1978 USA:	The development of computer aided design (CAD) and computer aided manufacturing (CAM) programs.
1979 USA:	Xerox Corporation introduced 'benchmarking' in order to compare features of their operations with those of competitors.
1984 USA:	The phrase 'total quality management' (TQM) began to be used. Goldratt and Cox's book *The Goal* is published, eventually translated into 16 languages, selling 1.8 million copies.
1987 Switzerland:	The International Organisation for Standardisation published the quality standards framework for ISO 9000.

1990 USA:	Richard J Schonberger outlined his ideas on supply chains.
1990 USA:	The principles of 'business process reengineering' (BPR) proposed by Michael Hammer. The book *The Machine that Changed the World* is published, which introduces the term 'lean manufacturing'.

Table 1: Major historical events contributing to today's operations management theory and practice

We explore the historical context again at the end of the unit when you analyse the article 'Roots', Resource Item 1.1. As we progress through the module, we also look at the contributions of many of the pioneers, who are mentioned in Table 1 and who have become part of today's operations management.

1.3 Continuing challenges for operations managers

There will be continuing developments and innovations and today's operations managers must respond to new challenges such as:

Global competition
Increasingly, products are traded internationally and components are sourced internationally. The continuing decline of the world market share of British manufactured goods illustrates the relentless rise of new manufacturing competence worldwide.

Developments in strategic management policies
The introduction of business process reengineering (BPR) in long-established organisations has resulted in managerial delayering and the need to develop new ways of working and communicating as there are less hierarchical levels.

Total quality management principles and certification quality
Many organisations have found it almost impossible to become partners in a supply chain without quality certification (BS 5750 / ISO 9000). This has created a need to rethink quality policies and staffing, and a rush to achieve certification.

Employee empowerment
The need to be more responsive to market needs has encouraged many companies to become more open and innovative with their staff. It was estimated by *Fortune* magazine that 50% of American companies will have self-managed work teams in place by the year 2000. For some operations managers this represents great opportunity, but, for others, great threat.

Privatisation

Throughout the former Soviet Union, Europe, Australia, New Zealand, and elsewhere, privatisation has brought and is bringing enormous change. In general, operations managers from former state-run enterprises have had to become much more customer-, and market-conscious than they were previously.

Complex external environments

The increasingly complex arrangements, quotas and legal requirements of trade between partner countries within the European Union is an example of the constraints that are imposed on the organisation by the environment. Consider another example:businesses involved in the deep-sea fishing industry are operating under increasing complexity imposed upon them from an economic environment which appears politically, financially and administratively hostile.

Incorporation of technological developments

Continual advances in materials technology, process modification, computing systems, automation and product design, impose increasing demands upon operations managers. Whilst some of these developments are internal to the company, many will arise in the external environment. Unless a business has some mechanism to scan the wider environment, it is likely to be unaware of the existence of technological change. Whole new sets of problems are being posed for operations managers when late adoption of new technology has resulted in a competitive productivity deficit which must then be speedily addressed.

Ecologically sound operations (green manufacturing)

The increasing emphasis being placed by the wider community and pressure groups upon careful use of the earth's resources and the detrimental effects created by businesses, has led to new approaches being developed. Inevitably, a process of significant change affecting resources involves the work of operations managers. Examples include the car industry, which is now designing its products with recycling in mind, and the chemical industry, where many plants have established low or zero emission goals.

Ethical business operations and conduct

As line managers responsible for the majority of people within many organisations, operations managers have to be involved in the development and application of codes of conduct, statements of values and ethical policies.

Ethical problems which confront the operations manager can be explored using frameworks. One such framework includes the following factors:

- magnitude of the consequences
- probability of the effect
- social consensus
- temporal immediacy (time scale of effects)
- personal and organisational proximity
- concentration of the effect.

(Elliott, 1996, Chapter 13)

Summary

In this section, we looked at a number of definitions of operations management and investigated its origins. We reviewed all the major historical events since 1700 which have contributed to the development of operations management theory and practice. Finally, we highlighted the continuing, and new, challenges faced by current operations managers.

SECTION 2

Frameworks for Operations Management

Introduction

In this section we will look at the partnership between operations and marketing, which is crucial to the success of an organisation. We then consider the common element they share. We will conclude with a list of 'universal' principles which we believe can make a big difference to any operations-based organisation.

Many organisations are involved in three fundamental activities:

- identifying potential customers, seeking to understand their needs, and persuading them to use the product or service

- providing the product or service efficiently and effectively

- managing the organisation's finances to ensure continuing success.

We can refer to these three activities as marketing, operations, and finance. Although the first and last activities are usually named in even a small organisation, it is comparatively rare, outside manufacturing companies, for the 'operations' function to be identified. Indeed, many people engaged in operations, from chefs to surgeons, from bank clerks to newsagents, not only have never taken a course in operations management but may well resent any suggestion that this is what they are doing there. We do not presume to specifically address the daily problems of chefs, surgeons, banking clerks or newsagents, nevertheless, these people share much in common with 'professional' operations managers. For instance, they need to work out their physical working environment, their daily schedules, their inventories, and who their suppliers will be. They also need to be concerned with the quality of their services or products.

Many organisations resolve such issues in an informal way. This may be adequate, however, an organisation of any size needs to take these three activities very seriously, whatever they are called.

Classically, in a manufacturing organisation, these three activities are in a state of tension. Thus marketing seeks to improve service and to offer a greater variety of product choice to the customer. Operations or production seeks to improve efficiency by reducing inventories and by longer runs of fewer products. This conflicts with marketing objectives. Finance seeks to minimise cost, by limiting inventories and by reducing expenditure on machines and staff. This conflicts with both marketing and operations objectives.

The classic contradictions between these activities are no longer as severe as was once thought. It is now often possible to have low inventories, high quality products, good customer service, high productivity, and relatively low investment in machines, with the use of just-in-time (JIT) inventory systems and other many flexible manufacturing systems. With the JIT inventory system inventory items arrive when they are needed in the production process and not held in stock.

Marketing and operations therefore are, or should be, equal partners in the success of the organisation. In this respect, they share several common reference frameworks although from different perspectives. We consider each in the following sections.

2.1 Porter's value chain

Every business takes in resources and completes some type of transformation process before passing on an output of goods or services to the customer. Each of the stages in this process adds value as resources are converted into outputs. The activities occurring in the value chain affect the costs quality and ultimately the profitability of the business.

Michael Porter (1985) suggested that every business should construct a **value chain**, which depicts the total value generated and added to its product or service. He analysed the business functions into primary and secondary activities. Through these nine activities the company can add to, or reduce, the total value of its product (Naylor, 1996). Porter identifies the five **primary activities** as those that are directly concerned with the product or service:

- inbound logistics
- operations
- outbound logistics
- marketing and sales
- customer services.

He sees these as links in a chain (Figure 1). The operations cover the actually making, or transformation, of the inputs into the product or service. The four essential **support activities** are:

- procurement – obtaining the required inputs
- technology development – basic research and design and development of products and processes
- human resource management – recruiting, training and managing personnel
- company infrastructure – managerial processes of planning, control, quality, finance, communication system.

The company's profitability will depend on the difference between the total value put on the product or service and the actual costs of doing this through the nine activities. Operations management has a key role in ensuring that these activities are carried out effectively and efficiently.

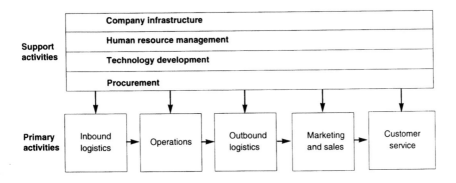

Figure 1: Porter's value chain

You will see when we view the value chain later, just how important the effects of applying operations management concepts and techniques are when a company is considering its profitability. This module will provide insight into how operations management is useful in many parts of a typical organisation.

2.2 Operations as systems

THE SYSTEMS VIEW

A system can be defined as a set of entities together with the relationship between them. This simple definition belies its importance for the operations manager, or for management in general. The point is that, although most organisations are arranged into departments or sections such as accounting, marketing, operations, and personnel, this is not the way that goods or services are made or delivered. Goods or services are made or delivered according to systems or processes which integrate these organisational entities. Having a **systems view** is important for an operations manager, because he or she must be able to see the whole process, from concept to completion. The entire process chain may include outside suppliers, service delivery and back-up, and the information flows that are required.

Systems can be described as having either **open** or **closed** features. These describe the extent to which communications and interactions occur freely across the system boundaries. Boundaries are not only physical, like the walls of a specific functional area, but can also be invisible, and represent, for example, the authority exercised by a manager. In today's business world, there is often a global dimension with international companies.

The diversity of boundary-crossing communications is increasing continually. A few years ago, people crossed boundaries physically all the time. The production manager walked down the corridor into the personnel department to discuss a recruitment need. The sales manager walked into the warehouse to talk to the distribution manager about a late dispatch of a customer's order. But today's communication and conferencing systems provide instant access and save on cost, journey and possible delay time.

An **open system** has few boundary regulations. Systems thinkers argue that every system requires inputs of resources to produce outputs of goods or services. Without these resources, the system will collapse. What is in debate is the level of control or restraint of freedom placed on a system boundary. How closed is it? A totally **closed system** exists only as a conceptual model. Whatever the level of insularity achieved by the most secure prison complex, it will be closed in one dimension only – the ability to retain inmates. Every day, staff, food, mail, visitors and finance move across the boundaries.

Systems and sub-systems can be categorised along the open – closed continuum, and recognised as a 'relatively-open' or a 'relatively-closed' system. There are costs and risks associated with all points on the continuum. The more controls in place on a boundary, the greater the cost. The more open a boundary, the greater the potential loss through theft or mishandling.

ACTIVITY 2

Think of a hospital. In what respects is it a closed system? In what respects is it an open system? Why does it need to be open in some respects and closed in others? Indicate operations management issues which arise when we look at these features.

What features did you explore? You might have thought about safety and security issues. Without boundary controls, patients and staff are vulnerable to theft or attack as access is gained to the hospital itself or to individual wards. At the same time, legitimate access for staff and visitors must be allowed. In normal situations, a relatively open system must be designed. In special cases, for example for intensive care or maternity wards, a relatively closed system will be required. From an operational management perspective there needs to be a system of control which minimises delays and operating costs, yet provides the appropriate level of security.

Other criteria that need consideration from an operations management perspective, for a well-designed system are:

Open aspects

must be available to all kinds of people

must be possible to walk into reception areas

wards need to be open to visitors

patients are normally free to leave at any time

ambulances can be near to wards

supplies can be brought in by lorries.

Closed aspects

restricted access to facilities must operate

schedules for admissions are required

only qualified personnel can be employed.

Throughout your studies it may be helpful to keep in mind the following diagrammatic representation of systems showing open and closed features (Figure 2). In systems design situations there is a tension between these two perspectives, and people working in the system under review often have strong views which the operations manager needs to reconcile!

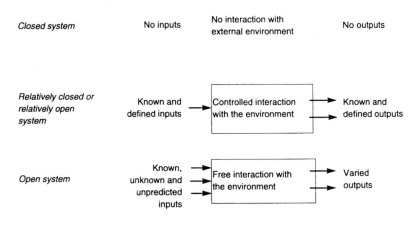

Figure 2: Open and closed system features

The boundaries around systems and sub-systems tend to be defined by the extent of managerial control over the resources being used. Free movement of resources and easy communications suggest a more open system. Restricted access and controls tend more towards a closed system. Closed systems are more expensive to maintain and will in extreme cases lead to the demise of the system as it is cut off from its environment and therefore from fresh inputs. Similarly the more closed a system is the more likely it becomes ill-adapted to the changing world around it.

Manufacturing and service industries, are greatly affected by influences arising in the external environment. As we see in Figure 3, there are many bodies and pressure groups which an organisation must take into account in its operational system.

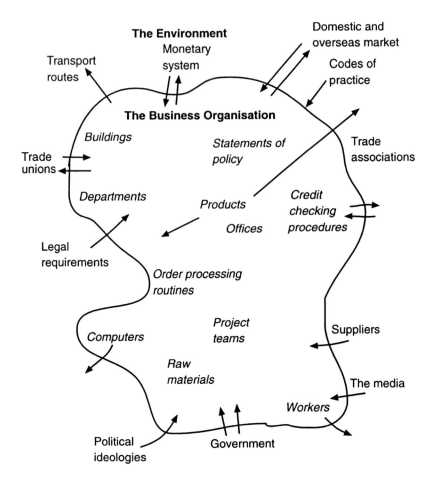

Figure 3: External influences on an organisation

Government legislation, backed up by regulations and officials, affect almost every aspect of the organisation. Working conditions, pay regulations, taxation, health and safety, quality, standards and official documents all need to be attended to. Trade union agreements on national pay bargaining, holiday entitlements and agreed procedures for handling disputes require handling. Societal groups exert considerable pressure upon particular businesses. For example, firms processing nuclear waste as a service to the electricity power generating industry make continual efforts to assure the public that there are no harmful side-effects or risk of leakages.

From an operations management perspective, the nature of the inputs and outputs, communications linkages, the skill and discretion of staff and the potential damage done by poor or inaccurate information flows, both internally and externally, should be recognised. The appropriate level of control, with economy in mind, must be built into the system.

OPERATIONS AS TRANSFORMATION SYSTEMS

Any operations system can be viewed as a composition of three major components with important communication linkages. Each component and the pathway itself is of interest to the operations manager.

If we need to design a new operational system or solve a problem in an existing system, the construction of a simple systems diagram showing these components greatly facilitates our understanding.

Each of the diagrams that follow (Figures 5-7) are developed from the basic input-transformation-output model illustrated in Figure 4.

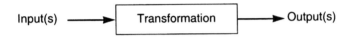

Figure 4: The basic input-transformation-output model

In operations management terms, **inputs** are resources which are introduced into the system in an organised and controlled way. These inputs include: materials, capital, equipment, personnel, energy, skills and time.

The **transformation process** consists of the use of manufacturing or service operations which change or employ the input resources to add value.

The **outputs** of the system include products and services with the right quality, in the right quantity and at the right time. There are other outputs which interest the operations manager also. There may be measurable amounts of scrap material, rejected finished product, unsatisfied customers, bad public relations, high labour turnover and untreated effluent.

In systems study, often called cybernetics, the transformation process is often referred to as the **black-box**. Whatever the system we are looking at, whether it is making a product or providing a service, it is the balance of input resources to the desired output and the associated control process which is of prime importance in creating a highly productive business.

A simple control link is shown in Figure 5.

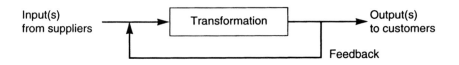

Figure 5: A simple control link

In this model, information is flowing back to the input end to ensure that the transformation stage is fully supplied with resources and, conversely, not oversupplied. **Feedback** loops are shown in these diagrams which model homeostatic (**steady state**) systems. Whilst **negative feedback** is essential for control, some systems need the facility of **positive feedback** to encourage growth. See the *Glossary* for more detail on these terms.

ACTIVITY 3

Consider a food supermarket. What problems would arise if there was no feedback control link between the sales output and the buying input for:

(a)   perishable commodities (e.g. fresh vegetables)

(b)   tinned food (e.g. soups)?

You should have concluded that:

(a) could result in too much food inside the supermarket, which could go bad and cause a health/hygiene problem; could provide difficulties on stock rotation resulting in waste; or could be empty shelves and lost sales.

(b) there could be empty shelves and lost sales; excessive purchases would tie up finance over a long period; excess stock would need warehousing and eventually would pass its 'sell-by' date.

You perhaps came up with some different but equally valid consequences, all of which indicate the need for a fast and accurate feedback control system.

In our studies we shall be considering the aspects of operations management which apply to a whole range of systems, learning how to forecast the input needs, control the transformation process with quality in mind and deliver the right product or service to satisfy the customer.

In practice, the feedback process grows in complexity, as illustrated in Figure 6. In this model, there is provision for passing information into both the input and transformation processes to improve control.

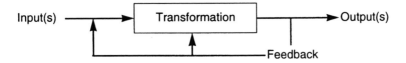

Figure 6: The feedback process

As models approach real-world systems they become increasingly complex to take account of other sub-systems within the business and, vitally, the external environment in which the business operates. This enables a system to be depicted as an adaptive and progressive system, rather than something which is static and deterministic. The model may begin to look like Figure 7. In our studies we will also be examining the wider environmental aspects of this model which are influenced by operations management strategy and application.

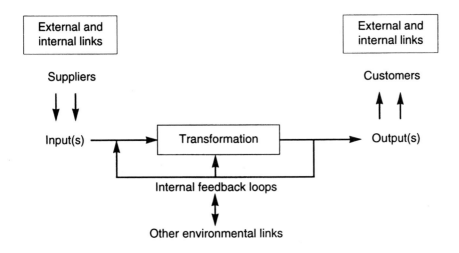

Figure 7: Internal and external links

Controlling systems

The control process is part of all management. If the system needs to be well balanced, to optimise resources and achieve outputs of a stipulated quantity or quality at a prescribed time, then the **negative** aspect of **feedback** is used for control.

Operations management techniques and procedures need to provide rapid comparisons with stated criteria, to enable a manager to dampen down or boost the output of the system. A profile, over time, could look like Figure 8, where the output shown could be for instance the volume of an item produced over a given period of time.

Output

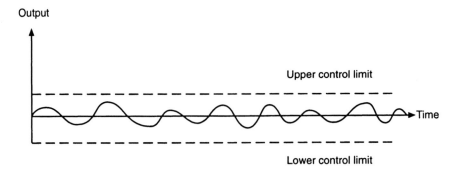

Figure 8: A system profile over time

If a growth system is required, for example, repeated product advertising to stimulate market growth, then **positive feedback** is used. A profile, over time, could look like Figure 9. (Note the explanations of feedback given in the *Glossary*.)

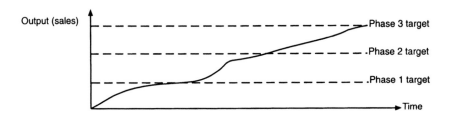

Figure 9: Profile of a growth system over time

2.3 Operations mix: the six Ps of operations

Like the marketing mix, the **operations mix** provides not only an easy-to-remember frame of reference but also an integrated package of the factors that should be considered together when designing a new or revised operation. The origin of the operations mix is not clear, but an early version was developed by Professor Keith Lockyer of Bradford Management Centre (1988). Like the marketing mix, it is the compatibility of the elements that is important. The elements of the operations mix overlap with those of the marketing mix, but with a different perspective. The elements are:

- **Product**. For convenience we refer to 'product' but 'service' could be equally applicable. In operations, it is the design and quality of the product or service that is important. Product design is the essential interface between marketing and operations. Marketing should be looking back at the external customer, and operations looking forward to the internal customer.We investigate product design in later units.

Recently, the technique of quality function deployment (QFD), which we will examine in Unit 6, *Quality Management*, has come into prominence for managing the interface between marketing and operations.

- **Process**. In the last section we saw how process involves the transformation of inputs into more valuable outputs. Suppliers, whether internal or external, provide the inputs and customers, whether internal or external, receive the outputs. In between customers and the process, and between process and suppliers, feedback should operate. Recently, in operations management, attention has been given to 'process' from the perspectives of quality and time.

  It is the underlying processes, which cut across organisational departments, that are the fundamental drivers of an organisation.Thus, the purchasing process does not involve only the buying department, it should also involve quality, finance, engineering, operations, and so forth. This process view of organisation has become integrated into management thinking as a result of BPR which you will meet in Unit 9, *Time Based Operations*.

  In recent years we have also learned how much potential there is for reducing time in a process by removing waste. Any process has six basic sub-processes: operations, transportation, inspection, delay, storage, and rework. Of these, only operations ultimately adds value for the customer. All the others are wasteful, and can and should be reduced or removed over time. Moreover, controlling the process is an important concern for operations managers through techniques such as statistical process control (SPC), You will look at this in Unit 6.

- **Place**. In operations, 'place' means location and layout. Finding the location is a classic problem of operations management, and one which we look at in Unit 3, *Process Design*. Having decided on the location, attention turns to layout of the factory or office. There should be a direct link with strategic issues, and with product and process considerations. Having decided upon the general layout of the factory or office, attention then turns to detailed workplace layout. Increasingly this is being done less and less by operations 'professionals' such as industrial engineers and more and more by the real experts of the workplace, the people themselves. They must of course, be given guidelines on how to approach the task, plus relevant data on topics such as ergonomics. You will look at some of these guidelines in Unit 3.

- **Programmes**. 'Programmes' in operations means the schedules and plans under which operations are carried out. In manufacturing operations, such programmes are fairly standardised ranging from the production plan, through the master schedule, and on to material requirements plans, capacity plans, and detailed shop floor schedules. We cover these topics in Unit 8, *Scheduling and Capacity*.

In project management, the programmes are covered by techniques such as critical path analysis. In service operation, programmes are equally important. Whatever the type of operation all programmes have features in common. They try to meet customer demands or requirements, and they must pay attention to resource (people, machines, material) availability or capacity. The programmes themselves must, of course, be compatible with all other elements of the operations mix.

- **Procedures**. Procedures covers 'how should it be done'. This is a traditional field of study for operations managers, with its modern origins in the work of Frederick Taylor and the founders of motion study, such as Frank and Lillian Gilbreth. Whatever the task, there is a best and safest way of doing it; the issue is therefore how this best and safest way is to be determined.

Today the trend is for operators to take over responsibility for work standards themselves. But this is very different from an abdication of responsibility on the part of the operations manager. Work standards are important for planning, costing, quality, and safety. They cannot be ignored.

- **People**. Last but not least comes people. People drive all the other five Ps, indeed their contribution is growing rather than declining. In the mid-1980s some managers and the popular press believed that the future of industrial work would lie largely with the computer controlled, lights out, unmanned factory. However this was a naive view; factories not only require maintenance, but more importantly the automated factory is also the non-improving factory. Today, improvement and change are the essence of operations. Operations management is ultimately about the management of people.

Like the marketing mix, the operations mix needs to be tailored to particular circumstances, with each element being seen in relation to the other elements. In other words, it is a system. The mix has to be appropriate to the chosen goals. We now turn our attention to those goals, again viewed from an operations perspective.

ACTIVITY 4

Most operations-based organisations are part of a 'supply chain'. They form one link in a chain of organisations which transform raw materials into finished products. Consider an everyday product such as:

- a sandwich, bought from a supermarket chain, or
- a newspaper, or
- a telephone.

Select one of these and draw out the chain which results in the final product reaching the customer. Then consider:

- what each stage requires from the previous stage
- if it is desirable to hold stocks (inventory) at each stage

- if it is desirable to hold stocks (inventory) at each stage
- what performance measures are critical at each stage
- what communication channels are used between each stage
- what distribution channels are used
- what quality requirements are needed at each stage.

A sandwich starts life in a wheat field. Wheat is harvested (seasonally), processed, stored as flour, moved to a bakery, made into bread, stored, moved to a sandwich maker, joined by other ingredients such as lettuce, butter, tuna, assembled, stored, moved to the supermarket, unpacked, placed on shelves.

A sandwich, of course, should be fresh. So some stages need to be processed very rapidly. In earlier stages there is greater emphasis on efficiency. Wheat is seasonal but sandwich eating is daily, so somewhere there needs to be a buffer inventory. Moisture and temperature need to be controlled, more tightly towards the final stages. Continuity of supply is critical; the farmer does not know where his wheat will end up but grows it in anticipation that there will be good distribution channels. Some of these distribution channels, such as ships, require long lead times to bring their services. Most stages have customers and suppliers. There is mutual dependence – improving the service not only benefits the provider but also the suppliers and customers. The whole chain is only as 'good' as its weakest (or slowest, or most expensive, or worst humidity-controlled) link. Somehow the preferences of end customers have to be communicated right down the chain, for example, brown not white bread, and tuna fish not beef. But, of course, the response cannot be instantaneous so there is risk and inevitable waste. Generally, the more information that flows along the chain, the easier it is to plan and control.

We can make similar comments about the other products. An unsold newspaper is almost worthless. A telephone has a longer shelf life, but not as long as it used to have. Again, marketing has a role to play between the customer and the designer.

Bear this activity in mind through the next few sections, and the rest of the module.

2.4 Dimensions of competitiveness

Operations management plays a key strategic role within an organisation. In his book *The Manufacturing Advantage*, Nigel Slack (1991) argues that there are five 'performance objectives' which enable an 'operations-based' advantage to be gained:

- doing things right results in a quality advantage
- doing things fast results in a speed advantage
- doing things on time results in a dependability advantage
- changing what you do results in a flexibility advantage
- doing things cheaply results in a cost advantage.

Any organisation competes on two or three of these dimensions. Modern approaches to strategy emphasise the concept of 'focus', a legacy of work done by Harvard Business School Operations Professor Wickham Skinner (1978). Each dimension or focus of competitiveness has direct implications for both marketing and operations.

The **dimensions of competitiveness** are: price, quality, delivery, speed, design and flexibility:

- **Price**. For any market there can only be only one lowest price competitor. What is as important as the lowest price is **margin,** that is, the difference between cost and price. Efficient operations can make a vast difference to the margin. Later we will explore the strategic implications of competing on productivity or on **price recovery,** that is, the difference between prices charged and resource costs. Cost reduction is one of the pervading themes of operations management, and is something that we shall meet throughout the module.

- **Quality.** Quality is one of the most significant factors of competitiveness. In Unit 6, you will learn about eight dimensions of quality, each of which has significant implications for both marketing and operations. Here we need only mention one dimension, **quality of conformance**, that is, the degree to which the product or service designer's specification has been met by operations.

  The advent of Japanese electronics and cameras on Western markets illustrated how markets which were previously price dominated could be transformed by the consumer's realisation that reliability and performance were significant new dimensions.

  Quality and price are linked in two ways. Higher quality usually means that a higher price can be asked; and, strangely perhaps, a higher-quality product can often mean lower cost though less waste, rework, and returns. We explore this further in Units 6 and 9.

- **Delivery**. Delivery time and delivery reliability are operations-driven dimensions with significant impact for marketing. Often being able to deliver ahead of the competition and with greater reliability can command a price premium. When the customer is another industrial company, delivery reliability can mean significant marketing advantage.

- **Speed.** Closely linked to delivery is speed. What is meant by speed in this context is reduced time to bring new products to market, or to design and make products to order faster than a competitor is able to do so. You should also recognise that new innovations in design such as 'simultaneous engineering' mean that speed is not necessarily a trade-off with quality and cost. We explore this concept later, and particularly in Unit 9.

- **Design**. Design is what adds 'that little something special' to a product or service. Design may be regarded as an aspect of quality, but it is so important to marketing and operations that we look at it separately. Good design is not just the work of an inspired artist. It requires co-operation from both marketing and operations; the former to crystallise customer requirements, and the latter to ensure its feasibility in practice. Good design, of course, can command a premium price and can have a huge impact on cost.

- **Flexibility**. A deliberate strategy aimed at flexibility is an increasingly important competitive advantage. In fact, flexibility is regarded as one of the few remaining 'order winners' (see the next section) (Upton, 1995). There are different forms of flexibility: flexibility to change easily from making one product to another within a standard range; flexibility to change volumes easily; and flexibility to introduce new products easily. We discuss these flexibilities in Unit 9.

2.5 Order winners, order qualifiers and the Kano model

For a particular product, in a particular market, during a particular time, some of these dimensions of competitiveness are more important than others. It is therefore useful to distinguish between so-called **order winners** and **order qualifiers** (Hill, 1993). An order qualifier is your ticket to enter the race. An order winner is what allows you to carry off the trophy. Order qualifiers are no less important than order winners.

An example of an order qualifier is the quality assurance standard ISO9000, now demanded by many international companies. An example of an order winner is the Apple computer's operating system.

An alternative way of looking at the competitive dimensions is through the **Kano model** (Joiner, 1994). Kano is a Japanese quality expert who believes that product characteristics can be classified into 'must be', 'more is better', and 'delighters'. We say more about this model in Unit 6. Here we note that some characteristics must be in place, others have the power to improve customer satisfaction as they improve (or reduce), whilst still others have the power to delight where they exceed customer expectations.

Whatever we call them, it is important for marketing and operations to have a thorough knowledge of, and agreement about, what the important dimensions of competitiveness are. It is useful to distinguish between markets and marketing. Markets, but not necessarily marketing, should be thoroughly understood by operations managers. As Skinner (1978) has pointed out, the focused plant, which concentrates its operations resources on a particular market, outperforms the unfocused plant.

Order winners one year may not remain order winners for another year. Evolution takes place as competitors seek to catch up and as technology develops. One way in which this evolution takes place is through the product life cycle.

2.6 Product life cycle

The **product life cycle (PLC)** appears to be a universal phenomenon, and we discuss it further in Unit 2. Marketers often identify four or five stages through which a product passes. The linking of marketing strategy with life cycle stages is well established. But operations also can be linked to the life cycle stages. It makes sense to combine both the marketing and operations implications of life cycle stages on one diagram, as in Figure 10 (see page 33). The product goes through development, growth, maturity and decline phases. Some products may move through the PLC in a few weeks, others may take decades. If you show a graph of volume against time, the characteristic shape of a PLC is an elongated S. In its development stage, small quantities will be produced and the emphasis is on design and innovation. As it reaches this growth stage, large quantities are produced at a smaller unit cost. This levels out in the maturity stage. You can see the implications for operations management at all stages of the life cycle as particularly process, procedures and delivery mechanisms must change.

Corresponding with each stage of the PLC, we comment on several factors of competitiveness. In addition, to make the link with the next section, we comment on **process**. Process in this context means the way in which operations are physically arranged and the appropriate selection of technology. We are not suggesting all products evolve through having to adopt particular technologies or layouts at various stages of their PLC. However, one particular choice of layout or technology will probably be compatible with marketing strategy at various stages of the PLC.

An operations manager should appreciate that he or she needs to adapt throughout the PLC. You should refer back to Figure 10 when you are reading each unit, as this figure integrates many of these concepts we deal with throughout the module.

2.7 Volume variety matrix and product process matrix

A most useful way of viewing operations management is through the **product process matrix** (Hayes and Wheelwright, 1984). Here product dimensions of **volume** and **variety** are arranged along the horizontal axis, and **process** is arranged on the vertical axis from project to continuous flow. This is shown in Figure 11.

Briefly, we can explain **process** types as follows. The **project** form of process brings resources to the project, rather than bringing the project to the place of work. A classic case is a civil engineering project, such as building a bridge. On a smaller scale, the launch of a new product has similar characteristics.

In a **job shop** work is organised around similar skills; in a factory all the lathes may be grouped together; or in an office all the accountants work in the same section. Typically the job shop undertakes a large variety of tasks with little similarity from day to day.

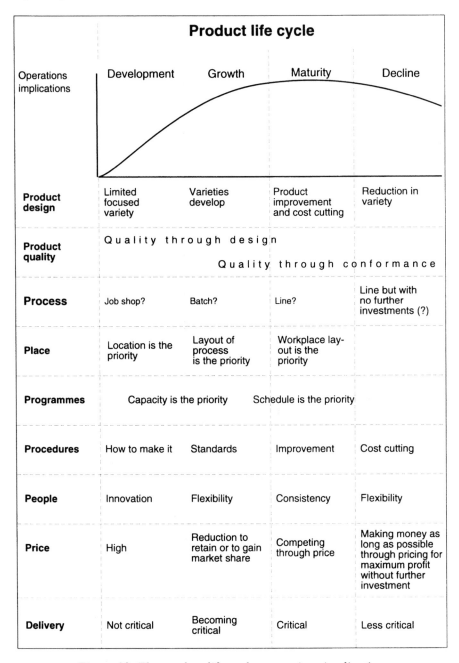

Product life cycle			
Operations implications	Development	Growth	Maturity	Decline
Product design	Limited focused variety	Varieties develop	Product improvement and cost cutting	Reduction in variety
Product quality	Quality through design		Quality through conformance	
Process	Job shop?	Batch?	Line?	Line but with no further investments (?)
Place	Location is the priority	Layout of process is the priority	Workplace lay-out is the priority	
Programmes	Capacity is the priority		Schedule is the priority	
Procedures	How to make it	Standards	Improvement	Cost cutting
People	Innovation	Flexibility	Consistency	Flexibility
Price	High	Reduction to retain or to gain market share	Competing through price	Making money as long as possible through pricing for maximum profit without further investment
Delivery	Not critical	Becoming critical	Critical	Less critical

Figure 10: The product life cycle: operations implications

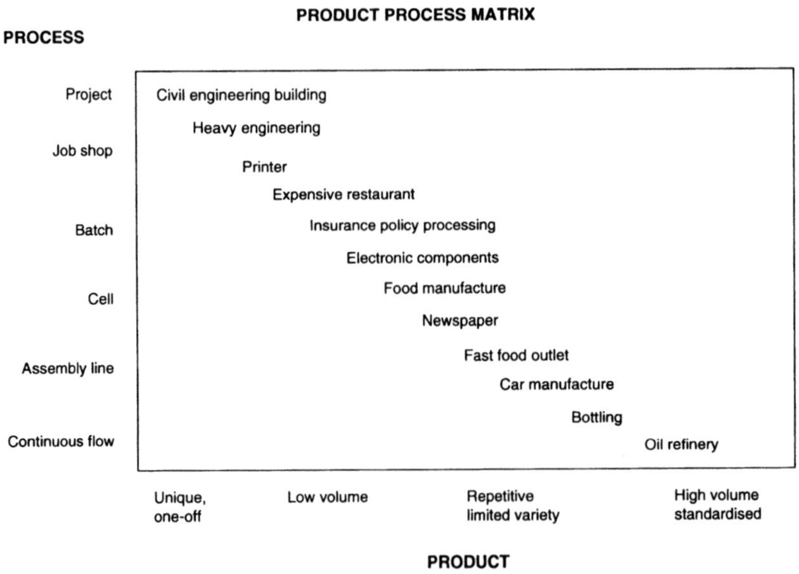

PRODUCT PROCESS MATRIX

PROCESS

Project	Civil engineering building	
	Heavy engineering	
Job shop	Printer	
	Expensive restaurant	
Batch	Insurance policy processing	
	Electronic components	
Cell	Food manufacture	
	Newspaper	
Assembly line	Fast food outlet	
	Car manufacture	
	Bottling	
Continuous flow		Oil refinery

| Unique, one-off | Low volume | Repetitive limited variety | High volume standardised |

PRODUCT

Figure 11: The product process matrix

In **batch** processes, the layout arrangement is similar to the job shop but more attention is paid to the flow of work. Here, as the name suggests, work is done in batches. In a factory, canning beans for several days may be followed by canning peas for several days. In an office, application forms for admission to university, for example, are processed in groups.

An **assembly line** takes specialisation further and tends to be more highly automated as is appropriate to higher volumes. The car assembly line is the classic case, but offices too may have assembly lines for cheque clearance. Finally, **continuous flow** processes found in the chemical industry. In this module we will work our way down the processes on the vertical axis, covering each type in some detail. It is important to realise that each position can be directly related to the dimensions of competitiveness.

A **cell** is a half-way stage between batch and assembly line. In a cell, all the machines necessary for a particular product or assembly are arranged in sequence close to one another so that 'one-piece flow' is possible. All machines in the cell are set up together to create the equivalent of one large machine. As soon as an operation is completed on one machine the product is passed to the next machine without having to wait for a batch to accumulate.

All types of organisation are arranged on the diagonal. Notice that there is a rough correspondence between the stages of the PLC as regards volume, and with the process remarks we made in the PLC Figure 10. Notice also that the regions at the top right and bottom left are blank. This is because they are mainly infeasible; it would be uneconomic to run an assembly line for one-off production or to operate a job shop for high-volume production. Having said that, note that pressures are continuing to build for low cost, which tends to be associated with assembly line or flow operations and for high variety. This is now beginning to be achieved through 'mass customisation' techniques, a topic that we cover in Unit 9.

We can also use the product process matrix to view appropriate approaches to scheduling, this is central to operations management. This is shown in Figure 12. The positions shown for the scheduling techniques are approximate, and overlap. We discuss critical path methods in Unit 5. We discuss Just-in-time (JIT) techniques in Unit 9. We discuss optimised production technology (OPT) in Unit 7 and material requirements planning (MRP) in Unit 4. You may also have covered simulation and linear programming in your previous studies in quantitative methods. You should note at this stage that different scheduling techniques are appropriate to different circumstances, and that, often, a combination of techniques is necessary to tackle a product/process combination adequately. It will be useful for you to return to this figure as you progress through the various units.

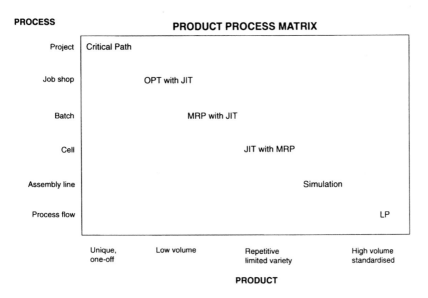

Figure 12: The product process matrix and scheduling

In Figure 13 the relationship between product, process and types of automation is shown. 'Flexible automation', meaning the integration of robots, automatic guided vehicles, computer numerically controlled (CNC) machines, together with computer-aided design (CAD) and computer-based materials management systems, have gained much interest over the past decade. Unfortunately, much of the potential has still to be realised and several companies have had problems by investing too early.

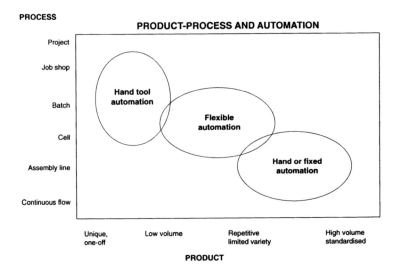

Figure 13: The product process matrix and automation

2.8 Quality and productivity

Increasingly, managers understand that quality and productivity are partners not alternatives. As Deming (1986) has pointed out, improved quality cuts defect rates, which mean less waste, which means improved productivity, which means less cost, which means reduced prices, which expands markets, which creates more work. Improving quality and productivity have rightly become a, (or perhaps the), central concern of operations managers.

Operations managers have realised that they cannot achieve quality and productivity goals by themselves. A total organisational effort is required. Quality received an enormous boost in the late 1980s with the widespread adoption of total quality management (TQM). This was probably one of the most significant developments for operations managers. The pursuit of quality in all its various forms, from design to conformance, from speed to product availability, is an underlying theme throughout this module.

PRODUCTIVITY

Like quality, and linked to it, productivity is a central concern of operations management. Productivity is of particular relevance to marketing and finance, as we show in this section. Although productivity can be defined in general terms as being the ratio of outputs to inputs, it is appropriate for us to begin looking at productivity by first looking at changes in profitability from one period to the next. (van Loggerenberg, 1988). An accountant would view a change in profitability from one period to the next as resulting from a change in revenues and/or a change in costs, as shown in Figure 14. Here, for example, an increase in profit results from an increase in revenues or a decrease in cost, or some combination of the two.

Figure 14: Profit change: the accountant's view (1)

Changes in revenue result from changes in product quantities and/or from changes in product prices. Likewise changes in costs result from changes in resource quantities (that is the numbers of people, machines, materials, and energy) and from changes in resource costs. This is shown in Figure 15.

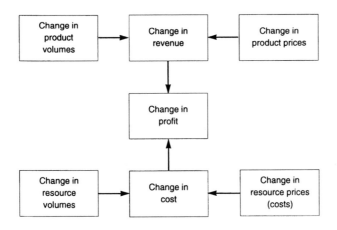

Figure 15: Profit change: the accountant's view (2)

This completes the standard accounting view. Management accountants will seek to understand deviations from budgets by variances in each of these four areas. Operations managers are generally more interested in productivity change. We may note therefore that a change in productivity results from changes in the ratio of product quantities to changes in resource quantities. This uses the familiar definition of productivity as being outputs/inputs. Likewise we can view a change in **price recovery** as resulting from a change in the ratio of product prices to changes in resource costs (or prices).

Thus **price over-recovery** reflects a situation where prices of products are increased more than the costs of resources, and **price under-recovery** reflects the situation where the organisation absorbs some of the cost increases and does not increase the cost of its products by as much as resource costs have risen.

We can now draw the complete **nine box diagram** (van Loggerenberg, 1988), as shown in Figure 16.

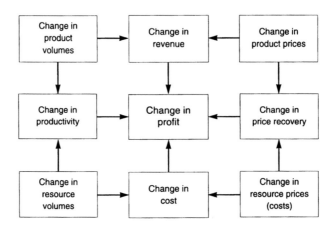

*Figure 16: Profit change: the operations manager's view, the
'nine box diagram' (after van Loggerenberg, 1988)*

Instead of seeking to explain changes in profit by the conventional accounting view of changes in revenue and changes in cost, a view more appropriate to the operations manager (and probably to the marketing manager also) can be given. This is that changes in profit result from changes in productivity and from changes in price recovery.

We can explore this further with the help of productivity grids (van Loggerenberg). In Figure 17, changes in productivity are shown on the vertical axis and changes in price recovery on the horizontal axis. No change takes place at the intersection of the two axes. A negative change in productivity is shown in the lower half of the figure; a negative change reflects a decline in the rate of productivity growth rather than an absolute decline in productivity.We can make the same comments about changes in price recovery with negative changes to the left of the vertical axis. Positive changes in profitability from one period to the next occur at any point above and to the right of the diagonal axis. Once again, a positive change means increased profit or decreased loss.

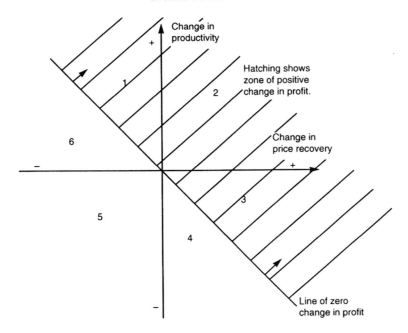

Figure 17: The productivity, price recovery grid (after van Loggerenberg, 1988)

Notice that there are three segments where positive changes to profit occur. In segment 2 both productivity change and price recovery change is positive. In segment 1 however, a negative change in price recovery is more than offset by a positive change in productivity. Clearly, this is a segment where competitive advantage is greatest. Prices are, relatively speaking, being cut whilst improved profits are being generated through productivity change. Remaining in this segment discourages competitors. The reverse is true in segment 3. Here increased profits are being generated through price increases which are offsetting a fall in productivity. Clearly, although increased profits are being made, this is the weakest position to be in. Remaining in this segment for too long represents an opportunity for competitors, particularly those whose productivity is superior.

Looking at the segments where profit change is negative, we can see a big difference between segment 6 where only a small adjustment in prices is called for, and segment 4 where the company is in considerable difficulty.

So, an operations manager, and probably a marketing manager, needs to know not just if increased profits are being made, but how those increased profits are being generated.

2.9 Universal principles

We have seen the differences in processes, automation and scheduling in the volume variety and product process matrix, we could ask if there are principles of operations management that apply across the entire matrix. Schonberger and Knod

(1994) provide one of the most useful lists of principles, applicable both to service and manufacturing operations. They contend that these principles can make a huge difference to any operations-based organisation.

A glance at the list of issues reveals great scope for the intervention of operations managers in company policy making and strategy. Here is their list of principles:

- get to know and team up with the next and final customer
- become dedicated to continual, rapid improvement in quality, cost, lead time, flexibility, variability and service
- achieve unified purpose via shared information and team involvement in planning and implementation of change
- get to know the competition and the world-class leaders
- cut the number of product or service components or operations and number of suppliers to a few good ones
- organise resources into multiple chains of customers, each focused on a product, service or customer family; create cells, flow lines and plants-in-a-plant
- continually invest in human resources through cross training (for mastery of multiple skills), education, job and career path rotation, and improved health, safety and security
- maintain and improve present equipment and human work before thinking about new equipment; automate incrementally when process variability cannot otherwise be reduced
- look for simple, flexible, movable, low-cost equipment that can be acquired in multiple copies, each assignable to focused cells, flow lines and plants-in-a-plant
- make it easier to make/provide goods or services without error or process variation
- cut flow time (waiting time), distance and inventory all along the chain of customers
- cut set-up, changeover, get-ready and start-up times
- operate at the customer's rate of use (or a smoothed representation of it), decrease cycle interval and lot size
- record and own quality, process and problem data at the workplace
- ensure that front line improvement teams get first chance at problem solving before staff experts
- cut transactions and reporting: control causes not symptoms.

Summary

In this section we looked at the partnership between operations and marketing, which is crucial to the success of an organisation. We considered the common reference frameworks they share. We began with Porter's value chain and the analysis of business operations into primary and support activities. We went on to consider the importance of a 'systems view' for operations managers. This view includes the whole process from concept to completion. We discussed open and closed systems and their features.

We then described the operations mix, the six Ps of operations, and the dimensions of competitiveness. We distinguished between order winners and order qualifiers within the competitive dimensions and mentioned the alternative Kano model.

We introduced the concept of the product life cycle and then dealt in some detail with the product process matrix. We highlighted the links between quality and productivity and looked at the analysis of changes in profitability.

We concluded with a list of 'universal' principles, applicable equally to all manufacturing and service operations, which we believe can make a big difference to any operations-based organisation.

SECTION 3

Operations Management in Manufacturing and Service Industries

Introduction

In this section we will look briefly at the functions of operations management in manufacturing and service industries. We will introduce the terms 'front office' and 'back office' and the concept of the 'moment of truth' in service organisations. We will highlight several service provisioning features: the inability to inventory; service availability; and ease of customer access.

The difference between manufacturing and service industries is largely a function of their kinds of output. Manufacturing organisations exist primarily to provide the market place with goods, which are tangible. The service provider meets needs in society but the outputs are largely intangible. In terms of the overall business structure however, there may be great similarities between manufacturing and service industries, although the deployment of resources will vary. Operations management skills and approaches are often woven into the daily working lives of functional managers who are continually concerned about the efficient use of resources under their control.

Some companies have executives with the title operations manager, or with the word 'operations' in their job title. Other companies give very different job titles such as: production manager, service manager, project manager, distribution manager or quality manager.

When we consider the job specifications of these posts, we can see that these managers are playing very significant operations management roles. The analysis of many managerial roles within organisations indicates that knowledge of and skillful application of operations management practice is essential for effective performance. Functional areas as diverse as marketing, finance, warehousing, distribution, human resource management, administration, customer liaison and research and development all require the input and control of resources to produce outputs of the right quantity, quality and at the right time. It is therefore important for both aspiring and existing business managers to study operations management. In developing skills in the approaches appropriate to their own personal area of responsibility, there is also a growing awareness of the implications which individual functional changes have for other parts of the business.

On a spectrum showing the manufacturer and the service provider at opposite ends, there is a whole continuum of combinations which can be seen in the business community. An example would be that of a fast-food catering business which would tend to be classified as in the service sector. Closer consideration however, could well show that underpinning the service counter activity, is a sophisticated manufacturing base. This produces the actual beefburgers, grows and shapes potato 'french-fries' and formulates its own speciality dressings.

In analysing the activities of service organisations, in operations management terms, two terms are often used. The **front office** activities concern the interface with the customer. This would include here the ambience of the premises, the quality of the staff attention, the speed of service as well as the food itself. The **back office** activities include the food cooking, storage and ordering, the provisioning of wrappings, staff, finance etc. The customer is unaware of most of these activities, and is unlikely to have contact with any other staff or functional area unless he or she is dissatisfied with the producer or the staff.

ACTIVITY 5

Consider a travel agent which arranges holidays for customers. Use the 'front office', 'back office' approach to the running of the business. Identify the activities which occur in each category in the agency.

Front office activities involve the shop itself:

- customer interface by phone or personally
- provision of brochures
- currency transactions and traveller's cheques
- insurance.

Back office activities would include:

- liaison with tour, holiday, airline companies and hotels
- negotiating package or hotel prices
- dealing with complaints and compensation
- promotion and marketing decisions etc.

In the provision of services, there is a point of encounter or **moment of truth** when the prospective customer meets the organisation, either face-to-face or by some other communication link, such as the telephone. A point of decision is reached when the customer decides either to continue or discontinue the process. For example, there will be a certain level of tolerance when waiting for service in a non-appointment men's hairdressing salon. A point is, however, reached when a decision to leave the premises occurs.

Many of you have probably had the experience of telephoning a service engineer and failing to get through. Usually an alternative engineer is contacted. The increasing use of the mobile telephone has to some extent eased this problem in recent years, because the engineer can answer the call from a remote location. In these situations, the special nature of service provisioning is obvious. Services are not tangible, special appointments are not always made and there can be some degree of inconvenience to the provider in setting up an arrangement.

Another feature of service provisioning is the inability to inventory the service. Once the train has departed from a station, no more revenue can be generated until the next station is reached, irrespective of seat occupation percentage. After about 10 p.m. in the evening, the seaside hotel is unlikely to get any more paying guests booking in for the night. Even if a sign is placed outside cutting the cost of an overnight stay by 50%, it is unlikely to bring in much more business and could be the cause of complaint by other customers who had agreed on the full price!

A significant change made in one part of a system will almost certainly affect other parts. The availability of the service where the customer either needs it, or can be attracted to using it almost on impulse, is important. A mobile ice-cream van in the right place, at the right time, selling quality ices at reasonable prices illustrates key operations management concepts. Associated with the provision of this facility will be planning, production, staff training, advertising and financial control. Remove any of these features and there is the potential for the failure of the business.

The simpler the ease of entry for the customer into the service, the better the chance of a successful deal or relationship. The more open the banking facilities, the greater the readiness of customers to use systems which provide automatic cash withdrawal and a bank statement. Traditional professions such as accountants and lawyers, both of which provide essential services to business and individuals, have been learning the benefits of opening up to prospective customers and removing some of their mystique and jargon. Many lawyers, for example, will allow their legal secretary or clerk to interrogate an expert system about a point of housing or inheritance legislation, to give guidance about the likely complexity and outcome.

The following list includes most kinds of services in which operations management plays a vital role:

- governmental: national and local
- educational: schools, colleges, universities, distance learning systems
- business support services: e.g. recruitment agencies, contract distributors, computing and software consultants, designers, printers, market researchers etc.
- medical care: national and private hospitals, surgeries, dispensaries
- selling: retailing, wholesaling, mail-order, door-to-door
- financial: auditing, banking, stocks and shares, insurance, capital investment
- personal: home deliveries (milk, newspapers, post, fast food), laundry, hair dressing, shoe repairing, film processing etc.

There are many common factors which are recognisable when comparing manufacturing and services in operations management terms. Where there is a different emphasis, it tends to pivot on the 'what' – 'how' relationship. Manufacturing tends to major on the tangible 'whats', whilst service tends towards the more intangible 'hows' of delivery.

Summary

In this section we looked at the functions of operations management in manufacturing and service industries. We introduced the terms 'front office' and 'back office' and the concept of the 'moment of truth' in service organisations. We highlighted several important service provisioning features and problems: the inability to inventory; service availability; and ease of customer access.

We identified service areas where operations management has a vital role to play and recognised the common factors when comparing manufacturing and services in operations management terms.

Unit Review Activity

Read the article 'Roots: the early pioneers', Resource Item 1.1. Taylor's ideas of scientific management can be regarded as the foundation for the discipline of operations management. Do you agree? Explain how his ideas and those of the other early pioneers contributed to more effective operations in manufacturing. How can these practices be applied to service industries? In answering this you will need to explain what operations management is, the transformation process, and the idea of the operations system.

Unit Summary

In this unit we introduced you to the study of operations management. We started Section 1 by pointing out that operations management has been practised since earliest times and indicated that it is concerned with the turning of the 'whats' of objectives into the 'hows' of execution and achievement. We then examined the origins of modern operations management and the historical events contributing to its development, concluding with a list of challenges that will continue to face operations managers.

In Section 2 we considered the various common reference frameworks shared by operations management and marketing. We examined the elements of the operations mix (the Ps of operations), the dimensions of competitiveness, order winners and qualifiers and the product life cycle. We discussed process types and the product process matrix view of operations management. We then highlighted the partnership of quality and productivity. Finally, we listed a number of principles which are crucial to the success of any operations-based organisation, whether service or manufacturing.

In Section 3 we looked at the functions of operations management in both manufacturing and service industries.

References

Barnett, H (1996) *Operations Management*, Macmillan, Basingstoke, 2nd edn

Cox, J, Blackstone, J H, Spencer, M S (eds) (1995) *APICS Dictionary*, American Production and Inventory Control Society, Falls Church, Virginia, 8th edn

Deming, W Edwards (1986) *Out of the Crisis*, MIT Centre for Advanced Engineering, Cambridge, Massachusetts

Elliott, B B R (1996) 'Ethical Issues in Operations Management' in Kitson, A and Campbell, R, *The Ethical Organisation*, Macmillan, Basingsoke

Gaither, N (1994) *Production and Operations Management*, Dryden Press, Orlando, Florida

Hayes, R and Wheelwright, S (1984) *Restoring our Competitive Edge*, Wiley, New York

Hill, T (1993) *Manufacturing Strategy*, Macmillan, Basingstoke

Joiner, B (1994) *Fourth Generation Management*, McGraw Hill, New York

Krajewski, L J and Ritzman, L P (1996) *Operations Management*, Addison-Wesley, Reading, Massachusetts

Lockyer, K, Muhleman, A and Oakland, J (1988) *Production and Operations Management*, Pitman, London, 5th edn

Naylor, J (1996) *Operations Management*, Pitman, London

Porter, M (1985) *Competitive Advantage*, Free Press, New York

Schonberger, R and Edward, K (1994) *Operations Management: Continuous Improvement*, Irwin, Burr Ridge, Illinois, 5th edn

Skinner, W (1978) *Manufacturing in the Corporate Strategy*, Wiley, New York

Slack, N (1991) *The Manufacturing Advantage*, Management Books 2000

Sperotto, F (1994) *In the Footsteps of Homo Industrialis*, PICSIE Press, Sandton, South Africa

Stevenson, W J (1993) *Production/Operations Management*, Irwin, Boston

Upton, D (1995) 'What makes factories flexible?' *Harvard Business Review*, July/August, pp. 74–84

Van Loggerenberg, B (1988) *Productivity Decoding of Financial Signals*, Productivity Measurement Associates, Pretoria

Waters, C D J (1991) *An Introduction to Operations Management*, Addison-Wesley, Reading, Massachusetts

Womack, J P, Jones, D T and Roos, D (1990) *The Machine that Changed the World*, Rawson Associates, New York

Recommended Reading

Barnett, H (1996) *Operations Management*, Macmillan, Basingstoke, 2nd edn

Naylor, J (1996) *Operations Management*, Pitman, London

UNIT 2
PRODUCT PLANNING AND POSITIONING

Introduction

Having begun our study of the nature of operations management and the integral role that it plays within both manufacturing and service systems, we now consider life cycles. As we have seen marketing and operations are linked through this product or service, and changes in this will affect the operations management function. This unit deals with the typical product life cycle, from concept to termination. In unit 1, you met the product life cycle, here we look at it in detail. We examine the nature of product and service life cycles and the appropriate system changes which accompany clearly recognisable phases and makes demands on operations managers. Throughout this unit, we tend to use the word 'product', however, many approaches are also relevant to a 'service'.

Objectives

By the end of this unit, you should be able to:

- understand the life cycle concept
- recognise the importance of product strategy
- appreciate the need for creativity in organisations
- follow the approaches of Research and Development (R&D)
- recognise the reasons for failure of good ideas
- understand the methodology of value analysis
- recognise the importance of the role of operations management throughout the product or service life cycle.

SECTION 1

Product Strategies

Introduction

In this brief section we will indicate the importance of a product strategy for an organisation and look at the relationship between market share and profitability. We will also look at the use of SWOT analysis in business decision making. This is obviously a very large area that you will cover in detail in your marketing and business strategy studies. Here we look at some key issues which are relevant to operations management.

Organisations exist to provide products or services which can be purchased by another organisation or an individual. Customer needs and preferences are constantly changing and at times can be very fickle. The continual advancement of knowledge and technology tends to render the product as obsolete, at least in the mind of the potential customer.

A basic rule in design would, therefore, be to design the product with both economy and quality in mind, which a customer will find attractive, be able to understand and quickly able to use with minimum risk and which delights him or her by its performance or flavour or durability etc.

In reality, few products promoted as 'new' are truly 'new'. They are usually evolutionary developments of products or services which have been around for some time. For example, the modern-day film industry had its origins in theatre, still photography, silent films, sound tracking, colour technology and video systems.

Collins and Porras (1995) claim that leaders of visionary companies concentrate primarily on building an organisation rather than on hitting a market at the right time with a visionary product idea. These leaders concentrate on building the organisational structures of a visionary company and when viewed retrospectively their greatest creation is the company itself and what it stands for, rather than the actual product or service it provided.

When a new product or service is recommended as a result of R&D, a great deal of groundwork will have been done already. The operations managers may have been involved, particularly in the applied research phase as the idea was turned into a possibility. Specialists from other functional areas will also have contributed on financial, marketing and human factors issues.

An organisation needs to develop a product strategy which integrates its mission with the strategies set out for its major functional areas: finance, marketing, operations and human resource management. A product strategy contains three elements which set down the markers for all personnel involved in product and service development:

- **Identification of the potential market segment and price range.**

For example, a fabric manufacturer may choose to operate at the luxury end of the market; a barber's shop may look for its customers from passers-by and offer a quick, cheap haircut.

- **Deciding whether few or many types of products or services are offered or carried.**

Many organisations offering a limited range to the customer, gaining a competitive edge by speed of response, delivery and price. For example, for fast-food delivery to your home you would expect to choose from a limited range menu. Other businesses gain advantage by offering immense variety, for example, the do-it-yourself (DIY) supermarket sells everything from a nail to a conservatory.

- **Deciding on the extent of product availability or service immediacy.**

This becomes a logistical problem which needs handling by operations management staff, as it is a function of the number of outlets, shops or warehouses, the opening hours, the operational and delivery systems, inventory and human resourcing.

1.1 Making decisions about the product and the market

Studies undertaken by the Boston Consultancy Group (Genus, 1995) show the relationship between market share and profitability. It formulated a law of experience by plotting the reduction in unit costs against the increases in cumulative output across a variety of businesses. The reduction in unit costs amounts to between 20 and 30% whenever cumulative output doubles. This is illustrated in Figure 1. If we plot the log of unit cost against cumulative output we obtain a straight line graph. This leads us to conclude that businesses that have the largest cumulative output and hence the largest market share will have the lowest costs. So our product strategy should be to capture as large a market share as possible. The rapid experience gained by employees reduces costs and thereby raises profitability.

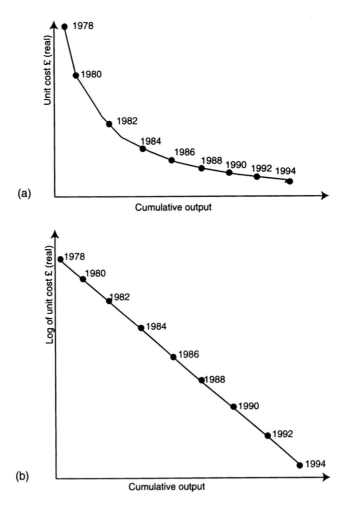

Figure 1(a) and (b): The experience curve (Genus, 1995)

ACTIVITY 1

What weaknesses can you identify in this 'law of experience'?

You might question some of the generalisations made:

- Is the law really so deterministic and predictable?
- What about the operations management techniques, skills and application level within organisations?
- How significant are creative breakthroughs?
- Is a range of 20-30% too broad for effective planning?
- To what extent does a changing external environment over time affect market share e.g. tax changes or trade embargoes?

The BCG developed their matrix further and classified products into problem child, star, cash cow and dog, depending on the market attractiveness and the product strength. The theory relies on this notion of the product life cycle. They also identified where investment should be made at particular stages on particular products. Another approach to determing product strategy is to construct a SWOT analysis. This concept – originally developed by the Boston Consulting Group as a TOWS analysis – is widely used in business decision making. The product concept has *strengths* and *weaknesses*; the external environment provides *opportunities* and *threats*.

A matrix like the one in Figure 2 is constructed to consider these issues as thoroughly as possible. The successful product strategy matches the product's strengths with the external environment's opportunities. Other strategies should be avoided as they have product weakenesses, or environment threats or both, and will not be successful.

External Environment

	Opportunities	Threats
Strengths	Match (Strengths and opportunities)	Avoid (Threats)
Weaknesses	Avoid (Weaknesses)	Avoid (Weaknesses and threats)

Product concept

Figure 2: SWOT analysis matrix

As you can see, the experience curve is not necessarily an instant answer to success and there are many other factors that come into play. Unit costs can be reduced as the output increases as the production process will probably change with the increased output. Recall the linking of the product life cycle and the process in Figure 10 in Unit 1. And a large market share gives you other advantages in pricing and distribution that affect profitability.

The BCG devised a matrix classifying products into problem child, star, cash cow and dog, depending on two parameters that they identified as market attractiveness or market growth rate and product strength or relative market share (Figure 3). In other words, an attractive market is a young growing market, and your product is strong in the marketplace if it has a large market share relative to your competitors.

For each product, we need to ask the questions: Is it in a growing market? and Is it the biggest seller in the market?

- If the product is in a growing market and is the largest competitor then it is classified as a **star**.

- If the product is in a growing market, but is not the largest competitor then it is classified as a **problem child** or question mark.

- If the product is not in a growing market but it is the largest competitor then it is classified as a **cash cow**.

- If the product is not in a growing market and is not the largest competitor then it is classified as a **dog**.

Check that you can identify these four categories using the matrix in Figure 3. The matrix is based on the concept of the product life cycle that you met in Unit 1. It also identifies what we should do with each type of product:

- **Build** to increase the market share so a problem child becomes a star.

- **Hold** to preserve the market share with a strong cash cow.

- **Harvest** to increase cash flow in the short term with a weak cash cow, a problem child or a dog

- **Divest** to sell off a problem child with no future or a dog.

Relative market share

Figure 3: BCG matrix

This is a very simplistic way of looking at product strategy, however, it does give us some basic guidelines and questions to ask.

Where a promising concept emerges, a strategy is developed which will ensure it has the maximum chance of ultimate success. Now read the article 'Strategic Innovation', Resource Item 2.1.

ACTIVITY 2

Using the article, Resource Item 2.1, identify types of product strategy that form part of an organisation's market strategy. Is innovation always the answer?

Positioning and scope are the key issues of market strategy. This links in with our breakdown of strategy into potential market segment and price range; product range; and extent and immediacy of product availability. Innovation is not necessarily the answer; the organisation needs to do what it can do well.

Once the final decision to proceed with a particular product or service is made, a range of appropriate operations management techniques should be available to move everything towards a smooth and efficient launch. We shall be looking in depth at some of these techniques in both this and later units.

Summary

In this section we looked at how organisations respond to changing customer needs and preferences through the formulation of a product strategy. We looked at the three key elements of the strategy: potential market segment and pricing; product range; extent and immediacy of product availability.

Finally, we considered the relationship between market share and profitability and the 'law of experience' and the use of SWOT analysis in business decision making.

SECTION 2

Product Planning Concept

Introduction

In this section, we look at the product planning concept and the use of a checklist to enable managers to make well-informed and consistent decisions during the development of a product. We consider the production engineering, R&D, marketing and financial aspects involved in the evaluation of a product.

2.1 Initial screening

Figure 4 shows the development of a product from initial idea to launch, with related inputs from the marketplace, research, etc.

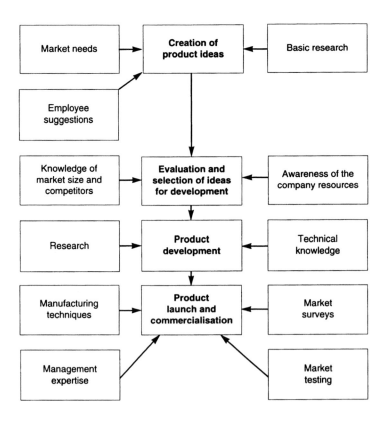

Figure 4: The product planning concept

The initial stages of product development may require the use of project network techniques to give a complete overview, with time schedules, of every activity which must be done before the launch of the new product or service into the market place (Unit 5). Forecasts will be required to identify potential output volumes and thereby enable the purchase of new machinery and materials. Processes and/or administrative systems need to be designed and the staff recruited and trained. The layout of the work area with health and safety, as well as efficiency in mind, must be planned. The work methods will need to be designed, payment schemes constructed, and quality standards clearly understood. Once the new product or service is operational, then control and feedback systems for inventory, quality and reliability will be essential to maintain high levels of efficiency and productivity.

In the process just described, we can see various phases. In practice, the first phase can be termed a 'pre-authorisation' phase. The ongoing R&D programme will produce possible ventures and projections about profitability. New ventures should be assessed and selected so that the organisation will maintain satisfactory profit and growth levels without exposing itself to unnecessary risk. BCG matrix and SWOT analysis should provide some help with the assessment.

Once a concept has been identified as having potential to meet company objectives, certain parameters need to be established:

● What will be the key parts in this venture for which special effort or resources must be made available?

● What are the potential markets, and how will the product or service be promoted in them?

● What are the major operational problems which have to be faced in completing this venture?

● How can the cost and time of this venture be minimised and controlled?

● When the venture is complete, how will it be commissioned, launched and then administered to satisfy the customers?

● In the event of lack of progress on this venture, what criteria should be used to change or abort it?

These procedures will help to ensure that, in a consistent way, the best possible ventures are selected for development. They will also identify and examine in advance potential problems and the likely duration with informed estimates of cost. The skills and techniques available in the discipline of operations management are invaluable throughout this vetting procedure. Many organisations use checklists to enable managers to make informed and consistent decisions during the initial screening process and the ongoing development of a project. Whilst economic factors are important, other qualitative issues must also be considered. Numerical evaluation, to pull together what are often highly subjective views, is common.

The use of a checklist is valuable because management must:

- recognise and examine potential problems which will arise
- estimate the size of the market and forecast likely returns
- determine the cost of development
- produce a time schedule for the project.

Figure 5 illustrates the importance of careful decision making at the earlier stages of product development.

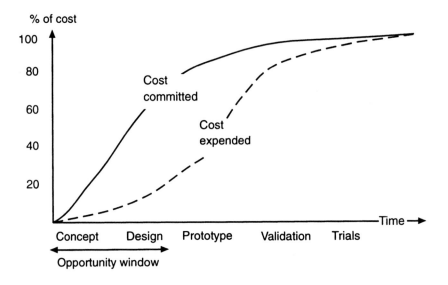

Figure 5: Costs committed and expended in the early stages of product development

During the stages of concept and design, the committed costs build up rapidly. These include manufacturing changes, production costs, quality and materials costs, labour costs, handling costs etc.

The role of the operations manager, and the information produced by the use of various techniques, are invaluable in many stages of a checklist evaluation.

A checklist should include the following features:

- Production and engineering factors
    - size of the business
    - raw materials and components
    - technical capability and competence
    - disposal of potential waste and by-products
    - location

- health, safety and risk
- product stewardship
- R&D factors
  - research team experience
  - patenting
- Marketing factors
  - product or service characteristics
  - market research
- Financial factors

We look at each of these groups of factors in turn, and examine the different roles of operations management. However, remember that as with all simplistic ways of dealing with complex issues, there is a danger of oversimplifying. A checklist is just what it says it is, it is there to remind you that all the key factors have been considered in the decision-making. It is not a magic list, where all the 'ticks' mean success!

2.2 Production and engineering factors

SIZE OF THE BUSINESS

Some products can be produced by companies which operate with low overheads and which are satisfied by making a small profit on each unit sold or service provided. Such companies are able to undersell larger companies operating in the same business area. However some R&D ventures can only be exploited by a large, technically sophisticated company which is at the leading edge of its area of business.

The operations management role here would be to appraise the concept carefully in the light of the ability of the organisation to make or provide the envisaged product or service at a profit. Some concepts will be discarded or perhaps sold off to more suitable organisations as a result. The suitability of existing plant or facilities must be evaluated, as must the availability of new plant or facilities if there is a need to provide them for the project.

RAW MATERIALS AND COMPONENTS

If the raw materials required can be readily sourced in the right quantities, at the right price and quality, this will provide a sound basis to justify the commencement of the development phase. The operations management role here will be to work with the purchasing specialists on quality standards, to assist in the rating and choice of suppliers, and to advise upon contractual and practical issues such as just-in-time (JIT) arrangements (see Unit 4). The ideal findings should be that the raw materials or components are readily available at an acceptable price and quality, and not subject to international trade embargoes or other company monopolies.

TECHNICAL CAPABILITY AND COMPETENCE

If the proposal is just a new variant on an existing product or service, it is likely that personnel, equipment and materials will already be in place and well established in the organisation. The operational management role will concern itself largely with the process of change and the determination of new standards. Where the proposal introduces new concepts, possibly involving new and little proved technology, evaluation is much more complex. Inevitably, with little background data, decisions will be made on what is factually available combined with the considered opinion of specialists. Here, a subjective approach like the Delphi technique may be helpful. We discuss this later in the module (see Resource 2.3). An up-to-date 'expert system' may also be used (see Unit 7).

The putting together of a design proposal will involve:

- performance requirements
- definition of the quality standards to be met
- clarification of the expected look and size of the product
- maximum selling price per unit of product or service
- time-scales and stages for development
- quantities of product or levels of service forecast
- specification of any safety features needed.

DISPOSAL OF POTENTIAL WASTE AND BY-PRODUCTS

The environmental response to the eventual introduction of an envisaged new product must be considered. It will be necessary to remove waste from a manufacturing site, or to discharge fluid effluent into the drains, or fumes into the atmosphere. Initial proposals which take account of the likely quantities and nature of waste need to be made. The operations management role in this will concern storage and safe materials-handling recommendations.

Where a service for the community is proposed, its acceptability must be carefully assessed. Environmental pollution can be viewed legally or ethically. Something can be banned or severely restricted if serious offence or inconvenience is caused to the general public or to local residents. Careful marketing can help to prepare the way for smooth introduction of the service.

Good conceptual environmental thinking makes a by-product of one process into a key component of another, perhaps entirely different, product. The creative thinking skills and ingenuity of operations management personnel can help in this process.

LOCATION

The site at which production is planned, or the service provided, can be evaluated (see Unit 3). Geographical location can be a critical factor in achieving ultimate financial success. If the site is suitable for the purpose, strategically near suppliers and/or customers, with all the necessary service provisioning, then the new venture will start from as good a base as possible.

When there is a need for management to evaluate the appropriateness of facilities and choose locations which will prove economically advantageous, the approaches and techniques of operations management greatly assist the decision-making process.

HEALTH, SAFETY AND RISK

Laboratory evaluation is necessary where toxic fumes, explosive fumes or corrosive effluent is expected to be part of a new process. Operational management decision making will be required on the best way of handling and controlling any unpleasant or potentially dangerous features. The advice of external specialists may be required (e.g. the emergency services) and the legal aspects identified. A hazard and operability study can be conducted by operations management staff. Resource 2.4 gives you some idea of this, but we do not need to go into detail here.

PRODUCT STEWARDSHIP

This involves responsibility for all the environmental issues associated with a product from the design, through development, manufacture, usage and ultimate disposal or scrapping. Whilst a company may be guided in some areas by legislation, there will be many aspects in which policies need to be designed and controls introduced. The major impetus towards the drive for better stewardship is caused by the desire to reduce company liability. In these days of increasing litigation, a company needs not only to have taken every reasonable precaution in the manufacture of the product, but also to show that it has acted responsibly throughout and taken the relevant health, safety and environmental issues fully into account.

2.3 Research and Development (R&D) factors

RESEARCH TEAM EXPERIENCE

A well-balanced, highly trained and experienced R&D team inspires greater confidence by senior company management. The members of the team need to be able to fully research their specialisms, nationally and internationally. There must be capability of undertaking the appropriate level of experimental and analytical methods, whilst maintaining open channels of communication with staff in other functional areas. The high level of experience necessary in some situations is rarely achievable within one organisation; this has consequently led to many kinds of partnership agreements.

PATENTING

If there is a company policy on patenting, a decision will need to be taken to investigate the likelihood of a successful application to the appropriate Patent Office. If this is possible, then the required documentation, and technical drawings must be produced and costs of the application met. There may be considerable waiting time before the granting of a patent, and there is no guarantee of a successful outcome.

Decisions regarding the timing and launch of the project become both sensitive and critical during this period. In a highly charged and rapidly developing competitive market, risks must often be taken. Operations management staff involved in the production, quality, inventory, and distribution of a new product will be active in evaluating each set of circumstances.

2.4 Marketing factors

PRODUCT OR SERVICE CHARACTERISTICS

It will be necessary for the marketing function to evaluate the new product or service in various ways. A start must be made on producing technical literature which will form the basis of the promotional push. Unfortunately, regular revisions may be requiried as the R&D work leads to modifications.

The information that is produced for 'the trade', may differ greatly from that made available for the customer. A new type of kitchen appliance, for example a cooker hood to extract fumes, will require instructions for the installer and a leaflet for the customer. The installer needs precise technical details and diagrams so that the appliance can be rapidly and safely installed. The customer needs a simple illustrated explanation of how the product works, how it must be maintained and what to do if it goes wrong.

MARKET RESEARCH

This special aspect of R&D is usually conducted by the marketing function, sometimes with the assistance of external consultants. It is possible to research the opinion of potential customers at any stage of R&D and to include the findings as part of the decision-making process. Information on the likely volume of sales and an acceptable selling price will influence actions taken by other functional areas. For example, there may be pressure on the operations managers to reduce the initial manufacturing or distribution costs, or to improve quality.

General marketing intelligence items which will be required are:

- state of the economy
- levels of business activity
- company take-overs, mergers and bankruptcies
- government policies and legislation
- restrictive practices and trade quotas
- availability and supply of raw materials
- current costs: materials, components and distribution
- time size of the market 'window of opportunity'
- availability of human and other resources
- possible changes in price levels
- future changes in technology
- organisation's policies and corporate plan.

2.5 Financial factors

The financial decision making during R&D will play a major and significant role. Each financial appraisal of an ongoing product development will build on the previous ones and will become increasingly detailed. Ultimately, the company is looking for a satisfactory return on the investment in an uncertain future. If it is available, sophisticated financial computer modelling can be used to provide this information. This approach allows the rapid production of a series of evaluations based on differing scenarios but using consistent criteria.

Summary

In this section, we looked at the product planning concept and the setting up of a range of parameters for a particular venture. Checklists enable managers to make well-informed and consistent decisions during the development of a product, however, they should be used with care. We considered production engineering, R&D, marketing and financial aspects involved in the evaluation of a product development.

SECTION 3

Product Life Cycle

Introduction

In this section we consider the product life cycle from an operations management perspective, from concept to termination. You met the product life cycle in Unit 1. Various creative thinking approaches will be described and we will outline the six phases in a value analysis approach. We begin with the R&D programme that leads us to the product life cycle itself.

3.1 Stages of an R&D programme

It is helpful, from an operations management perspective, to examine the R&D process as a series of stages. In reality the process is often more complex than this. Stages often merge, more than one product may be developed at the same time, or the sequence may be changed for good technical reasons and some iteration is inevitable. Figure 6 shows a suggested breakdown of the stages in typical sequence. Figure 7 identifies the three key stages in the product life cycle itself.

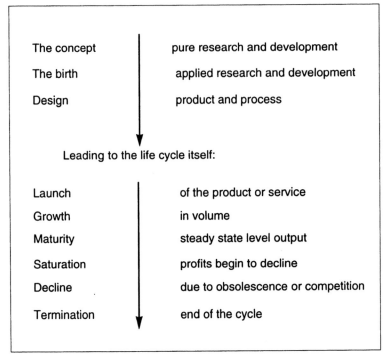

Figure 6: The stages of an R&D programme

THE CONCEPT

We can identify the differing roles of operations management throughout the life cycle. Manufacturers of high technology products are increasingly involving their operations managers in discussions with customers to construct new product ideas. This enables early consideration not only of the design of the product, but also of the processes which will be required to achieve the desired quality and quantity levels. Where requirements are found to be technically too difficult or expensive, it is possible to advise the customer quickly and agree a change to different, but attainable criteria.

The presence of operations managers greatly facilitates realistic determination of the likely product costing. Product planning can be undertaken with a great deal more confidence when customers seem to be talking in the same terms as the operations managers who will be charged with the responsibility of delivering the

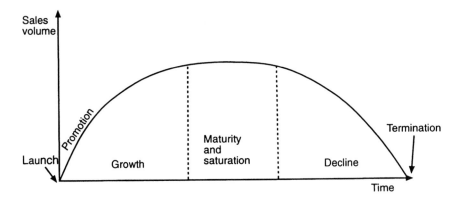

Figure 7: The product life cycle

product. Providing access to design and operations management staff tends to build confidence in the customer and to build more and stronger links across the boundary into the external environment.

The development process will need to be rigorously controlled, and operational management techniques such as network planning can assist in achieving this. There is always some reworking or various modifications required to achieve compatibility within the product or the components of a service. Few designs are entirely new or novel. The majority use familiar materials, styles and sizes, often in new combinations.

Careful and astute decision making during the development phase will result in acceptance of some issues at appropriate points rather than proceeding unnecessarily. Proceeding may lead to little being achieved, but costs will have been involved. If time targets are set out clearly, the minds of members of R&D personnel can be focused.

MORPHOLOGICAL ANALYSIS
The product or service may not be totally new, but is an amalgam of well-proven features put together in a new format. A creative thinking technique like morphological analysis is used to achieve this.

ACTIVITY 2

Study Resource 2.5 and use a morphological analysis matrix to create a new tooth cleaner using the following dimensions: form; function; context; users; and container.

You could have come up with something like the following matrix with a number of variables:

Dimension	Variables				
Form	paste	gel	powder	cream	solid
Function	polish	protect	clean	whiten	
Context	bathroom	travel	anywhere	morning	
Users	children	anyone	adults	elderly	pets
Container	tub	tube	bottle	spray	tin

This matrix provides a large number of possible combinations which can be researched. Some combinations will be physically impossible and therefore excluded, for example, a solid in a spray container.

A gel which genuinely whitens teeth, which can be discreetly used anywhere by the elderly out of a tube, could prove a good commercial proposition! Nothing however about it may be entirely new if and when it is ever launched.

Launch

When a completely new product or service is launched, the external environment may treat it as a novelty and demand may be slow to rise. Unit prices are relatively high and there are probably few competitors. At this stage the roles of marketing, in promotion, and technical services, in designing out any initial problems, will be vital. As demand rises, there is accelerated potential customer interest which must be tapped into using the principle of positive feedback to create a growth system. Operational management must gear up with this to satisfy the rising demand. It is essential that quality, timing and price criteria are met.

Growth

As the product or service becomes more standardised, there is a tendency for prices to fall and strong competitors begin to appear. Pressures exerted by the external environment lead to company mergers, or firms leaving the marketplace. These pressures may centre upon particular issues such as safety, price, quality, distribution or customer care. As the product or service becomes established, the best designs survive, are further developed and sales volumes rise.

Maturity and saturation

Eventually other manufacturers or service providers or importers come into competition in the market place, and a saturation level is reached. This level is unlikely to be raised however much promotion is undertaken, and only existing customers are served on a replacement or repeat basis. If, for example, on a product basis, 95% of the UK population owns a TV set, and this percentage has remained constant for the past ten years, it is unlikely to suddenly rise towards 100% ownership. Some households may not own a TV due to poverty, and unless they win on the National Lottery, are unlikely to be able to afford to purchase, licence and maintain a set. Other households choose not to own a TV set for religious or cultural reasons although they could afford one.

When a service is considered, we again see the questions of maturity and saturation emerging. Traditional daily milk deliveries to houses in the UK reached their peak in the post-war period between 1950 and 1970. The emergence of large food stores selling discounted milk has resulted in a rapid decline in the numbers of private delivery services. Some areas are no longer served, to the disadvantage of some potential customers.

The stages of maturity and saturation then portray a well-established product or service with its market share, but facing a growing number of competitors. The product or service is reasonably priced and gives satisfaction, but the problem of new market opportunities must be faced. Sales are bound to level off, unless there is a need for repetition or replenishment by existing customers. It is here that product strategy again becomes important.

Decline
In the final stage of a life cycle, when decline sets in, there are often attempts made to revitalise the product or service in order to prolong the life cycle. This is done by strategies such as: re-designing it, re-packaging it, improving the quality and reliability, reducing its cost, attempting to enter new markets or devising competitions with prizes to attract interest. After producing packets of mints in a virtually unchanged format for many years, a major manufacturer introduced two sister products to the market inside a six-month period, spearmint flavour and extra-strong mints.

If we construct the product life cycle curves of this strategy (Figure 8) , they show little halt to the decline of the traditional product but increasing sales of the new products to generate higher cumulative sales.

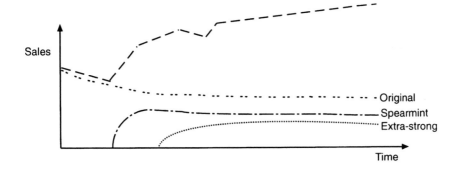

Figure 8: life cycle curves for competing mint products;
profit levels are indicated by the dotted lines

PRODUCT REJUVENATION

By considering the rejuvenation of a product or service, a company may find it possible to recover a lost market share and rebuild profit levels. New product or service ideas usually appear to be attractive and have greater potential. Whilst this will be true in many situations, the availability of a rejuvenation strategy operating alongside a development programme could have distinct benefits. Such a strategy would require senior management support, staffing and finance. Many issues will need careful analysis and ways must be found to turn decline into growth.

These issues include:

- precise identification of the reasons for the decline and the generation of proposals to halt this
- possibility of the external environment accepting the re-launch of a rejuvenated product or service
- need for market research to determine what the name or image of the business, product or service conveys to customers
- identification of gaps in the market-place and whether there are strong potential competitors for the business
- consideration of ways of adding further value to the product or service, ideally at minimal or no extra cost.

As you will see later in this section, the techniques of value analysis and value engineering are important in product rejuvenation.

Some very simple products or services do not seem to go through a life cycle in the way we have described. If there is a cycle it is a very long one which at least initially, suggests it could continue in the steady state phase virtually indefinitely. A paper clip, for example, is now available in different shapes, sizes and colours. It is however instantly recognisable as a paper clip, and performs the same function as the basic item, but at an increased cost. A service job, such as window cleaning, continues to be performed in much the same way as it has been done for generations. There has been experimentation with rubber blades and spray-on polishes, but the traditional chamois leather and bucket of water are still favoured, with cost, quality and speed in mind.

ACTIVITY 3

Can you think of a product and a service which was once well established, but now no longer exists or operates? Why is it no longer in favour or necessary?

There are many examples of obsolete products or services. Word processsors and computers have replaced typewriters; calculators have replaced slide rulers; tennis presses are no longer required to keep graphite rackets in. You will probably think of many other examples.

3.2 Product life cycle in greater detail

We have looked at the overall product life cycle. Now we look at it in more detail and see how the different functional areas including R&D and operations management are required to play differing roles at differing stages. It would be helpful at this stage to read the article 'Life Cycle Engineering', Resource Item 2.2, to get a useful overview. Don't be confused by the title, the article concerns life cycles themselves. Note that not all products have exactly the same life cycle profiles and normal company strategy would be to carry a range of products at any one time, each of which was at a different phase.

A car manufacturer, for example, would have some models being currently developed, some models in full production holding their share of a particular market, and other models in decline. A profile aimed at maintaining company profitability levels is shown in Figure 9.

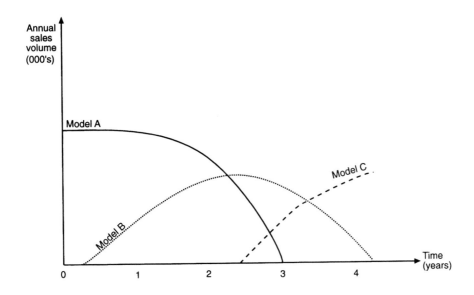

Figure 9: Profile of three overlapping car models

A similar principle would apply in a company which makes a range of different products. Seasonal factors may also be taken into account.

CONCEPT, BIRTH AND INITIAL DESIGN OF A PRODUCT OR SERVICE

These stages are undertaken in the context of the R&D functional area. This is the part of the organisation which co-ordinates effort towards increasing scientific knowledge and concentrating on product and process innovation. The success of an R&D function often depends upon a supportive organisational philosophy.

Three particular activities are recognisable in the R&D function of some organisations: basic research, applied research and development.

Basic research advances knowledge and may be largely conceptual. The researcher is aware of the general direction of the research and may be working towards stated objectives. Quite often discoveries are made by accident during the process. This is usually described by the term 'serendipity', a word reputedly coined in 1754 by Horace Walpole in his fairy tale *The Three Princes of Serendipity*. Serendipity is related to inquisitiveness and curiosity but also features 'good fortune'.

Many scientific discoveries have allegedly come about by chance or good fortune. For example, aniline dyes were invented as a result of a failed experiment to make quinine; hormone weed killers were discovered as a result of an investigation into the use of hormones to speed up plant growth.

Applied research takes the concept or innovation and moves it into the realms of potential commercial usage. This begins the process of turning the 'what' of pure research into a practical 'how'. New facets are often revealed which provide invaluable information. Every feature of the potential product or service must be brought into focus. Building sound business relationships with possible suppliers can begin as early as this phase.

Development takes the product or service up to and through the launch. Many modifications to the design may be required to develop acceptability to the customer or client. This often lengthy phase involves test marketing and the application of considerable production engineering skills in the case of a product, and possibly extensive system engineering, in delivering a service. The designer needs to achieve a result which meets the criteria of specification, cost, quality and delivery. All of these criteria are areas of interest to operations management staff.

The importance of good mutual understanding and co-operation between personnel involved in both R&D and other functional areas cannot be overstated. Figure 10 illustrates the interactions which occur.

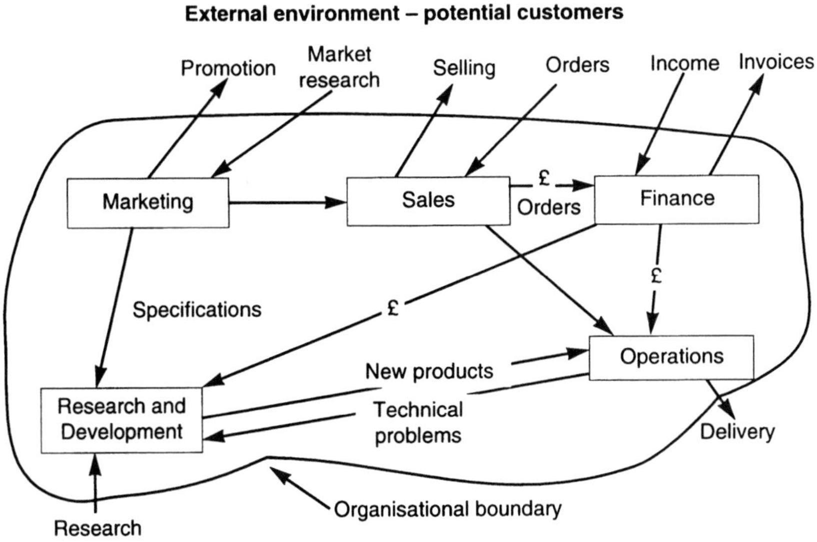

External environment – potential customers

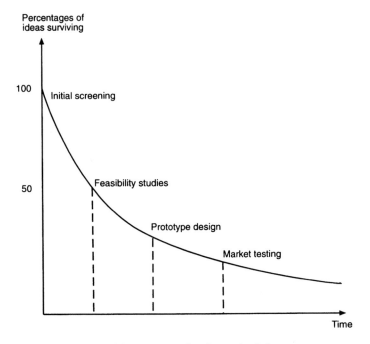

Figure 10: Systems diagram illustrating the communication processes which occur during an R&D project

Where the actual stages of R&D cover a long time period there is greater opportunity for the gradual elimination and termination of projects to occur. A decay curve illustrates this process (Figure 11).

Figure 11: An example of a typical decay curve

Regardless of the product itself, failure of an R&D programme can be because of one or more of the following reasons:

- lack of continuing financial support
- R&D staff are unable to handle the programme
- senior management require significant outcomes too quickly
- actual research facilities are inadequate
- friction between R&D and other functional areas
- poor quality management skills shown by the head of R&D
- no high level patron of R&D at board level.

There may be other reasons for failure depending on the product, the company or the environment. The benefits of successful R&D can be immense, but the risks of not being able to complete and commercially exploit something can prove to be a threat to the existence of an organisation. There must be a policy to exercise control in the context of uncertainty, with a framework provided for staff. An example would be:

- The board of directors, in consultation with the R&D manager and other senior functional managers, should draw up a time and expenditure budget for each individual project.
- The financial director or company accountant should introduce a regular reporting system covering expenditure on all items on both an individual and cumulative basis.
- Quarterly control meetings vested with the authority to make continuation or termination decisions on the project must be planned. Full consultation by staff and a review of progress must be part of this process.
- When a project is terminated, another is fed into the programme.
- Steps must be taken to maintain the staffing establishment in the R&D department.

We tend to think of R&D in the context of large corporations, however, it can also occur in small companies on a much less grand scale, where perhaps just one person is involved. The output of product R&D can lead to patenting, but this is itself fraught with complexities in a fiercely competitive international market. Some multinational companies, even apparently ethical ones, exploit loopholes in order to compete in the marketplace. Some countries apparently ignore the blatant, almost identical, copying of foreign products, in order to develop their own economies. Costs to the misled consumer are, of course, lower. Even if the cost of components and processing are identical, no contribution towards R&D costs needs to be built into the price. The implications for the original developer are obvious.

With these issues in mind, many companies are now foregoing the patenting procedures, even in developed countries. The time-scale involved, the divulging of essential details and the sophistication of modern industrial espionage means that immediate commercial exploitation is necessary to maximise financial returns.

With the right kind of launch and back-up, a great deal of revenue can be generated before copies begin to flood the market. As this happens the price will usually drop, sometimes very steeply. In the public mind there will be a continuing association of the product with the originator, which may be of continuing advantage.

Further design may be required in this development phase to fit the product or service to the needs of the marketplace, whilst ensuring that the organisation is capable of delivering or making it. This will be undertaken by designers, engineers, operations managers, market researchers and administrators.

The launch will be arranged by the marketing function with the full support of other functional areas. The operations managers, for example, will ensure that a stock of products is held, and a delivery system available. Accountants will be administering the financial aspects of promotion and launch. Office managers will have built up the staff levels to cope with the anticipated demand for a new service.

Let's take a closer look at several important approaches to product design and development

3.3 Value analysis

Value engineering and value analysis are procedures developed over the last 50 years for optimising the worth and cost of the functions or parts of a product or service. The value of something is seen as the provision at the least cost of an essential function or service, at the appropriate time and place, with the required quality and reliability.

Value engineering is concerned with building value into a product or service as it develops. Where this has been done rigorously, there will only be scope for later application of value analysis if certain factors change; for example, if new materials are developed during the life cycle of a long-running product or service.

Value analysis is concerned with challenging the value of existing and often well-established products or services, with a view to improving them.

The value of something has to be defined relative to other criteria. We value the refreshing qualities of an ice lolly relative to the weather conditions, the availability of a shop and our ability to buy one. Things can be more critical in value terms. A man dying of thirst in the desert would offer all he possesses for the ice lolly, which will keep him alive until other help arrives.

Designers using a value engineering/analysis approach see 'value' in four different ways: cost value, use value, esteem value and exchange value.

- **Cost value**: this is the total cost of producing the product or providing the service. It includes the cost of materials, labour, machinery and overheads which are required.

The value engineer will concentrate upon the provision of all the essential functions at the minimum cost relative to the quality level. The value analyst will identify the cost of providing each of the current functions. For example, the cost value of a quality ball-point pen is £4.

- **Use value:** this is the value of the properties and qualities built into a product or service expressed in minimum cost terms. For example, the use value of a ball-point pen is £0.10 (the minimum price of acceptable quality).

- **Esteem value:** this is the properties, attractiveness and scarcity of a product or service which create a pride in ownership or usership. It is the measure of the desire to own or use something special, rare or unique. It is what the customer is prepared to pay, and helps define the profit mark-up. Suppose the pen sells for £5, the esteem value of the quality pen is £5 – £0.10 = £4.90.

- **Exchange value:** this is the features of a product which make it exchangeable at a later date for something else, either money or another product. There may be appreciation over a period of time, for example, antiques, works of art; other products depreciate, for example, mass-produced cars.

  If there is a market created by collectors of quality 'old-fashioned' ball-point pens in 10 years time, our quality pen may have an exchange value equating to £10 at present values. If so, we can calculate the exchange value as: £10 – £5 = £5 appreciation.

In order to be attractive to potential customers, a product or service must satisfy a particular need. It must function efficiently and meet certain acceptable quality criteria. To be successful commercially, the product or service must be sold at a cost which provides a margin of profit, and which is affordable by customers.

There are many reasons why customers feel that something is of 'poor value'.

ACTIVITY 4

List reasons why you might say that a domestic product of your choice was of 'poor value'.

Suppose you had chosen a toaster capable of toasting two pieces of bread. You might see poor value if the toaster:

- has an electric flex which is permanently contorted
- achieves uneven browning on both sides of the bread
- has an ill-fitting crumb tray at the bottom
- has slots which do not cope with all sizes of bread
- has a frame which gets hot and can burn.

The customer rarely has the opportunity of using an appliance like a toaster before purchasing it. You might rely on consumer reports, or the recommendation of friends. Often, however, the purchase is made without any referencing and the problems are discovered through usage. A dissatisfied customer is unlikely to buy anything else from those particular manufacturers and could bring adverse publicity by word of mouth or through the media.

Perhaps the items relating to poor value arose from any of the following typical criteria?

- inadequate time allocated to design and development
- lack of skill in the design team
- ingrained attitudes at the company
- poor market research and consumer evaluation
- purchase of relatively cheap raw materials.

We can consider the provision of poor value services; think out the 'why?' question in detail.

ACTIVITY 5

Why might you describe work done by your solicitor in connection with your house sale or making a will as 'poor value'?

You might have listed the following issues:

- lack of urgency and general inertia, he or she would get back to you tomorrow
- inability to explain legal entities in layman's language
- flaws in printed legal documents, your name mis-spelt
- apparent non-availability of the solicitor when you needed him or her, they were 'in a meeting'.

VALUE ANALYSIS METHODOLOGY

We need to identify the 'value' of our existing product or service. We can do this with a value analysis methodology which can be undertaken in six phases:

- selection and setting of criteria
- information gathering
- critical examination and speculation
- evaluation and development
- reporting, planning and implementation
- review.

We now discuss each of these phases.

The whole process tries to answer five basic questions about the product or service:

- What *is* it?
- What does it *do*?
- What does it *cost*?
- What *else* will do it?
- What will that *cost*?

It also tries to overcome many ingrained habits within a design team. This is a challenge because there is often a tacit recognition of constraints which should really have been questioned a long time ago. These are often described as 'roadblocks' because no further progress can be made in a particular direction because it is assumed, perhaps wrongly, that there is no possible benefit in going along that particular route. Probably, at some time in the past, the proposition was true. The error is in the assumption that the environment remains static and constant.

STRUCTURE OF A TYPICAL VALUE ANALYSIS TEAM

One of the strengths of value analysis is the team approach. Usually a team leader is appointed to the project. The team leader may be a member of staff with the appropriate technical and human resource management skills, or an external consultant. The leader will probably be the only person who devotes full-time working hours to the project. The other team members will divide their time between working with the team and their normal functional duties.

The structure of a typical team consists of:

- team leader – line manager/designer/consultant
- designer
- operations manager
- quality manager
- purchasing officer
- technologist
- accountant
- marketing planner.

The team will only be able to function effectively if it 'gels' as a group, receives support from senior management, is able to meet regularly and relates to both suppliers and customers. Some projects will inevitably be more complex than others due to the nature of the product or service under investigation. This must be appreciated and the team entrusted with the responsibility of announcing results at an appropriate time. Usually complex projects yield the greatest cost-cutting potential when using the value-analysis approach. It is important that the team is well balanced and contains members capable of both analytical and creative thinking.

GUIDELINES FOR THE SELECTION OF PROJECTS

Value analysis concerns the investigation of existing products or services which ideally have been well documented over a period of time. Selection, either by senior management or the value analysis team, will probably be based upon the following criteria :

- high cost of product manufacture or service delivery
- current low profit margins due to market conditions
- increasing competition in the marketplace
- high reject or complaint rates
- major technical manufacturing or service delivery problems
- excessive manufacturing scrap or service time wastage
- inadequate or unsatisfactory performance
- unreliability
- customer difficulties when using the product or service
- problems on the supply of raw materials or components
- quality
- complexity of the design itself.

INTRODUCING A VALUE ANALYSIS PROGRAMME TO A COMPANY

This may be done initially by an external consultant. It can be done by an existing member of staff who has been trained in the value analysis approach, but this is difficult in a traditional, long-established organisation, because change can be painful. In a newer, more dynamic company, value analysis can be introduced quickly with rapid results. Whatever the prevailing conditions, care must be taken with the initial introduction. If the whole venture is handled badly, erroneous messages sent out, poor standards set, then the momentum and potential will be lost.

Whether the introduction is from within the company or from a consultant, the following steps should be followed:

- Provide senior management with information on value analysis and follow by a seminar
- Repeat the process for middle managers
- Set up short courses for middle managers from different functional areas. Work through case studies, examine potential projects within the company. Begin to develop certain value-analysis 'rules' or principles. For example, personal criticism of designers is avoided.
- Discuss the selection of potential team members and the time implications for current work within the functional areas. The tendency to put incompetent or 'spare' staff into the team must be resisted. Ideally, the team should contain a blend of youth and experience, both men and women, and above all, people with the right attitudes and abilities for the task.

- Approach any potential team members who are not middle managers and arrange introductory training for them.

- Train the team. This will involve a detailed consideration of the methodology, and the approach of value analysis. Examine further case studies possibly with the actual product itself. In the case of services, arrange field trips.

The team will practice problem-solving using both analytical and creative thinking techniques. Members will also need to develop skills in judicial thinking. Quantitative information, if correctly produced, is easy to compare and a decision easily made. Qualitative information is usually more subjective and much more difficult to handle. In a value-analysis project, the team will often be faced with decision making where there is quantitative and qualitative information. Members must learn how to deal with this.

Once the introductory and preparatory work has been completed, the team can agree a time schedule to begin its work on the first project. In practice, senior management usually allocates the first project to the value-analysis team. As time progresses, however, a good team begins to build on its successes and sets its own agenda, and chooses projects which seem to have the greatest potential benefit relative to the cost of undertaking them.

3.4 Methodology of value analysis: the six phase approach

Value analysis follows a basic six phase approach which links in with the product life cycle. We follow through each stage and examine the differing operations management role.

PHASE 1: SELECTION AND SETTING CRITERIA

There is a whole range of reasons why a particular product or service is selected for value analysis. A well-established team will probably take the responsibility for selection and go on to establish the criteria for the project. These are often referred to as the terms of reference, and may need to be consulted from time to time to prevent tangential movement or potentially excessive financial commitment. Amongst the typical terms of reference will be statements concerning the following:

- objective(s) to be specifically targeted
- desirable customer-satisfying features which need to be included
- current features which must be retained
- time factors for completion of the project
- financial constraints which exist
- person to whom the team sends its report.

It is vital to ensure that a value analysis begins only on projects which the team has the skills, scope and authority to handle. A file full of part-finished projects is very demotivating, as an R&D officer will be concerened about:

- accountability for the expenditure of time and skills
- resentment against other staff who are blocking progress
- little job satisfaction
- affect on career prospects
- general ineffectiveness.

PHASE 2: INFORMATION GATHERING

The late 20th century is witnessing an information and communications explosion as a result of new technology. The increasing use of the 'information superhighway' looks set to increase as more and more people become computer literate and begin to use e-mail and Internet in their daily work. In terms of research effort, there are not only gains in this process, there are the dangers of too much information, some of which may well be suspect.

The team must organise itself to compile all the appropriate information that is available about the product or service under consideration. Members may tend to operate within their own specialist fields, certainly to some extent. The engineer will dismantle the product into its components, and weigh, measure, classify and test everything. The accountant will look through past and present cost data to identify trends in particular aspects of cost etc.

Some teams make a positive effort so that members do not work too rigidly within their own discipline, recognising that it is easy to accept the status quo, without asking important, fundamental (but sometimes naive) questions.

The role of the team leader begins to be important during this phase. It is necessary to begin to set agendas, deal with contention or inertia within the team and keep overall momentum going. Within a short time a mass of data should be available for consideration. This will come from both internal sources within the company, from external sources such as suppliers and customers, and from research papers, academics and reports. Understandably, not everything will be compatible!

The kind of material gathered could be of the following types:
- annual production rates over the past five years
- current raw materials re-ordering arrangements
- details of staff labour costs of providing the service
- material costs for all components
- compiled lists of reported breakdowns by customers
- analysis of complaints by users
- samples of the product
- videos of the service provisioning
- quality standards: in theory and practice
- copies of accompanying documentation
- assembly times

- packaging samples and costs
- delivery and distribution arrangements
- promotion and marketing facilities and budgets.

All this data can only be assimilated through a series of team meetings and a process of collation and prioritisation. If this rather routine methodical work is not done properly, there is always the danger that rather circular paths will be taken. This will create delays on the project and add to the cost.

PHASE 3: CRITICAL EXAMINATION AND SPECULATION

Some insights can be gained by the team if members have been trained in method study and are capable of using the thorough and rigorous approach of critical examination (see Unit 7). When this is not possible the team will probably begin by defining the primary and secondary functions of the product or service.

For example, the primary function of gloss paint is to enhance appearance. The secondary functions may be to protect wood from the damp, make it easy to clean and to limit damage when furniture is moved around.

ACTIVITY 6

State a primary function, and several secondary functions for a product such as a screwdriver and a service like a taxi service.

Your answer probably included:

primary:	a screwdriver is for inserting screws
secondary:	removing screws
	mixing paint
	opening tins of paint
	testing circuits.

primary:	a taxi is for transporting you from A to B
secondary:	saving you from using your own car
	companionship when travelling
	helping you to handle heavy suitcases.

Or you may have given very different functions; this shows the value of the team approach, which results in a greater variety of responses.

Statements about function may require greater definition in order to become useful information for the value analysis team. Clothing the statement with quantitative detail from the material gathered from various sources can then be done.

For example, the primary function of a water heater is to provide hot water. When the team discover that it is designed to provide a maximum water temperature of 70 degrees Celsius, various perspectives on the nature and quality of the heating element can be gained.

Consideration of the need for all the functions we have identified can be stimulating, as can the need to introduce further functions and improve existing ones. Where large products composed of many components, or complex services embracing many sub-systems are involved it is usually necessary to handle the project in smaller parts.

For example: all the electrical aspects can be considered first, then the mechanical, finally the administrative issues; all the staffing organisation can be considered first, then the computer control system, then the documentation.

The analysis is gradually extended to include the costs of providing each function. It then becomes possible to link the value of each of these functions to the cost of providing it, and the adverse effect of omitting it from a revised design.

Speculation can be undertaken using a variety of creative thinking techniques designed to open up new perspectives. Techniques such as the following are regularly used:

- **Brainstorming** is a group technique used to generate a large number of ideas on a given topic in a set period of time. The team leader must sensitively use the appropriate level of control during the brainstorming session which lasts about twenty minutes. It is vital that participants feel psychologically safe, and that there is a strict 'no criticism or ridicule of ideas' rule. Failure in these areas will result in little creative thinking because of fear. Every idea is recorded for later evaluation, possibly using a scribe skilled in shorthand or audio/video recording. This latter approach can itself prove inhibiting as a permanent record of a spontaneous private session is permanently held and could be used in career advancement situations in later years.

- **Analogies** look for ideas which already exist in other products or systems which can be applied to the task in hand.

  The team can look for a:

  functional comparison, by asking the question, 'What else does the same as this does?' For example, in re-designing a food mixer, insights came from the examination of other mixing devices like a concrete mixer, a paint blender and a cocktail shaker.

  visual comparison, by asking 'What else looks like it ?' For example, in designing a new household dustbin, objects like jars, beer barrels and tea chests were considered to give ideas on shape, materials, external fittings, ergonomics and manufacturing technique.

  natural comparison, by asking 'How is this done in nature?' For example, observations on spiders provides data on synthetic fibres and construction technique. Radar was developed by considering how bats avoided obstacles, and waterproof coats by asking how a polar bear kept warm.

personal (role-playing) analogy can be used in certain complex situations which may have resisted other approaches, by asking each team member to imagine him or herself to be a key component in the current system or product. For example, in the design of a chemical spray to remove grease from inside an oven, one person plays the role of the grease, another the oven and another the user of the oven.

Many questions are asked of the participants:

Grease – how did you get on the oven sides?

– what keeps you on the side?

– how long have you been there?

– what don't you like?

– how would you get off if you wanted to?

Oven   – how often are you cleaned?

– what are you cleaned with?

– why does grease stick to you? etc.

● **Synectics** is a special form of analogy in which the team leader requires a deeper understanding of the psychology of the team. It has been defined as 'bringing things of different nature into connection'. It attempts to describe the psychological states which occur in a creative act. Tapping into team emotions and occasional irrationality by careful definition and re-definition of the problem often leads to new perspectives.

One aspect of synectics – *making the strange familiar* – is not far removed from analytical problem solving. When the mind is presented with something strange, the analytical approach breaks it down into ever smaller parts until is understood. The intensity of the study itself brings familiarity, and removes what may be perceived to be a threat to normality.

The other aspect – *making the familiar strange* – moves into the realm of the fantasy analogy. Whilst this has been traditionally tackled by stretching the imagination, group discussion and paper and pencil, there is an increasing tendency to use computer techniques to do this. The creation of virtual reality imagery allows exploration of concepts without the need to build a series of physical models. The pursuit of strangeness is an attempt to get new perspectives, a different view of people, needs, machines, systems etc.

A benefit of the exploration undertaken through synectics, is that the structuring and solving of problems which are outside the bounds of current technical ability, allows the team a degree of comparative ease when members mentally return into the real world of normality.

For example, a synectics group facing a question about public transport systems were encouraged to mentally distort the familiar double-decker bus into something strange. Instead of holding 70 passengers, a vehicle was required which held 200.

The team leader drew out ideas of vehicles which were three or four decks high, twice as wide, twice as long and a series of linked carriages. He or she then persisted with a set of questions which opened up the thinking further in problem-solving terms.

– 'How would this long vehicle get round corners?'

– 'How could fares be collected?'

– 'What about bridges?'

– 'How could loading/unloading be minimised?' etc.

Some of the insights gained enabled the team to see possible changes to double-decker bus design, staffing and operation.

ACTIVITY 7

In terms of 'making the familiar strange', examine issues which would arise in re-designing a ball-point pen so that it was twice as long but had its circumference reduced by half. The expected benefits would include longer life, reduced raw material usage and less scrap.

So what issues came to mind as you visualised this strange-looking pen?

How would I get it into my pocket/bag?

Could I grip it firmly?

Would it be rigid enough?

Could I accidentally injure myself with it?

Your list could be quite different, that would show the value of a team approach. You would then have to set about trying to solve such questions:

design bigger pockets/bags/pen-carriers

add a movable grip

make the case out of metal etc.

If you were wanting to design a slightly bigger or better pen, some of the answers would probably help.

- **Checklists** are used to stimulate the flow of ideas by forcing the team to answer a series of questions of the following type:

    – Is it the best shape and size?

    – What else can it be made to do?

    – Can anything be left off or out of it?

    – Can it be made safer?

– Can the system be made 'idiot-proof'?

– Is it robust enough?

– Can it cope with extra demands? etc.

All checklists suffer from the same problem. Many of the issues raised will not apply to every project, and the team needs to use considerable discernment to make the best use of their time.

Whichever techniques are used the objective is to examine the purpose and cost of each function. Caught up with this process will be the possibilities of making or providing the function cheaper, simplifying it or combining it with something else. A standard checklist may be used at this point to force the team to search out answers from the mass of data which is to hand. Questions of the following type must be answered to the satisfaction of the team leader. Where no answer is forthcoming, the speculation aspect is incomplete:

– Is there anything available which can do the job better?

– Can any part be made or replaced by a lower-cost method?

– Will standardisation of parts or procedures help?

– Could parts be bought instead of manufactured?

– Could aspects of the service be contracted out?

– How can quality be improved?

– Are the most suitable raw materials being used for the job?

– Could complex features be simplified?

It will be essential for the value analysis team to begin to consult widely from this point onwards. Technical and specialist advice beyond the capability of the team must be sought, with new angles being rigorously explored to prevent roadblocks being created. It must be recognised that not every member of staff is keen to further a process of radical change - if the change affects them personally. In fact, some people have a vested interest in covertly opposing change as it is either too uncomfortable or a threat to personal job security. The classical case of this behaviour is found in the person who is openly working in harmony with the proposals of the value analysis team, but who is subtly laying a false trail with their own expert knowledge. This trail eventually leads nowhere and soaks up time and energy, and a very reasonable proposal may eventually have to be abandoned. Other strategies involve the undermining of the credibility of the team in technical or decision-making terms through private comments to influential staff.

PHASE 4: EVALUATION AND DEVELOPMENT

This phase brings together many diverse ideas and physical components to produce a unified proposal. Regular comparison with the project terms of reference will be necessary to ensure a positive outcome.

Each potential feature of the new product or service will need to be appraised in financial, technical and human terms. The process of testing begins to further evaluate individual and combinations of features. It will not be sufficient to only consider responses from sources external to the company, but it will be necessary to work closely with all operational staff who will be associated with the venture if it is adopted.

Care must be taken to handle sensitively some typical responses which are heard in every new situation:

- 'I don't like the idea/design/colour/documentation etc.'.
- 'We tried this years ago, and it didn't work'.
- 'This is risky, its never been done before'.
- 'The staff will never agree to...'.

When a constraint or limitation on design is identified, it will be necessary to test it for validity. If valid, then it must be recognised and eventually incorporated into the proposal. To ignore it would jeopardise the possibility of a successful outcome. Actions which can be taken if a constraint occurs are:

- challenge it (question the authority who set or established the constraint, and seek to get it changed or removed by debate)
- neutralise it (produce a design which is not affected by the constraint)
- eliminate it (determine the reasons which underlie the constraint and remove them).

The amount and nature of testing and evaluation will depend upon the kind of product or service being developed. Some ventures will need to pass through a development system which will result in gradual modifications being made after operational and repair reports come in from the customer base. Other services or products will need to be as near correct as possible before launch.

The influence of the era of total quality management (TQM) through the 1980s led to the voice of the potential customer being added into the R&D process. The approach known as quality function deployment (QFD) is now widely used both in product and service development, whether through the conventional R&D or the value-analysis approach. We describe QFD in Unit 6, *Quality Management*.

The envisaged new situation may need to be evaluated using computer simulation to answer the 'what if?' kind of questions which will inevitably arise once a formal proposal is made. A re-designed product will probably be made up, certainly in model form, to illustrate important features. A service simulation can be video-recorded to enable discussion of features which may be difficult to convey in words.

In order to minimise the time taken from the product design to the product launch stages, it is necessary to begin to design the manufacturing system concurrently. This often involves the consideration of complex alternative factors and requires a team approach. Team members will require width of experience of the processing facility and skill in the use of operations management techniques. For some years concurrent design teams have worked in areas such as design for assembly and design for maintenance.

In process design, there is an increasing awareness of the importance to build ergonomic features into the product itself, the plant and equipment configurations, the work areas, the control and communication systems and the internal working environment. With good ergonomic design, less process training is needed, errors are less, quality is better and productivity is higher. The resultant user-friendly products are likely to give increased customer satisfaction and lead to an extended product life cycle time.

At this stage precise specifications can be produced. These are detailed descriptions of the product or service which will be given to the functional areas which will be charged with the responsibility of manufacture or provisioning. In the case of products, dimensions and manufacturing tolerances will be included together with details of any degree of standardisation of parts across a product range. The production of specifications enables most of the technical questions to be answered, and to ensure that, given the approval to finalise the project, the current or proposed facilities will be able to actually deliver the output.

3.5 Phases 5 and 6: product launch and growth

In understanding Phases 5 and 6 of value analysis, we return to the general R&D methodology, as the concluding aspects are identical.

At the conclusion of each project it is necessary to formally report to gain approval, plan the launch and prepare for ongoing review and maintenance.

The written and illustrated report is drawn up for the attention of the senior managers who authorised the project. A series of meetings may be required before a decision is made on adoption or rejection.

The power of the computer must also be recognised as a major contributor in the field of R&D today. A computer can be programmed to solve complex problems, search for new combinations, record all possible permutations and simulate conditions. Virtual reality allows the consideration of a whole range of experiences which the user of a product or service may have, and this stimulates change processes.

Computer-aided design (CAD) makes use of computer graphics. Once a product design is entered into the system and shown on the computer screen, it can be viewed in a range of ways. It can be rotated to allow viewing from other perspectives, split apart and examined in its parts, reassembled in different ways and enlarged or reduced in size. Eventually a technical drawing is produced, filed electronically and printed out in hard copy for the consideration of interested personnel in the organisation. The potential productivity of designers has accelerated with the development of CAD. Sophisticated design work can often be done in a fraction of the time it once took and is saved in a form which permits instant recall. A consistency in specification is easier to achieve and the opportunity to completely satisfy the customer with the design is increased.

The availability of these developments has brought R&D within the ambit of comparatively small businesses. Traditionally, such companies were unable financially to support a research programme, but could undertake a certain amount of ongoing development. Often R&D facilities and expertise were 'bought-in' from a commercial organisation or an academic institution.

PRODUCT LAUNCH

Once the new or re-designed product is ready for the marketplace, it is essential that there is close liaison between the marketing and operations functions. The marketing function will concern itself with giving the product or service the maximum advantage at the point of launch. Probably an overall plan produced by the operations staff using a network planning approach (see Unit 5) will be used to co-ordinate the overall focus. Operations management will be ensuring that the right quantities of product are available for sale, or the service is geared up to deliver, once the promotional push results in producing potential customers.

ACTIVITY 8

The marketing, operations and finance functions will play major parts in a product launch. Can you identify several possible problems which could arise due to poor communications between these functions?

Some typical problems are:

prices – there could be differences between what finance was happy with and marketing was quoting to customers.

delivery dates – operations could be gearing up for delivery dates much later than marketing want to secure orders.

manufacturing costs – operational delays might cause overtime working to meet delivery dates. The excess costs eat into the profit margins expected by finance.

Once the product or service has been developed and specified, it allows the marketing function the opportunity to work with the finance function to establish the second item in the classical marketing mix, the price. Figure 12 illustrates the components of this mix:

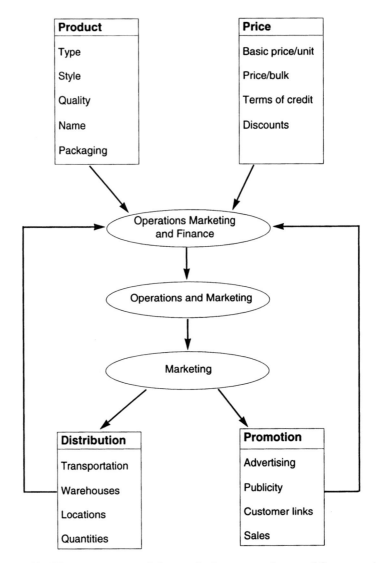

Figure 12: The components of the marketing, operations and finance mix

As a product is launched it must be appreciated that a customer will initially be attracted to it by the perceived benefits which ownership or usage will confer, rather than its specific features. In purchasing a CD-ROM system, there is a possible pride of ownership as well as having access to a vast amount of information. The ease of operation, which is a function of design features, becomes more important where there is a long product life cycle, increasing customer product knowledge and competition. Extra features or facilities built into the product or service become a promotional tool. For example, we use a modern optician's premises because we are concerned initially about the benefits of eye care. This desirable objective will hopefully be achieved by a quality service, with professional attention and modern equipment, which are the features of the practice.

It follows therefore that in a product launch the marketing effort must be geared up initially to sell the benefits of ownership or usage, moving on in later stages to concentrate upon features. Of course, if the company is well established, having its own recognised brand name, a product launch may centre upon promotion to an existing customer base.

Timing is a crucial feature of a launch and operations managers hold the key to success. The product for sale on a certain date must have been manufactured in adequate quantities. The manufacturing facility must have been set up, possibly months before, to achieve the output levels which forecasts demanded. Inventories must have commenced at the point of manufacture and at different sites from which distribution will occur. Physical materials handling will have been planned and undertaken, and all the quality aspects attended to.

When a service is launched, there are many aspects which have to be handled and co-ordinated by operations managers. The delivery system itself has to be balanced, resourced, tested and operational before the set date. Many different features need to work together smoothly to satisfy the first customers and give the impression of control and efficiency, even if there are teething troubles behind the scenes! Careful and detailed pre-launch planning is essential and the appointment of a project manager usually proves a great asset. For example, if a business letter translation service is launched in a centre of commerce then planning must cover the requirement to receive requests by post, fax and personal delivery. A fax machine operational on launch date with competent staff, and forms designed to take down a customer's requirements would be required in the pre-launch planning.

Failure by the operations managers to do, or oversee the completion of, any of these tasks satisfactorily will almost certainly negate the promotional efforts of the marketing and sales function, and impetus will be lost.

PRODUCT GROWTH

Given the essential criteria of a good product or service, strong promotional effort and an efficient back-up from the system, we can expect a growth in sales. Different or uneven rates of growth can bring problems for operations managers who would normally plan with some consistency.

ACTIVITY 9

What do you think causes uneven rates of growth and how could you handle this problem?

Uneven growth rates might be due to:

● seasonal factors

● economic factors (local, national or international)

- ambient conditions (e.g. weather).

- location

Forecasting information will be particularly useful in these circumstances, with comment from the marketing function on these issues:

Without accurate forecasts of demand, operations managers will be forced to take risks on the purchase of quantities of raw materials and components, on labour resourcing requirements and on warehousing and distribution contracts. In a service situation, there will be a risk of providing a service of variable quality and levelling uneven demand by queuing. Providing effective staffing levels throughout the working day or week to give each customer immediate attention can become too expensive. For example, a 'while-you-wait' car-tyre replacement business may fail because of needing too many staff to cope with lunch-time or after-work trade.

FORECASTING METHODS AND SIMULATION

Forecasts provided for operations managers will range from basic data of a qualitative nature to a range of techniques which grow increasingly sophisticated in quantitative terms. Don't be worried by the detail of some of these techniques. You cover them later in the module or in your quantitative methods studies. The approach used will depend upon the skills present within the organisation. Forecasting techniques include time series analysis methods, causal methods and simulation modelling.

Time series analysis methods

These methods are based on the idea that the history of past sales of the product or service, or a similar one, can be used for prediction.

- **moving averages** – in which a number of data points is averaged by dividing the sum of the point values by the number of points. Each point is of equal value.

- **weighted moving averages** – in which certain points which relate to circumstantial issues are awarded greater weighting than other points.

- **exponential smoothing** – in which data points equating to recent events are given greater importance weighting and then decline exponentially with age.

- **regression analysis** – which fits a straight line to past data using time as a factor.

- **trend projections** – which project a graphical trend line into the future.

- **Box-Jenkins** – a complex time-series analysis which relates a group of statistical models to data using Bayes's theorum of posterior distributions.

Causal methods

These try to understand the environmental issues surrounding the sales of the product or service and include:

- **econometric modelling** – in which a segment of the economy is expressed in mathematical equations so that it can be understood.

- **input/output modelling** – this focuses on industrial sales or level of service activity and the changes which can be expected due to changes occurring in linked areas of business.

- **leading indicators** – these sets of statistical data tend to move in the same direction as the subject but move before it. For example, an increase in interest rates affects mortgage demands from building societies and subsequently private house sales.

Simulation modelling

These are dynamic models which are programmed into a computer. The forecasting is undertaken after a series of assumptions are made. Optimum conditions can be achieved using a heuristical, trial and error, approach or can be calculated using operational research methods.

Once conditions are established to maintain a steady growth pattern, the reinforcement tendency of positive feedback (see Unit 1) will continue to bring results. Changes of strategy will be needed when the rate of growth begins to level off and the volume begins to plateau into the recognisable curve of steady state saturation level.

3.6 Saturation, decline and termination

SATURATION

This phase in the product life cycle is clearly recognisable provided a sound and responsive management information system is in place. Depending on the inertia built into the system by nature of the kind of product or service being provided, management should, sooner or later, be in a position to make important decisions.

With the advent of Electronic Point of Sale (EPOS) cash registers, it is possible for a sales manager of a chain of shoe shops to know exactly how sales are going across the country at any particular time. If an advertising campaign is being run to sell particular types of shoe at reduced prices, a cost-benefit analysis can be undertaken to check whether cheaper regional newspaper advertising improves sales to a greater relative degree than expensive commercial TV promotions. If so, repeat advertisement space can be rapidly booked in the effective publications.

Where saturation is occurring, the features of a Pareto curve (see Glossary) can be seen. This is the 80/20 rule that identifies that the bulk of something is made up by a small percentage. It is possible to double the advertising budget, but only achieve an extra 1% on sales. Quadrupling the budget would only produce a 1.5% increase on the plateau level, and could well use up more than the current profits! In such situations, it is necessary to go back to the R&D team. Hopefully there will be an ongoing series of product launches to maintain profitability levels, but a value analysis of the product or service could extend its useful life by reintroducing a modified version. This could have additional features, new styling and packaging and would be competitively priced relative to the other manufacturers or service providers.

Note that the saturation features of a market vary enormously according to the kind of product or service being provided. The catering industry, for example, recognises that people have to eat each day. However, if there are 20 cafes offering a three-course midday lunch to tourists in a small seaside town, the probability is that there is saturation. If there are only enough daily customers for, say, 10 cafes to make a profit, cost cutting, often resulting in poorer quality food, premises and service, will occur. Eventually there are closures or some cafe owners may look for a niche in the marketplace like ice-cream sales, either to subsidise the losses at lunchtime, or to change entirely.

Saturation is, however, very different for a product like a microwave oven. It is likely that eventually about 75% of domestic premises will own a microwave oven. What will be needed thereafter is an effort to meet the needs of the post-sales market situation. Repairs, spare parts and servicing are required with the expectation that a quality performance in these areas will result in a replacement sale eventually. This can be encouraged by a 'trade-in' agreement, which is used in both the 'white goods' trade and the new car market. Poor performance by operations managers whilst the customer is using the product, and needs help or service, will almost certainly result in the loss of potential repeat business.

DECLINE AND TERMINATION

There are two factors which contribute to the ultimate decline of a product or service. There is the competitive aspect, which is often now both national and global. The other factor is the obsolescence of a product or service through the advances of technology, changes in public taste, need or interest. We saw examples of technology earlier.

ACTIVITY 10

If the senior managers have tried unsuccessfully to revitalise the sales of a particular product or service, what steps do you think are open to them?

Once decline is recognised, senior management decision making is required as to whether the product or service can be:

- terminated immediately – which would upset customers, agents and suppliers

- phased out over a published time period – which means certain levels of complexity at the operational level, as new products or services are being simultaneously introduced.

- franchised – which could extend the useful life of the product or service but on a reduced scale, whilst still receiving some contribution towards overall profits.

- sold off – which could again extend the life cycle by placing the product or service in the portfolio of a company which may be linking it closely with one of its own currently successful lines.

Whichever decision is made, operations management staff will be involved in the subsequent actions.

Summary

In this section we examined the R&D process as a series of stages and took the product life cycle through its initial concept to decline and termination. In particular we discussed the six value analysis phases in some detail.

Unit Review Activity

Answer the following questions.

1 What are the three elements required in a product strategy?

2 How are the best possible ventures identified?

3 Why do designers need to think about waste, scrap, effluent and by-products?

4 Outline the stages of an R&D programme and product or service life cycle.

5 What issues need to be considered prior to the commencement of a product or service rejuvenation exercise?

6 List some of the reasons which cause the failure of an R&D project.

7 What are the four aspects of 'value' considered in a value analysis exercise?

8 What is the benefit in using a multidisciplinary team in a value analysis exercise?

Unit Summary

This unit has dealt with the typical product life cycle, from concept to termination. We examined the nature of product and service life cycles and the appropriate system changes which accompany clearly recognisable phases.

We began by considering the importance of a product strategy for an organisation, integrating the aims of its corporate plan and the strategies of its major functional areas. We then looked at the product planning concept and the use of a checklist to ensure well-informed decision making during initial and ongoing development phases, covering engineering, R&D, marketing and financial aspects.

The final section focused on product life cycles, starting with the stages of an R&D programme, and going through the six value analysis phases.

References

Collins, J C and Porras, J I (1995) *California Management Review*, 32, (2)

Genus, A (1995) *Flexible Strategic Management*, Chapman and Hall, London

Recommended Reading

Abell, D F and Hammond, J S (1979) *Stragtegic Market Planning*, Prentice Hall, Englewood Cliffs, New Jersey

Kotler, P (1991) *Marketing Management*, Prentice Hall, Englewood Cliffs, New Jersey, 7th edn

Porter, M E (1985) *Competitive Advantage*, Free Press, New York

Roome, N (1994) 'Business Strategy, R and D, management, and environmental imperatives' *Research and Development management*, January

Answers to Unit Review Activity

1 The three product strategy elements are:
   - potential market segment and price range
   - types and range of products or services which will be offered
   - how available the product or how immediate the service will be.

2 Use a checklist, followed by the appropriate level of analysis to clarify all the relevant details. For example:
   - What is the evidence of need for the product or service?
   - Which are the major markets?
   - How will launch and promotion occur?
   - When will key resources be required?
   - What are the operational/manufacturing problems?
   - What is the cost?
   - What is the time-scale? Etc.

3   This is essential on economic and environmental grounds. There is a cost associated with the production or generation of waste, and this should be minimised. Where it occurs, consideration will need to be given to its disposal (which will cost more money), its recycling back into the system, its conversion into something usable which can be sold or a straight sale of the waste to an organisation which can use it. Environmental issues are important for the neighbourhood and the planet. Legal obligations must be met.

4   The stages of an R&D programme:

- Concept – pure research
- Birth – leading into applied research
- Design – of product or service and process
- Launch – of product or service
- Growth – of sales through promotion
- Maturity – steady state
- Saturation – of market, profits decline
- Decline – obsolescence or competition
- Termination.

5   You may have included the following:

- What has caused decline?
- Will the environment accept a rejuvenated product or service?
- Are there any new gaps in the potential market?
- Who are the strong competitors?
- Can further value be added at minimum cost?

6   You may have included the following in your list:

- Lack of continued financial support
- R&D staffing problems
- Inadequate facilities
- Cross-functional friction
- Poor resource control
- Weak R&D management.

7   The four aspects of value are:

- Cost value – the cost of production
- Use value – the minimum cost of getting the job done
- Esteem value – the pride of ownership factor; the difference between the selling price and the use value
- Exchange value – whether something appreciates or depreciates over time relative to its conversion into cash or some other item.

8   You may have included the following in your answer.

A wide variety of perspectives can be explored. Inputs of specialist information are required and decision making will tend to be more precise. Creative thinking procedures generate more ideas.

UNIT 3
PROCESS DESIGN

Introduction

In this unit, we will consider various ways in which a company can focus its operations, together with the development of operational and facilities strategies. We will discuss the identification of appropriate processes, how locations are determined and the focus for each particular facility.

We will look at how integrated manufacturing or servicing systems are constructed and examine the layout of facilities and the advantages of each option for different types of business organisation.

Objectives

By the end of this unit, you should be able to:

- explain the important aspects of facilities provisioning
- be aware of the various ways a company can focus its operations
- understand longer-term capacity planning issues in organisations
- understand how facility sites are evaluated and selected
- understand how processes are arranged within facilities
- undertake simple layout planning procedures
- be aware of differing essential features in types of facility
- calculate assembly-line balancing percentages
- understand the importance of ergonomic design principles.

SECTION 1

Operations and facilities strategies

Introduction

Once the organisation has developed the product that it wants to launch into the market place, the operations manager has a key role in developing the processes for making and supporting the product. In this section, we look at some key issues that need to be considered in developing an operations strategy. Appropriate processes at appropriate locations and with appropriate capacity at an agreed schedule will need setting up. Features of the facilities and their focus will need to be identified, and with an international company, this identification will need even more attention.

We start by linking the product design to the provision of the facilities; this will obviously involve a fundamental decision about the process to be used. You may recall the product process matrix from Unit 1 which identified various types of process, their particular features, and the link with the product life cycle, as far as operations management is concerned. we then look at the issues of the facilities themselves. In the next section, We looked at capacity and strategies to achieve capacity management.

1.1 Linking design to facilities provisioning

There are many issues relating to company facilities that operations management needs to consider during an R&D programme. The design team will have consulted with operations management regarding the turning of 'whats' into 'hows', and built into the design will be factors allowing ease of manufacture, handling, packaging, use, storing, servicing, modifying and transporting. The use of concurrent engineering helps to minimise the problems associated with the move into actual production or use of the new service.

We saw in Unit 2 that there was an opportunity window early in the design process when little cost had been expended but overall financial commitments to the development were rapidly increasing. It is in this window that managerial control is vital to ensure the best possible use of all resources.

PROCESS TYPE AND FACILITIES

The operations strategy of an enterprise is aimed at achieving corporate goals through the effective provisioning and deployment of resources. Amongst the many issues which operations management must address are:

- identification of the appropriate processes which will be needed to achieve the required level of output of the planned goods and services at the right quality standard.

- decisions on the location of facilities (premises) and how the impact of each will be integrated and controlled.

- the focus of each particular facility with concentration on a specific process, product or market etc.

We consider these particular issues in this unit. Further important factors are dealt with in other units.

We need to consider both the traditional ways in which the organisation has handled and processed its products and services, and the possible alternatives which currently present themselves. The advancement of technology, computing power and evolving managerial expertise must not be overlooked. If, for example, the organisation has traditionally handled its processing by a jobbing approach, a move to batch processing may now prove to be more effective in resource utilisation terms. You will recall some of the key processes from Unit 1 when we discussed the product process matrix. Table 1, developed from original work by Hayes and Wheelwright (1984), links process and unit cost considerations. Unit costs, equipment and labour flexibility are high at the top of the matrix and low at the bottom.

The move from a jobbing shop system towards a continuous system brings a reduced level of flexibility within the organisation. Machinery, work stations, staff and materials handled tend to become increasingly specialised and dedicated towards achieving relatively narrow objectives.

Unit product cost	Jobbing shop	Process Batch	Mass	Continuous
Single high standard units	Personal insurance quotations			
Varied specifications medium volume		Lettering a fleet of commercial vans Making shoes in a range of sizes		
Varied but limited range of specifications high volume			House-to-house leafleting Car assembly	
Very limited range of specifications high volume				Telephone directory enquiries Oil refining

Table 1: Process systems

Some industries display a process life cycle, either as a whole or in parts of its operations. There is a build-up through the jobbing shop into batch and then finally into mass production. When decline sets in there is a retrenchment into smaller-scale operations, thereby completing the life cycle profile. Again you will recall this linking of the product life cycle with the process from Unit 1.

KEY FEATURES OF FACILITIES PROVISIONING

Note that many decisions on facilities recommended for or by the operational level in a business, must be sanctioned at board of director level. These decisions often involve capital expenditure and must form part of the long-range corporate planning procedure. Lead times on facility provisioning may range from a few months, for a new rented warehouse, to fifteen years for a new nuclear powered electricity generating plant. The potential capacity of the new facility when it becomes operational is of vital importance to the success of the business. Under- or over-capacity provisioning has many serious implications. Unfortunately, future facility needs are often very complex to analyse and authenticate with confidence.

We must ask three basic questions:

- How much capacity will be required?
- When will this capacity be needed?
- Where must facilities be sited?

ACTIVITY 1

List some potential problems which could arise if these three questions are not raised and responded to by a business going through a period of change.

You might have included in your list:

- if sufficient capacity is not provided, sales will be lost.
- if too much capacity is provided in a manufacturing facility, stock will build up
- too much capacity in a service facility will lead to staff idle time
- getting the timing wrong could waste promotional effort
- putting a facility in the wrong place could lose sales and could raise administrative and distribution costs.

1.2 Types of focus of facilities

We now consider the various ways in which an organisation can focus its facilities. It can do this by: customer, location, market, product or process.

CUSTOMER FOCUSED
Each facility makes a range of products or offers a range of services for a defined group of customers. The operations managers within the facility should find it possible to build close relationships with both suppliers and customers. This kind of focus has grown through emphasis given by a total quality management (TQM) approach and just-in-time (JIT) supply chains for example, vehicle component manufacturers and computer systems service contractors.

GEOGRAPHICALLY FOCUSED
Each facility is designed to produce the full range of company products or services to meet demand in a defined geographic area. This helps to overcome distribution

problems and possible quota limitations imposed by governmental agencies, for example, continental 'white goods' produced in the UK and franchised carpet-cleaning businesses.

MARKET FOCUSED

The facility operates in or near the centre of the market which it serves. Whilst this may be a geographic dimension in a manufacturing context to minimise distribution cost and time, it need not be so in service situations. The development of advanced computer networks, electronic data interchange, e-mail and satellite communications technology has opened up many new horizons for service industries. A service cannot be stored and speed of response is often required, for example, the credit rating of a potential customer.

PRODUCT FOCUSED

The facility mass-produces a particular type of product or service with few variations for a large market, for example, a canned food manufacturer or a mail order company.

PROCESS FOCUSED

These facilities concentrate on a few specialised technologies, and can often produce wide specifications and diversity from the limited range of resources employed. The product is usually designated for transportation and assembly into more complex products, often manufactured under another company's brand name. Within the service sector, professional firms attend to specific issues for organisations on a contractual basis, for example, nylon-crimping textile firms (throwsters) and financial advisers on taxation.

Many organisations can be identified which fit this framework. They are often described as 'general purpose' because they use many types of process to produce a wide variety of products for a continually changing mix of customers and markets. These companies are often entrepreneurial and opportunist and tend to operate in this way whilst they remain relatively small. With growth, there is a tendency to move towards a different kind of focus, a procedure which is commonly difficult and time-consuming.

ACTIVITY 2

Suppose you are a manager in a growing business which has a process focus. Your directors are proposing a shift over the next 12 months to a 'customer-focused' style. Suggest a strategy to smooth the transition.

You might have suggested a strategy which:

- builds closer relationships with suppliers

- builds closer relationships with existing customers

- actively seeks new customers

- takes a TQM approach

- develops a supply chain system with minimal stock

- reduces unnecessary variety

- carefully evaluates the existing plant efficiencies, etc.

As you can see, some of these issues are rather time consuming, so detailed planning of the changeover is essential.

Now read the article 'Developing and Introducing New Consumer Products', Resource Item 3.1. The article provides case material linking the product life cycle you learnt about in Unit 1 to the practical implications we are developing here. It will give you an idea of the complexity of launching a new product and the extent of the detail of planning and operations that is required.

We will come back later in the unit to have a closer look at both the process-and product-focused types of organisation. First, however, we need to look at the strategic issues affecting a business which operates internationally. An international company has additional problems that are not addressed by simply a product or a process orientation of its facilities.

1.3 International operations strategy

There are particular strategic issues that need to be addressed by a business which operates internationally. The starting point for the review, revision or development of a global operations strategy is the generation of a body of information, using questions like the following:

CAPACITY

- What total capacity is required globally?

- Do all products or services suit all markets?

- How easily can materials be moved across frontiers?

- Which markets are growing, steady, declining?

FACILITIES

- What facilities already exist, and in which countries?

- Which facilities duplicate the work effort of others?

- Do some facilities integrate with others in a supply chain?

- Are all the skills and resources available locally?

- What are the relative operating costs of facilities?

MANAGEMENT

- Are local, national or international staff used as managers?
- How are managers recruited, trained and developed?
- What is the comparative age profile of managers across facilities?
- What interchange or transfer of managers is possible?
- What are the designated/preferred management styles?

INTEGRATION

- Which communications language(s) are used?
- What electronic communication channels exist?
- How is productive effort planned and controlled across facilities?
- How are equitable quality standards achieved and maintained?

RESEARCH AND DEVELOPMENT

- Is R&D effort concentrated in one facility or across many?
- How are new products or services introduced to different markets?
- What patent laws exist in each country having a research facility?

STRATEGIC APPROACHES

You should appreciate that many organisations operate throughout the world using other local companies to support and administer their operations. The relationship between the organisation and its local partner could be as a joint venture, an alliance, or as part of a network.

JOINT VENTURE

A joint-venture approach is often employed when entry to a market is difficult. These difficulties may stem from government restrictions or attitudes expressed by potential customers. An existing local facility is sought, which may or may not already be operating within the same kind of business sector. This local facility will largely provide premises, plant, personnel and contacts. The international partner will provide product and service knowledge, managerial direction, operations management expertise, finance and brand image. The outcome of a successful joint venture will be that both companies share in the success of creating a niche in a market which would otherwise be unavailable to either of them. An example of a joint venture is the novel marketing approach taken by the Daewoo car makers seeking entry to the UK car market. Instead of opening up a chain of showrooms themselves, the company's interests are being handled by the Halfords chain of car repair and spare parts units. An interactive display screen and Daewoo adviser assists the potential customer in making a purchase. Servicing of cars is done by Halfords.

ALLIANCE

An alliance drawn up between international companies is often a successful strategy. This is an on-going relationship involving collaborative effort in all or some of the functional areas of business, for example, R&D, operations, marketing, communications. Partner companies may, for example, agree to manufacture each others' products, or deliver the others' services, within the geographic boundaries which they are geared up to serve. The transference which occurs between facilities within the alliance will largely be of knowledge. Mutual trust must be built up over a time period. Precise and accurate data flows are essential for this, assurances on the quality of performance and a building up of relationships between corresponding staff will build confidence.

NETWORKS

Networks of companies whose outputs of goods or services complement each other have been growing in recent years. Each business remains completely independent, but the synergistic effect of collaborative effort increases the overall impact beyond a level which the business could achieve by working on its own. A networking arrangement may exist to purchase raw materials or components in bulk, or to double the marketing or research effort. Some networks are of a supportive nature in which knowledge and experience can be shared. In some of these, companies are under no obligation to participate on all issues, and the facility can be used as appropriate. There is a danger however of the network disintegrating through the demotivation of major participants when others are disinterested.

Any of these approaches may lead to mergers or take-overs, with the parent company taking control over their local contact. This may also be considered as a primary strategy. If an organisation embarks upon any of these strategies rather than working on its own, questions about facilities and resourcing become paramount. The role played by operations managers will prove critical to overall success.

1.4 Facilities strategy

Once the issues raised on the organisational macro level have been resolved, in terms of the proccess and the focus of the facilities it is necessary to develop an integrated strategic plan. Here, we look at the development of a facilities strategy and important facility factors.

Facilities will usually relate to premises on a given site, however, this will not always be so. A facility could be a flow of information about weather conditions which will affect decision making. Another facility may be mobile, like a fishing vessel, whilst others will be owned and operated by different companies and are linked through some alliance or network. The integration of diverse elements to achieve efficient operations is never simple, but overlaying it with different languages, time zones and cultural perceptions make it a great deal more complex!

The following facility factors are important:

- capacity and range of product or service
- location and proximity to the marketplace

- the adequacy of the facility space
- nature of the equipment and process in each facility
- degree of sophistication of the administrative support systems
- relative unit costs per facility
- whether restrictions apply to particular facilities (e.g. noise)
- geographical dispersion of the facilities
- what communications linkages exist/are necessary
- any measures of productivity that are available.

Section 2

Capacity Management Strategy

Introduction

As 'capacity' is an important macro-level consideration when decisions are made on the number, nature and extent of facilities needed by an organisation, we need to define and understand what it means. This section will define capacity and a number of other capacity management terms, we will also discuss passive and active capacity management strategies.

2.1 Definitions

Capacity management is concerned with the matching of an organisation's resources with the demand placed on it. This is the most important, and difficult, problem and decision area of operations management. Capacity management decisions will provide a framework within which inventories and activities are planned and controlled.

Capacity may be defined as the maximum output of a system in a given time period and can be measured in a number of ways, depending upon the nature of the product or service provided by the organisation, for example:

- number of beds in a hospital
- number of bookable sessions in a squash club
- total work time available in man or machine hours.

As an operations manager you would also need to define capacity in terms of the length of time that a particular level of output can be sustained. Some organisations may be geared up to producing maximum high quality output on just one or two days per year, for example, a flower show or a fireworks manufacturer. Other businesses operate continually, adjusting for the seasons and changing customer demands, for example, umbrella/parasol makers and hospital accident wards.

ACTIVITY 3

Consider a university or college. Identify the way in which the activities change over the course of the year. What steps would need to be taken to ensure these activities were properly accomplished.

A university is driven by the 'academic year'. Before students arrive, administrative staff will have been concentrating on the application and entry phase. When students arrive at the start of the academic year the major effort with the incoming undergraduates is undertaken by academic staff. This is directed towards teaching them until the following June and then evaluating their performance. The administrators process the results and gear up for either the reappearance of the students or their exit from the system through the degree ceremony. To cope with the changes in capacity:

- Extra part-time administrative and lecturing staff can be employed at periods of maximum workload.

- Lecture rooms can be used for other purposes at certain times of the year, for example, summer schools or conferences.

- Computing staff and facilities can be hired out to businesses during slack periods.

2.2 Strategies

The strategy adopted in a given situation depends upon the relative emphasis placed upon the following objectives of operations management, which are often in tension:

- to achieve an efficient resource utilisation

- to provide a high-quality service response level.

Strategies available to management are of two kinds: **active** and **passive**. Active strategies involve attempts to influence the demand to smooth out the fluctuations over a given planning period. Passive strategies involve actions aimed at absorbing the demand fluctuations.

ACTIVE STRATEGIES

Active strategies which are available are:

- vary demand by advertising, reducing or raising prices
- delay orders during high-demand periods – making customers wait and risking a loss of custom
- mix and balance seasonal products.

PASSIVE STRATEGIES

Four passive strategies which are available to management are:

- maintain excess capacity – leads to higher overhead costs
- use inventory levels – high stock levels result in increased storage
  costs
    – low stock levels lead to poor service or loss of custom
- adjust capacity by – hiring or laying off workers
    – using overtime or idle time
    – subcontracting
- fix an upper capacity limit – relies upon customer loyalty.

'Produce-to-stock' businesses prefer to employ 'level' capacity aggregate plans producing at a certain level throughout the planning period for the following reasons:

- minimisation of:
    – costs of hiring or laying off workers
    – costs of overtime or idle time working
    – costs of locating and developing new sources of material supplies
    – costs of start-up and shut-down of operations
- only the most efficient productive machinery and staff is used
- supervision is simplified
- low scrap rates
- voluntary labour turnover and absenteeism may be lower.

The kind of problems which are faced by organisations which provide customised products or services are:

- production or service cannot begin until customers' orders are received. For example, tailoring bespoke clothes cannot begin until material has been selected, styles discussed and measurements taken
- it is difficult to specify the nature and extent of capacity required. For example, the supplier of carpets cannot keep rolls of every kind of carpet in the showroom, so some customer choices will be subject to a delivery delay

- finished goods inventory cannot be used to smooth the difference between level capacity and variable demand.

Strategies which can be employed to smooth the differences are:

- use backlog of orders, orders received but not dispatched
- use self-service systems to reduce pressure on the operating staff (only suitable for certain services)
- conversion of some services into standardised services
- incorporation of flexibility, use stand-by or casual staff
- use excess capacity.

2.3 Capacity and its features

An essential aspect of capacity management strategy is to match the capacity provisioning to the anticipated demand level. The concept of a **capacity cushion** is common, but must be carefully handled to minimise both cost and loss. The capacity cushion is equal to capacity minus average demand.

For example: production capacity per week   = 40,000 units

average demand per week   = 38,500 units

capacity cushion   = 1,500 units.

This will provide a margin to cope with trading fluctuations, staff holidays, machine breakdowns and material shortages. A positive cushion provides excess output above average demand with a view to everything balancing out over a longer time horizon. The perfectly balanced system would have no capacity cushion, and many companies have moved towards this ideal through the adoption of JIT arrangements with suppliers and customers. We examine the attempt to achieve balance within facility systems later.

In order to operate a capacity cushion with a degree of success, several heuristical, trial and error, rules have been developed by operations managers:

- Use a positive capacity cushion big enough to ensure there is no shortfall, for example, electricity supply, an expanding consumer product market, a motorway petrol service station.

- Limit the risk, but accept the chance of a shortfall. Use forecasts to plan outputs. Often used when the cost of excess output equates to the cost of lost orders through shortfall, for example, non-perishable products which are seasonal, fresh food market stalls

- Maximise the facility resources by planning for a marginal shortfall. This enables high utilisation of capital equipment and expensive resources, for example, process industries like steel making and oil refining, a vehicle haulage business.

To overcome the problems caused by variability, the concept of **best operating level** has been developed. This is the level of output at which the average unit cost is minimal. If output falls, unit costs will rise due to the apportionment of the overheads to a smaller volume. Likewise, when output exceeds the best operating level, unit costs also rise. This is due to the extra costs of labour (overtime pay) and the greater possibility of scrap and wastage due to the pressures on the system.

The term **design capacity** is used to describe the maximum output that can be achieved under ideal conditions.

The term **effective capacity** is the maximum output which can be achieved under given operational practicalities like breakdowns, absenteeism, shortages and quality specifications. It is less than the design capacity.

The **actual output** is a quantitative measure of what is produced in a time period. This may be a measure of units, customers served or in situations of variety, a total of the standard minutes (hours) produced. (see Glossary)

System efficiency is the ratio of actual output to the effective capacity:

$$\frac{\text{Actual output}}{\text{Effective capacity}} \times 100$$

System utilisation is the ratio of actual output to the design capacity:

$$\frac{\text{Actual output}}{\text{Design capacity}} \times 100$$

ACTIVITY 4

Calculate the system efficiency and system utilisation of a shoe repair shop with the following capacity:

Design capacity	=	15 pairs of shoes/day
Effective capacity	=	12 pairs of shoes/day
Actual output	=	10 pairs of shoes/day

System efficiency $\dfrac{10}{12} \times 100 = 83.33\%$

System utilisation = $\dfrac{10}{15} \times 100 = 67.67\%$

The **capacity utilisation rate** can also be calculated as a percentage:

$$\frac{\text{Effective capacity}}{\text{Design capacity}} \times 100$$

Note both numerator and denominator must be expressed in the same units, for example units/day, customers/hour, in this case, shoes/day.

Let's look at another example. Samples taken in a college faculty in mid-morning showed that there were on average 60 lecture and tutorial rooms in use out of the 80 available on each weekday of the academic year. Capacity utilisation rate is therefore:

$$\frac{\text{Effective capacity}}{\text{Design capacity}} = \frac{60}{80}$$

Capacity utilisation rate = 75%.

The inability to load rooms up to 100% utilisation must be recognised by the timetabler. There is in practice a whole range of reasons why this is not possible. There are changeovers between classes, non-compatibility of class sizes with rooms, scheduling of staff problems as well as basic cleaning and maintenance periods.

ACTIVITY 5

Calculate the percentage system utilisation and efficiency rates for a gents' hairdressing salon given the following data: the sole hairdresser works for 8 hours a day, 5 days a week and an average customer is 'in the chair' for 15 minutes; in a typical week, 112 customers had a haircut; the hairdresser uses 30 minutes of personal needs time per day.

We first convert the data into the same units: customers/week:

Availability/week =	40 hours
Each customer takes =	0.25 hours
Designed capacity 40/0.25 =	160
Customers/week =	112
System utilisation rate =	$\frac{112}{160} \times 100 = 70\%$

Organisations find that it is more efficient not to stretch the resources to the limit and hence the effective capacity is always less than the design capacity. In the case of our hairdresser, he or she recognises the fact that he or she will lose time each day due to 'personal needs'. This would include tea breaks and visits to the toilet. In reality, therefore, he or she sets aside 30 minutes per working day for these things, thus reducing the number of customers which he or she can attend to per day to:

$$\frac{7.5}{0.25} = 30$$

The business will therefore operate at an effective capacity of 150 customers/week. The actual output may be more or less than the effective capacity and the hairdresser may forego the personal needs time to attend to more customers if demand is high.

Therefore the **system efficiency** percentage is:

$$\frac{112}{150} \times 100 = 74.67\%$$

When the actual output is expressed as a percentage of the effective capacity it is called the **efficiency**.

2.4 Capacity planning

Organisations need to consider capacity planning and strategy issues on three levels:

- **long-term** aspects, which have already been partially considered, involving product and service provisioning and facilities
- **medium-term** aspects, often considered using the term **aggregate planning** or **aggregate capacity planning**, and involves a broad-brush overview which relates resourcing to projected output whilst taking appropriate constraints into account. The objective of aggregate planning is to determine the overall medium range (2-12 months) capacity requirement needed to satisfy the total expected demand without getting into great detail on specific products, services or staffing. For example, in an educational establishment the number of tutor hours required is calculated based on the number of staff hours required to teach on all the courses offered without getting into details of requirements of each course, subject by subject. We consider aggregate planning in Unit 8.
- **short-term** aspects, involving scheduling and control techniques, which we deal with in Unit 4.

Summary

In this section, we defined capacity and capacity management. We introduced the two main kinds of strategy, active and passive, and a number of other key terms and concepts: capacity cushion, design capacity, effective capacity, actual output, system efficiency, system utilisation rate and capacity utilisation rate.

SECTION 3

Facilities

Introduction

In this section, we will deal with the critical decision making associated with the size, location and number of facilities.

Managerial decisions on the nature and size of facilities operating within an organisation involve the investment of capital. These decisions are made as part of the long-range corporate planning cycle and as such facilities are provided, modified or reduced, constraints will thereby be imposed upon capacity planning in both the medium and short term.

Some facility provisioning requires extensive lead time. A new regional hospital can only be planned, built and fully operational after at least a five-year time horizon. Facilities strategic planning takes account of the forecasted capacity requirements, the time schedules of capacity needs, and the location and integration of the facilities.

3.1 Size of facilities

Economy-of-scale considerations will play a part in the decision making on facility size. Although larger-sized facilities are recognised as having the following advantages:

- fixed costs can be spread over a larger product volume
- building, rental or operational costs do not increase with the product volume in a linear relationship
- staffing requirements are proportionately less.

  We can also argue that there are also some diseconomies of scale which we need to consider, these are:

- internal organisational complexity leads to inefficiency
- distribution costs are greater
- major catastrophes (fires) are more significant.

In making recommendations on facility size, operations management staff will gather data which can relate unit costs to the effective capacity of the facility. Figure 1 illustrates optimum unit size.

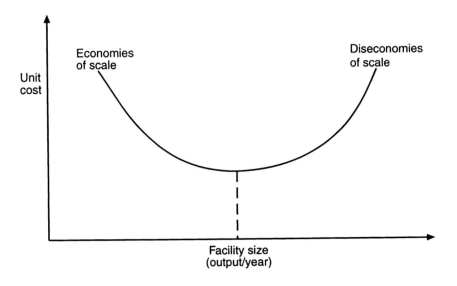

Figure 1: Optimum unit size

ACTIVITY 6

Plot the following data on graph paper to determine the optimum size of a single-storey facility relative to the unit cost. Plot £ unit/cost against cubic metres.

Unit/cost		Size (m)		
£	L	W	H	cubic metres
1.20	70	30	10	
1.30	140	35	5	
1.40	110	42	6	
1.50	122	25	5	
1.60	100	28	5	
1.70	80	24	7	
1.80	77	21	8	

Which dimension facility would you recommend?

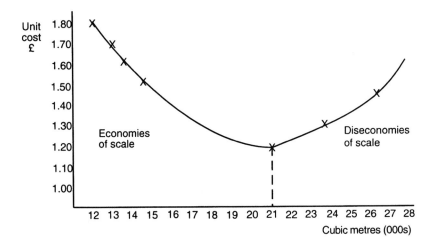

The graph bottoms at a unit cost of £1.20 which is ideal if the organisation can fully utilise a building 10m high. It has 21,000 cubic metres of space. The unit cost may rise substantially if only a 5m height can be used!

Decisions on the physical shape, and the equipping of the facility would also be part of the operations manager's recommendations.

3.2 Location of facilities

Careful consideration on locating facilities is given to competitive and technological factors and the criteria laid down by national and local government agencies.For example, Japanese companies have in the last decade been opening up manufacturing facilities in Europe and the USA in order to overcome trade embargoes, reducing delivery times and transportation costs. In the service sector, fast-food outlets and private hospitals have been opened up in strategically important locations far from the organisational administrative centre.

An additional factor carefully considered in location decision making is the trend in the manufacturing sector to operate JIT arrangements with other organisations (see Unit 9).

The development of increasingly sophisticated computerised manufacturing and service systems has decreased emphasis on the human aspects of operating a facility. Staff needed to run a facility tend to be multi-skilled: they can consult expert systems in difficult decision making and can be in constant contact with headquarters or area managers using current communications equipment.

FEASIBILITY STUDY OF POTENTIAL SITES

Certain technical issues will need investigating and clearly defining. In the case of land itself, with or without buildings:

- legal status and title to ownership must be established
- surveying expertise must be employed to assess the viability of putting up the required facilities. This involves technical analysis of soil conditions, drainage factors and load bearing factors
- local governmental officers will need to approve the suitability of the site for the type and volume of business proposed
- public utility managers must be consulted on the supply of water, gas, and electricity, and the removal of solid waste, effluent and sewage
- opinions of financial advisers and investors will be needed to appraise the quality of the investment
- forecasts of future needs will assist in assuring operations managers that growth can be accommodated
- architects need to give advice on the structure and condition of existing buildings.

Not all these issues are of equal importance in differing kinds of facility. In making decisions on which site to select, a mixture of quantitative and qualitative decision making will be required.

SINGLE FACILITY LOCATION

In locating a single retail store, fire station, school, dental practice or production unit, all of which need no or very little interaction with other similar facilities, consideration must be given to:

- staff availability
- staff costs
- proximity to the customers or clients
- enough space to house all operational, administrative and storage needs
- visibility.

The level of business generated from a single facility will depend largely upon its own operational expertise rather than from some other source. Quantitative decision issues include the costs of land, premises, ground rents, business rates, taxes, insurance and staffing. Qualitative aspects include an assessment of the acceptability to the local environment, the reaction from similar facilities already operating within the vicinity, the significance of any constraints imposed upon the facility, the supply of staff with adequate skills and the quality of the working experience.

Operations managers, in making a recommendation to senior management on the preferred single facility location, can use a points rating assessment system to compare the strengths and weaknesses of each option. There will be a degree of subjectivity in this. It will need to be undertaken by a small group of knowledgeable staff which can explore all the pertinent issues carefully. In some cases, individual categories may need to be subdivided further to arrive at a decision.

Let's consider an example. Several doctors working in an area intend to combine together to build and staff a group practice. There are two possible sites on a growing housing area which are available for purchase. One is situated adjacent to privately-owned housing, the other is in the middle of council built houses now administered by a housing association.

In order to make a decision the doctors must:

● decide the most important criteria

● gather all the comparative quantitative data relative to both sites

● collect together all the subjective (qualitative) perspectives

● choose a scoring system (e.g. scale: 1 high cost/undesirable; 10 low cost/desirable)

● process the information and make the decision.

A possible, simplified approach is shown in Table 2.

| Criteria | Points allocated (max. 10) | |
	Site A	Site B
Cost of building	7	5
Parking space	10	7
Security	5	4
Proximity to patients	8	9
Proximity to pharmacy	7	3
Ground rent (p.a.)	5	5
Room for expansion	8	6
Total	50	39

Table 2: Deciding on single facility location

Obviously care should be taken to ensure that the data used is strictly comparable and accurately calculated. From Table 2, we can advise that Site A should be selected.

ACTIVITY 7

The town council has to relocate a busy licensed taxi rank that has queuing spaces for 25 taxis. Identify five criteria which you should include in the decision about a new location.

You might have included the following criteria:

- space available
- accessibility to customers
- proximity to other facilities, shops, bus and railway stations etc.
- traffic congestion
- nearness to driver facilities: food shops, toilets etc.

3.3 Multiple factories, depots and warehouses

A major consideration when choosing a location for a new facility which will need to be integrated within an existing group of facilities, is the cost of transportation. We can use a special form of linear programming, known as the **transportation model,** to assess this. We then feed the results into the data on all the other important criteria. Often a weighted approach called **factor rating**, is used to consider all the aspects of the decision.

TRANSPORTATION MODELLING

There are certain assumptions which underpin transportation modelling:

- equitable items or volumes are transported
- only one route exists between facilities
- mode of transport is consistent
- constant transportation cost/unit is usable.

Operational research techniques involve paper and pencil, graphical and micro-computing methods of solution. A decision is made about which approach is to be used, and the form in which a solution is required, for example, volume moved to minimise overall costs and maximise profits.

A detailed consideration of transportation modelling is beyond our scope in this text. If we look again at 'factor rating', the results from the transportation modelling would provide support for at least one of the criteria which we listed for facility comparison. The procedure for undertaking factor rating is similar to the approach we suggested for single-facility selection, except that weighting factors are built into the list of criteria. Using our example of the new group practice premises, the doctors may decide to weight the importance of the factors as in Table 3.

Criteria	Weighting	Points allocated		Score	
		Site A	Site B	A	B
Cost of building	.30	7	5	2.1	1.5
Parking space	.20	10	7	2.0	1.4
Security	.15	5	4	0.75	0.6
Proximity to patients	.15	8	9	1.2	1.35
Proximity to pharmacy	.10	7	3	0.7	0.3
Ground rent (p.a.)	.5	5	5	0.25	0.25
Room for expansion	.5	8	6	0.4	0.3
Totals	1.00	50	39	7.4	5.7

Table 3: Weighting for criteria

The decision would be to still choose site A, but the introduction of the weighting factors can be significant in many situations. Care needs to be taken that the result is not manipulated by weighting certain criteria too heavily.

DECISIONS ABOUT THE SITE

The siting of a new facility in the context of others is a complex procedure. Integrating a facility amongst fifty others, presents a rather different set of problems than adding one facility to three others. If the facilities are predominantly warehouses it may be essential to handle particular types of product on each site rather than all the warehouses carrying a small amount of everything. Policy decisions will be required on such issues. Further discussion on the movement of materials between facilities will be provided later in the unit when considering materials handling and distribution.

3.4 Competitive retailing facilities

The revenue generating potential of a retail facility is raised or lowered according to the proximity of competing facilities. Departmental retail stores tend to be sited in city centre locations, whereas electrical, DIY, and carpet warehouses are often found on the edge of conurbations. Food supermarkets can still be found in city centres, but customer car parking and delivery problems have caused large retailers to move many stores out of town.

When planning a relocation or opening a new facility, decisions are often influenced by the belief that turnover increases proportionately with the size of the facility and is inversely proportional to the travel time to the facility. Consumer preferences however are fickle, and the relative costs of commodities sold relative to ambience and service quality are important factors.

Forecasts of the anticipated customer levels over typical weeks and the rate of service which can be provided to minimise queuing time need to be included in the list of decision criteria.

3.5 Emergency services facilities

The major utilities which fall within this category are the police, fire and ambulance services. Location decisions will be affected by potential response times.

In the cases of fire appliances, they will normally be standing ready at the fire station with a full crew in attendance. The distance to the furthest or most inaccessible part of the area covered will be known, and optimal routes will have been planned. Siting of the facility on a one-way road system would be undesirable and add journey time.

Whilst ambulances and police cars are also required to service an area, they will often be on patrol and given directions by radio. The return journey from the scene of a crime could result in a police car returning to police headquarters, but time may not be of the highest priority. In contrast, the ambulance may need to return at high speed, not to its base but to the nearest hospital which is able to provide treatment.

The level of service coverage given by emergency facilities to an area, as well as response times, are regularly debated. Inevitably there is a trade-off between provisioning, quality of service, cost and response times.

3.6 General service facilities

Many of the issues raised already will need to be addressed when other kinds of service facilities are provided. When a motoring organisation decides on facilities and resourcing, target response times to stranded motorists must be considered. A local council lorry called out to grit main roads when there is an unexpected drop in temperature, will need to be locally sited and have access to materials and loading equipment. A high street shoe repairer offering a 'while-you-wait' service will need to provide a waiting area and have enough capacity to meet the demand in the envisaged time period.

Summary

In this section, we looked at some key factors to be considered in the size, location and number of facilities.

SECTION 4
Layout principles within a facility

Introduction

In this section we will look in some detail at some layout principles that affect the arrangement of a facility. We will consider the advantages and disadvantages of product, process, fixed position, and cellular layouts. We will also consider special layout applications to retail service facilities, warehouses, and offices.

Finally, we will refer briefly to systematic layout planning and introduce the concept of business process reengineering (BPR).

4.1 Layout of facilities

Layout is the arrangement of a facility to provide working, service, reception, storage and administrative areas. The operation of a facility requires continual movement of resources, materials, equipment, components, staff and documents from location to location. Traditional techniques using templates, scale plans, string diagrams and travel charting have proved to be low cost methods of achieving either optimal or near optimal layout plans using a heuristical approach. Resource 3.2 illustrates one of the more interesting types of travel chart within a facility. These were developed by J A Apple (1977) and are called 'From-To' charts in the USA. A system measure of the amount of traffic between locations, often called **torque** is generated. Attempts are then made using logic and heuristics to compose a layout which will reduce the overall torque and minimise the amount of contrary-flow traffic. The simple matrix shown in Resource 3.2 illustrates the principle when facilities are laid out in a sequential fashion, for example, A B C D.

LAYOUT PROBLEMS

Poor layout of a new facility will greatly reduce the overall capacity and productivity levels, and could be technically difficult, expensive and upsetting to staff to revise. When the layout of a new facility is either poorly planned or designed, the following types of problem will surface:

- **'Bottlenecks' occur**

  These operational blackspots are unable to cope with the demands placed upon them. The backlog which arises compounds the situation. Bottlenecks are difficult to eradicate in practice when they are caused by expensive equipment which cannot justifiably be added to or by a physical constriction in the layout. Ideally therefore, care should be taken to minimise the potential for a bottleneck at the design stage of a facility.

● **Safe working practice becomes an issue**

Staff may suffer injury or be affected by the injurious effects arising from adjacent processes. Manuals of good working practice associated with particular types of equipment or activity can be consulted to minimise this risk. When the facility layout is actually set up, training programmes should be provided for staff. These will familiarise staff with potential hazards, protective clothing, legal requirements and action expected in an emergency.

● **Quality performance is impaired**

The provision of information on the quality standards which apply to the performance of all work within the new facility is essential. Training will be required on all new equipment.

● **Supervision becomes more difficult**

The physical dimensions of the facility, and the nature of its equipment and storage areas must be carefully considered when decisions are made regarding the number of supervisors or managers needed. Too few supervisors often lead to inefficiency and poor overall control. Too many supervisors add overhead cost and is overly bureaucratic. Placing supervisors' offices or desks in positions of working acceptability, with full visibility and ready access is not a simple exercise.

● **Staff motivation decreases**

When staff feel that they could achieve a great deal more if only the layout was more user friendly, didn't demand so much walking around, was cooler or warmer or better lit, then demotivation and general lack of interest can soon arise. Care at the design stage to build in appropriate ergonomic features (see Resource 3.3) will help overcome this tendency.

● **Costs of providing the service or manufacturing the product increases with a poor layout**

Determination of the times and costs of each process using work study techniques enables comparative evaluation, and an optimal layout to be provided. Existing layouts can be measured using one of the work measurement techniques we outline in Unit 7. Potential layouts can be simulated and synthetic times generated. Travel charting is a useful technique for comparing alternative layouts (see Resource 3.2)

ACTIVITY 8

Think of a facility you know well, for example, a shop, office, sports centre or library. Sketch a two-dimensional 'birds-eye view' of the layout. Identify a potential bottleneck; and a safety concern.

You might have selected a food supermarket. Part of the layout showing the bottleneck which occurs at one of the cash points is shown in Figure 2. The tail-back of the queue causes general congestion. Safety problems for customers are caused through loose boxes lying on the floor whilst fresh fruit is being loaded onto shelves.

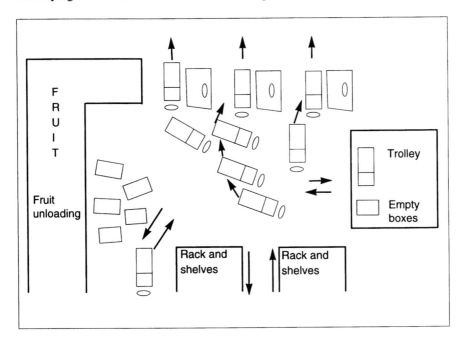

Figure 2: Supermarket bottleneck and safety problems.

4.2 Types of layout

There are three basic approaches to the laying out of facilities. These are traditionally described as **product, process** and **fixed-position layouts**. Note, however, that **hybrid layouts** have become popular within certain kinds of organisations. In these an attempt is made to obtain the best attributes of two or more approaches whilst minimising the disadvantages. The advent of cellular or group technology layouts, where machines, which are often computer programmed, are grouped into cells capable of undertaking similar manufacturing requirements, has brought new concepts into layout and the associated scheduling operations. In recent years, there has been growing expertise and sophistication in the layouts of retail facilities to improve the speed and efficiency of service.

PRODUCT LAYOUTS

This approach to facility layout will be most appropriate when large quantities of material, or a large number of people need to be moved smoothly through the system in an organised and efficient way. Product layouts are repetitive, standardised operations and although expensive to install, they are economical to use when supported by good planning systems. Only a few types of product or variants of one product will be handled by a product layout. In a service situation, customers are categorised and streamed into particular processing lines, so that successive customers are similar.

For example, a food processing company sets up a product line to produce 5,000 tins of baked beans per day; a hospital outpatients' ward receives 600 day patients and then streams them into areas served by the appropriate specialists and consultants.

In manufacturing facilities, product layouts are often called assembly lines. In setting up an assembly line, careful selection of equipment and balancing of adjacent operations is essential.

The advantages of product layouts are:

- high levels of output are achievable
- supervision, planning and control is comparatively simple
- high utilisation levels of labour and machinery are achievable
- minimum work-in-progress and materials handling cost
- staff training is reduced due to operational specialisation.

However, we need to recognise certain disadvantages which product layouts possess, and ensure that the choice of a product layout for a new facility will provide the greatest economic advantage. Disadvantages are:

- jobs tend to be routine and can prove demotivating
- inflexibility of the layout presents problems when change is necessary
- a breakdown on one work station soon results in the whole operation being halted.

A service product line would be a self-service cafeteria with an entrance at one end, food and drinks available along the line, with the payment till at the end of the line. If a product layout is appropriate, then decisions must be made on the physical location of each operation or work station. Consultation with plant, electrical and mechanical engineers, operations managers, safety officers and other staff who can make a contribution, regarding the actual physical sites for each operation within the facility. Various configurations can be considered. Simple paper templates and scale drawings can be used to model the facility. If the organisation owns computer simulation packages, sophisticated work can be done with a view to optimisation of the resources. The development of virtual reality techniques for commercial and industrial layout evaluation has immense potential. The **U-shaped product layout** takes account of the need to take completed product, or served customers, away at the same end of the facility as the operations began (Figure 3).

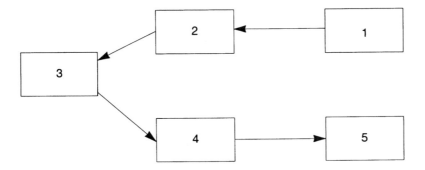

Figure 3: A U-shaped product layout

The **straight-line product layout** is probably the most common type encountered in manufacturing situations. The work stations can be linked by conveyor systems of various types, such as roller, moving belt or overhead conveyors. Where there is downward movement between levels, gravity roller conveyors can provide movement without energy cost.

PROCESS LAYOUTS

A **process layout** groups together all similar processes, forming them into a recognisable physical area referred to as a section or department. In a large retail store, there will be departments for items as diverse as food, clothes, electrical goods, gardening, sports, household goods etc. A textile firm may have carding, spinning, dyeing and weaving departments, plus an administration function, which itself will be subdivided into sales, accounts, personnel and training departments.

ACTIVITY 9

Consider an organisation which you know well, and identify the functional areas into which it is divided because of the grouping of special equipment or facilities.

Perhaps you chose a health and sports club. There are areas for outdoor sports, with special courts and equipment for tennis, five-a-side soccer, and netball. The indoor sports hall has areas marked out for several sports, although some areas double up for two or more sports. For example, it was not possible to play basketball and badminton at the same time. The swimming area is self-contained. The gymnasium, with training equipment and weight lifting facilities, is in a separate room. It has a process layout, although there is double use of some facilities.

Process layouts are much less likely to face a total shutdown situation than a product line, but manufacturing activity is much more complicated in planning and scheduling terms if maximum utilisation of resources is required. Materials tend to be moved around in batches, each accompanied by a detailed job card giving precise details or, in some cases, reference numbers so that a remote computer terminal can be consulted.

The advantages of a process layout are:

- general-purpose machinery or facilities provides flexibility
- a machine breakdown results in work being switched to another machine
- more varied work open to staff
- individual incentive schemes can operate well
- departmental group identity tends to be strong.

If a process layout is selected for a new facility, you should also recogonise the following potential disadvantages:

- communications and supervision often tend to present difficulties and careful design of these areas is essential
- level of individual resource utilisation is bound to be lower than a well-balanced product system, and this must be accepted by senior management.

For example, in a large retail store, for cost-centre purposes and to minimise customer queuing, every department has its own electronic cash register. The utilisation percentage of each cash register may be only from 5 to 10% over the working week. If only one cash register is provided for a whole floor at a recognisable cash point, there may be almost 100% utilisation, but increased customer queing.

In a manufacturing situation, a considerable amount of materials handling, with associated temporary storage of work-in-progress (WIP) is required, and a new facility must be planned accordingly. Aisles need to be of suitable width to allow for the turning circles of forklift and reach trucks, and storage areas must be clearly defined.

FIXED-POSITION LAYOUTS

Certain kinds of products are huge in size, or extremely heavy or have to be built on the site at which they must operate. In these cases, all the resources necessary to manufacture or construct the product must be brought to the site itself. Usually only a single product at a time is being manufactured to specifications which are unique and never to be repeated, for example, building a road bridge across a river.

A fixed-position layout may be used to produce a small number of repeat items over a consecutive time period. The effect of the learning curve will reduce not only operational times, but also the quantities and timing of resource delivery. For example, a shipyard may build several minesweepers over a few years to repeat specifications.

Planning and co-ordination of effort are key factors in efficient resource utilisation if a fixed-position layout approach is used. Often the techniques of project management (see Unit 5) are used for planning and control of all the activities necessary to complete the task. This can raise the costs of administrative effort above the equivalent costs with other types of layout. Set against this are certain finished product storage and distribution costs which do not occur.

Even the building of large products can be examined to see if parts can be manufactured elsewhere, transported and inserted into the structure at the appropriate point. Where this is possible, the project time-scale is reduced and the fixed-position layout complexity simplified.

A good example of a service sector fixed-position layout would be a hospital operating theatre. By careful planning everything is in its rightful and logical place prior to surgery. The patient then becomes the centre of focus until the surgery is completed with everything being brought to him or her. After completion, there is a need to clean, sterilise, tidy and replenish the resources within the facility.

In a restaurant, the dining area is the fixed-position layout. The customer is provided with service, everything necessary is brought to the table, hopefully with a satisfactory level of efficiency, quantity and quality. Once again after the meal there needs to be a tidying, resetting and replenishment process before the table can be used again.

ACTIVITY 10

Consider a fixed-position layout activity like building an office block. Identify three component parts which can be manufactured elsewhere and fed into the construction as components.

With an office block, for example, the following parts could be manufactured off site:

- double-glazed window units
- electricity control panels
- fire-alarm system components
- lift-system
- built-in office furniture
- security systems.

Figure 4 shows an example of a fixed-position layout.

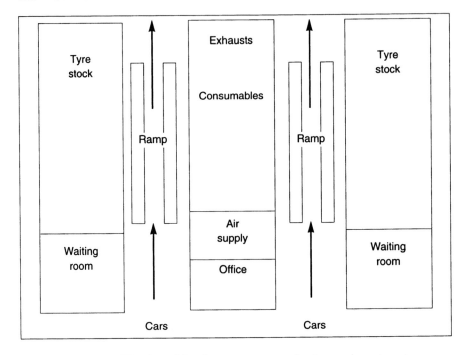

Figure 4: Fixed-position layout: a tyre and exhaust department

CELLULAR (OR GROUP TECHNOLOGY) LAYOUTS

In this type of layout, machines are grouped into a **cell** which is capable of producing items which require similar processing (see Unit 1 and Glossary). In reality, the cells become miniature product layouts which exclude the need for significant movement between operations and are finely balanced to minimise queuing. Many of the machines are automatic or robotic and computer programmed and controlled. This kind of layout is now widely used in metal fabrication, assembly work and computer chip manufacture and enables a small working group to have a degree of autonomy, decision making, variety of task and responsibility for quality. Components which need to be produced can be classified into either those with a similar design, or those which require similar processing stages.

The advantages of a cellular layout are:

- labour costs are low as few staff are needed to run a cell
- teams of workers quickly develop expertise through repetition
- reduced materials handling
- minimal set-up times are required
- planning of work within each cell can be left to the staff concerned
- performance of each cell reflects performance of staff.

Care should be taken when introducing a cellular layout into a new facility if the conceptual underpinning which is necessary for success is not already within the organisation. Training will be required on group working, the idea of the 'internal customer' in quality performance and the achievement of targets. Once the analysis of products and components has been done, machines will need to be grouped into cells. In practice, a team of between six and fifteen workers per working period is found to be optimal per cell to develop the close interpersonal relationships which are necessary. You need to remember these points whilst planning the cellular layout. The group may include maintenance or computing staff as well as production personnel.

Although developed in manufacturing industry, the cellular layout is now being introduced into the service sector. Groups of staff in the mail order, commercial banking and insurance industries are now organised in this way. In complex organisations such as hospitals, all varieties of layout may be seen.

4.3 Special applications

RETAIL SERVICE LAYOUTS

The fundamental principle underlying the layout of retail facilities is to maximise the profit per square or cubic metre of space. Assuming that the organisational policy is to provide a certain quality and quantity level of output, the design of a suitable layout in the new facility is essential. If the policy identifies minimal cost and maximum throughput, the resulting layout within the basic facility will probably require customers to perform a degree of sorting, sifting, and moving of cardboard as order pickers and shelf loaders normally do.

Such extreme austerity would, however, probably prove commercially unacceptable in a developed country due to competition, customer comparisons and the health and safety issues arising for employees. Whilst some large food retail and DIY facilities are little more than large prefabricated sheds on a bleak industrial estate, other facilities are attractively designed with many desirable features built in, based on good layout design.

The perspectives of sociologists and marketing specialists have combined to produce the so-called 'service-scape'. This concerns the experience created for the customer within the facility, and is designed to increase the desire to buy.

In laying out a retail facility, the route which a customer takes can to some extent be prescribed. In a small facility there may be only one route through, and it may prove difficult for a customer to return back against the flow. In a large facility, however, once initial entry has been gained, the customer is free to wander at will. The design of aisles, their widths, angles and intersections, are of importance both commercially and technically. For example, customers need to be encouraged to explore all the areas of the facility, which may promote some 'impulse' buying. It is also known that sales of items in special baskets at the end of aisles are higher than sales of the same commodity in its normal place on a mid-aisle shelf. The Ikea furniture store in London has created a large store but with a completely unidirectional flow, throughout all floors, for the customers to exit in one place.

The design of the storage baskets, racks and shelves introduced into the facility must also be considered. Safety must be paramount to avoid litigation from an injured customer or employee, but visibility and reachability are essential. The placing of items, which do not necessarily have a relatively high unit price but a high level of profitability, at a comfortably reachable level is common.

General ambient conditions of good lighting, air circulation and adequate warmth may be supplemented by the appropriate smells in fresh food or gardening areas. Such equipment needs to be designed into the facility, together with a closed-circuit TV security system and a fire-fighting sprinkler system.

Staff rooms, storage, and certain specialised service areas, should be carefully planned. Those areas to which customers do not have access should be discreet, and out of the way. A space designated for returned goods, complaints, trade or credit enquiries may be placed in a 'dead' part of the facility layout to bring customers into this area.

As part of the ambient design, labels, signs and symbols may be extensively used to enable the customer to make decisions without the need to seek help from a member of staff. Café areas and areas to leave children may also be designated.

ACTIVITY 11

Next time you visit a DIY warehouse or garden centre, take a leisurely walk around. Note the types of shelves, racks etc. used. Observe design of the aisles. Are they all of equal width? Note several display symbols which are used.

Perhaps you found that the aisles were of a right-angular nature, with a wide central aisle leading from the entrance. Side aisles were slightly narrower, leading to an aisle that ran around the perimeter.

Some signs indicated wallpapering, electrical goods, self-assembly kitchens and plumbing. Other signs were difficult to see due to the height of some shelves or used an unrecognisable logo!

In food retailing, a great deal of research regarding the arrangement of cash points has been undertaken. Cine film and video studies and time-lapse techniques have contributed to our understanding of customer behaviour, queuing patterns and the effects of layout design. Allied with computerised cash tills, cheque writing equipment, bar coding and scanning equipment, the actual customer processing time has decreased substantially.

When considering the total site area of the facility, there needs to be provision of a customer car park, possibly with a control/security barrier, a staff car park, unloading bays for lorries and safe traffic routing onto adjacent main roads.

WAREHOUSE LAYOUTS

A warehouse is a specialised kind of facility, in which commodities can be received, safely and securely stored, broken down into small unit loads, repackaged and dispatched. For perishable items, the layout design needs to promote a stock-rotation principle.

In many warehouses, costs are minimised by storing commodities as densely as possible. This is now facilitated by computerised control and bar-coding technology, which enables a random storage approach, rather than the use of defined areas for each separate commodity.

In laying out a new warehouse facility, attention should be given to the flow of items, aisle design, safe working practices, the mechanical handling equipment to be used, the degree and nature of any transformation processing which will be undertaken, the kind of pallets and racking required, the stacking height, the order-picking procedures and the despatch arrangements.

A mail order warehouse could be laid out to facilitate order picking in one of several ways:

- **customer route collecting**, allows the order picker to collect all the items needed for a customer whilst moving around a prescribed route through a warehouse. Where an automated guided vehicle is used, whether pulled through a sub-floor chain drag or operating as a battery-powered laser-guided vehicle, there will be a defined route. If pushing a simple trolley the picker covers the whole route progressively.

- **batch picking**, allows a quantity of like goods for different customers to be taken from a defined area and transported to a section in which they are consolidated into customer orders.

- **area picking**, requires the picker to obtain commodities without knowing who the customer is. The items are moved to an assembly area, often by conveyor, for consolidation into a customer's order. Data flows are by the use of remote computer terminals.

OFFICE LAYOUTS

As a result of the shift away from traditional shopfloor work towards service industry work in the UK over the past 20 years, a higher percentage of employees are today working in a facility which can be described as an office. In some cases, the office may be a desk in an open area, perhaps with a card index and a telephone. At the other extreme, the office may be a large complex, which is full of computing hardware, fax machines and TV conferencing linkages with remote sites.

In laying out an office or administrative facility in the past, three issues were paramount. There was a need to provide privacy, proximity and to reflect organisational hierarchical seniority. Within many organisations the two latter issues have been gradually dropped. The networked desktop computer has reduced the need for physical proximity. Using internal and external e-mail provides immediate written communication to back up work jointly done on the computer file. The development of leaner, flatter organisational structures through TQM and BPR procedures has swept away many divisive features. What are still required, however, within an administrative or office layout, are privacy areas for interview and consultation, and limited access areas in which resources are stored.

The traditional office layout provides the manager with a smaller private office, often with proximity to, and with a view of, the general office. The open-plan, or landscaped layout, is popular in some industries and service sectors. Staff of all disciplines and levels work at their own desks in a large room, screened only by plants and low furnishings. Walls are clad with sound-absorbing acoustic tiles, floors are carpeted and telephone bells muffled to provide a relatively quiet working environment. A typical layout is illustrated in Figure 5.

A development of the open-plan layout has been to design activity locations virtually on a cellular principle. This increases the mobility of staff as they move from workstation to workstation to complete whole tasks.

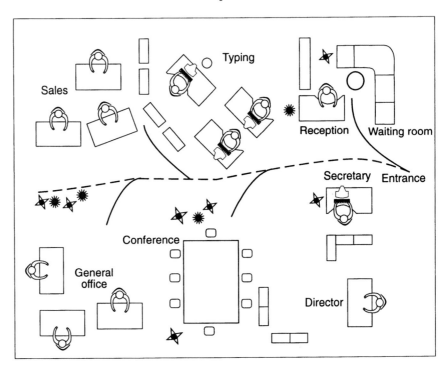

Figure 5: Open-plan office layout

4.4 Systematic layout planning

This approach to facility layout planning was developed by Muther (1970). He advocates the following methodology:

- Collect and analyse all the significant information about the processes which will go into the facility and select a type of layout: for example, product.

● Analyse the potential interactions between processes and seek to place those with frequent interaction nearest to each other.

● Construct a relationship (REL) chart containing codes showing the desirability or otherwise of proximity and the reasons.

● Estimate the space required for each process area.

● Evaluate alternatives using any appropriate technique, for example, travel charting (Resource 3.2); CRAFT (computerised relative allocation of facilities technique); CORELAP (computerised relationship layout planning).

● Convert the data into a two-dimensional layout using templates.

● Experiment heuristically to fine-tune the final layout proposal.

4.5 Business Process Reengineering (BPR)

The facilities currently being used by organisations and those likely to be required in the future come under scrutiny during the course of a reengineering exercise. BPR takes businesses one step further than TQM was able to and is in contrast to the traditional scientific, analytical management approach. Every major restructuring programme will have its advantages and disadvantages.

The important disadvantages for employees, are:

● retraining on jobs within the organisation

● facility relocation

● re-focusing and role change

● redundancy (or outplacement).

The employee advantages, however, are:

● new opportunities

● more meaningful and satisfying roles

● improved long-term employment prospects within a leaner, but fitter organisation.

We can define BPR in various ways:

● It is about starting again with a clean sheet, with a willingness to challenge existing power structures, assumptions and conventional wisdom. The objective is to find new ways of doing business.

● Rather than looking at narrow functions such as accounts, personnel and marketing, with BPR companies look at their business from the point of view of its outputs – what is delivered to customers, whether external or internal – and the steps that contribute to the process of creating those outputs.

● 'BPR is the fundamental re-thinking and radical re-design of business processes to achieve dramatic improvements in critical contemporary measures of performance, such as cost, quality, service and speed' (Hammer and Champy, 1993).

BPR attempts to identify those processes which add value to either the service or product. It then seeks to eliminate all the other processes from the organisation. Techniques like method study are, of course, of vital importance in assessing the productivity levels within the value-adding processes, and yet more efficiency gain can be achieved by studying them.

Organisations have been forced towards a radical overhaul of their operations by a number of factors in the external environment:

● opening up of global markets and labour sources

● intense competition for market share

● increasing customer demands for speed, quality and service

● need to cope with continual change.

Re-engineering requires courage and determination from senior management. Honest answers must be provided to questions like:

● Why do we do the job this particular way?

● Does this process add significant value to the service or product?

● Can technology be further used to achieve productivity gains?

In reality, these answers are not always readily available. Those responding to the questions may not be in harmony with the objectives of a BPR exercise. It is accepted that radical change is often a painful experience and is usually resisted either implicitly or explicitly. The answers given to these searching questions are not always exact, creative or unbiased, for the following reasons:

● fear of change, and one's ability to survive or cope

● desire to protect one's empire and staff

● changes to the present system or facility is a rejection of the original designer and his or her ideas.

Summary

In this section, we looked at the layout principles underlying the arrangement of a facility. We highlighted various layout types – product, process, fixed position, and cellular – and some of their advantages and disadvantages. We also considered special layout applications such as retail service facilities, warehouses, and offices.

Finally, we referred briefly to systematic layout planning and introduced, the concept of business process reengineering. We indicated the advantages and disadvantages of BPR for employees, the external factors which drive it and the questions that need to be addressed by an organisation undertaking a reengineering exercise.

Unit Review Activity

Answer the following questions:

1 How will a sound operations strategy for resource provisioning help in the achievement of corporate goals?

2 In what ways can organisational facilities be focused?

3 Describe the range of information needed for the review of an organisation's global operations strategy.

4 What is meant by capacity management?

5 Describe the ways in which a manufacturing facility can be laid out. Indicate the advantages of each approach.

6 Explain what BPR is.

Unit Summary

In this unit, we described various ways in which an organisation can focus its facilities, whether by groups of customers, geographically, by markets, products or processes. We then looked briefly at the strategic issues affecting businesses operating internationally.

We went on to note the importance of facilities and capacity management strategies and we defined a number of capacity management terms.

We discussed facilities, their size and location, and considered a range of facility types, from multiple factories to retailing and emergency services. We then examined different types of layout – product, process, fixed position and cellular – and some of their advantages and disadvantages, as well as special applications – retail, warehouses, and offices.

We concluded with a brief reference to systematic layout planning and an introduction to the concept of BPR.

References

Apple, J A (1977) *Plant Layout and Materials Handling*, John Wiley, New York

Hammer, M and Champy, J (1993) *Re-engineering the Corporation*, Harper Business Publications, London

Hayes, R and Wheelwright, S (1984) *Restoring our Competitive Edge: Competing through Manufacturing*, John Wiley, New York

Muther, R (1970) *Systematic Layout Planning*, Industrial Education Institute, Boston

Recommended Reading

Chase, R B and Aquilano, N J (1994) *Production and Operations Management*, Irwin, Homewood, Illinois, 7th edn

Dul, J and Weerdmeester, B (1988) *Ergonomics for Beginners*, Taylor and Francis, London

Grandjean, E (1988) *Fitting the Task to the Man*, Taylor and Francis, London

Answers to Unit Review Activity

1   The successful achievement of corporate goals will require effort from all parts of the organisation. Each part will use and consume resources (money, staffing, materials, machinery, premises, etc.). The use of an operations strategy will give the best chance of getting the balances and quantities of all resources right. For example: the distribution system will require strategic decisions on the mode of distribution (road/sea/air/rail) and the subsequent operational planning (unit loadings/depot locations/frequencies, etc.) then follows to optimise performance.

2   Organisational facilities can be focused:

● towards the specific customer

● relative to geographic considerations

● towards a particular market

● towards a particular product

● towards a specialised type of process.

3 There needs to be a considerable amount of sifting of data in order to extract information which will be pertinent for decision making. Such areas of interest could be:

- capacity considerations
- existing facilities
- current managerial structures and styles
- integration of effort and use of information technology
- nature of current R&D programmes.

4 This is the managerial skill used in matching an organisation's resources to the demands that are currently (or in the future, going to be) placed upon it. The aim is to achieve an efficient organisation in which there is a balancing of resources, from the input end, through the transformation system, to a successful product or service outcome. Sufficient flexibility should be designed in, so that significant fluctuations from the norm can be accommodated.

5 Product layouts are provided to achieve high volume, largely repetitive manufacturing facilities. All the processes required to make a particular commodity are provided in line formation, for example, car assembly lines. Amongst the advantages of product layouts are:

- high output levels
- control is relatively simple
- balancing leads to high resource utilisation
- minimal materials handling costs.

Process layouts include the grouping together of all similar processes or machinery. The advantages include:

- considerable flexibility in scheduling work
- machine breakdown problems can be overcome
- various types of product can be handled.

Fixed-position layouts are necessary when the product is large in size (for example, a power station electrical transformer), or must be made in a fixed location for example, a bridge. Advantages are gained through the planning of the whole manufacturing process, so that resources are provided at the right time and in the right quantity.

Cellular layouts have machinery grouped into 'cells'. Each cell is in effect a miniature product layout, dealing with very similar operations. After the initial capital investment, labour costs tend to be low, quality standards high. There are minimal delays due to setting-up requirements.

6 BPR is a fundamental rethinking and redesign of parts of businesses to achieve dramatic and cost-effective increases in performance.

UNIT 4
MANAGING DEMAND AND SUPPLY OF MATERIALS

Introduction

It is difficult to think of a business, either manufacturing or service, that does not use any inventory, sometimes called stock. In some types of business the amount of money tied up in inventory is very minor, but in a surprising number of businesses from supermarkets and restaurants, to bookstores and video shops, to builders and highway authorities, to distance learning MBA programmes, and to car and television manufacturers, inventory is a vital part of business operations. This unit considers the control of that inventory, from managing its demand to managing its supply. This is an important area for the operations manager: if there is no stock to sell, sales will be lost; it there is too much stock, money and warehousing are tied up. If there are insufficient supplies to make the stock, sales will be lost; if there are too many supplies; money and warehousing will be tied up.

Objectives

By the end of this unit, you should be able to:

- understand the components of demand management
- use various forecasting methods and know when to use them
- understand the difference between independent and dependent demand
- understand what materials requirements planning (MRP) is and where it is applicable
- perform MRP calculations
- use the basic economic order quantity (EOQ) and reorder point formulas
- know about other order quantity techniques
- know the limitations of the basic inventory formulas
- know what is meant by service level
- calculate safety stock levels
- use a number of time phased order point (TPOP) techniques
- understand the concept of ABC analysis.

SECTION 1

Demand Management

Introduction

Operations management is ultimately about serving customers who place demands on the organisation. These demands may be for products or services. This section deals with **demand management**, which is concerned with forecasting, influencing, promising and entering demands or orders. This is a central activity for both operations and marketing. Good demand management requires good co-operation between these two functions.

Demand management comprises three sub-areas: **order management**, **order service** and **forecasting**. These three functions are sometimes, but inappropriately, regarded as separate, but, as we shall see, there is much interaction. Their basic characteristics are shown in Figure 1.

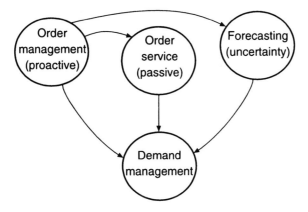

Figure 1: The three sub-areas of demand management

1.1 Order management

Order management is concerned with influencing, accepting, and translating requirements as placed by customers on a manufacturer or service provider. 'Influencing' means that order management is not passive but recognises that demands not only result from product attractiveness in the eyes of customer, as addressed by marketing and design, but are also influenced by expectations created as a result of actions and policies taken by operations. For example, customers may be discouraged by long queues or by unacceptable quoted delivery dates.

Pricing is the traditional mechanism for influencing demand. To maximise profit, but also to influence demand, prices tend to rise when demand rises and decrease when demand falls. Quantity discounts are widely offered.

With the advent of lean manufacturing, and of 'quick response' in the retail field (see Unit 9), as well as increased attention to cost competitiveness, many operations managers and marketing managers now recognise the importance of managing orders in ways which result in greater stability. Marketing has an important role to play in this. It may take actions which result in greater stability, for example, by encouraging off-peak demand, but it may also create instability, for example, by a promotion which is timed just when capacity is stretched or materials are in short supply. Sadly the latter type of event is still not unusual.

Marketing should not work independently of operations in sales promotions or making promises to customers. Equally, operations should not take actions which reduce costs at the expense of customer service. Both should have an interest in improved service and lower costs to customers. Co-operation through order management is one of the keys.

ACTIVITY 1

Think about the following common practices. Decide when, or if, each may be beneficial to customers and to the company:

- quantity discounts
- discounts for regular orders
- sales promotions
- incentives for salesmen which reward monthly sales performance
- information on advance bookings
- building or reducing inventories at financial year-end for accounting or tax purposes
- quoting longer delivery times.

You will realise that unilateral actions taken by operations, marketing, or accounting are seldom beneficial. Creating 'unnatural' demands may create short term benefit, but the longer term implications should be looked at. Many products, for example, toothpaste, have a finite maximum use, so creating a high demand one month may lead to decline in another. Much depends on market share. Some sales promotions result in large accumulations of inventory along the supply chain of retailer–distributor–manufacturer–supplier, resulting in more cost than the sales promotion brings in. Fuller *et al* (1993) suggested that only 25% of sales price promotions are profitable. Some companies such as Proctor and Gamble have moved towards a stated policy of 'everyday low prices'.

The traditional concept of quantity discounts is now being questioned by some manufacturing companies adopting JIT manufacturing methods (see Unit 9). JIT manufacturers tend to prefer regular demand to 'lumpy' demands and therefore are offering quantity discounts for regular orders rather than bulk orders.

Care must be taken when longer delivery times are quoted in response to increased demand. What may happen is that customers order earlier in response to longer quoted delivery lead times, thereby creating extra, but not real underlying, demand. The 'extra' orders in turn encourage the supplier to quote yet longer delivery lead times because the supplier does not have the capacity. A vicious circle develops. Extra demand may eventually trigger increased capacity investment in an attempt to reduce delivery lead times. When the extra capacity is installed and delivery lead times are reduced, orders collapse since the apparent increase was only as a result of increased lead times. This phenomenon has been named the 'lead time syndrome' by George Plossl (1985), and is shown in Figure 2.

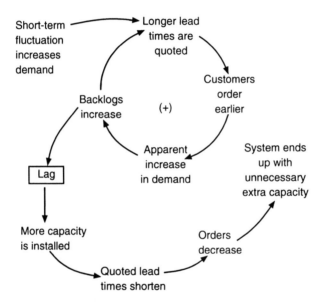

Figure 2: The 'lead time' syndrome

TECHNIQUES FOR ORDER MANAGEMENT
A number of techniques, both old and new, have been established to manage demand and orders more successfully. These include:

Establishing targets for order backlog and on-time performance
A target order backlog may help operations people stay within given bounds. A target order backlog means that a prescribed number of orders can be taken without delivery being made. Having too small a backlog may threaten the effective use of capacity, but having too large a backlog threatens customer service. Marketing and operations should agree on policy. A target for on-time delivery performance means that operations have a focused goal as they must deliver on time. Actions such as overtime may be authorised to meet the target.

'Consuming the forecast'

This indicates that for the immediate future, orders are more likely to be accurate than forecasts, but the reverse is true for the longer term. As orders come in they 'consume' the forecast. With time new forecasts are made.

Time fences

A time fence is simply a rolling time horizon within which plans are stabilised. Within the time fence, no new orders may be accepted which exceed the stated target, and the operations plan is fixed. We discuss this in detail in Unit 8, *Scheduling and Capacity*.

Available-to-promise logic

A standard feature in many manufacturing resource planning computer systems, this procedure compares orders taken with the production schedule and informs marketing of the difference. The difference between the two are orders that are **available to be promised** which will still meet the standard delivery times. Marketing is given a specific target to meet for several weeks into the future. Marketing should not oversell above the amounts available to be promised, otherwise quoted delivery dates will not be met.

'Variety as late as possible' and 'mass customisation'

We discuss these techniques, further in Unit 9, *Time Based Operations*. They allow a product to be produced in a standard way for as many steps as possible, whilst retaining flexibility and variety for as long as possible. Service examples include hamburgers or pizzas where the variety is added at the final stage to a standard product, and insurance policies that are pre-prepared but compiled to customer requirements. A manufacturing example is a built-to-order car, where the variety is made up from standard modules which are made well in advance of the order. This dramatically cuts customer delivery time whilst still providing the impression of uniqueness.

ORDER MANAGEMENT IN A 'QUICK RESPONSE' ENVIRONMENT

With the influence of time-based competitiveness and JIT, many manufacturing and service companies are attempting to become more responsive. Quick response implies being able to respond, along the supply-manufacturing-distribution chain, to customer demands in a short period of time. We consider this in detail in Unit 9, here we consider the implications for forecasting and order management. Prime examples of quick response are the retail fashion chain Benetton, which aims to respond to changes in demands for sweater colours within one week, and Caterpillar, which aims to supply any spare part for its bulldozers anywhere in the world within one day. Of course, such quick response requires considerable flexibility all along the supply-manufacturing distribution chain. Some implications for forecasting and order management are:

1   To be more responsive requires that the company truly understands its customers better. This includes understanding exactly what is needed, why it is needed, and when it is needed. For example, when Nikon expanded its camera business outside Japan, marketing and design staff spent time working at Western camera retailers and when Toyota decided to introduce the Lexus

range the design staff were sent to live in California to absorb the lifestyle of what was to be their future main market.

2 As a company becomes more responsive so the nature of the forecasting changes from long term to short term. Short-term forecasts use different methods and are inherently more accurate. In some environments, for example in supermarkets, electronic point-of-sale (EPOS) terminals enable retailers to know from minute to minute what sales patterns are developing. Retailers now know more about their customers than do manufacturers. In the UK, some supermarket chains may follow chains in the US where customer cards enable detailed profiles to be built up on individual customers, thus enabling even tighter forecasts and targeted advertising. Replenishments become demand-based 'pull' rather than forecast-based 'push'. With improved short-term forecast accuracy, coupled to an increased ability to respond faster, the need for large safety inventories decreases.

ACTIVITY 2

You or members of your family or colleagues may have store cards, for example, Tesco, or credit cards from known purchase analysers, for example, American Express. What do you think about the effectiveness of information gained on your purchasing habits? What might this information be used for?

Of course, opinions will vary about the effectiveness. Perhaps you only shop at Tesco for your wine and petrol supplies; or only use your American Express card on holiday, so any information to the analyser may be unhelpful. There is also the issue of data protection and unethical use of information. There is little doubt that where such information can legally be collected and analysed, the implications for marketing and for operations are vast. Many customers will show predicatable behaviour in their purchases, and the effect of offers and, say, in-store promotions can be easily monitored. Possibilities include personal special promotions, and less risk of new product introductions failing. *The Economist* 1995 reported that 20,076 new products appeared on the shelves of America's supermarkets and drugstores in 1994 compared with only 1,365 in 1970 and that less than 10% are expected to still be on the market in two years. Also, reduced uncertainty could lead to improved freshness and reduced inventories, which in turn may lower costs or improve profitability, and to more effective use of shelf space, which in turn may lead to increased variety.

1.2 Order service

Order service is the process of accepting customer orders, and entering them into the system for the use of manufacturers or distributors. It is a passive activity, but may make use of the available-to-promise logic we discussed in the last section. It may involve assisting the customer with the selection of options. Recently, with an increasing tendency towards customisation of products, 'configurators' have been developed which assist a customer in making a valid choice of product options, for example, a sunroof is not available on a convertible car. These configurators have the effect, hidden from the salesman and customer, of pre-specifying the appropriate bill of materials for the option, to make it easier for manufacturing to build the product. Don't worry about the term bill of materials, at this stage we discuss it in Section 2. Typical order service processes in make-to-order and make-to-stock environments are shown in Figure 3.

In a make-to-stock environment non customer-specific products are made and stored until demanded by customers. They are then 'picked and packed' either by customers (as in a supermarket) or by staff (as in a mail-order house). In a make-to-order environment products are either designed to customer requirements, such as with a bridge, or 'configured' to customer specification, such as selecting engine types or colours in a new car.

1.3 Forecasting

DEPENDENT AND INDEPENDENT DEMAND

If services or products can be obtained easily or made quickly using readily available skills or resources that are in plentiful supply, then there is little necessity to forecast. This is sometimes the case. As the risk of not having the necessary resources or time to carry out an activity increases, so the necessity to forecast increases. We are all involved in forecasting; housekeepers forecast future household requirements, builders order materials to avoid future delays, shopkeepers keep sufficient stock to satisfy anticipated demand, and manufacturers order components and raw materials to enable them to build products in time.

In anticipating future requirements, there are two circumstances, **independent demand** and **dependent demand**. Independent demand is demand that is unrelated to any 'higher level' item. This is typical of items purchased from shops; the demand for cornflakes is considered independent from the demand for soap. Such items are referred to as 'end items'. On the other hand, dependent demand is related to the demand for a higher level item. For example, the number of tyres that a manufacturer uses in building a new car is directly related to the number of end items, in this case cars, that are to be built. The number of cars to be built is an independent end item and this has to be forecast, but the number of tyres to be used is a dependent item which is calculated from the number of cars to be built. It would be silly for the car manufacturer to treat the requirements for tyres as an independent item unrelated to the number of cars to be built.

This distinction between dependent and independent demand is fundamental in operations management. Each has its own relevant theory, which we deal with in this unit. Forecasting and independent inventory management is appropriate for independent demand situations, and material requirements planning (MRP) is appropriate for dependent demand situations. We look at MRP in the next section.

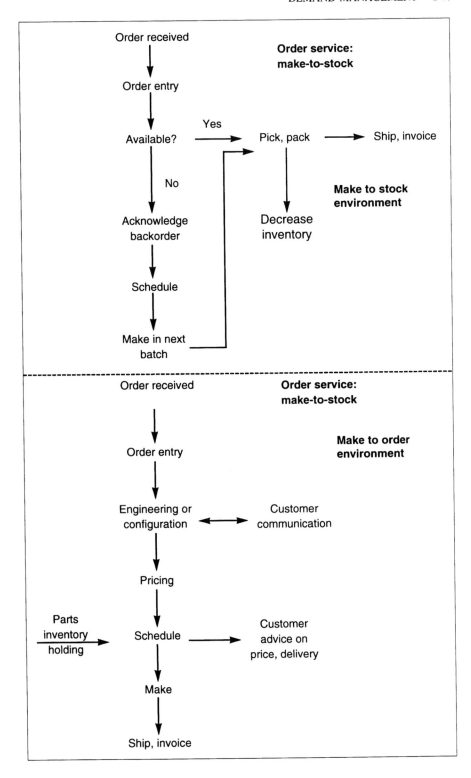

Figure 3: Order service in different environments

ACTIVITY 3

Consider the following items. For each, state whether you think it is a dependent or an independent item, and comment:
car tyres
boxes of cornflakes
milk
consulting services
hotel accommodation
textbooks
novels
electricity supplied.

You will realise that, very often, the categorisation depends on the circumstances. A tyre would be a dependent item for a car manufacturer, but an independent item for a quick-fit tyre supplier. Spare parts are often made to satisfy known end item requirements as well as to be used as spare parts. This dual requirement is easily handled in MRP (see Section 2). A textbook may be regarded as a dependent item based on the number of students, but the link is tenuous as not all students will buy a copy and the number of students is difficult to forecast, so many publishers would treat a textbook as an independent item. All other items are usually independent, but remember, do not forecast demand when it can be calculated.

FORECASTING TECHNIQUES

In operations management, we occasionally hear the statement 'the only thing you can say for sure about a forecast is that it will be wrong'. This statement sets the scene, however involved or rigorous a forecasting procedure may appear to be.

Broadly, forecasting techniques for operations management may be subdivided into **qualitative** and **quantitative** approaches as shown in Figure 4. But beware of selecting or relying on exclusively one or the other. Very often a final forecast will rely on both qualitative and quantitative inputs – one forming a check or validation on the other.

Qualitative forecasting techniques

Qualitative techniques rely on the judgement, intuition or experience of experts. They are used in situations of increased uncertainty, for example, a new product introduction, a new technology, a special event such as the Rugby World Cup, or to predict the impact on product sales of unusual developments such as the Gulf War. They may appear to be 'unscientific' but should not be regarded as a second-best alternative to quantitative techniques. We discuss four qualitative techniques: management consensus, Delphi, market research and historical analogy. However, there are several variations on each.

Management consensus

For this technique a small group of experienced managers are asked to give their 'gut feel' estimates. Senior managers accumulate a vast store of knowledge which

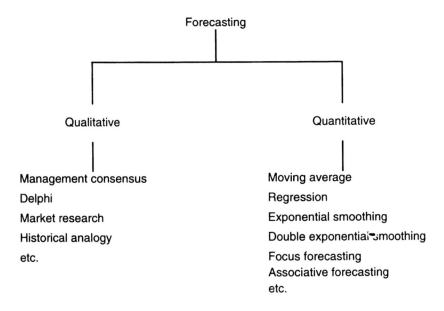

Figure 4: Qualitative and quantitative forecasting

this technique tries to tap into. Usually the group talks through differences in opinion until consensus is reached. Ideally, the group should be multidisciplinary, and should not feel constrained in expressing opinions. Several limitations of this technique are generally accepted. These include the risk of disagreement with a less well-informed but powerful manager, a 'hidden agenda' or personal power politics, and the phenomenon of 'group think'. (You may have met this in your studies on human relations.) Whatever forecasting technique is adopted, a forecast will usually have to be acceptable to management; so in this sense management consensus may be the most common forecasting technique of all!

Delphi

The Delphi method is a more structured form of group consensus involving outside experts who should have a special knowledge of the forecast area. Unlike management consensus, Delphi can be conducted by several experts who are located at different sites and may not even know the rest of the panel. Delphi is conducted over several iterations. Secret forecasts are collected from each panellist and the average determined. Panellists responsible for results which are significantly different from the average, are asked to either change their forecast to bring it in line with the group or to provide information on why they believe their original estimate was correct. Perhaps a non-conforming panellist has information not known to the others. Then all panellists are provided with the new information and the process is repeated until a sufficient level of consensus is reached. The technique is common for 'technological forecasting'. For example, by what date do you expect 90% of British university students to have their own Internet connections? How many electric vehicles will be in regular use in the UK by 2010?

Market research

You will probably have been exposed to market research in your marketing studies. It is a type of forecasting or statistical sampling and may involve quantitative data. It can take various forms: focus groups, consumer surveys (which itself can take many forms) and complaints analysis. Often, for forecasting purposes, the collected information is subjected to adjustment to correlate past experiences with anticipated developments.

Historical analogy

This uses past experience of special events as a guide to what may happen when a similar event takes place. For example, what will be the demand for Coca Cola at the next World Cup?

ACTIVITY 4

Consider the four qualitative techniques discussed. Rank them in terms of cost, time taken, and accuracy. Consider the suitability of each in forecasting expected use of a new technology, for example, high definition television, and a new service, for example, holiday booking via the Internet, without using a travel agent.

Management consensus is least expensive, often fast, but results may be highly variable depending on the experience of the managers and the degree of internal politics. Delphi can be moderately expensive, and a typical time to undertake is several weeks, especially if world experts are used. Results are variable but this may be all that is possible. Market surveys can prove very expensive and time-consuming. The survey instrument has to be carefully designed. They are good for short-term, less good for long-term forecasts. They are also most effective where participants understand the change, but can be useless for new developments. Historical analogy is low-to-moderate in terms of cost and time, depending on the degree of involvement by the company in the previous situation. Typically it has low forecast accuracy, but may result in some valuable insights into the wider problem.

QUANTITATIVE FORECASTING TECHNIQUES

In your previous studies on quantitative methods, you will probably have met some basic techniques of quantitative forecasting. We can make two general observations.

1   A good forecast should always be two numbers: the forecast itself and an estimate of the accuracy of the forecast.

2   The further ahead you forecast, the more difficult it is. However, for longer-term forecasts it will usually be good enough to forecast in terms of aggregated (or family) units. For example, looking a year ahead, it will usually be good enough to forecast how many Ford Mondeos will be sold, and it will be of less interest to know how many two litre cars are forecasted to be sold, and it will

be of even less use to forecast how many red two litre Ford Mondeos will be sold. In the short term, these more detailed figures will be of much more relevance. An aggregate forecast is in general easier to make than a more detailed forecast.

There are many quantitative forecasting techniques available, from basic, such as the moving average method, to highly sophisticated statistical techniques such as Box-Jenkins Time Series forecasting. Here we consider some basic but popular quantitative forecasting techniques: exponential smoothing, double exponential smoothing, focus forecasting, and associative forecasting.

EXPONENTIAL AND DOUBLE EXPONENTIAL SMOOTHING

Exponential smoothing is really a moving average technique, but one which gives a different weight to each period's data. The formula for exponential smoothing is:

$$F_t = F_{t-1} + \propto (A_{t-1} - F_{t-1})$$

where
F_t = forecast for period t
F_{t-1} = forecast made for period t-1
A_{t-1} = actual demand for period t-1
$\propto$ = the smoothing constant.

In words we can say:

New forecast = last period's forecast + $\propto$ (last period's actual demand – last period's forecast)

The second term in the equation is called the **error term** (last period's actual demand – last period's forecast). For a $\propto$ value of 0.1, the weighting of the error term will be:

0.1 for one period in arrears
(0.1)(0.9) = 0.09 for two periods in arrears
(0.1)(0.9)(0.9) = 0.081 for three periods in arrears
and so on.

This is where the term 'exponential smoothing' comes from. Past terms are exponentially weighted, that is, the weighting of 0.9 is raised to a higher power for each older period.

The value of $\propto$ ranges from 0 to 1. For an $\propto$ value of 1, of course, the forecast for the current period is the same as the demand for the current period, and for an $\propto$ value of 0, the forecast remains unchanged. This suggests that the value of $\propto$ should be adjusted according to the expected instability; where change is expected the $\propto$ value should be increased. In practice, an $\propto$ value of around 0.15 is usual.

One reason why exponential smoothing is popular is because it is efficient with respect to the amount of historic data that has to be held as only the last forecast needs to be retained, but the formula 'remembers' data stretching back indefinitely but with decreasing weights.

You will notice that exponential smoothing is fairly successful where there is stable data such as in Set A. A higher alpha value is not warranted. But, especially if you plotted a graph, you will notice that where there is a step change or trend, it is not so successful. A higher value is warranted.

Exponential smoothing is therefore used for items where demand is more stable, such as furniture or spare parts, but is not suitable where there are short-term changes such as in fashion goods. Where a trend is likely, a modification called 'second order exponential smoothing', or **double exponential smoothing**, is preferable. The formulas for this are:

$$FT_t = F_t + T_t$$

$$F_t = FT_{t-1} + \propto (A_{t-1} - FT_{t-1})$$

$$T_t = T_{t-1} + \beta (A_{t-1} - FT_{t-1})$$

where

F_t is the forecast including the trend and

T is the trend.

ACTIVITY 5

For each set of data given below, calculate what the exponentionally smoothed forecast would have been, and the forecast errors, for $\propto$ values of 0.2 and 0.5. Plot the results on graph paper and comment. The first few lines of the calculation have been worked out for you in each set. Go over these calculations and make sure that you get the same answers. Then complete each set.

Set A

Week	Actual Demand	Forecast ($\propto = 0.2$)	Forecast ($\propto = 0.5$)	Forecast Error ($\propto = 0.2$)	Forecast Error ($\propto = 0.5$)
1	200	200	200	0	0
2	210	200	200	10	10
3	190	202	205	-12	-15
4	215				
5	220				
6	215				

Set B

Week	Actual Demand	Forecast ($\propto = 0.2$)	Forecast ($\propto = 0.5$)	Forecast Error ($\propto = 0.2$)	Forecast Error ($\propto = 0.5$)
1	200	200	200	0	0

Set B continued

Week	Actual Demand	Forecast ($\propto = 0.2$)	Forecast ($\propto = 0.5$)	Forecast Error ($\propto = 0.2$)	Forecast Error ($\propto = 0.5$)
2	210	200	200	0	0
3	220	202	205	18	15
4	230				
5	240				
6	250				

Set C

Week	Actual Demand	Forecast ($\propto = 0.2$)	Forecast ($\propto = 0.5$)	Forecast Error ($\propto = 0.2$)	Forecast Error ($\propto = 0.5$)
1	200	200	200	0	0
2	200	200	200	0	0
3	230				
4	230				
5	230				
6	230				
7	230				

ACTIVITY 6

Using the data sets B and C below, calculate the double exponentially smoothed forecast. Use an $\propto$ value of 0.2, a β of 0.4, and an initial trend of 0. Plot the results on graph paper and comment. The first few lines of the calculation have been worked out for you in each set. Go over these calculations and make sure you get the same answers. Then complete each set.

Set B

Week	Actual Demand	Trend ($\beta = 0.4$)	Forecast ($\propto = 0.2$)
1	200	0	200
2	210	0	200
3	220	0.8	202
4	230	1.66	205.76
5	240		
6	250		

Set C

Week	Actual Demand	Trend ($\beta = 0.4$)	Forecast ($\propto = 0.2$)
1	200	0	200
2	200	0	200
3	230	0	200
4	230	2.4	206
5	230	5.08	212.7
6	230		
7	230		

This exercise will give you some practice at double exponential forecasting. You should also compare the results with the former sets. Here, of course, starting with a trend of zero makes the results less dramatic.

Focus forecasting

Focus forecasting is not really a forecasting technique but rather a simulation or trial and error procedure. It takes a set of simple forecasting rules, applies them to past data, finds out which of the rules would have worked best for the latest period, and then uses this same rule for the next period. The forecasting rules are all basic, such as last month's actual = this month's forecast, a two period moving average, and a three period moving average weighted 0.5. 0.3, 0.2. The remarkable thing about focus forecasting is that it has often outperformed more sophisticated models (see Vollman *et al*, 1992).

Associative forecasting

Associative forecasting links external information with internal information in an attempt to establish a relationship which can be used for forecasting. When a relationship exists it can be measured by a correlation coefficient. One example would be to link ice cream sales with temperature, and then to use long-term weather forecasts to forecast sales. The number of students registered at the university may be correlated with meals sold in the student canteen. Governments and research organisations publish various indicators on, for example, unemployment, inflation, and housing which may be correlated with company sales of relevant products or services.

FORECASTING AND THE PRODUCT LIFE CYCLE

Different forecasting techniques are applicable at different stages in a product life cycle. We will not discuss this in detail but merely point out that the stage in the life cycle is relevant to the choice of forecasting method. Consult Table 1 for details.

Forecasting technique	Stage in product life cycle				
	Start-up	Growth	Maturity	Decline	Termination
Exponential smoothing			X		
Double exponential smoothing		X		X	
Associative forecasting		X	X	X	
Moving average			X		
Time series forecasting		X	X	X	
Delphi	X				X
Historical analogy	X	X			
Market research		X		X	X
Management consensus	X				X

Table 1: Forecasting and the product life cycle

FORECAST MANAGEMENT

What are the consequences of a forecast that is too high or too low on the various functions. The marketing function often produces forecasts which are too optimistic. For marketing, the consequences are probably lower than for any other function. For accounting, however, the reverse is true. Too high a forecast might lead to an inability to absorb overhead resulting in a magnification of loss, but if the forecast is too low profit may well increase by more than the forecast error percentage provided that operations can respond. For capacity, there may be no implications or big implications, because fixed capacity is usually added in lumps. For personnel, there may be direct consequences relating to overtime, layoffs, or hiring. Too pessimistic a forecast may lead to distribution problems resulting in longer lead times and thus an inability to capitalise on the favourable conditions. All this tells us that forecasts must be monitored, with more attention given to more important items.

The attention given to a forecast should be a function of the **importance** of the item. Generally a manager will not have the time to pay attention to hundreds or thousands of forecasts each month. In Section 3, you will learn more about inventory classification methods, but here it is sufficient to know that A items are the most important, followed by B and C items. A items usually make up a small proportion of the units, but account for a large proportion of profit or cost. With an A item you would take particular care of the selection and review of the forecasting method, you might be prepared to pay for market research or expert opinion, and operations and marketing would probably discuss trends and changes in the marketplace. For a C item, you may be quite happy to let the computer produce forecasts using, say, exponential smoothing and only look at forecasts that appear to be going wrong.

All forecasts should be monitored for **accuracy**. You would like assurance that the forecasting method being used is producing acceptable results. When we discussed exponential smoothing we introduced the concept of the 'error term'. This is the difference between the actual and forecasted quantities for any period, multiplied by the smoothing constant. Clearly, if your forecasting system is performing well, you would expect the cumulative sum of this error term to tend towards zero. That is, you would expect some forecasts to be on the high side, and some on the low but these should roughly balance out. If the cumulative sum of the error terms tends to grow or decline steadily, there is obviously a problem with the forecasting method being used, and you should stop and investigate. This is known as *bias* and is defined as:

$$\frac{\Sigma\,(A_i\text{-}\,F_i)}{N}$$

What is needed is an automatic procedure to know when a forecast method is 'out of control'. There are several tracking systems, and we shall look at a basic one. In Unit 6, *Quality Management*, we will discuss the concept of statistical process control (SPC). Here, as with forecasts, there is 'natural variation'. In SPC, control limits are set up and the process is monitored. If a reading goes beyond the control limit, the process is stopped because quality is in danger. This is exactly the procedure used for monitoring forecasts. A tracking signal is established, where:

$$\text{tracking signal} = \frac{\Sigma\,(A_i - F_i)}{\Sigma |A_i - F_i|/N}$$

$$= \frac{\Sigma\,(A_i - F_i)}{\text{MAD}}$$

Where A_i is actual demand in period i

F_i is forecast demand in period i

The divisor in this equation is known as the *mean absolute deviation* (MAD). It is a measure of overall forecast error $= \Sigma \dfrac{|\text{Forecast errors}|}{N}$

Very roughly, the standard deviation is equal to 1.25 × MAD. Now in SPC the control limits are often set at plus or minus 3 standard deviations. So in the monitoring of forecasts, the trip point that is often used is a tracking signal value of 4. Thus, for each period, the tracking signal is calculated using the above formula. If there is no problem you would expect the value of the tracking signal to be low. If, however, it rises above a value of 4, a review of the forecasting method being used is called for. This may happen, for example, if a previously level series develops a trend.

Summary

In this section we have seen how demand management comprises three components: order management, order service and forecasting. Order management is concerned with influencing the timing of customer orders in order to assist operations management to avoid lumpy demand patterns, and to provide customers with reliable delivery dates. We have noted that marketing and operations each have an important role to play in this. Order servicing is concerned with efficient order entry. Forecasting uses qualitative and quantitative techniques to predict customer demands. The selection of the most appropriate forecasting technique depends on a variety of factors including the nature of the product itself and its position on the product life cycle. Forecasts must also be controlled, and we examined a tracking procedure to do this.

SECTION 2

Material Requirements Planning (MRP)

Introduction

In the previous section we noted that independent demands need to be forecast but dependent demands should be calculated. This section deals with that calculation or material requirements planning (MRP).

2.1 Background and need for MRP

Why has inventory management in general, and MRP in particular, become such a big issue? It is simply that, from the turn of the century for most manufacturing companies, the proportion of total product cost comprised of bought-in materials, components, and sub-assemblies has grown steadily. In manufacturing today it is not untypical for these to account for 60% of total product cost. In some industries, for example electronics, the proportion often exceeds 80%. It is a trend that is likely to continue. Over the past decade most car manufacturers, led by the Japanese, have put out an ever greater proportion of work to subcontractors. Subcontractors are now doing the same. It is really a question of focus – each manufacturer would like to (and with increasing technological specialisation can only afford to) do only what they are good at.

Early in the century a large proportion of costs within any factory were in direct labour. This was because more work was being done in-house than is often the case now and because there was less automation. This explains why Frederick Taylor and his scientific management school spent so much time on direct labour, and why much management accounting has until recently been so heavily biased towards direct labour. Today, generally speaking, the costs are in materials, which helps explain the advent of MRP we discussed here, and the interest in JIT and purchasing we discuss in Unit 9. In JIT manufacturing, managers are much more interested in keeping materials moving than in keeping labour busy, especially if that labour is producing excessive inventories that tie up the company's cash for a considerable time.

ACTIVITY 7

If most costs are now in materials, then control of materials becomes critical. Also, the opportunities for cost reduction are proportionally greater. Consider the following annual figures (see Meredith, 1992):

Sales	£1,000,000
Cost of materials	£ 600,000
Cost of direct labour	£ 100,000
Overheads	£ 250,000
Profit	£ 50,000

How can profit be increased to £75,000 per annum (a 50% increase)? Some options are to increase price, to increase sales, to reduce material costs, to reduce direct labour costs, or to cut overheads. Assuming all other ratios are kept constant, calculate the percentage changes required for each of these alternatives. Now comment on the alternatives.

Did the figures surprise you? If ratios are kept constant, sales need to increase by £500,000 per annum (or 50%), but the same result can be achieved by a cut of about 4% in materials! Increasing the price by 2.5% may look attractive at first glance, but may not be possible in a competitive environment. A 10% cut in overheads may also be considered attractive, which probably explains why so many companies have gone in for 'downsizing' in recent years. But this carries the risk of losing valuable expertise. The direct labour option is probably no longer feasible for many manufacturing companies; in manufacturing, direct labour has been squeezed continuously for most of this century – now there is not much left.

Typically, when MRP is introduced as a replacement for a reorder point (ROP) system, the savings in inventory are around 2 to 5% per annum with a one-off inventory cut of 25 to 35%. In a ROP system, inventory is ordered depending on the supplier delivery time. To cope with any short fall, a reserve or safety stock must be held. In our example, we can see the effects of such cuts on the bottom line profit. Some of this 2 to 5% reduction is due to the increased discipline that MRP requires. In addition, more savings in materials are brought about by improved design, value engineering, and purchasing procedures. We come back to this later.

2.2 MRP and bill of materials

In common with all inventory management systems, MRP sets out to determine what items to order, and when to order them. MRP is primarily found in manufacturing industries, but some service examples have also appeared. MRP has been used, for example, in hospitals and in high-rise buildings.

MRP uses a **bill of materials** or product structure to 'explode out' the requirements for lower-level materials and components. The 'net requirements' are determined by comparing the gross requirements with on-hand inventory balances, and 'offsetting' by the appropriate lead time. There are a number of new terms here, so let us take it slowly.

First, the bill of materials details the components that go into the 'end item' or final product. It is like a recipe for a cake; all the ingredients are listed. In some cases two or more ingredients are used to make an identifiable item which is then used in the cake. An example is the icing made up from icing sugar and water. We will use the example of a calculator. Figure 5 shows the traditional bill of materials structure and the indented bill of materials for a calculator. The indented bill shows what components go into what sub-assemblies, and how the sub-assemblies go into the final product. Each indentation represents a different level in the bill.

If you were going to make 100 calculators, and had no components on hand, and if you did not intend to make the calculators ever again, the bill of materials would be all that you would need. To calculate how many of each component you would need, you would simply multiply out by the appropriate quantities. This is called **exploding** the bill of materials. To do this successfully we need to know how many or how much of each component is needed to make one calculator. These quantities are referred to as **quantities per**. You will notice in Figure 5 that the bill of materials is structured on various 'levels': the end item, in this case the complete calculator, is referred to as 'Level 0', and each level down in the bill of materials has its own level number, increasing by 1 for each level. The resulting levels are written in on the bill of materials. A **component** at any level may have a **parent** on the level above. The quantities per for each component refer to the numbers required to go into the immediate parent item, not the end item. The quantities per are shown on the bill of materials, in this case in brackets.

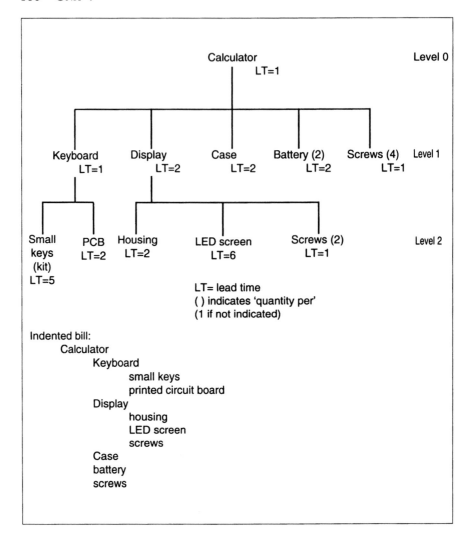

Figure 5: Bill of materials for a calculator

One other category of information is needed on the bill of materials. This is the **lead time** (LT in Figure 5). The lead time is the time required to obtain a component from an external supplier, or the time normally required to make a parent item assuming that you have the necessary component items available. The lead times are shown on the bill of materials next to each parent item. Sufficient time needs to be allowed to acquire component items from suppliers or to manufacture the parent items. Manufacturing lead times include the actual time to manufacture the batch of items, but also allow time for materials to be moved from process to process, time for waiting for the move to take place, and time to queue in front of a process waiting actual processing. This is referred to as **offsetting** by the lead times.

2.3 MRP calculations

It is usual in ongoing operations to have quantities of various components available in inventory. This information is kept in the inventory record file for each component. The MRP calculation process then explodes out the bill of materials to determine the gross requirements of each component item. The on-hand inventory (if any) of each component is then subtracted from the gross requirements to give the net requirements. This is called **netting**.

We will now work through our example of determining the material requirements for making 100 calculators, due for completion in week 10 (that is, 10 weeks from now). The calculation has been started in Figure 6.

Week	0	1	2	3	4	5	6	7	8	9	10
Calculator											
Gross requirements											100
Scheduled receipts											
Projected on-hand balance											0
Planned order receipts											100
Planned order releases										100	
Keyboard											
Gross requirements											100
Scheduled receipts											
Projected on-hand balance										0	
Planned order receipts										100	
Planned order releases								100			
Display											
Gross requirements											100
Scheduled receipts											
Projected on-hand balance										0	
Planned order receipts										100	
Planned order releases								100			
Case											
Gross requirements											100
Scheduled receipts											
Projected on-hand balance										0	
Planned order receipts										100	
Planned order releases								100			
Battery											
Gross requirements											200
Scheduled receipts											
Projected on-hand balance										0	
Planned order receipts										200	
Planned order releases								200			

Week	0	1	2	3	4	5	6	7	8	9	10
Small keys (kit)											
Gross requirements									100		
Scheduled receipts											
Projected on-hand balance									0		
Planned order receipts									100		
Planned order releases				100							
Printed circuit board											
Gross requirements									100		
Scheduled receipts											
Projected on-hand balance									0		
Planned order receipts									100		
Planned order releases							100				
Housing											
Gross requirements											
Scheduled receipts											
Projected on-hand balance											
Planned order receipts											
Planned order releases											
LED screen											
Gross requirements											
Scheduled receipts											
Projected on-hand balance											
Planned order receipts											
Planned order releases											
Screws											
Gross requirements											
Scheduled receipts											
Projected on-hand balance											
Planned order receipts											
Planned order releases											

Figure 6: Determining the materials requirements for making 100 calculators

We now explain MRP, usually shown in a standard format as in Figure 6.

The **gross requirements** line shows the total quantities of each component that are due for completion in any week. Normally the requirements are for the immediate week ahead, so we might standardise on a Monday morning, for example. Many modern MRP systems use days rather than weeks.

The **scheduled receipts** line shows the quantities of the item which have been ordered already, and which are scheduled to be received in a particular week.

The **projected on-hand balance** line shows, for each week out into the future, what the expected inventory holding will be. This line begins with the current inventory holding of the item.

The **planned order receipt** line shows the actual quantities that are planned to be received during future weeks. The difference from the scheduled receipt line is that planned order receipts have only been planned, they have not yet been released as orders. When they are released to suppliers or to manufacturing they become scheduled receipts. As planned orders they can be easily changed.

The formula for calculating planned order receipts is as follows for each period:

Planned order receipts =
    Gross requirements – Scheduled receipts – Projected on-hand balance.

A planned order receipt is required whenever the projected on-hand balance falls below the safety stock level (or zero if there is no safety stock).

The **planned order release** line shows the quantities that are planned to be released as orders to suppliers or to manufacturing. This line is exactly the same as the planned order receipt line and is offset by the appropriate lead time.

Before starting the bill of materials explosion process, we need to decide on the order in which calculations will be done. The rule is to proceed level by level through the bill of materials and not to start on any level before all items on the higher level have been completed. Where a component occurs at more than one level in the bill, calculation must be delayed until the lowest level at which the item occurs. This is why level coding is necessary. When a computer explodes out the bill of material, it first searches through all bills identifying the lowest level at which each component occurs.

Notice how planned order receipts of parent items are carried directly down to become gross requirements for component items. There is no lead time offset here. This is logical if we consider that as soon as one component is complete it is available to progress to the next stage of manufacture, and included in the lead time is time to move components from one process to another. Notice also that gross requirements make allowance for the 'quantities per'.

ACTIVITY 8

Complete the MRP record started in Figure 6 for 100 calculators required in week 10. Assume on-hand stocks of all components are zero.

You should obtain the following planned order releases:
200 housings in week 5
100 LED screens in week 1
200 screws in week 6, and 400 screws in week 8.
See completed record (Figure 7).

Week	0	1	2	3	4	5	6	7	8	9	10
Housing											
Gross requirements								200			
Scheduled receipts											
Projected on-hand balance								0			
Planned order receipts								200			
Planned order releases						200					
LED screen											
Gross requirements								100			
Scheduled receipts											
Projected on-hand balance								0			
Planned order receipts								100			
Planned order releases		100									
Screws											
Gross requirements								200		400	
Scheduled receipts											
Projected on-hand balance								0		0	
Planned order receipts								200		400	
Planned order releases							200		400		

Figure 7: Completed materials requirements for 100 calculators

Notice how planned order releases are carried down to gross requirements multiplied by the quantities per. Notice also that the calculation for screws is delayed until the lowest level in the bill where screws occur. The gross requirements for screws have to be carried down from two parent items, so the gross requirements are 200 in week 7 and 400 in week 9.

In real MRP environments there are some additional features: a master production schedule, saftey stock and batching. We look at each of these in turn.

A **master production schedule (MPS)** is established for each end item. This lists the planned requirement dates and quantities for the final products. There are often several scheduled requirements. In MRP terminology, the MPS 'drives' MRP. In our earlier service examples, the MPS would be patients with a particular complaint, or the schedule for completing each floor in the high rise building. We come back to MPS in Unit 8. For now, the essential relationships are shown in Figure 8.

Often, a **safety stock** of component items is held as a buffer against unexpected requirements or events. This is particularly true at the top and bottom of the bill of materials. Examples are late deliveries and quality problems resulting in defective items. Where there are safety stocks, the aim is to keep the on-hand balance at the safety stock level. Planned order releases must be adjusted accordingly.

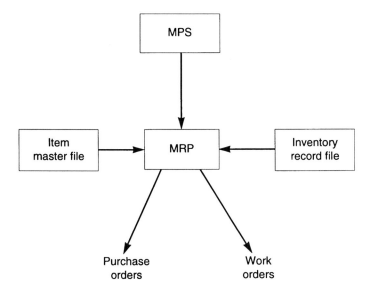

Figure 8: Master production scheduling and MRP

In manufacturing it is common to acquire and make products in specific **batch sizes** or **lot sizes**. Net requirements might indicate a certain quantity which is not a normal batch size. The normal batch size is then selected as a planned order release. Where no batch size is specified, you order the exact quantity required as above. This is known as **lot-for-lot**. Ordering or manufacturing in batches may result in on-hand quantities being higher than the safety stock or target levels, but this will be corrected the next time the explosion process is carried out.

ACTIVITY 9

Carry out the MRP explosion process for the calculator given the following master production schedule, safety stocks, and standard batch sizes.

The master production schedule calls for 100 calculators in week 6 and 200 in week 10.

On-hand balances are all zero except for the following:
500 LED screens
200 keyboards
500 screws.

Safety stocks are all zero except for LED screens, where safety stock is 100; order quantities are in multiples of 100, except for screws which must be ordered in batches of 1,000.

Your answer should agree with Figure 9. You will realise that MRP is a very error-prone process when done by hand. An error made at one level is carried down to all levels below. Fortunately, MRP is usually done by computer although it is useful to understand the calculation process.

Week	0	1	2	3	4	5	6	7	8	9	10
Housing											
Gross requirements				100				400			
Scheduled receipts											
Project on-hand balance				0				0			
Planned order receipts				100				400			
Planned order releases		100				400					
LED screen											
Gross requirements				50				200			
Scheduled receipts											
Projected on-hand balance	500	500	500	450	450	450	450	250	250	250	250
Planned order receipts											
Planned order releases											
Screws											
Gross requirements				100		400		400		800	
Scheduled receipts											
Projected on-hand balance	500	500	500	400	400	0	0	600	600	800	800
Planned order receipts								1000		1000	
Planned order releases						1000		1000			
Calculator							100				200
Gross requirements											
Scheduled receipts											
Projected on-hand balance							0				0
Planned order receipts							100				200
Planned order releases					100				200		
Keyboard											
Gross requirements							100				200
Scheduled receipts											
Projected on-hand balance	200	200	200	200	200	100	100	100	100	100	100
Planned order receipts									200		
Planned order releases								200			
Display											
Gross requirements							100				200
Scheduled receipts											
Projected on-hand balance	50	50	50	50	50	0	0	0	0	0	0
Planned order receipts							50				200
Planned order releases				50				200			

Week	0	1	2	3	4	5	6	7	8	9	10
Case											
Gross requirements						100				200	
Scheduled receipts											
Projected on-hand balance	150	150	150	150	150	50	50	50	50	50	50
Planned order receipts										200	
Planned order releases								200			
Battery											
Gross requirements						200				400	
Scheduled receipts		300									
Projected on-hand balance	0	300	300	300	300	100	100	100	100	0	0
Planned order receipts										300	
Planned order releases								300			
Small keys											
Gross requirements									200		
Scheduled receipts				1000							
Projected on-hand balance	0	0	1000	1000	1000	1000	1000	1000	800	800	800
Planned order receipts											
Planned order releases											
Printed circuit board											
Gross requirements									200		
Scheduled receipts											
Projected on-hand balance									0		
Planned order receipts									200		
Planned order releases							200				

Figure 9: MRP for MPS of 100 calculators in week 6 and 200 in week 10.

2.4 Requirements for successful MRP

Having worked through an MRP calculation, you should be in a position to understand the necessary prerequisites and assumptions. What factors need to be in place and in good order for MRP to be successful?

Of course the MRP calculation process is pure mechanics which any computer can be relied upon to get correct. What is more challenging for the operations manager is to obtain and maintain the correct information upon which the calculation depends. There are three requirements:

- bills of materials have to be accurate
- inventory records which reflect the on-hand balances need to be correct
- lead times need to be realistic and current.

Remember also that these three requirements are not independent; problems on one level of a bill of materials are carried down to lower levels.

Accurate bills of materials. Many manufacturing companies have hundreds or even thousands of products. Moreover, product designs are often updated to improve saleability, to reduce cost, to take advantage of new materials or different suppliers, or to comply with new legislation. At any one time several designers may be working on different aspects of a product. Keeping bills of materials up to date is a significant task. Fortunately computer-aided design (CAD) helps. Several CAD systems now have bill of materials capabilities. And product data management systems (PDMS) are beginning to be integrated into MRP systems. These control the release of different design versions, co-ordinate design changes, and display the same bill of materials in ways which are appropriate to manufacturing, purchasing, storepeople, quality control staff, and accounting all of which have different requirements. In more traditional environments it may be necessary to audit periodically a bill of materials against an actual product. We consider bill of materials structuring in Unit 8.

Accurate inventory records. A very high degree of inventory record accuracy is required for MRP. If a product has five components and each component has an inventory level accuracy of 90% (that is, 90% of the time when you think the component is available in the quantities that you require, it is in fact available) what is the probability of being able to build a complete batch? The answer is $0.9 \times 0.9 \times 0.9 \times 0.9 \times 0.9 = 0.59$ or 59%. Such performance would be totally unacceptable in today's competitive environment. Bearing in mind that most products have far more than five components, you will realise that for good MRP performance inventory level accuracies of 99% are demanded. Such levels of accuracy need good control, and a procedure called **cycle counting** is now becoming more common. Cycle counting should be considered essential for MRP. It is, however, more widely applicable than for just MRP, as you will see later under 'independent demand inventory management'.

Valid lead times. As we mentioned previously, the lead times built into a bill of materials comprise elements of process time, machine set-up time, move time between processes, queue time waiting for processing, and time to wait for movements to take place after processing is complete. MRP is only concerned with materials not process steps, so there may be several process steps within one lead time. The result is that actual process time is only a small element of total lead time. These time elements are estimates or averages for the typical batch. George Plossl, one of originators of modern MRP says 'lead time is what you say it is!' He considers that an urgent job can be moved to the head of a work queue, and the length of queues can be reduced by releasing less work to the factory floor. So his statement is an exaggeration, but nevertheless a useful reminder to take care with lead times. Certainly, increasing lead times can be dangerous. Some managers still believe that quoting longer lead times is a safe thing to do, yet often it is self-defeating as more work is released earlier, leading to longer queues, leading to longer lead times!

Lead times should be monitored very carefully. On the factory floor lead times should be shortened whenever improvements take place, and lead times from suppliers should be tracked and examined for opportunities for time reduction. We discuss this further in Unit 9.

2.5 Features of MRP systems

ITEM MASTER FILE

All stable data relating to a component part is kept in an **item master file**. This includes the unique part number, the part description, the supplier, the unit of measure, for example, units, hundreds of units, litres, or kilograms, the standard cost, and the standard lead time. There may also be information on the location(s) of the item in the warehouse, and the priority classification, whether it is an A, B, or C part.

REGENERATIVE AND NET CHANGE MRP

Over time, as events develop, an MRP bill of materials explosion becomes increasingly out of date. Just a few of the things that can happen are: materials are delivered late, work is completed late or early, components may be rejected for quality reasons, new orders come in, and a bill of materials may be updated. It becomes necessary to recalculate MRP. This is done in one of two ways: regenerative MRP (regen) and net change MRP. Regenerative MRP performs the full MRP calculation by wiping out all previous MRP records and starting again. It is a full bill of materials explosion. This is what you did when you performed the calculation. It is a time-consuming process for most manufacturing companies, taking several hours even on fast modern computers. It is often done over a weekend. By contrast, net change MRP recalculates only those portions of the MRP record that have been affected by changes. It is a partial bill of materials explosion, and requires less time. It is often done overnight. Today there are several 'on line' net change MRP systems. These perform a net change calculation immediately. However with several simultaneous changes taking place, on-line net change may not be possible so that an overnight update may also be required.

Computer-based MRP systems have features which enable them to be used more effectively. Standard features include: pegging, lot sizing, firm planned orders and 'bucketless' MRP.

Pegging. Standard MRP performs a top-down calculation through the bill of materials. What happens when events such as late deliveries or quality problems take place? There are consequences for higher level parent items which may be delayed. This is what pegging enables a material planner to do. The planner can trace upwards though the bill or bills of materials to determine exactly which batches will be affected. This information is useful to operations for rescheduling, to purchasing perhaps to delay the receipt of other components that can no longer be used as originally scheduled, and to marketing to inform customers of possible delays.

Lot sizing. In the previous examples we have used 'lot-for-lot' batch sizing. This means that we order exactly what our net requirements are. What happens if the net requirements are a non-standard batch size from a supplier, for example, calculator covers are only supplied in boxes of 100, or if ordering or delivery costs are high, making small batch quantities uneconomic? This is where lot sizing is used. There are several standard lot-sizing algorithms found on most modern MRP systems. These algorithms are also useful in independent demand inventory control, and we look at some examples in this section. For MRP purposes, however, these lot sizing algorithms are best only used at the lowest level of the bill of materials. If used at intermediate levels, small changes in the master schedule can result in dramatic changes in the sizing and timing of batches. When we work through some examples later in this unit you will appreciate this more easily. Increased schedule instability is something that most operations managers try to avoid. Lot-sizing algorithms are useful when placing orders for materials from suppliers, but should be treated with caution.

Firm planned orders. We have seen that the 'bottom line' in an MRP record is planned order releases. These are generated by the computer-based MRP logic. What happens if the planner wishes to override the computer system? For example, he or she may wish to consolidate several small batches into one large batch in order to reduce the total batch preparation or set-up time, or he or she may wish to override the standard lead time because at that time it is not appropriate, or he or she may wish to freeze the schedule of planned releases to prevent changes taking place when the next regeneration takes place. Firm planned orders (FPO) allow this to be done. An FPO fixes the planned order in quantity and time and is not overridden when the next MRP calculation is made. Instead, the computer undertakes the MRP calculation with FPOs as a constraint. FPOs are a very powerful mechanism for the planner to alter the schedule for the benefit of the company, and are widely used in practice.

'Bucketless' MRP. In the calculations so far we have assumed weekly slots or 'time buckets'. The word 'bucket' is used because all the demands or orders for the week are collected up into a single bucket, from which they are poured out during the week as required. This is the historic way of carrying out MRP calculations. But why be constrained to weeks? Why not just use the actual date of need? This is what 'bucketless' systems do. You would have noticed that in your manual MRP calculations many weeks retained constant data for a particular component. This is wasteful. Instead of working to given constant-length time buckets, the computer system only performs the calculations for days when things change.

2.6 MRP in practice

Although the concept of ordering just what is required when it is required has been around for a long time, modern MRP has only been around since the 1960s when computing power first made MRP calculations feasible and cost effective. But then manufacturing necessities were very different from today. For many companies today there is much greater emphasis on time and variety, so MRP has had to adapt.

Traditional MRP remains a good choice of manufacturing system where a company has complex products with deep, multiple-level, bills of materials. For example, in aircraft engine manufacture the final end product is made up of many sub-assemblies, which in turn have sub-assemblies themselves. Many have complex machining operations, undertaken in stages, and most are undertaken in-house. Moreover, many sub-assemblies are not made on a continuous basis, but periodically in batches. The batches surge through the factory in waves, rather than flowing though like a continuous stream.

By contrast car manufacture is no longer of this type. A car plant today is highly complex, but mainly assembly work. The manufacture of complex sub-assemblies such as engines and electrical systems is sub-contracted to 'first tier' suppliers, the majority of which are supplied by 'second tier' suppliers, and so on. The last thing you want in a car plant today is surge-type manufacture. MRP in this type of environment should be simply a question of generating the required materials. If we are not interested in intermediate sub-assemblies, a much shallower (that is, having far fewer or even one level) bill is all that is needed. Moreover, the netting process can be very disruptive to constant flow. This is because netting produces variable quantities and results in surges. The result is that 'lean manufacturing' in a repetitive environment is not comfortable with traditional MRP. MRP is still needed, but in a simplified form. We say more about this in Unit 9.

Of course, the materials management system has to be compatible with the organisation of manufacturing. As more and more companies change over to lean manufacturing philosophies, and cellular manufacturing, so their MRP systems need to change. In the mid 1990s, many manufacturing companies are in transition with their MRP systems finding that traditional MRP is too cumbersome but they are not yet organised to take advantage of more simplified MRP.

Likewise, small 'jobbing' manufacturers may find traditional MRP unsuitable. If the business of the company is to make a wide variety of products to order, and where there is very little similarity between orders, other than the basic manufacturing technology, then it is a waste of time developing complex bills of materials. Here the company simply generates the materials required from the design. It is the scheduling that is critical to business success, rather than the material requirements.

Is MRP USED FOR ALL TYPES OF COMPONENT OR MATERIAL?

MRP is most suitable for more expensive components. But most companies have large numbers of inexpensive components. At some point it ceases to be worthwhile to keep inexpensive components on an MRP system. Some common alternatives are to use the 'two bin' system which we describe in the next section, or to control parts in **kits**. A kit is a set of parts that is used together to make a component. If the same set of parts is always used, the whole kit can be treated as one component.

ACTIVITY 10

Consider the following businesses. For each state whether you think traditional MRP, simplified MRP, or no MRP is needed:

cigarette machine manufacturer

European Airbus

racing car manufacturer

McDonald's

hospital

washing machine manufacturer

pharmaceutical manufacturer

PC manufacturer

armoured personnel carrier manufacturer

chemical plant

make-to-order furniture manufacturer.

You will need to use your judgement and general knowledge in answering this question, but don't give up! The manufacture of cigarette machines and armoured personnel carriers involves complex machining operations on an on-going batch basis, ideal for traditional MRP. In the latter case, most armed forces are insistent that there is batch traceability, meaning that if something goes wrong they can trace back to the source of the problem. The same is particularly true in the case of pharmaceutical manufacturers, where absolute control of the source of ingredients and control of the progress of manufacture is an important requirement. Formula 1 racing cars would be classic 'jobbers' where the schedule is critical but where MRP is probably of limited use. On the other hand, in Britain some racing car manufacturers have regular but low-volume orders for standard products so traditional MRP may be what is required.

Many PC and washing machine manufacturers have moved away from traditional MRP and towards 'lean' concepts with simplified MRP. McDonald's could be an MRP user of the shallow bill type, but we would question the necessity with more simple products and a limited range. Spreadsheet-type explosion is probably good enough. There is also the question of freshness: to use netting may not be appropriate or batch traceability would have to be incorporated. Chemical plants do use MRP but of a specialised nature, suitably modified for the process industry. This is because the 'components' are not discrete items but may be measured in litres, any quantity of which can be drawn off.

Hospitals? Very unusual to use MRP, but a bill of materials covering a patient with a particular illness could be developed.

Summary

In this section we have seen that MRP is used for dependent demand inventory management which is common in manufacturing. Today MRP is widely used, and there are literally hundreds of MRP software packages available. The two main types of MRP are regenerative and net change. MRP involves exploding out a bill of materials and subtracting the on-hand balances to give the planned order releases. MRP requires strict discipline and accuracy in bills of material, in on-hand balances, and lead times to work well. We have also had a flavour of some of the techniques that material planners use in running real systems. These include firm planned orders to give stability to the material plan. In recent years MRP has evolved to meet the needs of faster and more diversified manufacturing, but the principles remain.

SECTION 3

Independent Demand Inventory Control

Introduction

You will recall that independent demand inventory control concerns 'end items' rather than components, parts, or ingredients. MRP is used for dependent demand. Independent demand has its own extensive body of theory, a small part of which we discuss here. This section will help you to understand the various types of inventory and why each is necessary.

3.1 Types of inventory

A common classification of inventory in manufacturing companies is: **raw materials, work in progress** (sometimes referred to as work in process), or WIP, and **finished goods**. These names are unfortunate. Raw materials gives the impression of commodities such as steel or plastic granules, but this is seldom the case; most raw materials are bought-in components. Work in progress is seldom in progress, in most manufacturing companies it is actually being worked on for less than 5% of the time, the remainder of the time is spent waiting to be moved or to be worked on. Finished goods may be finished by one manufacturing company, but most often finished goods are then passed on to another manufacturer or assembler.

In general, inventory is necessary:

- **to provide safety against uncertainty**. If a shop, restaurant, or manufacturer knew their customers, exact needs in terms of quantity and time, there would be no reason to hold finished goods inventories. Everything could be acquired, made and sold just in time. **Anticipation inventory** is held in expectation of future demands, and **safety stock** is held when there is uncertainty in quantity or timing.

- **to balance operations**. In manufacturing and service, most individual operations take different lengths of time. It is therefore inevitable that either less busy operations stop work from time to time or that inventories accumulate in front of longer operations. Often managers try to keep the longer or busier operations going without interruption, so to prevent them running out of work inventory is kept in front of these constrained operations. **Buffer inventory** is held between operations.

- **for economy**. For most people, it makes no sense to buy only the next day's requirements of food. In service, it makes no sense to buy only tomorrow's office requirements today. In manufacturing, it often makes no sense to manufacture and move products in batches of one – even though this might be the ideal way of manufacturing. **Cycle inventory** is held because products are made in batches rather than continuously. **Pipeline** or **in-transit** inventory is inevitable because products take time to move through a distribution network. **Hedging** inventory is held in anticipation of a future price rise.

3.2 Inventory decisions

All inventory management involves two questions, when and how much to order. There will often be other questions as well, such as who to buy from and where it is to be stored, but these are often one-off issues. When and how much to order involve regular reassessment. All the questions interact, however.

ACTIVITY 11

Consider domestic example where these four questions interact.

You might buy your groceries from the same supplier on a regular basis that depends on your usage and is in line with your storage space. A special promotion may influence you to buy early or in larger quantities than usual, but you would probably not buy in quantities that exceed your normal storage space, however inexpensive. A special offer may induce you to buy from a supplier who is not your usual one.

Note that all four questions interplay, but the first two are particularly closely linked. Generally we choose between ordering a little and often against ordering large quantities less often. Historically, the decision has been made by trading-off ordering costs with inventory holding costs for each item. In many situations it is far more complex, involving issues such as relationships with suppliers, loyalty, future demand, opportunity, storage space, quantity discounts, bulk discounts, total delivery costs, freshness, stockout costs, costs of surges and cash flow. Most housekeepers make good, but not necessarily optimal, purchasing decisions involving far more complex considerations than we will deal with in the following section. So treat the following apparent precision with caution.

WHEN TO ORDER

The 'when to order' question is largely decided by one of two possibilities. One possibility is to place an order when the level of inventory reaches a predetermined level which is fixed so as to allow sufficient time to acquire the product for its anticipated use. Another possibility is to review your inventory holdings at particular periods and decide whether or not to order. In the former case, the period between orders, known as the **review period**, is variable but the quantity ordered is usually fixed. In the latter case, the review period is fixed but usually the quantity ordered varies. Of course, you can also do both.

REORDER POINT (OR PERPETUAL) MODEL

The first option involves the reorder point (ROP). Assume that an inventory holding is continually depleted. The ROP is that level of inventory which is just sufficient to tide you over the period that it takes for your supplier to deliver. More precisely it is the forecasted demand expected during the lead time.

Of course the demand during the lead time may not materialise as we expect. If demand is lower than expected you will have inventory on hand when the new shipment is delivered. If demand is higher than expected you will experience a shortage or stock-out before the shipment is delivered. To allow for this possibility, safety stock is often held. As a result, the formula for the reorder point is:

$$ROP = DLT + SS$$

where

DLT = forecast demand during the lead time

= expected average demand per period $\times$ number of periods for lead time

SS = safety stock.

Figure 10 illustrates the 'sawtooth' pattern.

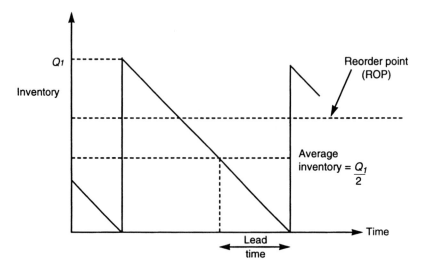

Figure 10: The ROP inventory model

A well-used variation of the ROP inventory model is called the 'two bin' system. Here each inventory item is literally kept in two bins, side by side. Inventory is drawn out from the first bin until it is empty. This is the ROP. There is sufficient inventory in the second bin to cover expected demand during the delivery lead time. It is a simple, visual system that is commonly used for low-cost C type items.

PERIODIC REVIEW MODEL

In many cases, it is more practical to order several items at the same time, as may occur where there is a common supplier. So it makes sense to review all items from the common supplier periodically and order just what is needed, if it is needed. Normally inventory is topped up to a target level, and for this reason this model is also known as the **min/max** model. Note that this type of inventory model is still widely used, for the following common situations:

- where individual transactions are difficult to record
- where shelf life is a problem
- where joint orders are placed with a supplier.

The first of these situations is, however, rapidly disappearing in supermarkets where there is increased use of point of sale terminals.

The question with a periodic system is how often should we make the review. Usually this is a practical consideration, perhaps coinciding with a scheduled order delivery cycle. On the other hand, we can calculate it from the economic order quantity (EOQ) we derive in the next section. Graphically, the situation is shown in Figure 11 where L is the lead time, R is the review period, and Q is the order quantity. Note that an order quantity determined at twice A must be sufficient to last through the review period and the next lead time. Notice also that the quantities are different for each review period.

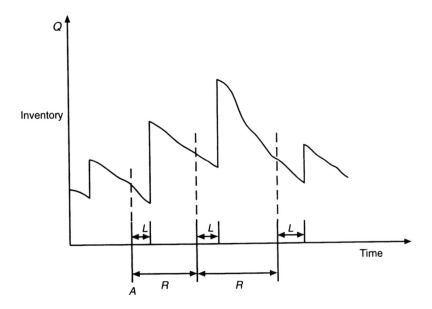

Figure 11: The periodic review model

The relevant formulas are:

Target inventory level *(M)* = Forecast demand during the lead time *(DL)*

+ Forecast demand during the review period *(DR)*

+ Safety Stock *(SS)*

Order quantity *(Q)*   = Target inventory level *(M)* – quantity on hand *(I)* – quantity on order *(O)*

= D *(R + L)* + SS – *(I + O)*

ACTIVITY 12

Calculate the target inventory level and order quantity, where:

the review period is 7 days

the delivery lead time is 5 days

demand averages 2 units per day

the safety stock is 4 units

the on-hand inventory is 15 units

the quantity on order is 6 units.

You should find it easy to use the formulas to get a target inventory level of 28 units with an order quantity of 7 units. In practice, these figures will often be modified depending on issues such as available shelf space, and special promotions of competing products.

3.3 How much to order: Economic Order Quantity

The EOQ is the classic formula in inventory management. It represents the optimal trade-off between the costs of ordering and the costs of holding inventory. The assumptions are that new inventory is delivered in batches, that there are no stock-outs, that demand is constant and continuous, and that delivery lead time is constant and known. Over time, inventory levels decline, but are replenished just in time to avoid stock-out. In the upper diagram below relatively large batches are ordered and delivered infrequently, in the lower small batches are delivered frequently. We can see that the average levels of inventory being held is very different in the two cases: high on the left, low on the right. On the other hand, the number of orders placed is low on the left and high on the right.

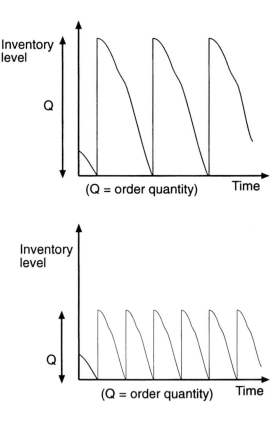

Taking the two cases as extremes we can draw cost curves as shown in Figure 12 below.

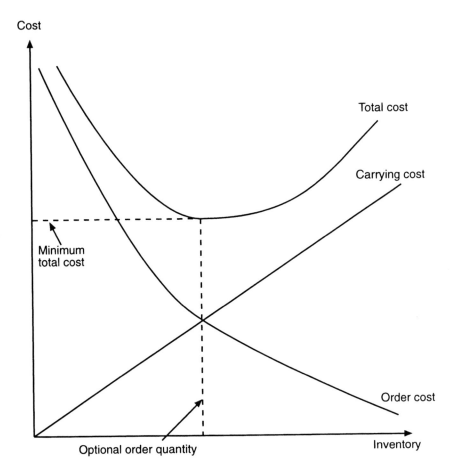

Figure 12: The Economic Order Quantity (EOQ)

The unit carrying cost rate, expressed as a percentage, comprises the sum of the cost of the capital tied up and the costs of holding inventory. The former includes the opportunity cost of the cash tied up, and the latter the costs of storage and control, the costs of insurance, and the costs of risk including that of obsolescence and possible pilferage. There are also less obvious costs including the cost of inspection, data processing and record keeping, inventory handling equipment such as racks and fork lift trucks, and the training of inventory control staff.

The monetary value of the carrying cost is equal to the average inventory held, multiplied by the carrying cost rate and the unit cost. If we assume that demand is constant, then the average quantity held will be equal to half the order quantity.

The order cost is the cost of placing a single order and comprises factors such as preparation of the order, receiving and inspecting, paying the invoice when received, and of supplier selection. The method assumes this cost to be constant irrespective of the number of orders placed. We can now write down the formulas for each cost as:

Carrying cost = $(Q/2)\ C\ I$

Order cost = $(D/Q)\ S.$

There is also the basic cost of the items which is constant irrespective of order size:

Item cost = $D\ C$

and so Total cost = Carrying cost + Order cost + Item Cost

$$= (Q/2)\ C\ I + (D/Q)\ S + D\ C$$

where

    Q = order quantity

    C = item cost

    I = annual carrying cost interest rate

    D = annual demand

    S = order cost per order.

The EOQ can be derived by equating the Holding cost and the Order cost, or by calculus, as shown.

By equating Holding cost with Order cost:

$$\frac{Q}{2}CI = \frac{D}{Q}S$$

$$2DS = Q^2CI$$

$$Q = \sqrt{\frac{2DS}{CI}}$$

By calculus:

$$\frac{d(\text{Total cost})}{dQ} = \frac{CI}{2} - \frac{DS}{Q^2} = 0$$

$$\frac{CI}{2} = \frac{DS}{Q^2}$$

$$Q = \sqrt{\frac{2DS}{CI}}$$

ACTIVITY 13

Complete the calculation for the EOQ for the following circumstances: annual demand 2,000 units, unit cost £10, order cost £50 per order, and carrying cost interest rate 25%.

$$\text{Then EOQ} = \sqrt{\frac{2 \times 2000 \times 50}{0.25 \times 10}} = \sqrt{\frac{200000}{2.5}} = \sqrt{80{,}000}$$

3.4 Limitations of the EOQ

Although the EOQ is one of the best known formulas in operations management, it is not easy to understand and it may be highly misleading. There are advantages and disadvantages with the EOQ.

First the disadvantages. Consider the elements of the formula: D is the demand. But what do we know about the demand? It is a forecast, so it is unlikely to materialise exactly. S is the order cost, assumed constant no matter the number of orders. That alone is a very questionable assumption. So is it better to use the marginal cost or the average cost? Most would agree the marginal cost is more appropriate in establishing the number of orders and EOQ. But others think the average cost should be used for more stable situations. Even if you agree to use marginal cost, then look back at the elements of order cost. Several are quite hard to establish accurately. Then consider I, the interest rate. This should be the future interest rate appropriate for the company; again it is a forecast and again it comprises several problematic elements. Then consider C, the item cost. What should we use here – the average cost, the replacement cost, the actual cost, or the future cost? Many think that replacement cost should be used, but not all agree.

So we have an uncertain quantity multiplied by uncertain cost, divided by an uncertain interest rate and by another uncertain cost! And then we assume that the average inventory is half the maximum, in other words, that demand is constant and continuous. This is the most serious assumption. In fact, if demand is non-uniform, the EOQ gives very poor results. Beware using the EOQ formula!

Does it have any advantages? Well, because of the square root sign, the EOQ is rather insensitive around the optimal point. This means that quite large percentage changes in the factors within the formula will result in only small changes in the EOQ. Try this yourself:

ACTIVITY 14

Using the same EOQ example, calculate revised EOQs, by taking each of the following changes one by one:

- annual demands between 500 and 4000 units in increments of 500

  (plot a graph of the resulting EOQs)
- an interest rate of 35%
- a unit cost of £12.50.

These exercises will give you a feel for the sensitivity of the EOQ.

ACTIVITY 15

What is the effect on the EOQ for each of the following:

an increase in price of the item

an increase in annual demand

a decrease in the applicable interest rate

a decrease in the holding cost.

You should be able to see the effects of these changes by looking at the EOQ formula. The point is that these changes often take place within a period of one year, so the conclusion is that the EOQ should not be regarded as static. Note that you can also use the formula the other way around: for instance, by knowing the normal order quantity, the current demand, the price of the item and the current applicable holding cost rate, you can calculate what these imply about the order cost. Then you can judge if the order cost is reasonable.

THE EOQ AND THE JIT PHILOSOPHY

We have seen that smaller EOQs directly affect the average level of inventory (see Figure 11). The JIT philosophy advises that we should try to keep inventory levels as low as possible and strive for a batch size of one. So, which approach is right? The answer is that both are right, but a shift in outlook is required. We can take the costs of ordering (or set-up in the case of manufacturing) as given and simply calculate the EOQ. Or we can work on the order costs (or set-up costs) so as to drive them down, and rethink the true costs of holding inventory. We look at the reduction in order costs and set-up costs in Unit 9, but here we will consider the JIT view of the holding costs of inventory.

So what is this JIT view of the true costs of inventory? JIT recognises that there are several additional costs of inventory. These are:

- **Lead time and responsiveness**. In factories, large batches contribute directly to longer queues. The longer the queue, the longer the lead time before another batch can be worked on, and hence the slower the responsiveness. A large batch, either made or ordered from a supplier, may have to cover requirements for a longer period of time. Near the end of the period, we would find that either we have been too optimistic leading to unsold products, or too pessimistic leading to shortages. It would be better then to make or order small batches more frequently which simultaneously reduces the inventory costs and decreases the forecast horizon. Of course, the key to this is to reduce order or set-up costs.

- **Quality**. The larger the batch size the less frequent inspections are likely to be. Also, there is an increased risk of spoilage with some categories of inventory. This means that there are likely to be more defectives.

- **Space**. Inventory occupies space in the warehouse on the factory floor. Not only is there the possibility that the space could be used for other things, but also that large accumulations of inventory often creates physical barriers thereby lengthening transportation distances, preventing visual controls, or inhibiting communication. These may have an impact on quality and lead time.

● **Control**. More inventory means more controls in the form of counting and in checking to ensure freshness.

● **Material handling**. With JIT, it is ideal to have, where possible, human-movable containers moving inventory between closely spaced operations, rather than using expensive forklift trucks to move large batches over longer distances.

Of course, you will realise that these points are mutually supportive. They may be hard to quantify, but we can say for certain that the JIT attitude leads us to conclude that the true costs of holding inventory are much higher than we thought they would be.

ACTIVITY 16

If we have simplified and rationalised to achieve lower order (or set-up) costs and if we have a new approach towards holding costs, what is the effect on the EOQ? In Figure 13 we show the traditional EOQ. Draw the revised JIT-based EOQ.

The JIT view lowers the order cost curve, and steepens the holding cost line. The result is that the EOQ point is shifted drastically to the left, towards the ideal JIT batch size of one. This is shown in Figure 14.

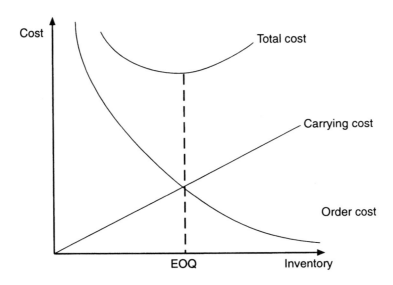

Figure 13: Traditional EOQ view

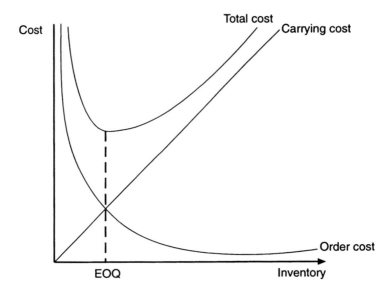

Figure 14: Revised JIT view

PRACTICAL CONSIDERATIONS

The EOQ is subject to a few practical considerations. Rounding means that the EOQ will probably be rounded off to the nearest convenient quantity. As we have seen in our sensitivity calculation this does not necessarily make a difference to the total cost. There may be limitations on shelf space, storage capacity, or vehicle delivery capacity which may make the EOQ impractical. The EOQ derivation does not include any consideration of availability of funds; a purchaser may simply not be able to afford to buy the EOQ in one order. The EOQ derivation does not consider shelf life; clearly if the EOQ implies a purchase interval which exceeds the shelf life it is impractical.

VARIATIONS IN THE EOQ FORMULA

You will appreciate that it is possible to allow for several limitations by adjusting the EOQ formula. There are a large number of possible adjustments and we will consider one possibility in the next section. Derivations may be found in one of the many specialist texts on inventory management (Silver and Peterson, 1985).

EOQ with replenisment taking place over a period of time:

$$EOQ = \sqrt{\frac{2DS(p)}{IC(p-d)}}$$

Where p = the relenishment rate (units/day)
d = the demand rate (units/day)

EOQ with shortages ('backorders') allowed:

$$EOQ = \sqrt{\frac{2DS}{IC}} \sqrt{\frac{IC + B}{B}}$$

where B is the penalty cost for each item supplied late.

Notice that where the backorder cost is large in comparision with IC, the value of the EOQ is similar to the standard case.

QUANTITY DISCOUNTS

Quantity discounts are popular between retailers and suppliers even though many manufacturers and retailers now recognise that when applied to end consumers the resulting surges in demand may be disruptive along the supply chain. Here we consider the implications of quantity discounts on order quantities.

The point at which quantity discounts are offered is known as the break point. At the break point there is a sudden discontinuity in the holding cost, because the item cost drops. Let us look at how the cost graph looks with quantity discounts (Figure 15).

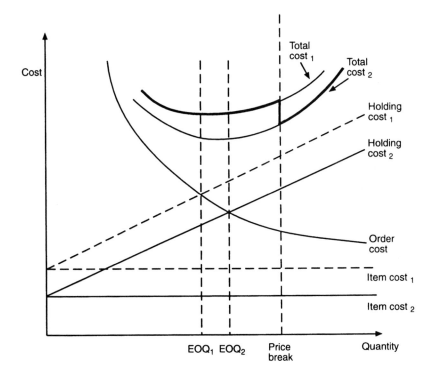

Figure 15: EOQ with quantity discount

From Figure 15, we can see the following:

- the total cost line has discontinuities at the price breaks
- the holding cost and item cost lines are valid only between certain limits
- it is difficult to be sure where the lowest total cost will occur, but it can be seen that it will occur at either the break point or at the EOQ minimum point.

The procedure for determining the lowest cost point involves using the former total cost equation, and evaluating the total cost at valid EOQ points and at break points.

3.5 Safety stock

We saw earlier that demand during the order lead time period can be faster or slower than expected. Of course, demand during the lead time is more likely to be closer to the average value than to outlying values. Several statistical distributions of demand are likely during the lead time, but it is almost invariably assumed that the demand during the lead time will be normally distributed. The normal distribution is characterised by a mean μ (called mu) and standard deviation σ (called sigma). Assuming that the lead time remains constant, the variation may be depicted in Figure 16 below.

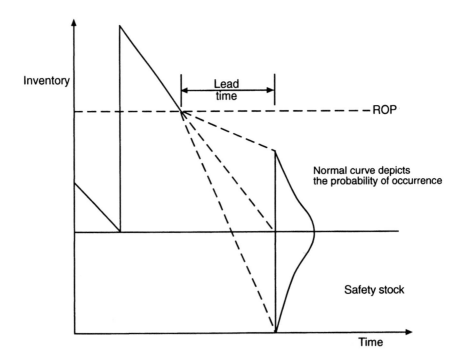

Figure 16: Safety stock and service level

As shown in Figure 16, safety stock is provided to cater for variation in demand. Demand will be more than average, of course, for 50% of the time. So if we define the **service level** as the probability of a stock-out during the lead time, then if we have no safety stock we would expect to have a 50% service level. We can calculate the necessary safety stock and reorder point to achieve more than a 50% service level by direct application of the formula used with the normal distribution:

$$Z = (X - \mu) / \sigma$$

$$X = Z\sigma + \mu$$

In inventory management terms, $ROP = SS + DLT$

where Z is the standard normal deviation

σ is the standard deviation of demand during the lead time

D is the average demand rate

T is the lead time

SS is the safety stock

so the service level = 100 % – stock-out risk.

You will recall from your earlier statistical studies that the Z value can be related to the area under the normal curve. The area under the curve beyond the Z value is the stock-out risk, as shown in Figure 17.

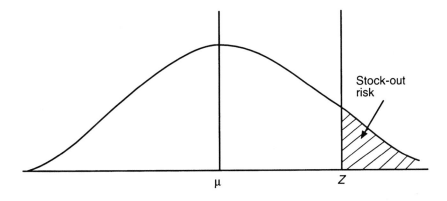

Figure 17: Stock-out risk

The Z values are available in standard tables.

ACTIVITY 17

Calculate the required safety stocks for the following service levels, when the standard deviation of demand during the lead time was found to be 10 units:

50%

70%

80%

90%

95%

99%.

The appropriate Z value for 50% is 0.00, for 80% it is 0.84, and for 95% it is 1.65. Make sure you see where these Z values come from, as different statistical tables show Z values in different ways. You will notice how safety stock levels have to rise very steeply to accommodate high levels of service.

OTHER MEASURES OF SERVICE LEVEL

You would probably have realised that the probability of a stock-out during the lead time is not the only way to measure service level. Other common measures include the following:

Items of orders shipped or delivered on schedule. This deals with individual items, each of which is measured separately. This is useful where multiple items are being shipped, and the number not included is measured. You might have experience of this in receipt of goods shipped from mail order companies.

Orders shipped on schedule. Here the concern is with complete orders rather than items. Unless the complete order is received in full, it counts as a non-delivery. Obviously it is less than satisfactory to receive three wheels per car, even if the item delivery performance is 75%.

Value shipped on schedule. It is useful to give priority to more expensive items. Periods without a stock-out or number of late orders outstanding.

3.6 Time phased order point

As we have seen, the EOQ has a number of shortcomings. Two principal shortcomings are the assumptions of constant demand and of constant order size. **Time phased order point (TPOP)** is a family of inventory techniques that address these issues. In this section, we examine only a few of the many TPOP techniques that have been developed. TPOP can be used in MRP and in independent demand inventory control. In MRP, TPOP is normally used at the lowest level in the bill of materials.

We will use the same set of demand data (shown in Table 1), holding costs, and order costs for each of the TPOP techniques we discuss. Assume that order costs are £10 per order placed, the unit cost is £2 per item, and the interest rate is 25% per annum. Over the 10-week horizon total demands are 1,450 units, which is equivalent to 7,540 units per year. Projected on-hand balance is taken at 400 units, and safety stock at 0 units, in each case. This means that the carrying cost is (£2 x .25) / 52 = £ 0.0096 per unit per week.

Week	0	1	2	3	4	5	6	7	8	9	10
Gross requirements		150	200	100	70	0	150	200	120	210	250
Scheduled receipts											
Projected on-hand balance	400	250	50								
Planned order receipts											
Planned order releases											

Table 1: Data for TPOP techniques

LOT FOR LOT

In the lot-for-lot procedure, a 'lot' or batch of the required quantity is ordered whenever inventory reaches the safety stock level. This usually results in many batches being ordered, but it does minimise the amount of inventory being held. The calculation is shown in Table 2 below.

Gross requirements		150	200	100	70	0	150	200	120	210	250
Scheduled receipts											
Projected on-hand balance	400	250	50	0	0	0	0	0	0	0	0
Planned order receipts				50	70		150	200	120	210	250
Planned order releases			50	70		150	200	120	210	250	

Table 2: Lot-for-lot calculation

Notice that this results in seven orders at £10 per order and a cumulative inventory total of 300 units, or a holding cost of £2.88. Total cost is £72.88.

ECONOMIC ORDER QUANTITY

In the EOQ TPOP procedure, the EOQ is calculated as before. You should check that this equals 550 units. Then, whenever the inventory level reaches the safety stock level, an amount equal to the EOQ is ordered. The order quantity remains fixed, but the order interval varies. This is shown in Table 3.

Gross requirements		150	200	100	70	0	150	200	120	210	250
Scheduled receipts											
Projected on-hand balance	400	250	50	500	430	430	280	80	510	300	50
Planned order receipts				550					550		
Planned order releases			550				550				

Table 3: Economic order quantity

Notice that this results in two orders at £10 per order and a cumulative inventory total of 2,880 units, or a holding cost of £27.64. Total cost is £47.64. Notice that seldom, if ever, does inventory get down to the safety stock level.

PERIOD ORDER QUANTITY

The period order quantity (POQ) technique is based on EOQ thinking, but also recognises the advantage of ordering for a set number of periods ahead. The order quantity therefore varies, but the order interval remains fixed. This has the advantage of bringing down the inventory levels to the safety stock level at the end of each order period.

First, calculate the EOQ at 550 units.

Now the average demand per week is 1450/10 = 145 units.

So the equivalent number of periods is 550/145 = 3.79 weeks. This is always rounded, so we will take four periods and order sufficient to cover this length of time each time an order is placed. This is shown in Table 4.

Gross requirements			150	200	100	70	0	150	200	120	210	250
Scheduled receipts												
Projected on-hand balance	400	250	50	220	150	150	0	580	460	250	0	
Planned order receipts				270				780				
Planned order releases		270				780						

Table 4: Period order quantity calculation

Notice that this results in two orders at £10 per order. The cumulative inventory holding over the 10 weeks is 2,110 units, or £20.25. Total cost is £40.25 over the 10 weeks.

LEAST UNIT COST

In the least unit cost (LUC) procedure, both the quantity ordered and the period of coverage may vary. The calculation is an iterative one which seeks to find the least cost per unit of ordering and holding. It is best set out in a table, as shown in Table 5.

Gross requirements			150	200	100	70	0	150	200	120	210	250
Scheduled receipts												
Projected on-hand balance	400	250	50	420	350	350	200	0	460	250	0	
Planned order receipts				470					580			
Planned order releases		470				580						

Table 5: Least unit cost calculation

When we get to week 3 it is necessary to obtain a planned order receipt. The question is, for how many periods should this cover? For simplicity, we will assume that the holding cost is accumulated only by the remaining inventory held at the end of a period. Thus if we order 50 units (just sufficient to meet the requirements for period 3), then inventory holding costs will be zero but order costs will be £10, or a unit cost of £0.20. If we order 120 units (sufficient to cover periods 3 and 4), inventory holding costs will be 70 units carried for 1 week or 70

(0.0096) = £0.67. Total cost is £10.67 or an average cost of 10.67/120 = £0.0889 per unit, and so on. Unit costs drop and then rise. We can therefore determine the least unit cost quantity, which turns out to be 470 units.

ACTIVITY 18

Using exactly the same data as previously, except where unit cost is £10 instead of £2, recalculate the TPOP tables in the space below.

Week	0	1	2	3	4	5	6	7	8	9	10
Gross requirements											
Scheduled receipts											
Projected on-hand balance											
Planned order receipts											
Planned order releases											
Gross requirements											
Scheduled receipts											
Projected on-hand balance											
Planned order receipts											
Planned order releases											
Gross requirements											
Scheduled receipts											
Projected on-hand balance											
Planned order receipts											
Planned order releases											
Gross requirements											
Scheduled receipts											
Projected on-hand balance											
Planned order receipts											
Planned order releases											

Notice that two orders are again placed at £20. Cumulative inventory holding is 2,330 units or £22.27. Total cost is £42.37.

You should be cautious about drawing conclusions about the best method. Much depends upon the order pattern and upon the costs. There is, of course, the carry over problem in making comparisons, that is, if we had added another one or two periods a different technique may have been more appropriate.

The completed TPOP table is given in Table 6.

Week	0	1	2	3	4	5	6	7	8	9	10
Gross requirements		150	200	100	70	0	150	200	120	210	250
Scheduled receipts											
Projected on-hand balance	400	250	50	0	0	0	0	0	0	0	0
Planned order receipts				50	70		150	200	120	210	250
Planned order releases		50	70		150	200	120	210	250		
Gross requirements		150	200	100	70	0	150	200	120	210	250
Scheduled receipts											
Projected on-hand balance	400	250	50	500	430	430	280	80	510	300	50
Planned order receipts				550					550		
Planned order releases		550					550				
Gross requirements		150	200	100	70	0	150	200	120	210	250
Scheduled receipts											
Projected on-hand balance	400	250	50	220	150	150	0	580	460	250	0
Planned order receipts				270				780			
Planned order releases		270				780					
Gross requirements		150	200	100	70	0	150	200	120	210	250
Scheduled receipts											
Projected on-hand balance	400	250	50	420	350	350	200	0	460	250	0
Planned order receipts				470					580		
Planned order releases		470				580					

Table 6: Completed TPOP table

Generally we would expect poor results using the EOQ TPOP technique simply because a basic assumption, that of constant uniform demand does not hold. The lot-for-lot procedure often outperforms the EOQ procedure where inventory costs are high and where demand is non-uniform. This is despite the fact that lot-for-lot is simpler. Lot-for-lot has become the standard procedure used in JIT systems.

The POQ is very popular with MRP systems. It gives good results, combined with simplicity and stability.

For costly A items, LUC is often an excellent choice. The iterative nature of the calculation is not a big issue for fast computers, and when performed for selective items of inventory. Often, LUC gives near optimal results. The optimal solution can be guaranteed by a technique known as the 'Wagner Whitin Algorithm' which involves dynamic programming, however, it is beyond our needs here.

3.7 Inventory control

In any operation keeping inventory, there will be items of different price and usage. It makes sense to control the inventory in relation to its importance. The way to do it is to make use of the Pareto Law that we also find in quality management, work measurement and purchasing. Remember that typically 20% of items make up 80% of the cost.

ABC CLASSIFICATION

In inventory management, we usually refer to the ABC classification to indicate that there are A, B and C category items. Typical class boundaries are to take the highest value 20% of items as the A class, the next 30% of items as B class, and the last 50% of items as C class. We would expect to find perhaps 80 to 90% of the total value concentrated in the A class items, and perhaps 5 to 10% of total value in each of the B and C categories.

There are different ways to classify items into categories. One very common way is to classify simply on the basis of unit cost. Another common way is to classify by annual monetary usage, that is, by unit price x annual number of units used. To categorise, rank the items in descending order of price or annual usage, and accumulate the unit price or annual usage respectively and then plot the result on a graph. Often the final classification is not done purely mechanically on the basis of calculation, but also incorporates special considerations, for example, an item that is about to be phased out, or a highly perishable item, or an item that is difficult to acquire, or a single high price item. In all these cases we might upgrade the classification because we would want to monitor the situation more carefully.

ACTIVITY 19

A list of items together with price, annual usage, and any special circumstances is given below. Classify them into A, B and C categories.

Item no	Price per item	Usage per annum	Remarks
234	1.10	1,000	
431	0.05	100	
455	0.17	400	
986	0.85	200	
554	0.37	1,500	long lead time
337	0.25	400	
707	15.86	10	
214	0.57	100	
118	0.15	2,000	phase out item

The class boundaries are somewhat arbitrary, but items 234 and 554 would certainly be A category and we could classify items 707 and 118 as A also.

Having classified the items, now what do we do? A items may be subject to more sophisticated control methods such as MRP or TPOP, whereas C items may well be controlled by a simple two -bin system. The security for A items may be tighter. For these two possibilities, a ranking by cost or price is appropriate. A items may be subject to a value analysis examination more frequently, or to review of supplier, or to review of lead times. For these reasons, a classification by annual usage is appropriate.

CYCLE COUNTING

A special case of inventory control is record accuracy. We discussed the importance of this under MRP, but the importance is no less with independent demand inventory control. The now almost universally agreed best practice is to use **cycle counting**. You should consider it mandatory for successful MRP.

Cycle counting uses the ABC classification. Then, A items are counted more frequently than B items, which are in turn counted more frequently than C items. Moreover, cycle counting involves counting a few items every day rather than a big, but invariably inaccurate, count once or twice per year. The latter procedure is known as the **annual stocktake**.

With cycle counting, a few personnel are given the specific responsibility for inventory accuracy and for counting. They know the stock locations exactly and they have the responsibility to track down any sources of error, not just to keep records up to date. These features are not found in annual stocktake procedures. Today most computer-based inventory management systems have a cycle counting feature which prints out a list of items to be checked every day. Then, by the end of the year for instance, A items will have been counted twelve times, B items four times, and C items once. Increasingly, external auditors are willing to accept cycle counting as a valid procedure thereby avoiding the necessity for the annual count. Cycle counting is one of the most cost-effective procedures in inventory management.

Moreover, there are times and events that should be incorporated with cycle counts and inventory record accuracy. For example, it makes sense to count the remaining items after a batch has been issued, because that involves the least amount of work. It is easier to count containers having a known number of items, so don't be in a hurry to unpack. Of course, an inventory record that indicates a negative balance should always be checked.

3.8 Measuring inventory performance

A common way of measuring inventory performance is by inventory turns. This is the number of times that inventory is turned around per year. It is measured by taking total sales and dividing by the value of the inventory. Inventory turns are widely quoted as a measure of manufacturing performance with some leading JIT manufacturers such as Toyota exceeding 80 turns per annum, and various divisions of Hewlett Packard exceeding 50 turns. But these are unusual figures; many car manufacturers still have less than 10 turns, many component manufacturers less than 5, and retailers around 20.

You have to be cautious about using inventory turns as a comparative measure. Some companies quote their inventory turn figures in relation to WIP and raw materials only and some exclude different categories of inventory. Spare parts are a common exclusion. It also depends upon how inventory is valued: first in first out, last in first out, replacement value, or actual value.

Other measures of inventory are days of inventory on-hand (this could be the number of days or working days) divided by the number of turns, and average age of inventory. The latter may be a more appropriate measure in businesses where freshness counts, but should still be treated with caution.

ACTIVITY 20

Accepting the limitations of inventory turns as a measure, obtain a few annual reports of leading companies (you may have some available in your library) and calculate their inventory turns. Try to compare similar companies. You may also like to calculate the inventory turns of utilities such as your local water company or of British Gas.

You will typically find turns of less than 10. But the number of turns in industry as a whole is beginning to creep up.

Summary

Inventory management is a huge subject and we have only just touched the essentials in this section. Inventory is a vital part of many businesses. Control of inventory offers tremendous opportunity for a business which has given low priority to this aspect in the past.

In this section, we looked at the basic inventory decisions: how much to order and when to order. We considered the classic economic order quantity method, which can be used to calculate how much to order, provided the assumptions underlying the formula are valid. Often, they are not.

We introduced two basic inventory control philosophies: the perpetual system and the periodic system; and a set of inventory management techniques, time phased order point, which is well-suited for non-uniform demand and for high-value items. We noted that all inventory management systems should incorporate ABC analysis and cycle counting. Finally, we briefly referred to inventory turns, a common way of measuring inventory performance.

Unit Review Activity

The article 'Inventory: Asset or Liability' Resource Item 4.1, raises a controversial issue, frequently discussed by management. Often marketing, accounting, distribution, production, and top management have different views on the topic. Read the article, and then summarise the arguments from the viewpoint of each of these managerial groups. Can these views be reconciled?

Unit Summary

This unit has dealt with two of the basics in operations: managing demand and managing inventory. These two are related: in general the better you can manage demand, the less inventory that you will need.

Demand patterns sometimes appear more random than they actually are. An operations manager should seek out the elements: underlying demand, trend, seasonality, and inherent variation. Some demand variation may also be self-imposed as a result of sales promotions, quantity discounts, salespeople's incentives, and the adjustment of inventories for tax or shareholder purposes. So whilst the forecasting techniques we have discussed are important, you need to realise that management has a role in promoting stability of demand and hence efficiency in operations.

We discussed inventory control techniques under two main headings: dependent and independent demand. Both cases have established techniques for calculating how much to order and when to order. In the former case, the classic technique is material requirements planning (MRP) which involves calculating the demand for components (such as car wheels) from the demand for the end item (the car). In the latter case, the classic technique is the economic order quantity (EOQ), which, however, has severe limitations in practice. Alternative techniques, such as time phased order point, were examined.

References

Cox, J F, Blackstone, J and Spenser, M (eds) (1995) *APICS Dictionary*, APICS, Falls Church, Virginia, 8th edn

'How to turn junk mail into a goldmine – or perhaps not', *The Economist*, 1 April 1995, pp. 81–82

Fuller, J, O'Connor, J and Rawlinson, R (1993) 'Tailored logistics: the next advantage', *Harvard Business Review*, May/June, pp. 87–98

Hackett, G and Caunt, D (1993) *Quantitative Methods*, Open Learning Foundation Blackwell, Oxford

Meredith, J (1992) *The Management of Operations*, Wiley, New York, 4th edn

Plossl, G (1985) *Production and Inventory Control: Principles and Techniques*, Prentice Hall, Englewood Clifts, New Jersey 2nd edn

Silver, E A and Peterson, R (1985) *Decision Systems for Inventory Management and Production Planning*, Wiley, New York, 2nd edn

Vollman, T, Berry, W and Whybark, D C (1992) *Manufacturing Planning and Control Systems*, Irwin, Homewood, Illinois, 3rd edn

Recommended Reading

Waters, C D J (1992) *Inventory Control and Management*, John Wiley, Chichester

Answer to Unit Review Activity

In short, traditionally, marketing would like much more inventory in order to maximise customer service and sales. Accounting often sees inventory as a asset, and potentially an asset that can be manipulated at the time of reporting of performance. However, accounting is often wary as inventory represents cash tied up. Of course, inventory is what distribution is all about. On the one hand, inventory represents a 'power base' for distribution, but in practice performance is often measured on factors such as inventory turns, customer service, and 'dead' stock. Production has recently come to regard inventory as a liability since it has been shown to have a direct negative impact on space, lead time, and quality. On the other hand, some production managers are still measured on machine utilisation which tends to encourage keeping higher levels of work in progress inventory. In Unit 9, *Time Based Operations*, we will see that it is possible to achieve low levels of inventory and high customer service simultaneously by adopting JIT and supply chain principles. Perhaps, then, the long standing controversy may finally be ending.

UNIT 5
PROJECT MANAGEMENT

Introduction

In this unit, we will consider the issues which arise whenever a project is planned and undertaken. We examine the logic principles underpinning the techniques used in project management. You will learn the basic principles underlying the technique of network planning.

We shall consider critical path methods, PERT, precedence diagrams and line of balance technique.

We will emphasise the use of the network planning approach for the effective control of resources during the planning and execution phases of projects. We will examine the role of operations managers and the importance of operational management techniques will be discussed in relation to cost/time aspects of a project. We consider how much help PC packages can provide in designing and controlling a project.

As a discipline, project management is continually developing, in this unit, we will refer to wider issues and applications. However, we have restricted them as appropriate for this module. A list of recommended reading is provided at the end of the unit if you wish to undertake further study.

Note that differing notations appear in textbooks dealing with project management techniques. Although the underlying principles are the same, you may find the different styles of presentation confusing. You should follow the notation and terminology given in this unit when undertaking the activities.

Objectives

By the end of this unit, you should be able to:

- explain what is involved in the planning of projects
- observe the significance of the resources and their inter-relationships in a project
- use network planning techniques to determine the critical path and project duration
- highlight the differences between the activity-on-arrow and the activity-on-node approaches
- calculate the various kinds of float which occur in a network and appreciate the significance of each
- design and calculate through networks
- appreciate why computer applications are widely used in network planning and be aware of the benefits and limitations of packages
- use the data produced from the network to plan manpower (and other resource) requirements

- draw Gantt charts and manpower load histograms for project control purposes
- understand why probabilistic concepts have to be introduced into many projects
- calculate the activity durations when the PERT weighting approach is used
- understand the 'line of balance' technique.

SECTION 1
Project Management

Introduction

In this section we will define, and look at the growth of project management, its techniques and key features, as well as the main participants in it. We will look at project life cycles and documentation and introduce the family of network planning techniques.

1.1 Growth of project management

The satisfactory completion of project work involves the organised utilisation of all the resources being used:

- money
- manpower
- machinery
- materials
- time.

Project management is concerned with the setting of clear objectives, using forward looking control procedures and sound decision making. A project is any task which has to be managed and which has a definable beginning and end, for example, constructing a building, recruiting a senior manager or launching a new product.

The processes of planning, scheduling and controlling all the resources required for completion of a project, involves the balancing of three factors, cost, quality and time, as illustrated in Figure 1. In this case we have an example of a project which has to be completed within a given timescale, with little emphasis given to costs or to quality.

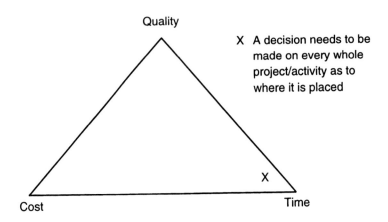

Figure 1: The balancing of cost, quality and time factors

There will always be a tension associated with the co-ordination of these three factors. The reduction of time taken on a task often results in reduced quality unless the method itself is changed. The raising of quality standards will often raise both cost and time.

Operations managers, who can precisely define methods and standard job times, are generally able to produce realistic data for use in project management. An experienced member of the operations management team should make an ideal project manager and be able to work in an independent way as a negotiator with all the personnel involved. He or she will be able to use a range of operations management techniques for either qualitative or quantitative selection of the activities and job methods to be used when sensitive decision making is required.

Project management has grown over the last few decades. Socio-economic factors have played a key role. The growth of international trade, increasing competition driving down unit labour costs and the increasing speed with which new products and service ideas must be converted into commercial realities, have all been contributory factors. Whilst mass markets exist for many products and services in which the factors of high volume, low cost and appropriate quality levels apply, there is also a growing demand for special customised products and services. These are often 'one-off' and require individual planning so that the resourcing cost is minimised.

> # ACTIVITY 1
>
> Identify two situations in which planning is required. One should be an example of manufacturing or processing high volumes of a commodity. The other should be an example of one-off service provision (like a concert or a wedding reception).
>
> List two similarities and differences which you feel exist between the two situations.

You might have chosen for your high-volume situation the planning required to harvest a seasonal crop on a farm, for example, strawberries.

This requires: plants; fields; fertiliser; staff attention whilst growing; water; cropping; packing; and financial planning and control.

For a 'one-off' service you might have chosen arranging a village festival.

This requires: fixing a date; location; facilities; staffing; financial management; publicity; and tidying up afterwards.

These are not exhaustive lists of the many things that have to be done to make these two projects a success, but already we can see certain common features emerging. There are also aspects which are very different! Some activities need to follow others in sequence, others can happen at the same time.

Project management techniques can be used to handle situations being driven by factors such as:

- increasing complexity of products and services
- sophisticated computing facilities within organisations
- availability of large knowledge data-bases
- rapid rate of technological change.

Project management is increasingly used because it:

- stimulates thought on tasks
- involves co-ordination of the work effort
- aims to minimise the cost of achieving the objective
- provides a good overall resource control focus
- minimises the project completion time
- leads to achievement on time, providing customer satisfaction
- lends itself to computerisation in complex situations
- leads to higher profit margins
- recognises and delivers quality standards

- can provide a secure and confidential framework where needed
- provides on-going reports which are easily understood
- gives opportunity for rapid re-scheduling.

In setting up a project, three fundamental criteria must be considered:

- end result of undertaking the project must satisfy the needs of the customer in terms of performance, cost and quality.
- authorised and agreed financial budgets must not be exceeded without good reason.
- actual progress will need to match the plan if the completion date is to be met. Delays on a major project can result in contractual cost penalties. This will not only reduce profits, but will also send out undesirable messages to potential customers.

A **project** is defined as a set of activities that has both a recognisable start and a definable ending which achieves an objective. Every project contains a number of clearly identifiable stages, each of which must be understood and controlled.

Project management is defined as planning, directing and controlling the resources needed to achieve a goal, whilst meeting the technical, financial and time constraints required.

Some examples of undertakings which are regularly handled on a project management basis include:

- organising conferences
- planning and running the Summer and Winter Olympics
- developing a new product
- reducing labour requirements
- building a bridge
- launching the space shuttle
- building a boat
- installing a new computer system.

The project manager needs to undertake the following steps:

- define the project, identifying all constraints and objectives
- determine the activities required and their times
- build a model of the process which will achieve success
- use the model to optimise all resources
- produce a project plan and denote calendar dates
- monitor progress and iterate through these steps as necessary.

You must appreciate that no project manager is an expert in the full range of managerial disciplines and techniques, and the skills of many specialists will be required in planning and controlling a project. Specialists in marketing, operations, management services, personnel and finance will all need to be consulted for information, and may well assist with the application of allied techniques such as:

- management by objectives
- management by exception
- probabilities and forecasts
- work methods and standard time values
- costing
- staffing levels and loadings
- quality, quantity and customer expectations.

Every project has a degree of novelty about it. Even if it is a 'repeat project'which has been done before there will probably be features which are beyond the control of the organisation.

ACTIVITY 2

What factors, which are beyond the control of staff, could affect a project?

You might have identified: the weather; illness in the workforce; trade union activity; shortages from suppliers; machinery breakdown; macro-economic environment; and actions of governments.

Different types of projects have different types and scales of such problems associated with them:

- Some projects must largely be completed out of doors on a particular site, for example, building a sports stadium. Huge capital investment is required and many sub-contractors will be involved.
- Some projects must be undertaken in a controlled environment by a small specialist team over a short time, for example, a heart surgery.
- Some projects will largely be of an administrative nature, like the design of a new security system for an office block. The task may take months but the installation might only take several days.
- A special kind of project is found in R&D. In pure research as you saw in Unit 2, a defined start can be made, and an objective broadly defined, but time-scales may vary.

1.2 Major participants in project management

PROJECT MANAGER

The project manager is responsible for the successful outcome of the project. He or she needs to be a good communicator and able to co-ordinate the efforts of people who will be making specific contributions, often in a teamwork capacity. The project manager should have the skills to develop plans using both manual and computer package techniques. He or she will need to be able to monitor the progress of the project and provide or authorise feedback in various formats to the line managers, accountants, technical staff and external contacts.

SENIOR MANAGERS

Senior managers make the final decisions on projects and have vested in them the authority to provide resourcing and give strategic guidance. They also provide essential lines of communication to staff of all levels who are involved in the project, and with suppliers, trade union officials and customers. Senior managers will also select staff who will spend part if not all of their working time in the project team.

CUSTOMERS

A project ultimately is designed to meet the needs of a customer. The customer may be an individual person wanting an extension to their house, or an organisation wanting something done, for example, an education authority wanting rough land turned into a school playing field and sports complex.

PROJECT TEAMS

A well-balanced team will need to be put together, and the project manager will probably be proactive in arranging this. The team should be able to provide a great deal of support for the project manager, with each member inputting specific skills and expertise. Liaison with external sources, suppliers and regulatory authorities will be necessary at times on most projects of any size.

When organising a project team, we need to remember the general principle of **unity of command**. Accountability and responsibility are always vital issues in project management, and the execution of the whole plan can flounder due to weaknesses in these areas. The publication of the organisational chart prior to the commencement of the project will greatly facilitate a smooth running process.

For a small project, an organisation chart may look like Figure 2.

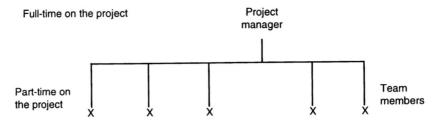

Figure 2: Organisation chart for a small project

For a more complex project, all staff may be seconded from their normal work to become effectively full-time participants, and another managerial layer may be inserted below the project manager for co-ordination purposes, as in Figure 3.

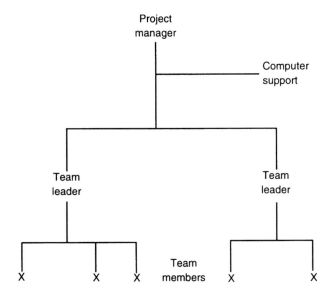

Figure 3: Organisation chart for a more complex project

Within the last 20 years, many projects have been managed on a matrix organisation basis, thereby reflecting the managerial style currently operating within a particular business. Lines of authority and responsibility are drawn both laterally and diagonally to overlay the structures shown in Figures 2 and 3.

The unity of command principle is usually amended to make team members answerable to two managers: their functional manager and the project manager. The project manager is not the owner of the complete project, but shares in the decision making with functional managers. This can lead to conflict and the degree of authority vested in the project manager may not fully match the level of responsibility. Sometimes the matrix can 'lose' information, exhibit inertia and lead to duplication. Proponents, however, claim that a matrix approach:

● more fully integrates team members

● has a greater degree of flexibility

● helps to overcome individual shortcomings, for example, in the project manager

● optimises the use of resources

● readily leads to group identity.

1.3 Project life cycles

As we saw in Unit 2, products and services tend to go through life cycles. A project can be viewed in the same way. One business, or part of a business, is providing a service for another. There will be finite starting and ending points, and the project itself will link them.

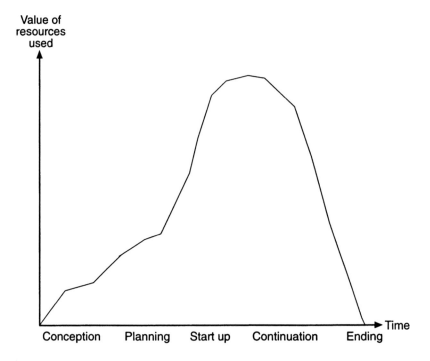

Figure 4: The project life cycle

Sometimes additional stages will be a feature of particular projects, for example, feasibility studies, to ensure the project is achievable, may be essential between conception and planning. When constructing a new motorway or airport runway, it will be necessary to undertake extensive technical simulations, resolve legal issues and consult with the public, before working plans can be drawn up.

1.4 Project documentation

Many projects run into difficulty through poor documentation and information flow. This leads to ineffective control, wastage and delayed decision making.

The documentation outputs from the project should be:

- easily understood
- in as simple a format as possible
- capable of highlighting concerns, for example, exception reporting
- strategically timed
- capable of presentation
- handling all appropriate information.

Typical documents which need to be designed before the project commences and used throughout are:

- project overview: including terms of reference, scope and scale, dates, costs, the project management approach used and any penalty clause conditions
- plans, schedules, working drawings
- management and milestone reports, for example, costs, problem-solving and progress
- stage agreements and conditions
- modification requests
- technical specifications
- files: electronic and hard copy.

1.5 Network planning techniques

One of the most powerful management techniques for project management is called **network planning**. A whole range of titles are given to the family of network planning techniques.

Basic titles:
> project network techniques (PNT)
> critical path analysis (CPA)
> critical path method (CPM)
> activity-on-arrow (AOA).

Special variations:
> precedence diagrams (PD)
> activity-on-node (AON).

Proprietary types:
> PERT (program, evaluation and review technique)
> GERT (graphical evaluation and review technique)
> PEP (project evaluation procedure)
> LESS (least cost estimating and scheduling).

Network planning identifies the **critical path activities** which must be rigorously controlled if the project is to be completed by an agreed date. Some commercial contracts carry financial penalty clauses which reduce the cost of the product to the buyer if delivery is late.

In practice, network planning is used:

- in **management by objectives (MBO)** programmes. Essential features of MBO are shared with network planning. A goal is set, a pathway identified and milestone review points established to monitor progress.

- as part of a **management by exception** process. This highlights the critical activities which could seriously affect progress. A network clearly shows relationships between these activities and other tasks which must also be performed, thereby providing scope for managerial decision-making should slippage occur.

- for detailed **cost analysis**. Cost scheduling can be undertaken to initially assess the costs of a project as various phases are reached. It is also necessary to control expenditure during a project, to ensure optimal use of resources, and to evaluate the effects of operational decisions during the project.

- in **manpower planning and levelling**. Efficient use of the labour force minimises both direct and indirect labour costs, cuts waiting (lost) time, reduces premium wage costs paid on overtime hours and ensures that the right numbers of suitably skilled staff are in place at the correct time. Later in the unit we look at the use of histograms in labour resource levelling.

1.6 Determining project activities

In any complex situation, the project team needs to find a method of identifying all the activities that are to be undertaken for the completion of the project. Information on the sequencing of activities and any possible variations from the norm must be identified. A work breakdown structure (WBS) can be undertaken. This is a top-down method which begins with the whole task and defines all the activities required. Having commenced with large activities, the analysis enforces division into smaller parts. Using systems analysis terminology, this is sometimes referred to as Level 1, Level 2, Level 3 etc.

A good WBS allows:

- activities to be considered and executed independently
- manageable size parts of the whole to be determined
- allocation of suitable activities to the correct staff
- improved monitoring and control during the project.

As an example, Figure 5 shows a maintenance service on a metal press.

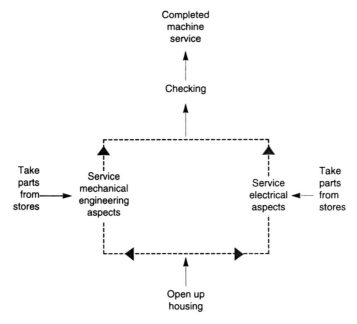

Figure 5: Activities involved in servicing a metal press

In this example we can see six activities which lead up to the completed service of a metal press in an engineering works. If this was a key piece of equipment in operational terms, then it would be necessary to minimise this non-productive period created by servicing (maintaining) the press. In such situations, the allied technique of work study will prove a powerful aid to the project manager. We discuss this technique in Unit 7.

ACTIVITY 3

Consider a job procedure with which you are familiar (e.g. arranging a party, arranging a holiday) and undertake a WBS to identify the activities required. What problems did you encounter?

You will have identified an individual procedure, but note that it is:

- easy to forget activities
- sometimes difficult to define sequences of activities
- often essential to consult with others who have greater expertise on aspects of the subject area
- possible to oversimplify the true situation.

Comparatively simple projects can be handled successfully using a paper and pencil approach to network planning. Complex situations demand a computerised approach and many software packages are now available. Some packages are capable of handling projects with several thousand activities. Others can only cope with 20 or 30 links. They all find the activities which lie along the critical path of the project and produce certain kinds of calculations for managerial action. The more sophisticated packages are capable of drawing the actual network itself and producing calendar dates, costs, bar charts and management reports. Unfortunately these systems are time-consuming to both learn and use. More details on packages for microcomputers are given in Resource 5.1.

In this unit we will concentrate on understanding the logic principles and symbolism used in producing a network. We then learn how to analyse a network and apply the information derived to the scheduling and control of a project.

1.7 Logic principles

First we need to determine all the activities which must be undertaken to successfully complete a project. In practice, this is not easy when a project manager is operating in new territory.

ACTIVITY 4

You have previously been project leader on local government projects which refurbishied vacated houses prior to their allocation to new residents. Now you are asked to lead a project to celebrate the founding of the city.

List several principles which would be applied in both types of project.

Identify two issues which would be significantly different.

Both projects have the following requirements:

  Manpower is needed.
  Costing is very tight.
  Time schedules are set by the council.

With the new project:
  Many non-council employees will be involved in planning the event.
  There may need to be an alternative 'bad weather' plan on the day.

You may have listed other factors.

Summary

In this section we looked at the growth of project management, its techniques and key features, as well as the main participants in it. We looked at project life cycles and documentation and introduced network planning and its family of techniques.

SECTION 2
Critical Path Method

Introduction

In this section, we will detail the various symbols and conventions used in network planning. We will look at how the network is numbered and constructed, and explain the concept, and the three measures of **float**.

In using a network planning approach to project management, we need to undertake certain steps. Firstly, we need to identify the type of network required and secondly, the amount of detail that we really want from the use of the technique.

We learn the basic principles of **critical path method (CPM)** and then go on to consider both **precedence diagrams** and **PERT**. In developing our ideas, we will concentrate upon a 'paper and pencil' approach.

2.1 Symbols used in network planning

Symbols are used to produce the arrow diagram, which is a logical construct used in network planning. Three types of symbols are used:

- **activities** are denoted by arrows ⟶

  The length and slope of arrow is immaterial, but the direction of the arrow indicates time flow. By convention time flows from the tail to the pointed head and from left to right on the paper. Activities take up time and other resources. This approach is referred to as **activity-on-arrow (AOA)**.

- **dummy activities** are denoted by broken arrows ┈┈┈▶

  These are not as common as normal activities, and are a logic device inserted into the network to show the relationships and dependencies of activities. They consume no time or other resources.

- **events** are denoted by ◯

  Events are also called **nodes**. They identify a point in time between two or more activities. In conventional networks, events take up no time or other resources.

  In precedence diagrams, time occurs on the node rather than the arrow. This is referred to as **activity-on-node (AON)**, and we return to this later in the unit.

Some events are recognised as having particular significance in the life of a project. The end of a phase may have been reached, or a decision is required based upon the prevailing circumstances. These events are referred to as **milestones**.

2.2 Logic conventions used in constructing the network

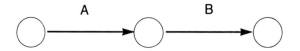

Activity A **must** precede activity B.

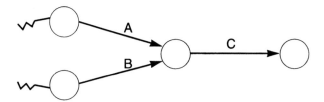

Activities A and B must both be completed before C can commence.

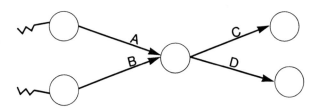

Activities A and B must both be completed before either C or D can be commenced.

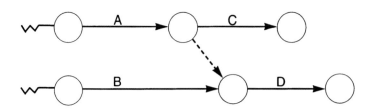

Activity A must be completed before C and D commence.

Activity B must be completed before D commences but it does not influence the start of C.

Note how the dummy activity, indicated by the broken arrow, is used to develop the logic.

If these conventions are followed any project can be put into a network format. There are however two common logic errors which must be avoided: **looping** and **dangling**.

- **looping**

    This is avoided by keeping the time flow from left to right.

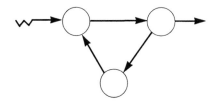

- **dangling**

    This is avoided by ensuring all events except the first and last have at least one activity entering and another one leaving them.

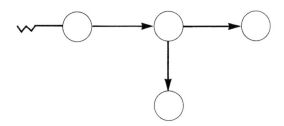

2.3 Subdivision of event symbols

Various approaches are taken to enable the arrow diagram to be evaluated. Probably the most common way is to divide the event symbol into three sections and observe the following notation:

Where:

N =   the event or node number.

E =   the earliest start time for the next activity.

L =   the latest start time for the next activity if the overall project completion time is to be achieved.

Various other notations are used, some of which appear rather untidy when the complete network model is drawn. For example:

where 10 is the earliest time, 17 is the latest time and 6 is the event reference number.

Another notation provides five pieces of information at each node:

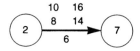

where   10 is the latest starting time
            8 is the earliest starting time
           16 is the latest finishing time
           14 is the earliest finishing time
           2 and 7 are the event reference numbers
           6 is the activity duration.

2.4 Numbering the network

In some simple networks, activities can be assigned letters of the alphabet A, B, C. Such approaches are however rather limited and a numerical system is much more flexible.

The event N is allocated following a general set of rules which will enable each activity to be precisely designated with a unique number. Therefore computer analysis of large numbers of activities can be speedily undertaken, and the potential for managerial misinterpretation of ongoing data is reduced.

Each activity can be referred to, for example:

Activity 15–20

The network numbering commences with low numbers on the left-hand side (the commencement) and proceeds to the highest number at the closing right-hand side event. It is common practice to leave gaps in the numbering system in all real project situations. This is to provide facility for the introduction of additional activities as the project unfolds. Failure to leave gaps involves renumbering and likely confusion in the accompanying documentation. Gaps in the early part of the network tend to be small whilst large gaps provide the facility for major changes or restructuring in the later stages of a project.

ACTIVITY 5

Construct a straight-line sequence for a project of writing a textbook and add some event numbers.

Activities included are: discuss and decide objectives

research material for first half

write first half

first half is reviewed whilst second half is researched

write second half

first half is amended whilst second half is reviewed

second half is amended

complete text is submitted to the publisher.

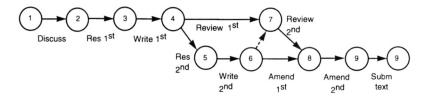

You might have made the event numbers consecutive if there were not going to be any changes to this network. You perhaps left some gaps to allow for, say, an additional review process. In some networks, you may see the start event numbered as zero. This is simply a convention which some project managers use.

In considering this example you probably thought about how long each of these activities took. You may have also wondered if the reviewing of the first half of the text took exactly the same time as the research needed for the second half. So we will revise the material and see what difference it makes to the sequencing of the project.

ACTIVITY 6

Construct the network for these revised activity details and number the events. The times given are in unit of a week, alphabetic references are given, as are the precedences. Two staff members work on this project X and Y. Precedence means it comes directly before.

How long can we expect the project to take?

		Time	Precedes	Staff
A	Discuss and decide objectives	2	B	X
B	Research material for first half	4	C	X
C	Write first half	5	D, E	X
D	First half reviewed	1	H	Y
E	Second half researched	4	F	X
F	Second half written	5	G,H	X
G	First half amended	2	I	X
H	Second half reviewed	1	I	Y
I	Second half amended	2	J	X
J	Text is submitted	1	none	X

This proved a bit more difficult. It is essential that we get the logic relationships right, otherwise later calculations will be erroneous.

This was the first network:

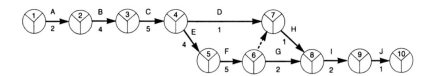

Route ABCEFGIJ adds up to 25 weeks.

Route ABCDHIJ adds up to 16 weeks.

Did you identify a problem with logic though? Staff member Y cannot begin reviewing the second half material until F is complete. This is where the logic device defined earlier, the dummy activity, is required.

This is the new network:

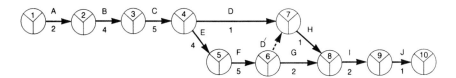

There is a new route now through the dummy: ABCEFDHIJ, this adds up to 24 weeks. It is essential that we account for all the logic issues and all the possible routes through the network.

OTHER WAYS OF INTRODUCING AND NUMBERING DUMMIES

On occasions two or more activities with different time allocations are structured between the same two events. This provides an opportunity to insert a dummy, which will itself be included in the calculations and have its own unique number.

The following example illustrates this:

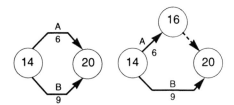

2.5 Determining activity times

The project manager will need to identify all the activities which must be undertaken to execute the project completely. Consultation with all who are knowledgeable about these activities is essential, and problems inevitably arise during the project if this process is treated superficially. Activities may be omitted or extra ones included to the detriment of the network.

The identification of all activities leads on to some form of classification in which each can be slotted into the work realm of particular managers. For example, activities under the control of a chief electrical engineer may occur intermittently throughout a six-month construction job.

The project manager will then personally meet all individual managers whose workforce is to be deployed on the project. This often involves sub-contractors also. At each meeting it will be necessary to:

- Confirm all the activities required from that source and amend the list if further things arise during discussion.

- Agree whether each activity is to be treated as a whole, or whether sub-division is desirable or possible.

- Agree activity sequencing and any variances which are possible.

- Precisely define the method of work to be adopted. This may mean a statement about work conditions/weather, machine performance and quality assurance. Resourcing factors must be determined in the light of the agreed method. For example, how many bricklayers are required for the task?

- Determination of the activity duration to be used in the network under the agreed conditions. Various approaches are adopted:

  - past records if similar jobs have been done before

  - work measurement, for example, time study synthetic data or predetermined motion time standards

  - estimation, preferably a system which involves some objectivity, for example, analytical estimating, comparative or category estimating.

Note that the process of agreeing activity duration times is often a sensitive one. Functional managers are thereafter going to be accountable to achieve these target times. There may only be a lot of work and worry associated with achieving a correct time with no hidden margins if anything goes wrong! Particular problems arise in green-field situations which have no past data to draw on. The development of state-of-the-art products as technology moves on is a prime example.

USING THE PERT APPROACH TO DETERMINE ACTIVITY DURATION TIMES

Sometimes activity duration times cannot be established using the normal deterministic methods. The activity itself may be subject to a degree of uncertainty and probabilistic concepts need to be introduced.

During the late 1950s the project managers of the Polaris missile programme were faced with complex problems in establishing activity durations because many of these activities were breaking new ground. The approach which was finally adopted by the US Navy has since been handed down to today's users. It is usually called the PERT approach after the full title of the network planning technique used: program evaluation and review technique.

Functional and technical managers are required to provide the project manager with three different time estimates for each of the activities that they are responsible for. These times may well have to be justified and so they must be based upon as much sound evidence as possible.

The three activity duration times provided are: **most optimistic, most likely** and **most pessimistic.**

Most optimistic duration time (O)

This is the shortest time in which the activity could be completed if everything goes exceptionally well. The manager should bear in mind that the chances of beating this time is no greater than one in a hundred.

Most likely duration time (M)

This time would be expected to be achieved on the greatest number of occasions if the activity was repeated many times under similar conditions. Statistically, this is known as the mode of a distribution.

Most pessimistic duration time (P)

This time estimate indicates the longest time which the activity will take if everything that can go wrong, does go wrong. Once again, the manager should not expect this desperate scenario to occur more than once in a hundred occasions.

A weighted average is determined using these three time estimates:

$$\text{activity duration time} = \frac{O + P + 4M}{6}$$

We look at how probability is used in the control of projects later in the unit.

ACTIVITY 7

When a network is numbered, gaps may be left in the numbering system. Why?

Consider the following project. Office equipment, desks, computers, filing cabinets, etc. are being transferred from one building to another 1 km away. The project is scheduled for three working days, Wednesday, Thursday and Friday. On Thursday, the lift in the receiving building broke down for five hours causing major delays on the network schedule. As the project manager you decide you must take alternative courses of action to get the project completed by 5.00 p.m. Friday. What could you do, and how would it affect the numbering of the network?

Gaps in the numbering are left to allow changes without a complete renumbering of the whole network.

With the office move scenario, it would obviously have been beneficial to leave gaps in the numbering. Let's look at some possible activity changes which might help:

- keep all the furniture moving and stock it near the base of the lift until it is required.

● reschedule activities to run through into Thursday evening.

● draft in extra personnel to complete the layout once the furniture is in the office.

If you adopted any or all of these activities, you would need to allocate an activity number and make a time assessment. The network could cope with the renumbering providing you had left appropriate gaps.

2.6 Constructing the network

The project manager, having collected all the relevant data regarding activities and their relationships, must then begin to construct the network itself. This involves a logical thought process if the network is a comparatively simple one using a paper and pencil approach.

Data should be in this kind of format for each activity:

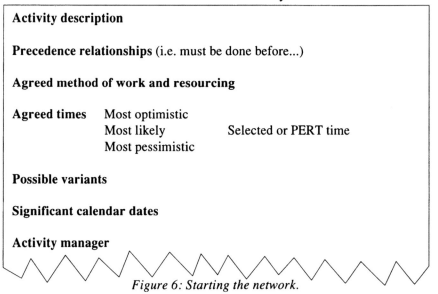

Activity description

Precedence relationships (i.e. must be done before...)

Agreed method of work and resourcing

Agreed times   Most optimistic
                   Most likely   Selected or PERT time
                   Most pessimistic

Possible variants

Significant calendar dates

Activity manager

Figure 6: Starting the network.

The next step is to identify the first activity or activities which must begin the project. Suppose we are modelling the construction of a building extension. Sketch on paper a circle near the left-hand side and draw the activity arrow from it, moving in a right-hand direction. At the arrow point draw another circle.

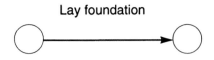

Lay foundation

Determine the next activity/activities which can begin once the initial activity/activities have been completed. Draw them in, beginning from the second circle (which represents an event). Do not close with an event until you are sure you have the logic correct. Continue the process until all activities are plotted and when checking the logic insert any dummy activities required.

For example, you probably have something like:

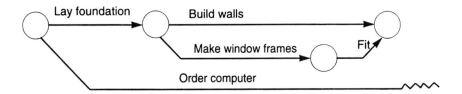

Suppose that this construction project began to shape up like this example:

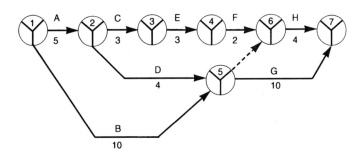

The longest route is through activities B and G, i.e. 1 – 5 – 7, a duration of 20 time units. This is known as the critical path route.

2.7 Entering activity times

Once the activities have all been entered, we usually call it an **arrow diagram**. Note you may need to construct a series of arrow diagrams if there are variances on methods and precedences.

The activity times are then added, by convention they go below the arrow.

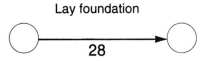

Sometimes when drawing a PERT network, the three time estimates are shown in this way:

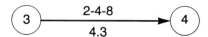

where the figure 2-4-8 represents the three time estimates and 4.3 is the weighted average.

2.8 Calculating the overall project duration

The project starts at zero. There must be a common time scale for all activities, for example, days, and relationships with calendar dates are determined towards the end of the whole analysis at the practical planning stage.

Enter zero in the bottom left-hand segment of the first event. Then by an addition process add through from event to event using the bottom left-hand segments. These are known as **earliest times**.

There is a rule which must be followed when more than one activity enters an event. The *largest total* is entered in the segment.

The final event will indicate the total time through the longest route. Again this is called the **critical path**.

The final time is now entered also in the right-hand segment of the final event. A subtraction process is then used to enter the right-hand segments, known as **latest times**.

The rule which must be followed when the tail of more than one arrow comes from an event is that the *smallest total* is entered. The latest time on the first event should end up as zero.

2.9 Float

Float, or sometimes called **slack,** is defined as the amount of time an activity can be delayed without affecting the duration of the project. Critical path activities by definition possess no float. The manager responsible for a critical path activity must ensure that it is completed in the allotted time. Failure to do this will extend the overall project duration, unless steps are taken at a later stage to claw back time which has been lost.

Float occurs on non-critical path activities and dummies. It is often possible to avoid having dummy activities in the critical path by careful modelling. If a dummy is non-critical, the float must be determined.

In appreciating the relationships within the network, note that time extensions of only a small amount on some activities will create a new critical path route and extend the network.

There are three measures of float, **total float, free float** and **independent float** each having special features:

- **total float is** the maximum time which is available to complete an activity. Knowing that an activity has a quantity of total float enables the manager to use discretion as to when the activity is undertaken. Faced with illness, machine breakdown, or departmental overload on certain days, the manager can schedule the activity to maximise the efficient use of resources. Many of the simpler texts on project management, only identify total float, calling it 'float' or 'slack'.

We can calculate total float:

Total float = Latest finish time for the activity (LF) – Earliest starting time for the activity (ES) – Duration of the activity.

For example:

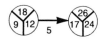

ES = 9 Duration = 5 LF = 24

Total float (TF)

$$= LF - ES - D$$

$$= 24 - 9 - 5 = 10$$

- **Free float** is calculated by considering earliest times. Many projects are organised and scheduled on earliest times to give the best possible chance of completion on time. The project manager needs to carefully monitor the progress of each activity as earliest time operation puts activity managers under some extra pressure. Not all non-critical path activities have free float.

We can calculate free float as follows:

$$\text{Free float} = \frac{\text{Earliest finish time}}{\text{for the activity (EF)}} - \frac{\text{Earliest starting}}{\text{time for the activity}} - \text{Duration}$$
$$(\text{ES})$$

In the above example,

Free float = EF – ES – D

$$= 17 - 9 - 5 = 3$$

- **independent float** is important when the project is being run on earliest times. Should an activity reach the next stage at the latest time possible, the independent float indicates whether it will be possible to complete it immediately and allow the following activity to begin on its earliest time, as scheduled. Sometimes the calculation results in a negative result. This indicates the degree of lost days still to be pulled back, but counts as zero days in control terms.

Normally in tabular analysis, negative data is shown as: 0 (– 5)

We can calculate independent float as follows:

$$\text{Independent float} - \frac{\text{Earliest finish time}}{\text{for the activity (EF)}} - \frac{\text{Latest starting time}}{\text{for the activity (LS)}} - \text{Duration.}$$

In the above example:

Independent float = EF – LS – D

$$= 17 - 12 - 5 = 0$$

Figure 7 illustrates these three types of float.

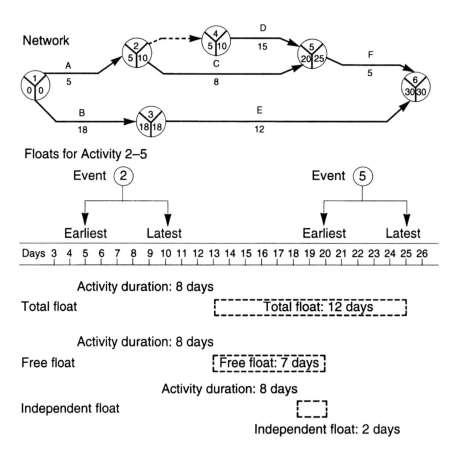

Figure 7: The three measures of float

ACTIVITY 8

Here are the details of a simple project, putting on a play, which we can use to construct a network in stages.

First, construct a network from the following data; determine the critical path activities; and calculate total, free and independent float for each activity.

Activity		Time (Weeks)	Precedes
A	Decide on the play	2	all
B	Print tickets	3	C
C	Sell tickets	3	–
D	Issue scripts to cast	1	E
E	Cast learn scripts	4	F
F	Rehearsals	3	G
G	Full dress rehearsals	2	–
H	Obtain stage props/equipment	2	F
I	Make costumes for cast	5	G

Hint: start every activity as soon as it is logically possible.

It helps to put this network together in stages. First, the logic:

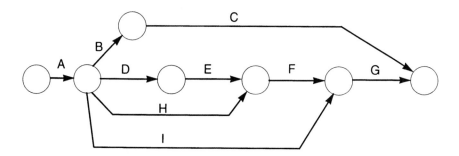

The logic diagram

Then add the numbers and calculate through, using the rules you met earlier in the unit.

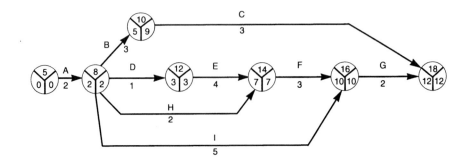

Calculated network

Finally calculate the floats and identify the critical path with no floats.

Remember how to calculate the different kinds of float:

Total float (T)	$=$	Latest Finish	$-$ Earliest Start	$-$ Duration
Free float (F)	$=$	Earliest Finish	$-$ Earliest Start	$-$ Duration
Independent float (I)	$=$	Earliest Finish	$-$ Latest Start	$-$ Duration

Tabular analysis

We can present the information in tabular form:

ACTIVITY	CODE	DURATION	START E	START L	FINISH E	FINISH L	FLOAT T	FLOAT F	FLOAT I
A Decide	5–8	2	0	0	2	2	0	0	0*
B Print	8–10	3	2	2	5	9	4	0	0
C Sell	10–18	3	5	9	12	12	4	4	0
D Scripts	8–12	1	2	2	3	3	0	0	0*
E Learn	12–14	4	3	3	7	7	0	0	0
F Rehearse	14–16	3	7	7	10	10	0	0	0*
G Dress Reh.	16–18	2	10	10	12	12	0	0	0*
H Obtain Props	8–14	2	2	2	7	7	3	3	3
I Costumes	8–16	5	2	2	10	10	3	3	3

* Critical path activities: project duration 12 weeks.

2.10 Using Computer Packages in Network Planning

Many real-life problems contain a large number of factors and activities. The resolution of the problem, with optimisation in view, lends itself to computerisation. In the past decade, many efforts have been made to produce programs which will rapidly handle network situations. Mainframe computer programs in FORTRAN were developed in large companies, for example, in construction and aircraft assembly. Specialist staffing was essential to write and run these programs and many project managers were unhappy that output was batched rather than in real time.

The development of microcomputers and associated packages has greatly renewed the interest in solving network problems, within a wide range of organisations. The added facilities of colour and graphics has enhanced the attractiveness of using the packages. Many PC applications concentrate mainly upon the calculation of the critical path duration and total float (slack).

We identify some features to look for in purchasing a network planning package in Resource 5.1.

2.11 Potential problems of computer applications

We can identify a number of problems with using computers in network planning:

- Computer paralysis: too much computer activity, too little real project management thought.
- Information overload: too much data or detail overwhelms staff.
- Dependency: project managers wait for computer reports before acting, rather than proactively avoiding problems.
- Biased reports: data is massaged to provide good reports.

Summary

In this section we described and illustrated the various symbols and conventions used in network planning. We looked at how the network is numbered and constructed, and explained the concept, and the three measures of float. We also considered the use of computer packages in network planning.

SECTION 3
PERT

Introduction

In this section, we will look in detail at PERT, a particular network planning technique that we introduced earlier. It is often difficult to establish the activity times, particularly when work of a particular type, or using a particular method has never been done before. Managers who will have to control parts of the project when work comes into their department or under their authority, are naturally keen to get the best possible time allowance for it. They are pragmatists and realise that they have to cope with staff absenteeism, holiday entitlements, machine breakdowns and material shortages. Having a little extra time on an activity seems like a good idea! The project manager will need analytical and persuasion skills to agree methods and times. A very legitimate question arises whenever estimates involving uncertainty are made. Will the project finish on time? The PERT approach can help answer this question.

3.1 Time estimates on networks

As we saw in Section 2.5, using the PERT approach to establish activity times generates three different duration estimates:

  M most likely duration

  O optimistic duration

  P pessimistic duration.

PERT uses the following weighted average to determine activity durations:

$$T = \text{activity duration} = \frac{O + P + 4M}{6}$$

3.2 Probability of duration

The probability distribution used in PERT is known as the **beta distribution**, which can assume a variety of shapes and allows M (called **the mode**) to fall anywhere between O and P. Note that M and T will only correspond in a normal distribution. The mode is the value that most commonly occurs.

A statistical measure known as the **variance** can be calculated. This is designated by the Greek letter σ:

$$\sigma^2 = \left(\frac{P-O}{6}\right)^2$$

The variance increases as the gap between O and P increases. Thus the greater the uncertainty of accuracy the greater the variance. A major use of variance data is in the determination of the probability of a project being completed by a given day or date.

We can construct a simple network from the following data:

Activity time estimates (days)		PERT	σ²	Precedes
Code	O M P	Mode		
A	1 2 3	2	4/36	All
B	6 7 8	7	4/36	E
C	1 2 3	2	4/36	F
D	1 4 9	4.33	64/36	G
E	3 4 5	4	4/36	H
F	2 3 4	3	4/36	H
G	2 6 10	6	64/36	H
H	2 4 6	4	16/36	-

Network model:

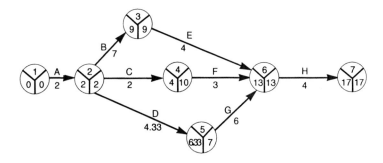

The critical path activities are A-B-E-H and the duration = 17 days.

If management wants to know the probability of the project being completed by day 20, the response can be calculated:

Activity	A	B	E	H	Sum
σ²	4/36	4/36	4/36	16/36	28/36 0.777

Thus σ = $\sqrt{0.777}$ = 0.882.

The probability of completion by day 20

$$\frac{P - O}{0.882} = \frac{3}{0.882} = 3.401.$$

Using a table of cumulative probabilities of the normal distribution curve, we can see that 3.401 gives a probability of .9997, that is, there is a 99.97% chance of completion by day 20.

Note that a negative result indicates the likelihood of it not being achieved.

Summary

In this section we looked at PERT and how this approach to network planning can help establish activity times and indicate whether a project will finish on time.

SECTION 4

Project Resources

Introduction

In this section we will discuss the allocation of resources to the network. We will highlight the use of histograms and Gantt charts by project planners and will also consider project control, project status and exception reporting. We will introduce the term **milestone** and look at project cost scheduling. We will describe the process of **crashing** activities on a network and mention briefly the control of variances. Finally, we will summarise the factors which can lead to project success or failure.

4.1 Calculation of load

The project manager will generally consider the allocation of resources to the network as the logic diagram is being produced. For example, it is not possible to run two activities simultaneously if both have to be done by the same staff, or if there is a demand on the same piece of equipment. Allocation of resources to the network is often called **loading the network**. Computerised techniques are available to handle complex situations, but the simple **Gantt chart** is widely used by project planners.

Amongst the problems involved with the loading of resources to staff, machines or departments are:

- **overloading**: too much work is required from the resource relative to the time available.

- **underloading**: too little work is available for the resource.

The objective is one of **full loading** but in practice we can only attain this in well-designed and balanced systems set up on management services and work study bases, for example a conveyorised product assembly line. In quantifying the duration of each activity in the network, it is advisable to use a standard time unit, and represent all activities in that unit or decimals of it. A standard hour (day or month) will have built-in allowances and performance statements.

For example: activity 19-37:   manually dig out 70 cubic metres of soil
   work standard: 7 cubic metres/hour
   working day: 8 hours
   duration: 10 hours, that is, 10/8 = 1.25 days of work.

In calculating what is attainable, we need to moderate the technically feasible target by reference to current factors such as:

- absentee rates

- holidays

- breakdowns and maintenance data.

Two problems arise when we calculate resource load:

- **optimisation**: What feature should be optimised? If maximum machine utilisation is achieved in the network, it is likely that other resources will be underloaded. Trade-offs are inevitable and must be explained in the planning documentation.

- **alternatives**; Activities in a network impinge upon each other. Choices have to be made regarding sequencing to achieve optimum efficiency. Three activities which can be carried out independently can be networked in six ways (3! or 3 factorial, 3 x 2 x 1); five activities have 120 alternatives (5 x 4 x 3 x 2 x 1).

4.2 Histograms and Gantt charts

Network loads can be represented as a histogram, with the length of each bar being proportional to the quantity of load. An example is shown in Figure 8.

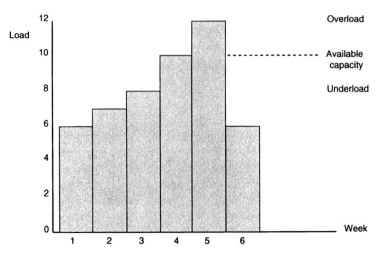

Figure 8: Example of a histogram

Gantt charts can be presented in various ways. Decisions need to be made about the data to be included once the network has been constructed and calculated. One chart may refer to the normal network, a second may refer to a crashing procedure. Charts will often be plotted on the earliest activity times and will indicate any of the types of float of particular interest. Many Gantt charts are plotted showing earliest times and free float and project managers are under pressure to keep to these times. An example is shown in Figure 9.

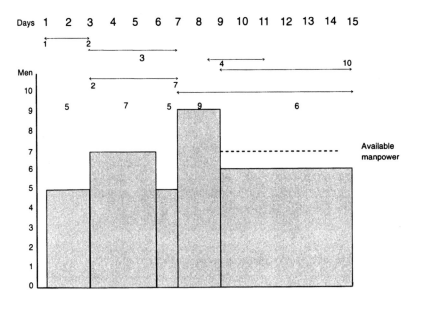

Figure 9: Example of a Gantt chart

SMOOTHING THE GANTT CHART

From Figure 9, you can see that problems of resourcing are going to occur on Days 7 and 8. The labour demands exceed the availability, and the project manager needs to resolve this issue to the best advantage. Usually budgets have been agreed at an earlier stage with operations managers. In the following example, the number of man-days has been agreed as indicated:

Activity	Duration (days)	Men	Man-days
1–2	2	5	10
2–3	4	4	16
2–7	3	3	9
3–4	2	8	16
4–10	6	5	30
7–10	9	1	9
		Total	90

Budgeted man-days: 7 men for 15 days = 105 man-days.

There are enough man-days but the distribution needs adjustment as no more than seven men are to be provided at any one time. One activity (3-4) requires eight men and this must now be carefully re-examined.

Careful consideration is given to the method, and discussions held with the managers concerned to see if there are alternative methods, or whether the 16 man-day requirement could be spread over four days instead of two. The relevance of float time will be seen at this stage, not only on the activity concerned, but also impinging other activities. In a fuller Gantt chart than this example provides, the three types of float can be shown. These will obviously change as activities are revised through consultation. The aim of the project manager will be to find a way of getting Activity 3-4 done within the budgeted man-days and to avoid an 'extra allowance' request due to manpower shortfall.

4.3 Project control

This is the next phase of project management and it is achieved by constantly monitoring the progress made on each activity. Constant referencing to time schedules and cost budgets is necessary, and the project manager will need to find the appropriate ways to act whenever signs of 'slippage' begin to occur.

In practice, monitoring of the progress of time is done by relating the actual start and finish times of each activity against either a time-scale relating to overall project duration or to actual calendar dates. The critical path activities are of prime concern, because uncorrected slippage will extend the project time. Of secondary importance are non-critical activities which possess small amounts of float. Slippage on these could cause them to go critical, and a whole new critical path develop. In this case, operations managers will need re-briefing on the changed status of later activities within their functional areas. The third level of importance are activities which contain considerable quantities of float. If independent float exists, for example, there will be scope to allow slippage and still operate the succeeding activity on the earliest time if required.

As part of this monitoring stage, regular management reports, prioritising activities which need to be done in terms of their float, will be required. Highest in the table are critical path activities which have no float, followed by those activities with ascending quantities of total float.

Simple projects can be drawn on to planning boards and progress can be recorded daily. If a computerised system is being used, the project manager must ensure that printed out material is intelligible to other managers and not in such copious quantities that it is set aside rather than acted on.

Figure 10 shows a further example of a Gantt chart.

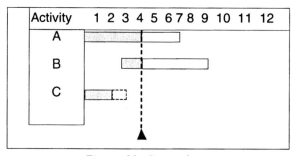

Figure 10: Gantt chart.

The following notation could be used:

Progress to date: ⬜

Work remaining: ⬜

Slippage or agreed extension: ⌐⌐⌐

Milestone dates: ▲

Gantt charts generated from computer packages have similar structures and are often based on the Lotus 1-2-3 spreadsheet package.

4.4 Project status reports

Project status reports are provided at both regular and pre-designated points in the life of the project so that corrective managerial action can be taken.

ACTIVITY 9

You are the project manager controlling the refurbishment of old shop premises into an up-market fashion boutique. A well-publicised grand opening is planned for 20 days ahead. It is apparent, however, that the builders have created a lot more dust, dirt and grime than was expected. The painters and decorators are due to start in three days time for their ten days of work. You reckon that there are six days of cleaning to be done. What possible actions can be taken so that the opening is not delayed?

Perhaps you could hire extra (contract) cleaners and possibly use them on a night shift.

You might consider cleaning up a particular area so the painters could make a start, allowing them to start on time. The cleaners would then move through ahead of the painters until the premises were clean. Some of the final tasks before opening could be approached differently; you apparently have a lot of float in the system, although perhaps you have 4 days' of carpet laying and shelf and rack building to schedule before the clothes can be displayed on the racks.

There are many options. A bar chart, with its associated network, allows 'What-if?' scenarios to be explored.

EXCEPTION REPORTING

Some projects are run on an exception-reporting basis. This only identifies activities on which managerial action is necessary to maintain scheduled progress. The management report shows the reference number of the activity, the amount of slippage, the effect upon overall project completion time, or the extent to which total, free or independent float can be used up.

Managerial accountability requires precise definition of the cause(s) of the delays so that other managers or customers can be accurately advised where necessary. A damage limitation process follows, led by the project manager. Ways need to be found to bring the project back into schedule by initially considering all the significant later activities. Challenging their resourcing and methods will often prove beneficial. This process is often a difficult one due to resistance from operational managers who know they may be required to execute an activity using new and untried methods. An alternative strategy when PERT principles have been used to determine the weighted average activity time, is to take steps over several sequential activities to pull the completion time towards the 'most optimistic' estimate.

4.5 Milestones

The term **milestone** is used in project control to describe events in the life of a project which signal the achievement of certain key stages.

ACTIVITY 10

You are using the project management approach to design a small business proposal which you aim to present to your bank manager. Can you list several key issues, or milestones, which would apply to this project?

Your milestones are likely to be:

- deciding your business idea by creative thinking process
- analysing your market research findings
- deciding on the location for the business
- carrying out your financial projections.

You probably included some different issues too. Notice how developments can often go in a number of directions after a milestone, depending upon your decision making.

Not all milestones need to be upon the critical path. Sometimes we can be dependent upon the efficiency of a contractor for the delivery of hire equipment, and have built in a margin to cope with late delivery through adverse weather conditions. The project manager is delighted to see the equipment arrive on time, happy to see it a day late, satisfied if it arrives two days late, when the network analysis shows there are five days of total float on the first activity which the equipment will be used for. Obviously, if the equipment arrives on time, it may be possible to pull activities forward and accomplish them early.

If a computer package is in use, it is possible to produce a management report consisting of a milestone listing. Various strategies can be employed to keep activities on schedule. One approach is to divide up the whole project into discrete phases and to ensure that every possible means is used to complete each milestone phase before the next phase begins. This is sometimes called **damming-up**.

4.6 Project cost scheduling

Cost control is necessary for a number of reasons. It assists in the financing of the project and recognises the points at which further finance needs to be injected. The project manager will be accountable for the on-going expenditure and this can be compared and reconciled against budgeted costs.

A cost schedule can be developed from the Gantt chart and milestone reporting intervals can be pre-determined. One approach which is used for control is to prepare a **cost-slope** for each activity. This can be used at the negotiation stage of project when a cost quotation is being prepared for the potential customer, as an overall project cost can be determined.

To undertake a cost-slope calculation for an activity requires the following factors:

- an agreed expected activity duration (in days/weeks/months)
- the budgeted cost of the activity, taking into account the costs of labour, equipment, materials and other resources.

The cost-slope is expressed in £/unit of time (e.g. £/day), by dividing the cost by the time. When all the activity cost-slopes are linked to the project calendar, a cost distribution graph can be drawn.

ACTIVITY 11

Calculate the activity cost-slopes for part of a project running between days 10 and 24 inclusively from the following data:

Activity reference	Cost (£)	Duration (days)	C-S
7-13	1875	15	
8-16	325	5	
9-18	1218	14	
10-19	873	9	
			Total cost per day £

Our calculations are

7–13	1875/15	=	£125/day
8–16	325/ 5	=	£65/day
9–18	1218/14	=	£87/day
10–19	873/ 9	=	£97/day
Total cost/day £		=	£374

This indicates the cash injection required over the 15-day period. A gross amount of £4291 will be required but spread differentially.

ACTIVITY 12

Develop this example further with this additional data:

Activity 7–13 begins at the start of day 1 and is completed by the end of day 15.

Activity 8–16 begins on day 2 and ends on day 7.

Activity 9–18 begins at the start of day 1 and ends on day 14.

Activity 10–19 begins on day 2 and ends on day 11.

Use a Gantt chart approach to calculate overall daily expenditure.

This is our Gantt chart and overall daily expenditures. We found that in this phase of the project the daily costs moved from £212 to £374 to £309 before returning to £212.

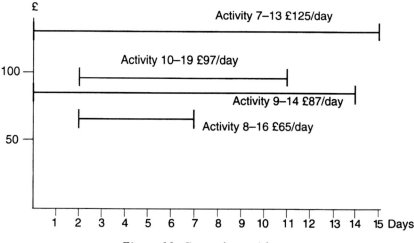

Figure 11: Gantt chart with costs

4.7 Crashing activities

The first overall project time established by a network may not be acceptable for a whole variety of reasons. There could be a commercial judgement relative to the acceptability to the customer or internal organisational reasons to do with resourcing or a clash with demands made by other projects.

If the duration is thought to be too long, the process of **crashing** the activities on a network is undertaken. More exceptionally, if the duration is rather shorter than the time available, **reverse crashing** can be used to open up activity times and reduce costs.

In order to reduce the overall project time the project manager will first identify the critical path activities and rank them in order of duration. The idea is that there would normally be greater scope for reducing time on an activity with a longer duration. The project manager would then examine the details of the activity at the top of the list and consult with the operational manager with whom the initial details had been agreed. If the PERT approach had been used there could have been later reflection on the estimates made and a revision is simply a matter of re-calculation. In most cases, however, the methods to be used, the resources involved and the relative costs will all need to be reconsidered. Other functional specialists from work study and finance may need to make inputs. Where a whole set of options develop it is possible to construct a cost/time curve and to make a selection in the light of the data produced.

4.8 Cost/time curve

The following data was produced whilst trying to crash an activity which involved sub-contracted printing and binding work:

Original
Printer 1 method 'A' £1200   8 days

Crashing Data
Printer 2 method 'A' £1150   7 days
Printer 2 method 'B' £1300   5 days
Printer 3 method 'B' £1620   3 days.

Plotting this data gives the curve as in Figure 12.

The project manager can then decide how much time reduction is needed on the project in the knowledge of the cost implications.

If a computer package is being used for this process it is then possible to revise the network data to take account of the new activity duration. This needs to be done for two reasons:

● to see when the target amount of reduced overall project time has been reached.
● to continually check which activities now lie on the critical path.

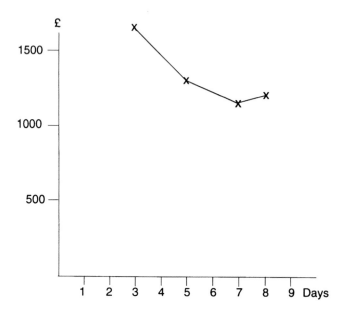

Figure 12: Cost/time curve.

You must appreciate that a degree of iteration is necessary and the project manager must ensure that time and energy are not being expended in attempts to crash activities which are no longer of critical importance.

Some computer packages are capable of producing a graph showing the overall project cost plotted against the duration. As changes are being made to activity times and costs, a decision can be taken about the whole project, to gain optimum economic advantage.

4.9 Controlling variances

Many projects are now agreed on the basis of either a fixed price or cost reimbursement contract. A **fixed price** contract contains a statement of the total agreed price, the delivery date and an identification of penalties which will come into operation should late delivery occur. Obviously it is possible for technical or political factors, which are beyond the control of any involved party, to arise during the life of a lengthy project. In such circumstances, further negotiations between clients, suppliers, contractors and sub-contractors have to be undertaken. The outcome is usually the production of a **change-order** which then forms that part of the overall contract. Note that many projects, particularly technological, creep up incrementally in cost due to a series of change-orders which become necessary. The final extra cost, whilst regrettable, is today usually a function of unforeseen factors outside of the control of the parties to the contract, rather than of poor planning.

The **cost reimbursement** (or cost-plus) approach requires the client to pay the costs incurred by a supplier or contractor plus an agreed profit margin percentage. This is probably what a householder enters into when a tradesman is employed to undertake a domestic job, for example, fit a new window. There is very little real control over what the tradesman actually does with his time, and even where an estimate has been given, it is difficult for the client to counter a demand for extra payment. In a more complex project, the client can receive extra payment demands which seem authentic, but which are retrospective and say nothing about the level of efficiency achieved.

4.10 Project success

We can consider a project as a success if it fulfils the objective criteria which were set. In reality, there are many criteria, and overall success is usually achieved as a result of numerous trade-offs. Some aspects of the project work out better than expected, and more than compensate for those aspects which were difficult to achieve. Typical success criteria would be time, cost, quality, profit and client satisfaction.

FACTORS WHICH LEAD TO PROJECT SUCCESS

A number of factors help to lead to project success:

- An initial careful definition of the objectives of the project, agreed by all the participants is essential.
- There should be commitment and involvement from all participants in the project. This will involve communication and information flows using appropriate channels such as: meetings, written reports, computer printouts on progress and cost, personal conversations, faxes, e-mails, video-conferencing.
- Appropriate planning and control systems must be used. Detailed provisioning and scheduling of resources will be essential to achieve optimal project conditions. A proactive stance can help in forestalling some potential problems, and feedback is vital to keep all participants fully informed on progress and modifications.

What can go wrong if clearly defined project objectives are not agreed between the project manager and the client? Any of the criteria could be emphasised wrongly, for example, the project manager wants to minimise time, but the client is much more concerned about cost; the project manager is concerned about the safety of staff. The client is unaware of the hazards of the job. The end result may not satisfy either party, for example a restaurant is built when a coffee bar is required. There are many more issues. How would you handle the actual specification process to ensure there were no misunderstandings?

4.11 Project failure

We can look at all project failures as the failures of systems. In Unit 1, we learned that a system can be viewed as an input of resources, a transformation to add value, and an output of goods or services. When a project fails to reach a successful conclusion, the cause could lie within any of the three aspects. Inadequate resourcing, poor planning and control, and an indifferent quality of output could all result in failure or non-acceptability.

Sometimes the project itself achieves a conclusion which is perfectly satisfactory in its own right, but which is unsatisfactory to the client. For example, the shop premises are built, but the late completion date has messed up all the plans the client had for new staff recruitment and the opening promotion.

FACTORS WHICH LEAD TO PROJECT FAILURE

The reasons for a failed or unsatisfactory project can be due to personnel, technical, financial, operational, legal or environmental factors such as:

- lack of support from senior management
- inadequate project management skills or experience
- poor communications
- rushed decision making
- inaccurate time estimations
- ignorance of legal or environmental stipulations
- too many ill-fitting significant changes during the project
- lack of managerial control.

Summary

In this section, we discussed the allocation of resources to the network. We highlighted the use of histograms and Gantt charts by project planners and considered project control, project status and exception reporting. We introduced the term milestone and looked at project cost scheduling. We described the process of crashing activities on a network and briefly mentioned the control of variances. Finally, we listed the factors which can lead to project success or failure.

SECTION 5

Activity-on-Node (AON) Technique

Introduction

In this section, we will describe the activity-on-node approach to project management. The development of increasingly sophisticated computer packages has led to increasing use of this technique. There are similarities in methodology to the work-balancing technique known as **precedence diagrams**, so these will be a good starting point.

5.1 Precedence diagrams

Precedence diagrams use the network planning symbols but the model produced shows the activities and their times on the node or event (activity-on-node). The arrows simply identify the relationships between the activities in terms of their logical sequences. The fundamental rule in scheduling the activities of the project is that no later activity can be undertaken before all the activities which lead into it by arrow have been completed.

NOTATION
We use the following notations:

A circle represents an activity ◯

The upper half is used to identify the activity with the order of operation reference number. The activity time can be shown either in the bottom half of the circle or outside the circle as in Figure 13.

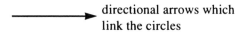 directional arrows which link the circles

Probably the major use of precedence diagramming is to solve efficiency problems in the setting up of work stations on product assembly lines. We look at a brief outline in this unit; other heuristical approaches are investigated elsewhere in this module.

METHODOLOGY
We follow a series of steps in creating the model as we did before:
- identify the number of activities in the project or process

- define the relationships between these activities in terms of what follows what, the precedences.
- investigate which activities can be undertaken using the same skills and resources in the same locations
- determine the standard times, known as SMs or SHrs (see Glossary)
- construct the precedence diagram model, building in the logic.
- establish any or all of the following factors from management:

  output required per period of time

  number of work stations desired

  target cycle time per unit of output

  if there are zoning constraints, for example, due to dust.
- discuss with operational staff the possibility of the splitting of activities into smaller components; the use of this data will be a secondary phase strategy.
- develop further managerial debate on objectives and the extent to which a **balancing loss** is acceptable. We cover balancing loss later in this module.

Let's look at an example!

On an assembly line, 11 activities need to be performed to assemble a domestic product. We want to construct the precedence diagram and then use it to look at the best way of using the work stations for maximum efficiency and productivity.

Activity:	1	0.27 SMs (precedes)	2,5,6,7,8,9,10,11
	2	0.12	4,5,6,7,8,9,10,11
	3	0.06	5,6,7,8,9,10,11
	4	0.16	5,6,7,8,9,10,11
	5	0.05	6,7,8,9,10,11
	6	0.13	8,10
	7	0.25	8,9,10,11
	8	0.35	10
	9	0.11	10,11
	10	0.21	11
	11	0.16	none

The following are key factors:

no zoning constraints

5 work stations required each staffed with one person, all of which can perform any activity

maximum work station time = 0.40 SMs

no subdivision of activities permitted.

PRECEDENCE DIAGRAM

We can now draw the precedence diagram as shown in Figure 13.

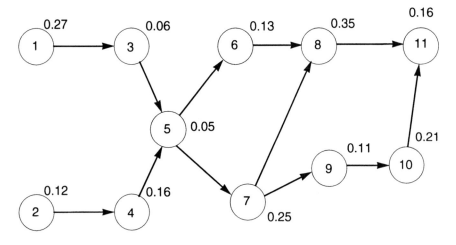

Figure 13: Precedence diagram for assembly line

POSSIBLE SOLUTION

We then need to break down the activities into the number of work stations, that is, 5.

work station			
	A activities	1,2	0.39 SMs
	B	3,4,5,6	0.40
	C	7,9	0.36
	D	8	0.35
	E	10,11	0.37

We can then calculate the output per hour, as the maximum work station time is 0.40SMs:

Output/hour $\qquad \dfrac{60}{0.40} \quad = \quad$ 150 appliances

Direct labour cost per hour: 5 staff @ £6/hr = £30

Our productivity will be the output per hour, divided by the cost of that output:

Productivity index $\quad = \quad \dfrac{\text{output}}{\text{input}} \quad = \quad \dfrac{150}{30}$

= 5 appliances/£1 direct labour cost.

5.2 Networks using AON

Different notation will be required within the nodal segments in order to calculate through the AON network.

Initially the nodes can be shown as   A B

They are then evaluated according to the times determined for the activity.

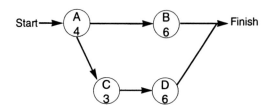

We need to identify a starting point for the project and a finishing point:

Start→ A 4 → B 6 → Finish, C 3 → D 6

Then we need to further sub-divide the node to enable calculation of the float time and to identify the critical path.

A typical convention is as follows:

ES	A	EF
LS	4	LF

where: ES is the Earliest Start time   EF is the Earliest Finish time
LS is the Latest Start time   LF is the Latest Finish time

All this data can be contained in a box shape or a large circle.

If we develop our simple example further:

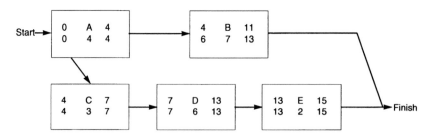

where: ES = earliest possible start time for an activity

EF = ES plus activity duration
LS = Latest finish time – activity duration
LF = Cumulative total – activity duration time.

The usual rules regarding situations where more than one path leads into a node apply (see Section 2). Float is calculated in the normal way.

ACTIVITY 13

This is a practice network for you to calculate using activity-on-arrow technique.

The directors of Sunrise Engineering Co Ltd are currently considering the feasibility of computerising the stock control procedures at their regional depots. It is likely that one depot at a time will be computerised and linked to the head office mainframe computer. The directors have decided to use network planning in this feasibility study.

Use the following data to: construct the network
calculate the project duration
identify the critical activities
calculate the float (T/F/I)

	Activity details	Duration (days)	Must precede
A	Pilot study of total needs	17	All
B	Pilot study of likely costs	26	E
C	Pilot survey of depot buildings	14	E
D	Arrange staff discussions	7	E
E	Project decision meetings	3	M, G, F, H, J
F	Appoint project leader consultant	49	N
G	Train depot staff	120	P
H	Appoint building contractor	24	I
I	Obtain building materials	17	K, L
J	Appoint electrical contractor	21	L
K	Alter depot buildings	77	N
L	Install cabling and power	29	N
M	Customise software, design forms	90	R
N	Install computer terminals	5	P
P	First test run	2	Q
Q	De-bug the system faults	11	R
R	Second test run	2	S
S	First commercial run	3	–

Why do the directors need to exercise rigorous managerial control of critical path activities?

Assuming a five-day working week, if the final managerial decision to proceed (activity E) was made on 20 May, and normal progress was maintained each seven-day week thereafter, when would the new system start?

First build the logic diagram:

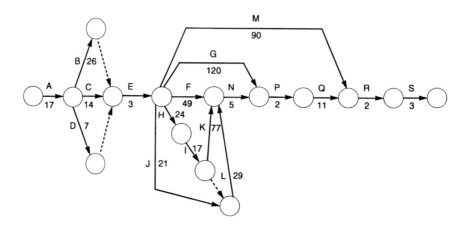

Then calculate the activity times and insert in the diagram, include dummy activities, identify the critical path:

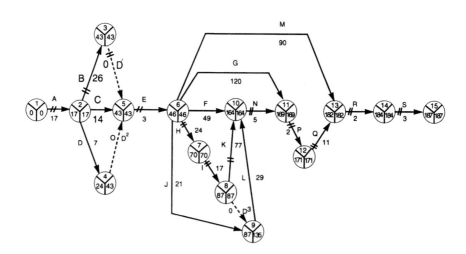

Critical path route is ABD'EHIKNPQRS, duration is 187 days.

Here are the float calculations:

Activity	Durn	ES	LS	EF	LF	TF	FF	IF
1–2	17	0	0	17	17	0	0	0
2–3	26	17	17	43	43	0	0	0
2–4	7	17	17	24	43	19	0	0
2–5	14	17	17	43	43	10	10	10
3–5	0	43	43	43	43	12	12	12
4–5	0	24	43	43	43	19	19	0
5–6	3	43	43	46	46	0	0	0
6–7	24	46	46	70	70	0	0	0
6–9	21	46	46	87	135	68	20	20
6–10	49	46	46	164	164	69	69	69
6–11	120	46	46	169	169	3	3	3
6–13	90	46	46	182	182	46	46	46
7–8	17	70	70	87	87	0	0	0
8–9	0	87	87	87	135	48	0	0
8–10	77	87	87	164	164	0	0	0
9–10	29	87	135	164	164	48	48	0
10–11	5	164	164	169	169	0	0	0
11–12	2	169	169	171	171	0	0	0
12–13	11	171	171	182	182	0	0	0
13–14	2	182	182	184	184	0	0	0
14–15	3	184	184	187	187	0	0	0

If critical path activities are not completed according to schedule, the overall project completion time will not be achieved. Any slippage which occurs early in the life of the project may be able to be clawed back if the directors crash activities later on in the network. Continual reporting, monitoring and appropriate cost-effective decision making by the directors is essential.

The system can start after 5 October. Did you calculate this, too?

The end of 'E' is 46 days into the project so your 141 remaining days begin on 21 May. The last day of 'S' is on 8 October, but this is the commercial run which began on 6 October!

Summary

In this section, we discussed the AON approach to project management. We began with precedence diagrams, which have similarities in methodology, then looked at networks using AON.

SECTION 6

Line of Balance Technique

Introduction

In this section, we will discuss **line of balance (LOB)**, a technique which extends the scope of network analysis. It is particularly suited to the scheduling and control of projects which are made in either fluctuating or repetitive batches. We study all activities which make up the final product and this is translated into an arrow diagram. A programme showing the quantities to be produced every week or month is also required.

Once we have constructed the LOB chart we can see where all phases of production should be at a particular review period, and the likelihood of the delivery programme being met. Current levels of production of each activity can also be compared with planned levels and corrective action can obviously be taken when imbalance is observed. Production levels above the LOB are regarded as safety stock or economic order stock but may indicate that greater than necessary costs have accrued.

6.1 Deriving the line of balance

We follow a series of steps in deriving the LOB:

- Draw a logic diagram of the process but show as many single event starts as there are separate departments.
- Number the events. It is advisable to work backwards. **The number of the last event will be the number of activities plus one**.
- Enter the activity times.
- Proceed to determine the number of weeks that each event is behind the finish of the last activity. This is done by taking the last event as 0 and working backwards, adding the duration of each activity cumulatively.
- Draw up a cumulative delivery schedule.
- Plot cumulative delivery against week number on the LOB chart and enter the departmental activities.

Consider the following example. A vacuum cleaner is being introduced in a new export market. An analysis of the activities shows:

Motor division

Purchase parts	1 week
Sub-assembly	3 weeks
Final assembly	1 week

Casting division

Purchase raw material	1 week
Cast	1 week
Fettle	1 week
Paint	1 week

Manufacture and assembly division

Purchase raw material	2 weeks
Internal manufacture	4 weeks
Purchase sub-assembly components	6 weeks
Assemble sub-assemblies	1 week
Final assembly	2 weeks
Purchase cartons	2 weeks
Pack for shipment	1 week

A manufacturing schedule was devised and actual output levels plotted against planned levels:

Week	Planned	Actual	Cumulative Planned	Actual
1	100	100	100	100
2	100	100	200	200
3	150	150	350	350
4	150	150	500	500
5	300	300	800	800
6	500	500	1300	1300
7	400	400	1700	1700
8	300	300	2000	2000
9	300	300	2300	2300
10	200	nil	2500	2300
11	200	300	2700	2600
12	100		2800	
13	100		2900	
14	50		2950	
15	50		3000	

The tabular analysis and the graph show that up to week 9 there was no deficiency. However, from week 10–11 deficiencies arise. The graph is quicker to interpret and shows the trend clearly. The chart does not show which division is responsible for the deficit, nor does it provide an early warning system. Line of balance is designed to provide these facilities (see Figure 14).

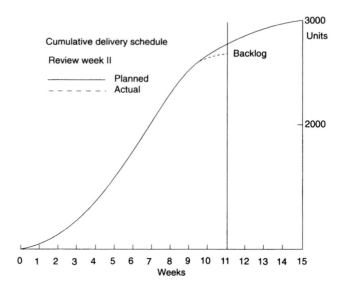

Figure 14: Cumulative delivery schedule (from information held by Bolton Business School and used by the author of this unit with permission)

We now draw a logic diagram (Figure 15) of the situation with as many single event starts as there are departments. Events are numbered and activity times inserted. It is then necessary to determine the number of weeks that each event is behind the finish of the last activity. Make the last event (15) as B = 0 and work backwards adding the duration of each event cumulatively.

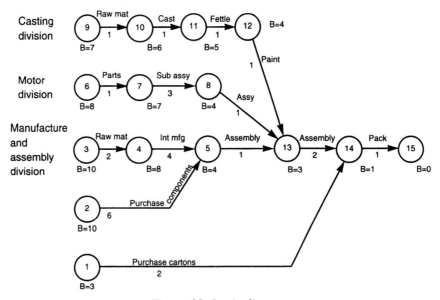

Figure 15: Logic diagram

The chart (Figure 16) shows that the planned output for week 10 will be short of units unless action is taken in the painting department in week 7. The LOB chart is here being used as an early warning system.

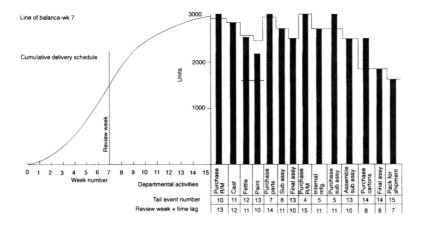

Departmental activities	Purchase R/M	Cast	Fettle	Paint	Purchase parts	Sub assy	Final assy	Purchase R/M	Internal mfg.	Purchase sub assy	Assemble sub assy	Purchase cartons	Final assy	Pack for shipment
Tail event number	10	11	12	13	7	8	13	4	5	5	13	14	14	15
Review week + time lag	13	12	11	10	14	11	10	15	11	11	10	8	8	7

Figure 16: LOB chart (from information held by Bolton Business School and used by the author of this unit with permission)

The chart can also be represented functionally. The purchasing department's responsibilities are shown in Figure 17.

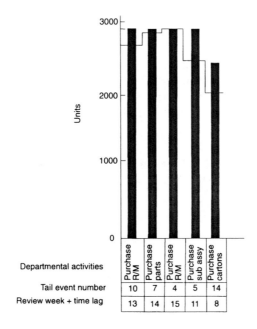

Departmental activities	Purchase R/M	Purchase parts	Purchase R/M	Purchase sub assy	Purchase cartons
Tail event number	10	7	4	5	14
Review week + time lag	13	14	15	11	8

Figure 17: Functional version of LOB chart (from information held by Bolton Business School and used by the author of this unit with permission)

In effect, we can say that any work which has been fettled will be ready for shipment in four weeks' time.

A cumulative delivery schedule is then drawn up. The cumulative delivery is plotted against the week number on the LOB chart (Figure 18).

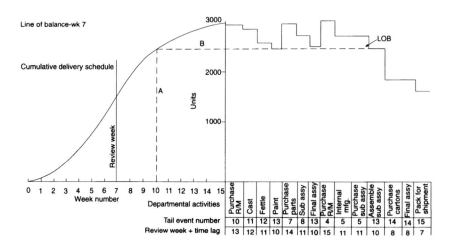

Figure 18: LOB chart for week 7 (from information held by Bolton Business School and used by the author of this unit with permission)

Consider the LOB chart for week 7 (Figure 18). The schedule demands a cumulative output of 1,700 units. The finished units produced in week 7 would have passed through the painting department in week 4. The logic diagram shows that it takes a further 3 weeks to complete the vacuum cleaner after painting. At the end of week 7 any finished units in the painting department should be ready for shipment at the end of week 10. The production level of each department can be determined.

Enter the review week on the chart. Consider week 7, and add for each department separately the number of weeks by which that department is lagging behind the finished product.

For each department erect a perpendicular (A) corresponding to that department's relative time-lag. The level at which the perpendicular meets the curve will indicate the planned cumulative level of that department, and it is recorded by drawing a horizontal line (B). This has been shown for the painting department.

Thus, a line of balance has been determined for all departments for week 7.

Enter in the actual units in each department by drawing bar charts. The number of units over the LOB is the extent of over-production. Any less is under-production. Computer programs are available for LOB. Once set up they can be easily manipulated to control production effectively. The table, over page, is what a sample print out might look like.

Departmental

Activity	LOB	Actual	Difference	Action
Purchase R/M	2900	3000	+100	Inform mgr
Cast	2800	2800	–	–
Fettle	2700	2600	–100	Inform mgr
Paint	2500	2200	–300	Inform mgr
Purchase parts	2950	3000	+50	Inform mgr
Sub-assy	2700	2700	–	–
Final assy	2500	2500	–	–
Purchase R/M	3000	3000	–	–
Internal mfg	2700	2700	–	–
Purchase sub-assy	2700	3000	+300	Inform mgr
Assembly sub-assy	2500	2500	–	–
Purchase cartons	2000	2500	+500	Inform mgr
Final assy	2500	2500	–	–
Pack for shipment	1700	1700	–	–

Summary

In this section, we discussed line of balance, a technique particularly suited to the scheduling and control of projects which are made in either fluctuating or repetitive batches. We looked in particular at the development and construction of LOB charts.

Unit Review Activity

Answer the following questions:

1 Detail the three factors which need to be balanced when planning a project.

2 List some of the reasons why projects are increasingly being handled using network planning techniques.

3 List the basic steps discernible in project planning.

4 Describe the three symbols used in critical path method.

5 How are activity times determined?

6 What are the three measures of float and how is each calculated?

7 How can a Gantt chart which highlights slippage on agreed stage dates be used for a project progress meeting?

8   What are precedence diagrams?

9   List some of the reasons why projects fail, either entirely or in part.

10   Detail some of the features you would look for when purchasing a computer network planning package.

Unit Summary

In this unit we examined the logic principles underpinning the techniques used in project management and emphasised the use of the network planning approach for the effective control of resources during the planning and execution phases of projects. We examined the role of operations managers, and the importance of operational management techniques was discussed in relation to cost/time aspects of a project.

References

Hall, O P (1989) *Computer Models for Operations Management*, IBM PC v 1, Addison-Wesley, Reading, Massachusetts

Recommended Reading

Harrison, F L (1995) *Advanced Project Management*, Gower, London

House, R S (1989) *The Human Side of Project Management*, Addison-Wesley, Reading, Massachusetts

Kleim, R L and Ludkin, I S (1994) *The People Side of Project Management*, Gower, London

Lock, D (1996) *Project Management*, Gower, London, 6th edn.

Nicholas, J M (1990) *Managing Business and Engineering Projects*, Prentice Hall, Englewood Cliffs, New Jersey

Page-Jones, M (1985) *Practical Project Management*, Dorset House

Reiss, G (1993) *Project Management Demystified,* F and F N Spoon

Spinner, M P (1993) *Elements of Project Management,* Prentice Hall, Englewood Cliffs, New Jersey

Answers to Unit Review Activity

1   Quality, time and cost. It is vital to identify customer expectations early in the process to draw up the terms of reference and contractual obligations. A high quality specification will require more resourcing time and cost.

2   Here are five major reasons:
   - work effort is co-ordinated across functional areas
   - a single comprehensive plan can be produced
   - optimal resource utilisation is targeted
   - an agreed completion date is established
   - sophisticated scheduling and progress monitoring is possible.

3   You should have included:
   - define the project
   - determine the essential activities and their times
   - build the network model
   - use the model to optimise resource usage
   - produce a master plan with scheduled dates
   - monitor progress, make changes to meet deadlines.

4   Activities are drawn as ───────▶ and require resources.

   Events are shown as ◯ . They do not use resources, and separate activities.

   Dummy activities are logic devices to show linkages and take no resources. They are drawn as ─ ‥─ ‥─▶

5   Activity times are determined by analysis, measurement and discussion.

   Past records, estimates and synthetic data may be available.

   Work measurement may be required.

   Comparative or analytical estimating can be used.

   PERT three-time estimating may be advisable.

6   **Total float**: is the longest possible time in which an activity which is not on the critical path can be completed.

TF = Latest finish time − Earliest start time − Activity duration

Free float: is used to run a project on an earliest possible time basis even with activities which do not lie on the critical path.

FF = Earliest finish time − Earliest start time − Activity duration

Independent float: is used to calculate slippage on non-critical activities when an earliest time plan is in operation.

IF = Earliest finish time − Latest start time − Activity duration.

7   Construction of a Gantt chart, by hand or from computer sources, will identify activities which are running behind (or ahead of) schedule. Decisions can be made about their significance and the technique of crashing is used, where appropriate, to recover lost time. Extra resources or new methods can be employed to advantage.

8   Precedence diagrams identify the sequence of occurrence of activities. They are widely used to undertake efficient balancing of work stations on a product assembly line to minimise time loss. A circle is used to denote an activity. Arrows are linkages.

9   You may have included these five reasons:
   ● lack of support from senior managers
   ● inaccurate activity time estimations
   ● poor project control
   ● unforeseen factors, for example, severe weather
   ● too many fragmented changes during the project.

10   You may have included these features:
   ● able to handle an adequate number of activities
   ● user-friendliness
   ● choice of CPM and precedence diagram modelling
   ● reasonable cost
   ● able to produce management reports and charts.

UNIT 6
QUALITY MANAGEMENT

Introduction

This unit deals with an area that has always been important, but which leapt to the top of many corporate agendas in the early 1990s. Quality is a huge subject that is even taught as a subject in its own right. So, necessarily, this is an overview of some of the more important concepts. Quality is a stimulating field, not just for experts, but for everyone in every organisation.

Objectives

By the end of this unit, you should be able to:

- appreciate the multifaceted views of what 'quality' means
- understand its importance and significance
- know some views of some leading figures in quality management
- know the basic techniques of quality management
- have an appreciation of the meaning of total quality management
- have an insight into some of the more advanced techniques and concepts, particularly as they apply to quality improvement.

SECTION 1

What is Quality?

Introduction

In May 1995 the BBC magazine *Top Gear* published the results of its second survey of customer satisfaction of car ownership in Britain. The survey was carried out in association with J D Power, a consulting company that has been undertaking similar surveys in the USA for 25 years. The results probably came as no surprise to those who have followed these surveys in the USA, but for Britain's 'home-grown' car industry, which has been making much of its progress on quality over the past few years, the results were almost certainly a disappointment. Of the top 20 most-liked cars in Britain none were 'home-grown' if we exclude the made-in-Britain Japanese cars by Toyota, Honda, and Nissan. The first European car on the list was a Mercedes Benz coming in at fifteenth place. The 'top' car was a Toyota Corolla.

The survey is interesting for the measures it uses. Performance is weighted 26%, problems encountered 23%, customer care 17%, warranty 15%, service costs 6%, and parts and service 13%. Of course, you may disagree with the findings. Your own measures of satisfaction almost certainly differ from those of J D Power. Then there are the intangibles. Writing in the *Sunday Times* of 23 April 1995, Jeremy Clarkson discussed the 'irrationality' of new car buyers, the vast majority of whom do not take test drives nor rely on road tests but are influenced by image and advertisements, many of which have no technical content at all. Most people feel they 'know quality when they see it', but if you ask them to be more specific, then the problems begin.

What is 'quality', and how do we make up our minds about what is a quality product or quality service? Many academics, consultants and market researchers, including J D Power, have attempted to answer this illusive but vital question.

In 1993, Mintel, a British market research organisation, undertook a survey of what customers value in products and in services. The top factors, in priority order, were:

Products	**Services**
Well made	Helpful staff
Safe to use	Efficient service
Value for money	Knowledgeable staff
Reliable	Clear pricing
Durable	Guarantees

It is interesting to contrast these with the views of academics. David Garvin, a professor at Harvard Business School, has identified eight 'dimensions' of quality which he maintains cover various meanings of quality held by managers and customers (1984). These are particularly appropriate in the product area. In the service area, Zeitham et al have extensively researched the 'dimensions of service quality' (1990). Their conclusions are:

Garvin's dimensions (in no particular order)	**Zeithaml et al's service dimensions (in order)**
Performance	Reliability (ability to perform the promised
Features	service)
Reliability	Responsiveness (willingness to help)
Conformance (to specification)	Assurance (knowledge and courtesy,
Durability	ability to convey trust, confidence)
Serviceability	Empathy (caring, individualised attention)
Aesthetics	Tangibles (appearance of facilities, staff)
Perceived quality ('feel', 'finish', reputation)	

ACTIVITY 1

How closely does the Mintel product survey match up with (a) Garvin's dimensions; (b) Zeithaml et al's dimensions?

There appears to be quite close agreement between Mintel and Garvin. One factor listed by Mintel but not by Garvin is value for money, although most customers would expect more on performance, features and probably several other dimensions if they paid more for a product. In other words, we are talking about expectations. In the following section we will discuss two views of 'quality'. We should stress once again that there is no one view used by everyone, but that each view increases our understanding of customers and their needs.

1.1 Two views of quality

JOHN GUASPARI

John Guaspari (1988), consultant and well-known author of a series of stimulating books on quality management, puts forward the view that:

$$\text{Quality } = S + E + e$$

Here '*S*' stands for **specifications**, and is to do with the closeness with which the product or service matches the specification or requirements. This is the traditional or 'engineering' view. Thus, for example, the required diameter of a shaft is given as 250 mm plus or minus 0.5 mm. This latter dimension is known as the **tolerance limit**. If the diameter of the shaft is between 249.5 mm and 250.5 mm it conforms to requirements, otherwise it does not. But this engineering view is applicable in service operations also: a service manager might specify that a telephone call must be answered before it rings four times, or British Rail customers are entitled to a discount if more than a certain percentage of trains run late. This aspect concerns internal controls; without such specifications there is less chance that a customer's expectations will be satisfied because the organisation will lack focus in its goals and operations.

'*E*' concerns **macro expectations**. A macro expectation is the expectation customers have for the type of product or service category under consideration. It is not brand-specific, but concerns the general expectations for that class of product. For example, today we would expect certain minimum standards of reliability, fuel economy, performance, safety features, instrumentation, and so forth, from any new car that we buy. This is a moving target. Sometimes, macro expectations derive from legal requirements such as the necessity to provide seat belts and an air bag. These macro expectations reflect the industry norm, and they might vary from country to country. In Germany, you expect the trains to be on time, in India this would be unrealistic. Clearly, an organisation cannot do much about macro expectations other than to ensure that they are understood by the organisation, and that at least minimum standards are achieved.

'*e*' concerns **micro expectations**. These are expectations that arise out of an organisation's communications and advertisements to potential customers, and also as a result of word-of-mouth communications from existing customers. The message here is that an organisation must not 'over-promise and under-deliver'. A customer is likely to be much happier to be offered a ten-day service on a broken-down personal computer and receive it back within seven days, than if a four-day service had been promised and it was repaired in the same seven-day period! Over the last few years a recurring theme in TV consumer programmes has been travel agents that have been taken to task by their clients over expectations built up in glossy holiday brochures. This aspect concerns the externally communicated message, and is largely within the organisation's own control. But it does require co-ordination and clarity of message between functions such as marketing, sales, operations, and service.

Both 'E' and 'e' are influenced by price. You would naturally expect better performance, better service, and a quieter ride from a Jaguar than from a Skoda. Yet in the BBC *Top Gear* survey a Skoda ranks higher in customer satisfaction than a Jaguar. Almost certainly this has to do with the high 'E' and 'e' that Jaguar customers have.

In Guaspari's view a good quality product or service is achieved where there is maximum overlap between 'S', 'E', and 'e'. This, of course, means that the product or service must conform to, or exceed, specification and expectation in design, operation, build and delivery, to both the external industry standards and expectations for the particular class and price, and must also conform to, or exceed, internally-generated specifications and communications. Quality can only be achieved by a 'total' effort involving everyone in the organisation, from design to manufacturing, and from suppliers to delivery.

THE KANO MODEL

A useful complementary model to Guaspari's is one proposed by Noriaki Kano (see Joiner, 1994). You may recall we mentioned this model briefly in Unit 1. Kano suggests that there are three categories of human perception: the *'must be'*, the *'more is better'*, and the *'delighters'*. This model is useful in both manufacturing where it has been extensively used in design, and in services. We can represent the Kano model as in Figure 1.

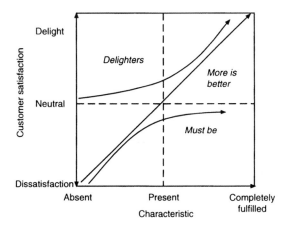

Figure 1: The Kano model (adapted from Joiner, 1994)

The *must be* category are those features and characteristics that we simply expect to be there. We hardly notice their presence, but definitely notice their absence. Thus we expect a restaurant to have fresh napkins and clean cutlery. We expect a CD player to be able to select any track. Students expect a lecturer to turn up for lectures and to have prepared reasonably well. If all expected features are there we will be reasonably contented, but hardly delighted. By contrast, if the features are absent we are likely to be quite upset and liable to complain.

In the *more is better* category, as the name suggests, the greater, or faster, or better the feature provided, the more we are satisfied. We can almost never have too much, or be fast enough. This might be the case with speed of room service in a hotel, with fuel efficiency in a car, with sound quality in a hi-fi system, or with manufacturing or delivery time. It is the extremes, however, that are important. In the middle range, roughly corresponding to Guaspari's macro expectations, where service or product performance is average, we are hardly impressed. But at low levels we are extremely unimpressed or unhappy, and at exceptional levels we are very happy, even delighted.

Finally, the *delighters* are features that are unexpected, and pleasantly surprise us. Generally, this is hard for a product to achieve, but may be an important source of competitiveness in services. In 1994, Marriott Hotels ran a series of advertisements telling of the exceptional levels of service undertaken by some of their staff, such as following a guest to the airport with an important item that he had left behind in the hotel. Delighters can be on different levels, ranging from remembering the name of a client at a hairdresser to an architect going out of his way to advise on possible and innovative alternatives, and then to check and continuously inform on the progress of building a house.

The Kano model can be thought of in much the same way as Maslow's hierarchy of needs, which you have probably met in your organisational behaviour studies. Lower level needs, such as safety and security, have to be in place before 'self actualising' targets become meaningful. In the Kano model case it is the *must be* category, and at least attaining a satisfactory level in the *more is better* category, that need to be in place before the *delighters* can make an impact. For example, if the bank has got your statement wrong you are not likely to be impressed by the standard of decor. The value of the Kano model is that it challenges an organisation to identify the various operations categories in relation to their products and services, and then to work on them appropriately.

ACTIVITY 2

Think of your business studies programme. List as many factors that you can think of that make a difference to the 'quality' of your learning experience at your university or college. Then classify them into *must be*, *more is better*, and *delighters*. It may be that you do not list any under the last category. In this case think of features or events that would *delight* you as a 'customer' of your university or college.

Under the *must be* category you will probably list factors such as a clear programme for each course, regularly scheduled lectures, good textbooks, access to the library, and good lecture room conditions. The *more is better* category might include access to relevant journals in the library, library opening hours, computer facilities, clarity of lectures, time for assignments, good lecture handouts, relevant time on the Internet, feedback from lecturers on assignments, fast assignment turnaround time and small tutorial group size. *Delighters* could include external visits, talks by practising managers, stimulating educational games used on the course, and personal help from a lecturer.

1.2 Customer expectations: moments of truth

Returning to the Guaspari concept, we noted that quality is the extent to which *SeE* overlap. We will now explore this further. The front line of quality is the interface between customer expectations and the operations of the organisation. Jan Carlzon, Chief Executive of Scandinavian Airlines System made this very clear by his simple but powerful concept of **moments of truth**. The concept was made even more popular by Albrecht and Zemke in their book *Service America!* (1985).

A moment of truth is that moment when a customer comes into contact with the products, systems, people, or procedures of an organisation and as a result leads him or her to make a judgement about the quality of that organisation's products or services. It is clear that many, even hundreds, of moments of truth are likely as a single customer interacts with a company. Carlzon emphasised that each one is a potential point of dissatisfaction, indifference, or delight. They all count, and good service results when all employees appreciate and work towards making the most out of each opportunity. This is where the Kano model proves useful.

In service organisations, the customer has little or no tangible product that remains after the service is complete. All that the customer is left with is a memory of perhaps hundreds of moments of truth, of which a few will count very heavily. This leads into operations. The problem from a quality management viewpoint is that most moments of truth take place away from the eyes of management, but in interaction with front line staff. So it is desirable to have a systematic approach to preparing for these events in advance. A moments of truth analysis should be constructed from two viewpoints, that of the customer and that of the operation. This can be most usefully done by drawing a circle. Albrecht and Zemke call this a **cycle of service**. Around the outside of the circle are written all the events experienced by a customer as he or she moves though the cycle, from the first enquiry to the last handshake or even beyond. These events are described from the point of view of the customer, not the organisation. Each is a moment of truth. The sequence, of course, ignores organisational boundaries about which the customer does not care. Then, within the circle, the corresponding actions taken by the organisation are constructed, including what are termed 'front office' operations, where there is direct contact with customers, and the supporting 'back office' operations. This leads to thorough, systematic preparation of operations.

ACTIVITY 3

Construct a cycle of service diagram for a car service. Follow the procedure given above. Consider both the external (customer) experiences, and the internal operations. Now compare the external moments of truth with your own experiences. Classify each action as a *must be*, a *more is better*, or a potential *delighter*. Then relate your diagram to your own experiences of a car service, and to your lasting impressions. Which moments of truth were positive, and which were negative?

A sample diagram is given below in Figure 2. Yours may well be very different.

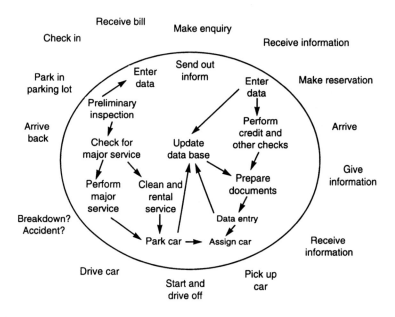

Figure 2: Cycle of service diagram for a car service

You should now ask how many of the activities are under the sole control of front line staff, how many are under management's control or influence, and how many are not within the organisation's control at all. These questions are important when attempting to improve your experience as a customer. A moments of truth analysis should also help to overcome the perception that 'no complaints is good news'.

ACTIVITY 4

If you have a tutorial group or seminar group, go around the room and ask for good and bad experiences with customer service and products. Ask the group members about their feelings towards the organisation concerned. Think of your own experiences.

You will often get interesting responses, some of them quite heated. Now compare these with the following research.

A US Technical Assistance Research Programs survey, reported in Desatnik and Detzel (1993), showed:

- 96% of consumers who experience a problem with a 'small-ticket' (i.e., low value) product do not complain to the manufacturer, but of these 63% will not buy again.

- 45% of consumers who experience a problem with a small-ticket service do not complain, but of these 45% will not buy again.

- only 27% of unhappy consumers of large-ticket (i.e., high value) durable products do not complain, but of these 41% will not buy again.

- 37% of unhappy consumers of large-ticket services do not complain, but of these 50% will not buy again.

- 13% of dissatisfied consumers tell their experience to more than 20 people.

- Each consumer whose complaint is satisfactorily resolved can be expected to tell eight other people.

- 92% of purchasers of small-ticket items and 70% of purchasers of large-ticket items whose complaints are satisfactorily resolved will go on to buy again.

The conclusion is that we need to make it easier to complain, and to encourage complaints! If customers can be made to express their dissatisfaction, they are more likely to remain valued customers.

1.3 Customer expectations: gap analysis

Of course it is not easy for management to pin down the causes of service failure or customer dissatisfaction. However, Zeithaml et al have provided an excellent framework for matching customer expectations with specifications by developing a model of what they term **service gaps**. The value of the model is that it provides insight into how customer expectations are developed, how operations specifications and communications are built up, and hence how gaps develop and how they may be closed or reduced. An adapted version of the model is shown in Figure 3 (over page).

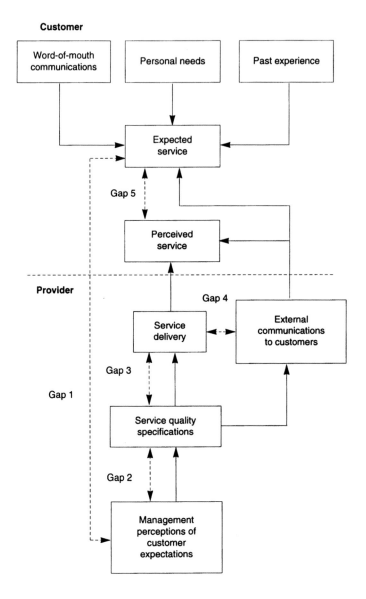

Figure 3: Conceptual model of service quality
(reprinted with permission from Zeithaml et al, 1990)

Gap 1 is due to management not knowing what customers expect. As we have seen with the SeEQ model, customer expectation is built up as a result of micro- and macro-expectations. In the Zeithaml et al model it results from management misunderstanding of the expected service which in turn stem from the four factors of word-of-mouth communication, personal needs, past experience and external communications (advertisements).

Gap 2 develops from having inadequate quality standards. This can result from management laziness or preoccupation with other activities, or from a belief that it is too difficult to set standards, or that such standardisation that does exist is inadequate. Yet, someone has to set the standards. If management does not, then operators have to do so by default; management should not then complain. In service operations, particularly, this can be quite a challenge. You must allow front-line staff the freedom to serve customers well, but within specified limits. This is sometimes called 'loose-tight' task specification.

Gap 3 is caused by a difference between what is specified and what is done. All sorts of possible factors are at work here, from behavioural (motivation, employee selection, teamworking, etc.) to technical (selection of, and training on, equipment).

Gap 4 results when performance does not match promises. There are several possible lines that can go wrong here: operations to marketing, marketing to customer, differences between operations in different branches, as well as a 'propensity to overpromise'.

Gap 5 is the difference between expected and perceived service, and the key to closing it is to close Gaps 1 to 4 and keep them closed. See Zeithaml *et al* (1990) for details of closing the gaps.

ACTIVITY 5

Brainstorm possible ways to close the gaps described. In each case, identify the function responsible in the organisation. Brainstorming is best done in a group if you can do this. You can get started on this activity by referring to the possible causes given in the last section.

Summary

In this section we have learned that quality has much to do with expectations. As John Guaspari says 'customers have all the votes'. But quality is also about getting the standards right, so that people delivering the products or services know what is expected of them.

Various authorities have produced models of the dimensions of quality. These are useful because they provide insight into the many facets of quality. Finally, we looked at a model which conceptualises the gaps that exist between an organisation and its customers.

SECTION 2

Some Quality 'Gurus'

Introduction

In this section, we will consider the contributions of some of the leading figures, or 'gurus', in quality management. They include Deming, Juran and Crosby.

2.1 Deming

Dr W Edwards Deming is probably the most revered figure in quality management. In the 1950s, Deming taught quality to the Japanese by insisting that top management attend his courses. They did, and prospered. Originally Deming taught statistical process control (SPC) to the Japanese and has always maintained that management must have an appreciation of statistical variation. Today Deming is mainly associated with quality management theories, particularly his **14 point plan**, the **Deming cycle** and his **deadly diseases** (1982).

Appreciation of statistical variation begins with the concept that very little in management is absolutely consistent, and that chance will account for a certain mount of **natural variation**. For example, a salesperson cannot sell exactly the same amount every month. He or she will have good and bad months, and the differences between good and bad are mainly explained by chance rather than by variations in skills. Therefore, merely to reward him or her for the good months, and to penalise for the bad, could be de-motivating and poor management. On the other hand, truly superior performance can produce sales which are significantly and consistently better. Here, special reward would be justified as would penalties in the case of consistently poor performance. Deming used to demonstrate this by asking people to draw coloured beads from a bowl. One colour represents poor performance and another colour good performance. Those people who draw the bad beads are castigated. Everyone quickly realises how unjust this is.

Management must distinguish between the natural variation and the significantly different variation. Deming maintains that many managers do not do this, and that performance suffers as a result. The two types of variation are known as **common causes** and **special causes** (or **assignable causes**). This is the basis of **statistical process control**, which we deal with later in this unit.

Common causes are inherent in the process but special causes are not, and these special causes need to be identified. Poor sales is one example but the same would apply to many other areas of both human-based and machine-based performance. For machines, this is the basis of SPC. Moreover, true performance improvement is very seldom within the sole power of an operator, salesman or supervisor. For example, a machine has natural variation and may be producing a certain percentage of defects. The operator can do little about it. Without management action or support, significant improvement can seldom be made. Deming's rule of thumb is that perhaps 80% of improvement requires management effort, while only 20% is actionable solely by front-line employees. Encouragements and incentives to produce better quality will have only limited results.

THE 14 POINTS

Deming's 14 point plan is a complete philosophy of management, not just quality management. Books have been written on the subject. Here we attempt only a brief summary.

1   There should be a consistent message about quality, throughout the organisation. It should not vary by department, by pressure of work, by time of the month, or by customer. Usually a clear statement is required from management, with actions that demonstrate that it means what is says.

2   The new age of quality requires a commitment continuously to improve. The competition is doing this; so must you in order to survive. Customers have increasing expectations about quality.

3   Switch from defect detection to defect prevention. Inspect the process than the product. Work to understand and reduce the natural variation in processes, the less the variation, the less the chance of defects.

4   In dealing with suppliers, end the practice of awarding business on price. Move towards quality of product, reliability of delivery, and willingness to co-operate and improve. In other words, build partnerships with suppliers. There should be advantages for both parties.

5   Constantly improve. Use the PDCA cycle (see the next section). Improvement is not confined to products and their direct processes, but to all supporting services and activities also.

6   Train in a modern way. Let employees understand the concept of variation, basic SPC, improvement, and the total approach to quality. The idea is to make everyone responsible for their own quality.

7   Supervision must change from chasing to coaching and support.

8   'Drive out fear' of improvement. Management must create the environment which removes all possibility that improvement in quality will somehow penalise operators, through more work, loss of jobs, financial loss, or whatever.

9   Remove any organisational barrier that prevents quality improvement. This means improved visibility between sections and also easier communications. Aim to remove any barrier that prevents the requirements and reactions of the customer being moved rapidly and without distortion to the point where action can be taken.

10 Don't have silly slogans that mean nothing. Don't have unrealistic targets. Remember, management has most of the power to make real improvements.

11 Work standards and numerical quotas should be eliminated. This is controversial, unless interpreted with the understanding of natural variation. Natural variation says that no standard or quota can be exact and without variation. If the natural variation is understood, the quotas and standards that are beyond the control of employees should not be penalised, nor rewarded, for undeserved performance.

12 Remove barriers that prevent employees having pride in their work. These barriers may include unrealistic quotas and time pressure, short-term requirements for profit rather than quality, lack of investment in the right machines or tools, individual incentive schemes based on output rather than group-based schemes based on quality and improvement, and lack of management support or consistency.

13 Train and educate. This follows from point 6 but emphasises that education must be widely based and continuing. Despite being point number 13, it is usually the starting point, after point 1.

14 Create an organisational structure that will support all the previous points. This is important because the 14 point plan is not a short-term implementation, but rather a long-term philosophy.

ACTIVITY 6

Take Deming's 14 points and apply them to your business studies programme at your university or college. Not all the points will be relevant, but discuss how your business studies programme could be improved if Deming's points were applied. Do this in a group if you can. Alternatively, consider their application in the organisation where you work.

Some quite radical ideas can come out of these discussions. They might include, for example, suggesting a curriculum that is continuously evaluated and improved, with student participation, no set deadlines for assignments, and a changed relationship staff and students. In the USA, it was reported in *Quality Progress* that some university departments are experimenting with the application of Deming's 14 points.

THE DEMING CYCLE (OR PDCA CYCLE)

Deming maintains that the **PDCA (plan, do, check, act)** cycle is a universal improvement methodology. Deming originally called the cycle **the Shewhart cycle** after the founder of statistical quality control, but it is now named after Deming himself. The idea is constantly to improve so as to reduce the difference in the requirements of customers and the performance of the process.

First **plan** what to do. This may be improvement in the design of the product and its features, or in the process which produces the product. Typically Pareto analysis (see Section 4 of this unit) is used to identify the most pressing need or problem. Then **do**. This means small-scale experimentation. Explore the problems, come up with possible causes, investigate them, identify the most likely ones. Then **check**. Try out what you have found to see if your ideas are valid. Then **act**. Implement widely if it is a success, or abandon if it is not. Where a new procedure is adopted, standardise it and make it part of the culture.

Note that the cycle is about learning and about ongoing improvement. You learn what works and what does not, in a systematic way. And the cycle repeats. After one cycle is complete, another is started, as shown in Figure 4.

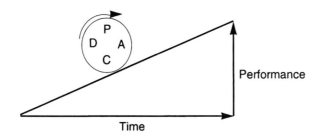

Figure 4: The Deming cycle

THE DEADLY DISEASES

The seven **deadly diseases** of quality, as Deming terms them, are a severe criticism of Western management and organisational practices. The first five are closely related. They are always worth considering, and re-considering:

1 **Lack of constancy of purpose** appears in Deming's 14 point plan. It is a reminder about inconsistent policy on quality, particularly as the end-of-period rush begins! The twin of this point is point 2.

2 **Emphasis on short-term profits** is a reminder to take a more consistent view, without being influenced by the end-of-period financial performance. And this may be brought about by point 3.

3 **Over-emphasis on performance appraisal and merit rating**, particularly when judged solely on financial performance. In our introductory section on Deming, we discussed variation. If variation is not understood, appraisal can be literally destructive. Deming is particularly worried by the emphasis on short-term results rather than on coaching and helping staff to develop their potential. This is made worse by the next two diseases, points 4 and 5.

4   **Too much staff mobility**, where managers do not get to learn the real problems and requirements of an organisation.

5   **Over-dependence on figures**, particularly financial, which can be massaged to look good in the short term, while the longer term suffers.

6,7   These last two points relate to **excessive medical costs** and **excessive legal costs**, which Deming believes are paralysing competitiveness. Some would regard these as being typically American problems, but they may be a foretaste of problems to come in Europe.

ACTIVITY 7

Not all managers agree with Deming. What are your views ? For example, do you favour performance-related pay? Deming does not. Some of your friends or colleagues may have examples of people who have been rewarded or promoted unjustly. How do you 'drive out fear' of job loss whilst improving quality and productivity?

The Ford Motor Company has been a committed Deming enthusiast for several years. Some Ford executives, including its then president, have cited the adoption of the Deming philosophy as being a principal reason for the turn-round in profits during the latter years of the 1980s.

2.2 Juran

Like Deming, Dr Joseph Juran (1979, 1988) is given credit for developing Japanese quality in the 1950s. His books on quality since then have had a profound influence around the world, and are so wide-ranging it is difficult to highlight particular contributions from the many that have been made. Perhaps the best known Juran concepts are his definitions of quality, the concepts of **breakthrough** and the **internal customer**, and the **quality trilogy**. Juran also was responsible for **Pareto analysis** as applied to problem solving, for work on the costing of quality, and for the idea of a **quality council** within the organisation.

Juran believes quality is associated with product satisfaction and product dissatisfaction. Both require consideration. **Satisfaction** occurs when a product has superior performance or features. **Dissatisfaction** occurs when there are deficiencies or defects in the product or in its service or support. Thus there are two dimensions, an external one concerned with matching customer requirements, and an internal one concerned with building the product or service correctly. Juran has proposed the well-known definition of quality as **fitness for purpose**. This is not as simple as it sounds. We need to ask, 'for whose purpose?', and 'what is the real purpose?'. There may be many possible customers, both internal to the company and external, who may use the product in different ways. Quality begins with a close understanding of who the users will be and how and where the product will be used. Without this customer orientation, good quality is not possible.

And what is an **internal customer?** Each person along the chain, from product designer to final user is both a supplier and a customer. Also, of course, the person will be a 'process', carrying out some transformation or activity. The process is subject to all the concepts of process control. Taking these together, this is what Juran calls the **three role model,** that is each stage is a supplier, a process, and a customer or user. So our customer orientation applies internally as well. At each stage there is the opportunity to improve the product, perhaps making it easier to handle, or fit together, or maintain, or update.

Juran emphasises the necessity for ongoing quality improvement. He maintains that this is only achieved through **project-by-project** improvement, in other words by a succession of small improvement projects carried out throughout the organisation. Projects may be suggested by management, by operators, by quality specialists or by Pareto analysis of existing problems. Juran was the first to name the **Pareto principle** and to describe it as a universal problem-solving methodology. The Pareto principle simply sets out to identify the 'vital few' as opposed to the 'trivial many' or the 'useful many'. This is the well-known phenomenon that there will always be a relatively few processes or people or defects or problems that take up most of the time or effort or cost. Hence it makes sense to identify these and to tackle them first. Pareto analysis is one of the seven tools, considered in Section 4.

Improvement projects can also be identified through costs and Juran was responsible for suggesting that **quality costs,** or the costs of not getting something right first time, should be recorded and classified. Money is the prime language of management, so that if the costs of poor quality are known this not only gets management attention but helps identify where effort should be made. For Juran, it is necessary for middle managers in the quality area to be able to translate the language of things into the language of money and vice versa. To do this we need a classification system.

Quality costs can be classified into:
- **failure costs:** both internal, such as scrap and rework; and external, such as guarantee claims and perhaps loss of custom,
- **appraisal costs**, such as inspection,
- **prevention costs**, such as education and SPC implementation.

Such costs can be obtained relatively rapidly by careful interviews or perhaps more accurately by a parallel accounting system, but in any case should be assembled in order to direct and evaluate progress on quality improvement. We deal with quality costs in Section 6

Project-by-project improvement is perhaps similar to the Deming cycle and leads straight into the quality trilogy. The **quality trilogy**, according to Juran, comprises

quality planning, quality control, and **quality improvement**. These can be seen as being parallel to the financial processes of budgeting, cost control, and cost reduction. Good quality management requires the quality actions to be planned out, improved, and controlled. We can view the process as achieving control at one level of quality performance, then planning to be better, project by project using various tools and techniques, then eventually achieving **breakthrough** to an improved level, and then once again controlling at the new level.

This series of actions will not take place by chance or by a series of unco-ordinated actions. Rather, they must be organised in a systematic way. This is where the **quality council** comes in. This body, typically consisting of senior managers, has the responsibility for co-ordinating the quality improvement actions and projects. They would, for example, set goals, identify needs, establish training, ensure measurements, such as quality costs, undertake co-ordination, and in general liaise between quality projects and top management.

In another parallel with the Deming cycle, the Juran **breakthrough sequence** sees the improvement process as taking two 'journeys': the 'journey from symptom to cause' and the 'journey from cause to remedy'. The first journey moves one from the problem to the 'diagnosis' and may be seen as parallel to the 'P'(plan) and 'D' (do) stages of the Deming cycle. Here we are concerned with identification, using, for example, Pareto, and with the generation of and testing of hypotheses as to what might be the contributing causes. The second journey moves the 'diagnosis' to the 'solution' and may be seen as parallel to the 'C' (check) and 'A' (act) stages of the Deming cycle. Here we select the appropriate cause, implement the necessary actions, and then replicate the improvements where possible in other areas.

More recently, Juran has spoken about **Big Q**. This is to emphasise that quality is not just the concern of production or even of total quality within the organisation, but extends further into the linkage between organisations, and includes all service organisations and operations.

2.3 Crosby

Like Juran, Phil Crosby (1979, 1989) has been a prolific writer on quality. Unlike Juran, who uses much quantitative and statistical techniques, Crosby concentrates on quality philosophy, particularly relating to management. Crosby's dynamic speaking style and stimulating writing style have gained him a large following.

Crosby is perhaps best known for his **four absolutes** of quality, his phrase 'quality is free', his 14 point plan which is different from Deming's 14 points, and his commonsense approach to a wide range of quality topics.

Crosby's four absolutes are :

1   **The definition of quality is conformance to requirements**. This very specific definition of quality leaves very little in doubt, which is probably what Crosby

intends. According to Crosby, once the requirements are specified then quality is judged solely on the criteria of whether it is met or not; aesthetics or feelings don't come into it. It is then the duty of management to specify those requirements very clearly, to say what they want, and this, Crosby believes, is one of the major failings of management. Of course, if management does not decide what is needed then by default, operators are going to have to make that decision for the company!

2 **The system of quality is prevention**. In other words, prevention is better than detection or appraisal. This is very much in line with the philosophy behind SPC; understand the process, look at what can go wrong, and take preventative actions before the process begins to deal with customers.

3 **The performance standard is zero defect**, or 'ZD', as Crosby calls it. Here Crosby is stating that nothing less than perfect quality has to be the aim. Setting targets below 100% is the start of a downward spiral. Of course, traditional quality management has taken zero defects to be uneconomic, and there should be a trade-off between prevention costs and failure costs. The Crosby view is now supported by a developing view that prevention costs, particularly where 'total quality' is in place, do not necessarily rise massively as we approach zero defects, but in fact rise by no more than failure costs fall. In other words, zero defect may well be optimal from a cost point of view, but again it comes back to getting the requirements right in the first place.

4 **Measurement of quality is the price of non-conformance**. Like Juran, Crosby believes in costing quality as a prime motivator for management. Here Crosby's famous phrase 'quality is free' is appropriate. As he says, 'it's not a gift, but it's free' or, in other words, if you put effort into improving quality it will more than pay for itself through improved productivity, reduced rework and claims, and improved customer satisfaction. Crosby classifies costs into:

● **PONC:** the price of non-conformance, all the costs involved in not getting the product or service right

● **POC:** the price of conformance, what it costs to do things right; prevention, detection, etc.

Crosby's **quality vaccine** can be related to the Deming 14 point plan. In typical stimulating style, Crosby's vaccine is preventive medicine for management against poor quality. The vaccine comprises practical advice on 21 areas, subdivided into five sections. The quality vaccine is in fact a succinct summary of what is needed for total quality management.

● The first section deals with **integrity**. This is really about taking quality seriously, from chief executive to every employee. If quality is taken as 'first among equals' – the others being marketing, finance, operations, and so on, then everyone understands that their own future and the future of the company will be judged on performance on quality.

● The second section deals with **systems** – for quality costs, for education, for quality performance, for review and improvement, and for customer satisfaction. All of these must be designed and put in place.

- The third section deals with the need for **communication** and for communication systems that will make clear the requirements and specifications, and which will communicate improvement opportunities within the organisation. Crosby often emphasises the importance of listening to customers, and to those front line employees who often know what is needed but perhaps have never been asked. Also external communications, in advertising, letters, and product information must convey a consistent message.

- The fourth section deals with **operations**, including working with and developing suppliers. Processes must be prepared prior to use and made capable, and process improvement must become the norm.

- And lastly, Crosby maintains that **policies** must be made clear and consistent throughout the organisation.

2.4 Other quality gurus

Several other people may qualify for the title of 'quality guru'. We will not discuss their contributions at length here but summarise a few points. For more details see Bicheno (1994).

Armand Feigenbaum, an American engineer, is known as the originator of **total quality control**. He referred to the **industrial cycle** which brings new products to market, and stressed the necessity for marketing, design, purchasing, manufacturing, production, inspection, packaging, distribution, and service all to play roles.

The late Kaoru Ishikawa is regarded as the leading Japanese contributor to quality management. His contributions are extensive but perhaps the most noteworthy are his total quality viewpoint, his work on statistical process control, his emphasis on the human side of quality, and his invention of the Ishikawa diagram and the use of the **seven tools** (see Section 4). He is revered as the father of **quality circles**, since it was he who furthered the concept of circles and popularised their practice in Japan.

Genichi Taguchi is a Japanese statistician and engineer whose concepts began to make an impact in the West during the 1980s. His principal contribution has been to our understanding of what specifications really mean, and how such specification can be translated into cost effective design and production. This is done by **Taguchi Methods** which we briefly discuss in Section 6.

Summary

In this section we discussed the contributions of leading quality management figures, principally Deming, Juran, Crosby. We also mentioned other quality 'gurus' like Feigenbaum, Ishikawa and Taguchi.

SECTION 3

Total Quality Management

Introduction

In this section, we will bring together definitions of quality and the views of the quality 'gurus', and gain an insight into how we can integrate everything into total quality management (TQM). We will look at two 'systems' of quality: the ISO 9000 standard and the quality awards. The ISO standard sets the framework for the procedures of total quality. The awards go beyond this, to consider the total picture and how quality should be related to the rest of the organisation.

3.1 Overview of TQM

TQM became popular in the late 1980s. It was widely adopted in service and manufacturing firms and probably reached 'fad' status in the early 1990s before slipping back on the list of corporate priorities. Nonetheless it remains an important development, the effects of which are likely to remain in all good organisations. TQM can be seen as a natural extension and consolidation of the views of the quality 'gurus' together with the realisation that poor quality does cost in terms of hard cash and loss of future market share, and that good quality can offer a definite competitive edge. All of the techniques and tools discussed in later sections are relevant to TQM. TQM integrates all of these, plus other concepts particularly from marketing and organisational behaviour.

TQM explicitly recognises that good quality is not the preserve of the quality department, nor is it even the responsibility of operations, but requires involvement across the board. The concept is of a **chain of quality** involving everyone and every process from product, or service, concept and market survey, to design, to engineering, to manufacturing, to packaging, to sales, to distribution, to field service. In other words, the complete cycle of service, all moments of truth, the closing of all gaps, and the perception that each link or process in the chain has as its customer the next link or process. It demands participation by all. It demands awareness of the costs of quality, not just departmentally but by process. And it recognises that quality is only as good as the weakest link.

This is truly a bold vision. It is also proven to be a most difficult vision to achieve, one that only perhaps one-third of companies have managed.

On a rather simplistic level we can contrast the TQM view with the traditional view by looking at Figure 5. The traditional view is inspection-based. Quality is seen as inspecting and controlling incoming materials and inspecting finished products. The TQM view, by contrast, begins with the customer, seeking to understand his or her needs and expectations, and designing quality into the product. It then works with suppliers so as to achieve component and material delivery of good quality without relying on receiving goods inspection. Finally, it controls the processes, through, for instance, SPC and process capability, but also through involving everyone and every process. This avoids the necessity for finished goods inspection. This is undoubtedly an oversimplified view of TQM, but it serves as a quick overview.

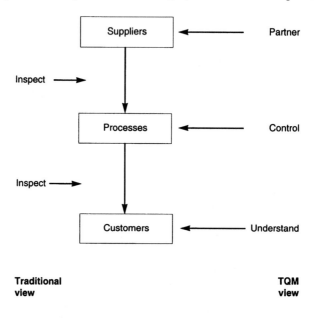

Figure 5: Flow process view of quality

THE OAKLAND MODEL

A more comprehensive conceptual view of TQM has been proposed by Professor John Oakland (1995) of Bradford Management Centre. The Oakland concept is shown in Figure 6. At the centre, is the **process chain**. This conveys several messages:

● quality should be seen as a customer-serving process rather than a department

● chains of linked processes go all the way from product concept to product delivery and beyond

● quality can only be as good as the weakest link in the chain.

Along a chain there are processes each with customers and suppliers, some of them internal some external. TQM is driven by teams, often cross-functional, rather than individuals who work together for improvement and control. The teams use 'tools' such as the seven tools we discuss in Section 4, and make use of 'systems' such as ISO 9000 and others particular to the organisation. Systems are linked to tools for policies regarding training, updating, and maintenance. And TQM requires top management commitment and indeed commitment by everyone. It requires a culture of insistence on standards, of continuous improvement, of support and 'no fear' as Deming would say. Further the quality message, including clear standards and specifications, must be clearly communicated. The Oakland model (see Figure 6) is therefore a concise way of tying together much of what we have discussed throughout this unit.

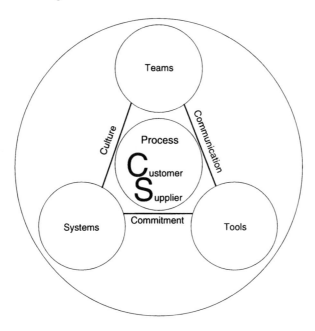

Figure 6: The Oakland TQM model: major features

Referring to the Oakland model (Figure 6), we will not deal with the 'teams' aspect in this unit, even though it is a vital part of TQM. The teams and organisational aspects are better dealt with in your organisational behaviour studies.

In the following sections, we will look at two of the 'systems' of quality: the ISO 9000 standard, and the quality awards. The ISO standard sets the framework for the procedures of total quality. The awards go beyond this, to consider the total picture and how quality should be related to the rest of the organisation.

These systems are best thought of in the order in which we present them. The ISO 9000 system sets the procedures in place, which can then be followed by wider considerations.

In Section 4, we look at some tools of quality.

3.2 The ISO 9000 system

The International Standard 9000 is now the world standard code of practice for quality assurance systems. Two common misconceptions must be cleared up immediately. Firstly, these are recommended standards for quality systems, they are not about actual product or service quality. It is possible for an organisation to be registered under ISO 9000 and still be producing products which are defective and not to customer requirements. Product quality is not necessarily better than that in non-registered companies. Secondly, the standards do not lay down a set of procedures to be followed. To some, especially smaller companies, ISO 9000 is unnecessary bureaucracy. But to many it is a way of demonstrating, internationally, that the company takes quality seriously and has thought through its quality system. It has become a marketing advantage and a trade facilitator.

What the standards do is to require conformity to documented practices specified in the company's own quality systems. The standards give the areas that need to be considered: the company installs its own most suitable response, documents it, maintains it, updates it, and guarantees that its own procedures are followed. Unannounced external audits are necessary to ensure compliance of the company with its own standards. Certification can only be awarded by an accredited third-party registrar. Certification would involve a company in (at least) preparing a written policy statement, writing a quality manual on its own systems and procedures, as well as making available all documents and controls as required.

The standards follow the logic of what is required to run a controlled business. To illustrate, consider the next activity.

ACTIVITY 8

The idea for this activity comes from the British Standards Institute. Imagine you are running a business for making and distributing orange juice from fresh oranges. You have contracts for the supply of oranges, and a laboratory which tests different formulations of juice from oranges from several countries. You would obviously like to have close controls on the product and processes. What controls and procedures do you consider necessary? Perhaps it would be helpful to construct a flowchart, or process chain, of the steps involved. Be as thorough as you can; consider all possibilities.

Your process chart would probably contain at least the following activities:
  draw up contracts with suppliers,
  decide incoming test procedures,
  formulate the mixes,
  carry out the mixing,
  keep records of what you have mixed,
  sample the mix,
  throw away poor quality product safely,
  pack,
  distribute,
  maintain the equipment,
  maintain the test equipment, etc.

Now compare your activities with what ISO 9000 would recommend you to do. This is summarised below.

Quality system requirements: summary of main sections of ISO 9000

1   Management responsibility

1   Policy: 'shall define and document its policy... and commitment...'

2   Organisation: 'the responsibility, authority, and interrelation, (particularly for those who initiate action, identify and record problems, initiate or recommend solutions, verify implementation, control conformance).

3   'Verification' (resources and personnel concerned with inspect, test).

4   A representative who shall have responsibility for maintenance of the standard.

5   'Shall be reviewed at appropriate intervals...'

2   Quality system: 'shall establish and maintain a documented quality system'.

3   Contract review: 'establish and maintain procedures' for contracts entered into.

4   Design

1   '...procedures to control and verify the design of the product...'

2   Design shall be assigned to qualified personnel.

3   Design input requirements shall be identified, documented. Incomplete, ambiguous, conflicting requirements shall be resolved.

4   Design output shall be documented (requirements, calculations).

5   Verification: shall plan and use competent personnel.

6   Design changes: establish and maintain procedures.

5   Document control

1   Document approval: maintain, distribute, destroy obsolete documents.

2   Document changes: procedures for review, keep master list, reissue.

6   Purchasing

1   General: ensure purchased material conforms to specification.

2   Assessment: Select suppliers on the basis of meeting requirements.

3   Data: documents shall contain data clearly describing the product.

4   Verification: purchasers shall be allowed to verify at source.

7   **Purchaser supplied product**: procedures established for verification, storage and maintenance of supplied product, and for damage reporting.

8   **Product identification and traceability**: where appropriate traceability from drawings, and from all stages of production.

9   **Process control**:

General: plan the production and ensure that processes are carried out under controlled conditions including documentation, monitoring, approval, criteria, standards.

Special processes: for processes where results cannot be verified, monitoring and records are required.

10   **Inspection and testing**

Receiving: incoming product is not used until verified.

In process: inspect, test, hold product until verified, identify non-conforming.

Final inspection: planned and carried out, not released until completed.

Test records: establish and maintain records which show that product has passed.

11   **Inspection, measurement and test equipment**

Control, calibrate and maintain equipment by whoever owned. Shall be used in a defined manner consistent with capability:

identify measurements to be made

identify, calibrate and adjust all equipment that can affect product quality

establish, document, maintain calibration procedures

ensure that inspection equipment is capable of required accuracy

show the calibration status on each piece

maintain records

assess and document the validity of previous inspections when calibrations are found to be needing adjustment

ensure that environmental conditions are suitable for testing

ensure that handling of test equipment is careful

safeguard test facilities.

12   **Inspection and test status of products**: shall be shown by suitable markings, stamps, tags, etc. Identify the authority responsible for release.

13 **Control of non-conforming product**: establish and maintain procedures. Non-conforming product shall be reviewed by documented procedures.

14 **Corrective action**: 'establish, document, and maintain procedures for':
investigating the cause of non-conforming material
analysing all processes, operations, complaints, potential problems
initiating preventative actions
applying controls to ensure preventative actions are taken
implementing and recording changes.

15 **Handling, storage, packaging and delivery**: establish, document, maintain records for each.

16 **Quality records**: establish and maintain procedures for identification, collection, storing, etc. Records of achievement shall be maintained. All records identifiable to the product involved. Readily retrievable.

17 **Internal quality audits**: a comprehensive system of planned and documented audits to determine the effectiveness of the quality system. Results documented and brought to attention of responsible personnel.

18 **Training**: procedures for identifying needs and providing for training. Training records kept.

19 **Servicing**: where there is servicing, records shall be maintained.

20 **Statistical techniques**: where appropriate, procedures established for process capability.

Note: this is summarised from ISO 9000.

How did this list compare? You can see that ISO 9000 could be regarded as just good business practice. Do you agree? Some do not! Notice that ISO 9000 expects you to improve, so it is compatible with the continuous improvement or Kaizen philosophy, with the Deming Cycle, and with Juran's breakthrough sequence.

3.3 The Baldridge and European Quality Awards

THE BALDRIDGE AWARD

The Malcolm Baldridge National Quality Award was established as a US Public Law in 1987 and is administered by the US National Institute of Standards and Technologies (NIST). The aims of the Baldridge are to:

● stimulate companies to improve quality
● recognise achievement in quality
● establish guidelines for self-evaluation
● publicise successes in quality and learn from the winners.

The real purpose of the Baldridge is to educate. It is not an alternative to ISO 9000, which addresses many of the same categories, but you should regard them as complementary.

Although the Baldridge is a competition for US companies it has become perhaps the most comprehensive statement on just what total quality really means and requires. As such the framework can be used by any company, US-based or not. Many British companies use Baldridge as a measure of their TQM efforts, even though they are not eligible to enter the competition. Awards are made in three categories: manufacturing, small business, and service, and are presented by the President of the USA. For US companies, there is considerable prestige and market advantage in winning, or even reaching the site visit stage, but entering itself forces a comprehensive discipline for the company and commitment by management.

The award is structured around four basic elements, seven areas, and 28 categories, which should form a dynamic relationship. 1,000 points are identified. A brief summary follows:

The driver
1   Senior executive leadership. This examines the personal commitment of senior management to quality and customer focus. Customer focus is expected to be integrated into everyday leadership, and leadership should demonstrate a concern, amongst others, for ethics and public health and safety.

The system
2   *Information and analysis.* This examines how information is used to support prevention-based quality. Information must be timely and reviewed regularly. Benchmarking must be done and kept up-to-date.

3   *Strategic quality planning.* This examines the process of planning for, and retaining, quality leadership. Quality plans must be integrated into business plans, and measures to track performance of both the company and its suppliers kept.

4   *Human resource development and management.* This examines how human resourcees are planned and managed as part of quality. How are employees involved, and how they are educated, trained, and recognised? Their morale is also considered. Performance measures must be in place, and attention given to ergonomics, health and safety.

5   *Management of process quality.* This covers the processes used in design, production, support, supplier management, and quality assessment. The conversion of customer needs into products and services must be demonstrated. Prevention must be emphasised, and continuous improvement must be used.

Measures of progress
6   *Quality and operational results.* This examines the measurement system applied to products, services, suppliers, business processes, and operating

results. Quality levels in these areas must be compared with competing companies.

The goal
7 *Customer focus and satisfaction.* This important area covers the company's knowledge of, interaction with, and commitment to customers. The methods used are examined, and how customers feel about the company in relation to its competitors.

THE EUROPEAN QUALITY AWARD (EQA)
The European Foundation for Quality Management (EFQM), a consortium from leading European companies, launched a European version of the Baldridge in 1992 (EQA). Like the Baldridge, the EQA is an interesting definition of just what is needed for total quality. The EQA differs from the Baldridge in as far as it sees TQM having an impact, not only on business results, but also on customer satisfaction, employee satisfaction, and eventually an impact on society. The first winner of the EQA was Rank Xerox.

The EFQM categories are subdivided into the **Enablers** and the **Results** and are as follows:

Enablers	**1993 Points (max.)**	**Area**
Leadership	100	behaviour of all managers
Policy and strategy	80	mission, values, vision, direction
People management	90	management of company people
Resources	90	management, utilisation, preservation
Processes	140	all value adding activities
Results		
Customer satisfaction	200	perception of external customers
People satisfaction	90	people's feelings about the company
Impact on society	60	perception amongst the community
Business results	150	business performance

The awards have not been without their critics. Phil Crosby has entered a debate which has ranged across several magazines and journals, including *Harvard Business Review* and *Quality Progress*. Crosby claims that the Baldridge is positively detrimental, resulting in diverting attention away from improving the lot of customers to being more concerned with the internal procedures and documentation necessary to win the award. Crosby's critics say that by undertaking all the steps required for the award, customers will ultimately benefit, and anyway the award is really about good business practice. Whatever the arguments, it is a fact that the number of organisations entering the Baldridge competition is sharply down from the heydays of the early 1990s. It will be interesting to follow the trends of the EQA. Perhaps you could investigate yourself; it is bound to be controversial for several years to come.

ACTIVITY 9

Read the article 'The straining of quality' (Resource Item 6.1) for an update on the progress of TQM. After reading the article, consider whether TQM is destined to be yet another management 'fad' or something permanent and substantial.

It might be easy to conclude that TQM has become, or will soon become, just another 'has-been' management concept. But remember that the companies discussed in the article are all world leaders in quality: most companies are nowhere near achieving the quality levels of, say, Motorola. The article is also interesting because it ties in with topics we discuss in Unit 9, *Time Based Operations*.

Summary

In this section, we have brought together definitions of quality, the views of the quality 'gurus', and integrated them into TQM. 'Total' in TQM means *total* processes, *total* people, *total* materials, and *total* ongoing improvement. TQM demands participation by teams, using tools and systems. Some specific systems or models were looked at, namely ISO 9000 and the Baldridge and European Quality Awards.

All this rests on 'culture, commitment, and communication', factors that we briefly looked at in the meaning of quality and gap analysis.

In the next sections, we will expand upon some of the tools and concepts referred to in the Oakland model.

SECTION 4
Seven Tools of Quality

Introduction

This section introduces the **seven tools of quality**, which were originally assembled by Kaoru Ishikawa for use with quality circles. In this respect, and referring to the Oakland total quality model, tools are used by teams in relation to the quality process chain. The seven tools, when used together or even individually, are a 'first line' attacking force for quality improvement. They are taught to a large proportion of operators in Japan and are now increasingly used by operators worldwide.

The seven tools are widely used in service and manufacturing. Each year the National Society for Quality through Teamwork holds its national conference in Britain. Teams from a wide variety of companies make presentations. The use of two or more of the seven tools is cited in virtually every presentation.

We present the tools in the order in which they are commonly used, although many variations are possible.

4.1 The process chart

The **process chart** lists every step that is involved in the manufacture of a product or in the delivery of a service. It has long been used by work study officers, who usually use special symbols to indicate 'operation', 'delay', 'move', 'store', and 'inspect'. We look at these issues in detail in Unit 7. The process chart helps identify wasteful actions, and documents the process completely. Good communication is an important reason to do this. The systematic record helps reveal the possible sources of quality and productivity problems. Two important variations of the process chart are the flowchart and the **cycle of service** diagram, that you met earlier.

It is a good idea to draw the process chart using the standard symbols (see Figure 7) because this aids clarity. The chart can be plotted against a time scale if time is critical. Process charts should also be used to document a process after it has been changed. This serves as a future record and can be used for 'auditing' the process, to see if it is still being carried out in the way it was designed.

Many companies already have process charts. If they are available, beware! There are often differences between the 'official' process charts and the way things actually happen in practice. The team or analyst should take the time to follow through a number of products, services or customers, documenting all apparent wastes and noting any major problems that occur. Often several actions and 'rework loops' unknown to management will be discovered. But it is not the purpose of the chart to be used for 'policing'. Often a team will draw up a chart for their own use and is not obliged to turn it over to management.

Some process charts can be very long and complicated. If so, break them up into sections of responsibility. Also use a hierarchy, with the overall process shown in outline and the detail on several sub-charts.

In the service sector, process charts can be made more effective by dividing the page into two halves. On one half, show those actions where there is direct interaction with external customers. On the other half, show actions that are entirely internal. For example, in the process chart of checking a guest out of a hotel, the front desk sequence of actions are shown on the left and the accounts office actions on the right. The two halves are, of course, linked by the complete sequence of events.

A **flow chart** is similar to a process chart and is often used when there are decisions involved. The symbol for a decision, a diamond, would lead to branching as a result of different decisions. Flow charts are often used with computer systems and usually do not include the standard process chart symbols. However there is no reason why these symbols should not be combined.

Whether using a process chart, a flow chart, or a cycle of service, these charts are best assembled using a team approach, preferably the people who are 'front line'. Using the charts, the team can begin systematically to document the nature of quality problems and defects. This leads onto the next tool. Examples of a process chart and a flow chart are given in Figure 7.

4.2 Pareto analysis

Pareto analysis is known by several names including **ABC analysis** and the **80/20** rule. Whatever the name, it is one of the most effective yet simple tools available. Pareto analysis recognises the fact that, invariably, a small number of problem types account for a large percentage of the total number of problems that occur. The name 80/20 is representative of this; perhaps 80% of all problems are due to 20% of all the types of problem that occur. Often 90/10 would be more typical. The name ABC is also a good one. This suggests that the range of types of problem be classified into A, B, and C categories, designating their importance. Pareto analysis is also good practice in many other fields of management, for example, inventory control, forecasting, marketing, and personnel.

It makes good sense to tackle the most pressing problems first; the 'vital few' as Juran calls them. When these are successfully eliminated or reduced, of course, another problem will head the list. So now tackle that one. And so on. Continuing in this way is an effective on-going improvement methodology.

Standard process chart and flow chart symbols

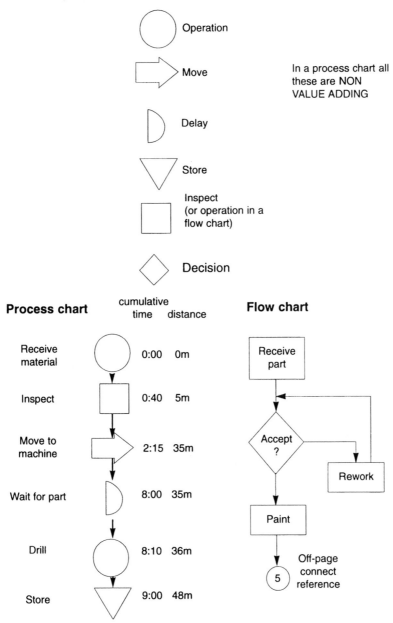

Figure 7: The process chart and flow chart

Pareto analysis begins by ranking problems from highest to lowest. Then the cumulative number of problems can be plotted on the vertical axis of the graph. Along the horizontal axis are arranged the problems in descending order. You can see that the resulting graph rises rapidly then tails off to an almost flat plateau (see Figure 8). Now it is easy to pick out how many problems need top priority attention.

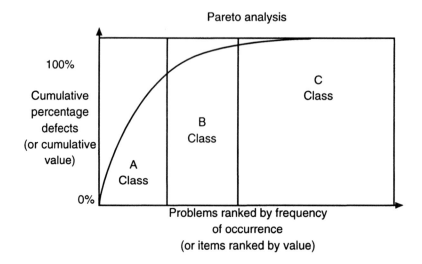

Figure 8: Pareto analysis diagram

Now the team has used the process chart to list and classify the problems, and Pareto analysis to identify the most serious problems. In the next stage, the team would begin to explore possible causes and their solution.

4.3 The Ishikawa diagram

The Ishikawa diagram, also known as the **cause and effect** diagram and the **fishbone** diagram, is used to brainstorm out possible contributing causes of a particular problem or defect. It follows directly from the Pareto diagram, with the most pressing problem becoming the spine of the 'fish'. An example is shown Figure 9. The name 'fishbone' clearly represents the shape of the diagram.

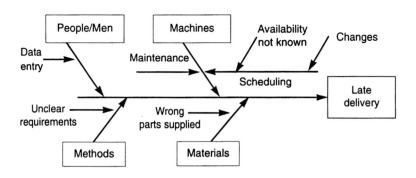

Figure 9: The Ishikawa fishbone diagram

As you can see, contributing causes are written on the diagram, arranged in a hierarchy. Hence the name cause and effect. If you experience some difficulty in starting off the diagram, use the '4 Ms' (men/people, machines, methods, materials) as four initial 'bones'. Usually the diagram is built up by one person writing in points on it while team members contribute their ideas.

ACTIVITY 10

Brainstorm ways in which your business studies programme or any course or class that you are currently taking could be improved. Enter them on the Ishikawa diagram.

You do not need to use the 4 Ms framework as the main fishbones. You could, for example, use lectures, seminars, materials, and back-up (for example, library, computers). The Ishikawa diagram offers a concise and visual way in which contributing causes can be documented on one diagram. It requires only seconds of instruction in order for any employee to understand.

A variation on the Ishikawa diagram is the **CEDAC** diagram, originally developed by Fakuda. CEDAC stands for **cause and effect diagram with addition of cards**. It is the same Ishikawa diagram except that cards, containing notes and ideas on each particular cause, are added to the diagram. Usually there are slots made for each cause, giving access to a pocket into which cards are placed. This addition is very useful because it allows elaboration on the thinking. The diagram can be kept on display, and as further information or thoughts are acquired, they are added to the pockets. This prevents 'reinventing the wheel'. Fakuda has developed the CEDAC concept into a complete improvement methodology. Here, a team brainstorms out possible improvements, writes them up on cards, and places them on the left side of each fishbone. When the idea is implemented it is moved to the right side of the fishbone. Thus, we maintain a visible record of ideas already implemented and to be implemented.

Now with the range of possible causes identified, it is a good idea to firm up on the information that is available. This is where the next tool comes in: the histogram and measles chart.

4.4 The histogram and measles chart

The **histogram** has much in common with the Pareto diagram. It is used to show graphically the relative number of occurrences of a range of events. Using vertical bars, it plots frequency on the vertical axis against events, arranged one after the other on the horizontal axis. You should already be familiar with histograms from your studies in quantitative methods.

Following from the Ishikawa diagram, data is collected and classified according to each of the causes suggested. This data is shown on a histogram, from which the most important causes should be apparent. As with the Pareto diagram, it is then clear which causes require further investigation.

Histograms can be used to collect data as it happens. For example, a flip chart is set up right at the work station. As problems occur they are written down on the flip chart. When the same problem recurs, a tick is placed next to that problem. In effect this is building up a histogram. In this case, the histogram is lying on its side, but that does not matter. The problems with the most ticks are obviously the most frequently occurring and most urgent problems. Such a flip-chart histogram has the great advantages of being easy to use, visible for all, and up-to-date.

A special form of histogram, with similarities to the flip-chart procedure, is **the measles chart**. Here, defects or problems are simply plotted on an engineering drawing, blueprint or map at the location where the problem occurs. The accumulation of marks on the drawing gives an excellent impression of where the problems lie. It avoids numerical or written description and may lead to the rapid identification of related problems. A symmetry of the defects may indicate a process problem, but a lack of symmetry may indicate a maintenance or wear problem. There are extensions of this technique: times can be written in; or different symbols used for different operators. Measles charts are widely used outside of manufacturing. Traffic police and engineers use them to pinpoint accident black spots, and for example, a theme park could use them to track litter problems, complaints, and areas where children tend to get lost. The histogram and measles chart are shown in Figure 10.

The histogram helps identify likely causes. The next stage requires some experimentation to find out how that cause can be eliminated. The next set of tools, **run diagrams**, is appropriate.

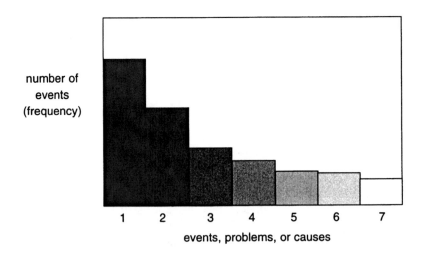

number of
events
(frequency)

events, problems, or causes

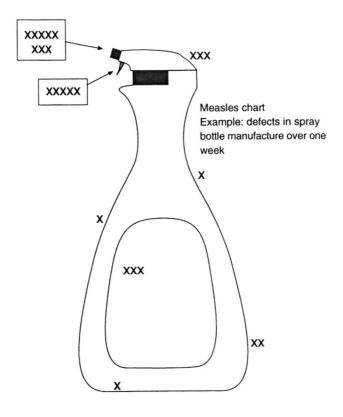

XXXXX
XXX

XXXXX

XXX

Measles chart
Example: defects in spray
bottle manufacture over one
week

X

X

XXX

XX

X

Figure 10: The histogram and measles chart

4.5 Run diagrams

Run diagrams are used to explore relationships between events and time, and between problems and causes. They are used for basic experimentation, to find out when and how problems arise and how problems can be rectified. Despite sounding rather scientific, they are often simple but very effective, and certainly within the capability of most operators and front-line personnel.

The run diagram is simply a graph of the number of events plotted against time. For example, a record can be kept of the number of complaints over time. This may reveal that complaints occur at the beginning of the month or at a certain time of day. If defects produced on a machine are plotted against time, we may discover that most defects tend to occur when the machine has been used for some time (hot?) or just after the tea-break (carelessness?). A common use for a run chart is to detect slow trends, that is, a gradual increase or decrease. For this, the charts have to be maintained over a long period.

ACTIVITY 11

Consider the three run diagrams shown in Figure 11 below. They show weights taken from a breakfast cereal filling line. The vertical bars show the range (minimum to maximum) of weights taken from batches over the course of a few days. What do they suggest to you? What are possible reasons?

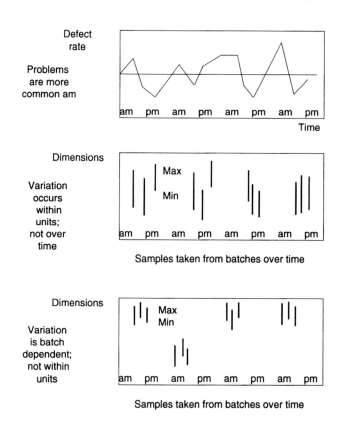

Figure 11: The run diagram

It is surprising the amount of information that we can glean from such a simple tool. In the first diagram, problems occur predominantly in the morning. So this is where to look: could the problem lie with the morning shift or with machines that run worse when cold? In the second and third diagrams, the length of bars represents the spread of a sample of readings. In the second diagram, there does not seem to be much difference by time of day, but there does seem to be quite large variation within the samples. This indicates process instability, perhaps due to wear-out or lack of training. In the third case, once again there is little difference between time of day and there is also only small variation within the samples. But here the problem lies with differences between batches so this could suggest differences between raw materials used or incorrect set-up. From these examples, we can see that run diagrams can be useful in pointing where to look and where not to look.

4.6 Correlation diagrams and stratification

The **correlation diagram** is used for more specific experimentation. Usually defect level, or some other measure of performance, is plotted on the vertical axis and the 'experimental variable' on the horizontal. An example would be rejects against temperature. Perhaps as temperature rises rejects fall, but then around a specific temperature rejects begin to increase again. This could either be found out by a specific experiment involving deliberately varying the temperature, or by simply counting rejects and taking the temperature from time to time in the normal course of operation.

Very often no relationship or correlation is found. So something else has to be tried, perhaps first temperature, then pressure, then temperature divided by pressure, and so on. In services, perhaps we are investigating customer wait time against number of servers, or customer response time against quantity of information displayed on a screen. Eventually, and with intelligent guesswork, good relationships can be found. This detective work can be a lot of fun, and front line people are often good at it because they appreciate the real factors that make a difference. Normally an attempt is made to hold other factors as constant as possible while one factor at a time is varied.

We can calculate the measure of correlation, called the **correlation coefficient** by formula. You will have met the formula, and associated tests, in your quantitative methods studies. The measure is also 'built in' to many scientific calculators. However, it is always preferable to plot the results on graph paper and to judge the relationship visually.

Often we use both run diagrams and correlation diagrams. First we use a run diagram for more general analysis and to see if time of day or month has an effect. Then we follow with a correlation study for the specifics. There are other possibilities as well. A common one is the matrix, where, for example, errors are recorded in a matrix which shows operator names along one axis and types of error or time of day along the other axis. This would reveal, perhaps, that different operators are good at different things or have different error-prone periods.

Stratification simply means splitting the data into groups and plotting the results on graphs. For example, defect data against time may appear to have no particular pattern, but when data for individual operators or machines is plotted the situation may suddenly clarify. Clearly there is often a large number of ways in which data can be separated out; by operator, machine, material, time, batch, product, customer, location are just a few. But once a team knows about stratification they are likely to make good suggestions about how it can be separated. Of course, this means that care has to be taken in the first place about how the data is collected. It is a learning process. Correlation and stratification are illustrated in Figure 12. Note that in diagram c there appears to be no correlation when the results from two machines are shown together. In diagram d by stratifying the results there is a correlation between defects and temperature for machine A.

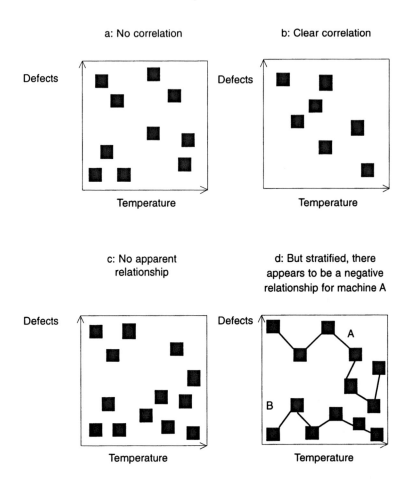

Figure 12: Correlation and stratification

Run diagrams, correlation diagrams and stratification have the effect of identifying what are termed 'special causes'. These are the events or defects which cannot be explained by natural variation of the process. We deal with this topic in *Section 5*.

4.7 Check sheets

The last of the seven tools is there to maintain the level of quality attained by the application of the previous tools. This is the straightforward yet effective tool of **check sheets**. A check sheet simply details the correct procedure. This correct procedure must be verified or audited at specific intervals.

There are several forms. 'Aircraft-style' checks would be carried out at the start of every shift or the start of each new batch, as an airline pilot would do before setting out. A process diagram, placed next to the machine or service counter, details what should be done and may advise what action to take in special circumstances. Whatever the form used, the philosophy is to have the correct procedures laid out and available at the workplace, not in some remote office. McDonald's is a service organisation that makes extensive use of check sheets.

One special form of check sheet, used by Toyota, is a sheet containing perhaps 50 questions that ask operators if particular events are taking place, for example, 'Do you have to reach to grasp a control?' and 'Do you have to take more than two paces to collect parts?'. If an affirmative answer is obtained, this indicates that there is potential for improvement, and the operator is challenged together with his or her group to suggest possible improvements. We discuss this further in the Unit 9, *Time Based Operations*.

ACTIVITY 12

The point about the seven tools is that they are a set. In an earlier activity you considered how to improve your business studies programme, or a class or course, using the Ishikawa diagram. Now extend this by considering how each of the other tools could be used for improvement. This may require some speculation.

There are a few possibilities. The process diagram could be used in its 'moments of truth' form to trace through your experiences. We could have an overall chart, and more detailed charts to do with a typical course, an exam period, accommodation, library, etc. Pareto could be used to highlight your complaints or concerns in some of these areas. Suggestions to alleviate the top-most concerns could then be brainstormed using Ishikawa. Run diagrams could trace assignments due, complaints, grades, books on loan, and others against time. Correlation diagrams could study the relationship between seminar attendance, course marks, and exam marks. A measles chart on where students and lecturers live might prove revealing. We might then ask what check sheets are now provided, and what should be provided.

Summary

This section discussed the seven tools of quality. The seven tools form a basic problem-solving and quality-improvement kit. Ishikawa put them together as a set to be used by quality circles, or for team problem solving. The aim was to make them accessible to enable everyone in the organisation to use them. The participation by everyone is at the heart of TQM.

Section 5

Statistical Process Control (SPC)

Introduction

Statistical process control (SPC) aims at achieving good quality during manufacture through prevention rather than detection. It is concerned with controlling the process, or machine, which makes the product. If the process is good, then the products will automatically be good. So the process or machine which makes the product is inspected rather than inspecting the product itself. This is really proactive management – inspecting and controlling the process before the event, rather than reactive management – inspecting the product after the event.

SPC is not, of course, the full answer to total quality. A poorly designed product can conform to all manufacturing requirements, but still fail to convince customers that it is a quality product. SPC is just one of the tools in the total quality toolkit, although it is a major tool.

Perhaps confusingly at first, the best way to find out what is happening to a process is to take measurements of the products that the process is producing. Of course you do not need to look at every product that is produced. Instead you take samples and use statistics to judge what is happening to the process. This is why it is called **statistical process control**. It may appear that we are inspecting a few of the products coming out of the process, but in fact it is the process that is being inspected and controlled.

SPC is undertaken through the use of charts on which the performance of the process is plotted. If the process starts to go wrong it can be stopped in good time before many or any defectives are made. We begin by examining the types and content of these SPC charts.

5.1 Variables charts

There are two main types of SPC chart: variables and attributes. A **variables chart** measures some characteristic that is variable along a scale, such as length or the number of scratches. It is something that can be measured. An **attribute chart** is used where there are only two possibilities: pass or fail, yes or no. With an attribute, a judgement is made rather than a measurement taken.

The main variables chart is the **average and range chart**, also known as the **x bar and R chart**. This is actually two charts, one tracks the average measurement of the sample taken, and the other the range of the sample, that is the maximum minus the minimum value. Both are necessary. For example, the average of a sample of five may be fine, but the range could be unacceptably wide. And the range could be small, but located in the wrong place; that is it has an undesirable average. So typically, from time to time throughout the day, the operator will take, say, the five most recent products produced and set them aside. This is a **sample**. The particular product dimension is measured and the average and range values of the sample calculated. These two results are plotted on the chart, usually by the process operator. The chart indicates if the process is acceptable. If it is acceptable work continues. If not, work stops to investigate. This is SPC in practice.

Refer to Figure 13. Note the rotated normal distribution shown next to the average chart indicating the expectation that samples will be normally distributed and that the upper and lower control limits correspond to plus and minus three standard deviations. Notice that both the average and the range charts have an upper and a lower 'control limit'. These limits are the bounds beyond which unacceptable performance is indicated.

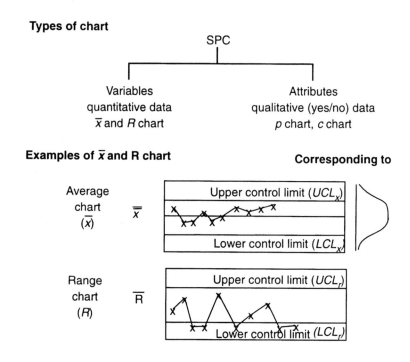

Figure 13: Statistical process control charts

NATURAL VARIATION OF THE PROCESS

This brings us to the concept of **natural variation**; you met this earlier in our discussions on Deming. Every process has natural variation. In other words, it is impossible to make any product with absolute consistency. The inconsistency will be caused by chance variations, however small, in, perhaps, the material, tool wear, positioning of the piece, speed of the machine, actions by the operator, and so on. These are called **common causes**. This variation can be measured and, using statistics, its spread can be predicted. It turns out that the spread follows the normal distribution, irrespective of the type of process. This is a consequence of the central limit theorem. Therefore if points are plotted which fall outside the distribution, then **special events** are occurring. The special events are assignable to unusual or unexpected changes or events, which may cause defects to be produced. This knowledge is very convenient for two reasons.

First, if the variation does not follow a normal distribution then we know that some special event is taking place. The special event may be an untrained operator, a change in the type of material, tool or bearing wear-out and so on. These special events can, with perseverance, be tracked down and the cause eliminated.

Second, the spread of a normal distribution can be measured by calculating the control limits. The formula is given in Figure 14. It turns out that within these limits which equal plus or minus three 'standard deviations' on either side of the process average value, lies virtually all of the natural variation. So if an operator takes a measurement and finds that it lies outside these control limits, then it is virtually certain that something has happened to the process. The process is then referred to as being **out of control**. The process should be stopped and the situation investigated.

Be careful to distinguish between: the **control limits** (which are a characteristic of the process and are set at plus and minus three standard deviations from the average), and the **tolerance limits** (also known as the specification limits) which are set by the designers or engineers. Ideally, of course, the control limits should lie within the tolerance limits, and a designer should take into account the normal variation of the process when designing a product.

SETTING UP THE CONTROL CHART

A chart should ideally be set up for each process, that is for each machine, making a particular type of product. (Pre-printed SPC charts are available from some quality societies or in books, and these make data entry and chart plotting very easy.) When setting up a chart it is important that there is consistency, so you should take samples over a representative period of time. You will need to decide on a sample size and the number of samples. Typical numbers are a sample size of 5 and at least 25 samples. For each sample calculate the average ('mean') and the range. Refer to Figure 14. Then calculate the average of the averages, and the average of the ranges. Now you will need to look up the control limit factors for the sample size you have used. If you have used a sample size of 5, the factors are given in the Figure 14. Now use the formulas in Figure 14 to calculate the control limits. When these are drawn in you can begin to use the charts for control purposes. You will have to decide what is a reasonable interval for samples to be taken. Generally, the higher the 'Cpk' value, the less frequent does the sampling have to be. We discuss Cpk, or capability ratios, later.

x and R charts

Assume samples of the size 3 are taken
the readings are x^1, x^2, x^3

$$\overline{x} = \frac{x^1 + x^2 + x^3}{3} \quad , \quad R = \text{largest } x - \text{smallest } x$$

These two values are plotted on the charts
To set up the chart, take 20 (minimum) random
samples, each of sample size (say) 3
Calculate $\overline{x}$ and R as above, then

$$\overline{\overline{x}} = \frac{\overline{x}^1 + \overline{x}^2 + \overline{x}^3 + \dots + \overline{x}^{20}}{20} \quad \overline{R} = \frac{R^1 + R^2 + \dots + R^{20}}{20}$$

These give the average (x and R) lines on the chart
Then calculate the control limits using the formulas

$UCLx = \overline{X} + A^2 \times \overline{R}$ $UCLr = D^4 \times \overline{R}$
$LCLx = \overline{X} - A^2 \times \overline{R}$ $LCLr = D^3 \times \overline{R}$

where the values A^2, D^3, D^4 depend on the sample size

Sample size	A^2	D^3	D^4
3	1.023	0	2.575
4	0.729	0	2.282
5	0.577	0	2.115
6	0.483	0	2.004
7	0.419	0.076	1.924

Figure 14: Calculations for mean and range charts

CHART INTERPRETATION

There are other criteria, apart from falling outside of the control limits, that indicate an out of control condition. These other criteria can be identified by operators, or automatically where SPC data is entered by computer, so that early action can be taken. Let us consider the logic. With natural variation occurring you would expect measurements to be spread more or less evenly on either side of the average value. To be more precise, with the standard deviation known, you would expect a certain proportion of measurements to fall within plus and minus one, two, and three standard deviations of the average value. If this does not occur, again there is an indication of trouble. As an example, the probability of a measurement falling above the average is, of course, 50%. The probability of two successive measures above the mean is 25% ($.5 \times .5$). And the probability of three successive measures above the mean is 12.5% ($.5 \times .5 \times .5$). Four successive measures above is 6.25%, and so on. If we get to seven successive measures above the average the probability is less than 1%, and we could reasonably conclude that something strange (a special event) has taken place. The other criteria are linked with the probabilities of successive measurements falling beyond a particular number of standard deviations.

The interpretation of process control charts is a skill that can be developed. Particular chart patterns are indicative of particular problems that may be developing. Some indications of the possibilities are given in Figure 15.

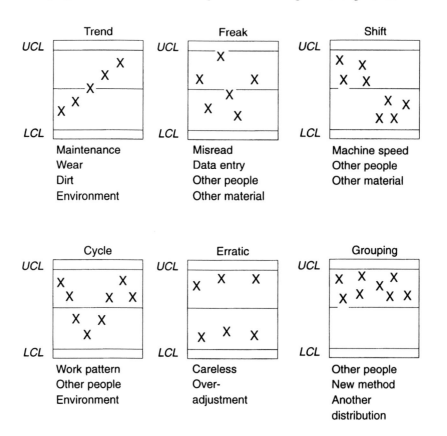

Figure 15: SPC chart interpretation

5.2 Attribute charts

It is not always possible to measure variables. Some defects, such as scratches, tears, and holes are either there or they are not. The products either pass inspection or they do not. There are two basic types of **attribute chart: *p* charts and *c* charts.** *p* charts are used where there are batches of product and the percentage that are defective can be determined. *c* charts are used where there are a number of possible types of defect associated with a particular product, for instance the number of scratches or stains or dents on a table.

With attributes only one chart is plotted, not two, as with the average and range chart. But the basic concepts of controlling variation, of taking samples, of setting up the charts, and of interpreting them, remain. Only the formulas are different. Formulas for p and c charts are given below.

$$\bar{p} = \frac{\text{number of defectives in all samples}}{\text{total inspected in all samples}}$$

$$UCL_p = \bar{p} + \sqrt{\frac{\bar{p}(1-\bar{p})}{n}}$$

$$LCL_p = \bar{p} - \sqrt{\frac{\bar{p}(1-\bar{p})}{n}}, \text{ or zero whichever is greater}$$

c Charts

$$\bar{c} = \frac{\text{number of defectives in all samples}}{\text{number of units sampled}}$$

$$UCL_c = \bar{c} + 3\sqrt{\bar{c}}$$

$$LCL_c = \bar{c} - 3\sqrt{\bar{c}}$$

ACTIVITY 13

For each of the following examples, select the appropriate control chart:

1   time to run a computer exercise
2   number of paint defects on a wall
3   diameter of a wheel
4   bags of cement used to pave 100 square metres
5   time spent in the queue at a bank
6   proportion of fridges sold requiring work under guarantee
7   number of complaints received in a hotel
8   proportion of students attending lectures
9   time to reply to an enquiry
10 number of enquiries per period

The following flow chart is a guide for your answers:

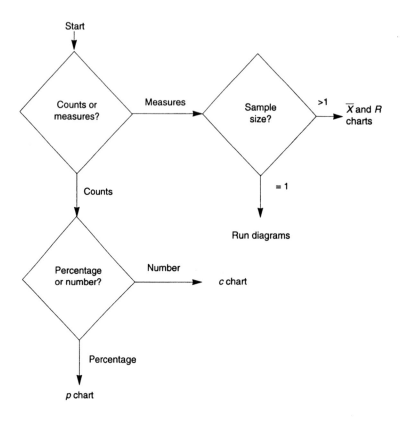

5.3 Process capability

Being 'in control' indicates that measurements taken from items coming out of the process follow an expected pattern (the normal distribution). But being 'in control' does not necessarily mean that the process is making good quality products. The process may be producing consistent products with small variation all of which are below the specification (i.e. consistently bad). So there is another requirement. This is referred to as **process capability**.

Process capability refers to the match between the location of the upper and lower process control limits (*UCL* and *LCL*) and the specification limits *USL* and *LSL* (also known as tolerance limits *UTL* and *LTL*). The location of the process control limits is due to the natural variation of the process that makes the product. The specifications of the product, on the other hand, are given by the designer of the product. These are two distinctly separate issues, but they must relate in order to produce quality products.

It is important that we don't measure process capability before the process is in control. In other words, if there are assignable causes and special events to be sorted out, this must be done first. These assignable causes are by their nature unpredictable, and have an unpredictable effect on the process control measures. This is illustrated in Figure 16.

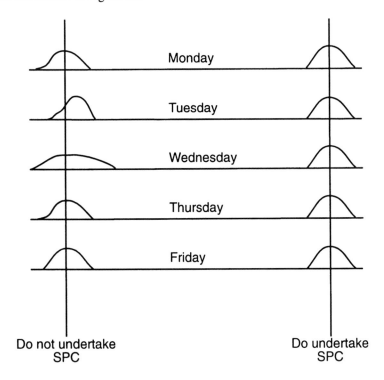

Figure 16: Process capability study

Process capability is measured by two ratios: 'Cp' and 'Cpk'. The Cp measure simply compares the specification (or tolerance) spread with the process spread. Clearly if the natural spread of the process is wider than the spread of the specifications, the Cp ratio is less than 1, then defectives are certainly going to occur. Defectives will 'seep out'; this is a way to remember the ratio names. But we need to also be concerned with where the process spread is located in relation to the specification limits. We could have a small process spread located outside of the specification limits, even though the Cp value is acceptable. So Cpk is needed.

Cpk is the smaller of two ratios:

$$\frac{\text{(upper specification limit} - \text{process average value)}}{\text{half the process spread}}$$

or

$$\frac{\text{(process average value} - \text{lower specification limit)}}{\text{half the process spread.}}$$

Half the process spread is, of course, equal to the upper control limit minus the lower control limit. Refer to Figure 17 below.

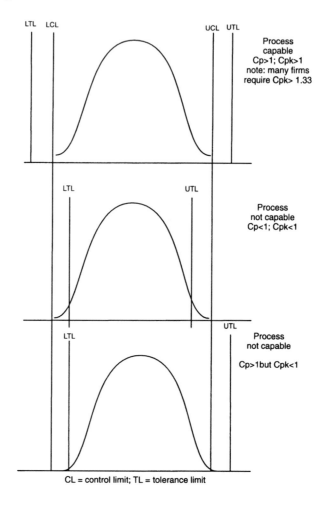

CL = control limit; TL = tolerance limit

Figure 17: Process capability diagrams

In practice, many companies, such as Ford, insist on a Cpk value of at least 1.33 before the process is regarded as 'capable'. So 'quality capable' means that the process or machine is both 'in control' and has a Cpk value of at least 1.33. As the Cpk value goes above 1.33, the likelihood of defects declines so the need to take more frequent samples decreases. It is always a good idea to seek to improve Cpk values even if the value of 1.33 has been reached. This can be done by many means including improved maintenance, better tool wear monitoring, closer working with suppliers, and improved training.

5.4 Six Sigma

Six sigma is a concept and aim developed by the Motorola Company but now adopted by many others. Motorola defined it as: 'a measure of goodness – the capability of a process to produce perfect work'. The six sigma concept is about the aim of making all processes in a chain highly capable; that is achieving a capability index of at least two. Six sigma is the number of standard deviations from the average setting of a process to the tolerance limit. In statistical terms, this translates as 3.4 defects per million opportunities for error. At Motorola this concept has been extended to every function in the company, where everyone is considered to be both a supplier and a customer. For such levels of quality, both design and manufacturing must play a role.

'Sigma' is the symbol that is used for the standard deviation of the normal distribution (σ). In statistical process control, when samples are taken from a process the readings are expected to stay within plus or minus three standard deviations of the mean. If a sample is taken which plots outside of these limits the process is said to be 'out of control'. It should then be stopped and investigated. There is still a small chance that an in-control reading will be taken outside of these limits. If however the tolerance limits are set by the designers at plus or minus six sigma, then it is highly likely that a deviating process will be stopped well before defects are made. Six sigma aims to set tolerance limits at six standard deviations from the mean, whereas the normally expected deviation of the process is three standard deviations. This gives a capability index of two.

To give you an idea of six sigma standards of performance, we estimate is that it would be equivalent to only two spelling mistakes in a business studies class of 30 students in all written assignments and examinations over a period of a year.

When Motorola announced its six sigma programme, such levels of process capability were rare. Most product manufacturing chains were found to have quality levels at five or even four sigma (which is still a good standard not achieved today by many companies). Expressing the company goal as six sigma indicated a clear aim. It also acts as a guide to priorities, because those processes with the lowest sigma ratings could be targeted first and all new products (for example, Motorola's Keynote pager) would have six sigma as the target quality level.

Motorola has attacked the six sigma objective through a variety of means, but team involvement and design of experiments have been particularly important.

5.5 Alternatives to SPC

Traditional SPC is widely, but not universally, applicable in manufacturing. In this section, we will consider two techniques that may be used either as alternatives or supplementary to SPC.

PRE-CONTROL

SPC is more suited to longer production runs where a large number of samples can be taken over time. Unfortunately this is not the case with many JIT systems. Also, particularly with JIT, it is important to verify as quickly as possible if a changeover has been undertaken correctly and the process is capable of producing good quality parts. One possibility is to use **pre-control**, originally developed by consultants Rath and Strong.

The procedure is as follows:

1 Divide the tolerance (or specification) band (i.e. the area between the upper and lower tolerance limits) into four equal bands. The middle two bands are the green zone (and should be coloured green on a chart). The two outer areas are called the yellow zone. Beyond the tolerance limits is the red band.

2 Following changeover (to check capability): measure five consecutive units. If all five are in the green zone, the process is in control. Production can start. If even one is in the red zone, the process is not in control. Production must not start. Reset the process. If one is in the yellow zone, a 'special cause' may be present. Take another sample of five. Better still, investigate. If two consecutive readings fall in the yellow zone, adjust the process and restart the measurement process.

3 During production: take samples of two consecutive units. If even one unit falls in the red zone, stop production and investigate. Return to Step 2. If both units fall in the yellow zone, stop production and investigate. Return to Step 2. If one unit falls in the yellow zone and one in the green, continue. If both units fall in the green, continue.

4 Sample six pairs between set-ups. (e.g. for an hour-long batch, sample approximately every 10 minutes).

The method is obviously very simple. Pre-control charts can be printed ahead of time and no statistical training is necessary. Implementation is immediate. However, critics have pointed out that pre-control is based on tolerance limits, not on process variation as is the case with SPC. As such the method relies on these tolerances being carefully set during design. Some statisticians have pointed out that a sample size of two may simply be inadequate. Nevertheless, the technique is statistically based and is likely to be reliable under many circumstances. Bhote (1991), who has been a strong advocate of pre-control, has pointed out some weaknesses in SPC, and claims that SPC is very antiquated. Bhote claims that pre-control has overtaken SPC in popularity in Japan. Pre-control is illustrated in Figure 18.

FAILSAFING OR 'POKAYOKE'

Pokayoke, or **failsafing**, is about adding devices to machines and processes in order that defects are simply not made. Although we could argue that failsafing has been used for a long time, it was the late Shigeo Shingo that popularised the concept. 'Pokayoke' is a Japanese adaptation for 'foolproofing' or, rather, 'mistake proofing'. Shingo believed that today, in an era of defects measured in parts per

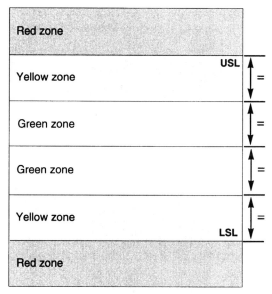

For process capability, 5 successive units must be in
the green zone. For production, take samples of 2
units (dividing inter-setup time
by 6)
If 2 units in green zone, continue
If 1 unit in green and 1 in yellow, continue
If 2 units in same yellow zone, stop and adjust
If 2 units in opposite yellow zones, stop
If 1 unit in a red zone , stop

Figure 18: Pre-control zones

million, statistical quality control and inspection is no longer appropriate. Hence a
pokayoke device aims to:

- carry out 100% automatic inspection, done by the process or the next
  process
- stop the process, or give a warning, if a defective is found.

Although Shingo's classic textbook *Zero Quality Control* (1986) gives details of
scores of pokayoke devices, most of the devices themselves have to be developed
by the ingenuity of in-plant personnel. Essentially, after an actual or potential
quality problem is identified, a device must be invented that checks every part for
the defect. This is often done by a limit switch detector or by a physical barrier. An
example of the former is a switch that is tripped when a part is added to a packing
case. Unless the switch is tripped the conveyor carrying the case simply stops. An
example of a mechanical device would be one that prevents a part with an excessive
dimension slipping through. When such a part is found it is channelled off, thereby
tripping a switch which stops the machine or gives a warning. Another variation of
pokayoke is the 'constant number' type. Here an automatic counter prevents
progress to the next stage unless the exact number of steps have been taken or parts
have been added.

Pokayoke systems should be operated on two levels. At the first level, defectives are simply prevented from proceeding. At the second level, where such stoppages or warnings recur, these should be recorded and the underlying cause of the problem identified.

ACTIVITY 14

Take an everyday process such as making tea or getting ready to go out. Which activities can be failsafed and how?

In doing this it is useful to begin with a process chart to detail all the steps involved. Then it is up to your imagination. Part of tea making might already be failsafed by an automatic kettle. You may also use tea bags, sugar sachets and milk catering packs, all to ensure exact quantities. You could use an alarm to notify when the exact length of time required for the tea to brew has been reached, and so on.

There is, of course, no limit to the number or location of pokayoke devices that can be employed. While manufacturing examples abound, service applications are certainly possible, ranging from cooking times in a fast food restaurant to warning systems for goods which are past the 'sell-by' date. Chase and Stewart (1994) have studied failsafing in service industry, with an approach beginning by identifying possible failure points, and then going on to failsafe them.

It is now the experience of many organisations that once the concept is understood by employees and a few examples developed, a large number of innovations are possible from employees, not necessarily confined to engineers and technicians, who relish the challenge of invention. Pokayoke comes down to education, support for innovation, and reward for enterprise.

Summary

This section has examined SPC, a powerful family of techniques for preventing defects. Today many manufacturers, and some retailers, demand that their suppliers have implemented SPC.

SPC involves setting up a chart and monitoring the process to detect if a shift has taken place. If it has, the process should be stopped. Whether it is stopped before defects are made is determined largely by the capability index. Many companies today are striving to improve their process capability.

A recent innovation relating to SPC is pre-control, based on tolerance limits rather than process variation. Shingo has argued that SPC is not good enough where parts per million defect levels are being aimed at, and recommends the use of failsafing or pokayoke in these situations. Pokayoke is yet another alternative with wide and growing applications in both manufacturing and service industries.

SECTION 6
Some Improvement Techniques

Introduction

Today it is not good enough merely to control quality or even to prevent defects from occurring. Continuous improvement is a necessity. In this section we will consider five of the most useful concepts for continuous improvement.

6.1 Cost of quality

Cost of quality (CoQ) aims at the financial quantification of all activities involved in the prevention and rectification of defects. The idea is that if the locations and magnitudes of quality related costs are measured and brought to the attention of management, this will be a powerful force for directed improvement. Cost of quality analysis may range from one-off estimates to a complete parallel accounting system. Traditionally, quality is measured by a series of ratios. The problem is that these are seldom comprehensive and lack common units. Ratios should be supplemented by costs, which should be publicised throughout the organisation. CoQ can provide specific cost justification data for a management considering the question of quality 'hype' against quality benefit.

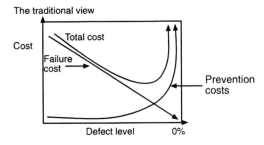

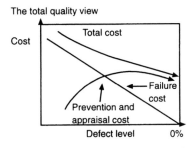

Figure 19: The cost of quality: traditional and total quality views

The conventional quality costing categories are:

- **prevention costs**: the costs of measures to prevent defects from taking place. This would include training, pokayoke, and capability studies and improvement (see SPC).

- **appraisal costs**: costs incurred in the detection of defects. This would include testing and inspection.

- **internal failure costs**: all failure costs incurred by internal customers. The costs incurred to rectify defects and failures internally, before the product or service reaches an external customer. This includes costs of scrap, rework, and all internal activities incurred through 'not getting it right first time'.

- **external failure costs**: all failure costs incurred by external customers. The costs incurred to rectify products and services after they have reached external customers, including returns, warranty claims, complaints, field repair, and perhaps lost custom.

As you saw earlier, Crosby (1979) groups the first two as POC (price of conformance) and the second two as PONC (price of non-conformance). For simplicity we can refer to the first two as **prevention costs** and the second two as **failure costs**.

Traditionally, prevention and failure costs have been seen as a trade-off. This is shown in the top diagram in Figure 19. Total costs are the sum of failure costs and prevention costs. Failure costs are thought to decline steadily, perhaps linearly, as quality improves. But as the defect level decreases, particularly as it nears 0% or perfect quality, prevention costs begin to rise very steeply, perhaps exponentially. The result is that there is an 'optimal' quality level, where total costs are minimised, which is below perfect quality (or above 0% defects). This trade-off thinking is now considered to be dangerous; it means that perfect quality is not only not the aim but actually undesirable. It becomes the excuse for not seeking to 'get it right first time'.

The total quality view is different. This is shown in the bottom diagram in Figure 19. Here, while failure costs continue to decline steadily, prevention costs tend to level out, at least above a certain level. The belief is that with 'total quality' everyone participates, quality becomes the natural way of life and not an 'extra'. Prevention requires initial but not continuing investment, and as a result costs stabilise. Total costs continue to decline all the way to the level of zero defects, so that the optimal is reached with perfect quality.

ACTIVITY 15

Do you believe that costs can actually decline with near perfect quality?

Students and quality professionals often have difficulties with this concept. Quality in this context must be defined as performance to specification or fitness for purpose. It probably does not apply to Kano's delighters. It is more likely to be true with product quality than service quality. But, as Crosby points out, if you disagree with the concept, how many babies is it acceptable to let die, and how many faults is it acceptable to send out on a new car?

The diagrams in Figure 19 are conceptual and have seldom been proved or disproved in practice. One point in favour of the total quality view is that the costs of failure are really unknown in terms of lost reputation and future custom. Therefore, if anything, failure costs are understated and may at least match the prevention costs.

The real point is that cost of quality analysis does set out to quantify what poor quality actually costs. The results, in many organisations that have implemented CoQ, are often **shock treatment**. The cost of not getting it right first time is typically in the range of 20% to 25% of turnover. So the savings that can be achieved by improving quality are very large, and the associated investment often more cost effective than the costs of increasing turnover, including marketing and capacity acquisition.

CoQ pinpoints the sources of quality costs. Specific budgets can then be set and controlled. Juran, the early pioneer of cost of quality, sees CoQ as an essential feature of his 'trilogy'. Quality becomes a closely managed function, using money rather than having quality as something that is desirable but really of low priority.

Some more advanced CoQ systems now incorporate cross-coding, so that some of the costs that are booked into the normal costing system are cross-linked to appropriate CoQ categories. This is not an exact science, and many of the problems that are found in cost accounting, such as the appropriate allocation of overheads, also found in CoQ. But exactness is not the issue; it is the trends, approximate magnitude, and locations that are important. When setting up these parallel costing systems it is useful to go further than just prevention and failure costs by identifying the source of the defect; operator error, equipment problem, material problem, specification problem, procedural problem, supplier problem or communication problem.

Many organisations do not yet undertake CoQ on a regular ongoing basis. Instead they rely on specific CoQ assessment studies. Here detailed questioning is the norm, usually making use of the process diagram, Pareto analysis, Ishikawa diagram, and histogram.

CoQ can be seen as closely related to the 'Seven Wastes' we discuss in Unit 9. The real aim is not merely to keep on reducing the costs of (poor) quality but to go on reducing the costs of all wastes. Defects are but one of the seven wastes. Some companies have now begun to cost wastes, either directly or through new cost accounting systems such as **activity based costing** (ABC).

6.2 Benchmarking

The Benchmarking Centre defines **benchmarking** as: 'the continuous, systematic search for, and implementation of, best practices which lead to superior performance'. In essence, it aims to compare a range of performance criteria with what the best in the business is achieving. It is a guide to necessary present performance and to future requirements if the organisation is to be 'world class'. It is about knowing yourself and really knowing the competition: where they are weak, where they are strong, and where they are going. To an extent, benchmarking is an alternative to 'cost plus' budgeting, and to productivity targeting by simply 'matching inflation'. It is outward looking rather than inward looking. It is concerned with tracking performance, not just taking snapshots. Think of the on-going Deming cycle. And, like several other techniques discussed here, it is equally applicable to products and to services.

Of course, benchmarking has always existed. People and organisations have always compared themselves to others. But it was the Xerox Corporation that appears to have pioneered **competitive benchmarking**. It was the systematic and comprehensive way in which Xerox set about making benchmarking a competitive weapon that has brought this technique into prominence. Robert Camp of Xerox is responsible for much of the thinking, and has written the definitive book (1989).

Types of benchmarking include:

- **internal** (where one branch is compared with others)
- **competitive** (as per Xerox, comparing with the toughest competitors)
- **functional** (where similar processes are compared with non-competitors)
- **generic** (where basic processes found in any business, such as human resource practices, are compared).

Benchmarking can be seen not just as a technique on its own, but as one of a mutually reinforcing family. The insights from benchmarking are useful if not necessary for quality function deployment. For value management it can help identify what is technically possible. Benchmarks help bridge the credibility gap. It identifies which Garvin's dimensions of quality that a competitor is competing on. And systematic measurement is part of any quality improvement process, such as the Deming cycle or the Juran trilogy.

We begin with the understanding that a single measure of performance is rarely adequate. Just as several instruments are necessary to monitor and control the performance of a car or plane, so it is with any organisation. Now recognise that to be competitive in quality and productivity, steady inward-looking progress may not be enough. But of course we do not go out to benchmark everything possible. It must be a directed search.

WHAT TO MEASURE

Robert Camp states that benchmarking is 'first a goal setting process'. You have to know what to benchmark, and, as with much of quality management, this brings you right back to the customer. Identify your customers, present and future. Now you can begin to assess their needs and the core processes. These are the areas where the organisation absolutely needs to perform well, and where unique advantages can be obtained. Garvin's dimensions are useful as an aid. The areas can be assembled by a team using brainstorming or the Ishikawa diagram.

There may be a particular interest in targeting areas that are known to be important, such as costs or complaints or geographical areas. Staff policies, salaries, and personnel policies on training, recruitment, and the use of people at work may be relevant. There may be some standard productivity or quality measures which are prevalent in the industry, such as cars per employee per year in the car industry. However, beware of being too specific on what should be measured. The idea is to concentrate on processes first and measures of performance second. You now know what you wish to benchmark, your next step is to identify who to benchmark.

It is a good idea to think through the information collection procedure, in particular who will be responsible and where it will be centred. The latter has to be clearly communicated so that if information is obtained from or by an unexpected source, it will still go to the right place. It will often be necessary to dedicate people, part time or short term, to information collection.

WHO TO MEASURE
The aim of competitive benchmarking is to find the 'industry-best' performance, and where appropriate the 'world-best' performance. The toughest competitors now and in future are often known or easy to shortlist, so a search can be more focused. But do not close your mind to the possibility of world class performance from a new or unexpected source. Benchmarking is an on-going process.

HOW TO MEASURE
We assume that internal benchmark information is relatively easy to obtain. Now comes the external information. There is a huge number of potential sources of benchmark information. But it must be ethically collected and secured; benchmarking is not stealing, nor passing on potentially valuable information obtained from one source to another. For partnership benchmarking, you have to be prepared to give and take; not just take. For competitive benchmarking some possibilities are: a library database search, commercial press-cutting databases, specialist industry reviews in newspapers or journals, specialist surveys, for example by *The Economist Intelligence Unit*, trade magazines, conference papers and proceedings, market research, special surveys, factory visits and evening meetings of relevant societies, annual financial reports and published accounts, trade and sales literature, quotations from the companies themselves, management consultants and academics.

Many benchmarking exercises will involve actual use of competitor products, including one-way viewing through mirrors of customer usage, and full technical disassembly.

USING BENCHMARKS
Benchmarking is not static. It aims at projecting future trends. When the internal and external benchmarks are assembled, analysts can begin to assess the critical question of whether the 'gap' between our own and competitor performance is widening or narrowing. This leads to the establishment of areas for priority action. Competitive benchmarking can become a management philosophy in itself, the aim is to remain or achieve 'industry-best' position in the particular niches identified as important. As soon as one set of improvements has been implemented, it all begins again. It's the Deming cycle.

6.3 Design of experiments

Design of experiments (DoE) is a family of techniques which enable a quality professional to identify rapidly the most important variables in new product design or process improvement. DoE has a long history, going back to Sir Ronald Fisher in 1930, but popularised and refined by Taguchi, Box, and, more recently, by Dorian Shainin (see Bhote, 1991). DoE has until recently been the province of professional statisticians, but the effect of the work of the above named people, has been to open up DoE (somewhat) to non-statisticians.

Let us say that we suspect a number of variables (say temperature, pressure, metal thickness, length of time processed etc.) has an influence on the quality level of a product. Traditionally these would be explored one variable at a time whilst maintaining all the other variables constant. Where there are several variables, say 13, each of which has three possible settings or 'levels', this becomes totally impractical as over 1.5 million trials would be needed. The optimal combination could be missed, especially if there are significant 'interactions' between variables, for example, drink alone or drugs alone may be survivable, but in combination they could be fatal.

The DoE answer to this problem is to use an 'orthogonal array', combined with Analysis of Variance, (ANOVA: a straightforward statistical technique that you may have covered in your quantitative methods studies) to identify the correct combinations. In our example, in fact, only 27 trials would be necessary. This procedure was popularised by Taguchi who took it out of statistical specialisation to become a procedure that many engineers could use. Taguchi orthogonal tables are available in books such as that by Peace (1993).

A simple version of Taguchi works like this. Consider that you are investigating the flow of liquid through a membrane. The goal is to maximise the flow. First, identify the relevant factors; this may be done by brainstorming or experience. Say there are three: thickness, viscosity, and temperature. Each factor can have two 'levels', for example, thick/thin, low/high. Four trials would be necessary and the orthogonal array would be as shown in Figure 20. Notice that between any two columns each combination of levels occurs the same number of times. Undertake the trials, measuring flow each time. Analysis of variance is now used to calculate the percentage contribution of each factor. This identifies the critical factor(s) to watch. In some cases it is necessary to undertake further analysis to examine the interactions between factors.

There is no doubt that DoE is essential to achieving world-class levels of quality in manufacturing, such as the six sigma programme. For improvement, DoE is an order of magnitude more powerful than the basic seven tools.

	Thickness	Viscosity	Temperature
1	Thick	Low	Low
2	Thick	High	Medium
3	Thin	Low	Medium
4	Thin	High	Low

Figure 20: An orthogonal array for flow through a membrane involving 3 factors, each with 2 possible levels, 4 trials would be involved, as shown

SHAININ TECHNIQUES

Despite considerable support, not all companies have achieved success through the Taguchi approach. It is still quite complex for the non-statistician. More recently, Dorian Shainin has further refined and simplified DoE. His methods involve even more 'engineering judgement' than those of Taguchi, and are not accepted by all purists. An additional problem is that the Shainin methods have in general not been written up to the extent of Taguchi's approach, and are also subject to copyright. Nevertheless, the Shainin techniques deserve considerably more attention than they have been given.

The Shainin approach to DoE uses a series of methods to identify what is termed the 'red X' (the critical factor, or top problem) or the 'pink X' (a likely or important factor). The three basic methods are:

- **the multi-vari chart** (a more sophisticated form of run diagram)
- **components search** (a four-stage procedure used where there are interchangeable components, which involves identifying good and bad products, disassembling them and reassembling from components taken from good and bad products, then retesting)
- **paired comparisons** (used when there are no components, which involves carefully observing and noting all differences between several pairs of products, one good and one bad in each pair, to give a strong clue as to the problem).

Quite often these methods will reveal the red X directly. If not, then, having identified the pink Xs, we move onto 'variables search' and 'full factorial' analysis. These are similar to the orthogonal array and ANOVA approach, but have been modified by Shainin.

A more complex example would be to compare two university courses taken by the same students, but having very different average marks. We could list many of the attributes: lecturer, textbook, amount of quantitative material, lecture times, tutorials, examination, coursework, etc. side by side and make a qualitative comparison of differences. This would help identify the 'pink Xs', being the reasons for the discrepancy in marks.

ACTIVITY 16

A very simple, perhaps over-simple, demonstration of the components search method involves taking two ball-point pens, one of which has no ink remaining, and is thus 'defective'. If you know which is the 'defective' one, you can make a list of all the visible differences, one of which will be that there is no ink. This is then a 'pink X'. Another demonstration involves identifying the good and defective pens, and marking each component as 'possible good' and 'possible bad'. Then disassemble them, interchange the two parts and reassemble. Once again test and note possible goods and possible bads. There will only be one part, the empty ink carrier, that is twice identified as bad.

Finally, the **B versus C** tool is a simple but effective 'paired comparison' method to determine if a better (or B) process is truly better than a current (or C) process, given a level of risk of being wrong. As an example, consider the case of three random samples taken from a current C process and three random samples taken from a possibly better B process. If the results are arranged in order from best to worst, and if the three best are all from the B process, then B stands a good chance of really being better. But if, for example, the two best readings are from B but the third best is from C, then there is a greater risk in concluding that B is really better. The B versus C tool extends this type of analysis to the case where there is known variation in the current process. This is really a refinement of a statistical test for the difference between two means, but requiring far less data. Such a test has wide application in quality management: from comparing two processes or methods, to comparing customer opinions about two products or services.

DoE fits in well with quality function deployment (QFD), which we deal with in the next section. In QFD, a set of 'technical specifications' (the columns in a QFD matrix) are set against the customer requirements (the rows in a QFD matrix). DoE is a powerful way to test which of the technical specifications has the most influence or is most sensitive.

6.4 Quality Function Deployment

Quality function deployment (QFD) is a tool used to aid the product design and development process. Customer needs are identified and systematically compared with the technical or operating features of the product. The process brings out the relative importance of customer requirements which, when set against the technical features of the product, leads to the identification of the most important or sensitive technical characteristics. These are the technical characteristics which need development or attention. Although the word 'product' is used in our descriptions which follow, QFD is equally applicable in services. Technical characteristics then become the service characteristics.

Perhaps a chief advantage of QFD is that it is carried out by a multi-disciplinary team who are all concerned with the particular product. QFD is then the vehicle for these specialists to attack a problem together. QFD is, therefore, not only concerned with quality but with the simultaneous objectives of reducing overall development time, meeting customer requirements, reducing costs, and producing a product or service which fits together and works well the first time. The mechanics of QFD are not rigid and can easily be adapted to local innovation.

QFD is also referred to as the **house of quality**. This is because of the way the matrices in QFD fit together to form a house-shaped diagram. A full QFD exercise may make use of several house of quality diagrams, forming a sequence which gradually translates customer requirements into specific manufacturing steps and detailed manufacturing process requirements. The most simple QFD exercise would use only one house of quality diagram which seeks to take customer requirements and to translate them into specific technical requirements.

In addition, a QFD exercise may spin off (or 'deploy') a whole hierarchy of house of quality exercises. This would happen where a new product is being considered. The first exercise would consider the product as a whole but subsequent exercises may involve consideration of individual components. For instance, a complete new car could be considered at the top level but subsequent exercises may be concerned with the engine, body shell, doors, instrumentation, brakes, and so on. Thereafter the detail would be deployed into manufacturing and production.

HOUSE OF QUALITY DIAGRAM
We now explain the essential composition of the basic house of quality diagram. Refer to Figure 21.

CENTRAL (OR RELATIONSHIP) MATRIX (CM)
The central matrix lies at the heart of the house of quality diagram. This is where the 'what is required' is matched with the 'how to do it'. Each customer requirement (the what) is systematically compared with each technical characteristic or design feature (the how). The nature of the relationship is noted in the matrix by an appropriate symbol. The team can devise their own symbols; for instance, numbers may indicate the relative strength of the relationship or simply ticks may suffice. The relationships may be positive, neutral or negative. This matching exercise is carried out by the team based on their experience and judgement. The idea is to clearly identify all means by which the 'whats' can be achieved by the 'hows'. It will also check if all 'whats' can in fact be achieved (insufficient technical characteristics?), and if some technical characteristics are not apparently doing anything (redundancy?).

CUSTOMER REQUIREMENTS (CR)
The usual starting point for QFD is the identification of customer requirements or the 'voice of the customer'. These are entered into the rows to the left of the central matrix. Information on customer needs may be obtained from a variety of sources and this may be a major exercise in itself. Customers may be present or future, internal or external, primary or secondary. All the conventional tools of marketing research are relevant, as well as techniques such as complaint analysis

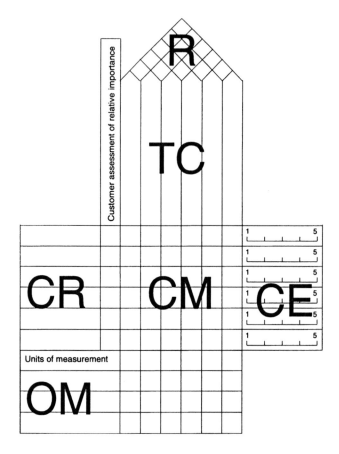

Figure 21: Quality function development: house of quality

and focus groups. Customers may include owners, users, and maintainers, all of whom have separate requirements. After collection comes the problem of how to assemble the information before entering it into the column. It helps to think in terms of a hierarchy; on the primary level are the broad customer requirements, secondary requirements add the detail.

Marketing would have responsibility for assembling much of the customer information, but the team puts it together. Marketing may begin by circulating the results of surveys and by a briefing. Thereafter the team should brainstorm out the customer requirements, but not the technical features as short phrases.

In a real study, the number of apparent customer requirements may be very large. There is the temptation to shorten the list by grouping. This may be reasonable, but an important requirement is to preserve the 'voice of the customer'. The team must not try to 'second guess' or to assume that they know best what is needed.

RANKINGS OR RELATIVE IMPORTANCE OF CUSTOMER REQUIREMENTS

When the customer requirements are assembled onto the matrix on the left of the house diagram, weightings are added to indicate the importance of each requirement. Weightings are established by market research or focus groups, or failing these the team may determine rankings by a technique such as **pairwise comparison**. Each requirement is compared with each other. The most important of the two requirements gains a point, and all scores are added up to determine final rankings. The rankings may be listed in a column immediately to the right of the relationship matrix.

COMPETITIVE EVALUATION OF CUSTOMER REQUIREMENTS (CE)

Each customer requirement may then be examined in terms of customer perceptions. For each customer requirement, a group of customers may be asked to state how they perceive the present performance of the company's product as against those of competitor products. The aim of this part of the exercise is to clearly identify the SWOT (strengths, weaknesses, opportunities, threats) of competitor products against your own. The competitive evaluation is placed in a row to the right of the customer requirement rankings.

TECHNICAL CHARACTERISTICS AND ASSOCIATED RANKINGS (TC)

Customer requirements, weightings and competitive evaluations are displayed from left to right across the house. The corresponding technical characteristics (or design features), rankings, and competitive evaluations are displayed from top to bottom across the house. Immediately above the central matrix are listed the technical characteristics of the product. These characteristics are stated in terms that are likely to have an impact on the customer requirements.

Immediately below the relationship matrix appears one or more rows for rankings such as cost or technical difficulty or development time. The choice of these is dependent on the product. These will enable the team to judge the efficiency of various technical solutions. The prime row uses the customer weightings and central matrix to derive the relative technical characteristic rankings.

Next below the relationship matrix comes one or more rows for competitive evaluation. Here, where possible, 'hard' data is used to compare the actual physical or engineering characteristics of your product against those of competitors. To the right of the relationship matrix we can judge relative customer perceptions, and below, the relative technical performance.

The bottom row of the house, which is also the 'bottom line' of the QFD process, are the target technical characteristics. These are expressed in physical terms and are decided upon after team discussion of the complete house contents, as we describe below. The target characteristics are, for some, the final output of the exercise, but many would agree that it is the whole process of information assembly, ranking, and team discussion that goes into QFD which is the real benefit, so that the real output is improved inter-functional understanding.

ROOF OF THE HOUSE (R)

The roof of the house is the technical interaction matrix. The diagonal format allows each technical characteristic to be viewed against each other one. This simply reflects any technical trade-offs that may exist. For example, with the hamburger case (see Figure 22) , bun size may have to be compatible with beef size. These have a positive relationship; increasing the bun size increases the beef size. These interactions are made explicit, using the technical knowledge and experience of the team.

USING THE HOUSE AS A DECISION TOOL

After assembly of the customer requirements, customer rankings, competitive data, technical characteristics, and technical competitive measures, work on the house begins by completing the main relationship matrix and the technical relationship matrix. The full team should be involved because this is a major learning stage.

In the central matrix, customer requirements are compared with technical characteristics. The extent to which each customer requirement is matched by each technical characteristic is judged. Go through the matrix, cell by cell. Using the hamburger example in Figure 22, ask, for example: to what extent does the meat in a hamburger meet the requirements for nutrition? The answer will be high (write in 9 points), medium (write in 3 points), low (write in 1 point), or not at all (write in zero). In some cases a negative is possible (write in minus 3). Then, for each cell, multiply the point score by the weight for that row (the customer requirement ranking). Write this figure in the top right-hand of the cell. When complete, add up the top right-hand figures for each column. This gives a weighting which reflects the ability of each technical requirement to meet each customer specification.

Matrix Analysis

Example: design of a hamburger to customer preferences

Begin with a focus group to determine customer requirements and relative weightings. Then perform the analysis in a QFD matrix.

Customer requirements	Customer preference weighting	Features			
		Beef	Bun	Lettuce	Ketchup
Moisture	1	0 0	0 0	1 1	9 9
Flavour	3	9 27	0 0	0 0	3 9
Nutrition	3	9 27	3 9	0 0	0 0
Visual appeal	5	9 45	1 5	1 5	1 5
Value for money	5	9 45	1 5	0 0	1 5

Weighted scores	144	19	6	28

Conclusion: Concentrate attention on beef and ketchup

Figure 22: Ranking matrix: hamburger example

When all cells have been completed, the matrix is examined. A blank row indicates that a customer requirement is not met. A blank column indicates a redundant technical feature. The main matrix shows the required technical characteristics that will need design attention. The costs of these can be seen with reference to the base rows. This may have the effect of shifting priorities if costs are important. Then the technical trade-offs are examined. Often there will be more than one technical way to impact a particular customer requirement, and this is clear from rows in the matrix. And it may also be that one technical alternative has a negative influence on another customer requirement. This is found out by using the roof matrix. Eventually, through a process of team discussion, a team consensus will emerge. This may take some time, but experience shows that time and cost is repaid many times over as the actual design, engineering and manufacturing steps proceed.

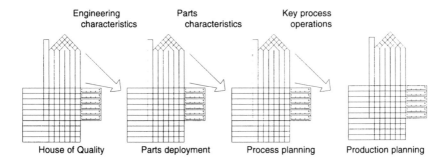

Figure 23:Deployment

The bottom line is now the target values of technical characteristics. This set can now go into the next house diagram (Figure 23). This time the target technical characteristics become the 'customer requirements' or 'whats', and the new vertical columns (or 'hows') are, perhaps, the technologies, the assemblies, the materials, or the layouts. And so the process 'deploys' until the team feels that sufficient detail has been considered to cover all co-ordination considerations in the process of bringing the product to market.

QFD may be used in several stages in order to 'deploy' customer requirements all the way to the final manufacturing or procedural stages. Here the outcome of one QFD matrix (for example the technical specifications), becomes the input into the next matrix which may aim to look at process specifications to make the product (Figure 23).

ACTIVITY 17

Use QFD to analyse your local library service. To do this properly you will have to:

● survey customer requirements, including ranking them
● list the technical characteristics (i.e. the services offered)
● undertake benchmarking or comparisons with other libraries
● complete the central matrix and roof
● identify areas of strength and weakness
● make some recommendations.

6.5 Kaizen

Kaizen is the Japanese name for continuous improvement. As such it is a vital part of total quality. It brings together several of the tools and techniques described in this unit and a few others. Kaizen was made popular in the West by Maasaki Imai (1986). According to Imai, Kaizen comprises several elements. Kaizen is both a philosophy and a set of tools.

PHILOSOPHY OF KAIZEN

Quality begins with the customer. But customers' views are continuously changing and standards are rising, so continuous improvement is required. Kaizen is dedicated to continuous improvement, in small increments, at all levels. Everyone has a role, from top management to shop floor employees. Top management must allocate the resources and establish the strategy, systems, procedures and organisational structures necessary for Kaizen to work. Middle managers are responsible for implementing Kaizen. They must monitor performance of the continuous improvement programme, and ensure that employees are educated in the use of the necessary tools. Supervisors are responsible for applying Kaizen. They must maintain the rate of suggestions, coach, and improve communications at the workplace. And shop-floor employees must make suggestions, learn new jobs, use the tools, and generally participate in continuous improvement activities individually and in teams. Imai's book has several examples of how this philosophy works its way down the organisational hierarchy in Japanese companies.

Imai believes that without active attention, the gains made will simply deteriorate. But Imai goes further. Unlike Juran, who emphasises 'holding the gains', Kaizen involves building on the gains by continuing experimentation and innovation.

According to Imai there are several guiding principles that include :

● questioning the rules (standards are necessary but work rules are there to be broken and must be broken with time)

- developing resourcefulness (it is a management priority to develop the resourcefulness and participation of everyone)
- get to the root cause (don't solve problems superficially)
- eliminate the whole task (question whether a task is necessary; in this respect Kaizen is similar to BPR, that we discuss in Unit 9)
- reduce or change activities (be aware of opportunities to combine tasks).

TOOLS OF KAIZEN

Kaizen incorporates several tools but the most well known are the **5 Ss**, the **5 M Checklist**, and the **5 Whys**.

The **5 Whys** is a simple but effective technique developed at Toyota and strongly associated with JIT manufacturing. It involves asking 'why?' over and over again, typically five times, so as to get to the 'root cause' of the problem. This avoids 'solving' the problem at the superficial level.

The **5 Ss** are five Japanese words beginning with S covering aspects of housekeeping. Many Japanese believe that this is the foundation for quality and productivity. Some British companies taken over by Japanese companies have experience of this fundamental belief. When Sumitomo took over Dunlop, apparently the first six months were spent on these five Ss. The 5 Ss correspond to:

- cleanliness (operators/staff must be responsible for keeping their own equipment clean).
- orderliness (put equipment away in the right place, in the right condition when not needed)
- tidiness (a place for everything and everything in its place)
- organisation (removing unneeded items, laying out the workplace, tools, equipment, and inventory)
- discipline (doing all this every day, not periodically).

Nissan has an audit procedure to check on these aspects. We will meet these 5 Ss again when we discuss total productive maintenance later in this unit.

The **5 M Checklist** is intended to ensure that all five factors: men (people), machine, material, method, and measurement, are considered in any process improvement or problem solution. The 5 Ms are often incorporated in constructing cause and effect diagrams as the basic fishbone framework.

Summary

In this section we have reviewed a selection of more advanced quality improvement techniques: cost of quality, benchmarking, design of experiments (DoE), quality function deployment (QFD) or the house of quality, and kaizen. QFD is a technique that integrates several others. All of these techniques provide an essential background to our next section.

SECTION 7

Reliability and Maintenance

Introduction

Reliability is a concept very closely associated with quality. You will recall that reliability is one of Garvin's **dimensions of quality**, and for many people, reliability figures strongly in any set of desirable product characteristics, for example, remember the *Top Gear* survey we discussed in Section 1.

Maintenance, in turn, is closely associated with reliability. Often without good maintenance procedures there will only be poor reliability. Reliability and maintenance are vast subjects in themselves and often involve high levels of statistics. In this brief section, the aim is to introduce you to the topics rather than to make you a reliability and maintenance expert. Like many other areas of operations management, maintenance has undergone a revolution over the past decades with the influence of Japanese methods. Total productive maintenance (TPM) philosophically has much in common with TQM.

7.1 Reliability

Reliability is defined as 'the probability of a product performing its specified function under prescribed conditions without failure for a specified period of time'. (*APICS Dictionary*, 1995). The word is also in common use in relation to a duration of time without failure.

In reliability theory, the 'bath-tub' curve is well known, and probably fits with your own experience. It is shown below in Figure 24.

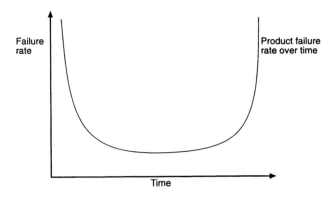

Figure 24: The 'bath-tub' curve of reliability theory

Notice that the axes are failure rate against time, not failures against time. Infant mortality or **burn-in** failures are often the result of defects undetected during manufacture. It is common for many types of electronic equipment, particularly where high reliability is required, to be subjected to a 'burn-in' test period before leaving the factory. The system is run through a number of cycles often subject to increased temperature. The idea is to make any defective products fail, before they reach the customer and are therefore much more expensive to repair.

Random failures are a function of product design. Finally, **wear-out** failures are a function of design and, of course, wear and age.

Although the bath-tub curve is common, this is not the only mode of failure.

RELIABILITY STATISTICS

We will not say much about this, but a brief insight is useful. The exponential distribution, shown in Figure 25, is by far the most commonly-used reliability distribution.

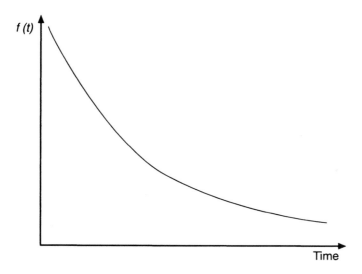

Figure 25: Reliability statistics – exponential distribution

The probability density function of the exponential distribution is

$f(t) = \lambda e^{-\lambda t}$ where

λ = failure rate

and the Reliability is $Rt = e^{-\lambda t}$

This is fortunate, because the exponential distribution has some special features, which are :

● mean and standard deviation are equal; thus it is relatively easy to obtain. This is known as the **mean time between failures** or **MTBF**, an important figure in reliability calculations.

● approximately 63% of the values fall below the mean, which means that there is a 37% chance of survival beyond the MTBF.

ACTIVITY 18

A photocopier has a MTBF of 50 hours. What is the probability that it will work perfectly for 2 days, or 16 hours?

The failure rate is 1/50 = 0.02 per hour, so:

$$e^{-\lambda t} = e^{-(0.02)\,(16)} = 0.73 \text{ or } 73\%$$

SYSTEM RELIABILITY

Many products or systems have hundreds or thousands of components. The whole system fails if one component fails (a common problem, but fortunately becoming less common with PCs), then this is known as a **series system** (Figure 26). The reliability of such a system is the product of the sub-system or component reliabilities. If there are three components with reliabilities, for say 1,000 hours of operating life, of 0.98, 0.95, and 0.99, then the system reliability is:

0.98 x 0.95 x 0.99 = 0.9216 or 92.16%

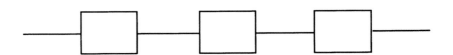

Figure 26: A series system

ACTIVITY 19

Work out the system reliability for 100 series components each with a reliability of 0.995, or 99.5%. Low isn't it ?

Sometimes sub-systems are arranged in parallel for reliability reasons (Figure 27). This happens with, for example, 'hot back-up' computer systems. Here, the system fails only if both sub-systems fail.

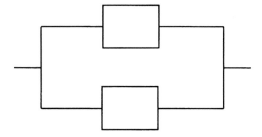

Figure 27: A parallel system

Here the relevant formula, for two components, is:

$$R(s) = R_1 + R_2 - R_1 \times R_2$$

so, for two components, each having a reliability of 0.95, $R(s) = 0.9975$.

7.2 Maintenance

Here we will concentrate only on total productive maintenance (TPM). The term productive is used because we wish to gain productivity, not just concentrate on maintenance. TPM, like TQM, has been one of the great ventures of the past 10 years. It has much in common with TQM, namely the involvement of all the maintenance task, not just the specialists. Like TQM, TPM relies on team involvement. TPM is very relevant to JIT manufacturing, but its principles are not confined to manufacturing.

TPM begins with the idea of **six big losses**. These are

- breakdown losses
- set-up and adjustment losses (delaying the start of work)
- idling and minor stoppages (due to necessary minor adjustments)
- reduced speed losses (unable to run at full speed)
- start-up losses (pre-production breakdowns)
- quality defects (as a result of imperfect equipment).

ACTIVITY 20

Apply these six big losses to your car, when you are just about to set off for an important appointment. What could you do about them?

Breakdown is obvious. Set-up losses might involve seat and seatbelt adjustment, or delays when you have forgotten to put fuel in. Idling and minor stoppages might involve a headlight or brake-pad failure. Reduced speed may be caused by cumulative imperfect maintenance or poor tuning. Start-up losses may be due to a flat battery, or having to scrape ice off the windscreen. Quality defects are probably not applicable here, but of course would be in manufacturing or service. What could you do? You could call your local garage, or an emergency repair service if you are a member; or you could take greater care, and check beforehand. This is what TPM does: it makes operators and staff aware of the losses and puts them, as far as possible, in charge of their own processes. Like TQM, TPM is a do-it-yourself (DIY) methodology: 'ownership' of the machine or process is fundamental.

The role of the maintenance experts is to teach the DIY activities, being responsible only for the more complex tasks, including maintenance information systems. This is a feedback loop. As staff take over more maintenance tasks themselves, so the maintenance staff have more time to train, track, and improve.

To do this, there are the five Ss, which should guide all staff, as we listed earlier:

- cleanliness (operators/staff must be responsible for keeping their own equipment clean).
- orderliness (put away in the right place, in the right condition when not needed)
- tidiness (a place for everything and everything in its place)
- organisation (removing unneeded items, laying out the workplace, tools, equipment, and inventory)
- discipline (doing all this every day, not periodically).

And finally, the five pillars of TPM are then :

- adopt improvement activities aimed at the six big losses
- improve existing planned and predictive maintenance
- establish a level of self-maintenance and cleaning carried out by the operators (using the five Ss)
- improve the skills of operators and maintenance staff
- initiate prevention techniques.

The associated techniques of TPM are numerous, and some can only be mentioned here. They include aircraft-style checks (a start-of-shift checklist used by all, like that used by pilots), condition monitoring (where, for example, oil and vibration is monitored to give early warning of problems), full use of senses (humans are very sensitive to changes in vibration and sound, so get the operators to report when they detect a change), and maintenance information systems (to keep track of faults and costs). Many of the problem-solving techniques we discussed under quality are highly relevant to TPM also.

ACTIVITY 21

Many lecturers and presenters rely on maintenance staff for the good operation of overhead projectors, and then complain when things go wrong. This is not TPM! What might you do if TPM was considered part of the job? Brainstorm out some ideas, preferably in a group. (The idea for this exercise comes from Tom Willcox & Peter Willmott, 1994.)

You will probably come up with quite a few sensible actions, including keeping spare bulbs handy, getting training on how to change bulbs, cleaning the glass afterwards, and checking and testing before the lecture starts. You would be familiar with the manual. Then you might record the approximate length of time that the bulb has been switched on, to allow timely replacement, and you might monitor the temperature with a thermometer, even carry out studies as to the maximum length of time to switch on for. By knowing the costs of components, you might recommend scheduled maintenance or replacement, etc. All very different, but all easy, and all possible.

Summary

In this brief section, we have learned something of the meaning of reliability and looked at the basic formulas used for prediction and management. We have looked at the effects of placing components in series and parallel. Finally, we looked at total productive maintenance (TPM), observing the similarities with TQM as both emphasise involvement and empowerment of staff.

Unit Review Activity

Read the article 'Getting the numbers right', Resource Item 6.2. Identify the approaches BT uses to promote TQM in the company. What are the benefits to the customer?

Unit Summary

In this unit we looked at quality – an area that has leapt to the top of many senior management agendas over the past decade. First we looked at the meaning of the word 'quality'. There are several dimensions, such as reliability, performance, conformance and perspectives, such as macro and micro. Quality is a changing target. Quality must begin with the external customer, but internal customers are also important.

The views of some of the quality 'gurus' such as Deming, Juran and Crosby were examined. These people have had a considerable influence, not only on product and service quality, but also on management in general.

We looked at TQM, noting that it involves all functions, all people, all products, and all processes from design to delivery. We looked at a well-known standard, ISO 9000, and at various quality awards, which form a useful checklist for the support infrastructure for quality. Prevention, rather than detection, was seen to be a consistent theme. A 'cost of quality' exercise makes this explicit by tracking the costs of failure and the costs of prevention and detection.

We examined a small selection of tools and techniques for quality. Many of these tools have applicability well beyond that of simply improving a product. An example is statistical process control, which can also be used in areas such as forecasting, inventory control and cost accounting. Finally, in a brief section, we looked at reliability, an area closely linked to quality.

Acknowledgement

Portions of this unit, both text and figures, were taken from John Bicheno, *The Quality 50*, PICSIE Books, Buckingham, 1994. Permission to copy is acknowledged.

References

Albrecht, K and Zemke, R (1985) *Service America!* Dow Jones Irwin, Homewood, Illinois

Top Gear (1995) Annual Survey of Customer Satisfaction, BBC *Top Gear*, May

ASQC (1987) *Guide for Reducing Quality Costs*, American Society for Quality Control Press, Milwaukee

Bhote, K R (1991) *World Class Quality*, AMACOM/ASQC, New York, Chapter 15

Bicheno, J (1994), *The Quality 50*, PICSIE Books, Buckingham

British Standards Institute, BS 5750 / ISO 9000 (1993); BS 6143 (Part 2, 1990 and Part 1, 1991)

Camp, R (1989) *Benchmarking*, ASQC Quality Press, Milwaukee

Carlzon, J (1987) *Moments of Truth*, Harper and Row, New York

Chase, R B and Stewart, D M (1994) 'Make your service fail safe', *Sloan Management Review*, Spring

Clarkson, J (1995) *Sunday Times*, 23 April

Cox, J F III, Blackstone, J and Spenser, M (eds) (1995) *APICS Dictionary* (8th edn), APICS, Falls Church, Virginia

Crosby, P (1979) *Quality is Free,* McGraw-Hill, New York,

Crosby, P (1989) *Let's Talk Quality*, McGraw-Hill, New York

Deming, W E (1982) *Out of the Crisis*, Cambridge University Press, Cambridge

Desatnik, R L and Detzel, D H (1993) *Managing to Keep the Customer*, revised edn, Jossey Bass, San Francisco

Garvin, D (1984) 'What does product quality really mean?', *Sloan Management Review*, Fall, pp. 25–43

Guaspari, J (1988) *The Customer Connection*, AMACOM, New York

Imai, M (1986) *Kaizen: The Key to Japan's Competitive Success*, McGraw-Hill, New York

Joiner, B (1994) *Fourth Generation Management*, McGraw-Hill, New York

Juran, J (1979) *Quality Control Handbook*, McGraw-Hill, New York, 3rd edn

Juran, J (1988) *Juran on Planning for Quality*, The Free Press, New York

King, B (1989) *Better Designs in Half the Time*, Goal/QPC, Methuen, Massachusetts

Mintel (1993) *Quality Assurance and the Consumer*, Mintel

Oakland, J (1995) *Total Quality Management: Text with Cases*, Butterworth/Heinemann, London

Peace, G S (1993) *Taguchi Methods: A Hands-On Approach*, Addison-Wesley, Reading, Massachusetts

Shingo, S (1986) *Zero Quality Control: Source Inspection and the Pokayoke System*, Productivity Press, Bedford

Watson, G (1992) *The Benchmarking Workbook*, Productivity Press, Bedford

Willmott, P (1994) *Total Productive Maintenance: the Western Way*, Butterworth/Heinemann, Oxford

Zeithaml, V P A and Berry, L (1990) *Delivering Quality Service*, Free Press, New York

Recommended Reading

Balbridge evaluation packs, NIST, Route 270 and Quince Orchard Road, Administration Building A537, Gaithersburg, MD20899, USA

Levitt, T (1972) 'Production line approach to service', *Harvard Business Review,* Sept-Oct

Naylor, J (1996) *Operations Management,* Pitman, London

Zeithaml, V P A and Berry, L (1990) *Delivering Quality Service,* Free Press, New York, Chapters 4–7

UNIT 7
PRODUCTIVITY METHODS AND MEASUREMENT

Introduction

In this unit we will concentrate on methods for improving productivity. In particular we will consider one of the key resources of an organisation, its workforce. In this unit, we will look at issues which impinge upon effective **workforce management** from an operations management perspective. We will examine Japanese and Western organisations to learn about factors which lead to employee motivation and commercial success. We will identify the inputs of resources which are utilised in manufacturing, administrative and service systems and we will consider the concepts of productivity measurement and improvement. Finally we will introduce important productivity-raising techniques used by many operations managers: method study and work measurement.

Objectives

By the end of this unit, you should be able to:

- understand workforce management practises in Japanese and Western organisations
- identify resources used by organisations
- define productivity
- choose appropriate productivity raising approaches
- understand the analytical problem-solving methodology of method study
- use the techniques of flow process charting and multiple activity charting
- critically examine key aspects of a job with a view to overall improvements
- use several creative thinking techniques in your search for change
- pull together all the varied aspects present in new method proposals
- appreciate the complexities involved in the installation of a new method
- understand the necessity to maintain the new system so that we continue to attain the correct levels of productivity
- understand how work measurement is undertaken
- explain the significance of the standard time value and the uses of time values in payment schemes and in capacity planning.

SECTION 1

Workforce Management Perspectives

Introduction

In this section we will look at European and Japanese approaches to management and the deployment of human resources.

1.1 European perspectives

In their research undertaken across Europe, Lessem and Neubauer (1994) examined the approaches and styles adopted by managers faced with changing situations and differing cultural mixes. They identified four levels of managerial expertise:

- **attribute-based managers**. These individual managers endeavour to cope with both behavioural and attitudinal changes which are occurring across different organisations and countries.

- **model-based managers**. These senior managers need to handle complex institutional structures and diverse organisational concepts across international frontiers.

- **idea-based managers**. This group of managers develop economic and philosophical ideas about the recovery or growth of a company or a whole industry from a complex set of factors.

- **image-based managers**. These managers seek to influence the external environment – where the customer or client is – either regionally, nationally or internationally.

Within this framework it is possible to see the integral nature of operations management to business enterprise and execution. We will see the problems associated with change. Where productivity needs to be raised, changes in work practices and pay systems may need to be made and wholesale restructuring may become essential. Our concerns from an operations management perspective centre around the first three of these managerial categories in this unit. We cover the image-based manager at the interface with marketing in the units on product design and distribution.

As many of the modern operational management practices have been taken on and fine-tuned to perfection by Japanese business, we look first at the Japanese perspective.

1.2 Japanese perspectives

Japanese economic competitiveness has been founded upon four major factors:

1 Complex systems are managed in simple ways.

This helps to minimise the conflicts which exist between human needs and the requirements of the organisation. Having a harmonious workplace is a vital feature of the Japanese work ethic. The company makes a total commitment to the employee and expects loyalty. It shares knowledge with them and appreciates their ideas and contribution. The employee is involved in the design and operation of the process.

2 There is a clear focus on the human resources available.

This is demonstrated through the drive for quality, the consideration given to employee needs, the emphasis upon teamwork and co-operation and the careful selection of compatible people to fit into the system.

3 The need for high productivity, high quality and precise completion dates is emphasised.

There is a commitment to continuous improvement in the drive to reduce costs.

4 Consensual decision-making is designed into each job (the 'ringi' system).

This is based on a bottom-up strategy, which uses the greater number of people, rather than the top-down approach, which uses only one or two senior figures to make the decisions. Where possible, decisions are made as low down the organisational structure as possible as a result of this empowerment process.

There is a need for vision to define where the business is heading, and to clearly communicate intentions and objectives to the employees. The Japanese value the importance of a cohesive system in which everything fits well. One of the problems which Western businesses have experienced is that it is difficult to attach part of the Japanese approach to a typical European company. For example, quality circles may operate nominally but produce few results due to the fears possessed by the staff. The JIT system needs a chain of suppliers who are similarly interested in quality, reliability and timing in order to minimise stock costs.

A cohesive system correlates the talents of the employees with the organisational objectives and creates an internal environment which allows the development of greater potential.

In order to achieve this, it is necessary for:

- each member of staff to commit themselves to self-development
- each manager to coach his or her staff to maximise his or her potential
- the organisational climate to stimulate the learning process.

This structure is illustrated in diagrammatic form in Figure 1.

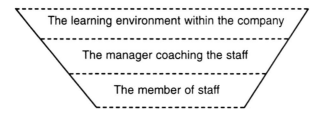

Figure 1: Japanese management approach

The company is seen as a learning organisation, with career development, job performance and skills development opportunities. Appraisal schemes exist to check that all is well, to review the past and set targets for the future. It is the responsibility of management to provide an appropriate environment in which learning can occur. Well-designed jobs underpinned by proven procedures lead to job satisfaction, a motivated workforce and high productivity levels.

With all this in mind let's have a closer look at what productivity is, and some of the techniques which can be used to raise it.

Summary

In this section we first looked at European approaches to management and the deployment of human resources. We then looked at the Japanese approach.

SECTION 2

Productivity

Introduction

In this section, we will define and discuss productivity, how it is measured and techniques for increasing it.

2.1 Definitions

Productivity is the **ratio** between **output** and **input.** We can also define it as the quantitative relationship between what is produced and the resources used. Thus:

$$\text{Productivity} = \frac{\text{Output of goods and services}}{\text{Input of real resources}}$$

Productivity is therefore different from production, which is concerned with volume. It is possible to increase the volume of production and yet decrease productivity.

HOW PRODUCTIVITY IS MEASURED

In practice, productivity is often expressed in terms of different indices, for example:

Labour index = output per employee hour

Material index = output per ton of raw material (or some other measure)

Capital index = output per £1,000 of capital invested.

The basic reasons for the calculation of specific indices are:
- simplicity
- comparison purposes, to observe trends
- in some situations certain indices are of overriding importance, for example, material utilisation would probably be of paramount importance in the diamond-cutting trade.

HOW PRODUCTIVITY CAN BE INCREASED

Productivity can be increased by getting:
- more output from the same input
- same output from less input
- more output from less input
- considerably more output from a little more input
- slightly less output from considerably less input.

Let's consider some examples. A farmer uses better seed and fertiliser to increase corn yield from the same piece of land; costs rise but he or she gets proportionately more return. A tailor finds he or she is able to cut out 11 blouses from a roll of cloth instead of 10 using a different method.

Other definitions include:

1 'A measure of the efficiency with which resources are converted into the products and services that people need.'

2   'Output per employee hour, quality considered.'

3   'The continual improvement of the efficiency of an organisation which results in increasingly efficient use of the materials, labour, plant and machinery available.'

ACTIVITY 1

Use a matrix approach to compare these definitions of productivity:

Are all the definitions saying exactly the same? What differences are there and why?

Definition No.	Quantitative	Resources	Output	Input	Employee hours	Quality
1	√	√	√	√		
2			√		√	√
3	√	√	√	√	√	

ACTIVITY 2

What measures of productivity could you use if you were an operations manager working in:

● a hotel

● a bank

● a firm making video cameras.

You might have considered the following measures:

Hotel:

meals served per day per member of kitchen staff

bed linen laundered per week per member of laundry staff

cost of providing guest rooms relative to revenue generated.

Bank:

successful deals relative to number of enquiries

ratio of customer complaints relative to throughput of business

number of cheques processed per employee per day.

Video camera manufacturer:

output per direct operative per day

ratio of rejects to perfects.

2.2 Resources

Productivity concerns inputs. The inputs include a variety of resources: money, materials, equipment and people. Figure 2 illustrates the flow of input into a productive unit and the flow of output, the product or service.

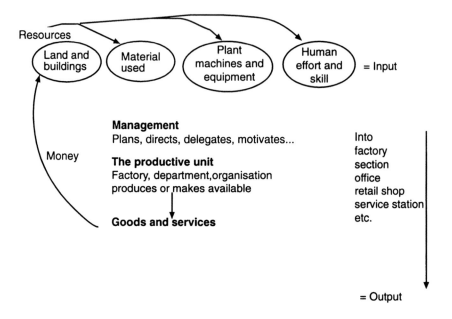

Figure 2: Diagram of the productive unit

FACTORS AFFECTING PRODUCTIVITY

The factors affecting productivity, can be grouped into three main categories:

- **Government policies**: which play an important part in establishing the conditions under which firms operate. Financial policies affect interest rates and therefore the cost of capital and its availability. Tariffs and import quotas are factors which have to be considered prior to investment decisions being taken.

- **Geographical factors**: which affect the availability of indigenous sources of raw materials or fuel. Transportation charges inevitably increases cost.

- **Managerial skill**: which in the final analysis is responsible for the efficient use of all the resources in its control. The degree, or absence, of management skill will greatly affect the productivity of the enterprise through its output.

2.3 Productivity-raising techniques

There are a variety of techniques we can use to increase productivity.

- **Work study:** one of the main productivity-increasing techniques designed to help management to make better use of all resources. It pays close detailed attention to actual productive operations. In many organisations the discipline is called 'management services' or 'organisation and methods'.

- **Capital investment:** productivity can be raised by the injection of capital to purchase new equipment and modernise old. To be effective, capital is often required on a large scale and the results are long term.

- **Simplification and standardisation**: often a matter of basic design coupled with a determination by management to reduce the number and variety of products and equipment. Specification and design can often be simplified.

- **Quality standards**: sometimes unrealistic, with designers and engineers demanding a quality which is far higher than the work requires. The specification of an appropriate quality standard can reduce unnecessarily high costs.

- **Material utilisation**: productivity can be raised by improved control of materials, with regard to purchasing, storage, usage, issuing and transportation, simplification of product design can also affect material costs.

- **Use of plant and equipment**: careful and detailed planning by management is essential to ensure maximum utilisation of expensive plant and equipment. The design and implementation of effective maintenance systems are a particular help in raising productivity.

- **Research and development**: essentially a long-term way of raising productivity. Existing techniques of production are improved and new processes developed, often at considerable capital cost. The results are frequently long term.

- **Use of manpower**: In many situations manpower represents a substantial element of cost. Effective use of manpower is only achievable through good planning based on accurate data, and adequate supervisory control. Many of the above techniques will also have implications for the use of manpower.

ACTIVITY 3

Having carefully looked at the diagram of the productive unit in Figure 2, convert this into an appropriate diagram for your college or university.

You may have produced something like this:

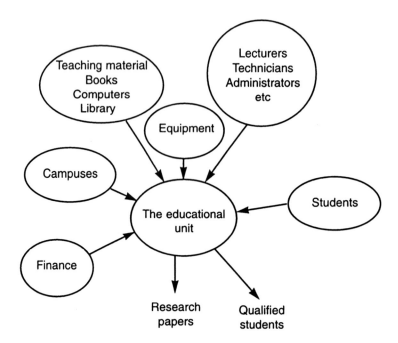

Were your ideas similar? Naturally we are trying to model a complex and dynamic system using paper and pencil, and there is a limit to the detail which we can introduce into the model. In practice you would ensure that the model included all the issues which were important for your particular study programme.

Summary

In this section we began by defining productivity, how it is measured and, in broad terms, how it can be increased. We also examined factors affecting it and we ended with a review of techniques for raising productivity.

SECTION 3

Job Design

Introduction

In this section we will discuss job design and the effects of new technology in the workplace. We will look at strategies for coping with changes and problems arising within the working environment.

3.1 Nature of job design

The careful identification and arrangement of tasks which together build up into a portion of work is called **job design**. For this to be a success in terms of productivity, we must add a further dimension. We need to match the job itself and the individual charged with the responsibility of performing it. The closer the match, the greater will be the motivation of the operator to achieve the objectives laid down in terms of quality and output.

One of the increasingly important factors since the Industrial Revolution has been the degree to which machinery and technology lays down rigid criteria for the performance of at least part of many operations. The move away from craft work into mass production factory systems increasingly drew in the skills of machine-design engineers, electrical engineers and, latterly, computer programmers as technology advanced. Some of the earliest attempts of formal job design were undertaken in the late 1800s by F W Taylor and F B Gilbreth. The approach they pioneered, that of breaking down existing jobs into components called **elements**, and of composing new job routines by building up these elements, is still the method largely used today. The approach led to job specialisation, with a narrow range of component parts, high levels of repetition, minimum training needs and expected high productivity attainment.

The introduction of computer-controlled machine tools and robots into the workplace has resulted in a steady decline in high-volume, routine, monotonous jobs with little stimulus for operator motivation. Administrative jobs within both the manufacturing areas and the office block have moved in the same direction. Routine clerical procedures, job cards, clock cards, worksheets, bonus calculations and quality control sheets have disappeared with the spreading of computer terminals throughout organisations. The result is that those staff who remain tend to have been pushed to the margins of the process. In the manufacturing section they look after the input supply of materials or components, internal storage arrangements and the despatch or distribution of the product. Wider control processes accessed from a computer terminal have been assigned to various support services, for example, health and safety or security. Administratively, staff concentrate much more time now on public relations, customer complaints and quality assurance certification systems, rather than routine clerical work.

3.2 Problems

The fast-changing nature of jobs has presented new types of problem to those involved in job design. Method-study specialists, for example, have not had to contend so much with the effects of physical fatigue in the performance of work but have been faced with combating the extremes of mental fatigue, or complete boredom, in some cases.

ACTIVITY 4

Surveillance systems have been installed in many situations to promote safety and security. Imagine that you are employed to move the cameras, watch the screens and take action where needed in these dissimilar locations: a Premier League football ground; a shopping mall.

What do you think are the problems associated with concentration and motivation? Are there any similarities or differences between the two situations?

The problems are likely to be:

Concentration: at the football ground, the game itself is an attraction and you could miss crowd incidents at moments of excitement in the goalmouth. In the shopping mall, there may be so little incident for long periods you could go to sleep!

Motivation: at the football ground you may be motivated to concentrate on some of the opposing team's 'fans' when watching the crowd for vandalism. In the shopping mall, you could be motivated by financial rewards offered by stores for the arrest and subsequent prosecution of shoplifters.

3.3 Strategies

A number of strategies can be introduced into the design of jobs which are aimed at overcoming the sort of issues we have just been considering. These include **job rotation, job enlargement** and **job enrichment**.

JOB ROTATION SCHEDULES

Staff move to different kinds of work either at set intervals or at the discretion of their supervisor. In a supermarket, for example, a full-time member of staff might expect to spend a third of each 7.5 hour working day in each of the following sections: cashpoint, pricing labels and stock control, loading shelves. Rotation of this kind increases interest, provides variety, widens skills and reduces boredom. From the perspective of management, a more flexible workforce is established, there will be less chance of claims arising for medical conditions such as Repetitive Strain Injury (RSI) and, hopefully, labour turnover will be reduced. Staff may develop an awareness of the value of the internal customer concepts advocated by the TQM approach, and feel a more significant member of a quality circle, as a result of rotation.

Problems can arise in a job rotation arrangement when successive types of work are not at the same skill level. Staff may be under- or overstretched for at least part of the time.

JOB ENLARGEMENT

Appropriate principles can be introduced into the job design process. The aim is to provide the operator with a larger, more significant role relative to the accomplishment of the whole job. The range of tasks given are generally pitched at the same level. This horizontal expansion can be augmented by some vertical dimensioning, for instance in the area of quality checking. An example would be the university lecturer whose original job description centred upon a balance between teaching and research. The work contract was redesigned to include income-generating consultancy, and the quality aspects of new degree proposals.

JOB ENRICHMENT

This is the most comprehensive of the approaches to job design. Much greater emphasis is put upon vertical expansion of work and upon empowering the operator. Self-directed and self-managed teams can be set up and given almost complete responsibility for the accomplishment of the task. Sometimes external liaison with suppliers, customers and legal authorities is undertaken. The work may, on the other hand, be undertaken by one member of staff who has received sufficient training to be able to handle it. An example could be a telephone enquiry about planning permission requirements received at the town council offices. The member of staff interrogates the expert system and gives the caller a preliminary opinion. The staff member then follows this through with a more extensive search, discusses the matter with colleagues, and then word processes and despatches the final decision to the enquirer. If further correspondence ensues, then the member of staff concerned tends to handle it.

In summary, therefore, job enlargement involves a variety of skills, meaningful overall objectives, a degree of autonomy and feedback.

The restructuring of jobs has often led to the need for organisational redesign. When jobs begin to span boundaries, managerial control and accountability becomes more complex. Organisations, or specific divisions within them, may be redesigned along matrix principles rather than the more traditional functional or line and staff structures.

With regard to staff motivation, Herzberg's and Maslow's theories of motivation contend that the kind of points we have been discussing will have little effect unless the basic needs of the staff are being met. This indicates the need for good organisational policies, practices and systems to be in place.

Needs hierarchy theory suggests that workers have a complex set of strong needs which can be placed in a hierarchy and which are underpinned by the following assumptions:

- a satisfied need does not in itself act as a motivator. The fact that another need soon emerges, which itself needs satisfying, causes the drive.
- several needs affect the behaviour of a worker at any one time.
- lower level needs in the hierarchy (which are physiological and security-based) must be satisfied first.
- there is an increasingly wide range of options available to satisfy higher-level needs (affiliation, esteem and self-actualisation).

Later theorists have adapted the work of Maslow. Clayton Alderfer (1972) suggests that there are three sets of basic needs:

- **existence needs** (material needs which are satisfied by food, air, water, pay)
- **relatedness needs** (interpersonal relationships)
- **growth needs** (personal development opportunities).

The implications of these theories to the job designer are obvious, assuming that they model the behavioural realities of the workplace in motivational terms.

Summary

In this section we looked at the features of job design and the problems facing those involved with it as a result of changes in the modern workplace. We considered some of the possible strategies for resolving such problems.

SECTION 4

Problem Solving using the Method Study Approach

Introduction

Job design and redesign often surface as a result of problems in the workplace. As a student of operations management, therefore, you need to look at the question of problem solving using the well-proven approach known as **method study**. We will look at each step in the basic six-step method study procedure in turn and highlight related considerations and techniques

As we saw in Unit 1, the origins of modern work study lies in the era of 'scientific management', which was beginning to gather momentum about a century ago. The names of F W Taylor and F B Gilbreth are always associated with the development of the foundation techniques used in work study. Although many advances have been made since their time through the work of others, or through technological advance, the underlying principles and methodological approach are of great value to the operations manager in job design, problem solving, the setting of standards and motivation of staff.

4.1 Objectives of method study

The objectives of undertaking method study are to:

- eliminate unnecessary work
- reduce unnecessary fatigue
- improve processes and procedures
- improve layouts and methods of materials handling
- make better use of manpower, machines and materials
- improve working conditions
- improve and simplify design
- improve and maintain quality.

These objectives are achieved by collecting the facts, exposing them to searching critical examination and redeveloping methods. Method study is not a science but a systematic and creative way of thinking. It provides a channel for the inventive ability which exists in all organisations. The method study practitioner is not necessarily the inventor or originator of new methods but rather an evaluator of ideas.

4.2 Methodology

The classical analytical problem-solving methodology includes the following steps:
- define
- analyse
- search for alternatives
- evaluate
- decide/specify
- cause acceptance
- initiate/implement
- follow up.

The operations manager who chooses to use this methodology will probably find it helpful to concentrate thinking within the guidelines of the well-proven six-step approach of method study. Generations of problem solvers have used the six steps and learned the order by using the mnemonic **SREDIM**, which stands for **Select, Record, Examine, Develop, Install** and **Maintain**.

We refer throughout this unit to definitions included in the document produced by the British Standards Institute, entitled *'Terms used in work study and organisation and methods'*, BS3138, 1979. (Note: BS stands for British Standards Institute, 3138 identifies the document.)

Here are two important definitions with their reference numbers:

- *10001 Work Study – the systematic examination of activities in order to improve the effective use of human and other material resources*

- *10003 Method Study – the systematic recording and critical examination of ways of doing things in order to make improvements.*

In the following pages we will generally only refer to the definition reference number rather than repeating the document number. There is a definition for many factors in the methodology. They are shown in italics.

Method study is:

- diagnostic (it determines faults}

- remedial (it improves situations)

- constructive (it sets standards for control).

4.3 The basic procedure

The six-step approach, SREDIM, is:

- **Select** — the work to be studied

- **Record** — all the relevant facts about the present method by direct observation

- **Examine** — those facts critically and in ordered sequence, using the techniques best suited to the purpose

- **Develop** — the most practical, economic and effective method, having due regard to all contingent circumstances

- **Install** — that method as standard practice

- **Maintain** — that standard practice by regular routine checks.

You should learn these six steps.

Method study seeks to achieve:

- equal results at lower cost

- better results at same cost

- better results at lower cost.

The relationship between method study and the associated technique of work measurement is shown in Figure 3 (over page). The final result is higher productivity.

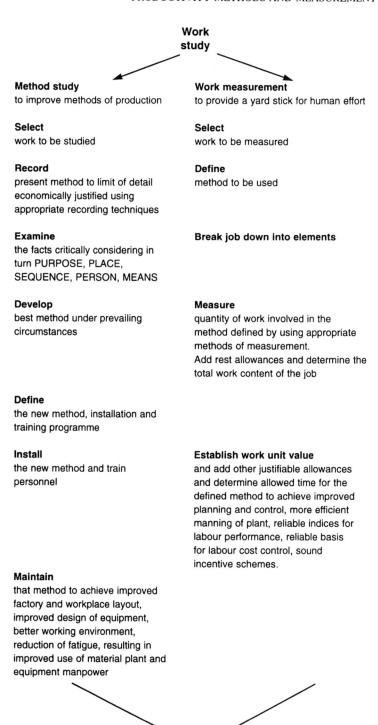

Work study

Method study
to improve methods of production

Work measurement
to provide a yard stick for human effort

Select
work to be studied

Select
work to be measured

Record
present method to limit of detail
economically justified using
appropriate recording techniques

Define
method to be used

Examine
the facts critically considering in
turn PURPOSE, PLACE,
SEQUENCE, PERSON, MEANS

Break job down into elements

Develop
best method under prevailing
circumstances

Measure
quantity of work involved in the
method defined by using appropriate
methods of measurement.
Add rest allowances and determine the
total work content of the job

Define
the new method, installation and
training programme

Install
the new method and train
personnel

Establish work unit value
and add other justifiable allowances
and determine allowed time for the
defined method to achieve improved
planning and control, more efficient
manning of plant, reliable indices for
labour performance, reliable basis
for labour cost control, sound
incentive schemes.

Maintain
that method to achieve improved
factory and workplace layout,
improved design of equipment,
better working environment,
reduction of fatigue, resulting in
improved use of material plant and
equipment manpower

Higher Productivity

Figure 3: Relationship between method study and work measurement

---

ACTIVITY 5

List the reasons why ideally work measurement standards should be set after method study has been undertaken.

If work measurement is undertaken first:

- time standards are fixed on poor methods
- product/service pricing will be higher
- it will be easy to earn high bonuses
- system changes will prove difficult
- many inefficiencies are overlooked
- training will be given on low target outputs.

Each of these factors can prove a major obstacle to later work efficiency.

We now look at the six steps of the methodology in more detail.

4.4 Step 1: Selecting the work to be studied

31003: The process of choosing by systematic means, a specific problem to be solved, or an area of work to be studied.

This is the initial step in the basic method study procedure. Often there is opportunity for the work study practitioner to make decisions on which areas of work are likely to be the most rewarding, and to establish priorities for study work.

In making such decisions there are three aspects which must be taken into account:

- economic considerations
- technical considerations
- human reactions.

ECONOMIC CONSIDERATIONS

These are usually the most important, as method study is concerned with economic use of resources. The need for improvement in a process is not always apparent. It is often the case that existing methods are defective but are accepted simply because they have been long practised and unchallenged. Some jobs, like those with a short-run expectancy and no repeat orders in hand, are economically unattractive, even though methods are poor.

Jobs requiring methods investigation are indicated when they display features like the following:

- the job is a production bottleneck
- there are movements of material over long distances between processes
- lack of balance in labour-intensive teamwork jobs
- highly repetitive, long-running orders have never been method studied before
- poor production planning, which results in too much work-in-progress
- a high reject rate
- wide variations in quality of work
- high labour turnover
- excessive amounts of overtime being worked
- unsafe working practices
- very high relaxation allowances required
- inefficient use of resources (manpower, materials, machines, space)
- improvements envisaged by the operator by means of a suggestion scheme.

TECHNICAL CONSIDERATIONS

There are two areas to be taken into account when selecting work for study:

- The skill, competence and training of the work-study practitioner to handle this particular assignment.
- The technical limitations of the process itself must be borne in mind so that new methods are not 'invented' which will prove unworkable. Specialist technical expertise must often, therefore, be sought, so that investigations are not commenced which have to be abandoned for technical reasons at a later date, with no beneficial outcome.

HUMAN REACTIONS

It is difficult to predict human reactions to work study. There are sometimes strong mental and emotional reactions to investigations into a particular area of work. Very often these feelings lie dormant until changes are formally proposed. Adequate communication is the most helpful way of reducing tensions and suspicions.

Knowledge of local personnel and conditions, together with early consultation with management, trade unions and operators, all help to take human reactions into account at the select stage.

Work study cannot be imposed on operators. Nor can it effectively succeed without the co-operation of supervisors, who are usually the first link between the practitioner and operator at the commencement of work study.

4.5 Step 2: Recording the facts

After selecting the work to be studied, it is essential to *record* all the relevant facts of the existing method. The success of the whole procedure will probably depend on the accuracy with which the facts are recorded.

There are many ways of recording the detail contained in a particular sequence of events. One method is the detailed long-hand account, which is tedious both to produce and comprehend. Consequently a wide range of recording techniques have been developed to cater for the recording of all types of work. These can be broadly classified into:

- charts (for process and time records)
- diagrams and models (for path of movement records)
- written descriptions
- photographic and video techniques.

The graphical or pictorial presentation of data is found to be invaluable to the methods investigator who must study situations, which are often complex, in a systematic way. At a later stage in the investigation it will again be necessary to explain the proposals and these charts and diagrams will be very helpful.

Some recording techniques are easier and cheaper to apply than others in a given situation. Obviously the skilled investigator selects the right tools for the job like any craftsman does. A checklist of relevant data is often found helpful in ensuring that essential background details are not overlooked.

A TYPICAL CHECKLIST

- product/operation or service
- investigation proposer
- reason for the proposal
- suggested limits of the investigation
- job particulars:
    - Output per week?
    - What percentage is this of departmental output ?
    - How long will the job last?
    - Will output levels increase or decrease ?
    - Staffing levels: direct/indirect/administration?
    - Job evaluation grades and pay levels?
    - What are the individual operative output levels?
    - How is payment made?
      (team work, piece work, premium bonus, basic pay etc.)?
    - When were any existing targets or standards set?
    - Has the job any unpleasant or injurious features?
- **Equipment**
    - What equipment is used?
    - What equipment efficiencies are achieved?
- **Layout**
    - Is the existing amount of space adequate or excessive?
    - Which pieces of equipment would be difficult to relocate?
    - Are aisles clearly defined?

● **Product or service**

- Are there frequent changes calling for design modifications?
- Can the product be modified for easy manufacture?
- Can the service be simplified?
- What quality is specified?
- When and how is the product inspected?

● **Savings potential**

- through reduction in the 'work content' of the product or service
- through better equipment efficiency and utilisation
- through better use of labour
- through reduced scrap or wasted time.

In this unit we shall be concentrating on developing skills in two of the work study recording techniques which are of major interest to operations management staff:

● flow process charting
● multiple activity charting.

You have already met these techniques in Unit 6. Additional techniques can be found in the books listed as recommended reading at the end of the unit.

PROCESS CHART SYMBOLS
32003: Symbols used for recording the nature of events.

The five symbols in most common use today were developed by the American Society of Mechanical Engineers (ASME) in 1947.

1   Operation   ○

Indicates the main steps in a process, method or procedure.

Usually the part, material or product concerned is modified or changed during the operation. An operation always takes the material, component or service a step towards completion.

Examples: machining an article; a chemical reaction; screwing a nut to a bolt; unpacking a parcel; tying a knot.

2   Inspection   ▢

Indicates an inspection for quality and/or a check for quantity.

An inspection does not take the material, component or service further towards completion. It simply verifies that specified operations have been done correctly.

Examples: testing yarn; counting rows; checking a part with micrometer; using a spirit level against a wall.

3   **Transportation**

Indicates the movement of workers, materials or equipment from place to place.

Examples: material carried to bench; walk to stores; part moved by conveyor.

4   **Delay (or temporary storage)**

Indicates a delay in the sequence of events.

For example, work or worker waiting between consecutive processes, or any object laid aside temporarily without record until required.

Examples: material awaiting hoist; operative awaiting material; castings awaiting machining.

5   **Storage**

Indicates a controlled storage in which material is received into or issued from a store under some form of authorisation, or an item is retained for reference purposes.

Examples: document in filing cabinet; tools in stores awaiting issue; goods in warehouse.

Note: the difference between $\rbrace$ and $\triangledown$ is that a formal requisition or chit is usually required to get work out of storage, but not out of temporary storage. Delays of more than 24 hours are usually classified as storages.

COMBINED SYMBOLS

When two activities are performed simultaneously, for example, when an inspection is carried out whilst an operation is being performed, then one symbol can be superimposed on another. The activity which seems to be the most important is shown as the outer symbol.

The way the symbols are used on different types of process chart can be seen in Figure 4.

Symbol	Process chart			
	Outline	Flow process chart		Two handed
		Man type	Material type	(or operator)
○	Operation	Operation	Operation	Operation
⇨	–	Transportation	Transportation	Transportation
▢	Inspection	Inspection	Inspection	–
▽	–	–	Storage	Hold
D	–	Delay	Delay	Delay

Figure 4: Flow process and process chart symbols

FLOW PROCESS CHARTS

32004: A process chart setting out the sequence of the flow of a product or a procedure by recording all events under review using the appropriate process chart symbols.

An outline process chart does not show what occurs between operations and inspections. The flow process chart, however, does cover this part of the procedure by use of the additional symbols, transport, storage and delay.

The flow process chart enables systematic analysis to be made of all the events in a process, with the consequent elimination, reduction or combination of operations, inspections, transports, delays and storages.

Two examples of flow process charts follow: study them carefully.

The first is buying a train ticket (Figure 6, see page 363); the second records unloading goods in a warehouse (Activity 6, Figure 7, see page 365).

Note the conventions for dealing with repeat situations and numbering up in symbol series, as shown in Figure 5, (see page 362). Note also the use of standard times. This is the time that it actually takes to do a task and an 'allowance' as the operator cannot work at exactly the same pace throughout the working day. The standard time can be measured in minutes (SMs) or hours (SHrs).

We look at this in more detail in the next section.

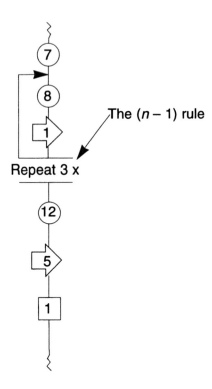

Figure 5: Convention for repeat situations in a flow process chart

This part of a flow process chart shows the repeat convention bracket.

Activities operation 8 and transport 1 occur four times in the work situation charted. The number used in the repeat line is always one less than the total as the first occasion is plotted on the chart, (hence the (n–1) rule).

Flow process chart
Process: Buying a ticket and proceeding to train
Person type: Passenger
Chart begins: Walk to indicator board
Chart ends: Walk to train
Charted by:
Date   2/2/

Present method

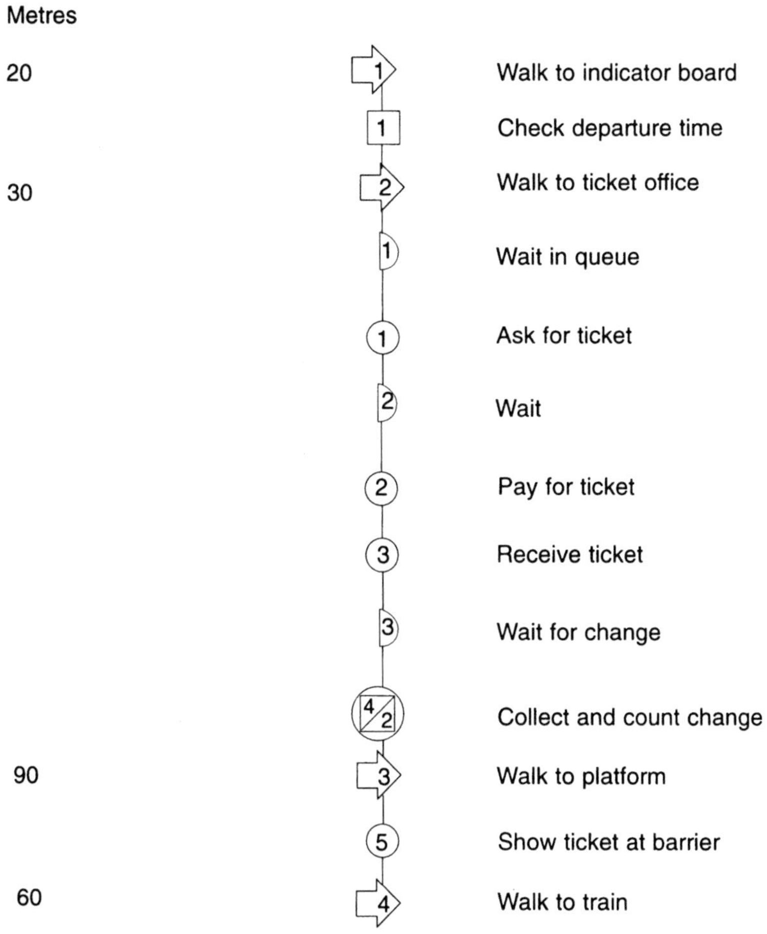

Metres

20	Walk to indicator board
	Check departure time
30	Walk to ticket office
	Wait in queue
	Ask for ticket
	Wait
	Pay for ticket
	Receive ticket
	Wait for change
	Collect and count change
90	Walk to platform
	Show ticket at barrier
60	Walk to train

	Summary	Distance
Operations	5	
Inspections	2	
Transports	4	200m
Delays	3	
Total	14	

Figure 6: Buying a train ticket flow process chart

ACTIVITY 6

Add the process chart symbols to this flow process chart. Hint: the numbers will give you clues!

Flow process chart (m/c-type)
Work sequence: Fork lift truck driver's routine
Raw materials warehouse: Sunrise Engineering Co
Chart begins: Driver on truck in storage area
Chart ends: Driver on truck in storage area

Standard minutes (SMs)	Metres	No.	Description
.40	40	1	Driven to loading bay area
.50		1	Wait whilst dock leveller is fitted
.10	10	2	Driven into back of 20 tonne lorry
.25		1	Lift stack of 3 pallets each with 4 x 50 kg Alum billets
.50	50	3	Driven to billet storage
.33		2	Put down stack of pallets
			Repeat 65 times
1.25		2	Wait whilst driver signs lorry driver's documents
.62	60	134	Driven to manufacturing manager's office
1.70		3	Wait whilst driver gets instructions
.40	42	135	Driven to battery recharger
.20		133	Attached to recharger
.25		1	Voltage tested
.20		134	Detached from recharger
.45	48	136	Driven to storage area to await next job

Summary Symbol	Total	Time	Distance
○	134	38.68	–
D	3	3.45	–
⇨	136	41.47	4150
□	1	.25	–
Totals	274	83.85	4150

Flow process chart (m/c-type)
Work sequence: Fork lift truck driver's routine
Raw materials warehouse: Sunrise Engineering Co
Chart begins: Driver on truck in storage area
Chart ends: Driver on truck in storage area

Standard minutes (SMs)	Metres		Description
.40	40	1	Driven to loading bay area
.50		1	Wait whilst dock leveller is fitted
.10	10	2	Driven into back of 20 tonne lorry
.25		1	Lift stack of 3 pallets each with 4 x 50 kg Alum billets
.50	50	3	Driven to billet storage
.33		2	Put down stack of pallets
			Repeat 65 times
1.25		2	Wait whilst driver signs lorry driver's documents
.62	60	134	Driven to manufacturing manager's office
1.70		3	Wait whilst driver gets instructions
.40	42	135	Driven to battery recharger
.20		133	Attached to recharger
.25		1	Voltage tested
.20		134	Detached from recharger
.45	48	136	Driven to storage area to await next job

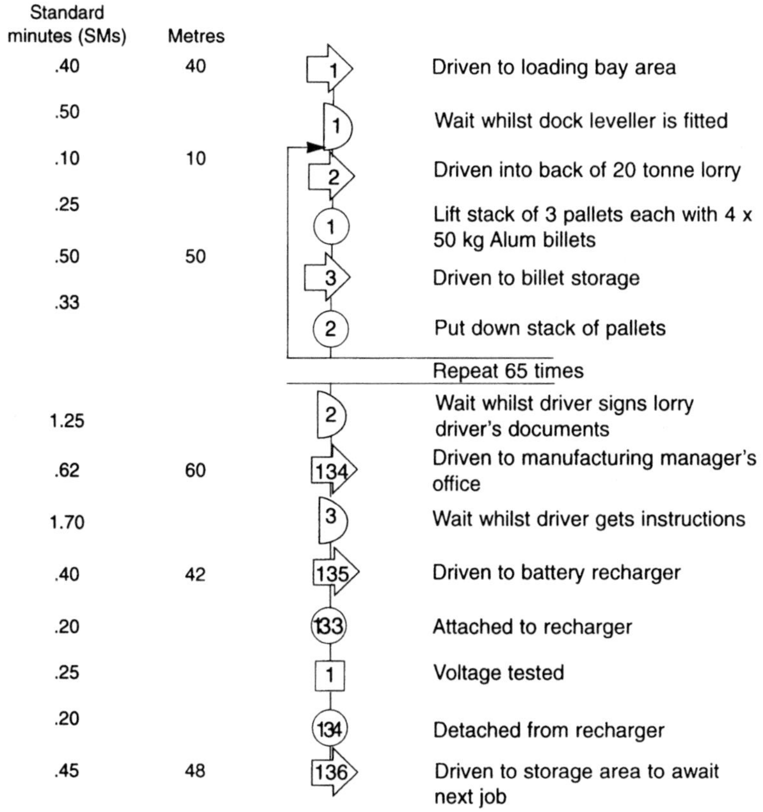

Summary Symbol	Total	Time	Distance
◯	134	38.68	–
◗	3	3.45	–
⇨	136	41.47	4150
▢	1	.25	–
Totals	274	83.85	4150

Figure 7: Completed flow process chart for unloading goods in a warehouse

ACTIVITY 7

Complete this flow process chart.

Flow process chart
Task: Counter service in a fast-food restaurant
Type of chart: Person   Present method

		Metres
Take customer's order (oral/aural)	①	
Walk to bag storage hopper	⇨ 1	4 m
Select correct size bag	②⃠1	
Walk to hamburger heated cabinet		2 m
Pick up hamburger		
Place hamburger in bag		
Return to counter		2 m
Put down bag		
Walk to chip hopper		3 m
Pick up scoop		
Pick up container		
Scoop chips into container		
Put down scoop		
Walk to counter		3 m
Put down container of chips		
Ask customer for payment		
Receive exact payment		
Check payment		
Open till		
Put coins into correct sections		
Close till		
Push order across counter to customer		

Summary

○	16	
□	3	
◗	0	
⇨	5	14 m

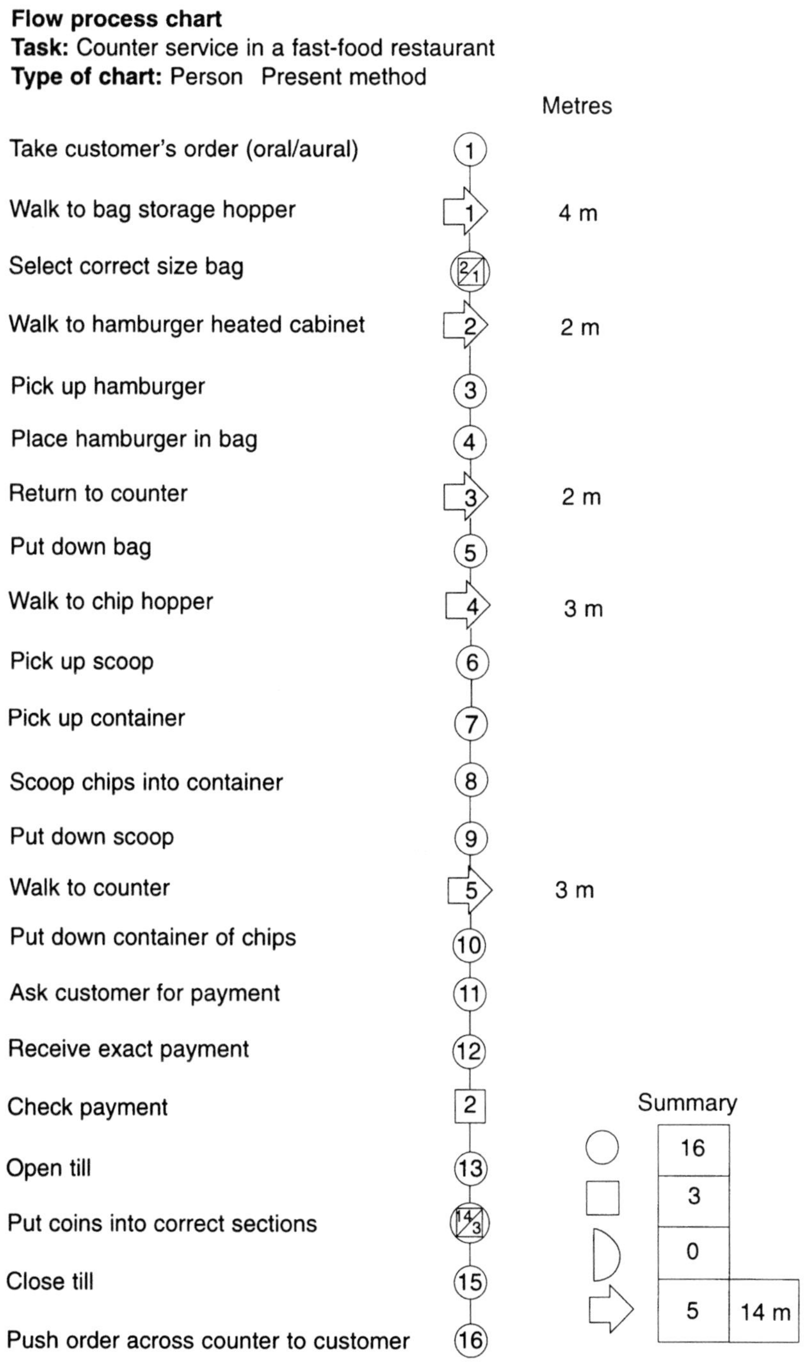

Flow process chart
Task: Counter service in a fast-food restaurant
Type of chart: Person   Present method

		Metres
Take customer's order (oral/aural)	①	
Walk to bag storage hopper	⇨1	4 m
Select correct size bag	②1	
Walk to hamburger heated cabinet	⇨2	2 m
Pick up hamburger	③	
Place hamburger in bag	④	
Return to counter	⇨3	2 m
Put down bag	⑤	
Walk to chip hopper	⇨4	3 m
Pick up scoop	⑥	
Pick up container	⑦	
Scoop chips into container	⑧	
Put down scoop	⑨	
Walk to counter	⇨5	3 m
Put down container of chips	⑩	
Ask customer for payment	⑪	
Receive exact payment	⑫	
Check payment	2	
Open till	⑬	
Put coins into correct sections	⑭3	
Close till	⑮	
Push order across counter to customer	⑯	

Summary

○	16
□	3
D	0
⇨	5 14 m

Figure 8: Completed flow process chart for serving a customer
in a fast-food restaurant

MULTIPLE ACTIVITY CHARTS

32017: A chart on which the activities of more than one subject (worker, equipment or material) are each recorded on a common time-scale to show their inter-relationship.

In a situation where there are two or more related activities being carried out in close association with one another, requiring a balance to be achieved, multiple activity charts are the most suitable recording technique. Each separate group of activities is shown in bar form alongside all other related activities against a common time-scale.

Construction

There are a series of steps you go through to construct a multiple activity chart:

- Prepare a flow process chart for each operative or machine involved in the process.
- Activities recorded must then be grouped into convenient 'elements' for time study.
- Sufficient time study observations must be taken so that an accurate elemental time can be obtained.
- A start is then made on the drawing of the chart by setting out in bar form the activities of the leading operative or machine together with the time scale. The work cycles of other operatives or machines are then plotted in adjacent bars using the same timescale.
- The different sections within each bar should be colour coded, and the amount of effective work per cycle calculated as a percentage.

Design

An example of a multiple activity chart is given in Figure 9.

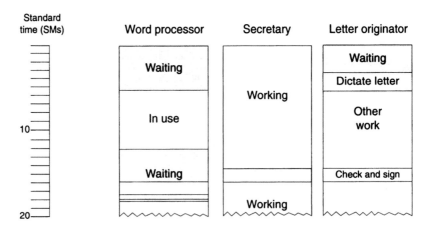

Figure 9: Multiple activity chart for producing a letter, originated by a manager, and typed by a secretary using a word processor

Application

A multiple activity chart may be used to record activities in the following types of situation:

- one operative running one machine
- one operative running several machines
- several operatives running one machine
- several operatives running several machines
- a team of operatives
- a bank of machines.

It is essential that the multiple activity chart shows a representative section of the work being studied. The pace of the operation is controlled by the operative or machine whose job has the greatest work content.

Examination of the multiple activity chart will show the possibilities of elimination, change of sequence, combination and simplification which exist. For example, in the case of a man-machine relationship it may be possible to:

- install an additional machine
- introduce extra 'inside cycle' work to increase the operative utilisation percentage
- simplify loading and unloading procedures to minimise stopped time between operating cycles.

ACTIVITY 8

Construct the multiple activity chart for the following procedure.

Servicing a car

Three mechanics are required. A new lubricating machine requiring two men to operate it has just been installed. The following duties, with times in standard minutes, are performed on each service.

Mechanic 'A' washes and waxes the car (50), whilst 'B' changes the plugs (20) and changes the oil and filter (40). 'C' has commenced by changing the points (10). Mechanics A and C then use the lubricating machine (40), whilst 'B' drains and refills the radiator (10), and then tunes the engine (30).

Finally, 'C' checks the lights (20) whilst 'A' adjusts the brakes (30) and 'B' checks the tyre pressures (10).

The service is then complete. The normal working day is eight hours plus two hours overtime.

Ignore any constraints on sequencing. If you are technically minded do not worry about the 'logic', and assume that this is a typical car service.

Here is our solution:

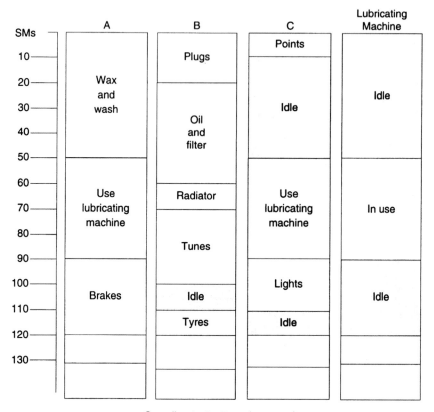

Overall output = 5 services per day

Figure 10: Multiple activity chart for three operators servicing a car

Note that a range of calculations can be developed from multiple activity charts. eg. operator occupation %s, machine utilisation %s , productivity indices, balancing loss %s

4.6 Step 3: Critical examination

3400: The systematic analysis of information about a problem, procedure or activity, by which it is subjected to exhaustive challenge with regard to need, simplification, combination, sequence and alternatives.

PURPOSE

The purpose of critical examination is to determine the true reason underlying each event and to draw up systematically a list of all the possible improvements for later consideration and possible incorporation into a new and more effective method. This step is the crux of the basic procedure of method study and is dependent for its effectiveness on the accuracy and completeness of the recording of the present method.

Every aspect of the work being studied must be critically analysed in the light of the information recorded, much of it written on to critical examination sheets.

The whole examination procedure requires exhaustive collaboration with everyone who can offer useful information, and full use must be made of all sources of technical information. When examining the recorded facts of a process it is important that a systematic approach is followed from start to finish. The examination involves focusing on one step of the process at a time. The charting and subsequent analysis provide the work study officer with detailed facts about a process and the underlying reasons for each item on the chart. The work study officer is then in a position to review the process as a whole and again making full use of consultation, can seek the alternatives which will be the basis of any new methods.

GENERAL APPROACH

Critical examination requires, above all, the correct attitude of mental self-discipline, in which the following guidelines should be followed:

- Facts must be examined *as they are*, not as they appear to be, should be, or are said to be.
- Preconceived ideas which often colour the interpretation of facts must be ruthlessly discarded.
- All aspects of the problem must be approached with a challenging and sceptical attitude. Every detail must be examined logically and no answer accepted until it has been *proved* correct.
- Hasty judgements must be avoided.
- Hunches should be committed to paper and then put away for consideration later in the study.
- New methods should not be considered until all the facts about the existing method have been exposed by systematic examination.

CLASSIFICATION OF OPERATIONS

Although transports and delays may, on the surface, appear to give the greatest scope for improvement, the best results are achieved by studying certain **operations** first.

Operations can be classified as:

- **make ready operations:** These are preparatory 'operations' concerned with the preparation of material, plant or equipment, which enable the actual work to be done.
- **key operations:** These represent the actual performance of work that adds value to the product and which normally result in a change in the properties or characteristics of the material.
- **put away operations**: These are concerned with the placing aside or clearing up after the 'key' operations.

The greatest room for improvement lies in eliminating the key operations for if this can be done, the 'make ready' and 'put away' operations associated with them will be eliminated, as well as corresponding delays and transports. Even if the key operations cannot be eliminated, questioning them *first* (where, when, how, etc.) offers the best chance of generating worthwhile alternatives since they constitute the framework around which the job as a whole is built up.

EXAMINATION PROCEDURE

A thorough critical examination consists of three main stages:

- examination of the operation as a whole.
- detailed analysis of the key operations and/or inspections (known as the 'key concept')
- final analysis, where justified, of the 'movements', 'delays' and 'storages' arising from the second stage of the examination.

DETAILED CRITICAL ANALYSIS

This part of the procedure is the heart of method study and consists of a searching or detailed analysis of the key operations and inspections. Each of these key operations and inspections is treated separately for the purpose of critical analysis and is subjected to a systematic questioning procedure.

The examination is achieved by means of two sets of questions: the **primary questions** to establish the facts and the reasons underlying them, and the **secondary questions** to indicate the alternatives and consequently the possible improvements.

PRIMARY QUESTIONS

34006: The first stage in which the fundamental need for performing, each activity recorded, and its place, sequence, person and means are questioned and justification is sought for each reply.

The following are the primary questions under their respective headings:

Purpose: the questions **What is achieved?**, **Is it necessary?** and **Why?**, challenge the existence of the activity. If these questions show that an operation can be eliminated, it is not necessary to ask the remaining questions.

Place: the questions asked under this heading are: **Where is it done?** and **Why then?**

Person: the next questions refer to the person performing the activity. They are: **Who does it?** and **Why that person?**

Means: finally the means of carrying out the activity are challenged by asking **How is it done?** and **Why that way?**

The first question, **What is achieved?** is worth spending a lot of time on. We are critically examining an activity. The activity has an end-result – the achievement. We are here questioning *purpose*, and *purpose* is a way of expressing the *need* to achieve a particular *result*.

Critical examination is a logical way of generating new ideas. It will succeed only if the user has the courage and determination to follow up the implications of the answers to the questions asked.

SECONDARY QUESTIONS

34006: The second stage, in which the remaining essential activities are subjected to further questions to determine alternatives and to select those which are practicable and preferable.

We are questioning the need for the (precisely-stated) results of an activity and asking: **What else could be done or achieved?**. Having completed the questioning of purpose, we can then proceed to consider place, sequence, person, etc. in the same way. For instance, **Where is it done?**, **Why there?** lead naturally to **Where else could it be done?**, similarly with **When else?**, **Who else?** and **How else?**

In all cases, the primary questions should be answered carefully and factually, in precise terms, covering all aspects. Alternatives can be easily generated by applying simple logic questions, for example, '*not* there' implies somewhere else, hence, **Where else might it take place?** Similarly, '*not* then', '*not* that person', '*not* that way' will be found to imply whole ranges of alternatives based on **When else?**, **Who else?** and **How else?** A guide sheet is often found to be helpful and is included as Resource 7.1.

As in all brainstorming approaches of this type, any alternatives generated should at first be listed uncritically. Only later should they be subjected to evaluation and tests for practicability and preferability. In the value analysis technique, a team approach at this stage is normal practice, and there is evidence that the same is desirable in method study at the critical examination stage. In the team approach, it is absolutely imperative to obey the rule 'no criticism of ideas' as they emerge, otherwise inspiration dries up.

Evaluation

Strictly speaking, when alternative possibilities have been generated for a particular activity (under What else could be done?, When else?, Where else? etc.) the critical examination is at an end and the evaluation or development stage starts. 'Selection for development' is sometimes included as part of critical examination, however. This is an assessment of the possibilities and is generally separated into short-term and long-term changes. The questions **What should be done?**, **Where should it be done?**, etc. are used to indicate this selection.

SUMMARY OF CRITICAL EXAMINATION

We can summarise the sequence of the examination to which each job and then each activity is subjected as follows:

Purpose	What is achieved?
	Is it necessary? Why?
	What else could be done?
	What should be done?
Place	Where is it done?
	Why there?
	Where else could it be done?
	Where should it be done?
Sequence	When is it done?
	Why then?

When else could it be done?
When should it be done?

Person   Who does it?
Why that person?
Who else could do it?
Who should do it?

Means   How is it done?
Why that way?
How else could it be done?
How should it be done?

Modern practice is to use a guide sheet as shown in Resource 7.2. A line is drawn across when each section is completed. An example of a partly completed guide sheet for a particular activity, in this case, packing goods into a carton, is shown in Resource 7.3.

ACTIVITY 9

Why is the 'key concept' useful? Why not begin improvement by elimination of waiting time?

The 'key concept' focuses attention on fundamental aspects of the job. If we thoroughly undertake critical examination on these aspects we will probably find that many ancillary aspects will be eliminated or changed. If we concentrate initially on reducing or eliminating waiting time, we will not be examining the major issues and the scope for productivity improvement is limited.

Creative thinking techniques can be used during the critical examination stage of a method study investigation. You studied some of these in Unit 2. A further approach, heuristical thinking, can be useful.

HEURISTICAL THINKING

Heuristic means discovery. It was originally used to study the methods and rules of discovery and invention. It follows a 'trial and error' approach.

The heuristic calculation of an answer to a problem follows this pattern:

- decide the solution required
- calculate a result from the known data
- is the result anything like the requirement?
- recalculate to bring the result nearer to requirement
- continue recalculating until the solution is reached.

Let's look at a mathematical example:
square root of 24 is required
$5 \times 5 = 25$
similar, but too high
try, $4.8 \times 4.8 = 23.04$

too low
try, 4.92 × 4.92 = 24.10 etc., etc.

Heuristics can be used to handle ill-structured problems. We need to consider the present situation, and the kind of situation which we want to reach. We prepare a solution and compare it with the objective. Deficiencies are examined and another trial solution attempted. Heuristic reasoning is good in itself but if you are a thorough problem solver you may prefer the analytical approach when you can do this. An example of someone using a heuristic approach is the central heating installer. The task is to connect two pipes already installed with a further piece of pipe, which goes around an awkward bend. An analytical approach would demand a careful measurement of the situation, and then a drawing from which a suitable piece of pipe could be cut and bent in the workshop. Hopefully the piece of pipe would fit exactly. The heuristic approach would mean that the installer took a piece of pipe approximately of the right length and commenced to bend it to shape. By trial and error the right shape is reached and the pipe then cut to length and fitted it into the system. Here, the heuristic solution may achieve perfectly satisfactory results, in much less time.

ACTIVITY 10

Use the brainstorming technique we outlined in Unit 2 with several colleagues if you can. Spend 15 minutes generating ideas on a topic. Here are two possible topics:

- How could a local petrol station improve its public image?
- How could a college or university promote its courses?

How many ideas did you achieve? For the petrol station, you probably thought of considerations like:

- paint the premises
- improve customer service
- sell a range of motor accessories
- have a do-it-yourself facility etc.

If you achieved 40 or 50 ideas, some may be very similar. You would probably need to classify the ideas in some way, for example, staffing, equipment, facilities, quality etc.

4.7 Step 4: Developing the new method

Critical examination is closely linked with the development stage of the basic method study procedure. Amongst the points which will have been established are:

- Activities which are vital to the achievement of the objective.
- Sequences of vital activities which can be contemplated.
- Those activities which can be completely eliminated.
- Combinations of vital activities which are possible.
- Full range of alternatives with short- and long-term preferences.

The process of developing a new method consists of the formal evaluation of the possibilities available and the selection of the solution which best meets the objectives established at the beginning of the investigation. In development work it is essential to:

- work with facts, not opinions
- work on causes, not effects
- work with reasons, not excuses.

Possibly the best way to develop a new method is to select an ideal proposal to cover each essential activity, and then to obtain compatibility by minimal amounts of compromise on each proposal. The solution may, even then, be rejected in favour of something less attractive but cheaper and easier to implement.

The use of specially-designed development stage sheets (see Resource 7.4) is found helpful by many method study practitioners. A whole series of critical examination sheets are prepared prior to moving into the development stage. Remember that some degree of iteration may be necessary. You may need to go back to earlier stages before moving forward through the methodology again.

PROCESS OF DEVELOPMENT

Consultation

During the process of recording and examination the method study practitioner will have had a considerable amount of dealings with persons involved with various aspects of the task. At the development and evaluation stages, the process of consultation must continue until the practitioner is satisfied that the proposals are valid and realistic and can be put in a report for submission to line management. The groups of people likely to be involved in consultation over new method proposals would be:

- Line management, at the appropriate level for particular points.
- Technical specialists, who will give advice where design, quality or manufacturing changes are proposed.
- Works engineering personnel, where machine or layout modifications are desirable.
- Operatives and their representatives, particularly when trials and evaluations need to be performed.

Departmental layout

Features of departmental layout will need consideration.

- Realistic proposals must be translated into a practical and detailed layout. The specific use of each square metre of floor space should be stated. The access to all work stations must be planned.

- Workplace storage areas need to be carefully designed.

- Consideration should be given to the nature of each process in the layout. If any have undesirable features which cannot be eliminated, effort should be made to minimise the effects of such features. For example, dust migration can be prevented by extraction or localised by plastic curtains. Sound can be baffled by carpeting offices.

- Ergonomic aspects must be built in.

- Gangways should be logically planned and provide access to and from all work areas. Selected width should relate to the nature and volume of traffic.

- Floor loading capacities should be borne in mind.

- The location of mains services (drains, steam, water, gas, electricity etc.) should be taken into account.

Envisaged equipment

It is necessary to specify the type and quantities of work tables, trucks, racks, conveyors, containers, tools, jigs and fixtures, desks, computer terminals, lockers, filing cabinets etc. required in the new system. Trade literature will usually be consulted and the advice of outside suppliers, with quotations and delivery times, will normally be sought.

Personnel matters

Personal matters will need consideration.

- Where working methods are changed, estimates of any effect in staffing levels must be made. Work measurement data will be particularly useful in this connection.

- Specific plans for dealing with labour which is superfluous to requirements must be drawn up in conjunction with the personnel function. The kind of options normally open are: transference within the firm or group; reduction by natural wastage; encouragement and help in finding alternative employment. In the case of redundancy, payments would obviously be a cost set against savings.

- Plans for training operatives in the new working methods must be prepared.

Organisational changes

Fundamental changes will result in a need for revision of the system of recording and controlling output. Alterations to the paperwork and supervisory arrangements must be proposed in such circumstances.

In order to be realistic, a proposal must satisfy the following:

- **safety regulations**. There must be no short cuts at the expense of operator safety, or infringement of factory or office legislation

- **quality standards.** Changes must not detract from quality standards laid down by specification

- **stringent trials, tests and evaluations.** These must satisfy all concerned of the validity of the proposals

- **desired output levels.** The original terms of reference must be kept in mind when assessing realistic output potential

- **additional resource constraints.** There must be the possibility of the required resources being made available.

4.8 Step 5: Installing the new method

By following the basic procedure of method study, the stage is eventually reached at which an improved method is ready to be discussed by all parties concerned. A formal report will have been prepared and circulated in advance of any arranged meeting. When a meeting is arranged, obviously any agreed negotiating procedures existing in the firm must be followed.

In situations where method changes are being proposed, various levels of management, operatives and their unions would normally be represented.

Four separate phases in the installation stage can be discerned: **selling the proposal, preparing for installation, commencing the new method** and **initial monitoring.**

1 'SELLING' THE PROPOSAL

The stage of convincing all parties concerned about the advantages of adopting the proposed method is often called **selling.** Approval must be gained from the various people in the organisation affected by the proposal. The method study practitioner must convince management that he or she is competent and that real benefit will accrue from the proposal. He or she must convince the operatives and their trade union representatives that the work is factual and unbiased, and that the proposal will make easier and safer working procedures. Often, a method proposal is presented as part of a package, in which monetary matters are also raised for discussion.

Many questions will be raised during the discussions and the method study practitioner must be prepared to deal confidently and squarely with all matters. Lack of enthusiasm or a weak presentation will not commend the method proposal.

2 PREPARATION FOR INSTALLATION

A method proposal may require complete acceptance before any real preparation for installation can be undertaken. Machinery and plant may need to be purchased or structural alterations made. In such cases, once final decisions have been taken it may prove expensive to alter or cancel the plan at a later date.

The nature of some method proposals, however, permits a provisional acceptance on behalf of the parties concerned. There is often an undertaking that regular review meetings will take place in the weeks immediately following installation, and minor changes to the method made, as the need arises, with the consent of all parties.

The preparation stage can be viewed in three aspects: **planning, arranging** and **rehearsing.**

Planning

- One person only should be responsible for installation planning and all persons concerned should be aware of the identify of that person.
- Actual dates for each stage of installation should be fixed and published.

Arranging

- All layouts must be checked in detail to ensure all the necessary plant, tools and equipment are available and services laid on.
- Old stocks of raw materials and bought-out parts must be progressively reduced, and the build-up of new supplies continued as the installation date draws near.
- New control systems must be set up.
- Arrangements must be made when a change of shift working is involved.
- Training in new methods must be provided, away from the working area if possible.

Rehearsing

Rehearsals enable operatives to familiarise themselves with the new method, and various management specialists to check that their requirements are also likely to be met, for example quality controllers, who will want to be certain quality standards are going to be maintained, and plant engineers, who will want to ensure that no unsafe working practices are being introduced. Rehearsals or trial runs are often arranged outside normal working hours.

3 COMMENCEMENT OF THE NEW METHOD

- Physical changes of layout and stocks are best done just before the commencement of the method. Loss of output is minimised if comparatively simple changes are made over the weekend or more complex changes are made during the works' shutdown period.
- Close supervision is essential during the first few days to ensure all persons concerned are co-operating and to give immediate decisions on snags which arise.
- Where any minor modifications have to be made in the early days with mutual agreement, they must be incorporated in the work specification.
- Adequate stocks of materials and a free flow of containers, crates, trucks etc. must be maintained.
- There must be close liaison between the method study practitioner and relevant staff to ensure that installation strictly follows the prescribed plan.

4 INITIAL MONITORING

- Devise and operate a performance monitoring system. Feed in data on a daily basis. This will be simpler if standard times and an incentive scheme are also being introduced with the method. Calculate daily performances on individual and group bases and feed back information to the department concerned.

- Determine the new levels of lost time, breakdowns, scrap and rectification and compare with the original system. Get such levels as low as possible.

- If an incentive scheme is being introduced, ensure any geared features operating during the lead-in period are applied, and reflected in wage payments.

- Collate and list all data obtained from the new system in readiness for discussion at the review meetings.

4.9 Step 6: Maintaining the new method

The installation stage ends with the new method operating smoothly at the expected output levels. The working practices at this stage should square up exactly with the details given in the work specification. (See example in Resource 7.5.)

An agreed working procedure can only be maintained by constant vigil on the part of the work study function. In almost any working environment, changes can occur within a comparatively short period, which will radically affect safety, quality and speed. The variations from standard practice which thereby arise, must be noted and evaluated.

Changes can occur in three main ways:

- deliberate alterations with good reason
- gradually and without intention
- deliberate but unauthorised changes by either operator or supervisor.

An efficient review policy will highlight such changes. The frequency of review will depend on the nature of the work.

DELIBERATE ALTERATIONS WITH GOOD REASON

If changes of this nature are discovered by the review, when the working practices are compared with the work specification, the work study practitioner will:

- ascertain who authorised the change
- stress to that person the need for communication with the work study department on such matters, *before* any change is made
- investigate the effect of the change
- consult with all concerned on the findings and either revert, or amend both work specification and standard times.

The effect of the review will make management 'method conscious'. The introduction of a formal system which indicates proposed or likely changes in advance to the operations management staff should be introduced. A suitable form to cover method changes can be designed and provided to appropriate staff and functional areas to record these method changes. An example is shown in Resource 7.6.

CHANGES WHICH OCCUR GRADUALLY AND UNINTENTIONALLY

These kind of changes are often minute and almost imperceptible. For example, the oiling or servicing of a clamp makes operation easier. The repair of a bench results in new tool locations. These changes, when observed, must be evaluated and assessed. If beneficial, they must be formally incorporated into the work specification, and adjustment made to the standard times. If detrimental, there must be reversion back and an explanation given. If obvious 'gaps' have appeared in the system, which are undesirable, the practitioner must consider how they can be plugged.

DELIBERATE BUT UNAUTHORISED CHANGES

Deliberate but unauthorised changes may be carried out by:

- operator
- technologists
- supervision
- maintenance staff.

These changes, when observed, must be highlighted. The role of supervision must be stressed. The authority for change when a work studied specified job needs amendment is an agreement between the work study department, supervision and operator representatives that attention is required.

ACTIVITY 11

Explain why we need to use the SREDIM methodology in an iterative way when solving real-world methods problems.

We often find we do not have enough information to proceed satisfactorily. When critically examining, we may need to iterate back into the record stage to gather more information on some aspect of the method which we had overlooked. Another situation could arise when we are selling the proposal to the staff concerned. If just one or two points need rethinking before acceptance, we will need to iterate back into the develop stage or even further back into the critical examination stage, before finding new aspects to fit into the proposal.

4.10 Failure of projects

There are a number of reasons why some method study assignments do not lead to a successful application. It is fair to say, however, that if the detailed methodology is followed carefully through all stages there should be a high level of probability of a successful outcome. Where particular difficulties are identified during the assignment, they can either be addressed, or the assignment suspended or aborted.

Here are some of the reasons why a completed assignment is never actually installed:

● circumstances have changed since the study began
● management dislikes certain features in the proposal
● opposition from the staff who are involved
● unwillingness of management to provide resourcing.

ACTIVITY 12

Think through each of these four reasons and give a practical example of each.

Here are some examples:

circumstances: a large, long-running customer order has been lost; competitor has gone bankrupt; government regulations have changed

management dislike: the proposal recommends higher staffing in order to maximise usage of an expensive machine

staff opposition: the prospect of retraining, relocation or redundancy is feared

lack of resourcing: management will not supply money for an essential computer package to be bought.

Once a new system has been successfully installed, it is essential that maintenance is undertaken. Failure to do this will lead to a loss of efficiency due to general slippage which can occur in many directions. The next piece of method study undertaken to resolve the new problems will be more difficult both to undertake and to install.

Summary

In this section we examined in detail the contribution of work study to job design, problem solving, and to setting standards and motivating staff. We considered each of the six steps (SREDIM) in the method study approach and related considerations and techniques.

SECTION 5

Work Measurement

Introduction

Having established the need for sound, safe and productive work methods, we now consider the time content of jobs. This factor needs careful determination because it can be applied to many issues. Its importance was realised centuries ago, and recorded details of time studies undertaken by Leonardo da Vinci (Italy) and Jean Perronet (France) exist. We will look at the basic procedure of work measurement and then at the techniques of time study, activity sampling, predetermined time motion standards and analytical and comparative estimating. We discuss briefly financial incentive schemes.

Clandestine time studies were being undertaken in the UK in the 1790s in the pottery industry for production planning, and Charles Babbage, the Cambridge University mathematician, was an industrial adviser on time study and cost accounting in the 1830s. The whole concept of precise and detailed time study was brought into focus through the work of F W Taylor (USA) in the late 1800s. The philosophy which underpinned Taylor's work can be summarised:

- developing a science for each element of a person's work to replace guesswork
- selecting best worker for each particular job
- training, teaching and developing each worker in the job
- improving management/staff co-operation
- apportioning of work to allocate equal shares of responsibility to both management and staff.

Although many of Taylor's objectives were not fully achieved in his lifetime, and there have been many critics of his approach, it is interesting to relate them to the business situation today. The last two in the list given, for example, sit very comfortably in a total quality framework.

The article 'Roots', Resource Item 1.1, gives further information about the work of some of the pioneers in this field.

5.1 Methodology

10004: Work measurement is the application of techniques designed to establish the time for a qualified worker to carry out a task at a defined rate of working.

Work measurement provides management with a means of measuring the time taken to perform of an operation so that ineffective time can be highlighted. It is used for:

- comparing the effectiveness of different methods
- balancing the work of team members
- determining operator machine loadings
- providing planning and scheduling data
- providing cost estimates, delivery dates, selling prices
- setting standards of machine utilisation
- designing incentive schemes to stimulate labour performance
- providing data for a labour cost control system.

Work measurement provides the basic information necessary for all the activities of organising and controlling the work of an enterprise in which the time element plays a part.

Work measurement techniques in use are:

- time study
- activity sampling and rated activity sampling
- predetermined motion time standards
- analytical and comparative estimating.

THE BASIC PROCEDURE

As for method study, a systematic six-step approach is used:

1   **Select** the work to be studied.

2   **Record** all the relevant data relating to the circumstances in which the work is being done, the methods and the elements of activity in them.

3   **Measure** each element in terms of time over a sufficient number of cycles of activity to ensure that a representative picture has been obtained.

4   **Examine** the recorded data and element times critically to ensure that unproductive or random elements are separated from productive elements. Examine the recorded times of each element and determine a representative time for each.

5   **Compile** a time for the operation which will provide a realistic standard of performance and will include time allowances to cover suitable rest, personal needs, contingencies etc.

6   **Define** precisely the series of activities and method of operation for which the time has been allowed and issue the time as standard for the activities and methods specified.

We use a methodology like the six-step approach in applying work measurement so that we will work efficiently. It is easy for many important details to be missed which will invalidate the actual standard minute value. For example, we may include elements which really need to be excluded, or undertake work which is already on file, having been done before.

5.2 Time study

Once the work has been selected for study, the time study practitioner has to decide which technique is appropriate. If the approach selected involves time study, the following steps must be undertaken:

- Obtain all relevant details about the job, the operator, the machine and its environment, together with a complete description of the method.
- Attend to the normal industrial relations courtesies which should precede all study work.
- Make a number of fairly broad-detail time study observations of the main parts of the job.
- Decide on an appropriate elemental breakdown and define breakpoints.
- Select appropriate study periods.
- Undertake a series of time studies, and measure the time taken by the operator to perform each element. Assess working performance levels for each completed element of work.
- Ensure work study covers all aspects of the job.

The practitioner then analyses this work measurement data to produce information in the form in which it is required, for example as a basis for an incentive scheme. A special kind of stop watch is normally used for time study, although many practitioners are now being trained in the use of computerised time study boards. The advantage of these systems is the greatly reduced analysis time following study work. Times are normally recorded in 1/100ths of a minute (deciminutes or centiminutes). Care should be taken in describing time values in terms of the unit used, for example 0.60 centiminutes is equal to 36 seconds.

TIMING METHODS
- **Flyback analogue-type watch:** The hands return to zero every time the central plunger is depressed. The slide on the side of the watch is used to start and stop it.
- **Flyback digital-type watch:** Often this watch has a built-in memory function and will show cumulative times.
- **Computerised study board systems.**

TIME STUDY PROCEDURE
Before undertaking a time study, various courtesies need to be attended to. These involve discussions with personnel concerned and their supervisors. Time study must not be undertaken secretly. All data should be available for inspection and verification.

Prior to time study, the operation must be broken down into elements.

*42003: an **element** is a distinct part of an operation selected for convenience of observation, measurement and analysis.*

*42002: a **breakpoint** is the instant at which one element in a work cycle ends and another begins.*

Jobs are broken down into elements for a variety of reasons:

- Variations in operator speed and effectiveness can be more accurately assessed over short periods.
- Relaxation allowances can be more accurately determined.
- Productive and unproductive work can be separated.
- To enable appropriate frequency factors to be applied to repetitive elements in the compilation of a standard time value.
- Elemental times can be used in the compilation of synthetic standard times, and in analytical estimations.

Different types of element are recognised:

*42007: **repetitive elements** occur in every work cycle of an operation.*

*42006: **occasional elements** do not occur in every work cycle of an operation but may occur at regular or irregular intervals.*

*42004: **constant elements** are elements for which the basic time remains constant whenever it is performed.*

*42005: **variable elements** in which the basic time varies in relation to some characteristics of the product, equipment or process, for example, dimensions, weight, quality etc.*

*42010: **manual elements** which are performed by the operator.*

*42011: **machine elements** which are automatically performed by a power-driven machine (or process).*

*42008: **governing elements** which occupy a longer time than that of any other element which is being performed concurrently.*

*42009: **foreign elements** are elements observed during a study which, after analysis, are found to be an unnecessary part of an operation.*

ACTIVITY 13

Think of a domestic activity which you know well, divide it into elements and classify each one into a type.

You might have thought of mowing the lawn. The following elements are all repetitive, constant, manual types:

take the key from the hook in the kitchen

go to the garden shed

unlock and open the shed door

pick up the mower

carry mower onto the lawn

unwind the electric cable

walk with the plug to the power socket

switch on the power

walk to the mower

start the mower

mow the lawn, etc.

If in the autumn, perhaps you needed to rake off the leaves first, this would be an occasional, variable, manual type.

RATING

Whilst timing a job, the work measurement practitioner also 'rates' the performance of the operator. Accuracy in rating comes from specialised training using films of typical work sequences and wide practical experience. Many organisations keep their practitioners in line with the use of 'rating clinics' at regular intervals. These are often set up and administered by the local college or university. It is also common for trade union representatives to be included in these clinics so that meaningful discussions about working performance can be held.

Normally a rating factor is written alongside each element of effective time recorded on the study sheet.

*41018: **rating** is the numerical value given to a rate of working.*

The practitioner may take into account, separately or in combination, one or more factors necessary to carry out the job such as: speed of movement, effort, dexterity, consistency.

*41025: **standard rating** is the rating corresponding to the average rate at which qualified workers will naturally work, provided they adhere to the specified method and provided they are motivated to apply themselves to their work.*

If the standard rating is consistently maintained and the appropriate relaxation is taken, a worker will achieve standard performance over the working day or shift.

The practitioner must bear in mind the following issues whilst rating:

- a representative motion pattern for performing the elements of work
- the speed of movement which would be present if the operative were suitably motivated

● effort must be considered from a range of speeds which could be expected under varied conditions, for example, walking on the flat, walking unladen uphill, walking with load uphill, etc.

It is important in rating that only the effective speed at which the operation is performed is judged. Trained operatives should not vary in effectiveness. It is obviously possible to work very fast yet include in the motion pattern many undesirable and overelaborate movements which thereby reduce effectiveness. Highly skilled operatives may appear to be working slowly yet, because every movement is effective they will complete the task in a relatively short time. Consequently, the skills and method of a job should be properly understood by the observers so that accurate assessments of effective speed can be made.

RATING SCALE

As with all scales of measurement certain fixed points must be established. Two points are quoted in connection with the rating scale. The lower fixed point is the expected speed and effectiveness over a time period from a worker, skilled and accustomed to his task, who is not working under any particular incentive, monetary or otherwise. This is commonly likened to a 3 mph walking pace and known as **normal performance**.

The upper fixed point, called **standard performance**, has already been defined. It is the speed and effectiveness expected from a skilled and experienced operator working in good conditions and suitably motivated. The performance level attained is likened to 4 mph walking pace.

Figure 11 shows the BSI rating scale.

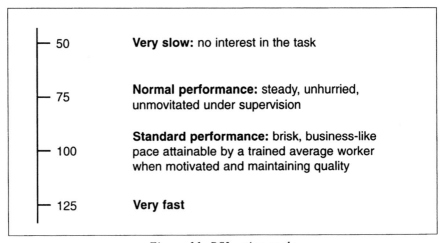

Figure 11: BSI rating scale

With practice a high degree of accuracy can be obtained and ratings are normally taken throughout a range of studies so that minor errors will tend to be cancelled out.

ACTIVITY 14

Take a pack of playing cards (52). Deal into 4 piles on a table.

1   Collect up cards and go through the process several times.

2   Use a digital watch or stopwatch to time yourself doing this task over ten cycles of dealing, taking the reading as you place down the last card. (Do not time the collecting up.)

3   Record your times.

4   Deal at an even pace throughout the whole cycle of 52 cards.

5   Vary your speeds so that you get a range of times.

6   Put an asterisk alongside the time or times which seem to be nearest to your perception of standard performance (100 rating).

You should have an asterisk alongside one or more of the times.

The internationally agreed benchmark time for this task is 0.375 minutes (22 seconds) for a 100 rating. The benchmark for a 75 performance is 0.50 minutes (30 seconds). How well did you do?

Construct a table, filling in the time data for different ratings:

Rating	Decimal Minutes	Seconds
50	.75	45
55		
60		
65		
70		
75	.50	30
80		
85		
90		
95		
100	.375	22
105		
110		
115		
120		

BASIC TIMES

On completion of a time study, the times recorded for each element are adjusted by means of the rating to give the **basic time** for each element. We can extend this to basic minutes (BMs).

43023: the time for carrying out an element of work at standard rating.

It is calculated in the following way:

$$\text{Basic time for an element} = \frac{\text{Observed time} \times \text{Rating}}{100}$$

For example, OT = 0.30, R = 90
Basic time = 0.27 BMs.

ACTIVITY 15

Calculate the basic times from the following data, total and average.

Rating	Observed time	Basic time
95	0.45	
110	0.39	
80	0.52	
65	0.62	
105	0.39	
Average elemental BMs =		Total _____

Your calculation rounded to two decimal places should be:

                0.43
                0.43
                0.42
                0.40
                0.41
                ____

Total   2.09
Average BMs 0.42

Note that when working with decimal minutes it is usual to round to two decimal places. With hours (BHrs), three or four decimal places is common.

DETERMINING A REPRESENTATIVE ELEMENTAL BASIC TIME

Normally, a number of readings will be taken of each element occurring in the work sequence. Sometimes there may be hundreds of readings on certain repetitive elements. Each observed elemental time is extended by its rating to give the basic time. A time study analysis sheet can be used to group all the basic times for the same elements.

A decision is then taken as to how a representative elemental time can be established. In many cases, a straight average can be taken. It is advisable, however, to scrutinise the list of basic times carefully to eliminate any which are grossly out of line because of abnormal circumstances, before taking the average.

Some practitioners plot the basic times in the form of a histogram and produce a distribution curve. The median is calculated and used as the elemental basic time.

Where an element is variable with respect to a particular feature, for example, **weight** or **size** of product, graphical analysis is necessary to produce a range of basic times relative to that variable feature.

For example, consider a simple two element job.

Time study sheet extract is shown in Table 1.

Element	Rating	Observed time	Basic time
1	90	.30	.27
2	100	.40	.40
1	100	.27	.27
2	110	.38	.42
1	100	.28	.28
2	70	.56	.39
1	120	.23	.28
2	100	.41	.41
1	70	.40	.28
2	100	.40	.40

Table 1: Time study sheet extract

Time study analysis sheet extract is shown in Table 2.

Basic Minutes	
Element 1	Element 2
.27	.40
.27	.42
.28	.39
.28	.41
.28	.40
Total 1.38	2.02
Occurrences 5	5
Average BMs 0.28	.40

Table 2: Time study analysis sheet extract

RELAXATION ALLOWANCE

*43025: **Relaxation allowance (RA)** is an addition to the basic time to provide a qualified worker with a general opportunity to:*

- *recover from the effort of carrying out specified work under specified conditions (fatigue allowance)*
- *allow attention to personal needs*
- *recover from adverse environmental conditions*

The amount of the allowance will depend on the nature of the job.

The levels of allowance given in Table 3 are intended to enable an average and suitable worker to maintain a 100 performance over the whole of the working day, without becoming more than ordinarily tired. The assessment of relaxation allowance must never be included in the rating assessment. The allowances are awarded under six categories to each element on the relaxation allowance sheet.

The total RA for an element is added as follows:

- personal needs (A)
- effort (B)
- posture (C)
- eye and mental attention (D)
- abnormal conditions (E)
- monotony (F).

$$\text{Standard minutes} = \text{Basic minutes} \times \frac{(100 + RA\%)}{100}$$

If the total RA% for a job as a whole adds up to, say, 20% of the total basic time for the job, it is a strong indication that the method should be carefully reconsidered.

We do not claim that the relaxation allowances in Table 3 are absolutely correct, but by using the table and awarding the allowances elementally, we can be sure of two things:

- the relaxation allowance is reasonably adequate
- the allowances given for comparable jobs are identical.

Personal needs
A constant allowance is given to cover purely personal needs and tea breaks.

Effort
This allowance is given to compensate for cumulative muscular fatigue resulting from the use of the muscles in lifting, pushing or pulling loads. We choose the allowance after taking into account:

- the intermittence or continuity of handling
- the ease or difficulty of handling – compactness, bulkiness, rigidity or floppiness of the load
- the proportion of the element during which the worker is under load.

Posture

This allowance is given when the work is done other than in the normal sitting position. But remember that a seated worker may have to reach with body assistance. This would be classified as other than 'normally seated'. The proportion of the element time spent standing, crouching, bending or reaching will influence the award.

Eye and mental attention

Some jobs, even under conditions of good lighting, will cause eye strain and in a few jobs there is some mental strain involved. In deciding upon the size of this allowance it is useful to slot the element in question into a scale running from zero for work similar to tossing a small object into a packing case, to 10% for, say, fitting a hairspring in a wrist watch. The element being considered may fall perhaps nearer to the zero end of the scale than to the half-way mark.

The important thing to remember is that if there is an award under this category, its purpose is to enable the worker to leave the job for a time and still produce a 100 performance at the end of the day.

Abnormal conditions

Awards may be given to compensate for the hindrance caused by having to wear special clothing, excessive heat or cold, excessive humidity or fumes, and a poor environment. Up to 20% may be awarded under this one category in a very exceptional case. It is worth calculating which is the cheaper alternative; to allow the abnormal conditions to continue and to pay for them as non-productive time in the form of an allowance, or to pay to have the conditions improved and not give an allowance.

Monotony

Awards under this category can be made for highly repetitive work, for example in light assembly work.

Guide to relaxation allowances

Table 3 (see page 394) is an example of a widely used guide, which can be used for either male or female operatives.

ACTIVITY 16

Consider two types of jobs you know well: in administration (office); in manufacturing (manual).

Evaluate each job in relaxation allowance % terms using the guide in Table 3.

Category	Heading	Description	% Allowance range
A	Personal needs		6
B	Effort	0–2.2 kg (Seated light assembly work)	5
		2.21–4.5 kg (Walking unloaded)	6
		4.51–6.7 kg (Light manual work)	8
		6.71–9.0 kg (Sawing plank of wood)	11
		9.1– 11.3 kg (Climbing upstairs unloaded)	14
		11.4–13.5 kg (Shovelling coal)	18
		13.6 (Digging heavy soil)	22
C	Posture	Sitting work	0
		Standing work	2
		Crouching/kneeling work	5
D	Eye and mental attention	Toss small object into large crate	0
		Inspect finished garment	5
		Fit hairspring to watch	10
E	Conditions	Special clothing e.g. light overalls (0–5) Diving suit	0 / 5
		Thermal conditions e.g. normal heat or cold	0
		Outdoor work	3
		Furnace or cold store work	5
		Atmospheric conditions humidity, fumes etc	0–5
		Environment noise, dirt, poor light etc	0–5
F	Monotony	Little	0
		Medium	2
		High (repetitive short cycle work)	5

Table 3: Relaxation allowances

How did the two jobs compare? Did you line them up something like this?

Category	Office clerk	Machine operator
A	6	6
B	5	8
C	0	2
D	3	0
E	0	2
F	0	1
Totals	14%	19%

Remember, however, that RA% is normally added per element, not as an overall amount. Some parts of a machine operator's job when he or she is 'machine minding' may only receive a small amount of RA.

OTHER ALLOWANCES

In some work situations additional allowances will be added to the basic time. Detailed explanation of such allowances is beyond our scope here.

For definitions of these allowances consult the British Standards document BS 3138, *Glossary of terms used in work study and organisation and methods.* All definitions quoted come from this publication.

SUMMARY OF TIME STUDY PROCEDURE

- Convert the 'observed' times for each element into 'basic' times.
- Compile study basic times on an analysis sheet.
- Select appropriate elemental times using averaging, graphical or other statistical approaches.
- Determine the amount of relaxation and other allowances required for each element.
- Establish the frequency with which each element occurs in the work cycle.
- Compile a 'standard time value' for the job.

STANDARD TIME

Figure 12 may help to clarify the way in which the different allowances are applied.

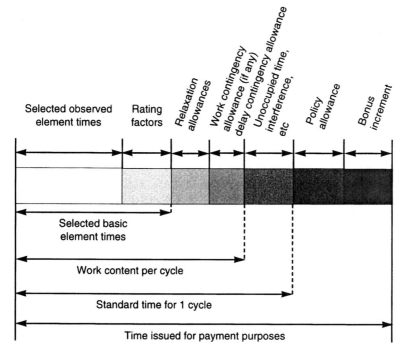

Figure 12: Calculating the standard time with different allowances applied

5.3 Activity sampling

This technique, which was devised by Tippett in 1934, consists of taking a series of instantaneous observations at random times to gather data about the activity levels in a situation. Certain statistical concepts underpin the technique. These are primarily associated with the laws of probability and the properties of the normal distribution curve.

To undertake an activity sampling survey, we follow these steps:

- Select the subject area and identify the features to be observed.
- Design a suitable recording form.
- Determine the number of observations which will be required for a pilot study using the formula:

$$N = \frac{4P(100 - P)}{L^2}$$

where

P = estimated % occurrence of a main activity (or non-activity)
L = accuracy required (known as the confidence limits).

- Obtain and group enough random times to cover the work periods to be studied over a representative phase of the work process.   Insert these random times on the recording form and arrange the studies.
- When studying, it is necessary to observe the subject(s) at the random time, and to record what is happening at that particular moment.
- When the study is complete, all recordings are totalled up for each category and the accuracy determined using:

$$L = \pm 2\sqrt{P(100 - P)/N}$$

where

P = actual % occurrence of the category

N = total observations made on the whole study.

If the accuracy achieved is outside of the required range, then recalculate N using the revised % for P. Undertake any additional studywork, add on, recalculate etc.

Date: 4 January	Section	Department
	Administration	Computers
Random Time	Category	Notes

Random Time	A	B	C	D	E	F	G	Notes
7.21			1					
7.38				1				
8.09			1					
8.58								
9.40		1						
10.01		1						
10.29			1					

Let's consider an example that concerns the utilisation of the forklift truck in the Parts and Raw Material Warehouse of Sunrise Engineering Co. Ltd.

Pilot study
Estimate of utilisation (given by manager) 35%, that is 65% idle.

Accuracy required: ± 5%.

No. of readings: $N = \dfrac{4 \times 35 \times 65}{5^2} = 364$

A pilot study of 375 readings was decided on, spread over three weeks, 125 readings per week were taken.

Recalculation
Working % found to be: $\dfrac{140 \text{ readings}}{375 \text{ total}} \times 100 = 37.5\%.$

Accuracy $L = \pm 2 \ \sqrt{37.5\,(100-37.5)/375} = \pm 5\%$

This is within the accuracy range required so the 37% utilisation can be accepted.

Utilisation range = (37% − 5%) to (37% + 5%), that is, 32 to 42%.

If you are statistically inclined, we can say that there are 95 chances in 100 that the true working % lies between 32% and 42%. This is based upon the formulas derived from the normal distribution curve and relates to the area enveloped by two standard deviations.

RANDOM TIMES
There are many tables of random numbers available. They have usually been produced by a computer. Random numbers are essential for an activity sampling exercise, but they must first be converted into clock times. This can be done by using the random numbers shown below:

Random hours covering 07.00 to 18.00 (7.00 am – 6.00 pm)

```
07 17 09 14 16 11 15 12 11 13 17 07
17 08 17 13 07 08 13 09 07 11 09 08
07 17 13 10 08 07 14 14 13 08 10 13
10 09 08 08 11 16 08 17 17 14 15 15
09 11 15 11 09 08 16 08 08 16 15 12
11 09 09 10 11 07 07 15 08 10 10 09
08 13 12 17 11 11 16 09 16 13 15 11
13 09 15 09 17 10 15 16 15 13 12 10
09 11 13 11 09 15 16 12 11 10 08 16
```

Random minutes (00 – 59)

```
02 49 59 26 39 45 12 32 18 56 10 03
22 02 43 19 23 55 39 05 09 17 44 52
00 01 03 34 38 27 29 26 24 44 15 54
31 26 10 06 11 05 47 41 01 23 53 42
26 13 16 01 51 43 07 42 21 05 24 57
34 56 36 31 41 17 44 50 25 52 02 03
45 07 16 18 42 51 33 55 43 20 46 54
23 09 21 01 04 23 08 04 23 52 38 01
17 43 07 38 19 54 40 40 36 54 07 58
14 04 50 10 11 25 36 00 39 37 59 59
34 16 05 29 25 28 30 32 35 58 02 51
35 08 52 47 52 10 05 36 02 48 17 31
```

- Decide the number of readings required per working period, for example, between 08.00 – 12.00 and 13.00 – 17.00.
- Select the number of readings required from the random hours table, for example, 20 readings 09, 13, 08, 11,...
- Select the number of readings required from the random minutes table, for example, 20 readings 02, 22, 00, 31,...
- Compile a list of times, for example, 09.02, 13.22, 08.00, 11.31...
- Put the times into logical order and add to the study sheets.

RATED ACTIVITY SAMPLING

This technique includes a rating assessment with the instantaneous samples taken, and is often used to determine elemental times within a job.

5.4 Predetermined Motion Time Standards (PMTS)

This method of determining standard time values is widely used in administration, manufacturing and maintenance situations. Time values for human movements at standard performance level (100) have been built up from the analysis of hundreds of film and video studies of work routines. From these studies, times have been categorised and published in tabular format. The practitioner needs to be able to analyse the method of the job in a certain way and then use the data provided.

One popular PMTS approach is known as MTM (Methods-Time-Measurement). In fact there are a series of MTM systems which vary in complexity:

MTM 1 which is extremely detailed

MTM 2 which is a useful compromise

MTM 3 which uses rather broader definition.

Many proprietary types of pre-determined time standards are available. These have been developed by research establishments and consultants for particular applications, for example, office work, engineering craft work etc.

To become a competent practitioner in pre-determined motion time standards, you would need to obtain qualifications through a specialised course.

Some organisations use PMTS as the vehicle for producing all time standards as there is a problem associated with taking of time studies. Other businesses use both PMTS and conventional time studies.

5.5 Estimating systems

We give the definitions of the two main techniques, but fuller explanation is beyond the scope of this unit.

*41005: **Analytical Estimating** – this is a development of estimating in which the time required to carry out elements at a defined rate of working is estimated partially from knowledge and practical experience of the work concerned and partially from synthetic data.*

*41006: **Comparative Estimating** – this a technique in which the time for a task is evaluated by comparing the work in it with the work in a series of similar tasks (benchmarks), the work contents of which have been measured. The arranging of tasks into broad bands of time is referred to as slotting.*

5.6 Financial incentive schemes

We can use standard minute values to determine output potential. Let's look at an example. A word processing operator working in a mail order business deals with outgoing customers' orders and after time study, a value of 8.42 SMs per order has been calculated.

As the operator works an 8 hour day (480 minutes) his or her supervisor knows that he or she should be able to deal with:

$$\frac{480}{8.42} = \text{57 orders per day}$$

This is provided he or she works at standard performance (100 rating level) and only takes the allocated amount of allowance time.

We can calculate the number of operations required at different times of the year as seasonal demands vary. For example, in the spring build-up of summer business, 600 orders per day are being handled.

This needs $\dfrac{600}{57} = 10.53$, that is, 11 operators working.

We can also calculate a performance level if a financial incentive scheme is applied.

For example, an operator produces 51 orders/day.

Performance is $\dfrac{51 \times 8.42 \times 100}{480} = 89$

This can be equated in financial terms to a level of bonus earnings. Specific financial scheme design is beyond our scope in this unit. However, you **should** carefully consider the following general comments on incentives.

BASIC PRINCIPLES FOR A SUCCESSFUL FINANCIAL INCENTIVE SCHEME

If a financial incentive scheme is to operate successfully, the following conditions should be realised:

- There should be complete frankness and honesty on the part of management.
- The scheme should be equitable between employer and employee, and should ultimately contribute to the benefit of both.
- The scheme should be acceptable to the employees and so operated that they will have confidence in it.
- The scheme should be simple to understand and operate, and an adequate write-up should be provided for the operation.
- The incentive should be substantial (a weak incentive is useless).
- A person's reward should be related to factors (quantity, quality, etc.) which they control.
- Notification of bonus earnings should be prompt, daily or weekly for preference.
- There should, in general, be no arbitrary limits to the amount of bonus that may be earned.
- The scheme must provide just penalties for substandard or spoiled work.

- Operators should not suffer any loss of earned bonus due to causes beyond their control, for example, waiting for materials.

- In no circumstances may a rate or time be altered once it has been set, unless there has been a clerical error, a change in the method of doing the job, or full agreement with the people involved.

- The scheme should be applied individually wherever possible: if it must be applied to a 'group', the 'group' should be as small as possible.

- All standard times should be accurately determined.

- The scheme should be designed to assist supervision in their day-to-day management.

- Complaints and queries should receive prompt attention.

Summary

In this section we considered the time content of jobs. We looked at the basic six-step procedure of work measurement and then at the techniques of time study, activity sampling, pre-determined motion time standards and analytical and comparative estimating systems. We ended with a brief look at financial incentive schemes.

Unit Review Activity

Answer the following questions.

1   Define productivity.

2   Identify the key factors which affect productivity levels.

3   How will better material utilisation improve productivity?

4   What is meant by job enrichment?

5   Recall the six basic steps of method study.

6   Write down the symbols used in constructing a flow process chart.

7   Why is the identification of 'key' operations necessary when we are undertaking critical examination?

8   Why is it vital to maintain an interest in the ongoing performance of a new system of work?

9   Why should job times ideally be established *after* methods have been specified?

10 Write down the principles which underpin a well-designed financial incentive scheme.

Unit Summary

In this unit we looked at issues which impinge upon effective management from an operations management perspective. We began by examining features of Japanese and Western organisations to highlight factors which lead to employee motivation and commercial success. We identified the inputs of resources which are utilised in manufacturing, administrative and service systems and considered the concept of productivity measurement and improvement. Finally we introduced and discussed important productivity-raising techniques used by many operations managers: method study and work measurement.

You can probably see now why there is a close relationship between the methods employed to achieve an objective and the time value allocated to the task. Ideally standard time values should be allocated to the task. These time values should be related to sound and efficient work methods which have been carefully designed and clearly specified to maximise job satisfaction and output quality. In such circumstances, with the appropriate managerial skills and resourcing, an organisation can expect to be able to operate at high productivity levels.

References

Alderfer, CP (1972) *Existence, Relatedness and Growth: Human Needs in Organizational Settings*, Free Press, NewYork

Hellriegel, D, Slocum J W and Woodman, R W (1989) *Organizational Behaviour*, West Publishing, New York

Lessem, R and Neubauer, F (1994) *European Management Systems*, McGraw-Hill, New York

Recommended Reading

Alkhafaji, A F (1995) *Competitive Global Management*, St Lucie Press, Florida

Currie, R M (1977) *Work Study*, Pitman, London

International Labour Office (1980) *Introduction to Work Study*, Geneva

Lorriman, J and Kenjo, T (1994) *Japan's Winning Margins*, Oxford University Press, Oxford

Answers to Unit Review Activity

1   Productivity is the quantitative relationship between what is produced and the resources used.

$$\text{Productivity} = \frac{\text{Output}}{\text{Input}}$$

2   Government policies; geographical factors; managerial skill.

3   If more effective supply chains are organised which reduce inventory levels, storage and handling costs and possible material wastage rates are reduced.

4   This is one of the approaches which can be taken when a job is redesigned. The emphasis is on the empowerment of the staff concerned to undertake responsibility for a much more significant part of a job or, in some cases, the whole job itself.

5   Select the work to be studied.
Record the facts.
Examine the facts critically.
Develop an alternative.
Install the new method.
Maintain the new method by regular checks.

6   Operation   ◯

Inspection   ▢

Transportation   ⇨

Storage   ▽

Delay   D

7   The starting point of critical examination is the consideration of 'key' activities. Sometimes the answers to the questions suggest the whole job should be abolished or radically changed. In which case, examination of other activities will be pointless.

8   Changes to methods occur in various ways over a period of time, and unless these are evaluated there is a tendency that the standard time values will become 'slack' relative to the actual amount of work undertaken. This will affect costings, accuracy in planning and the effectiveness of financial incentive schemes.

9   It is likely that standard times established on unspecified methods will prove 'slack' in practice and lead to excessively high costings, poor planning, unsafe working practices and low staff productivity levels.

10 Some of the main principles are:
    ● equitability between employer and employee
    ● simple to understand and calculate
    ● there should be a sufficiently strong incentive
    ● the factors which lead to incentive payments are understood and within the control of the staff involved.

UNIT 8

SCHEDULING AND CAPACITY

Introduction

It is difficult to think of a business in either services or manufacturing that is not concerned with scheduling and capacity. Scheduling is about the timing of work and the order in which it is to be done. Capacity management is concerned with making sure that the operations unit has sufficient resources to carry out the work when needed. These two areas are interrelated and both involve trade-offs. This unit aims to make you familiar with the thinking and techniques of capacity and scheduling.

Objectives

By the end of this unit, you should be able to:

- understand the hierarchical nature of scheduling and capacity evaluation, and be able to apply it to service and manufacturing operations
- identify the differences between capacity and load, forward and backward scheduling, push and pull scheduling, and finite and infinite scheduling
- understand the aggregate planning process, in particular level and chase plans
- understand the importance of master scheduling in manufacturing and its equivalent in services
- undertake basic capacity evaluation calculations
- undertake basic scheduling of jobs though a series of workcentres
- understand the issues of sequencing
- understand the basics of queuing theory.

SECTION 1

Definitions and Concepts

Introduction

In this section we will first cover the basic definitions and concepts relating to scheduling and capacity. We will then distinguish between capacity and load and cover the fundamental concepts of push and pull, finite and infinite, and backward and forward scheduling. Finally, we will introduce the important concept of a bottleneck and show how this and related optimised production technology (OPT) concepts have significant implications, not only for factory managers, but also for general management.

A schedule is simply a plan which sets out when activities are due to take place and usually where they will be performed and by whom. Detailed schedules have planned start and end dates. You have already met one specialised type of schedule when we discussed project management in Unit 5, and in this unit we will discuss more general cases. Schedules come in many forms: some formal such as semester times or class timetables, or train timetables, or scheduled football league games, or manufacturing schedules; and some less formal such as when you plan to sleep and work, to have your car maintained, or to start your dissertation. Scheduling is pervasive. It is found in services, in government, in manufacturing, and in domestic situations.

ACTIVITY 1

Consider a register of bookings held by a hotel. What does it contain?

Scheduling is in such common use that this question would seem to be obvious. But in scheduling terms, a hotel booking register contains arrival and departure dates and room allocations. Overbooking has to be avoided. Available capacity must be checked before a booking is accepted. The hotel would try to allocate rooms to suit the group size. The booking plan rolls forward in time, and becomes the basis for several other plans, such as room service, staffing and restaurant seats as the arrival times get closer. A good schedule will satisfy guests and make good use of available facilities.

1.1 Scheduling in service industries

Schedules are everywhere in service industries. All transport services have schedules such as flight schedules or bus timetables. Hotels and restaurants take reservations. Doctors take bookings. Universities have terms and timetables. Newspapers have deadlines. Shops have opening hours. Telephone companies have tariffs which depend upon time of calls. All of these schedules set the framework for operations. They form the basic organisational building blocks allowing all subsequent operations to be derived. A schedule also creates the link between customers and the organisation; each side knows they have to meet the schedule or risk failure. Airline passengers cannot be late for a flight and expect to be well served, and the airline must deliver the plane in a reliable condition with crew, meals and fuel or risk going out of business.

1.2 Scheduling in manufacturing industries

In manufacturing, schedules are often more formalised. For many manufacturing companies the basic schedule is known as the master production schedule (MPS) which forms the link between customers and the organisation, but which also provides an important interface between operations, marketing, personnel, and finance. George Plossl (1983), manufacturing guru, considers that the MPS is 'management's handle on the business'. We will study several schedules in this unit.

1.3 Capacity

The common English usage of the word **capacity** is in terms of volume. Thus the capacity of a jug is 1.5 litres, and so on. In operations management, however, capacity is usually expressed as a rate. Thus the capacity of a bank is 100 customers per hour or the capacity of a machine is 40 standard hours per week. However, capacity is often difficult to be accurate about. It depends for example upon:

- **mix of customers or products**. In a bank, the capacity of 100 customers per hour makes an assumption about the average amount of work that a transaction will involve.

- **efficiency of the operation**. In the bank, the assumption would be made about the skill level of staff. If the bank was staffed one day by trainees, the capacity would not be the same. We define efficiency later.

- **utilisation of resources**. In the bank, if some cashiers are often called away to do other work, then their utilisation would drop and with it the capacity of the banking hall. We define utilisation later.

Notice that even in situations where you may think you know the capacity, for example, 'the capacity of this cinema is 300 people', you may often be talking about the volume. In operations terms, the capacity of the cinema would depend upon the length of films, the number of shows per day, the changeover time between shows, and the time taken per day to clean and maintain the cinema.

It is useful to distinguish between:

- **theoretical capacity,** the total capacity for the envisaged mix of customers or products

- **demonstrated capacity,** based on historical records

- **calculated capacity,** the theoretical capacity adjusted for utilisation and efficiency.

1.4 Load

It is important to distinguish between **load** and **capacity**. This is often a source of confusion because 'load' can be closely linked with the common English usage of capacity in terms of volume. Load is the amount of work that has accumulated within an operation. A well-known diagram, variations of which you can see in many texts, explains this difference and is shown in Figure 1.

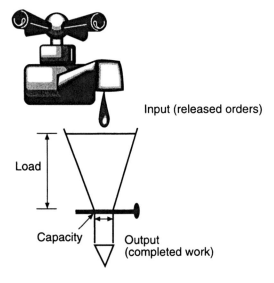

Figure 1: Load and capacity

We can see the interrelationships between several important operations concepts in this figure. Thus to decrease the lead-time we must either let less work into the system (limit the number of people coming into the bank so that once inside the queues are shorter), or increase the capacity (put on extra cashiers). We cannot decrease the lead time by allowing more work into the system.

1.5 Scheduling and capacity: push and pull scheduling

The **pull system** has become very popular in managing operations since the advent of JIT methods. The history of pull scheduling is much older, however, than JIT. Pull systems simply replace what has been used by the next process, and having replaced that product, then do not go on to make or send further products until the next process again uses up a product. It is the system found in many supermarkets, whereby goods taken off the shelf are replaced by the same quantity that was removed. This pull can go back right along the logistics chain to manufacturer, to supplier, and to supplier's supplier.

Pull may sound like common sense. However, it has been the exception rather than the rule until recently. The **push system** simply moves items from one process onto the next whether or not that next process is capable of handling them in the short term or not. Thus files accumulate in baskets, work piles up in front of students, and work accumulates in front of factory workstations.

A pull system acts as an automatic regulator of capacity. It prevents overload. But it does assume that operations are repetitive, which they are not always. We look at pull systems in Unit 9, *Time Based Operations*.

1.6 Scheduling and capacity: finite and infinite scheduling

In many textbooks scheduling is treated separately from capacity. The reason possibly concerns the historic limitations of calculating power, but today this makes less sense. Schedules should, wherever possible, be drawn up bearing in mind the limitations of capacity. In this unit, we will attempt to keep the two together.

When we discussed material requirements planning (MRP) in Unit 4 we ignored capacity requirements. We simply assumed that all necessary capacity would be available. You will also recall that, with MRP, we not only established planned order release quantities, but because we used lead times we also established a rough schedule. MRP is therefore an **infinite** scheduler. It is also a push scheduler because, having launched work onto the factory floor, work is moved irrepressibly on to the next workstation irrespective of the queue of work that may be waiting in front of that workstation. Infinite scheduling does have the advantage of viewing the load to be placed on various operations assuming that the lead times are exactly as planned. Overloaded and underloaded operations and periods are thus easy to pick out. A manager may then be able to assign extra staff or machines.

Since the mid-1980s, in manufacturing, **finite scheduling**, which schedules activities within capacity bounds, has been a major growth area. More calculation is required because overloaded periods or operations have to be rescheduled onto less busy ones, but it does have the considerable advantage of producing more realistic or achievable schedules than infinite scheduling techniques. Sometimes, however, work cannot be smoothed out in this way. The demand for cinema seats will always be high on Saturday evening and the capacity cannot be adjusted in the short term, so other means, such as increasing prices, may have to be tried. We discussed these methods in Unit 4.

Typical plans produced by infinite and finite scheduling are shown in Figure 2.

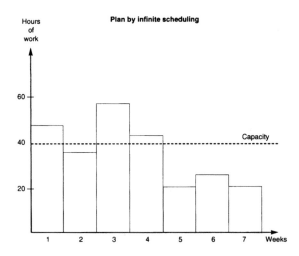

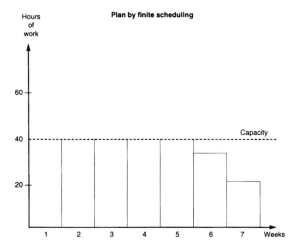

Figure 2: Finite and infinite scheduling

In the two diagrams in Figure 2 the week-by-week load, as imposed by the MPS on a particular workstation, is shown. Alternatively, you could think of the figures as representing the amount of assignment work that is due to be done by a student over the next few weeks. In the first case, no allowance has been made for capacity, and scheduling is infinite. You will notice that in some periods the workstation or student is overloaded, but is underloaded in others. After a period of time the load tends to tail off, simply because insufficient orders have been thus far obtained. This infinite scheduling does give an idea about when the busy weeks are, and during those weeks either overtime will have to be worked or some work will have to be delayed. In the second figure, the scheduling has been undertaken strictly in accordance with planned capacity. Overloads are not allowed. This finite schedule probably gives more realistic completion dates, but under- or overloads are not as apparent. Also customer due dates of need are not necessarily coped with.

1.7 Scheduling and capacity: backward and forward scheduling

In producing a schedule, whether finite or infinite, there are basically three methods: **backward**, **forward**, and **hybrid**, which uses both backward and forward.

MRP, which we dealt with in Unit 4, uses backward scheduling. We start with the target completion date and then calculate the latest times that components have to be received by and work has to start by, in order to finish on time. Backward scheduling is very common in everyday life. You may fix the time for dinner, and then plan backwards when you need to start cooking the various dishes.

Forward scheduling is also popular. You might forward schedule the many things that need to be done to renovate an old house. You use forward scheduling because money and available time are finite. If the completion date was the priority and funds and resources were unlimited, backward scheduling may have been preferable. Forward scheduling is also popular in manufacturing scheduling, particularly in the case of finite scheduling of resources which are in short supply. If there is a 'bottleneck' process, for example a paint line, then the rest of the factory can only work at the rate dictated by the bottleneck, so it makes sense to forward schedule on this resource. We discuss this in the next section.

ACTIVITY 2

Why do forward and backward scheduling produce different answers?

In scheduling there is often slack time. You will have experience of this in calculating the forward and backward passes in critical path analysis. The backward pass or schedule gives the late starts, the forward pass gives the early starts. Times correspond on the critical path only. In any task, in service or manufacturing, where a network can be used to describe the necessary sequence of events to complete the task, on all paths other than the critical path, different results will be obtained from a backward or from a forward schedule. In manufacturing there are time elements such as move, queue, and wait between operations but only set-up and run times are scheduled. As we shall see there is considerable uncertainty about these 'in-between' time elements.

1.8 Capacity bottlenecks and OPT principles

A **bottleneck** has always been thought of as something that delays progress. In manufacturing, the significance of bottlenecks was highlighted with the publication of *The Goal* by Eli Goldratt and Jeff Cox (1986). This novel has become a bestseller in the area of production management, largely because of its easy-to-read but thought-provoking style. The book follows the adventures of a plant manager, Alex Rogo, who has problems with his factory, but is guided by a reluctant consultant, Jonah, who forces Alex to think through some fundamental issues, using the so-called **Socratic approach**. The book should be read, not only by production managers, but by everyone in operations.

In *The Goal*, the OPT principles are gradually revealed. OPT, which stands for **optimised production technology**, is a computer package for finite scheduling. The OPT principles, however, are independent of the software, and are a powerful set of ideas. More recently, Goldratt has extended the principles into what he terms the **theory of constraints** (ToC) which he claims, with justification, are far more widely applicable.

Goldratt makes a distinction between bottlenecks, which limit the amount of money that a system can make, and **constrained critical resources** (CCR) which are near bottlenecks or temporary bottlenecks. Bottlenecks can be of different types: machine, material, marketing, financial, human, or managerial. The OPT approach begins by attempting to identify bottlenecks and CCRs.

The principles are directly relevant to scheduling and capacity. They are:

1   **Balance flow, not capacity.** For too long, according to Goldratt, the emphasis has been on trying to equate the capacity of the workcentres through which a product passes during manufacture. This is futile, because there will inevitably be faster and slower processes. Instead, effort should be made to achieve a continuous flow of materials. This means, for example, eliminating unnecessary queues of work in front of non-bottleneck workcentres, and by splitting batches so that products can be moved ahead to the next workstation without waiting for the whole batch to be complete. This principle can be expanded to cover the case of variation. For instance, two successive machines might have the same capacity, but the output from the machines would not necessarily equal the capacity if there is a high degree of variation, say due to breakdown stoppages. A breakdown on the first machine may result in the second machine becoming starved of work, thereby losing effective capacity.

2   **Utilisation of a non-bottleneck is determined not by its own capacity but by some other constraint in the system.** A non-bottleneck should not be used all the time or overproduction will result, and therefore the capacity and utilisation of non-bottlenecks is mostly irrelevant. It is the bottlenecks that should govern flow.

3   **Utilisation and activation are not synonymous.** This emphasises the point that a non-bottleneck machine should not be 'activated' all the time because overproduction will result. Activation is only effective if the machine is producing at a balanced rate, this is called **utilisation**. Notice that this differs from the conventional definition of utilisation, which ignores capacity of the bottleneck.

4   **An hour lost at a bottleneck is an hour lost for the whole system.** Since a bottleneck governs the amount of throughput in a factory, if the bottleneck stops it, it is equivalent to stopping the entire factory. The implications of this for maintenance, scheduling, safety stocks, and selection of equipment are profound! It also has deeply significant implications for cost accounting.

5   **An hour saved at a non-bottleneck is merely a mirage.** In effect, the time saved is worthless. This also has implications for the areas we mentioned in point 4.

6   **Bottlenecks govern both throughput and inventory in the system.** A factory's output is the same as the bottleneck's output and inventory should only be let into a factory at a rate that the bottleneck is capable of handling.

7   **The transfer batch may not, and on many occasions should not, equal the process batch.** A transfer batch is the amount of work in process inventory that

is moved along between workstations. Goldratt says that this quantity should not necessarily equal the production batch quantity that is made all together. Instead, batch splitting should be adopted to maintain flow and minimise inventory cost. This applies particularly to products that have been already processed on bottleneck machines; they are then too valuable to have to wait for the whole batch to be complete. Note that MRP makes an assumption at odds with this principle, in assuming that batches will always be kept together.

8   **The process batch should be variable, not fixed.** The optimal schedule cannot, or should not, be constrained by the artificial requirement that a product must be made in one large batch. It will often be preferable to split batches into sub-batches. On bottleneck machines, batches should be made as large as possible between set-up (changeover) operations (thereby minimising set-up time), but on non-bottlenecks batches should be made as small as possible by setting up machines as often as possible so as to use all the time available. This suggestion is the fairly radical view that batches not being processed on bottlenecks should be split and the machine set up again for other product batches, to such an extent that the non-bottlenecks become near-bottlenecks.

9   **Lead times are the result of a schedule, and cannot be predetermined.** Here Goldratt disagrees with the use of standard pre-specified lead times such as those we find in MRP. As we have already seen, and will see more of in this unit, the amount of wait and queue time is an uncertain and large proportion of total lead time, and so to estimate it beforehand is dangerous. However, as we have seen with MRP, it is often necessary to get materials there on time.

10   **Schedules should be assembled by looking at all constraints simultaneously.** In a typical factory, some products will be constrained by production capacity, others by marketing, and yet others perhaps by management inaction. It is important to know which constraints are affecting performance in any part of an enterprise. If, for example, you have a production constraint, it would be foolish to expend more effort on marketing.

These ideas continue to have an important influence in scheduling and capacity management. They are highly relevant to JIT production (Unit 9) and more will be said about them later in this unit under finite scheduling (Section 2.10).

ACTIVITY 3

You can set up an exercise to illustrate several of the OPT principles. You will need six people, although you can do it with 4 or 5, six sets of dice, and a lot of matches or Lego bricks or something to represent products. Production passes along the line of six people. Each round, each person throws a dice. The value obtained is the amount of production by that person during that round. You can only produce if you have materials to work on, as provided by the previous workstation. What do you predict will be the average production coming out of the last process, once production is established?

You might think it will the average of the dice throws, namely 3.5. Is it? No! This activity illustrates the interdependence of a sequence of operations which is quite common in manufacturing. Relate this back to the OPT principles.

ACTIVITY 4

Now arrange the game so that the fourth operator has a constant capacity of two units. What will happen?

Work will pile up in front of this operator. Goldratt suggests that the way to manage such situations is to run the 'drum, buffer, rope' principle. The **drum** is the drumbeat at the bottleneck which governs the rate at which money can be made. Marketing has the task of maintaining a constant flow of orders to keep this bottleneck running. The **buffer** is a quantity of inventory, or safety stock held in front of the bottleneck to ensure that it never runs out of work. This safety stock should be thought of as a time buffer rather than an inventory buffer. The type of work may vary, but the length of time over which the bottleneck is protected should remain constant. The **rope** forms an imaginary connection between the bottleneck workcentre and the first workcentre. The rate at which work is let into the line is thereby directly related to the amount of work coming out of the bottleneck.

Summary

In this first section, we have covered basic definitions and concepts relating to scheduling and capacity.

We have noted the crucial distinction between capacity, that concerns the output rate that can be achieved under current conditions, and load, the amount of scheduled work due to be done.

We also covered the fundamental concepts of push and pull scheduling, finite and infinite, and backward and forward scheduling. We use these in the next section.

Finally, we introduced the important concept of a bottleneck, and showed how this and the closely related OPT concepts have important implications, not only for factory managers, but also for general management.

Section 2

Scheduling Systems

Introduction

In this section, we will trace the history of MRP (material requirements planning), show how it has developed into MRP II (manufacturing resource planning) , and then into finite capacity scheduling and enterprise resource planning (ERP). We will also attempt to show how these established manufacturing frameworks can be of use in service industries.

We will work our way down the formal closed loop system in manufacturing and show how the concept is applicable to services, at least as a framework. We will look at aggregate plans in service and manufacturing and then master scheduling. We will go on to deal with more detailed scheduling and sequencing and finally introduce queuing theory.

2.1 Evolution of manufacturing systems: an overview

As we have seen, MRP involves backward infinite capacity scheduling. The result of exploding out the bill of materials is a schedule not just of order releases to external suppliers, but also a broad-brush internal manufacturing schedule, mapping milestones in project management. Modern MRP was conceived in the 1960s with the advent of less expensive computer power. MRP evolved into **manufacturing resources planning**, or MRP II, during the following two decades and has now evolved further into **enterprise resource planning** (ERP). In tracing the evolution refer to Figure 3, which shows a typical representation of **closed loop manufacturing.**

In this figure you will notice that scheduling activities are shown on the left-hand side, capacity checks on the right. Each level of planning has a corresponding capacity check. The planning process moves from long term, shown at the top, to short term, shown at the bottom. Some arrows are shown as two-way to indicate that where the capacity check reveals a potential problem, the plan is revised.

At the top level is the **production plan** or 'aggregate plan'. The plan is prepared in terms of family or aggregate units. The aim is to achieve the right economic balances between customer service, inventories, and the use of resources. This plan has to be subservient to the strategic, marketing, and finance plans. It is usually prepared at least a year in advance, to allow sufficient time to acquire the necessary resources, such as people, space and equipment, in order to carry out the plan. The Production Plan commonly sets monthly production targets.

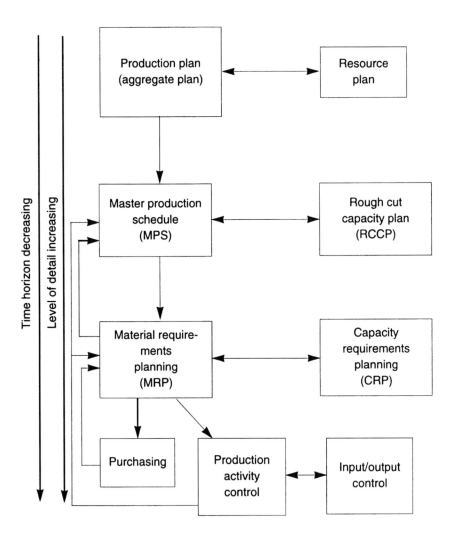

Figure 3: Closed loop manufacturing

Next comes the **master production schedule** or MPS. The MPS states the target completion dates for actual products, and must be subservient to the objectives of the production plan. The MPS must be prepared sufficiently in advance to allow time to acquire the components or materials, and to make the products. The MPS is often stated in terms of weekly requirements.

We dealt with the **material requirements plan** (MRP) in Unit 4. MRP is 'driven' by the MPS. MRP concerns the scheduling of component items, and with the timing of completion of major sub-assemblies. Finally, the **production activity control** or detailed scheduling module deals with the actual sequencing of work from process to process on a day to day, or even hourly, basis.

An MRP requires a well-managed MPS if it is to have any practical use. 'Well managed' implies the discipline of not changing the schedule once actual manufacturing has begun, and of creating as much stability as possible in the period immediately prior to actual manufacture. Too much change within this period destroys the philosophy of orderly manufacturing that MRP seeks to achieve. Thus, the concept of 'time fences' developed. Within the time fences only limited changes would be permitted. We will discuss this later. But time fences alone cannot solve the problem. The MPS must also be **valid**, meaning that it is not overloaded from a capacity point of view. Releasing too much work to the factory floor simply increases the amount of inventory on the factory floor, or 'work in progress' and increases lead times.

A valid MPS therefore requires a **capacity check**. This is achieved by **rough-cut capacity planning** (RCCP). RCCP is concerned only with key workcentres or machines that are known or suspected to be critical from a capacity point of view. It is concerned with those workcentres that are most heavily loaded with work and which as a result are likely to cause delays. A 'workcentre' is simply a convenient grouping of one or more machines or assembly operators which can be considered for the purpose of capacity calculations. A workcentre may range from a single process to a whole cell or department charged with producing a particular family of products or services.

We will look at the mechanics of RCCP in more detail later. Simply, the aim of RCCP is to ensure that the MPS has sufficient capacity to allow the planned production to take place. Where it does not, either the MPS or the capacity must be adjusted. This capacity adjustment could be achieved by, for example, working overtime.

With a valid MPS, and continuing improvements in computer power, further modules of the standard manufacturing system were developed:

- **purchasing module**, charged with sending out orders, documenting, receiving and controlling the flow of orders, was developed. This is the natural extension of the basic MRP module, using planned order releases.

- **capacity requirements planning** (CRP). As we have noted, the MRP module itself produces an outline schedule of when work is due to start. CRP uses this outline schedule and calculates the capacity implications for all important workcentres. This calculation is done using the detailed product routeings which describe the exact sequence in which a product is manufactured. Once again, where overloads are found, adjustments will be necessary, this time to the MRP, or if necessary, to the MPS.

- **production activity control** (PAC) module. With the MRP validated for capacity through the CRP process, it now becomes worthwhile for the manufacturing system to produce the detailed schedule of times of exactly when the operations to be performed by each workcentre on each batch of work that MRP has scheduled is due to take place. And once again, a check is kept on capacity, this time by **input-output control** which monitors the amount of work that is due to go into a workcentre. And of course, the MPS must be linked to the longer term production plan and to its capacity management equivalent known as the resource plan.

Further, all these modules would work together in a dynamic way not only rolling ahead through time but also making adjustments when events do not work out exactly as planned. This set of modules working together became known as **closed loop manufacturing**, and was state of the art in the early 1980s. The complete closed loop manufacturing concept is shown in Figure 3.

ACTIVITY 5

What are the prerequisites for closed loop manufacturing to work well?

Your experience with the MRP calculations in Unit 4 should convince you of the necessity for accurate data. This implies good inventory records, (via cycle counting), accurate bills of materials, and realistic lead times. It also requires, as we noted above, that the MPS in particular is not overloaded. (There is sufficient capacity to be able to make the MPS using the existing resources.) Even today, some 15 years after closed loop manufacturing became 'state of the art', there are still many manufacturing companies battling to achieve these requirements.

MOVING TOWARDS MRP II

From the early 1980s, more developments have taken place. If the whole closed loop manufacturing process is in place, if schedules have been validated against capacity, and the system and data is continually updated, then what we have is no longer just a manufacturing control system but also a model of the operations of the company. Moreover, it is a model which extends well into the future. It seems reasonable to add simulation capabilities to be able to ask 'what if?' questions, to link the purchasing module with accounting, and to link the production activity control module with costing systems. What started off as an inventory control system some 30 years ago has evolved into a full manufacturing management system. This is now known as **manufacturing resources planning (MRP II)**.

Today there are hundreds of MRP II systems on the market, ranging in cost from perhaps £500 to over £1 million. All major computer manufacturers support MRP II packages; some support several. The choice of an appropriate system has become quite a specialised field in itself, and is aided by manuals and 'expert systems'. (For example, *But Smart!* is a PC-based expert system for the evaluation and selection of manufacturing software, and is produced by Expert Buying Systems of Vancouver, WA, USA, and BDO Seidman's *Comprehensive Guide to Manufacturing Software* is a long-established publication.)

From the mid-1980s and into the 1990s, evolution has continued in three directions:

- **Finite scheduling** has been incorporated and MRP II has developed further into enterprise resource planning. Finite scheduling uses the framework produced by MRP and then calculates detailed schedules bearing in mind the finite limitations of workstation capacity.

- **Enterprise resource planning (ERP)** is an extension of MRP II which uses a common database for the entire organisation. All the MRP II modules are in place with ERP but the common database extends to accounting and finance, to personnel and payroll, to maintenance, to quality control, and into integration with computer-aided design systems. The concept is shown in Figure 4. A popular European example of ERP is the SAP system, a German software package.

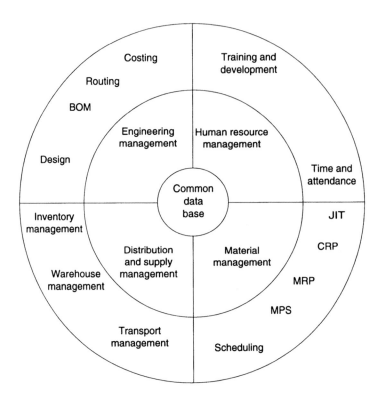

Figure 4: Enterprise resource planning (adapted from Brown, 1995)

- **Manufacturing execution systems (MES):** have evolved rapidly to enable the rapid and easy updating of factory operations. They also assist with activities which are not normally part of MRP II, such as time and attendance, quality control, and labour allocation. These typically use a combination of bar code scanners, portable data entry devices, and data entry terminals to give supervisors or team leaders up-to-the-minute information. These MESs are typically not part of the MRP II system, but augment MRP II and finite capacity scheduling systems. MES systems are often provided by a different supplier to that of the MRP II system. A representation of an MES is shown in Figure 5.

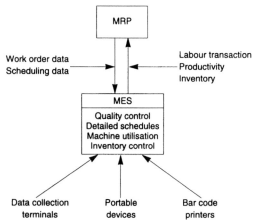

Figure 5: A manufacturing execution system
(adapted from Swanta and Parish 1995)

This section would not be complete without mention of JIT methods. Much of the evolution described in the preceding sections took place over the last 30 years in the USA. Organisations such as APICS (the American Production and Inventory Control Society) and BPICS (its British equivalent, now renamed the Institute of Operations Management) were instrumental in fostering its growth. Some might argue that in the West, we became too blinkered in our approach to manufacturing, believing that computers would solve it all. In Japan, however, a parallel stream developed over the same period. This was the JIT philosophy, much of the credit for which should go to the Toyota engineer, Taiichi Ohno. JIT concentrates on the elimination of waste, including improved layout, quality and maintenance. It seeks to control work in process inventory, not by computers, as is the case with MRP II, but by visible control systems such as *kanban*. JIT emphasises simplicity, where MRP II was developing evermore complex systems. The two philosophies met in the mid-1980s. For a while, there was much argument. Today, however, the strengths and weaknesses of each are recognised. Broadly, MRP II is good for planning and JIT is good for execution. Any manufacturing company would now be best advised to seek an appropriate blend of each. We say more on this topic in Unit 9, *Time-Based Operations*.

2.2 Closed loop concept as a framework for scheduling and capacity in services and manufacturing

Although the closed loop framework we presented in the last section is not directly applicable in service industry, nor in fact is it applicable in all of manufacturing, it is nevertheless useful as a framework for much of services and manufacturing. The module names may change, but much of the framework remains. We will continue to use the idea that at each level capacity is considered side by side with planning or scheduling.

The closed loop framework, in common with several planning processes, has the characteristic of beginning at a high, aggregate level and progressing down to more detail. With this change in detail goes a change in time horizon as shown in Figure 6. As the time horizon decreases, the level of detail increases.

At the top or aggregate level, we make the assumption that we can sort out schedules and resources at lower levels nearer the time when more detail is known. For example, a bank might decide on the broad levels of staff needed to meet the forecasted long-term demands. Training would be carried out in good time to meet the average requirements. But on the day that work is actually required to be undertaken, the actual demand may vary widely from the average. Short-term adjustments will be required, involving say moving people from cheque clearance to cashier work. In car manufacture, it is good enough for long-term planning to work with the forecasted number of cars to be built, without having to know about colours and options.

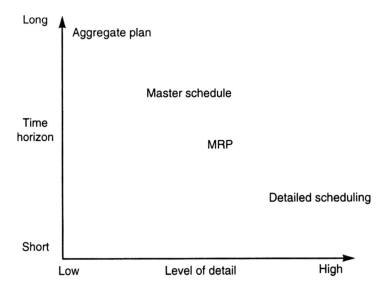

Figure 6: Closed loop operations: level of detail and time horizon

We will consider each of the scheduling and capacity modules in some detail, but before we do so it is worth having a look at how the framework may be applied in a service industry. Consider the case of a hotel. The production, or aggregate, plan comprises those activities concerned with deciding if the hotel should close during the off-season, when the high season should be, and what staff will be required throughout the year. At this level, the schedule is considered together with the capacity plan. The 'master schedule' in a hotel is the reservations book, which is checked for capacity against available rooms. In a hotel there is no MRP as such as it is not manufacturing a product but nevertheless the hotel must ensure that it has sufficient food, linen, bathroom supplies and so forth for the estimated number of guests. Thereafter, equivalent to production scheduling or production activity control, the detailed schedules must be developed for room make-up, for staffing the front desk, for the planning of meals and room service. This detail includes exactly who will do what and when it is due to be done. And finally, equivalent to input/output control, checks have to be maintained to see, for instance, if the delays in room service are acceptable and, if they are not, have resources moved to alleviate the problem.

ACTIVITY 6

For each of the following services, describe the activities which are equivalent to those given in the closed loop framework:

a fire brigade

a restaurant

an insurance company.

You would have had to use your imagination here, and there is no one right answer, but your answer should look something like Table 1.

MRP II / ERP module	Fire brigade	Restaurant	Insurance company
Production plan / resource plan no. of engines,	plan covering: area served, size, staff, max no. of fires handleable	plan covering: opening times	plan covering: number of field and support staff and working hours
MPS	rota of staff on duty; also fire prevention	table bookings, menus	requests for policy advice
MRP or inventory plan	equipment which must be available to cope with max. demand	food and drink provided for bookings and menu	standard policy pack
Detailed schedule	who will be on duty and the allocation of duties between staff		which salespeople will call on which customers and when

Table 1

We will now consider the various modules in Table 1 in greater detail. We will consider each from a service and from a manufacturing perspective.

2.3 Aggregate plans in services and manufacturing

The **aggregate plan** or **production plan** is 'aggregate' because it is usual to plan for 'families' of products or customers without worrying about the detail breakdown. A hotel might plan for the number of guests, not worrying at this level whether male or female or child. A car manufacturer uses a particular model, such as a Ford Mondeo, without worrying at this level about engine options, colours or whether saloon, estate or hatchback. A brewer might plan in terms of hectolitres of beer, not worrying at this stage about brands or packaging. Aggregating demand is good enough for the longer or medium term. In fact, it is more than good enough; it is desirable because we would like to keep our options open for as long as possible. You are bound to get forecasts for saloons, estates, and hatchbacks incorrect, but you are more likely to be accurate in forecasting the total numbers.

There are two classic or pure aggregate plans, the **level plan** and the **chase plan**. These two plans are at the extremes, with many mixed plans in between. The two types of plan are shown in Figure 7.

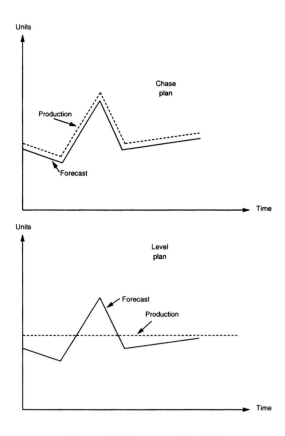

Figure 7: Chase and level plans

In the level plan, resources, or the capacity rate, remain fixed and excess demands must be taken up by keeping inventory, by back orders or by late deliveries. In manufacturing, the rate of production remains constant. Inventory accumulates when demand exceeds the production rate and declines when the production rate is less than demand.

The chase plan is the reverse: here resources, or capacity, change in line with forecast demand variation. In manufacturing, the level of inventory remains more or less unchanged even though the rate of demand changes.

In services, of course, inventory cannot be stored so a level plan may have to accept customer delays, or a varying rate of customer service. The correct level plan would aim to achieve the right compromise between lost customers at peak times and efficient use of resources. If excellent customer service is the objective, it may be necessary to provide sufficient capacity to cope with peak demand. Some services find it difficult to offer a chase plan. For instance, a cinema or a hotel has fixed resources in seats or rooms. Yet, it may still be possible to have fewer shows or to close down part of the hotel in line with demands. In a hotel this is not much of a problem, but a cinema has greater difficulties because demand variation is more volatile, depending on the popularity of individual movies.

ACTIVITY 7

What are the advantages and disadvantages of each of the two classic capacity plans? You might think in terms of people, quality and money in answering this question. Put yourself in the position of an employee, a manager, a customer and a supplier to answer this.

As an employee, you may feel more comfortable about working at a constant level rate throughout the year. Quality may be better as a result. For a manager, operations would be less complicated because there are few disruptions, but you may be concerned about the high level of inventories at one time of the year and low levels at other times. For a customer, the type of plan adopted does not matter as long as you get good quality products on time. With normal fluctuations, however, the delivery rate is likely to be better in the off season but there may be a risk of 'stockouts' in the high demand season. The level plan may not be possible with perishable or seasonal goods. A supplier may also prefer the stability of demand.

The reverse is true for the chase plan. As an employee, you may be laid off during periods of low demand. On the other hand, temporary staff may be taken on during periods of high demand. As a result, quality may suffer. However, inventory levels would remain constant throughout the year and generally there would be a saving in inventory because large quantities would not need to be accumulated. Generally, then, from a finance perspective, it is a trade-off between incurring more cost on inventory in the level plan and the costs of change with the chase plan.

Generally, we can write an equation for the costs of capacity plans as follows:

Total cost = resource costs at normal rates + cost of overtime + cost of subcontracting + cost of inventory + cost of late deliveries + cost of capacity rate changes.

The cost of capacity rate changes involves the costs of lay-off, hiring, training and any resulting quality penalties.

Spreadsheets are useful in calculating aggregate plans. A spreadsheet allows a manager to evaluate a large number of options between the chase and level plan extremes. Analytical optimisation methods using, for example, linear programming (LP) formulations for aggregate planning are beginning to be more widely used as the friendliness and power of LP packages improves. You have probably met linear programming in your earlier quantitative methods studies.

Notice that the problem sets out to minimise total costs subject to various constraints as is usual with LP. In this case, the constraints are the abilities to meet demands, and to limit the amounts of overtime and inventory. Various other constraints could be added such as limiting the amount of subcontracting, setting a minimum workforce level, and specifying the maximum age of inventory.

ACTIVITY 8

What are the drawbacks of using an LP formulation, as opposed to using a spreadsheet (apart from the availability and cost of software!)? And what are the advantages?

The key point is that many of the cost and constraint functions are non linear. For example, capacity or warehouse space may only feasibly be added in chunks. This means that either LP needs to be treated with caution or you should consider using more advanced mathematical programming such as mixed integer programming. On the positive side, you will recall from your earlier studies that a computer solution to an LP also generates sensitivity or 'shadow costs'. This is very useful information to a planner operating in more sophisticated, high-cost environments.

GRAPHICAL APPROACH TO AGGREGATE PLANNING

The graphical approach is popular because of its clarity, something that we cannot say about the mathematical programming approach. This is important because such medium-term capacity planning is best done in a multi-disciplinary team setting, with representatives from operations, marketing, finance and personnel.

Refer to Figure 8 which sets out an aggregate or production plan. Notice that we are plotting **cumulative** units against time. The units are, of course, expressed in aggregate or family terms. We will assume that the appropriate planning horizon is one year. The starting point is the forecast demand for the planning period ahead.

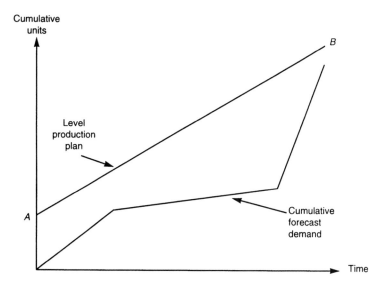

Figure 8: Graphical aggregate planning

You will note that demand is not constant throughout the period, but is low during the mid section. Then consider the beginning and ending inventory positions. At the start of the planning period there might be a certain quantity of inventory in stock. This quantity is shown by point *A*. Then consider the desired ending inventory position at the end of the planning period. This quantity will be established by management to meet demand uncertainties. If there was no starting inventory but a desired ending inventory, then assuming that the company meet all demands, the total quantity to be produced would be the total cumulative demand plus the ending inventory quantity. Therefore, a level or constant production plan (which, of course is shown in cumulative units) can be represented by the straight line which joins points *A* and *B* as shown in the figure. The slope of the line represents the production rate. Of course, the company may not wish to produce at a constant rate all year. So any series of lines which start at point *A* and end at point *B* represent possible production plans. As long as the production plan line remains above the cumulative forecast demand line, no inventory shortages will occur provided the forecast is correct. One such plan is shown in Figure 9.

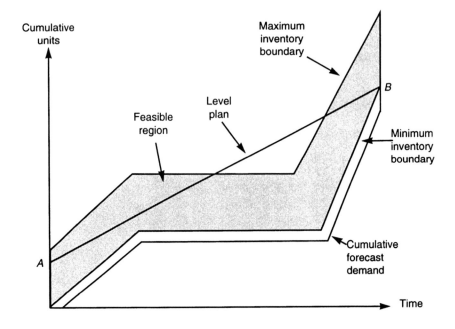

Figure 9: Aggregate planning showing inventory envelope

In the service industry, where inventory cannot be held, the approach may be simplified but a graphical approach is still an attractive proposition. In a hotel, for instance, the plan may use bedrooms as the unit of capacity, and the plan could determine the number of bedrooms to be kept open. In an office situation, the aggregate units could be the number of insurance policies to be dealt with or the number of orders to be processed.

You should realise that the vertical distance between the cumulative demand line and the production plan line represents the inventory being held at any time. This is because (initial inventory + cumulative production) – (cumulative demand) = inventory holding. In Figure 9 notice how inventory accumulates when demand falls below the production rate. If we have constraints or requirements concerning maximum and minimum levels of inventory, we can represent these as an envelope drawn in above the cumulative demand line. The former may be due to maximum warehouse space, and the latter due to a required minimum level of safety stock. Once again any production plan joining A and B is feasible so long as it remains within the envelope. Referring to Figure 9, we can see that a level plan is no longer feasible.

In Figure 10, various other constraints can be added:

- maximum and, or minimum rates of production can be represented by slopes of lines, that is, the maximum number of units that can be produced, and the minimum number of units per period. These are shown in Figure 10, and could represent, for instance, the desired maximum and minimum staffing levels. The significance of these maximum and minimum rates is that, in joining points *A* and *B*, no line or production plan must have a slope steeper than the maximum rate nor shallower than the minimum rate.

● the maximum age of inventory can be represented by a maximum horizontal line drawn to the left of the forecast demand line. Think of it this way: if the company stopped production at the beginning of the planning period, inventory would run out in a period represented by the length of the horizontal line drawn from the starting inventory position to the point of intersection with the cumulative demand line. A constraint of maximum age of inventory therefore represents an envelope drawn by a horizontal line representing this length drawn to the left of the cumulative demand line.

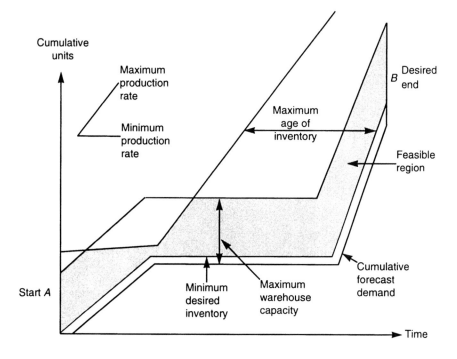

Figure 10: Aggregate planning showing all constraints

Now we can put all these constraints together and draw in the complete 'feasible region' in Figure 10. Any line joining points A and B and staying within this region is feasible. The relative merits of the various plans can then be discussed by the planning team. Try the following exercise yourself.

ACTIVITY 9

Draw the feasible region. Find a feasible plan which achieves all requirements but which also involves the least number of production rate changes. You should use graph paper for this exercise.

Forecast demand:		
	1st quarter	2,000 units per month
	2nd quarter	4,000 units per month
	3rd quarter	3,000 units per month
	4th quarter	4,000 units per month

Beginning inventory	2,000 units
Desired end inventory	1,000 units
Maximum inventory holding	3,000 units
Minimum inventory holding	1,500 units
Maximum average age of inventory	2 months

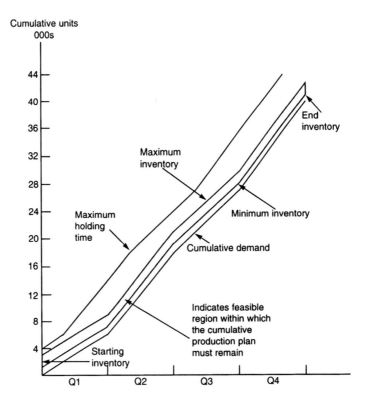

Figure 11: The solution to Activity 11

You will have noticed that, at the aggregate or production planning level, scheduling and capacity is considered simultaneously. This is normal for production or aggregate planning, but is usually not the case for lower level, more detailed plans.

An aggregate plan or production plan is usually prepared once per annum, but at the next level, scheduling and capacity planning may be prepared on a rolling monthly basis. This is our next consideration.

2.4 Master schedule in services and manufacturing

The **master production schedule** or **MPS** derives from the aggregate or production plan, but also integrates more detailed forecasts and customer orders. This is shown diagrammatically in Figure 12.

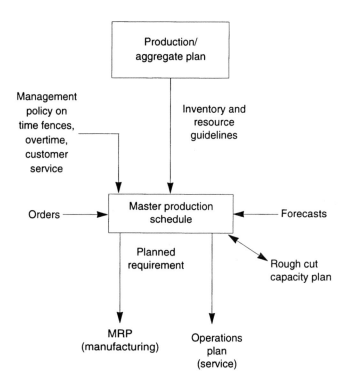

Figure 12: Master scheduling

As we mentioned earlier in this unit, the master schedule is 'management's handle on the business' (Plossl, 1983), and is the document that integrates operations, marketing, personnel, finance and personnel. The master schedule process in a manufacturing company would normally be carried out by a 'master scheduler' in consultation with managers from all the departments mentioned. In many manufacturing companies, there is a master schedule meeting once a week, always attended by operations and marketing, and by other functions when necessary. Increasingly, master scheduling is being delegated to sub-factories, or cells.

In services, the equivalent of the master schedule may be done less frequently or less formally, but it remains critical to the productivity of the organisation. In services, the 'master scheduler' could be a hotel front-desk assistant, a nurse at a surgery, a garage receptionist, or a departmental secretary in a university department. Often service managers do not realise the critical nature of their work. For example, when an unskilled garage receptionist takes car service bookings, he or she is committing the resources of the garage to meet the perhaps unspecified requirements of customers. It is not surprising if customer requirements are not met on time or to specification. This suggests that the 'master scheduler' should have some knowledge or appreciation of actual operations and also what is required by customers. The master scheduler or equivalent should also have an estimate of the load implications of various orders or jobs, otherwise dissatisfaction, either from customers or management, is inevitable. Barber shops have, for instance, increasingly adopted booking arrangements. This is their master schedule. If the time to cut hair is underestimated, customers could experience long waits, but if times are overestimated, idle time on the part of the hairdresser will result.

WHAT TO MASTER SCHEDULE
Master scheduling should be carried out at the most effective level, bearing in mind the most constrained or scarce resources. Thus in a hotel the master schedule is the room bookings made by guests, in a doctor's surgery it is the doctor's working time, in a university it is the lecture room slots or perhaps the time of a top professor who is in constant demand, and for a publisher the target dates for the publication of various books. The master schedule sets the overall plan from which other activities are derived. You would not master schedule invoicing, or a cleaner's time, or acquisition of stationery; these are activities that depend upon the master schedule.

In manufacturing, where to master production schedule is guided by the type of environment and the characteristic shape of the bills of materials. Characteristic shapes of bills and their appropriate scheduling levels are shown in Figure 13.

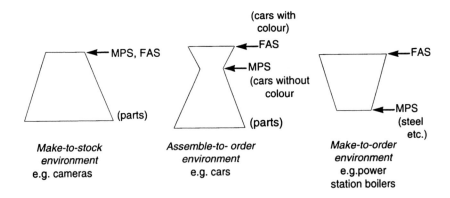

Figure 13: Bills of materials shapes and where master production scheduling and final assembly scheduling (FAS) is done in various environments

In the case of make-to-stock manufacturing, the shape of the bill of materials indicates that a few standard end items or products are made from many components. This is the case, for instance, with a range of calculators. MPS takes place at the end item level, and all component requirements are determined by MRP from the target completion dates of the end items. Recall the example in Unit 4. In the case of assemble-to-order, the characteristic bill of materials is hour-glass shaped. This is the case where the end item is basically the same, but variety is controlled by customers' requirements. Good examples are cars and computers. The basic unit is master scheduled, but customers determine, for instance, the colour of the car and the options. The master schedule drives the basic operations but final assembly is driven by a related plan, known as the **final assembly schedule** or FAS. In a pure make-to-order environment, the final end products are not known. Detailed scheduling is only possible when orders come in. A forward-looking MPS can only be done on the expected use of components and raw materials.

We will illustrate master scheduling in a make-to-stock environment with reference to Figure 14. The table looks much the same, and indeed has many similar features to those we discussed in MRP.

Weeks	0	1	2	3	4	5	6
Forecast demand		200	200	200	200	200	200
Actual orders		230	150	160	80	50	0
Projected available balance	300	70	320	120	320	120	320
Available to promise		70	90		270		
MPS			400		400		400

Figure 14: Master production scheduling example

A **demand time fence** is set up after two weeks, and a **planning time fence** after four weeks. On-hand quantity at the start of period is 300 units. The master-scheduled planned quantity is 400 units.

Notice the following:

● There are **time fences**: a demand time fence and a planning time fence. The demand time fence is normally set to correspond with the actual time to manufacture the product. In other words, inside the demand time fence work has commenced on making the product. Of course, within the demand time fence the scheduler would like as little disruption as possible and the schedule is regarded as **frozen**. The planning time fence is set to correspond to the time to acquire the most important components and to build the product. Within this time fence the aim would be to minimise disruption but still to allow flexibility. Normally the master scheduler is authorised to make changes within this period only under certain pre-specified conditions. Between the time fences the schedule is regarded as **slushy**. Beyond the planning time fence, the computer can make changes automatically, and the schedule is regarded as **liquid**. In this period the consequences of schedule changes are minimal.

● Second line of the table details the **item forecasts period by period** out into the future. These may be actual forecasts derived by methods that we discussed in Unit 4, but may reflect the objectives of the production plan to, for example, build up inventory at particular times of the year.

● Third line lists **orders actually booked**. Of course, these tail off with time. In the first few periods, actual orders may exceed forecasts. As orders come in they are entered into the master planning system, and are said to 'consume' the forecast.

● Fourth line details the expected **on-hand balance** week by week. This line is calculated in the following way:

within the demand time fence:

$$\text{projected available balance} = \text{prior period on hand balance} + \text{MPS} - \text{customer orders}$$

after the demand time fence:

$$\text{projected available balance} = \text{prior period on hand balance} + \text{MPS} - \text{(greater of) orders customer orders or forecast.}$$

● Fifth line of the display shows **available to promise (ATP)**. These are literally the remaining items that marketing can promise to customers in each period, knowing that they will be delivered on time. This line is calculated as follows :

for the first period:

available to promise = on hand balance + MPS – sum of customer orders before the next

MPS

for subsequent periods:

$$\text{available to promise} = \text{MPS} - \text{sum of customer orders before the next MPS.}$$

Notice that available to promise is not listed in every period. If it were it would be misleading because availability is dependent upon cumulative demand.

● Sixth line is the **actual MPS**. An MPS item is needed whenever the projected available balance would otherwise fall below zero or below the safety stock quantity. Within the planning time fence, the MPS is 'firmed' by the master scheduler by the creation of firm planned orders. (You will remember from our discussions on MRP that firm planned orders are not overwritten by the computer system when a regeneration update takes place.) This introduces stability into the manufacturing schedule.

ACTIVITY 10

Complete the MPS record shown in Figure 15 below.

Weeks	0	1	2	3	4	5	6
Forecast demand		300	300	300	250	250	250
Actual orders		220	370	280	260	80	70
Projected available balance	400						
Available to promise							
MPS							

Figure 15: Master production scheduling example

Demand time fence = 2 weeks; planning time fence = 4 weeks; on-hand quantity at start of period = 400 units; MPS quantity = 500 units.

Your answer should agree with Figure 16. This has a few variations from the earlier example. One problem is that one available to promise quantity is negative. This, of course, makes no sense so we adjust the quantity by subtracting the negative quantity from the next available to promise quantity, and reducing the ATP to zero.

Weeks	0	1	2	3	4	5	6
Forecast demand		300	300	300	250	250	250
Actual orders		220	370	280	260	80	70
Projected available balance	400	180	310	10	250	0	250
Available to promise		180	0		10		
MPS			500		500		500

Figure 16: Master production scheduling example

YIELD ANALYSIS: A 'MASTER SCHEDULING' AID FOR SERVICES

Today, in many service areas, there are rarely standard prices. Airlines offer a host of prices depending on, for example, period of advance booking and whether or not a Saturday night is included. Train fares vary dramatically with time of day and whether a discount card is used. Hotels offer weekend deals. These offers attempt to make the best profit from demands for available capacity. This is what **yield** is all about.

Yield analysis divides up total available capacity into blocks which are sold off at the most competitive rates. For example, a hotel might be confident that it will sell 30% of its weekday capacity to the passing trade at premium rates. The remaining 70% of capacity might be targeted 50% to tour operators and 20% to conference traffic. Having projected these demand splits, the hotel would then be prepared to sell up to 50% to tour operators, but would be reluctant to sell more than this because it could foresee that it could probably sell the remainder more lucratively. **Yield management** defines the categories of demand, forecasting the split of demands, judging the probability of filling each type of demand, fixing prices which will maximise profit, and then managing demand for capacity in line with the targets. There may be more complex rules. For example, past experience may suggest that unless conference capacity is taken up by a week before the due date, it is more profitable to offer this capacity to tour operators.

2.5 Rough Cut Capacity Planning in services and manufacturing

Recall that the MPS should be checked for capacity against the **rough cut capacity plan**. This is sometimes an iterative procedure, necessitating going back and forth between the two. In services, however, MPS and **RCCP** is often done simultaneously. In can be done automatically, for example, when all rooms are taken, the hotel is full and it will not accept any more bookings. In other instances, for example airlines, deliberate overbooking is allowed in the expectation that a certain number of passengers will fail to turn up. This sometimes goes wrong, you may have been offered an incentive to take a later flight. Seat reservation strategies are worth millions of pounds to airlines, some of which have developed complex decision procedures to help with the problem. In a popular restaurant having more than one sitting, capacity evaluation involves making an estimate of how long it will take to finish a meal. These service examples illustrate that much capacity evaluation relies upon experience and learning. We need to make sure that this learning does in fact take place, for example, by recording the percentage of 'no shows' or the length of dinner sittings, so that judgements can be made on up-to-date information.

RCCP evaluates the MPS against key resources. The first question is therefore: 'what is a key resource?' In practice this is not a difficult issue. A key resource is a person, machine, or skill or other bottleneck or constrained resource which is in short supply. Usually it is expensive or difficult to acquire.

There are two common ways in which RCCP can be undertaken; using a **bill of resources**, and using a **load profile**. Both methods are 'quick and dirty' (see Woolsey and Swanson, 1975), but at this level, that is usually good enough. Since it is only a rough evaluation, there is a tendency to err on the safe or generous side.

RCCP BY BILL OF RESOURCES
The bill of resources is the simpler method. Here each master scheduled item has a list of key resources that it is associated with, together with the amount of time consumed on each resource by one master scheduled item. Although probably an unrealistic example, one hotel guest may 'consume' 1.1 beds (some will demand single accommodation) and one-tenth of a restaurant waiter per night. So 100 guests booked in will require 110 beds and 10 waiters per night. This is then compared with the availability of beds and waiters. If we replace beds, waiters and nights with minutes spent on a centre lathe, on a press, and days respectively we

have the more realistic factory equivalent. As a result of multiplying the MPS by the time each product is expected to spend on each bottleneck or constrained resource, a load will result which is then compared with the available capacity. In the bill of resources method, the week in which the MPS item is due for completion is assumed to be the same week in which the constrained resource is to be used. This may not be realistic, but is often considered good enough.

Take an example where the master scheduled items due for completion are 180 units in week 3, 300 units in week 4, and 600 units in week 5. If there is one constrained resource (say a centre lathe), on which each unit spends 10 minutes, then the rough cut capacity plan would show 30 hours in week 3, 50 hours in week 4, and 100 hours in week 5. If the factory works two shifts or 70 hours per week, there is a potential problem in week 5, as shown in Figure 18.

LOAD PROFILE APPROACH

The **load profile approach** uses the same sort of data as the bill of resources but offsets by the appropriate lead times. For instance, in the above example, perhaps the centre lathe is used for 2 minutes per unit one week before completion, and for 8 minutes per unit two weeks before completion. The total time per unit is the same 10 minutes. In between using this key resource, the master scheduled item is made using non-key resources that we need not worry about. Thus the load profile for the above example is given in Figure 17 below.

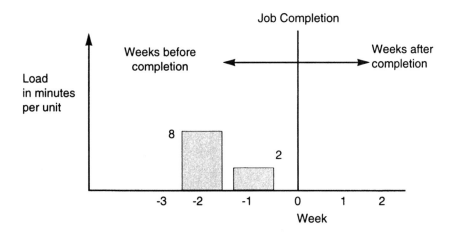

Figure 17: Load profile for centre lathe example

Figure 18 shows the load calculation for the same example using a bill of resources and load profiles.

Week			0	1	2	3	4	5	
MPS						180	300	600	
Bill of resources unit						10	10	10	Simple
Total load (mins)						1800	3000	6000	multiplication
Total load (hours)						30	50	100	approach
Load profile 1				1440	360				
Load profile 2					2400	600			Load profile
Load profile 3						4800	1200		approach
Total load (mins)				1440	2760	5400	1200		
Total load (hours)				24	46	90	20		

Figure 18: Load calculation using bill of resources and load profiles

Now we should compare this load to the available weekly capacity of 70 hours. We notice that there is still a capacity problem, but the week in which it occurs has shifted.

ACTIVITY 11

Using the load profile calculation that we have just looked at, what should now be done, assuming that there are no other MPS items scheduled to be routed through the centre lathe?

We now have a number of choices. We can work 20 hours of overtime in week 3. But we are already on double-shift working, so getting staff to do this may present a problem. We would also have to consider the impact on costs, and the effects on maintenance, if maintenance takes place during the third shift.

Or we could complete the work one week late. We would have to check the impact with marketing.

Or we could do 20 hours of extra work early, during the week before. This looks a possibility, but we would have to check if the necessary materials will be available ahead of schedule.

These are typically the types of consideration that a master scheduler would have to make on a daily basis.

Having validated the master schedule we are now ready to move on to material requirements planning. Refer back to the overall closed loop figure (Figure 3) if you are unsure of the sequence.

2.6 MRP in services and manufacturing

Material requirements planning (MRP) was developed for batch manufacturing inventories, and we dealt with it in Unit 4. We also noted earlier in this unit how MRP results not only in planned order releases for material, but also forms a rough manufacturing schedule.

MRP is suitable where a bill of materials can be developed, and where such bills are used over and over again. Materials are central to the scheduling task because, as we noted in Unit 4, that is where much of the costs lie. Few services are of this type, but we noted earlier that MRP has been used in hospitals and in a multi-storey building. However, there are many service industries that have material requirements that depend upon the MPS, but where it would be unusual to have a formal bill of materials. Examples are restaurants, hospitals, printers, and university bookstores. In the latter, the MPS is simply the schedule of courses to be run. Many service industries simply do not have inventory requirements, so in these cases this technique would not be relevant and they would go directly from the master scheduling equivalent to detailed scheduling.

The characteristic deep bill of materials structure is also not found in projects and in pure job shop operations (where a bill of materials would seldom be re-used), and where the critical resources are usually people or machines. In high volume repetitive manufacture much of the cost is in materials, and so it is appropriate to use a bill of materials, but here the emphasis should be on flow or JIT rather than on intermittent operations. The standard multi-layered bill of materials is replaced by a single-level bill not suited for scheduling operations.

We have already discussed MRP in Unit 4. Before moving onto to detailed scheduling, however, we should consider **capacity requirements planning (CRP)**, the capacity evaluator to MRP. Refer again to Figure 3, closed loop manufacturing.

2.7 CRP and line balancing

CRP, like MRP, is found only in certain types of manufacturing industry, particularly in batch manufacture where deep bills of material are appropriate. Like MRP, CRP uses infinite scheduling. Even in such batch manufacturing environments, however, CRP is gradually being superseded by finite capacity scheduling. In high volume environments, it is not or should not be found. Instead, **line balancing** is the way to manage capacity.

The MRP and CRP stages are generally not found in the service industry. Detailed CRP calculations are long and tedious. The 'bottom line' of CRP is that it produces loadings for all key workcentres, allowing the planner to make adjustments. CRP does not produce the final schedule of the exact sequence of jobs to be progressed through a workcentre, this is our task of the next section on sequencing. Nor does it recommend which jobs need to be rescheduled in the case of capacity overloads.

2.8 Sequencing in services and manufacturing

After master scheduling, and as we have seen for some manufacturing companies, after MRP and CRP, we have **detailed scheduling** or **sequencing**. This is also known in some manufacturing companies as **dispatching**. Here we determine the exact sequence in which jobs should be undertaken in order to achieve some objective such as minimising cost, maximising customer service, or making best use of facilities.

Everyone is involved with sequencing almost every day. A cook has to sequence food preparation and cooking in order to bring the entire meal together. Students face sequencing decisions relating to which assignments they need to work on next. You probably have to sequence your activities at weekends to fit shopping, reading, preparing meals, and so forth around events which have fixed slots such as a sports match or a television programme. In all of these, it may be inappropriate or inefficient to simply undertake jobs on a strict first-in, first-out basis.

Let us consider an example. A book printer has four main activities: setting, printing, collating and binding. All books have to go through this sequence. You cannot bind a book before it is collated. Some textbooks involve a lot of time on setting, art books have to be specially bound, and the printing time depends on the number of pages in the book and the print quantity. Just as in project management, no activity can start until the previous activity is complete. If the printer has organised the work well, the equivalent of master scheduling will have been done, resulting in the quotation of realistic delivery times and no undue overloading of constrained critical resources. The printer often has a backlog of work; at the beginning of a particular week the following jobs are outstanding, each operation having been allocated an estimated time for completion:

Job	Time in hours to:			
	Set	Print	Collate	Bind
1	7	3	3	2
2	2	5	10	8
3	16	4	2	5
4	5	10	1	12
5	4	2	9	7

ACTIVITY 12

What is the order in which the jobs should be done? You can address this question by drawing a Gantt chart. Remember Gantt charts from Unit 5, *Project Management*. One possibility is to simply do them in the order in which they have been received. Try this out. The Gantt chart has been started for you below in Figure 19.

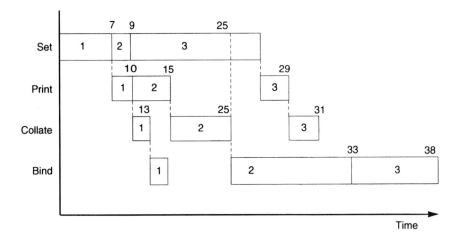

Figure 19: Partial Gantt chart for printer example

What is the overall completion time? Can you improve on the sequence to shorten the overall completion time? Try it out below.

Figure 20: Blank Gantt chart

ACTIVITY 13

You have probably achieved a dramatic improvement in overall completion time by using commonsense. Now think of the logic of what you have done. Which jobs should be scheduled first, and which last, and why?

You will probably realise that it is a good idea to start the shortest jobs first, in order that the second and subsequent activities get going as soon as possible. Also, if there is an exceptionally long final activity, that job should be scheduled as early as possible. This is to allow other jobs to catch up, and to avoid having to do one very long activity on its own at the end.

This type of problem is very common in manufacturing, and also in services. But the optimal solution is difficult to obtain except in some specialised circumstances. In the previous example there only 5! ($5 \times 4 \times 3 \times 2 \times 1 = 120$) possibilities, all of which can easily be enumerated. But if there are 10 jobs the number of possibilities has grown to 3.6 million, and 20 jobs would take the fastest computer on earth centuries to evaluate. The complexity rises even further if the sequence can be altered between processes. The formula is then:

$$(n!)^m$$, where n is the number of jobs and m is the number of processes.

Complete enumeration is impractical, and optimisation routines are very complex. But we can present a 'quick and dirty' (Woolsey and Swanson, 1975) method for this type of scheduling problem, which does not guarantee an optimal solution but usually gives a good solution. This is based on your own commonsense observations above.

For each job, determine a fraction as follows :

- Compare the time taken on the first process with the time taken on the last process.
- If the time on the first process is less than the time taken on the last process, the fraction is assigned a numerator of –1; otherwise it is assigned a value of +1.
- The denominator of the job fraction for each job is the minimum of the sum of the first two process times, or the next two processing times, or the next two, or (and so on) until the sum of the last two processing times.

Then, arrange the jobs in ascending order, from smallest to largest.

ACTIVITY 14

Try Woolsey's method on the earlier printing problem, and calculate the time to complete all the jobs

---

The job fractions are :

   job 1 : + 1/5
   job 2 : – 1/7
   job 3 : + 1/6
   job 4 : – 1/11

job 5   : $-1/6$

and the suggested best sequence is job 5, job 2, job 4, job 3, job 1.

How did this compare with your 'by inspection' solution? This method does not necessarily give the optimal solution, but it probably gives the best ratio of answer to time expended. Finding the true optimal solution is lengthy, and calculation time rises dramatically with the number of processes and jobs.

A SPECIAL CASE: *N* JOBS ON TWO PROCESSES

One special case is where any number of jobs have to be scheduled through only two processes in strict sequence. If you face this unusually simple scheduling problem, you can use 'Johnson's Rule' to get the optimal solution. You can probably derive this from your commonsense observations concerning the print shop problem:

- Find the shortest processing time (remaining) for any job on any process.

- For the job found, if the shortest processing time is on the first process, schedule that job first on the first process. If the shortest processing time is on the second process, schedule that job last on the second process.

- Cross off that job and begin again.

ACTIVITY 15

Consider an accounting firm which has six urgent jobs each involving report preparation, followed by word processing. Report preparation depends upon complexity, but word processing depends upon length. Estimated times in hours are as follows:

	Preparation	Word processing
Job 1	8	3
Job 2	24	5
Job 3	4	4
Job 4	10	8
Job 5	14	6
Job 6	3	1

1   Which job order minimises total processing time? Using Johnson's Rule you should get:

job 3, job 4, job 5 , job 2, job 1, job 6.

2   Draw the Gantt chart for this task below (Figure 21), to get the overall processing time. You will still find unavoidable gaps. *Figure 21: Johnson's Rule Gantt chart*

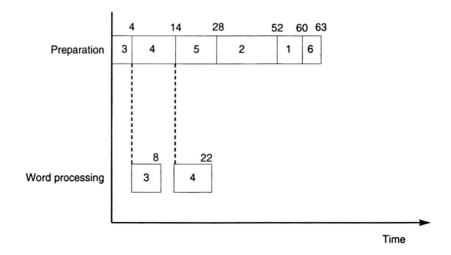

Figure 21: Johnson's Rule Gantt chart

SINGLE-PROCESS SCHEDULING IN SERVICES AND MANUFACTURING

We have seen that the **multiple-process scheduling** case is complex. We will return later to see how multiple-process scheduling has been developed into what we term **finite-capacity scheduling**. In the meantime let us look at the case of scheduling jobs through a single process.

Single-process scheduling is useful to know about, especially in service operations. Many services are of this type: a solicitor faces the problem of which clients to deal with first, a photocopy shop routinely has this same problem, as does a secretary, a student, a person working in a travel agency, and many others.

Let us look at the case of single-process scheduling by referring to the following case. Here 10 jobs (or clients) have to be dealt with by a single process (solicitor, photocopier, secretary, etc.). Each job has an estimated time and a desired completion date. To make things easy, all times are expressed in days:

Job	1	2	3	4	5	6	7	8	9	10
Days to do job	20	12	5	11	21	22	4	18	5	20
Target completion	40	20	92	42	68	74	93	108	110	105

There are many 'rules' according to which the jobs can be sequenced, but we will examine just a few common ones. These are the **due date rule** (nearest due date first), the **shortest processing time** rule (shortest job first), and the **sequence to minimise the number of late jobs**.

ACTIVITY 16

Using the above figures, arrange the jobs according to the due date rule and according to the shortest processing time rule. For each case, complete the tables below. Find the number of late jobs and calculate the total number of late days. The first calculations have already been started for you. Comment on your findings.

Period	1	2	3	4	5	6	7	8	9	10

Due date rule

Job order	2	1	4	5						
Job time	12	20	11	21						
Accumulated time	12	32	43							
Due date	20	40	42							
Days early (+) late (−)	8	8	−1							

Shortest processing time rule

Job order	7	3	9	4	2					
Job time	4	5	5	11	12					
Accumulated time	4	9	14	25						
Due date	93	92	110	42						
Days early (+) late (−)	89	83	96	17						

Figure 22: Single-process scheduling rules

You should have found that, in the case of the due date rule, there were four jobs done early and six jobs done late. The total number of days late was 78.

In the case of the shortest processing time rule, six jobs were early and four late. The total number of days late was 164. You should notice that, although the number of jobs late was less, those jobs that were late were very late in comparison with the due date ordered jobs. These results are typical.

ACTIVITY 17

When is it appropriate to schedule by shortest processing time and when by due date?

Shortest processing time has the effect of completing the maximum number of jobs in the least possible time. Formally, this rule minimises the sum of the waiting times. Woolsey refers to this rule as the **before the auditors' rule**, meaning that for cash flow or inventory reasons you may wish to complete as many jobs as soon as possible. If your performance is measured on how many jobs you have completed, this is the method to choose. On the other hand, some of those customers that are late are going to very late so you need to watch these. You will probably have noticed that there is a tie between two jobs having equal job times. Commonsense would indictate that you do the one with the shortest due date first.

The due date rule has the effect of minimising the maximum lateness. This rule is appropriate if there are large penalty costs payable for late work. The later the job, the greater the penalty. If it is inevitable that you will have a few late jobs, make sure you know the type of penalty applicable before deciding on which jobs to do first.

And now we will consider how to minimise the number of late jobs. The procedure is :

1   Arrange the jobs in due date order.

2   Accumulate the completion times, starting with the first job, until you find a late job.

3   Inspect all the jobs up to and including the late job and find the job having the longest processing time. Move this job from the list so that it becomes the last job.

4   Once again accumulate the completion times. If none are now late, stop. If a job is late and it has not previously been moved, go to step 3. If it has been previously moved, stop.

ACTIVITY 18

Carry out this procedure to minimise the number of late jobs for the 10 jobs given earlier. The task has been started for you in Figure 23. Determine the number of late jobs, and the total days late.

	1	2	3	4	5	6	7	8	9	10
Minimise late jobs										
Job order	2	1	4							
Job time	12	20	11							
Accumulated time	12	32	43							
Due date	20	40	42							
Days early (+) late (−)	8	8	−1							

Rule								
Job order	2	4	5	6	3	7	10	8
Job time	12	11	21	22	5	4	20	18
Accumulated time	12	23	44	66	71	75	95	113
Due date	20	42	68	74	92	93	105	108
Days early (+) late (−)	8	19	24	8	21	18	10	−5

Rule						
Job order	2	4	5	3	7	10
Job time	12	11	21	5	4	
Accumulated time	12	23	44	49	53	
Due date	20	42	68	92	93	
Days early (+) late (−)	8	19	24	43	40	

Rule
Job order
Job time
Accumulated time
Due date
Days early (+) late (−)

Figure 23: Schedule to minimise the number of late jobs

You should find that there are now eight jobs on time and two late. The jobs that are late are jobs 1 and 6. The total days late is 140, this figure is between the numbers for the due date rule and for the shortest processing time rule. Of course this rule will make the maximum number of customers happy, but those two customers whose jobs are late are likely to be very upset.

From the above we can see that there is no 'rule for all seasons' in sequencing. It depends on what you wish to achieve. As an operations manager you may meet conflicting requirements from marketing (emphasising delivery?), from finance (emphasising throughput? or efficiency?), or from PR (emphasising fairness?). Unfortunately, you often cannot make everyone happy. Many managers do not realise that there are definite choices to be made, and assume that everything is possible. If you, as an operations manager, do not make the choice, somebody else will have to.

2.9 Line balancing

In repetitive manufacturing, products move down an assembly line on a powered conveyor. Alternatively, products may move through a cell containing several machines. In either case there are no batches, and a product moves on to the next workstation as soon as operations are complete at the prior workstation. The capacity problem is therefore different to that found in batch manufacturing. What is required is to share out the work between successive operations such that the time taken by each operation is in line with the required capacity. For instance, if 60 products per hour are required, then each workstation should have a 'cycle time' of one minute. The total assembly task has to be split up into one-minute chunks. The one-minute chunks of work would probably remain constant for several weeks or months, before it is considered necessary to rebalance the line.

There are several line balancing algorithms which are used by industrial engineers. Industrial engineers need to estimate the length of time taken for each small assembly task, before attempting to allocate the work between operators. This forms part of the assembly line layout problem which we discussed in Unit 3, *Process Design*. Today, however, greater emphasis is being placed on operator participation in line balancing. Thus, for example, at Toyota, Vauxhall and Opel, operators use what is termed a **NUMMI board** to work out exactly how the assembly task will be carried out by members of each team. (NUMMI was the name of the joint Toyota/General Motors venture in Fremont, California.) Detailed timings of work elements is the responsibility of operators, as is the elimination of waste in the assembly task. On the NUMMI board operators accumulate the individual work element times which must add up to less than the desired cycle time.

We discuss this topic on cellular manufacturing in Unit 9.

There is no doubt that timing is still required for line balancing and for standards, but the traditional industrial engineer/work study officer who timed people with a stopwatch is no longer appropriate or acceptable in many Western companies.

2.10 Finite scheduling

In Section 1 of this unit we discussed the OPT principles and mentioned the book, *The Goal* by Goldratt and Cox. Here we will build upon those ideas and relate them to **finite scheduling**. This takes account of capacity constraints. You will recall that MRP is an infinite scheduler as it takes no account of capacity but it does rely on rough cut capacity evaluation and on CRP.

Finite scheduling has evolved rapidly since 1984. Today there are several dozen finite scheduling packages on the market. The algorithms used are often a commercial secret, but we will consider the principles associated with one of the original packages, namely OPT, which was the brainchild of Eli Goldratt. These principles have applications in service as well as manufacturing. In fact, Dr Goldratt has continued to develop these ideas into what he now terms the **theory of constraints,** which he maintains represent a new theory of management!

Central to the theories developed by Goldratt are the concepts of **bottlenecks**, **capacity constrained resources**, and **non-bottlenecks**. A true bottleneck is a resource 'whose capacity is equal to or less than the demand placed upon it'. It limits the amount of money that an organisation can make. A non-bottleneck, on the other hand, is 'any resource whose capacity is greater than the demand placed upon it'. In between lie capacity constrained resources, defined as 'any resource which, if not properly scheduled and managed, is likely to cause the actual flow of product through the plant to deviate from the planned product flow' (Srikanth and Cavallaro, 1995). By definition, therefore, there must be at least one bottleneck in every organisation. However, the bottleneck may be a capacity bottleneck, a market bottleneck, a material bottleneck, a managerial bottleneck, amongst others.

As we saw earlier, 'an hour lost at a bottleneck is an hour lost for the system' but 'an hour lost at a non-bottleneck is merely a mirage'. These simple-sounding statements have profound implications. It means that many traditional costing and performance evaluation systems are outdated. From a scheduling viewpoint it means that bottlenecks must be treated differently from non-bottlenecks. Bottlenecks must be kept working without delay. Consider the three diagrams below in Figure 24, X represents a bottleneck and Y a non-bottleneck:

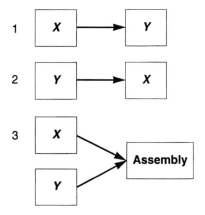

Figure 24: Scheduling with bottlenecks and non-bottlenecks (adapted from Srikanth and Cavallaro)

In diagram 1, a bottleneck operation feeds a non-bottleneck. This means that the non-bottleneck will be idle from time to time, and this is nothing to worry about. However, products that have passed through the bottleneck are valuable because they have had bottleneck time expended upon them. So the non-bottleneck should process the products as soon as possible so as to recoup the investment. Do not therefore send products through a bottleneck, and then let them lie in finished goods inventory. This would be a misuse of valuable bottleneck time.

In diagram 2, a non-bottleneck feeds a bottleneck. Once again the non-bottleneck should have excess time. If there is no set-up involved in the non-bottleneck it should be used only as required to feed the bottleneck. However, if there is set-up involved, then the non-bottleneck should be set up as often as possible, without disrupting the bottleneck, so as to produce smaller batches and thereby minimising inventory investment. Safety inventory should be kept in front of the bottleneck to ensure that it never runs out of products to work on. On the other hand, no inventory should be kept in front of the non-bottleneck because it has excess capacity and idle time is free, but inventory is not! A bottleneck should seek to maximise the batch size, and minimising the lost time due to set-up, but at non-bottlenecks batches should be as small as possible to minimise inventory. This implies that at non-bottlenecks batches will be split into smaller batches.

In diagram 3, a bottleneck and a non-bottleneck both feed an assembly operation. The bottleneck should be protected by safety stock placed in front of it as before, with none placed in front of the non-bottleneck. The non-bottleneck must ensure that it works at a rate that will keep the assembly task working at the same rate as the bottleneck. In order that this is guaranteed, there should be a safety stock of products from the non-bottleneck held in front of the assembly task, but there should be no safety stock from the bottleneck operation held in front of the assembly operation.

Most manufacturing and service operations, however complex, can be constructed by combining these three elements.

Finite scheduling software uses these principles to construct schedules. Many finite schedulers rely on MRP to provide the basic framework and to identify which are the bottlenecks, non-bottlenecks, and capacity constrained resources. Although the algorithms used are confidential to the companies using them, several finite schedulers use the principle of forward finite scheduling on the bottlenecks and near-bottlenecks, and then backward scheduling on non-bottlenecks. At bottlenecks, batch sizes are maximised by combining batches wherever possible, but at non-bottlenecks batches are often split both to fit in with finite requirements and to minimise inventory. In the OPT approach, as you saw earlier, the procedure can be described in terms of the **drum**, **buffer**, and **rope**. The **drum** is the master production schedule which sets the pace of production in line with finite capacity. **Buffers** are time buffers, rather than inventory buffers, which aim to hold a certain time period's worth of work in front of bottlenecks and near-bottlenecks. The amount of time buffer depends upon the assessed risk of problems such as delays. And the **rope** provides a link between bottleneck workstations and 'gateway' workstations (i.e. first operations), so that the amount of work let into the system matches the amount going through the bottleneck, thereby limiting inventory build-up. This is a type of pull system.

Whatever finite scheduling system is used, there is still a basic decision about the priorities of jobs to be loaded. This makes no difference if there is adequate capacity, but where there is a shortfall in capacity the issue arises. The advantages and disadvantages of single-process scheduling are relevant. Modern finite scheduling software allows a user to specify between these options and others, such as customer priority. Many also allow the scheduler to freeze jobs in place in the schedule, to forward or backward schedule, and to specify the period within which the schedule must be made finite. For example, it is more difficult to achieve a finite schedule for each day rather than over a whole week. Modern finite scheduling software usually has powerful graphic displays which allow the scheduler to try various options before committing the factory. Several 'Windows'-based finite scheduling packages are now available, which are often run as a supplement to the MRP II system.

Finally you will remember from our MRP discussions how critical accurate information was to the success of MRP. Accurate information is even more onerous in the case of finite scheduling. Not only do the capacities of all workcentres have to be defined, but product routings must be reasonably accurate, as must all the individual timings of set-up, run and move times. Several finite scheduling packages allow the user to differentiate between major and minor set-up times (i.e. set-up between families and within a family of products), but to do so requires all these times to be known or estimated. The result is that data collection to support finite scheduling is a formidable task for many companies.

2.11 Manufacturing scheduling in a repetitive environment

In repetitive manufacturing environments, often associated with assembly-line manufacturing, such as cars, the principles of JIT scheduling apply. We deal with these principles extensively in Unit 9, so we mention just a few points here.

The closed loop framework is still relevant. The hierarchy we discussed earlier generally applies, but with some modification. We would expect to find a production plan, resource plan, master production schedule and rough cut capacity evaluation. The master production schedule would be expressed in terms of production units, but without the detail of customer-specified options. We would also expect to find MRP, although not with deep bills of materials. Since the task is essentially one of final assembly, all that we need is to acquire the necessary parts in time rather than to build them up into sub-assemblies first. A 'single-level' bill of materials structure may be all that is necessary. Capacity requirements planning is replaced by line balancing. Production activity control is replaced by **final assembly scheduling (FAS)**, which includes the customer-specified options.

Mixed model scheduling is becoming the preferred way. Mixed model scheduling aims to send a repeating sequence of mixed products down the assembly line rather than producing batches of the same product. This allows a steady rate of work all day, rather than one speed for one batch and a second speed for another batch. Also material flow to the line is regular throughout the day.

Undercapacity scheduling is also being adopted. This allows for a certain amount of unscheduled free time at the end of each shift. The idea here is to allow for unexpected disruptions or delays and thus to make sure that the schedule is achieved, no more and no less. If all goes smoothly then the free time is used for team improvement activities and cross-training.

2.12 Queuing

Throughout this unit we have attempted to point out similarities and differences between manufacturing and service operations. In this last section we will consider, briefly, a topic of special applicability in service.

Queuing (or **waiting lines** as they are known in the USA) is an everyday occurrence. As it is a major source of dissatisfaction in service systems, it is worth knowing a little about it! The theory of queuing has been extensively studied. Queuing can involve extensive statistical work, which is not appropriate here.

The most widely studied type of queuing is referred to as **Poisson Exponential** queuing. This means that arrivals are assumed to follow the Poisson distribution and service time, while it is happening, is assumed to follow the **negative exponential distribution**. The Poisson distribution applies to a completely random arrival pattern, and has been found to approximate reality in a wide variety of situations such as customer arrivals, vehicle breakdowns, and accident occurences. The Poisson distribution is completely described by its average. So if you know the average rate of (say) customer arrivals, for example in customers per hour, then the distribution will give you the probabilities of different numbers of customers arriving per hour. Poisson tables are available in any statistics textbook. The exponential distribution is closely related to the Poisson. This is not a statistics text, so we will not go into these distributions further except to say that assuming Poisson/Exponential is a very reasonable assumption for many queuing situations where there are random arrivals and normal service. But, clearly, they do not always apply. For instance, if football supporters arrive in busloads, the arrival pattern in front of the ticket office is unlikely to be Poisson.

Assuming that we have Poisson queuing, it is only necessary to know the average arrival rate in units per time period (usually represented by the symbol λ), and the average service rate in units served per time period whilst serving is in progress (usually represented by the symbol μ). Although the derivations are quite involved, the formulas themselves are very simple, at least for the case of single server queues. They are:

Mean waiting time in the queue = $\dfrac{\lambda}{\mu\,(\mu - \lambda)}$

Mean number in the queue = $\dfrac{\lambda^2}{\mu\,(\mu - \lambda)}$

Mean time in the system (i.e. queuing plus being served) = $\dfrac{1}{\mu - \lambda}$

Mean number in the system = $\dfrac{\lambda}{\mu - \lambda}$

Probability of n customers in the system = $\left(1 - \dfrac{\lambda}{\mu}\right)\left(\dfrac{\lambda}{\mu}\right)^{n}$

To illustrate: if the average arrival rate is two per minute, and the service rate is three per minute (that is an average service time of 20 seconds), then

Mean waiting time in the queue is 0.667 minutes

Mean number in the queue is 1.333

Mean time in the system is 1 minute

Mean number in the system is 2.0

Probability of one customer in the system is (0.33) (0.67) = 0.22.

The ratio λ/μ is known as the **utilisation factor**, and given the symbol ρ (rho). Queuing theory predicts queues that will grow indefinitely when ρ approaches a value of 1.0. In practice, a queuing system is fairly ineffective when ρ has a value exceeding about 0.75.

ACTIVITY 19

To show that queue performance is highly dependent upon the value of the utilisation factor, ρ, calculate and plot the values of the four means in the last section by keeping the service rate constant at three per minute but varying the arrival rate from two per minute to 2.8 per minute in increments of 0.2.

Although the formulas given are strictly for single channel, single server queuing, you can get an impression of the effect of adding an additional server on queue performance by doubling the service rate and recalculating. The effects of adding an extra server are quite dramatic if the utilisation factor is high. Do a few sample calculations to see for yourself. You can also frequently observe this effect in practice in a bank or supermarket when an additional teller or checkout person opens. Next time you are in a queue in a bank or supermarket, look out for this effect.

Today with automated machines dispensing tickets, cash and drinks, a constant service time is becoming more common. Fortunately there are a few simple formulas for the case of Poisson arrivals and constant service.

Mean waiting time in the queue = $\dfrac{\lambda^2}{2\mu \,(\mu - \lambda)}$

For multiple-channel queues the formulas become very complex. In practice, multiple-channel queues are usually studied by simulation modelling for which there are several easy-to-use packages.

MANAGING QUEUES

Without even knowing any queuing formulas, or having a simulation package available, many managers are able to manage queues quite satisfactorily by adapting to situations as they develop. It makes sense, for example, to adopt one or more of the following queue management strategies:

- Alter the number of servers as demand increases. You will see this in operation in banks and supermarkets today. When the queue builds up, a person working at another job stops doing that particular job and opens another serving point. Tesco has recently made much of its stated policy to do just this. Of course, it implies that workers have been cross-trained.

- Adopt single queues. There is nothing quite as annoying as finding that you have ended up in the slowest moving queue, and that other customers who have entered after you are served before you. Fortunately, single queuing is becoming more commonplace.

- Consider the possibility of a streamlined server. Although this may conflict with the previous point, having a server dedicated to more simple transactions (such as basket only, cash only at a supermarket) will usually improve customer satisfaction.

- Inform customers about the expected length of wait. This is adopted in Disneyland and other theme parks and also by traffic authorities. It may have the effect of persuading some customers to come back at a less busy time. Also, psychology suggests that the notices should be pessimistic. If you expect a half-hour wait, and get through in 20 minutes you are likely to be less unhappy.

- Make sure that people entering a queue need to be there in the first place. For instance, in a post office, is it necessary to queue for a form when it could be made available on a rack.

The psychology of queuing is almost as important as the operations aspect. David Maister (1985) has assembled seven principles of queuing. These are:

- unoccupied time feels longer than occupied time
- pre-process waits feel longer than in-process waits
- anxiety makes waits seem longer
- uncertain waits seem longer than known waits
- unexplained waits seem longer than explained waits
- unfair waits are longer than equitable waits
- the more valuable the service the longer people are prepared to wait
- solo waits feel longer than group waits.

This suggests several actions: provide information; give queues a video to watch; have an efficient priority system, and so on.

Summary

In this section, we have worked our way through the formal closed loop system found in manufacturing. We have attempted to show how much of the closed loop concept is applicable in services, at least as a framework. At the top of the framework we looked at long term aggregate (or production) planning. In services and manufacturing, aggregate plans deal with how resources will be employed, and how much capacity is appropriate. The classic plans are the level plan and the chase plan. Both involve trade-offs that must be understood; fixing the correct level of capacity is challenging in service and manufacturing. In a manufacturing firm, the MPS is the key interface between operations, marketing and finance and all three parties should be involved in master scheduling policy formulation. In services the 'master schedules' are plans such as timetables, bookings, and appointments. It forms the basis for ongoing operations, so we should be careful about delegating this critical task. Yield management is an interesting guideline in services.

Then we looked at more detailed scheduling and sequencing. In manufacturing operations, we noted the growing use of finite scheduling and mixed model scheduling found in repetitive operations. With reference to sequencing we learned that there is no one best way: we must understand the objectives. Finally, in a section on queuing theory we learned the importance of the utilisation ratio, in avoiding unduly long queues, but we also noted the importance of the psychology of queuing.

We should consider scheduling and capacity side by side, level by level. As with many thing, good preparation ahead of time helps avoid detailed problems later on.

Unit Review Activity

Read the article 'JIT and MRP II could make beautiful music together' (Resource Item 8.1). This article ties together topics we dealt with in this unit, Unit 3, *Process Design*, Unit 6, *Quality Management*, and Unit 9, *Time Based Operations*. The article emphasises that an integrated approach is likely to be more successful. You will benefit by reading the article again after Unit 9. In the meantime, consider whether the integrated approach described is likely to apply in all manufacturing environments.

Unit Summary

In this unit we have looked at scheduling and capacity. These two related areas are more common than is generally realised. We all schedule and take account of capacity almost every day, although not of course in as formal a way as we presented in this unit. Scheduling concerns priorities.

In capacity considerations, we learned a fundamental distinction between load, how much work is released to the factory or office, and capacity, the ability of the factory or office to handle the work. Capacity and load must be kept in balance. Releasing more work does not mean that more completed work will come out the other end. Knowing your capacity and load situation is fundamental to good scheduling, and hence to good customer service. This requires that you have good data on how long each item of work will take at each stage.

An important fact of scheduling, not appreciated by all managers, is that there is no such thing as the one best schedule. Schedules for maximising cash flow, for minimising average lateness, and for maximising the number of jobs on time, may all be different. The unit looked at methods for these and others.

We looked at both push scheduling, where work is sent on to the next stage as soon as it is finished at the previous stage, and at pull scheduling where work is only accepted when it can be handled. This is the method used in JIT manufacturing. We also looked at OPT rules, which relate to the management of bottlenecks, and which are making a big impact on related fields such as cost accounting.

We then considered scheduling and capacity as part of a wider framework including 'master scheduling'. In manufacturing, the MPS is a prime tool for control of the business. The service equivalent of the MPS is, for instance, the reservation book at a hotel and the appointments book at a surgery. Compiling a successful MPS has to be done bearing in mind the available capacity.

References

APICS (1991) *Material and Capacity Requirements Planning: CPIM Reprints*, American Production and Inventory Control Society, Falls Church, Virginia

Blackstone, J H (1989) *Capacity Management*, APICS/South-Western, Cincinnati

Brown, R (1995) 'In search of the total solution', *The Performance Advantage*, American Production and Inventory Control Society, June, pp. 46–51

Cox, J F, Blackstone, J H and Spenser, M S (eds.) (1992) *APICS Dictionary*, 7th edn,, American Production and Inventory Control Society, Falls Church, Virginia

Goldratt, E and Cox, J (1989) *The Goal*, Gower, Aldershot

Lovelock, C (1994) *Product Plus*, McGraw-Hill, New York

Maister, D (1985) 'The psychology of waiting lines', in Czepiel, J A, Solomon, MR and Surprenant, CF, *The Service Encounter*, Lexington Books/D.C. Heath, Lexington, Massachusetts

Plossl, G (1983) *Production and Inventory Control: Applications*, Prentice Hall, Englewood Cliffs, New Jersey

Plossl, G (1985) *Production and Inventory Control: Principles and Techniques*, 2nd edn, Prentice Hall, Englewood Cliffs, New Jersey

Schonberger, R, and Knod, E M Jr., *Operations Management*, 5th edn, Irwin, Homewood, Illinois

Srikanth, M L and Cavallaro, H E Jr., (1995) *Regaining Competitiveness: Putting The Goal to Work*, North River Press, Great Barrington, Massachusetts

Swanta, W and Parish, R (1995) 'Putting data to work', *The Performance Advantage*, APICS, May, p. 24

Woolsey, R E D and Swanson, H S (1975) *Operations Research for Immediate Application: A Quick and Dirty Manual*, Harper and Row, New York

Vollman, T, Berry, W and Whybark, DC (1992) *Manufacturing Planning and Control Systems*, 3rd edn, Irwin, Homewood, Illinois

Recommended Reading

Adler, P (1993) 'Time and motion regained', *Harvard Business Review,* February, pp. 97–108

Answer to Unit Review Activity

Refer back to Unit 1, Section 2.7 where we discussed the Product-Process Matrix. Here we emphasised the positions of various scheduling techniques on the diagonal of the matrix. We noted that in environments of higher, more repetitive, volumes, JIT is increasingly applicable. Here we see the detail.

UNIT 9
TIME BASED OPERATIONS

Introduction

This unit aims to introduce some of the newer developments in operations management. The areas covered in this unit have been at the forefront of management attention over the past decade and are likely to remain priority areas for some time. They are united by the concepts of **time compression** and **waste reduction**.

Objectives

By the end of the unit, you should be able to:

- understand the significance of the just-in-time (JIT) philosophy
- identify the core JIT techniques
- know the importance of lean operations and the core techniques
- understand the importance of time in operations management
- identify the fundamentals of business process reengineering
  and its potential impact on all types of businesses
- understand the significance of the design and purchasing functions
- understand the significance of supply chain management and logistics
- understand the principles of the partnership approach to supply management.

Most of all, we hope you will have a sense of the excitement in the areas we cover. Most of the topics discussed are so new that they still offer ground-floor opportunities to both companies and graduates to achieve success.

Those of you who are interested can consult the articles identified in the References and Recommended Reading for further detail.

SECTION 1

A History of Time

Introduction

In this section we will look at the history and significance of time based operations, including the origins and development of the just-in-time (JIT) system. We will consider some conceptual frameworks: the **five zeros** and the **manufacturing trilogy.**

In the 1950s, Taiichi Ohno, Toyota's Chief Engineer, was sent to America to study production systems at General Motors. He was not impressed. But what did impress him were American supermarkets. Ohno (1988) took note of how products removed from the shelf by customers were replaced by staff. He thought that would be a good way to build cars, thus the JIT system was born.

In the early 1980s, Toyota once again was linked with General Motors. By this time GM was beginning to experience a loss of market share to Japanese cars, but was not unduly worried. GM believed that automation was the correct response, but nevertheless thought that something could be learned from the Japanese.

Toyota was attempting to get a toe-hold in American manufacture. An opportunity arose at GM's Fremont, California plant which had outdated equipment, a history of difficult labour relations, and was about to be closed down. A joint venture between GM and Toyota was established at Fremont, known as NUMMI. Within two years the NUMMI plant became one of the most productive in General Motors. Initially, GM refused to believe the results and continued on their automation strategy, which was eventually to cost them billions of dollars and lead to the dismissal of the Chief Executive Officer. You can read the whole fascinating, sad history of this episode, showing the politics and prejudice, in *Managing on the Edge* by Richard Pascale, 1990. Eventually, the message came through: automation alone is not the answer, but involving the workforce, eliminating waste, and ongoing continuous improvement, could well be. The JIT system had come to America.

Between the 1950s and 1980s, Toyota assembled the JIT system, later to be renamed **lean manufacturing**. The chief architect of this system was Taiichi Ohno. He was an integrator as well as an innovator. He successfully combined concepts such as the supermarket pull, cellular manufacturing, (originally developed in the former Soviet Union), quality (from Deming and Juran), set-up reduction (from Toyota consultant, Shigeo Shingo), and supplier partnership (supposedly learned from Marks and Spencer), to form a world-beating system.

In one sense, Henry Ford was the first JIT manufacturer. He was able to convert raw materials such as ingots of iron into complete Model T-Fords within the space of 60 hours, an achievement no modern car manufacturer has been able to match. He was the father of modern mass-production, a system which was paramount in car manufacturing until the arrival in the West of lean manufacturing (or JIT) a decade or so later. The difference, of course, was that model T-Fords were all alike – 'you can have any colour you like as long as it is black'. Toyota's achievement is that it has been able to match Ford's levels of productivity, but with much greater variety.

The JIT system has been the basis for a broad set of developments in operations management over the past 10 years. These include **lean manufacturing, mass customisation, business process reengineering, total productive maintenance, agile manufacturing,** and **quick response** distribution systems. These can collectively be termed **time based operations management**.

1.1 Conceptual frameworks for time based operations

A good way of looking at just-in-time is through the **five zeros**. This was suggested by Archier and Serieyx (1987) in their book *The Type 3 Corporation*. They are:

- zero paper
- zero inventory
- zero downtime
- zero defect
- zero delay

However, the five zeros require wider interpretation: **Zero paper** does not simply imply holding all data in computers but rather simplicity and visibility – is it necessary to keep it at all, and if it is, what is the best way to make it accessible to all? **Zero inventory** implies minimal levels of inventory and minimal idle inventory. **Zero downtime** applies particularly to bottlenecks but also to flexibility and reliability of all processes. **Zero defect** applies all along the chain of quality that we discussed in Unit 6. And **zero delay** applies to design time, manufacturing time, and to distribution time. It concerns minimising not only manufacturing time, but also the time required to bring new products to market. All five are desirable because all represent removal of waste and complexity. We may never achieve zero in all five or even in one of them, but they represent a vision of world class operations of the future, pointing the way and showing the hazards. The five zeros are illustrated in Figure 1.

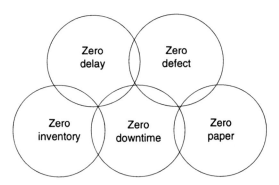

Figure 1: The five zeros

Yet another useful view is by Robert Hall (1987), one of the early Western pioneers of JIT, who refers to **the manufacturing trilogy: JIT scheduling, total quality (TQ),** and **total people involvement (TPI)**. According to Hall, this is like a three-legged stool: if one element is not present the whole system fails. Perhaps it is useful to recall Juran's **quality trilogy** at this point: **quality planning, quality control** and **quality improvement**. These three elements are applicable within each of Hall's trilogy: an expanded version of the Hall trilogy is shown in Figure 2.

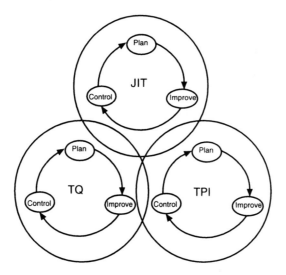

Figure 2: Expanded Hall trilogy: JIT (just-in-time); TQ (total quality) and TPI (total people involvement)

JIT can be viewed on at least three levels, as shown in Figure 3. At the core, JIT is to do with scheduling: co-ordinating operations so that they take place literally 'just-in-time' to be ready for the next stage. The 'next stage' applies all the way from raw material to final customer, and is not limited to the manufacturing firm itself. Each stage is synchronised with the next so as to avoid unnecessary delay. The concept of **flow** is central to JIT scheduling. In particular, we are concerned with the flow of materials; where much of the cost in today's manufacturing plants lies in materials. To many manufacturing managers, this scheduling view of JIT *is* JIT.

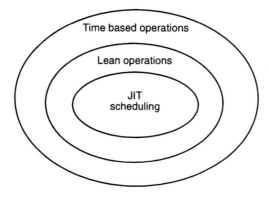

Figure 3: The JIT hierarchy

JIT scheduling requires a whole set of techniques to make it effective. And to ensure that it remains effective, it requires a dedication to continuous improvement and to the elimination of waste. This is the second level. Ohno believed that the **total Toyota production system (TTPS,** his phrase for JIT) was an all out attack on waste, and defined seven types of waste. According to this view, waste is everywhere, and everyone needs to be able to recognise it and to participate in its elimination. It is convenient to refer to this second level as **lean manufacturing** or **lean operations** to avoid the confusion with JIT scheduling. Perhaps it may better be termed **lean enterprise.** Lean manufacturing was a phrase coined by the researchers in the MIT study of the world car industry, which resulted in the best-selling and stimulating book *The Machine that Changed the World* by Womack et al, 1990. The machine is the Toyota production system.

But we may think of JIT in wider context, which is referred to as time based operations. This extends the JIT (and total quality) concepts of scheduling, waste elimination, participation and continuous improvement to not only the whole enterprise but also to the enterprise and its partners. All are increasingly involved in time based competitiveness, a phrase coined by Stalk and Hout (1990) in their classic book *Competing Against Time.* This time based view is the context into which concepts such as business process reengineering, quick response distribution, and mass customisation fit.

In the sections which follow we will use this hierarchy. First, however, we will briefly consider where JIT is applicable. Of course, JIT started in repetitive manufacturing, particularly the car industry, and is now a cornerstone of that industry. Over time, however, it has been found that various techniques, strongly associated with JIT, are applicable outside repetitive manufacturing. Moreover, repetitive manufacturing does not necessarily mean high-volume manufacturing; we can make one item a month and still make use of repetitive principles. And beyond this, as we have noted, much of the lean manufacturing philosophy has been found to be applicable in service industries. Beware, therefore, of managers who claim that 'JIT is not applicable to our business'. Perhaps they are referring to JIT scheduling, but they would almost certainly be wrong to dismiss the JIT or lean philosophy out of hand. In manufacturing, during the mid-1980s several articles appeared along the lines 'JIT or MRP – Which is Right for You?'. Today such articles would be considered to miss the point, which is that both are applicable in most manufacturing environments, but it is the emphasis that may well be different. MRP and MRP II are most applicable in batch manufacture, JIT is most applicable in repetitive manufacture. We can illustrate this by reference to the product process matrix, which we discussed in Unit 1 (Figure 4).

In this figure we note that different scheduling techniques are applicable to different industries. In batch manufacturing, MRP II supported by JIT techniques is most appropriate: but for repetitive manufacturing, JIT techniques supported by MRP (not necessarily MRP II) is more appropriate.

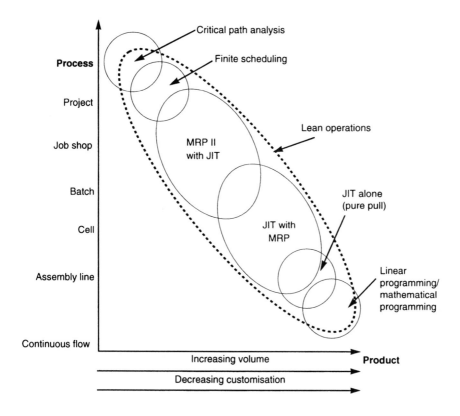

Figure 4: Product process matrix and scheduling

Summary

In this introductory section, we have learned something of the history and significance of time-based operations. A three-level hierarchy is a possible viewpoint with JIT scheduling at the core, then lean operations, then time based operations or the lean enterprise.

We looked at a number of frameworks: the manufacturing trilogy comprises JIT, total quality, and total people involvement. The five zeros (paper, downtime, inventory, defect, delay) is a useful way of setting the agenda for world-class operations. And the product process matrix shows JIT scheduling to be most applicable in the repetitive area, but the lean philosophy has much wider applicability.

SECTION 2

Just-in-Time Operations

Introduction

In this section, we will look at JIT scheduling, which aims to produce at a rate to meet customer demand, no more, no less. We will consider traditional **push systems** and the **kanban-based pull system** and how JIT scheduling should work together with MRP in a complementary way, not as an alternative.

2.1 JIT scheduling

We begin here with the narrow view of JIT. Traditionally, many managers have believed that to have good levels of customer service requires high levels of inventory. Another traditional view is that, to maximise efficiency, it is necessary to produce in large batches. These two traditional views fit together well, and for years have been the foundation for manufacturing scheduling. Take the hypothetical case where four products, A, B, C, and D, are manufactured on the same machines in a factory. The time taken to make each product is similar. Following the traditional approach, the four products are made in large batches over an eight-week period as shown in Figure 5.

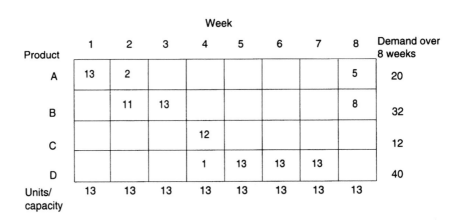

Product	1	2	3	4	5	6	7	8	Demand over 8 weeks
A	13	2						5	20
B		11	13					8	32
C				12					12
D				1	13	13	13		40
Units/ capacity	13	13	13	13	13	13	13	13	

Figure 5: Traditional scheduling

ACTIVITY 1

What is the average inventory level for product A, assuming that demand for the product is uniform, and starting inventory is nil? What problems do you foresee? And what would be a better solution?

You should notice that the demand for product A averages $20/8 = 2.5$ per week. Notice that product A is made in a large batch of 15 units at the beginning of the period but is not made again until week 8. By the end of the first week there is an accumulation of ($13 - 2.5 = 10.5$ units). During the second week net usage is 0.5 units, so end of period inventory is 10 units. At the end of each week over the next 5 weeks, the inventory levels are 7.5, 5, 2.5, 0, and 0. During week 7 there is a shortage which is remedied during week 8. Assuming backorders are allowed, at the end of week 8 inventory is back at 0. Average inventory is ($10.5 + 10 + 7.5 + 5 + 2.5 + 0 + 0 + 0)/8 = 4.43$ units.

The problem is that, although the average inventory level is quite high, there is still a stockout position. This is quite typical for longer-term forecast based systems. A forecast is made and production takes place to meet the forecast. Near the end of the forecast period, the company finds that they have produced either too much or too little. So the company has to either apologise to its customers about late delivery, or finds itself with excessive and perhaps expensive stock.

This is not the JIT way. JIT scheduling aims to make at the customer's rate of demand, no more and no less. This is shown in Figure 6.

Product	Week 1	2	3	4	5	6	7	8	Demand over 8 weeks
A	3	2	3	2	3	2	3	2	20
B	4	4	4	4	4	4	4	4	32
C	1	2	1	2	1	2	1	2	12
D	5	5	5	5	5	5	5	5	40
Units/ capacity	13	13	13	13	13	13	13	13	

Figure 6: JIT scheduling

Here we make some of each product each day. Again you can calculate inventory levels; it turns out to be ($0.5 + 0 + 0.5 + 0 + 0.5 + 0 + 0.5 + 0)/8 = 0.25$. We have no stockouts and we have less risk. We have less risk because we do not need to forecast so far ahead because we are making every week, so it is likely to be more accurate. If our forecast does turn out to be wrong, at least the product will be made again next week. So, overall, we have achieved an apparent contradiction, at least according to traditional thinking: lower levels of inventory and better customer service.

The key to this is being able to produce small quantities economically. This may require the full range of JIT techniques we discuss in the next section. At least it requires reduced set-up (changeover) time, and probably improved layout and good quality management. Note that this involves an 'engineering' approach to the problem rather than a 'mathematical' approach. In other words, the problem is addressed through reducing set-up and improving layout, rather than through finding a better forecasting method and an optimal scheduling strategy.

Having established the principle we can now consider JIT scheduling in practice.

2.2 Pull, synchronisation and kanban

JIT is about flow: parts, sub-assemblies and products flow like a river system whose volume matches the demand rate. Gradually, the tributaries erode the loops in the river and find short-cuts, so the lengths decrease, and problem rocks and rapids are worn away. With time, dams and lakes (equivalent to accumulations of inventory) along the routes are made to disappear, so that the water is not delayed in its flow.

Flow can be regulated by the use of **kanban.** Kanban is Japanese for card or sign. It has come to mean a signalling system to limit overproduction. The easiest form of kanban to imagine is the kanban square.

Squares are painted on the floor between two workcentres along a manufacturing or service route. The service equivalent of a kanban square could be an 'in-basket'. Each square or in-basket would hold a designated number of parts or files, let us say one per square as an example. When workcentre A has finished making a part or finished with the file it is placed on the kanban square from which workcentre B draws the parts or files for its operation. An empty square is the authority for workstation A to make another part or to process the file. When all the squares between workcentres are full, workcentre A has no more authority to make parts and so must stop work. Obviously, in this case, workcentre B has sufficient work to get on with so there is no point in workcentre A producing more parts or files. Parts or files are thus **pulled** by the next workstation only as needed.

Imagine now a whole string of workstations with kanban squares between them, as shown in Figure 7. A problem, such as a breakdown or quality problem, in any downstream workcentre will result in all 'upstream' workcentres stopping work within a short while, as intermediate kanban squares become full. Notice also that the speed with which the whole line can work is automatically governed by the speed of the slowest workstation. If all workstations are working below full capacity (a common situation in JIT production), then the rate at which the line will work is governed by the demand rate.

The result of this simple system is that not only is production regulated but also problems and bottlenecks become visible without delay. This allows for continuous improvement and waste elimination, the subject of our next section. We can contrast this with the traditional 'push' system whereby each workcentre works on any parts available and, upon completion, simply pushes them onto the next workstation. Figure 7 illustrates the push and pull systems.

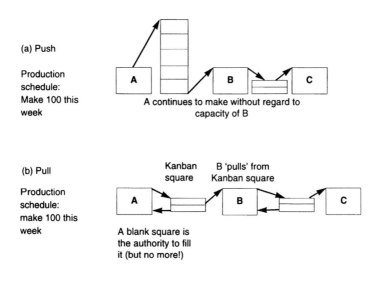

Figure 7: Push and pull

ACTIVITY 2

Think about the consequences of a push system on inventory, lead time and visibility where there is (a) a large imbalance between workcentres, and (b) where there is easily sufficient capacity. If you have time, you can simulate these two systems. Set up a group of your friends with instructions to 'produce' a product at different rates. You can use Lego bricks or paperclips as products. Run it with both push and pull. Measure the output of the line in both cases. Then have one process stop work, from time to time. Notice how easy or difficult it is to spot problems.

You will notice that inventory is likely to accumulate in front of those workstations where capacity is limited, but disappear in front of faster workstations. The problem is that queues of work can become excessive, leading to longer lead-times. Also, should a breakdown occur, this will not become apparent for some time because the feeder workstations will simply continue working. In the push system, therefore, there is a real possibility of overproduction. A more subtle point is that the push system may in some circumstances lead to less production as a bottleneck becomes starved of work from time to time as a result of disruption in earlier workstations. The point is that this is more difficult to notice, and so to take timely action. In the push system it is the **gateway** or first workstation that ultimately controls the amount of work going through the system. If this is out of line with demand, then production will be out of line. In a pull system it is the last workstation, whose rate of production should be easier to link with actual demand.

In JIT production only the main final build is scheduled, with all sub-assemblies and components being pulled in as needed. Kanban can take many forms. Kanban can be used internally within a factory or externally between a factory and its suppliers. Kanban squares stop upstream production when the square is full. Kanban cards are attached to containers and are returned to the feeding workstation when the container becomes empty. The cards move in loops between successive pairs of operations and are used in strict sequence.

Note that kanbans always operate between a pair of workstations, they do not follow a product through the sequence of manufacture; the latter is known as a **jobcard**. **Priority kanbans** are used like cards, but colours may indicate increasing urgency to make a particular part. Parts are pulled in the sequence green, yellow, red and are replenished in the reverse order. **Ping-pong ball kanbans** are used to signal the start of making a part which will be completed just in time to be inserted. **Electronic kanbans** can be transmitted over longer distances and may include the possibility of altering batch quantities. Variations include **faxban**, using a fax machine, and **EDI** (electronic data interchange) messages, which link company computer systems.

Kanban is suitable for any type of repetitive manufacture, but there are two main types of kanban. The **product type** signals for an identical part to be replaced; the **sequence type** signals that a workstation is ready for more work, but the actual part to be made is determined by product card or by broadcast. The broadcast system is used, for example in car plants, where several assemblies need to flow together in exactly the right sequence. A broadcast launches each branch in exactly the right sequence. Figure 8 illustrates some of the kanban variations.

NUMBER OF KANBANS AND PROBLEM IDENTIFICATION

Although there are formulas available for this purpose, the number of kanbans in a loop is, in practice, usually decided by judgement based on stockout risk, part cost, and material handling considerations. For example, you would not be prepared to make excessive trips to replenish a low-cost item, so the number of kanbans would be low and the kanban quantity high. A heavy item, necessitating a forklift truck, would have a low kanban quantity, with the number of kanban cards determined by space and cost considerations. Normally, a manager would start loose with a relatively high number of kanbans and sufficient inventory to avoid risk, and then gradually tighten the system by removing kanbans. Removing a kanban, of course, automatically cuts the amount of inventory between a pair of workstations. This leads us to discuss the famous 'river' analogy shown in Figure 9. As the inventory reduces, so 'problems' are exposed.

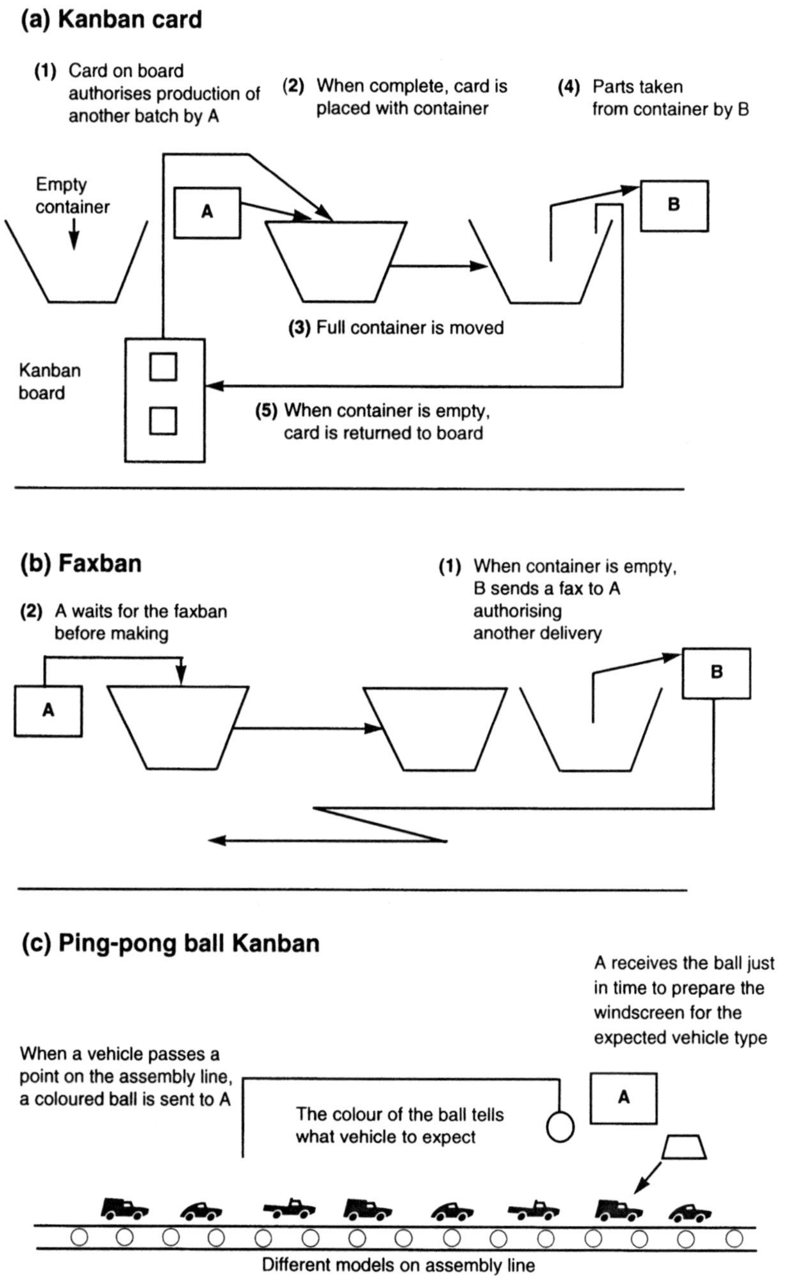

(a) Kanban card

(1) Card on board authorises production of another batch by A

(2) When complete, card is placed with container

(4) Parts taken from container by B

Empty container

A

B

(3) Full container is moved

Kanban board

(5) When container is empty, card is returned to board

(b) Faxban

(1) When container is empty, B sends a fax to A authorising another delivery

(2) A waits for the faxban before making

A

B

(c) Ping-pong ball Kanban

A receives the ball just in time to prepare the windscreen for the expected vehicle type

When a vehicle passes a point on the assembly line, a coloured ball is sent to A

The colour of the ball tells what vehicle to expect

A

Different models on assembly line

Figure 8: Kanban variations

Most manufacturing systems have problems which are covered up by inventory. For instance, a stoppage as a result of poor maintenance may go unnoticed because of the extra inventory held in front of the next workstation. Deliberate reduction of inventory results in a 'win win' situation: either you find that you are able to run unaffected with tighter inventory, or you expose a problem 'rock' – not just any rock, but the most pressing one. According to JIT thinking this is good news as the priority for continuous improvement problem-solving efforts has been indicated.

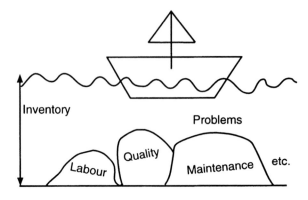

Figure 9: Uncovering waste

Kanban is linked with the 'visibility' principle which aims to make operations visible for all to see. For example, a kanban board hung with kanban cards each indicating a need to replace a previously used quantity, is a very graphic display of the production situation at any moment in time. Simply by walking past, a supervisor or manager has an excellent impression of the backlog of work. Moreover, by its nature, it is always up-to-date.

In a large factory, with hundreds or even thousands of parts controlled by kanban cards, the number of kanban cards hanging on a board can be quite significant. Material handlers use the cards as the authorisation to bring parts to the required workstations from the warehouse or from feeding workstations. A problem for the material handlers or previous workstations may then be knowing the priorities. This can be dealt with in various ways. Some GEC factories have adopted a colour coding system; a green kanban indicates an authority to replace parts, but with low priority. Yellow indicates higher priority. Finally, when a red kanban card appears this indicates that the next workstation requires parts very urgently. Feeding workstations replace parts authorised by the red kanbans first, then by the yellow, and then green. In replacing the parts they may decide to make or supply a batch which replaces the red, or the red and yellow, or the red, yellow and green. Operators make the best decision on the spot. At Vauxhall Motors in Luton, the kanban boards are electronic in as far as they 'remember' the oldest remaining cards on the board, and indicate this by a flashing light. This ensures a first in-first out replacement service.

KANBAN AND MRP

As we have already noted, the question of JIT versus MRP is largely a spurious one. It is more a question of taking the best of each, depending on circumstances, and of making suitable adaptations. A traditional manufacturing system uses work orders to push production through the factory. MRP releases the work orders and tracks them through the factory, attempting to keep completion due dates valid. As events take place so the MRP system becomes increasingly out of date, requiring a regeneration or update. By contrast, with a JIT pull system there are no work orders and work is pulled through from workcentre to workcentre under kanban control. MRP is still used for planning, but execution is controlled by the visibility of kanbans. The procedure is shown in Figure 10.

(a) Traditional push

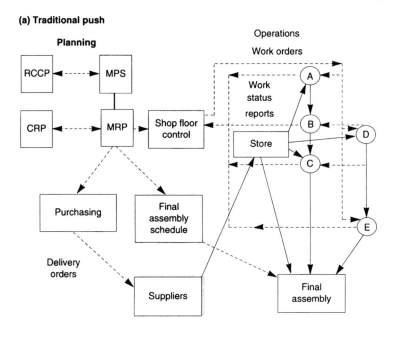

(b) JIT pull

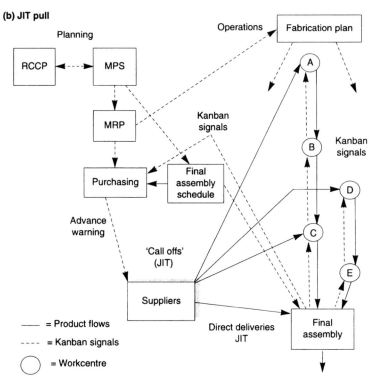

Figure 10: Traditional push and JIT pull systems

Updating of the MRP system is not needed as frequently because it is not being used to control manufacturing. In fact, where JIT is well developed, including where there is good quality and good supplier relationships, an MRP II system can be massively simplified to the extent that 'netting' is not required and 'gross only' explosions may be all that is necessary. Also, capacity requirements planning (CRP) and the detailed scheduling module (known sometimes as production activity control) may simply be unnecessary. Many companies have drastically cut their MRP systems as a result of implementing JIT. Examples are Hoover in South Wales, Ackermann in Milton Keynes, and an example often cited by Tom Peters, Titeflex in the USA. The modified procedure would then be as shown in Figure 11.

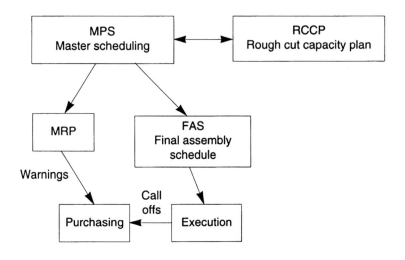

Figure 11: MRP in a JIT environment

2.3 Final assembly scheduling under JIT

A JIT final assembly schedule should be developed with the underlying principle of making, as far as possible, some of each product every day, or if not every day, every second day, and so on. Scheduling 500 units once per quarter produces about the same output as one unit per hour or eight per day (single shift), but the implications, plantwide, are very different.

ACTIVITY 3

What are some of the implications of 'some every day' for the entire factory, its layout, its people, its maintenance schedules, its material handling, its machines, and its thinking?

You will probably be able to add to this list, especially if you can discuss it with colleagues. For the entire factory there would be big implications for inventory. You would make and ship, rather than make, store, and ship. This would affect not only space but the number of people in warehousing. The entire distribution chain would be affected, with implications for marketing and finance. Marketing would be able to respond to market changes more rapidly. The layout would have to change; instead of moving large batches between workcentres perhaps by forklift truck or conveyor, you could perhaps move small containers by hand, so cells become more likely. Operators would probably have to be more flexible; and their jobs would be much more varied on a day to day basis. Maintenance would have to be more reliable. And the selection of appropriate machines would change from a preference for one machine being able to make large batches quickly (because many products would use the same machine over a three month period) to several smaller machines, perhaps permanently set up, where speed of production would not be as important.

We will consider how we construct this kind of schedule. To move towards regularity, we first classify the product line into **runners, repeaters,** and **strangers;** these are terms used by Lucas Industries. Runners get their own dedicated facilities or cells. Repeaters, items with regular demand, should be fitted into regular slots in the schedule, for example, make product XYZ every Tuesday. Strangers fit in around the regulars. Try for a constant repeating sequence, even if quantities vary. In fact, we run our lives around a runners, repeaters, and strangers schedule. Runners are ongoing activities such as heartbeat, repeaters are regularly occurring activities such as breakfast and sleeping, and strangers are the different activities that we do every day. The repeater activities take place every day but not exactly at the same time or in the same quantity. For instance, we sleep every night but may go to bed later on Saturday night and sleep in on Sunday. This form of organisation is so natural that we hardly think about it. It brings order to our lives. We know not to telephone friends at 3 a.m. and the family assembles for dinner at the same time each day without being told. What we don't do is to go for 'efficiency'. For instance, we don't decide that in order to save setting the table and washing up we will have breakfast next month for three days continuously!

A good JIT schedule is a boring schedule. Everyone knows that on Tuesday and Friday mornings we make a particular product: the suppliers know it, and deliver just-in-time, the changeover crew knows it and has all tools ready, the supporting operations know they must finish in time, and so on. Phil Crosby calls this 'ballet, not hockey'. With ballet, we rehearse and get things right, then repeat the performance the same way every time. So it is with JIT scheduling. With hockey on the other hand, every game is different. This is interesting, but it is not basis for operations very good management.

JIT scheduling is made easier as manufacturing lead time is reduced, and as manufacturing flexibility is increased. This is where all the tools and techniques we discuss in the next section come into play. If manufacturing lead time is a few months it is difficult to forecast, to avoid over- or under-production, and to adjust schedules to the changing needs of the marketplace. But if lead time is a week, it is not nearly as difficult. Many companies, by reducing lead-times, have changed from being make-to-stock manufacturers to become make-to-order manufacturers.

All parts of the manufacturing sequence should be synchronised. This means that all parts move forward at the same rate of production. Where there are set-up times involved, these too must be synchronised and regularised. For instance, final assembly scheduling may proceed at a regular ongoing rate of 100 units per day, but a supporting operation having a long set-up time might produce a batch of 500 units per week on the same day each week.

ACTIVITY 4

Consider the case of a breakfast cereal manufacturer. Every day cereal is sent out in various types of packaging. But each type of cereal is not made every day; instead it is made in batches. Try to envisage the process. How should manufacturing and packaging be scheduled?

According to JIT thinking, it would be preferable to make each type of cereal in the smallest quantity that is economic. It would also be desirable to regularise this production as far as possible, making different cereals in the same sequence according to demand. Packaging would be continuous, perhaps packaging some of every type and container every day. The quantities packaged would pull demand through from manufacture; if one cereal became more popular more would be made, but the sequence and approximate time slot would remain fixed. Likewise, packaging materials would be pulled in from suppliers as demanded and packaging suppliers would be given overall targets. Where demand for a cereal or packaging type is high enough, facilities could be dedicated, otherwise lines would be shared. In this way, flexibility is maintained. It is not necessary to know exactly the packaging destination of each product. For this type of product we would not adopt full mixed model scheduling. But, for example, in TV set manufacture, each set coming down the assembly line might differ in detail specification (say for different markets) but all sets made on the line would belong to the same basic family.

With JIT final assembly scheduling, the aim should be to balance material flows and capacity, not just capacity as is common in batch scheduling. You will recall capacity considerations in Unit 8. This means trying to ensure that, as far as possible, material flows evenly. So it is not desirable to produce one type of product in the morning and another type in the afternoon (which would result in uneven material flows), but rather to work towards **mixed model scheduling** so that, as far as possible, the sequence remains constant all day by alternating between the products being manufactured.

ACTIVITY 5

Develop the best mixed model sequence for a situation where the product mix is 4 As to 3 Bs to 2 Cs to 1 D.

Of course the best sequence will contain 4 + 3 + 2 + 1 = 10 products. The As should be spaced apart as far as possible. Begin with this first. This gives:

A _ _ A _ _ A _ _ A.

Now fill in the Bs, spacing them as far apart as possible. This gives:

A B _ A B _ A B _ A, and so to A B C A B D A B C A.

When the sequence repeats however there will be two As next to each other, so a better sequence may be:

A B C A B D A B A C, A B C A B D A B A C, etc.

This is a simple example. Real-world examples, in addition to having many more products, would need to balance not only the sequence but also the amount of work that making each product entails. For instance, if items A and C both involve lengthy assembly times, it may not be acceptable to have these two in sequence. Algorithms have been developed to help solve this line balancing under mixed model scheduling problem.

To support JIT scheduling, there are a number of wider requirements:

● There must be a good, and valid, Master Production Schedule and Final Assembly Schedule. A valid MPS means that it has been checked out for capacity using rough cut capacity planning, as we discussed in Unit 8. This should be supported in a make-to-order environment by time fences which stabilise the plan. As we move towards the actual date of commitment, so the plan is firmed. The plan should in turn be communicated to suppliers. For instance, suppliers would be given advance warning of the intended volume and mix for next month, they would also be given an updated more detailed plan for the next two weeks, be given the exact sequence for next week, and finally the sub-assemblies would be called off by kanban to allow sufficient time for JIT delivery.

● The organisation must establish policies that work towards demand stability, or at least do not encourage demand instability. Plateaus, or level schedules, of stability may be established, as shown in Figure 12.

● **Under capacity scheduling** is often practised whereby the master production schedule will allow for a few surplus hours each week. The prime purpose of this is to make allowances for things that might go wrong and to ensure that the schedule is met – no more and no less. If nothing goes wrong, the spare time can be productively used for improvement activities.

● A schedule should be controlled by **linearity** which measures the deviation from a constant daily target, and, at bottlenecks, by input/output control. Where manufacturing cells have been established the detailed scheduling task may be decentralised, giving control to the team running the cell.

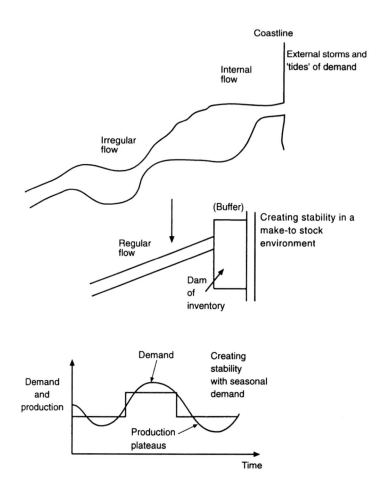

Figure 12: Creating production stability and regularity

Summary

In this section we looked at JIT scheduling, which aims to produce at the customer's rate of demand, no more and no less. JIT scheduling with small batches produced frequently achieves both low inventories and high levels of customer service. However, this is only made possible by the integrated use of a range of techniques that we discuss in the next section.

Traditional push systems were seen to encourage overproduction, but the kanban-based pull system regulates flow to that of the most constrained resource. Kanban can be implemented by moving from 'loose pull' to 'tight pull', thereby exposing problems. This is a 'win-win' approach. Kanban can also be applied in service environments, such as office in-baskets.

JIT scheduling should work together with MRP: it is complementary, not an alternative. MRP II however, should be simplified in a JIT environment. The concept of runners, repeaters, and strangers is useful in establishing JIT schedules. Mixed model scheduling aims to balance both time and material flows: it is now widespread in car manufacturing, but has much wider applicability. Many service environments can benefit from JIT scheduling principles. For instance, a bank or insurance company can have runner or dedicated operations, repeater operations which should be done at regular intervals about the same time each day and stranger operations which are fitted in around the regular slots.

SECTION 3
Lean Operations

Introduction

In this section we will look at the concept of waste and at the range of techniques which make JIT manufacturing or lean operations feasible. We will consider lean techniques in two stages: those providing a foundation and those providing for execution and ongoing improvement. We will end by looking at the applicability of lean techniques to service operations.

3.1 Lean operations and waste elimination

We now move to the next level in the JIT hierarchy: level 2 or the wider view of JIT. In the narrow context it is appropriate to speak of JIT, but in the wider context a more appropriate term is **lean operations**. This is the term we will use. The use of kanban and the scheduling techniques discussed in the last section may be effective on their own in some repetitive environments, but in most environments it will be necessary to employ the full range of supporting techniques. However, merely implementing the techniques as a once-off activity will not be effective for long, as products and environments change. As we have noted, Taiichi Ohno believed the essence of the total Toyota production system was an 'all out attack on waste'. The concept of waste elimination and continuous improvement should be seen as integral to all the techniques of lean manufacture. These are our topics in this and the next section.

The significance of lean manufacturing, especially in the car industry, was highlighted by Womack et al in their seminal book *The Machine that Changed the World*. In a series of fascinating graphs and tables they point out order of magnitude productivity and quality differences between lean manufacturers and traditional mass manufacturers. We cannot fail to grasp the message that to survive in the car industry, and probably in many other industries also, it is mandatory to adopt lean principles. Waste elimination, continuous improvement, and time compression techniques are at the heart of lean operations.

THE SEVEN WASTES

Consider that there are only two possible states for people and machines: work and waste! Waste is anything that does not add value for the external customer. Waste elimination is best thought of as the converse of continuous improvement. As we have noted from the views of Taiichi Ohno, lean operations are strongly associated with both waste elimination and continuous improvement. So, if you appreciate the seven wastes you should also appreciate lean operations in its wider context. Ohno compiled a list of seven categories of waste. They are:

- **The waste of overproducing.** This implies producing too many products, too early or just-in-case. Ohno believed that this was the most severe of all the wastes. Kanban, of course, is an important weapon, but the Toyota belief is that to produce to the customer's rate of demand requires an in-depth understanding of customers which goes well beyond simple forecasting or market research.

- **The waste of waiting.** Lean operations are about 'keep-it-moving' manufacturing. Any time that materials are not moving, or are waiting or queuing, is waste. The idea is to maximise the value-adding time. Of course, this is an enormous challenge for most factories where products are often being worked on for perhaps 1% of total time. Likewise, any employee whose time is not being productively employed represents waste. You may think that this conflicts with the waste of overproduction, but it does not; what it means is that an employee should be gainfully employed either producing or in improvement activities. There should always be a reserve list of things to do, such as cleanup or quality improvement.

- **The waste of transporting.** Your customers do not pay you to move products around the factory floor. Like the waste of waiting, this may be virtually impossible to eliminate, but you should go on trying. Ever more compact layouts, simplified materials handling and closer suppliers are the implication.

- **The waste of inappropriate processing.** 'Using a steam hammer to crack a nut' is an alternative way of expressing this waste. It means that we should not select or use a machine or process that is too fast, too big, or too variable for the task in hand. Importantly, it also implies a preference for using several smaller machines rather than one big machine. Toyota factories are famous for their use of low-cost automation, and for their immaculately maintained, but often older, machines.

- **The waste of unnecessary inventory.** 'Zero inventories' is a phrase often associated with lean operations. Of course, it is not possible to manufacture with literally zero inventory, but remember that all inventory – stores, buffers, large batches, their control systems and people – is waste. The ideal is to finish each stage just-in-time to go into the next stage.

- **The waste of unnecessary motions**. Ergonomics has always played an important role at Toyota. This waste addresses all motions where, for instance bending, reaching, or exertion is involved. It also addresses all unnecessary motions involved with, for example, unwrapping parts, lifting parts onto a machine, and excessive turns in tightening a nut.

- **The waste of defects**. Last but not least is the waste of scrap and poor quality. This is taken in its widest context, including rework, unnecessary inspection, and all consequences of 'not doing it right the first time'.

At Toyota everyone, in every function, is made aware of waste. This is done by several means. One example is waste checklists where operators receive a list of questions, based on the seven wastes, and are asked to go through the list asking each question as it applies to their own workstation. As a result, an operator will normally identify at least 20 areas for improvement. Ongoing improvement activities are never short of application areas.

ACTIVITY 6

We have discussed the seven wastes in a manufacturing context. But they apply in services also. Compile a corresponding 'seven wastes of service'.

Most service wastes do not need to be renamed. The first waste may be renamed something like 'the waste of non-required service', and the waste of inappropriate processing may become 'the waste of inappropriate service'. Of course, in service, there is at least as much waste as in manufacturing (probably much more), but the emphasis on priorities may change. In service, as in lean manufacturing, some overcapacity is necessary or inevitable for good customer response time. Is this overcapacity a waste? Think about this, referring back to the OPT principles you met in Unit 8.

Examples of the application of waste reduction in both service and manufacturing operations is given in a most stimulating way in the book and British television series *Sid's Heroes* (Joynson and Forrester, 1995).

3.2 Lean operations supporting techniques

It is convenient to group the family of lean operations techniques into two stages, shown in Figures 13 and 14. Some would argue, quite legitimately, that some lean techniques are not specific to lean operations or to JIT. This would be correct, but in lean operations all are necessary. The first stage is concerned with building the foundation for lean operations. The second stage covers those techniques necessary to actually run lean operations.

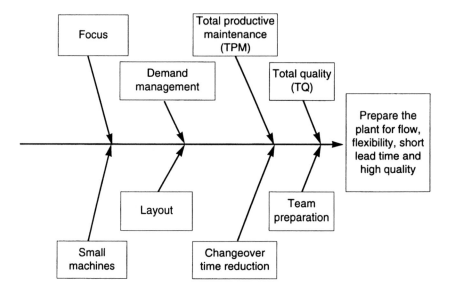

Figure 13: Lean operations Stage 1

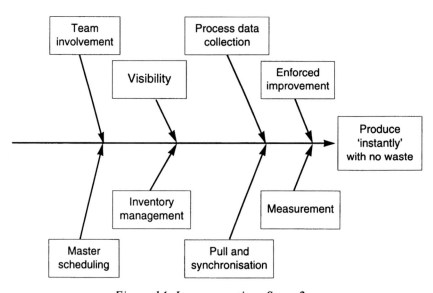

Figure 14: Lean operations Stage 2

3.3 Lean operations – Stage 1

FOCUS

The concept of the **focused factory** was first proposed by Wickham Skinner of Harvard Business School whose research showed that focused factories outperform unfocused factories. For lean operations the consequences of this finding are no less important. In fact it has been said that the Japanese retaught the West the importance of focus. Focus means having consistent policies with regard to production operations, quality, lead time, labour, machines, and so forth consistent in one cell. By contrast it is difficult or impossible for an operations manager within one unit to have to cope simultaneously with demands for short lead times and long lead times, for high volume and low volume, and for products requiring high skill and low skill. However, there are some areas that were once considered to be trade-offs or alternatives which lean thinking has largely destroyed: namely, cost, quality, and time. Today we know that for many operations, far from being trade-offs, these three are mutually supportive. We saw this in the cost of quality section in Unit 6; we will say more about the time dimension below.

DEMAND MANAGEMENT

As we discussed in Unit 4, **demand management** tries to ensure stability of schedules. This is achieved by several means: appropriate incentives for regularity not quantity, good information from customers via electronic point of sale and customer/supplier partnership, and a redefined role of marketing to understand customer needs and requirements in detail, good information to customers on delivery promises, policies which squeeze out inventory along the supply chain thereby communicating true demands (which are usually more regular) rather than false demands due to changes in inventory policy or accounting exercises (which result in surges being magnified).

TOTAL MAINTENANCE

As we discussed in Unit 6, **total productive maintenance** aims to keep machines and equipment available when needed at the lowest cost. If products are to be produced just-in-time they cannot be held up due to poor maintenance. This is achieved through operator participation in all maintenance and housekeeping activities. In fact in three areas, quality, maintenance, and set-up, the lean philosophy calls for maximum participation by operators in the routine aspects whilst saving specialist skills for more difficult tasks and for coaching the operators. An important concept is that of ownership; if operators are responsible for their own machines and workplaces then quality and productivity will improve.

TOTAL QUALITY

As we discussed in Unit 6, **total quality** is one of the legs of Robert Hall's manufacturing trilogy. Defects, of course, are one of the seven wastes. Total quality makes JIT possible by making operations more predictable and reliable. But JIT is also a strong facilitator for improved quality. Almost invariably quality improves as lean operations are implemented.

ACTIVITY 7

Why do you think quality tends to improve with JIT? Draw on your knowledge from this unit, and from Unit 6, *Quality Management*.

You might be able to think of several reasons:

- **Smaller batches:** with smaller batches, problems become apparent more quickly. And if there are quality problems, the quantity to be reworked is smaller.
- **Regularity:** small batches also mean greater repeatability. If you are making the same product every day rather than every month, fewer errors are likely.
- **Reduced lead time:** if quality problems emerge the reasons for the problem would be more recent. Operators can recall what happened, to make sure that the cause is eliminated.
- **Quality-at-source:** under this principle, operators are encouraged to take responsibility for quality themselves and not to knowingly pass on defectives.
- **Line-stop:** a classic Toyota technique, this allows operators to stop the assembly line rather than pass on defectives.
- **Failsafing or pokayoke:** a technique that has developed alongside JIT. The modern pokayoke innovator, Shigeo Shingo, was a Toyota consultant.
- **Improved visibility:** one of fundamentals of JIT simplicity, the aim is to make schedules and problems visible for all to see.
- **Compact layouts:** improve communication, thereby improving quality.
- **Total maintenance:** usually has a positive impact on quality through better machines, tools, and workplace cleanliness.
- **Kanban:** often reduces pressure to overproduce.

SMALL MACHINES

The small machine principle is one of the least recognised lean 'facilitators'. The overall principle is to use the smallest machine possible consistent with quality requirements. Several small machines instead of one bigger, faster one allow flexibility in layouts, reduction in material handling, less vulnerability to bottleneck capacity problems, less vulnerability to breakdowns, and through phasing of purchases, improved cash flow combined with more frequent technology updates. The principle extends also to self-developed machines and old machines. Small machines generally have better MTTR (mean time to repair) which is important in lean operations.

A closely-related concept is that of self-developed machines, the motivation for which is neatly summarised by the phrase 'at its worst when new'. Why? New machines are not necessarily made quality-capable and they usually do not come with added-on pokayoke devices. Under the lean philosophy it is desirable to set up mini cells combining several process steps to make unit flow possible. To do this low-cost automation can be added to machines (for example, activating several machines by one action) or added onto machines (for example, automatic ejection). Another variation is combined operations where several machines are set to work together – this ranges from simple multi-drills working together to a robot serving a few machines – but note that lean operations strive to simplify so don't use a robot for material handling when a purpose-built chute can be adapted with a little ingenuity.

The use of old machines and small machines is governed by the sunk-cost principle. That is, once a machine is acquired the costs are effectively 'sunk' irrespective of what the cost accounting system may say. We should be concerned only with minimising costs that are still to be incurred. Therefore utilisation is not important unless it is a bottleneck operation. It is better to have a machine stand idle than to have it make parts that may not be required. Many lean organisations use small and particularly old machines that are permanently set up even though they may be used for a small part of the day. It is the lack of delay and throughput that counts. With several small machines it is easier to achieve the aim of having them work at the regular rate of demand – the ideal is to achieve uniform flow, not surges. Also, small machines should be thought of as flexible resources to be moved at short notice, or even daily to the point of demand. Small machines can sometimes have wheels.

AUTOMATION AND LEAN OPERATIONS

According to lean thinking, the prime reason for automation is quality. But the principle is not to automate until waste has been squeezed out and tasks and material handling are as simple as possible. After quality comes speed and flexibility, this is particularly the case in service. Thereafter, automation may be considered for reasons of the the the three Ds (dull, dirty, dangerous) or the three Hs (hot, heavy, hazardous). To automate to save labour may be foolish because automation has no ability to improve. If automation is necessary, try to make sure it is of the small and flexible variety.

LAYOUT

We discussed layout in Unit 3, so here we will merely contrast some differences in thinking with traditional layout. Lean layout is a more dynamic concept than traditional manufacturing layout. We expect to move machines and people more often to satisfy demand, achieve steady flow, and minimise the waste of material handling. Layout is a key JIT facilitator because it makes small-lot or even one-piece flow possible. By contrast, with non-JIT layouts there is no option but to move parts around the plant in surging batches. So the overriding principle is to move machines and processes closer together, as soon as the opportunities arise. Opportunities always arise when buffer stocks are reduced, when process steps are reduced, when new machines are acquired, and with new designs.

Housekeeping, is a concept closely related to layout, at least from a lean viewpoint. It is noteworthy that the first action taken by several Japanese companies that have taken over European companies has been a major effort at housekeeping. It creates the environment for lean operations. First, there should be time allowed for housekeeping, even a few minutes each day. This is part of operator ownership and responsibility at the workplace. Housekeeping is judged on **cleanliness, orderliness** (concerned with the detailed location of tools, where parts are stored before and after processing, and how workplace handling is done), and **tidiness** (everything located and available in the designated place). Housekeeping incentives should be given. These are usually awards and recognition rather than cash. Housekeeping is at the core of lean operations, as Ohno of Toyota says, 'management begins at the workplace'.

Layout support concepts include machines on wheels (whenever possible as a matter of policy); the small machines concept; human movable containers (also know as 'egg crate' containers, which help avoid the necessity for extra space for material handling equipment and also facilitates rapid stock counting). Lineside delivery, once acceptable supplier quality has been achieved, avoids double handling and double storage space, and is made easier by having multiple access points around the building. This is something that can be achieved steadily if it is the clear policy. The use of gravity feeds encourages one piece flow and is made possible when distances are short.

Good individual workplaces help build into good overall layouts, so good workplace design is another important principle. Improved quality of life at the workplace is achieved through good lighting, ergonomics, noise abatement and carpets. In lean organisations it is genuinely believed that these are worth the investment through better quality and productivity, Toyota is once again the classic example. Improving workplaces involves countless changes so can only be done in practice by operator participation with specialists and not by specialists. Line balancing is achieved and improved little by little with the aid of the pull system and visibility rather than historic mathematical 'optimisation'. You will recall the discussion of the Toyota approach to line balancing, using the NUMMI wall from Unit 8.

For many companies, cells are at the heart of JIT and lean operations. As we noted in Unit 3, cells may be organised according to GT (group technology) principles, where the aim is to make a family of parts that share common manufacturing processes. The cell comprises a group of unlike machines that are able to make a complete part. These are located very close together, almost touching, and are often arranged in a U shape, to allow good communication and to minimise material handling and operator walking. Often parts are flowed around the cell in batches of one without intermediate queuing. The number of operators that man the cell is varied so that output will match demand. This is known as shojinka or people-flexible layout. Typically, an operator tends more machines as volume decreases. The effect is to create apparent automation, but with low cost and flexibility. This is known as **autonomation**. Cells are often designed by inspection based on process commonality. Small machine principles play an important part. Ultimately cells can become semi-autonomous, controlling their own schedules, inspection, and inventory. This is in turn totally compatible with self-directed work teams, illustrating once again the manufacturing trilogy.

Lean layout is non-static and continuous improvement should be applicable. One way is to use flow length monitoring whereby the total manufacturing process distance through a part or whole route is recorded and displayed prominently. The idea is to encourage continuous reduction through participation. Related to this is process chart analysis, particularly to identify and reduce those steps that do not add value, for example, inspection and storage. Many cell layouts now incorporate meeting and rest areas for the team, where performance charts should be on display. Waste checklists are distributed to all operators asking them to examine their own locations for wastes such as bending, walking to fetch tools, making more than one loosening turn, etc. At the heart of layout improvement lies the awareness that layout should be dynamic, taking every opportunity for reducing the flow length.

CHANGEOVER (SET-UP) REDUCTION

Reducing set-up times or changeover times not only increases capacity but also allows flexibility and smaller batches, as we saw in the earlier section on JIT scheduling. It is often the key in making JIT production possible. Over the past 15 years, hundreds of UK companies have shown that reducing set-up times is possible and inexpensive if time and priority is given to it. Note that changeover times should be defined as the time from the last piece of one batch to the first *good* piece of the next. Also, reducing changeover applies to operations that do not necessarily involve breaking down and setting up a machine. So the principles apply, for instance, to changing over assembly lines, to maintenance and to truck loading. The late Shigeo Shingo has written the seminal work on set-up reduction (1985). He calls it SMED, single minute exchange of dies, (single minute meaning less than 10), he maintains is very often possible even for set-up that used to take several hours.

ACTIVITY 8

The oft-cited classic case is the changing of four wheels on a Grand Prix car. How can a Grand Prix team change four wheels in around eight seconds? Factories have learned a lot from this. Think of the principles that makes this possible.

A brainstorming exercise would probably lead you to many of the ideas that have enabled Toyota and many others to reduce set-up times, often from hours to minutes. A changeover reduction programme often begins by classifying activities into **external** and **internal**:

- **External activities** are those that can be done while the previous batch is still running. With these, the maximum amount of preparation is done before the changeover. It is helpful to locate tools and dies, and cranes, ready for the change; perhaps dies can be located on roller conveyors to simply roll in and out. For example, if heat is involved, change into protective clothing early. After tackling the external activities turn attention to internal activities.

- **Internal activities** can only be done while operations are stopped, and so are on the 'critical path'. First see if any internal activities can be made external. An example may be preheating a die. The sequence of internal activities must be very carefully thought through in advance. See if any activities can be done simultaneously and if so use a team. Improved jig, tool, and fastener design helps, so it may be worth setting up a value engineering exercise to look at these aspects. Really fast changeover may require investment – but don't spend until all else has been squeezed out. Remember the quality side – the aim is to get the first perfect piece as fast as possible. Rapid testing and 'foolproofing' may be appropriate. The team should be accountable for pre-checking tools and dies.

There are some facilitator techniques which aid changeover analysis:

- It always helps to video a changeover and ask teams to view it and brainstorm improvements.
- The use of Fakuda's CEDAC (cause and effect diagrams with addition of cards, discussed as one of the seven tools of quality in Unit 6) is useful to organise ideas, some of which may not be affordable immediately.
- Sequencing (that is the order in which batches are made) can make a difference since some changeovers are minor depending on the previous setting. (For example, it takes less time in moving from white to black paint, than vice versa.) It helps to maintain the sequence even if lot sizes vary.
- Try to maintain regularity. If a certain changeover takes place at about the same time each day, everyone is forewarned. Otherwise have a clear signal (lights? siren?) in good time to warn of a changeover.
- Set-up operations should be a maintenance priority. Don't be delayed by a tool that was broken before the changeover started. Wheeled changeover trolleys with all the necessary equipment are becoming common.
- To facilitate production to the required quality as soon as possible, pre-control SPC charts are useful (see Unit 6). These short-run charts enable quick verification of the set-up by providing simple, visible rules.

Finally, the fastest changeover is no changeover. Can a machine be dedicated? Notice the relevance again of the small machine principle, we discussed earlier.

ACTIVITY 9

Is set-up reduction relevant to service? Think of some examples.

The answer is yes! Let's consider one example: garbage collection vehicles suffer considerably from breakdown problems due to the non-homogeneous nature of the material collected. To minimise stoppage time, one local authority applied the principles of set-up reduction. The most common types of failure were analysed and repair crews trained to deal with them in situ rather than having to bring the vehicles in for repair. As in factory set-up, the maximum amount of pre-preparation is done beforehand. Tools and equipment have been adapted for quick change.

Crews practice. The result has been a reduction in the total fleet size because vehicles no longer spend as much time in maintenance workshops and don't have to be brought in for the most common faults.

You could probably brainstorm several other applications from changing hotel rooms to checking in at an airport.

TEAM PREPARATION

People, as we have noted from Hall's trilogy, are an essential part of JIT and lean operations. You may well think, 'Yes, of course', and go on to think that there is no difference between people management in traditional factories as opposed to JIT factories. This would be wrong. Lean operations, in common with total quality, requires everyone to participate in continuous improvement. Toyota is famous for the expressions 'bring your brain to work', and 'the real aim of the TTPS (Toyota's acronym for lean operations) is to create thinking people', and we have already noted innovations such as the NUMMI wall, TPM, set-up reduction, and, of course, total quality. It is worth spending some time on people issues. In particular, when we talk of people in lean operations, we really mean teams of people.

We start with people policy, a prime principle is to hire the whole person – his or her skills, brain, all the senses, and all the potential. The aim is to hire people who are willing to contribute in a complete way. Most will need to be team players. The implications are that participation has to be built in, which in turn implies that there should be information sharing. Progress displays, newsletters and briefings help make lean improvements possible. Peter Wickens of Nissan has written on how the company aims to achieve line and staff equality on benefits, facilities, conditions of employment, and even parking, which fosters teamwork and communication, creates job security and 'drives out fear' (1987).

But participation cannot include people improving themselves out of a job, so efforts must be made to retrain operators, and marketing must play a role in taking full advantage of the new opportunities made possible. Nortel (formerly Northern Telecom) has gone to lengths to explain to operators the difference between productivity gains, for which no operator should lose his or her job, and losses as a result of market changes (that no company can guarantee). An increasing number of companies implementing lean operations have adopted a 'minimum specs' – job concept whereby job descriptions are only outlined, leaving innovation and development to the individual. In others, flexible job contracts, whereby people agree to work a set number of hours per year, but monthly hours may vary, are becoming more common to fit in with the JIT ideas of minimal inventory and working to the market rate of demand.

'Capacity through people' is the belief that capacity can be increased not only by extra machines and space, but also through people having ever greater and more flexible skills and through process improvement. Developing people is often more cost-effective than buying physical plant.

Rewards and incentives under lean operations must not compromise quality, overproduction or any other wastes but should encourage improvement. An individual bonus system based on output is in general not compatible with the lean philosophy. However, gainsharing, with benefits shared on the basis of improvements, is increasingly found.

The team concept is one of the most important developments accompanying lean manufacturing. This begins with operators that are multi-skilled and multi-functional. They operate several processes, set up machines, carry out routine maintenance, check quality, and participate in improvement activities in their own area and in other areas. Teams are easier to set up where there is a clearly identifiable product and area. Many teams are now evolving towards self-direction, where team leaders are elected by, and responsible to, the team not the company. At the same time former supervisors become coaches who decide with rather than for teams. Coaches are chosen by, and are responsible to, management. This enables the organisation to become flatter and leaner as many middle management roles are taken over by teams. Flat organisation in turn means improved communication, both vertically and laterally. It also means flexibility, simplicity and improvements which are just not possible at the same rates in traditional organisations.

The JIT (or lean manufacturing) approach to using teams has not been without its critics. Christian Berggren (1993) has been one of the more outspoken critics. In essence, he claims that the true facts about Japanese lean production are not widely known and that it is a highly regimented system that only the young can possibly maintain. He favours a return to the long-cycle Volvo type of production. Womack et al (1990), on the other hand, maintain that lean manufacturing is far more stimulating through its emphasis on continuous improvement.

3.4 Lean operations – Stage 2

VISIBILITY

The **visibility principle** is at the core of operations that have to take place just in time. This principle is a major departure from black box or computer-based production management. It is not that computers are unnecessary with lean operations, they are necessary, but the belief is that the best control takes place when the immediate past and future can be seen. Visibility does mean a change in management style – from reading figures remotely to 'management by walking about'. It is also called 'management by sight'.

Visibility can be classified under several headings:

- **Quality**: visibility means the use of lights and sound to highlight problems as they occur. In Unit 4, we studied the seven tools; here they are applied and made visible on the factory floor. Problem Pareto charts located on the shop floor allow operators to record problems as they take place. Successive occurrences gain extra ticks on the chart so it is clear to an improvement team what to work on. One variation is the measles chart or defect location diagram. Fishbone charts also belong on the factory floor as do SPC charts. Of course, all these charts are prepared by teams, thereby encouraging the team to take ownership of problems occurring in their own area.

- **Schedule**: visibility aids the schedule by making the status clear. So painted stock locations give an immediate indication of problems and the current inventory situation. Kanban cards, when hung on a board next to the workstation, indicate any backlogs. Electronic counts coupled with displays indicate status and help avoid manual counting, and bottleneck tag cards indicate those jobs that should enjoy priority because bottleneck idleness must be avoided.

- The famous display signs at Toyota are the overhead 'Andon' boards. These large electric displays are prominently located so they can be seen for many metres along the assembly line. If a problem occurs at a workstation, a siren sounds and the workstation number and type of problem is lit up. Problem types may be quality, maintenance, part shortage, tooling, and so forth. The prominent location of the displays mean that the potential hold-up is noticed right along the assembly line. When the board lights up, the appropriate people immediately investigate. If the problem is not solved or alleviated within the manufacturing cycle time of the assembly line (typically less than three minutes) then the line will stop. When the operator switches on the display a clock starts running in the control office. The response time to solve the problem is monitored. The idea is not to chase operators but rather to know where and how severe the stoppages are that are occurring so that appropriate remedial action can be taken.

- **Company performance**: other areas for the visibility principle include displaying company performance on sales, quality, profit, and output for all to see. Such displays are sometimes regarded with cynicism in British factories, but in many Japanese factories the management believes that not only are the workforce interested in such information, but that the company has a duty to inform the workforce.

- **Operator skill charts**: this is one form of display board which is increasingly being seen in British factories, which shows the current skill capabilities of each operator. The chart lists operators' names along one axis and job categories along the other axis. The intersecting squares show the operator's skill at the job, ranging typically from novice to trainer. These are useful to reallocate operators to changing areas of need, but also have a motivational effect in encouraging operators to learn more skills. Again such charts belong on the shop floor not in a supervisor's office.

- **Daily communication**: with regard to keeping teams informed, daily communication through the organisation is made easy by team briefings, layer by layer, through the organisation. Nissan, for instance, begins each shift with a short team meeting to review the problems of yesterday and to inform about targets and possible problems to look out for today. The team's performance should be on display in its own meeting areas. Also, the office locations of managers, engineers, designers, even cost accountants, deliberately near to the factory floor fosters understanding, communication and response. For instance, at Hewlett Packard's Bristol factory the production manager sits in a glass-fronted office right in the centre of the factory. At other HP factories, designers can only get to their offices by passing through the factory floor, and there is only one common tea area where factory operators take refreshment with designers, schedulers and sales people.

PROCESS DATA COLLECTION

Process data collection is the principle of collecting and making use of the data and techniques immediately at the process or workplace. This is a concept closely related to the visibility principle. Much of process data collection involves the use of electronic devices, but regular manual recording is also very effective. Used well the principle revolutionises shop floor management. You might recall from Unit 8 about the recent growth of manufacturing execution systems (MES) to supplement MRP II. This is the lean operations version, but it has much in common with MES.

Some examples include the following:

- **Bar codes:** in inventory and scheduling, bar codes avoid identification errors and assist with replacement stock records.
- **Delay clocks,** which accumulate lost time, allow real-time schedule updating and decision making. Automatic counting of made parts or production cycles gives an ongoing measure of performance and relieves operators of the need to count.
- **EDI** allows schedules and inventory to be updated automatically between external supplier and user. Rekeying is eliminated, but so too is delay and error.

With machines, automatic condition monitoring, for example, of temperature, pressure, vibration, dimensions, gives an early warning of problems. Run hour recording gives automatic data on the set-up/run/idle mix and can also assist with maintenance. Such devices can include pressure sensors indicating when a pallet or storage space is not in use (perhaps triggering ordering), or when a jig or fixture is not being correctly used. Status displays automatically monitor activities such as process strokes, tool status, and even inventory levels. They may be combined with run hour recording to trigger, for instance, tool changes or maintenance.

Quality is a well-established area for process data collection, with many operators active in shop floor statistical process control (SPC). For JIT batch sizes, precontrol may be preferable. Pokayoke devices which incorporate either automatic stop or warnings, and which demand immediate action, can lead to virtually defect free items being passed to the next stage. Operator performance on quality is ideally judged by operators themselves, rather than by quality inspectors. Refer to Unit 6 if you have forgotten about some of these.

ENFORCED IMPROVEMENT

We have already seen that the lean philosophy is strongly associated with waste reduction and continuous improvement. We have already discussed some of the relevant concepts such as the seven wastes, kaizen, and the five whys. We also discussed the river-flow analogy whereby problem rocks are uncovered as the water (inventory) level drops. Here we will attempt to bring these together by stating that improvement must not be left to chance but must be **forced** to take place. Robert Hall has spoken about regarding the factory as a laboratory in which continuous experimentation takes place (1987). That is the spirit that should be conveyed here.

Improvement is the lean way of life. But rapid improvement can only be achieved through full participation. At the heart of lean improvement lie four basics:

- First, make everyone continuously aware of the seven wastes.

- Second, encourage everyone to have a questioning attitude and to use the five whys.

- Third is kaizen which is a belief and methodology associated with many small, ongoing improvements made by teams and consolidated, rather than a few big improvements made by 'experts'.

- Fourth is continuous follow-through; one improvement always leads to another which in turn leads to another, and so on.

Management has the task of making improvement the natural state, and not leaving it to chance. The pace has to be encouraged by, for instance, process visibility which displays critical factors (for example, set-up times, response times) over which staff have a close influence. Audio-visual warnings of problems (by, for example, the Andon board) demand an immediate response in a lean environment. Under lean-type thinking, when failures or stoppages do occur, the costs of lost time should be apportioned to those departments responsible, not as punishment, but to recognise where help is needed and what it is worth. Improvement can also be forced by deliberate inventory withdrawal and by the use of check sheets. The level of suggestions made at some Japanese plants is staggering to Western observers, often running to dozens of improvements per employee per year.

The question of rewards for improvement varies according to company culture and origin. Generally, Japanese companies do not give monetary rewards, believing that improvement is part of everyone's job. They do, however, give non-monetary rewards, especially recognition, tokens and perhaps parties. At one Toyota plant no monetary rewards are given but the plant holds a once a year dinner to which people (and their partners) who have made substantial contributions are invited. At the dinner a draw is held and one person wins a new car. At some Japanese companies, tokens or badges are given. This idea does not tend to go down well at British companies. Instead, monetary rewards are more common. Britain was unique in having tax incentives for profit-sharing, but take-up of this concept has been slow. More generally, the concept of **gainsharing**, whereby savings above budget are shared between the company and its staff, appears to be attracting interest after a gestation period stretching back at least 40 years.

INVENTORY MANAGEMENT

To some, JIT and lean manufacturing is all about inventory reduction. But, as we now realise, this is an unduly narrow view. As Richard Schonberger (1982), the well-known JIT author, maintains, reducing inventory is like eating ice cream for the food value: there is some, but it's generally not why you do it. Ongoing reductions can only really be achieved if there is a new attitude about inventory. For managers this is that inventory means: cash tied up, reduced opportunities to identify wastes, reduced flexibility, and a bar to improved quality. Importantly, cutting inventory cuts the cumulative lead time by reducing the queues. This means more accurate scheduling and improved customer service. People actually feel better, work better, and communicate better in a cleaner environment with less inventory lying around. You will recall that in Unit 4 we showed how the JIT views of cost of inventory and of set-up reduction combine to drive the economic order or batch quantity towards one.

To reduce batch sizes it helps to establish a linkage with changeover times. So, if changeover time is cut by 50%, the number of changes or batches should double, with, of course, appropriate cuts in batch size. Buffer stocks and safety stocks should also be cut as improvements take place in quality and maintenance.

JIT and lean operations cannot continue without good inventory control and this topic could be considered as a JIT prerequisite. Bill of materials accuracy and stockholding accuracy needs to be good, as with MRP. However, many companies have found that inventory accuracy improves with JIT. This is because there is less inventory, greater visibility, and inaccuracies are noticed much faster. Throughout, all storage locations should be designed on the visibility principle-making detailed reporting unnecessary. It is wasteful to attempt to track inventory in detail within a factory, particularly when it moves through rapidly. So, often, it is adequate to record only what enters and leaves. This is known as the **four wall inventory system**. With low defect levels, **backflushing** is desirable. Upon completion of products, backflushing updates the inventory records by deducting all parts that are assumed to have been used.

Thus far we have considered only the advantages of JIT. Is there a downside? *The Economist*, (1992) looks at some disadvantages. Of course, traffic difficulties can result from many small deliveries. But, small batches do not necessarily have to be delivered in small vehicles. One large vehicle may be able to pick up small quantities from several suppliers located in the same area, before making the final trip to the factory. But being stuck in traffic is as much waste as inventory stuck on the factory floor. Waste elimination and continuous improvement still applies so you have to work out the best compromise. Perhaps you need to create a buffer warehouse which receives deliveries in larger but regular quantities from suppliers, and which delivers JIT to the assembly line. And, of course, you would not risk JIT delivery from a supplier susceptible to disruption.

ACTIVITY 10

A manufacturer accepts delivery in batches from a supplier every two weeks. Parts are first unloaded, entered into the materials management system, moved to a 'quarantine' area and then inspected by quality control before being placed in the warehouse from where they are delivered to the assembly line via work orders. The supplier sends in a monthly invoice, which has to be checked and reconciled before payment. Comment.

There is a lot of waste! Eliminate receiving, reduce batches, get the supplier to inspect (or at least inspect before off-loading), deliver direct to the line, and consider the possibility of self-billing, kanban control, etc.

3.5 Lean operations in service industry

In this section we consider the wider application of JIT. The concept of flow and waste is not confined to manufacturing. An article on the Karolinka Hospital (*Financial Times*, 1994) identifies a number of JIT principles and techniques.

JIT, of course, has its roots in manufacturing. But, increasingly, JIT and lean principles are found in the service industry even though they may not be recognised as such by service industry managers, many of whom have only a vague notion of JIT and lean principles. As we will see in the next section, JIT, lean operations, time-based competitiveness, business process reengineering, mass customisation, and total quality have all become mixed up. It no longer matters what it is that is being done is called; what matters is how effective it all is. In this section, we will discuss the use of a few JIT and lean concepts in the service industry.

The JIT scheduling concept of regularity has wide potential in service operations. In banking it is common to have regular slots for work; for instance, cheques are sorted at regular intervals. The same principles apply widely in magazine publishing where there are regular deadlines that must be met at the same time each month. The proofs must reach the editor's desk by a certain time each month, so that the editor is ready to receive them, the printer is ready to perform various tasks, and the supplier knows that paper must be delivered by a certain date. All this establishes a routine. This brings order without having to make a new plan each month. In a British investment bank, considerable cash flow savings were achieved when cheque clearance was changed from 'batch production' (with batches moving between sections) to 'flow production' (where now there are no batches but cheques move one at a time between sections situated close together). Kanban is also widely applicable. An in-basket can in fact be regarded as a kanban square, enabling the introduction of a pull rather than a push system. As in a factory, this has the advantage of making bottlenecks and hold-ups more visible. A full in-basket should signal to the feeding operation that there is no point in adding to the work and that perhaps it would be more effective to do other work or to assist the bottleneck. McDonald's is a kanban user: hamburgers, Big Macs and cheeseburgers are only made when there are vacant slots on the chute. Failsafing is also used; audible signals or automatic switch-off are used to ensure consistency. And of course, JIT delivery of foodstuffs is not only good for the business, but also for customers.

The lean operations concept of waste reduction, and its converse, continuous improvement, is of course widely applicable. Toyota uses the seven wastes in all areas, not just in manufacturing. In service, continuous improvement is more closely associated with total quality in general, and with kaizen in particular, than with JIT or lean operations.

Several lean techniques are directly relevant in service. We have already noted how Ohno observed the supermarket system at work. Today this pull system extends back right along the supply chain. Here we mention a few more techniques out of many possibilities:

- **Cellular layout**, rather than departmental layout, can have dramatic results. One example is a local authority where building plans approval, formerly taking weeks as the plans move around between departments such as the building inspectors, structural engineers, town planners, health department, and sometimes traffic engineering, is now routinely done within hours as some representatives from all these departments have relocated themselves into a cell.
- The lean design concept of **variety as late as possible** has wide application in insurance where standard policies are made up and necessary special clauses added as necessary.
- The **changeover reduction principle** of making the maximum possible preparation before the changeover is not only applicable to a Grand Prix pit stop, but is simply good practice to ensure good customer service in restaurants, at hotel reception desks, at university registration and for all meetings.

In TR Fastenings, we can identify several JIT and lean concepts: cellular layout, JIT delivery direct to the line, JIT scheduling (including lot splitting), single source suppliers, as well as waste reduction and teamwork (Collins, 1992). Extensive examples of the use of JIT and lean operations in the service industry are given in Schonberger and Knod's book *Synchroservice!* (1994).

Summary

In this section we looked at the concept of waste and at the range of techniques which allow JIT manufacturing or lean operations to be feasible. This is the level 2 or wider view of JIT. We looked at the classic seven wastes of Toyota, noting their wide applicability in manufacturing and service. We also looked at the lean techniques, which were grouped into two stages. The first comprises those techniques that lay the foundation (such as focus, cell layout, set-up reduction, total quality, total maintenance, and operator training), and the second comprises those techniques which allow execution and ongoing improvement (such as visibility, process data collection, enforced improvement and inventory management). Many of these techniques have features in common. All emphasise simplicity and visibility, all try to shift responsibility from experts to operators, and all are never fully implemented but require continuous improvement.

We concluded that understanding waste and continuous improvement is at the heart of lean operations. Finally, we noted the applicability of lean techniques in service operations.

SECTION 4

Time-Based Competitiveness

Introduction

In this section we will introduce time-based competitiveness, an important field of activity for operations managers. We will follow this through from design to distribution, considering also the integrating philosophy of business process reengineering (BPR).

We will note the impact of technologies such as computer aided design/manufacture (CAD/CAM), electronic data interchange (EDI) and electronic point of sale (EPS) terminals on time compression and their potential for improving customer service. Finally, we will examine supply chain management and quick response logistics.

4.1 Development of time-based competitiveness

Time-based competitiveness has developed out of JIT manufacturing to have a big impact on manufacturing, service, and distribution. Undoubtedly the seminal work was George Stalk and Thomas Hout's *Competing Against Time* (1990). In this work the authors cited many examples of companies that have benefited through time-based strategies. For example,

- Wal-Mart, the American discount store, has customer delivery times of about 80% less than those of competitors and as a result enjoys a profit advantage of 36% against the industry norm of 12%.

- Atlas Door, a manufacturer of industrial doors, has lead times of about 66% less than those of competitors and as a result enjoys a profit advantage of 15% against an industry norm of 5%.

ACTIVITY 11

We know that customers are prepared to pay for improved quality, but how about for reduced time? Try to validate Stalk and Hout's findings locally. Find some comparable shops, selling, say, furniture or domestic appliances, or insurance companies. Ask about their delivery times, or claim settlement times, and prices. Then, if they are quoted companies, try to find out about their profitability. Alternatively, think of a few examples where reduced time attracts a premium price.

Concorde is an obvious example. So too is the speed of computers, the Channel tunnel, and fast cars. You can probably come up with others.

ACTIVITY 12

Why should profitability improve as time is cut?

We have covered this before! Often there is a direct relationship between time taken and quality levels, but in the opposite way to what many people think. Generally quality improves as time is reduced. Reducing the time to make a product leads to less work in process and quicker detection of any problems that may have arisen. Defective processes can be stopped sooner and the amount of rework is reduced. The same effect is found in services; reducing the time often improves the feedback and leads to improvement before what has taken place is forgotten.

But overhead also reduces. Think of a project having to support a head office administration, with ongoing costs per month. If the project is completed sooner and another one begun, less overhead is accumulated. Then there is inventory; the longer it lies idle the more it costs. A sensational example occurred when Britain worked a three-day week as a result of power cuts, and output actually increased! Although this probably could not be sustained.

As a result of their research, Stalk and Hout (1990) have proposed a number of **rules of response**:

- **the 0.05 to 5 rule,** which highlights the fact that on average the proportion of time that value is being added to a product or service, is between 0.05% and 5% of the total time spent in the system.

- **the 3/3 rule**, which states that the 95% to 99.95% of time that a product or service is idle, is split into three components each accounting for one-third of the time. The three components are: completion of the batch that the product or service is part of; physical and intellectual rework; and management decision time. As a result, working harder has little impact, but working smarter and on the right activities can have a dramatic impact on time and cost.

- **the 1/4 – 2 – 20 rule**, which states that for every quartering of the time required to produce a product or service, productivity will double and there could be a 20% cost reduction.

- **the 3 x 2 rule**, which expresses the advantage of time-based competitors: a growth rate of three times the average with twice the profit margin.

Stalk and Hout identified what they call **the main sequence**, which is the critical path of value adding activities in product development. Their **golden rule of time based competitiveness** is never delay an activity on the main sequence by an activity not on the main sequence. This may sound like a restatement of traditional project management principles, but it is surprising how often this principle seems to be ignored. You may like to reflect on these rules, and on the golden rule, say, in relation to the time required to obtain a passport.

4.2 Design for manufacture and simultaneous engineering

Design requires special mention in the lean and time-based operations context. Design is potentially one of the most powerful tools for lean manufacturing. The organisation of design is also crucial for time competitiveness as it brings new products to the marketplace quicker.

Lean design necessitates close co-operation between a number of departments: design itself, engineering, quality, marketing, and manufacturing. The best JIT or lean companies find ways to bring these groups together to solve what should be a mutual problem. The whole process is known as **simultaneous engineering** (or concurrent engineering or simply concurrency in the USA).

A basic technique is **options and parts reduction** which is about limiting variety through controlled design and increased commonality of parts. Techniques include the use of a group technology (or GT) coding system and database to first check if existing parts can be used before a new part is designed. This of course can have a dramatic impact on inventory management. An associated aim is to try to cut out long lead time parts. Pareto analysis is a good way of identifying those product options that have low demand and may cause more disruption than they are worth. These products could then be cut from the product line. Value engineering, using functional analysis and creativity, is a powerful technique used in achieving similar product functionality with lower cost. And of course contact with the 'voice of the customer' helps ensure no redundant requirements and that all real requirements are incorporated, benchmarked, and prioritised. A central technique for this is quality function deployment. Today this highly sophisticated business and design-options software is available to aid designers produce products with the 'optimal' balance between variety and the costs of variety. For example, allowing an option may have a knock-on effect on other parts and costs, whilst increased capability in other parts may allow many more options to be offered at low cost.

Design for manufacture aims to design in quality and manufacturability. Simultaneous engineering involves a 'rugby scrum' approach putting together a team from design, manufacture, development, quality, suppliers, and others such as marketing, to reduce the 'over the wall' mentality. This means that each department 'throws' their completed work over the wall, not caring what the next department does to it, because it is 'not our concern'. The process of developing the product is then seen as more important than functional departments. Going further, some companies, for example Honda, require designers to work as operators for a week or so each year. Others, such as Hewlett Packard, attempt to locate the design team close to the shop floor, and to have common refreshment areas. The aim is to reduce time and cost.

Design and redesign can be a long process unless specific trade-offs are made between time and performance, cost, and development. To improve performance requires extra time but diminishing returns usually apply, so time cut-off and review points (known as 'gateways') are established. The same comments apply to cost reduction. The important thing now is to consider these trade-offs specifically, rather than to leave it to the 'gut feel' of engineers as previously. Additional development may have to wait for another product generation, once the development target is reached.

Computer-aided design (CAD) is vital today for both better design and for time compression. Advanced CAD systems can allow simulation, where a mathematical model of the product can be tested, before prototyping or manufacture. Another approach is 'early prototyping', to test products with customers, which may be better than waiting for 'design perfection'. Emerging technologies include stereo lithography, which enables a designer to obtain a full scale plastic part representation directly from CAD, literally in a matter of hours rather than having to wait for a 'mock up' which formerly took weeks.

Supplier involvement in design recognises that with established suppliers, where there is a climate of trust and perhaps 'co-destiny', the suppliers should be used as experts in their own areas of component or process speciality. Early consultation is necessary, sharing certain future product information with trusted suppliers. A particular technique is 'open specs' where the designer only gives the broad requirement and allows the supplier to innovate, cut costs, and use the latest technology. Increasingly, some suppliers are being asked to design and supply whole product 'corners', not just component parts. This means that first-tier suppliers increasingly have the responsibility to work with second-tier suppliers to supply a complete sub-assembly which can be inserted directly into the final product.

4.3 Time charting and analysis

Time charting and analysis can be used in reducing manufacturing lead times, in reducing product development times, or in improving the turnaround in most service industries. The procedure has much in common with the use of the seven tools of quality, but is worth specific mention here because the aims go well beyond the removal of quality problems.

The critical path technique (CPA), we discussed in Unit 5, has been used for over 30 years for project management, essentially to arrange the time co-ordination of a variety of activities. Versions of CPA allow for 'crashing'; that is, the deliberate reduction of project time by using additional resources. This is a trade-off; less time for more cost. But in time charting and analysis, the aim is to reduce time without an additional cost penalty or in fact to reduce both time and cost. Time charting and analysis begins by assembling a process chart or a critical path diagram which details all the steps involved in producing the product or service. Often in manufacturing, but also in services, there is an **official process chart** (what should happen) and a **real process chart** (what actually happens). Also process charts, where they are kept, are often out of date. In any case, the aim is to get the real time process chart. This can often be achieved by following through a product or service and detailing all the steps and times, including delays and storage, and distance covered.

Now the questioning begins. The aim is to reduce time and waste. It is essentially a creative process. Preferably the people involved in the process should be used in its analysis and improvement. Bold thinking is a requirement, not piecemeal adjustment.

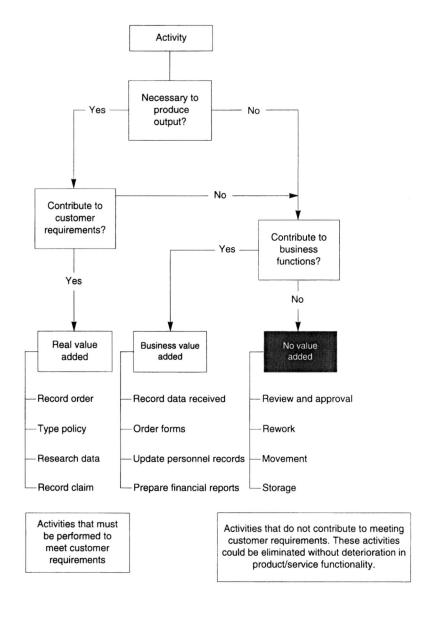

Figure 15: Value-added assessment (from Harrington, 1991).

The basic step is to examine the process flow chart and to split the activities into those that add immediate value for the customer and those that do not (Figure 15).

The idea, of course, is to achieve the added value of the product or service in as short a time as possible. Therefore try to make every value-adding step continue from the previous value-adding step, without interruptions for waiting, queuing, or for procedures which assist the company but not the customer. This is Stalk and Hout's 'main sequence'. There are several guidelines:

- C an the non value-adding steps be eliminated, simplified or reduced?
- Can any activity that delays a value-adding activity be simplified or rescheduled?
- Are there any activities, particularly non value-adding activities, that can be done in parallel with the sequence of value-adding activities?
- Can activities that have to be passed from department to department (and back!) be reorganised into a team activity? Better still, can one person do it? (What training and backup would be required?)
- Where are the bottlenecks? Can the capacity of the bottleneck be expanded? Do bottleneck operations keep working or are they delayed for minor reasons? Are bottleneck operations delayed by non-bottleneck operations, whether value-adding or not?
- What preparations can be made before the main sequence of value-adding steps is initiated so as to avoid delays (for example, preparing the paperwork, getting machines ready)?
- Can the necessary customer variety or requirements be added at a later stage, for example, making a basic product or service but adding the colour and sunroof as late as possible?
- If jobs are done in batches, can the batches be split so as to move on to a second activity before the whole batch is complete at the first activity?
- Can staff flexibility be improved so as to allow several tasks to be done by one person, thus cutting handing-on delays?
- What is the decision-making arrangement? Can decision-making power be devolved to the point of use? Can the routine decisions be recognised so that they can be dealt with on the spot? (Perhaps computer-based expert systems can be used.)
- Where is the best place, from a time point of view, to carry out each activity? (Can the activity be carried out at the point of use or contact, or must it really be referred elsewhere?)
- Do customers enjoy a 'one-stop' process? If not, why not?
- If problems do develop, what will be the delays and how can these delays be minimised?
- Is it possible to move inspection points so that they occur earlier? Better still, can a process step be failsafed?
- What availability of information will make the value-adding sequence smoother or more continuous? (Is there more than one source of information, and if so can this be brought to one place? A common database perhaps?) The old data processing principle is to capture information only once and let everyone use the same data.

● Can the time taken for value-adding activities be reduced? This involves breaking down a value-adding activity into more detailed activities, some of which would be non value-adding. For instance, preparing a meal might be considered to be a value-adding activity, but this activity itself may involve wastes such as moving around the kitchen. A more detailed analysis is advantageous for repetitive activities.

The JIT philosophy together with Stalk and Hout's contributions laid the foundation for some of today's most fashionable operations management theories, which are briefly discussed in the following section.

Is time-based competitiveness all good news or is there a downside? Stalk and Webber (1993) make several important points: avoiding the temptation to make time an end in itself (thereby producing too many product generations without allowing time to profit); and failing to link new product development with strategy and with marketing. This has been particularly prevalent in Japan. But, as a result, Japanese companies such as Toyota and Sony are trimming their product ranges. Daiichi is given as an example of a time-based competitor that is linking this time-based prowess to customer service.

4.4 Business Process Reengineering

Business Process Reengineering (BPR) came on the management scene in 1990 with a classic article in *Harvard Business Review* by Michael Hammer entitled 'Reengineering work: don't automate – obliterate'. Hammer claims that BPR is as radical a view of management as was Adam Smith's, but many disagree. In fact BPR can be seen as a natural development from ideas such as JIT, systems analysis, time based competitiveness and total quality.

For Thomas Davenport (1993), BPR (or process innovation as he calls it) should be seen as providing the breakthroughs in an alternating cycle with kaizen or continuing improvement activities. This is shown in Figure 16.

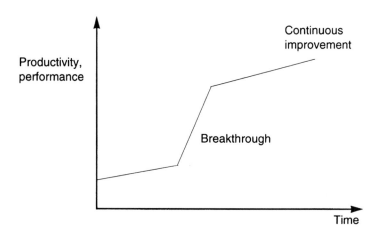

Figure 16: Breakthrough and continuous improvement

These breakthroughs can be dramatic. In one example, quoted by Hammer, Ford in North America employed about 500 people in their Accounts Payable department. A comparison with Mazda revealed that they employed only five people to do a similar task! This led Ford to a fundamental questioning of the business processes involved. Before reengineering, an order was placed, parts were delivered, the data entered into a computer system, invoices were received, invoices and internal documentation were matched, and payment made. After reengineering, parts were ordered for delivery in a specific time window. If they arrived in this window, payment was automatically made; if they did not, the parts were refused. No matching, no complicated controls and also reduced inventories. Ford was able to reduce staff by 75%, compared with an estimated 20% cut had the original plan gone ahead. Further partnership arrangements with suppliers will lead to even further reductions.

The essence of BPR sees the organisation as a set of processes which together achieve the core business objectives. A process is a system of activities which lead to the satisfaction of a customer by producing a particular output. Instead of viewing a company as a series of functional departments, such as marketing and finance, often each with their own objectives, BPR looks at the core processes in the organisation and reorganises and simplifies accordingly. Most organisations will have less than eight core processes: the essence of what the organisation does. Internal customers form a logical chain focusing on external customers; they do not look upwards to serving the boss, but sideways to serving the customer. The lack of a process view may help explain why so many good organisations, with good people, and good product ideas, fail to perform well. They are bound by the organisation. BPR is not matrix organisation, or automation, or more effective information technology, or even, as some would have us believe, an improved form of computer systems analysis.

Rummler and Brache (1990) recommend that all organisations considering reengineering should be analysed, not according to the traditional functional organisation chart, but instead into three levels: the organisation, the process and the job. Functional departments are simply there for organisational convenience, but all real work is done in cross-functional processes and it is these that need to be clarified, designed and managed. This is shown in Figure 17. At a university, for example, the core processes include admissions, teaching, research, accommodation and administration. All of these are cross-functional: for instance, the admissions process normally involves the admissions office staff, departmental tutors, finance department, housing department and public relations. If the process has not been specifically designed, delays and errors are likely to be common.

To an extent, BPR has been 'captured' by information technology professionals who tend to see it as the latest version of corporate information systems analysis. For them, BPR is about defining processes in terms of 'IDEFo' diagrams (a modification of flowcharting developed for the US military), and incorporating technologies such as work flow software and EDI. This is an unfortunate misrepresentation, as Hammer himself suggested in the title of his classic 1990 *Harvard Business Review* article. Thomas Davenport has presented a more balanced view. He believes that 'the new industrial engineering' involves viewing and using

	Goals	Design	Management
Organisation level	Organisation strategy	Organisation design: functions, flows fit with strategy	Appropriate functional goals and measures
Process level	Core process definitions and goals	Design of the business processes	Process goals and measures
Job level	Job goals and standards	Job design logic and environment	Job goals and measures (knowledge, skill, rewards, standards)

*Figure 17: The business process hierarchy
(adapted from Rummler and Brache, 1990)*

established concepts, such as those we mentioned earlier, as well as traditional work study and industrial engineering, in the light of developments in information technology.

Once the core processes have been identified, and the goal of each defined, we ask the simple yet radical question what are the minimum necessary activities to achieve this goal?, ignoring existing functional departments. This can, and has, led to massive reorganisation, large staff cuts, and also to dramatic reductions in lead time and improvements in customer service.

PRINCIPLES OF REENGINEERING

According to Michael Hammer (1990), the principles of BPR are:

- **Organise around outcomes, not tasks**. Instead of organising a job around departments or persons, each with their own responsibility, think about what the objective of the process is. Many of us have had the experience of being shunted from department to department in order to complete the task. Customers are not interested in the departments, they are interested in the outcome. So don't set up the process for the convenience of the organisation, set it up for the customer! This may mean radical redesign; perhaps one person should do the whole task.

- **Have those who use the output of the process perform the process**. Here Hammer is suggesting that, with the help of suitable information technology, it is no longer necessary to have, for example, centralised purchasing, accounting, personnel and so forth. One consequence is delay as different functions have different priorities. These tasks can be done by the users of each service themselves. It is time to cut the red tape; indeed cutting the red tape may be essential for survival. This, of course, fits in very well with the concept of self-directed work teams discussed under JIT. The point is that, with the help of computers, expert systems and distributed databases such thinking is increasingly possible.

● **Subsume information processing work into the real work that produces the information.** People who produce the information should also process it. So, again with the help of computers, functions who produce, sell or order should process the information themselves rather than handing it on to accounting or marketing or purchasing. Treat geographically dispersed resources as though they were centralised. Again this is made possible through IT. A company should be able to get the advantages of both centralisation and decentralisation simultaneously, thus ending the classic argument. An example is purchasing: let cell members be responsible themselves, but let them work through a system which aggregates orders, thus gaining economies of scale.

● **Link parallel activities instead of integrating their results.** In bringing a new product to market, for example, the traditional way is for each function (marketing, design, engineering, manufacturing and so forth) to work in sequence. Hammer suggests working in parallel, again with the aid of computers.

● **Put the decision point where the work is performed, and build control into the process.** The distinction between those that do and those that control is increasingly outdated, according to Hammer. This principle is not only about appropriate empowerment, but also creative management and once again computer systems. We should recognise that front-line staff often take decisions that have huge impacts. For this they need support, training and IT decision tools such as expert systems.

● **Capture information once and at the source.** The economics of information have changed, according to Hammer. Once, when information was difficult to transmit and store, it made sense to collect it several times. With modern IT this is no longer the case.

ACTIVITY 13

Compare Hammer's principles we have outlined with the principles developed from Stalk and Hout and Harrington (1991). Identify similarities. Make up a 'master list'. Also, compare Hammer's principles with what you have learned about JIT and TQM.

You will probably be able to justify the view that BPR is a natural outgrowth from earlier developments, but with greater emphasis on information technology. But is it *all* about IT? Clearly not.

IMPLEMENTING BPR

To implement BPR usually involves a fundamental examination of company systems. Once the framework suggested in Figure 17 has been worked through, detailed flowcharts or 'process maps' can be drawn. Two maps should be drawn for each process: an **is** map and a **should be map** (detailing the ideal state). (Note the similarities to work study that we discussed in Unit 7.) One difference between conventional flowcharts and process maps is that with the latter the logical sequence of activities is arranged in sequence and set against organisational departments arranged as rows. It is thus a cross-departmental view. The detailed changes at the jobs level can then be worked out to fit in with the processes.

Unlike kaizen, which emphasises continuous incremental improvements, BPR goes for the step-function leap in performance. BPR starts with a blank sheet of paper, kaizen with existing processes. BPR is top-down management driven, kaizen relies upon operator initiatives. BPR and kaizen should be recognised as partners.

Davenport suggests starting with a 'vision statement' about how the process will work. This progresses to identifying key process characteristics, followed by suitable performance measures and critical success factors. Finally, potential barriers to implementation are identified. And every process should be benchmarked. This sets the scene. Thereafter design alternatives are brainstormed, the feasibility and risk of each evaluated, and the chosen design 'prototyped' (simulated and tested). Finally a 'migration strategy' (possibly including a pilot study) is worked out.

Of course, BPR is not just technique. To be successful a complete change in culture is required, from departmental thinking to process thinking. That is the really hard part!

ACTIVITY 14

Compare BPR, JIT, simultaneous engineering and TQM in terms of the following dimensions: improvement (continuous or breakthrough), goals (improve quality, reduce time, reduce cost, reduce inventory, etc.), and organisational focus (teams, departmental, process, cells, etc.). Construct a matrix and fill in the cells.

Perhaps you have produced something like this:

	Improvement	Goals	Organisational focus
BPR	breakthrough	productivity time/speed	process organisation-wide
JIT	continuous but breakthrough may also take place	manufacturing leadtime waste reduction cost, quality inventory not a goal but the means	cells process
SE	continuous, occasionally breakthrough	time to market cost	inter-departmental
TQM	continuous; but Juran also sees 'project by project' break- through	quality service cost	organisation-wide process

4.5 Mass customisation

Mass customisation is a recent term stemming from a book of the same title by Pine (1993). It, too, incorporates many lean or time-based concepts but extends the thinking into the high-variety market. The aim of mass customisation, as the name suggests, is to get the best of both worlds: the cost benefits of mass production together with the variety benefits of customisation. Pine believes that this problem can be tackled by concentrating on one or more segments along the **value chain**. The value chain is a concept used by Michael Porter and frequently used in the context of organisational strategy. You may recall this from Unit 1. The value chain comprises the elements of product development, production, marketing, service and delivery.

● The first method of customisation is to have standardised products but to customise by concentrating on marketing and service. Examples are IBM, who had a fairly standard system in their IBM 360 computer but customised software and support services, or a hotel chain that has a ranges of standard offerings but targets each range at a particular market segment. Care must be taken, however, in the development and production areas to bring to the market products with sufficiently wide appeal but which are nevertheless capable of being segmented.

● The second method is to have customisation of products and services addressed at the design stage, and then targeted through appropriate marketing. Examples are an adjustable razor or adjustable car seats where the customer makes the necessary changes from a standard product, or cube furniture where the customer assembles exactly what is required from standard units. Again, from an operation viewpoint, it is the principle of understanding the customer, appropriate design, and focused manufacturing.

- The third method is to provide point-of-delivery customisation. Examples are photo shops that develop on-site rather than sending away, and in-store personal computer customisation. The trade-off is time against cost. These are the small-machine, small batch size, focused factory concepts at work. A pull system might also be more appropriate, as for example the computer manufacturer who pulls appropriately-sized screens, disk drives, and so on, as they are consumed.

- The fourth method involves the full process chain, and is in line with quick response that we discuss in the next section. This would apply, for example, in fashion distribution but also in customised heavy engineering. Here time is of the essence, so design time is tackled though simultaneous engineering and variety as late as possible, production may be tackled though cellular manufacturing, order processing may be tackled through BPR, and delivery through simplification of the distribution system.

- Finally, mass customisation may be approached through modularisation. Pine lists several types but most would be familiar to the experienced lean practitioner. Modularisation would include **component sharing and swapping** (where a common platform is used for a range of watches or calculators), **cut to fit modularity** (where a made to measure suit is made up from standard panels), **mix modularity** (where for example different engines could be fitted to the same type of car, and where customers are offered options such as a sunroof), and **sectional modularity** (where a customised kitchen can be made up from many standardised components some of which may be supplied by contractors with whom there is no formal contract).

ACTIVITY 15

Identify some examples of mass customisation in local products and services.

Examples you might have thought of include modular degree courses that allow students to combine course modules to create their own degrees, the take away pizza restaurant that can produce a large variety of products simply by using different combinations of a few ingredients, or the increased use of theming of pubs to attract particular client groups.

4.6 Agile manufacturing and the agile enterprise

The term **agile manufacturing** appears to have first been used by the Iacocca Institute at Lehigh University which has been seeking ways in which US manufacturing can best respond to the Japanese. The emerging thinking appears to be to combine lean and mass customisation philosophy with high technology and also to integrate manufacturing across the enterprise so as to create the manufacturing equivalent of TQM. Suppliers and distributors become part of the package. Read the article 'The use of time', Resource Item 9.1; it summarises some key features of current manufacturing technology.

4.7 EDI, EPOS and bar coding

EDI enables direct computer-to-computer communication. This can be extended where a bank is linked into the **value added network** to allow automated payment. This term is used where there is a whole network of companies using EDI. On one level, this **paperless trading** cuts time and improves accuracy by avoiding rekeying. Clerical staff may be saved, and transactions are less expensive than by mail, telephone or fax. Cash flow also improves. But on another, more strategic level, EDI opens up other opportunities such as the ability to link intra-company communications with external companies, to search for prices and suppliers more easily, to improve forecasts where EDI is linked to EPOS and to other information systems. It is possible, for instance, for manufacturers to write the master production schedules of their suppliers directly. EDI has until recently exclusively involved word processing, but now interchange of graphical design data is possible.

One of the problems with EDI has been standards. A supplier may find itself having to work through several EDI networks with different message standards. In Britain, Tradanet is a VAN (Value Added Network) used by several retailers. The German car industry uses one standard and the British another (Odette). Several networks operate in the USA. Attempts have been made to create a universal standard, and EDIFACT is slowly emerging but some industries have decide that they do not have the time to wait.

EPOS terminals which scan **bar codes** to produce itemised bills are a familiar feature in most supermarkets. Once again, they can be used far beyond their obvious advantage of improved data accuracy and customer service. They enable an up-to-date record to be kept of inventory and product usage – a tremendous marketing advantage. The implications are a shift in balance of power away from suppliers, who used to have most of the information about product popularity and the success of promotions, towards the retailers. In Britain and the USA, some supermarket chains are now encouraging customers to use personal cards, which has the potential to link detailed transactions to particular customers and so to target promotions to specific customers.

The real potential is realised when all three technologies are linked. Over the last decade, Tesco has been able to approximately halve the number of distribution centres, whilst the number of suppliers and turnover has more than doubled. The vast majority of their suppliers now deliver to the nearest distribution centre rather than direct to the supermarkets as previously.

4.8 Supply chain management and quick response

It is natural to expand out the concepts of JIT flow to the supply and distribution chain. This area, known as **logistics**, is currently a top priority for operations in many companies. The area has been given considerable impetus by developments such as EDI and EPOS terminals. We discussed the advantages of supplier rationalisation in Unit 6. Of course, many manufacturers are themselves suppliers and have been caught up in the rationalisation process. Another trend, which has had a slow gestation, is the realisation of the profit potential of tied up inventory and the advantages of trading off lower inventories against higher cost, but faster, distribution.

Another factor which until recently has been recognised by comparatively few companies is that of more focused channel selection. For many firms, until recently, all goods were sent along the same distribution channels irrespective of the needs of customers. This is known as **channel averaging**. But customers are different. Consider beer: supermarkets require bulk delivery (hopefully at a discount), shops often do not have available space and would prefer more frequent deliveries in small quantities. Some stores want support from their distributors in promotion, and shelf stocking, others do not. Then there are pubs and restaurants, again with a different range of requirements. All this suggests differentiation and tailoring of supply channels.

There are three basic elements of **quick response** (quoted in Hammond and Kelly, 1990):

- consumer testing to narrow product selections to the right products for the right markets;
- implementing an efficient information pipeline;
- instituting short-cycle (or JIT) replenishment.

Quick response logistics seems to have developed at about the same time on both sides of the Atlantic, in the late 1980s. In Italy, Benetton the fashion chain, working with a network of suppliers, developed a logistics system capable of meeting the inventory needs of any store within 48 hours. The philosophy is that, given the fickle demands of the fashion market, it is more effective to pull according to need than to try to hold 'just-in-case' stock at stores. Sweaters are kept 'in grey', dyed according to need and shipped to arrive within 48 hours. The network of suppliers shares information and distributes work to ensure the necessary quick response. In the USA, quick response developed out of initiatives by Wal Mart and the apparel industry. This makes full use of EDI and EPOS, and rationalisation of supply channels. Once again the idea, in common with JIT philosophy, is to pull requirements as needed with minimal lead time, rather than holding large safety stocks.

Manufacturers in a quick response system see themselves as a part of a chain, with the customer regarded as simply the next workstation with kanban cards in between. Operations must be carried out just-in-time with maximum flexibility. Levi Strauss, the jeans manufacturer, is a well-known partner in the Wal Mart quick response system and is able to make tiny batches of any size and style with minimal lead time, thereby avoiding the necessity to keep finished goods stock. And Wrangler has implemented **DSD** or **direct store delivery** to about 5,000 jeans outlets, thereby simplifying the supply chain and allowing immediate response to changing customer preferences. A quick response system also includes, naturally enough, rationalisation and streamlining of purchasing, quality assurance and inspection, supply, and payment.

ACTIVITY 16

You will recall we discussed the P:D ratio in Unit 1. What is the effect of quick response logistics on the P:D ratio, and what must be done to achieve these benefits?

Clearly, quick response aims at a P:D ratio of substantially less than 1 all along the logistics chain. The 'customer delight' that this results in allows stores to ask higher prices, as pointed out by Stalk and Hout. Also, of course, there are substantial inventory savings not only in direct inventories but also indirect in as far as wasted stock is reduced. This was a prime motivation for Benetton who, like others in the fashion business, is faced with end of season discounting in order to clear unwanted stock. Of course, to achieve these benefits requires partnership co-operation between parties along the logistics chain, as well as internally between functions. Some techniques that are increasingly found in JIT logistics, including quick response, are:

- **Milk runs**: instead of collecting a large load from a supplier (say) once per week, smaller part loads are collected from a range of suppliers situated close to one another, on a daily basis. Milk runs can also be used for distribution.
- **Cross docking**: instead of an intermediate warehouse acting as a storage centre, the concept is that it acts more as a sorting centre between incoming and outgoing vehicles, with goods being held literally for only hours and often not going into storage at all. The critical requirement is to arrange the timing of incoming and outgoing vehicles.
- **Continuous route moves**: shipping takes place in a never-ending chain of vehicles where, as they unload from a supplier, they then immediately take on a load due to go to a customer near to the supplier.
- **Shipping container marking**: bar coding of containers, used in conjunction with EDI, pre-verified quality and pre-labelling. When a container arrives there is no need for a retailer to open, check and sort the contents so that goods can be moved directly onto the sales floor
- **Stockless warehousing**: vehicle trailers are used instead of a building, and 'mechanical horses' (the cab section of the vehicle) merely interchange full trailers for empty ones. Once again, there are critical requirements for timing and co-ordination.

Quick response logistics requires a new co-operation between production planning, procurement and distribution, which were formally three distinct functions. For instance, the linking of procurement planning and distribution planning makes it possible to share vehicles and containers to make possible two-way usage, or continuous route moves. Of course, as we have already seen in Unit 6, the linking of production planning and procurement is becoming the norm with supplier partnerships. **Commodity teams**, comprising cross-functional representation from marketing, accounting, manufacturing, quality and production planning are increasingly being used to select and develop supplier partners. And linking production planning with distribution makes better communication with industrial customers possible, thereby allowing intermediate safety inventories to be reduced. All three functions need to work much more closely for effective logistics.

The evolution of the supply chain may be viewed with reference to the four stages illustrated in the set of diagrams in Figure 18 (pages 514–15).

In Stage 1, the initial, traditional, stage:

- Delivery lead times are long, and customers often expect to wait for many types of product.
- Inventory is managed by reorder point methods and safety stocks; however, despite high levels of safety stock, stockouts still occur because sometimes several warehouses go through their reorder points within a short period of one another, leading to excessive overload at distribution centres.
- Safety stocks are held at each stage.
- There are large variations in response times along the chain, and large variation in the amounts of inventory held as the different independent players along the chain vie for their own advantage. Waves of inventory surge through the chain in response to reorder point systems and large deliveries, combined with lack of forward visibility at locations along the chain which are remote from the customer.
- Receiving dock inspection is the norm, further adding to delays and to supply chain disruption as defective items are discovered.
- Supplier relationships are adversarial. As a result there is much waste in managing suppliers and in delivery.
- Marketing at retailers tends to act unilaterally without reference to the ability of the supply chain to respond. As a result several promotions fail because of shortages.

In Stage 2, control is attempted:

- Inventory is managed by distribution requirements planning (DRP). This is a form of MRP applied to distribution, where forecasts and time phasing is used. The planned order releases from warehouses become the gross requirements for the factory, thereby avoiding unexpected stockouts and allowing more stable, planned production. Alternatively, double reorder point is used. (Here an advance warning of an impending order release is given when inventory falls below a higher, warning level.)
- The supply chain is forecast driven, rather than reactive.

Stage 1: Independence

Suppliers

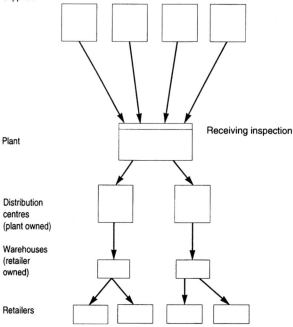

Plant

Receiving inspection

Distribution
centres
(plant owned)

Warehouses
(retailer
owned)

Retailers

Stage 2: Control

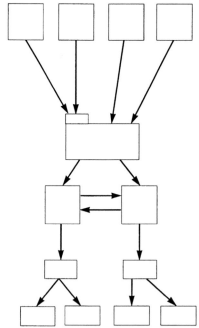

Stage 3: Partnership and rationalisation

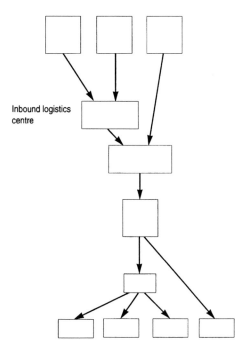

Inbound logistics
centre

Stage 4: Lean/quick response

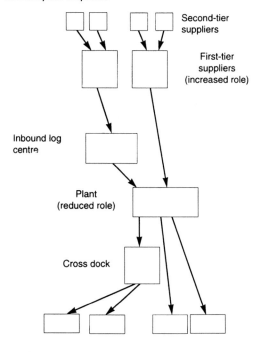

Second-tier
suppliers

First-tier
suppliers
(increased role)

Inbound log
centre

Plant
(reduced role)

Cross dock

Figure 18: Logistics development

- Links may be established between distribution centres and warehouses, so that a shortfall in inventory in one area of the country can be compensated for by an excess in another.

- In-house JIT operations begin at various factories. With this comes the recognition of the advantages of having extra capacity for flexibility and speed of response.

- JIT also leads to demands for smaller delivery quantities. Initially this may have a detrimental effect as receiving docks become congested with orders and too much in-house inspection.

This leads to Stage 3, partnership:

- With increased JIT recognition, a supplier base rationalisation begins.

- Supplier evaluation begins, with suppliers being judged on quality and long-term cost potential, rather than short-term price.

- Some single-sourcing may begin.

- JIT becomes more established within the factories. Some may reduce lead times sufficiently so that they are able to move from make-to-stock to make-to-order. As a result, there is less forecast dependence.

- Longer-term contracts begin. This allows some manufacturers to begin to work with suppliers on quality problems. Prevention based strategies, such as SPC, become more usual.

- Inbound logistics centres are used. Here suppliers that are not yet on JIT deliver to an inbound warehouse from which deliveries are made on a JIT basis to the manufacturer.

- Small parts supply is consolidated by third-party organisations that take over responsibility for a large proportion of inexpensive parts, resulting in a huge reduction in the supplier base.

- Milk round collection from suppliers begins.

- EDI is established.

- As partnerships become established, safety stocks along the supply chain are reduced.

- The need for intermediate distribution centres begins to be questioned. Simplification of the network becomes a priority for quick response and for cost reasons.

This leads to the 'final' Stage 4: integrated/quick response systems:

- Second-tier suppliers are brought in. First-tier suppliers become responsible for increasing percentages of final products.

- Value-adding networks are common. EDI and EPOS are common, and information is shared right along the supply chain, some of it instantaneously.

- Safety stocks are minimal, right along the chain. Instead, the chain relies on quick response and flexibility. Safety stocks are only held at the end of the chain to cope with short-term variation in customer demands.

- Receiving dock inspection has been eliminated. Each element along the chain is responsible for delivery of perfect quality.

- As suppliers, and suppliers' suppliers move into JIT, so the need for in-bound logistics centres decreases. Third parties may be used for milk round collections.

- 'Variety as late as possible' is the norm right along the chain. Manufacturers and suppliers are flexible, have extra capacity, and are only willing to commit themselves to final assembly when actual demands are known.

- Cross docking rather than warehousing takes place.

- There are far fewer distribution centres.

- Synchronisation of supplier and manufacturer schedules is the norm. Here what is produced today by a supplier is moved immediately to the manufacturer and immediately worked on. There are no intermediate buffers.

- Demand management principles are applied. There is acceptance of the dangers of uncoordinated promotions.

- Purchasing procedures have been simplified through the use of business process reengineering.

ACTIVITY 17

Read the article 'Supply chain revolution' (Resource Item 9.2) from APICS – *The Performance Advantage*, January 1995 (pp. 43-8) and note what accounting and marketing principles are increasingly important in managing supply chains.

The article traces the evolution of supply chain management and distribution in the USA. Similar patterns are now emerging in Europe. You should have picked up how market (or channel) segmentation is developing, how more sophisticated accounting is needed, and how promotions and 'everyday low pricing' is being integrated with operations. You should also have noted the increasing role of technology in the supply chain.

Summary

In this section we have demonstrated that time-based competitiveness is now a wide and important field of activity for operations managers in manufacturing and service. It extends from design (simultaneous engineering) to manufacturing (JIT) to distribution (supply chain logistics). The process view, as in BPR, is an integrating philosophy to all these areas. The process view promises to be one of the great advances of the 1990s, not only for operations management but in business and government also.

We have noted that technologies such as CAD/CAM, EDI and EPOS are an essential element of time compression. Such technologies go far beyond the mere automation of labour, but open up new horizons for improved customer service and responsiveness. But there are dangers also, such as too much variety too quickly.

Finally, we considered the evolution of logistics (Figure 19) and the implications for competitiveness, summarised in Figure 20.

Functional view	Process view
Forecast demand	Forecast variability
Warehousing	Cross docking
Safety stock	Make to replenishment
Blind contracts	Communication all along chain
Push	Pull
Slow response	Quick response
Standard products	Products to customer specification
Supply chain	Demand chain

Figure 19: The evolution of logistics

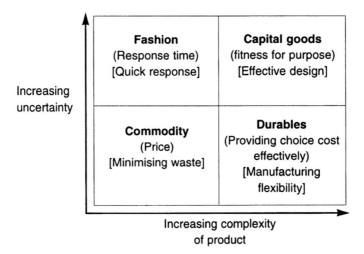

Note: Round ( ) brackets indicates order winners, square [ ] brackets indicates critical competenees in logistics.

Figure 20: Understanding order winners and critical competencies in logistics (adapted from Miles 1994)

SECTION 5

Suppliers and Purchasing

Introduction

In this section we will look at the changing role of suppliers and the importance of the purchasing function, as well as supplier partnerships, in reducing costs, improving quality and saving time. We will look at **single sourcing** and **network sourcing** within supplier partnerships.

5.1 The background

'For AT&T, it's an expressway to $1 billion in cost reduction by 1997' and 'Purchasing is by far the largest single function at AT&T', reported Shawn Tully (1995) in an article in *Fortune*. Many manufacturing companies are outsourcing an increasing proportion of their work so as to concentrate on core business whilst gaining from the expertise of suppliers both in design and manufacturing cost. The importance of time-based operations (JIT scheduling and time to bring new products to market) has also been significant. To these ends, most car manufacturers are now working closely with not only their immediate suppliers, but with suppliers' suppliers. World class performance requires world class foundations, which means working more closely with a more limited range of suppliers.

We have discussed the concept of a synchronised flow of materials all along the chain of organisations, from raw material supplier to final customer. This long-term aim can only be considered if there is a degree of co-operation between organisations along the supply chain. In the last section on logistics we saw how this might operate. Total quality also implies a partnership with suppliers. As we have seen in Unit 4, purchased materials constitute a significant and growing proportion of total costs in most manufacturing companies.

Traditionally, suppliers were seen as adversaries. In many companies, until recent years, the game began with the design specification and the calling for quotations to supply the specified parts. Contracts would be awarded on the basis of the lowest price, so there was a real incentive to cost cut, and to compromise on quality. Having won the contract, the game continued by arguing the price upwards on the basis of increased labour or material costs. Sometimes this was accepted but both sides would try to keep their options open. For the supplier, this meant not revealing any internal problems, quality or otherwise, and for the purchaser, this meant always looking around for an alternative source of supply, and keeping contract periods short. Purchasing often closely guards its area of competence, and in any case there seems no necessity to involve others. Purchasing is reactive. World-class competitiveness cannot be obtained on such a basis, so an alternative had to be found.

5.2. Supplier partnership

Japan was where the alternative was found. In essence, the Japanese partnership approach begins with the recognition that both sides have much to gain from building an ongoing relationship. Both sides bring expertise to the table. The supplier is often an expert in a particular technology or component area. The purchaser often brings a greater knowledge of the end market and expertise in quality management. The purchaser then does not specify the components to be supplied in as great a detail as previously, but allows the supplier to innovate to cut costs and improve quality. A long-term relationship is built, and the supplier is then prepared to invest in order to achieve these two aims. Both sides work together conscientiously to reduce costs and improve quality. This may include actions such as sharing of production schedules, working together on quality problems, and cutting unnecessary bureaucracy in the purchasing and payment procedures.

To co-operate more closely in this way means that, of necessity, there has to be fewer suppliers. So existing suppliers are examined, and the better ones get more business whilst the less good ones are dropped. The relationship is stable. The prime source of contact is through purchasing, but several other departments become involved with their opposite numbers. Design talks to design, quality to quality, marketing to marketing, engineering to engineering, and so forth. Purchasing is proactive. There is trust because both sides have too much to lose. But, contracts can still be lost or not re-awarded after the initial period, although both sides would seek to avoid this. Preference would be given to established suppliers to supply new components, simply because such a lot of effort goes into establishing the partnership.

From a JIT or total quality viewpoint, the ideal is to receive components from suppliers which are delivered directly to the point of use, at the latest possible moment, with perfect quality and no need to inspect, and packaged and presented in such a way that the parts require the least non-value adding handling. Clearly this is not achieved overnight. Initially the customer firm may be involved with 100% receiving goods inspection. Then, as the partnership develops, the supplier would take over the 100% inspection task, with the customer doing sampling inspection. Gradually, with help from the customer, the supplier would implement prevention-based strategies such as SPC and failsafing with the customer doing even less sampling inspection. Finally as process capability improves and confidence increases, the customer would cease receiving inspection. All the while, efforts would be in progress to simplify the documentation of purchasing and payment, and also to squeeze out intermediate inventories by close communication of schedules and the sharing of market information.

In the mid-1980s, Japanese car manufacturers in Britain shocked local component suppliers by expecting a year-on-year price reduction. They also demanded an 'open book' approach to product costing. This was a complete change to the usual adversarial approach. But, at the same time, the Japanese were prepared to send their quality people and engineers into their suppliers to assist in obtaining the required quality levels and cost reductions. If savings beyond the target levels were achieved, they would often be retained by the suppliers even though the savings had been achieved with outside assistance. Supplier partnership has been a major growth area in the 1990s. Most major companies are continuing to reduce their supplier base as the partnership concept expands. The *Fortune* article cited earlier reports that purchasing is beginning to attract some of the best young executives, a significant change compared with the 1980s. The purchasing function is increasingly seen as a central co-ordinating role in manufacturing and supplying, as Figure 20 illustrates.

Each function in the manufacturing firm talks to their opposite number in the supplier firm, but the main, formal link is through the two purchasing functions.

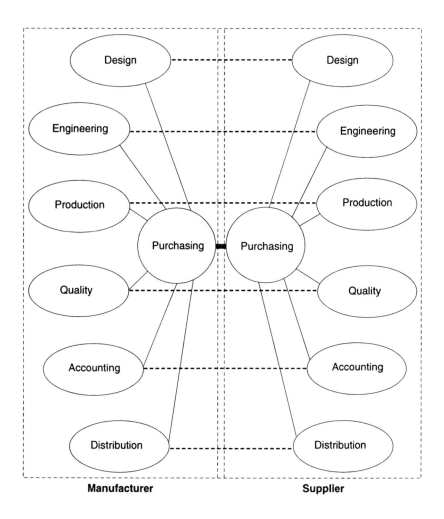

Figure 20: Purchasing's new role (adapted from Robert Hall, 1986)

Single sourcing has become a hotly debated topic, often associated with the Japanese approach. Under this concept, there is only one supplier for each component. This is in contrast to a **sole supplier** who is the only supplier capable of supplying a particular component due perhaps to patents or technology. Advocates of single sourcing cite British and American examples where Japanese factories have developed single source agreements. Critics maintain that there is too much risk of dependency, either on price or due to the risk of disruption through fire or strike action. The truth is probably somewhere in-between. Many Japanese plants do have single source suppliers but claim that there are simply insufficient good suppliers around, and that they would prefer if possible to have a few good alternatives. Other Japanese plants operate a mixed strategy. One plant may well have a single source supplier for a particular component, but other plants will use another supplier for the same component, thereby getting the best of both worlds. Certainly, for major components, it has become popular to require a supplier to set up a facility, often dedicated, within minutes from the main plant. This allows close co-operation on design and facilitates just-in-time delivery. This is especially applicable for first-tier suppliers.

Recently, beginning in the car industry, but now expanding out, the concept of two-tier supplier management has developed. Here the end product manufacturer wishes to become more focused on what they do best, and does not want the bother of co-ordinating and assembling scores of components. The first-tier supplier is expected to assume the role of assembling what is termed 'corners' or major sub-assemblies. For example, once the end manufacturer was prepared to assemble wheels, tyres, suspension, brakes, and cabling to form the complete unit. Now the first-tier supplier is expected to do all of this and to deliver the whole unit just-in-time to the final assembly plant. This presupposes a high level of partnership management. A network develops with the end user co-ordinating and developing both first and second-tier suppliers.

Of course, the partnership concept is not applicable to all types of purchased materials. Our discussion certainly applies to A items and perhaps to some B items. **Commodity** items, where there are no particular quality problems and where there are many suppliers and where quantity discounts are applicable, may be subject to centralised purchasing, but there would still often be efforts to reduce the supply base.

Richard Lamming, in his book *Beyond Partnership* (1993), has proposed a four-stage model tracing the development of supplier relationship from traditional to partnership/Japanese. He then goes on to explain the fifth, emerging stage, that he terms lean supply. The five stages are summarised in Tables 1 and 2 (pages 526–27).

5.3 Network sourcing

Peter Hines (1994) of Cardiff Business School has studied what he terms **network sourcing** in Japan and has proposed a 'ten force partnership model' to explain the effectiveness of purchasing in Japan. He uses the term network sourcing to indicate the complex web of relationships that occur in the supply process, not only vertically between end products and its suppliers, suppliers' suppliers, and so on, but also horizontally between suppliers that deal with more than one customer. A supplier may well have 'asset specificity' (that is, machines that are dedicated to a particular customer) that applies to several customers. His ten forces are:

1   The overall network of purchaser-suppliers is driven relentlessly by the consumer's changing needs and tastes. Customers are continually demanding better products, more features, higher quality, and lower prices. This forces all parties in the network to continuously innovate and improve, or be left behind.

2   As a result, customers or assemblers need to spend time developing their supplier's capabilities in terms of quality, flexibility, delivery, and cost. Peter Hines has shown that profit margins between customer and supplier are closer in Japan than appears to be the case in the West, indicating a willingness to share risk and opportunity and to be more truly partners.

3   The third force follows from the second and involves a spread of benefits and knowledge amongst several parties in an interactive network of suppliers and customers. What a supplier may learn from one customer benefits not only that customer but may also benefit other customers. Yet the supplier would learn other things from other customers which in turn would benefit the first customer. Thus as suppliers become stronger and more knowledgeable so the benefits are shared. Overall, everyone gains. This is one reason why Japan has such strong suppliers which benefits themselves, their customers, and the country.

4   A system of 'supplier associations' is the next force. Supplier associations are clubs of suppliers, working sometimes within a common industry or sometimes sharing a common customer. They tackle problems together and share knowledge between themselves. This goes well beyond mere factory visits but may include joint task forces and sharing of engineers and other staff, sharing the costs of training and educational materials, and benchmarking of processes. Where a supplier association is established by a customer company, that company will provide time and resources

5   The fifth force involves 'rivalry to find a favoured network position'. Japanese companies favour the concept of single-source suppliers, but they also favour developing and using several suppliers having common skills and capabilities. One of each group would be selected to supply a part for one product for the duration of that product's life. But another similar component going into another product made by the same assembler would be supplied by a second supplier. The performance of each supplier would be judged over the lifetime of the product, and when another product comes to market the contract is awarded to the best supplier. In this way, competition is maintained between suppliers whilst still benefiting from the advantages of single sourcing.

Table 1: The four-phase model of customer-supplier relationships

Model	Nature of competition	Basis of sourcing decisions	Role of data/information exchange	Management of capacity	Delivery practice	Dealing with price changes	Attitude to quality	Role of R&D	Level of pressure
Traditional before 1975	Closed but friendly; plenty of business	Wide; enquiries; lowest bid; price-based	Very restricted; minimum necessary	Few problems: some poor scheduling	Large quantities; buyer's choice: steady	General negotiation (annual); a win/lose game	Inspection: arguments/ *laissez-faire*	One-sided: either assembler or supplier	Low-medium: steady; predictable
Stress 1972–85	Closed and deadly; chaotic	'Dutch Auctions'; price-based	A weapon; one-way; supplier must open books	Spasmodic: no system to deal with chaos	Unstable; no control; variable; no notice of changes	Conflict in negotiation; a battle lose/lose	Aggressive campaigns; SQA, etc.	Shared, but only for cost reductions	High/ unbearable, volatile
Resolved 1982 onwards	Closed; some collaboration strategic	Price, quality and delivery	Two-way: short-term e.g. forward build	Gradually improving: linkages appearing	Smaller quantities; buyer's demands stabilising	Annual economics plus; negotiation; win/lose	Joint effort towards improvements	Shared for develop-ments	Medium: some sense of relief
Partnership/ Japanese 1990 onwards	Collaboration; tiering; still dynamic	Performance history; long-term source; costs	Two-way: long-term e.g. knowledge of costs	Coordinated and jointly planned	Small quantity; agreed basis; dynamic (JIT)	Annual economics+ planned reductions; win/win?	Joint planning for developments	Shared: some black or grey box	Very high: predictable

Factor	Lean supply characteristics
Nature of competition	Global operation; local presence Based upon contribution to product technology Organic growth and merger and acquisition Dependent upon alliances/collaboration
Basis of sourcing decisions	Early involvement of established supplier in new vehicle Joint efforts in target costing/value analysis Single and dual sourcing Supplier provides global benefits Re-sourcing as a last resort after attempts to improve
Role/mode of data/ information exchange	True transparency: costs, etc Two-way: discussion of costs and volumes Technical and commercial information Electronic data interchange *Kanban* system for production deliveries
Management of capacity	Regionally strategic investments discussed Synchronised capacity Flexibility to operate with fluctuations
Delivery practice	True just-in-time with *kanban* Local, long-distance and international JIT
Dealing with price changes	Price reductions based upon cost reductions from order onwards: from joint efforts
Attitude to quality	Supplier vetting schemes become redundant Mutual agreement on quality targets Continual interaction and *kaizen* Perfect quality as goal
Role of R&D	Integrated: assembler and supplier Long-term development of component systems Supplier expertise/assembler systems integration
Level of pressure	Very high for both customer and supplier Self-imposed Not culturally specific

Table 2: The lean supply model of customer-supplier relationships
(from Lamming, op. cit. p. 194)

6   The sixth force is 'creative tension between co-operation and competition'. Here several suppliers who are otherwise competitors (or may be members of the same supplier association) cooperate amongst themselves to remain ahead of outside competitors in terms of technology and quality. This may involve joint research or development projects. An example quoted by Hines is that of the development of car wiring harnesses which kept the business within a selected group of suppliers. The suppliers collectively benefit.

7   Stemming from the sixth force is the ongoing threat from new entrants, or the eighth force.

8   The threat of substitute products. The seventh and eighth forces both keep suppliers 'on their toes'.

9   The ninth force, probably more applicable to Japan, is the availability of cheap finance and the support given to small and medium-sized business by banks and finance houses. This may be due to the complex system of cross-ownership in Japan.

10 Finally, the government plays a role by creating an environment for development. This is well established in Japan; in Britain it is beginning to happen with support from the Department of Trade and Industry.

Summary

In this section we reviewed the changing role of the purchasing function and the evolving nature of supplier partnerships. We ended by looking at the effectiveness of purchasing in Japan, through the use of 'network sourcing'.

In the 1990s, many manufacturers began to realise the importance of the purchasing function and of supplier partnership as important weapons for cost reduction, quality improvement, and time reduction. The traditional adversarial way of dealing with suppliers is giving way to a mutually beneficial partnership. This means a reduction in the number of suppliers, often single sourcing for each part type. Suppliers are increasingly being called upon to deliver, just-in-time, not components as previously but whole assemblies. This in turn means co-operation with second-tier suppliers.

Lean supply means the reduction of waste all along the supply chain. JIT, total quality, and BPR principles are all relevant.

Unit Review Awctivity

Read the article 'The kindergarten that will change the world' (Resource Item 9.3) from *The Economist* of 4 March 1995. (This article is a part update on activities at Toyota which were described in the book *The Machine that Changed the World*.) List the methods that Toyota is employing to remain competitive in the face of the rising value of the yen.

Unit Summary

In this unit we have examined a variety of related approaches to operations which have come into prominence over the past 10 to 15 years. A central, unifying theme has been time reduction, but this has been combined with improved levels of quality, greater variety, improved service, and a reduction in wastes of all forms including inventory. Traditionally these factors were seen as alternatives or trade-offs, but the realisation now is that several of these factors can be achieved simultaneously. This quest for achieving low cost, high quality, greater variety, and improved service all at the same time is likely to challenge operations managers for years to come. In so doing, an increased level of participation by the whole workforce, as opposed to managers and specialists, will be necessary.

Modern time-based operations can be traced back to Henry Ford, but it was Toyota's Taiichi Ohno who brought about the JIT system which combined time reduction with variety. The JIT movement has spurned several offspring including (arguably) total quality, mass customisation, supplier partnership, and business process reengineering. These approaches are now beginning to be seen in the service sector where much of the battleground of business in the early part of the 21st century will, no doubt, lie.

References

Archier, G and Serieyx, H (1987) *The Type 3 Company*, Gower, London

Berggeren, C (1993) *The Volvo Experience*, Macmillan, London

Collins, P (1992) 'Admin JIT – method study comes of age', *Management Services*, December, vol. 36, no. 12

Davenport, T H (1993) *Process Innovation*, Harvard Business School Press, Boston, Massachusetts

Davenport, T H and Short, J E (1990) 'The new industrial engineering: information technology and business process redesign', *Sloan Management Review*, Summer, pp. 11–27

The Economist (1992) 'I want it now', 13 June, p. 90

The Economist (1995) 'The kindergarten that will change the world', March 4, pp. 81–82

Hall, R (1994) 'The Implementation of Zero Inventory/Just-in-Time' *Financial Times,* APICS, Falls Church, Virginia

Hall, R (1987) *Attaining Manufacturing Excellence*, Dow Jones Irwin – APICS, Falls Church, Virginia

Hammer, M (1990) 'Reengineering work: don't automate, obliterate', *Harvard Business Review*, July/August, pp. 104–112

Hammer, M (1994) 'Hammer defends reengineering', *The Economist*, 5 November 1994, p. 96

Hammer, M and Champy, J (1993) *Reengineering the Corporation*, Nicholas Brealey Publishing, London

Hammond, J H and Kelly, M G (1990) *Quick Response in the Apparel Industry*, Harvard Business School Case 9-690-038

Harrington, H J (1991) *Business Process Improvement*, McGraw-Hill, New York

Hines, P (1994) *Creating World Class Suppliers*, FT Pitman, London

Joynson, S and Forrester, A (1995) *Sid's Heroes: Uplifting Business Performance and the Human Spirit*, BBC, London

Lamming, R (1993) *Beyond Partnership*, Prentice Hall, Englewood Cliffs, New Jersey

Miles, RT (1994) 'Supplying the demand chain', *37th International Conference Proceedings, San Diego, California, Oct 30-Nov 4*, APICS, Falls Church, Virginia

Ohno, T and Moto, S (1988) *Just in Time for Today and Tomorrow*, Productivity, Stamford, Connecticut

Pascale, R (1990) *Managing on the Edge*, Simon and Schuster, New York

Pine, BJ II (1993) *Mass Customization*, Harvard Business School Press, Boston, Massachusetts

Rummler, G and Brache, A (1990) *Improving Performance*, Jossey Bass, San Francisco

Schonberger, R (1982) *Japanese Manufacturing Techniques: Nine Hidden Lessons in Simplicity*, Free Press, New York

Schonberger, R and Knod, E (1995) *Synchroservice!*, Irwin, Homewood, Illinois

Shingo, S (1985) *A Revolution in Manufacturing: The SMED System*, Productivity, Stamford, Connecticut

Stalk, G and Hout, T (1990) *Competing Against Time*, The Free Press, New York

Stalk, G and Webber, A (1993) 'Japan's dark side of time', *Harvard Business Review*, July/August, pp. 93–102

Tully, S (1995) 'Purchasing's new muscle', *Fortune*, 20 February, pp. 45–51

Wickens, P D (1987) *The Road to Nissan*, Macmillan, London

Womack, J P, Jones, D T and Roos, D (1990) *The Machine that Changed the World*, Rawson Associates, New York

Recommended Reading

Bicheno, J (1991) *Implementing JIT*, IFS

'Custom-made. Direct from the plant' (1994), *Business Week,* 19 December

Harrison, A (1992) *Just-in-Time in Perspective*, Prentice Hall, Hemel Hempstead

Schonberger, R (1994) 'Human resource management lessons from a decade of total quality management and reengineering', *California Management Review*, Summer, pp. 109–123

Answer to Unit Review Activity

This short article brings together much of the material discussed in this unit. You should have noted the following: supplier co-operation, kaizen or continuous improvement, the role of design, the role of value engineering, the role of factory layout and ergonomics, and the emphasis on a cross-functional approach involving design, engineering, purchasing and manufacturing. Significantly, however, you will have noted that the factory producing the new RAV4 has a lower level of automation than found at many factories, but despite this the new plant is perhaps the most efficient vehicle plant ever built.

RESOURCES

▷ RESOURCE 1.1

Dr CA Horn,
*Management
Services*, January
1991, vol. 35 no 1,
ed. David Charlton,
Institute of
Management
Services, pp. 28–33.

Roots: the early pioneers

In the century that has passed since the first efforts of what we now know as the scientific management movement began, a great deal has been written about it. Some of it is adulatory, some hyper-critical and much of it merely obscure. 'Among the makers of the modern world Taylor is rarely mentioned and yet he has made as much impact as Marx or Freud.' Great praise and from the lips of one of the most persuasive of modern management publicists, Peter Drucker. Perhaps a new appraisal and an attempt to place the movement in context is justified. The following is abstracted from the book 'Essays in the Development of Modern Management' by Dr C A Horn, published by the IMS in conjunction with Beacon Publications.

The problem is no easy one, and each will interpret the material differently. The more it is studied the more one is likely to be confused by the contradictions. Taylor enjoyed a two-volume biography by Copley, but it was in the main written after his death by one not particularly close to him and the work is rambling and uncritical. His associates suffer from similar treatment at a reduced length, although for the Gilbreth's *Cheaper by the Dozen* does much to improve an image that would be less attractive if one solely relied on the more formal biography. A spate of books and articles on certain aspects of the scientific management story, often enough highly critical, contain much information and testify to the impact the movement made by its very existence. The first balanced appraisal is perhaps that of H B Drury, *Scientific Management: a history and criticism*, which dates from 1915 and contains a good account of how the name was coined, and its instant attraction.[2]

It arose from an attempt to prevent the eastern railroads from achieving the consent of the Interstate Commerce Commission in 1910/11 to a rate rise to compensate for the rise in wages they had just granted. The lawyer Louis D Brandeis led the attack on the railroads arguing that the methods of

scientific management could save them a million dollars a day. The impressive name and the factual arguments had been put together less than a month before in the apartment of one of the principal advocates of scientific management, H L Gantt. F B Gilbreth, H V Sheel and R T Kent had also taken part along with Gantt and Brandeis. They had rejected such suggestions as the Taylor system, functional management, shop management and efficiency. Taylor had himself used the term scientific management as early as 1903 without giving it any particular significance. However, on this occasion, due to the nature of the circumstances and Brandeis' eloquence, it caught on. Magazines gave it great coverage, colleges and universities throughout America began to devote attention to it; a congressional committee was convened to consider its place in government institutions; city authorities began to debate its adoption and a Society for the Promotion of the Science of Management was set up.[3] The movement had taken off.

Just what sort of a society had all this taken place in? Who were the people involved and precisely what did they achieve? Although there were corresponding movements elsewhere in the world they were more limited than the American effort. American society in this period was intensely optimistic, individualistic and self-confident. It was engaged in opening up a continent and exploiting the business opportunities that arose from that situation. It is necessary to understand this to appreciate the attitudes that pervaded the scientific management group. If you did not like your employer the proper thing to do was not to combine and oppose him but to leave and go elsewhere. 'Go west young man, go west' was the advice of one of the shrewdest observers of the American scene. This philosophy, modified to some degree by time and experience, explains much of Taylor's attitude towards unions and individual employees.

The expansion of the railroads, the change from wrought iron to steel, the tariff barriers against foreign produce, required a greatly expanded engineering industry. The skilled labour for it was in limited supply and in the view of many, tainted by trade unionism. Immigrants there were in plenty, often willing to work hard and long hours, but lacking in skill. The need for standardisation, the breakdown of complex tasks into simple ones was obvious. Scientific management came at just the appropriate time. The wonder is that it took so long to achieve recognition. That may be due to the character of the promoters who often did not possess as many of the persuasive arts as they might have. This is particularly true of Taylor.

Frederick Winslow Taylor (1856–1915)

Undoubtedly the most important of the group, Taylor was also the most controversial. He often hinted, and his disciples said that he had risen from near poverty and a labouring job to the position of chief engineer of a large company in six years, and this entirely through his own efforts. In fact, he was born into a prosperous middle class lawyer's family in Philadelphia, and was destined to follow his father in his profession. At school he early displayed that mixture of stubbornness, ability and application that was to be such a marked feature of his later life and incidentally as a side line was to make him a national tennis champion. It may also have been partly responsible for his early death at the age of 59.

After an education partly in Europe, he developed an unspecified eye complaint that made it necessary for him to abandon study for the law. However, it did not apparently hamper him in any way in the pursuit of his chosen career of engineering, since he immediately entered into an apprenticeship as patternmaker and machinist. As this was at least as much a strain on the sight, a good deal of speculation has since taken place as to whether the illness was merely a device to justify his actions in taking up what was a comparatively low-status occupation.[4]

Nevertheless, Taylor, on the completion of his apprenticeship went to work for the Midvale Steel Company in 1878. No doubt Taylor's energy and ability did much to ensure his rise but in fact he was a close friend and ultimately the son-in-law of one of the major proprietors. His biography makes it clear that the intention was that they should ultimately control the firm. In these circumstances his varied experience and rapid progress is more easily understandable.[5] Similarly, he appears to have obtained his master's degree from the Stevens Institute by evening study on a course that he himself partly influenced.

Leaving Midvale Steel in 1890, when the possibility of ultimate control no longer existed, Taylor worked for three years as general manager of the Manufacturing Investment Company, a firm of paper fibremakers, and five years as a consulting engineer. For most of this period he was equally engaged in the efforts to raise the status of the engineer in America through the American Society of Mechanical Engineers. It was these combined experiences that led to his first important publication in a paper to that body in 1895: 'A Piece Rate System'. Taylor's differential system which offered two, sometimes three, rates for a particular job according to the speed at which it was performed was really carrying to its logical conclusion what many of his contemporaries such as Towne and Halsey in the USA and Denny and Rowan in the UK, were attempting to do, namely to manipulate the payments system in such a way as to induce the operative to work harder and indeed to break his control of the pace of work.

Ultimately Taylor joined Bethlehem Steel Company, then one of the largest companies in the United States, in 1898. In the next controversial three years he put into practice many of the ideas of production management that he had thought out before. In addition with Maunsel White, he developed the applications of high speed steel that so much reduced the time taken to cut metal and therefore made his management methods so important. The results are set out in two papers to the ASME – *Shop Management* (1903), published in book form in 1910, and *The*

Art of Cutting Metals (1906). The former, which includes for the first time the term 'Scientific Management', remains the work on which Taylor's reputation ultimately depends, but the latter was of much more interest to his contemporaries. Like other features of Taylor's work it is obscured by conflicting statements. Taylor and White certainly did not discover Chromium Tungsten steel. They in fact used commercial tool steel. What they did was to show how the new alloy steels could be used to cut metal at rates several hundred per cent faster than had been possible before; they had opened a way to a revolution in machine shop practice. Incidentally, and this is probably Taylor's contribution rather than White's, they had upset one of the most hallowed precepts of the machinist's craft: the belief that the proper cutting speed was the one that maximised the life of the cutting edge of the tool. Not so, said Taylor: tools can and should be reground systematically; what they should maximise is the amount of metal removed during the unit of time, and cutting speeds should be set accordingly. That speed was in fact when the tools were at the highest speed possible without melting.[6] Taylor's biographer says that he made nothing from high speed steel, but in fact from the patents that arose from its applications he made a great deal – $100,000 for the English rights alone. It was during his stay at Bethlehem that Taylor organised what is perhaps his best known feat, the loading of pig iron. It cannot have been of great importance to him or the company, but beyond displaying his relentless attachment to details it has perhaps provoked more than any other incident in his life, attempts to point out the inconsistencies in much of what he said and wrote and which for many throw doubt on his claims to be truly 'scientific'.[7]

Taylor left Bethlehem in 1901, in controversial circumstances, and thereafter devoted himself to consultation and lecturing in the interests of scientific management. He visited the UK to address a joint meeting of the ASME and the Institute of Mechanical Engineering in 1910. As frequently happened his audience was more interested in high speed steel rather than his views on management. It was in that year also that his methods were used in evidence before a congressional committee to oppose the rise in railway rates, by suggesting that 'scientific management' would make them unnecessary.

Such fame as Taylor had achieved was partially dissipated in 1911 over the Watertown Arsenal affair, in which efforts to introduce his system into a government organisation led to a strike, union opposition and ultimately to a congressional investigation. The result was much bad publicity, increasing antagonism with trade unions, and the banning of stopwatches and premium bonuses from government institutions. Taylor however continued to work and to receive the support of a growing band of friends and disciples until his death in 1915. In later life, much of his reputation depended on the adoption of his system by such firms at the Tabor Manufacturing Co, a Philadelphian plant making machinery and employing about 100 men and The Link Belt Company with 750 employees, both run by personal friends of Taylor. He continued working until his death.

Carl George Lange Barth (1860 – 1939)

Barth has been described as the earliest, ablest and closest associate of Taylor.[8] But also as a 'first generation immigrant with a fine contempt for American technical education and practice, given to immodest assertions of his own competence and ill-concealed contempt for the knowledge and abilities of his employers. He was dogmatic, self assertive and obstinate, but a faithful disciple of Taylor!'[9] Both these statements have sufficient truth to explain much of Barth's own career and the nature of the trouble he provoked on Taylor's behalf.

After serving an apprenticeship in a navy yard in his native Norway, Barth emigrated to the USA in 1881. He then worked for William Sellars, rising to be chief draughtsman in 1895. Sellars was for some of this time part owner of the Midvale Company and here Taylor made Barth's acquaintance. Barth was a particularly competent mathematician and as such joined Taylor in 1899 at Bethlehem. His principal contribution to the Taylor system was the construction of a slide rule to calculate the speed and feed of machine tools. He was to publish numerous articles on these topics in the next 20 years.

He left Bethlehem soon after Taylor's dismissal and worked successfully as a consulting engineer with Tabor and Link Belt, the two showpieces of the Taylor system. He was personally chosen by Taylor to install the system into Watertown Arsenal in 1911 and his personal characteristics bear some responsibility for the disastrous furore which resulted. Copley says: 'Some of the biggest businessmen this country has produced had the lesson taught to them, that Carl Barth courts no one.' This may have been true, but it was a dangerous attitude to adopt in the face of a strongly entrenched craft union and a suspicious congress. This, combined with his outspoken ridicule of conventional religion, even more than what appeared to be his anti-union views, angered the devout labour members of the Commission on Industrial Relations, investigating scientific management.[10]

Subsequent to Taylor's death Barth taught for some years on scientific management at the University of Chicago. As the most intense and most orthodox of Taylor's followers, he played a leading part in the organisation of the Taylor Society, although his own dominant concern with machine-shop management somewhat limited the spread of scientific management to other fields. He was responsible for much of the antagonism that grew up between Taylor's followers.

Henry Lawrence Gantt (1861–1919)

H L Gantt is perhaps the member of the Taylorite group who is least remembered. His charts of course are used, but little of his philosophy is understood or respected. Yet he was in many ways the most perceptive of the group, particularly with regard to the impact that his work had on the operative.

Born into a southern family that lost its affluence in the Civil War, Gantt was forced to make his own way in the world. He was educated at the McDonough School, a practical establishment run on military lines, and between studying for his degrees, joined its faculty. It was probably here that he absorbed the notions of community service that were so prominent in his later life.[11]

From 1887–93 he worked at Midvale Steel Co partly under Taylor but ultimately as superintendent of the casting department. He subsequently worked at Bethlehem and from 1902 onward as an independent consultant. Like Emerson, he was far less dogmatic that Taylor and much more willing to introduce his improvements piecemeal and as far as the client cared to go. This was anathema to Taylor and led to coolness between them. It also led Taylor to intervene to prevent Gantt undertaking the work at Watertown Arsenal, although he had already carried out the preliminary surveys and would have been much more sensitive to the needs of this particular situation.[12]

Gantt had already diverged from Taylor in the production of a task and bonus system which was not as punitive as differential piecework and increasingly he began to devote his time to service to the community. Although scientific management tended to increase the control of the worker, Gantt was critical of the growth in autocracy that was involved. He was also doubtful about the effects on the autocrat. 'We are clinging to an autocratic system under the mistaken notion that it at least was good for the autocrat. The fact is that it is not. Democracy is better for all of us.'[13]

Ultimately Gantt declined to work for any firm that did not subscribe to these objectives and apart from his work for the emergency shipbuilding programmes, retired to his farm. He died suddenly in 1919.

Frank Bunker Gilbreth

The Gilbreths, for F B Gilbreth was much assisted by his wife, Lillian, were not part of the small group most closely connected with Taylor, yet they were influenced by him, as they generously acknowledge. After a good education, F B Gilbreth declined to enter Massachusetts Institute of Technology, but preferred an apprenticeship in a building firm. Between 1885-95 he rose to be chief superintendent of the company. He was responsible for several technical innovations concerned with the design of scaffolding and in concrete constructions. Unlike the group which surrounded Taylor so closely, Gilbreth acquired his experience in an industry that was highly unionised and was much more concerned to accommodate his methods to this situation than were the others.

From 1895 onward Gilbreth ran his own contracting business in Boston and was able to take advantage of the many devices he had developed to speed up work. These included special adjustable scaffolding, the use of pallets for bricks and the introduction of much more standardisation than was common in the quality of both bricks and mortar. By so doing he was able to raise individual output from 1,000 to 2,700 bricks per day. An easy system of counting the bricks was introduced, combined with the inevitable bonus system. This led him on to the search for the one best way with which he will always be associated.

Gilbreth gradually changed over to the role of management consultant. He met Taylor and came to believe that he was the greatest man he knew and that the advent of scientific management was the most important thing that had happened in his lifetime.[14] Ultimately estrangement developed between the two as Gilbreth came to devote more and more time to his ideas on micromotion and Taylor began to display once again that morbid suspicion that was such a prominent part of his relationship with any independent colleague or subordinate.

On the Gilbreths' part, they came to feel that the innovations that they developed in micromotion study were undervalued. Taylor and Barth's stopwatch methods seemed to be almost 'rule of thumb' beside them. In their view, it was impossible to maintain the notion of 'scientific' study and still adopt what appeared to them to be crude methods of measurement. A break came in 1913 when Taylor suggested Hathaway to replace Gilbreth in the middle of a contract. The Gilbreths were reticent

about their views[15] and ultimately they came to see Taylorism as something corrupted by the Rigidity of the disciples. 'True Taylor philosophy has suffered in the hands of Mr Barth and many other loyal friends of Mr Taylor.'[16]

Increasingly, however, he came to devote his interests to 'the one best way'. He was particularly successful in assisting with the rehabilitation of maimed soldiers in the war and continued his interests in scientific management until his death in 1924.

Harrington Emerson 1853–1931

Emerson, like the Gilbreths, was always a stage removed from Taylor. Like Gantt too, he followed the path of moderation in that he was willing to introduce the methods of scientific management piecemeal in accordance with the limitations of the situation. This, on some occasions, could be determined by the employer's pocket, the breadth of his ideas or the opposition of organised labour.

Emerson was the son of a university professor born at Trenton, New Jersey. Much of his education was obtained in Europe, and indeed he followed a university career until 1882. His career then turned to banking and consultancy, followed by work for the Burlington Railroad and in glass manufacturing. His most notable contribution was the reorganisation of the engineering shops of Atchison, Topeka and Santa Fe Railroad between 1904–7. This included the introduction of the inevitable bonus plan, standard costs, planned maintenance and machine accounting. Emerson's methods tended to be flexible, even pragmatic, and although he acknowledged his debt to 'Shop Management' he always maintained his independence from them claiming to have used stopwatches, camera studies and slide rules many years before either Taylor or his associates.[17]

His most important contribution however was to be his appearance in the Eastern Rates Case (1911) in opposition to the rise of rail Charges. Based on his experiences on the Santa Fe he was able to claim convincingly that the railroads could save a million dollars a day by the adoption of the principle of scientific management. This is perhaps the action that launched scientific management to a general rather than a specified audience and as such Emerson made a considerable contribution to its future.

Emerson's later career contained the same mixture of pragmatism as before. He adapted the work of Gilbreth; when functional management upset the traditionalists, he justified the old system but supplemented it by advisers. Some of this adaptability verged on black magic. He used phrenology for the scientific selection of workmen and boasted that it prevented labour agitators from being selected.[18]

Ultimately his strong moral tone overlaid much of the system. The word 'efficiency' came in his usage to have a highly moral connotation.

He retired in 1923 but lived for another eight years, much given to moralising and endeavouring to justify certain aspects of an ethical nature, which was sorely needed at a time when scientific management was under heavy attack from the unions and other institutions concerned with the welfare and development of the individual.

The Other Americans
Of course there were many more than the small group linked with Taylor who were concerned to promote a more scientific approach to management a century ago. Of these perhaps, H R Towne (1844–1924) deserves a mention for the development of his payments system. Oberlin Smith (1840–1926) for his scheme for parts classification. A Hamilton Church (1866–1936), a British immigrant, for his work on costing methods, and F A Halsey (1856–1935) inevitably for yet another bonus scheme. Sandford E Thompson (1867–1949) might be considered for his work on Time Study for Taylor.[19] One could continue for a very long time listing the many who played some small part in improving managerial methods at this time in America. Essentially their viewpoints were the same as Taylor's, a concentration on individual initiative and reward, in an organisation that was tightly controlled and

in which a 'scientific' (a belief that measurement is a central feature in any activity) approach was adopted.

The United Kingdom
By the time that Taylor was operating, Great Britain was being widely challenged for her position as the workshop of the world. Yet as the first industrial nation she had been responsible for many innovations from stopwatches onward. John Marshall's Leeds factory contained much of the tight control associated with the Taylor system more than 70 years before him. Charles Babbage (1792–1871), a mathematician, was concerned with time study and aware of some of its unreliable features. By the end of the century however the UK was slipping steadily behind its rivals. There were, however, exceptions. Much work had been done on cost accounting by Garcke and Fells. Their book *Factory Accounts* (1887), was to pass through seven editions by 1922 and to remain the most important British contribution to improved management in that period. The notion of a machine-hour rate, discounted cashflow (but not by that name) and other innovations all appear in its successive editions. Yet the work was initially much criticised by the established accountancy bodies. Salter Lewis and F G Burton both produced valuable works on the commercial organisation of the factory at the turn of the century. Useful as they were, they lacked both the influence and the platform that the American scientific managers were to achieve.

On the production side Hans Renold of Renold Chain was perhaps the first firm to introduce scientific management into the UK in the years after 1910. Renold, Swiss by birth, had earlier worked with Hamilton Church but discarded much of his work as cumbersome and developed his own system by experience adapted by an intelligent appraisal of the value of the work of others. Again many more could be mentioned but what was lacking was the widespread acceptance of new methods with energy and enthusiasm.[20]

The Europeans
Although Walter Rathenau (1867–1922)

and others made substantial contributions to the development of scientific management, it is perhaps Henry Fayol (1841–1925) who stands as the obvious choice for his contribution to scientific management. Looking at the organisation from the top towards the bottom his view is from a different angle than that of the American pioneers. Yet posterity has given him the quiet compliment of according his organisational structure the title of 'the classical theory'. It is in fact the organisation of the army of the great Napoleon modified here and there, but still recognisable. It is due to Fayol that we grant it the universal accolade, which no subsequent demonstration of superior German military organisation has ever shaken. From the basis of this type of organisational viewpoint it is understandable that Fayol saw Taylor's functional foremanship as 'unsound and dangerous'. In this case it is Fayol's ideas that largely prevailed.[21] Trite as they may seem, Fayol's description of what a manger does – forecasting, planning, organising, co-ordinating and controlling - are still as good a breakdown as any subsequent explanation.

What were their achievements?

The American pioneers in particular had certain things in common. Most tended to come from families that had seen better days, but were still not too poor to give their children a reasonable education. Thus frugality and incentive went side by side, and where they were not present they could be invented. It has also been suggested that they had strong, high-minded mothers and weak fathers, but whether this has any significance is beyond the scope of this essay. Further they were primarily concerned with production or operating and each had some form of bonus system as a principal part of his repertoire. The latter point cannot be overestimated, the engineering industry in Europe and America was changing from the one-off craftsman's world to the standardised system of today. Bonus systems were therefore appropriate to it. In England, much less affected by scientific management than America, the

proportion of machinists on piecework rose from 11 per cent in 1886 to 50 per cent in 1914.[22] The changeover was much more dramatic elsewhere.

But what of Taylor, in particular, since without him the movement would indeed appear as Hamlet without the Prince of Denmark! Taylor's innovations were the differential piecework system, shop management including the ideas of functional foremanship and standard costing and finally the art of cutting metals.

Taylor's long term reputation really depends on his contribution to management methods, ie his second period. Not so, however, for his contemporaries. Drury makes it perfectly clear that the differential piecework system was what really interested them.[23] It certainly bears the hallmark of Taylor's personality, since it carries the whole contemporary thinking on incentives to an extreme but logical conclusion. The punishment for the tardy and incompetent combined with substantial rewards to the successful. Today it appears highly objectionable, but was welcomed by many of Taylor's contemporaries who were considered philanthropists as well as hard businessmen, for example, the Cadbury family in the United Kingdom.[24]

Similarly at a later date, and particularly during his English visit, it was the art of cutting metals that retained the interest of his contemporaries. References to his work on management aroused much less interest, even disappointment.[25]

Yet it is this that provides the lasting monument to the group. The thoughtful planning, the revised accountancy, the notion of functionalism, all find a place in every organisation that has the slightest claim to effectiveness. Few managers, however pragmatic, would admit to being influenced by the notions of scientific methods. A large part of this is the work of Taylor and his disciples. It is true that they were acting in the spirit of their age, the first which 'bestowed on science all the awe that it had taken from God', but its adoption and popularisation was a formidable task. By 1915 only about 1.3 per cent of American wage earners worked under scientific management, although a larger proportion were affected by some part of it. What was originally developed to assist production has now been adapted for much wider ends. Drucker argues that the need today is to do for the knowledge worker what Taylor did for manual work and the manual worker. Whether this is true or not, the influence of these notions is all but universal, only the extent of Taylor's contribution is in question. Yet in any informed discussion of this topic it would be surprising if Taylor was not the first name to be mentioned, or nearly so.

But there is the other side of the coin which is scarcely less influential. Taylor's relationships with individual workmen and, more particularly, trade unions, have left a legacy of hostility and suspicion that is deep rooted. Numerous quotations from Taylor stress his concern for the workman as an individual; his criticism of the lack of ability and co-operation of managers to ease the worker's burdens.[26] But with the best of intentions Taylor's attempts to deal with the workers as individuals were and are contrary to trade union principles, notably that of the collective bargain. Drury makes it perfectly clear that where Taylor's system entered, trade unionists left and unionism decayed. After an extensive survey at the end of Taylor's life he could only say 'In one case at least the collective bargain has been utilised!'. Small wonder if unions were hostile to such a situation and since in the long run the worker has preferred the collective bargain, they have been able and willing to impose restrictions on many of the methods considered.

If the two sides then had good reason to be suspicious of each other, was the competition between them entirely fair? Taylor's friends have always stressed his straightforward, honest nature, suggesting that he was incapable of duplicity. Careful investigation has revealed that he was not above advising on how to destroy unionism by, for example, setting up dummy competitive non-union shops.[27] Gilbreth alone seems to have sought union co-operation, and not very effectively. This legacy of union hostility has persisted to some degree alongside the major contribution and given the movement its two-edged reputation and made dispassionate surveys more difficult. Yet both aspects are unquestioningly part of Taylor.

The Inter-War Period

The First World War unloosed a cataclysm that few had foreseen and none had made plans to deal with. Established governments collapsed and were replaced by revolutionary or radical ones. Many of the major armies had, at some stage, mutinied in the face of impossible demands and frightful casualties. The problem of maintaining loyalties whilst requiring sacrifices was a major one. The more so since the authorities making such demands appeared incompetent and, in many cases, corrupt. At home the need for production created new organisations, staffed of necessity by those who had little previous experience of factory work, and hence little attachment to existing practices. The demands of the situation overrode established authority and enabled problems to be solved without too much reference to old precedents.

Scientific management was not the last to be affected by all this. Previously it had been largely the concern of American engineers engaged in production. True, Taylor and Gilbreth had visited the United Kingdom and Gilbreth had been to Germany before the war. They were, however, little known or regarded outside their own country. The war changed that. Scientific management, often linked with Fordism, made good catchphrases for politicians struggling to improve the condition of workers and reduce the antagonism between classes. Politicians as diverse as Gramschi, the communist and Mussolini, the fascist both saw the possibilities in Italy. In Russia, where classes had been officially abolished, Lenin was only too willing to adopt Taylorism for the benefit of the proletariat. The famous sentence of Taylor to the Congressional Commission of Enquiry regularly appeared in the literature of the time. 'Now in it essence scientific management involves a complete mental revolution on the part of the working man ... and it involves an equally complete mental revolution on the part of the management side ... The great revolution that takes place in the mental attitude of both parties under scientific management is that both sides take their eyes off the division of the surplus as an all important matter and together turn their attention towards increasing the size of the surplus.'

References

1   Drucker, P (1976) 'The Coming Rediscovery of Scientific Management', *The Conference Board Records*, June, p26
2   Drury (1918) *Scientific Management: a history and criticism*, 2nd edn, pp15–24
3   (1953) 'The Society for the Promotion of the Science of Management', *Exploration in Entrepreneurial History*, May, vol. V, p244
4   Haber, *Efficiency and Uplift*, chapter 1
5   Copley, *Frederick W Taylor*, vol. 1, p117
6   Aitken, *Taylorism at Watertown Arsenal*, p30
7   *Taylor's Pig Tale*
8   Urwick, *The Golden Book of Management*, p81
9   Aitken, op cit, p82
10 Haber, op cit, p35
11 Rathe, *Gantt on Management*, pp239–281
12 Aitken, op cit, pp79–84
13 Rathe, op cit, p18
14 Haber, op cit, p38
15 (1957) *Competition in Scientific Management, Business History Review XXXI*, Spring, pp23–33
16 Haber, op cit, p42
17 Drury, op cit, p128
18 Haber, op cit, pp56–57
19 Urwick, L (1956) *The Golden Book of Management*
20 Renold, C, *Joint Consultation over Thirty Years*, p14
21 Fayol (1949) *General & Industrial Management*, UK edn, p68
22 Jefferys, *The Story of the Engineers*, p129
23 Drury, op cit, p67
24 Cadbury, E (1914) 'The Case For and Against Scientific Management, *Sociological Review*, April, pp99–125
25 Urwick & Rech, *The Making of Scientific Management - Volume 1*, p34
26 Drucker, op cit.
27 Nadworny, *Scientific Management & the Unions*, pp21–22

▷ RESOURCE 2.1
D Jan Eppink,
Journal of Strategic Change, June 1995, Vol. 4, 155–160

Strategic Innovation

Professor Eppink's article deals with the need for strategic innovation as a counter to slack economic conditions. It discusses:
● the various types of strategic innovation
● how much innovation is desirable
● the important issue of how much is possible.

1.   Preface

For many companies the economic climate will not be improving. In some sectors of the economy growth is decreasing or even absent. It is noticeable that competition from Eastern European countries has increased; not only in bulk goods, but also in the supply of parts and components. This puts the profit margin of many companies under pressure. It is also noticeable that many countries in the West are relocating their production divisions to these countries: this relieves the pressure on the profit margin but lowers the rate of employment in these areas. The economic growth in Asian countries does not improve this picture.

Against this background a cry for improvement can be heard, preferably a strategic improvement. In answer to this cry many authors have come up with very useful suggestions; others seem to restrict themselves to 'voodoo'. Most important is that a company realises that drastic changes are vital.

In this article an explanation will be given of the types of strategic innovation. Subsequently, the question will be answered of how much innovation is possible and how much is desirable. The drive behind the innovation and the role of language in this will be discussed.

2. Types of strategic innovation

Mintzberg once pondered:If planning is everything, maybe it is nothing.

The same question can be asked about the use of the words strategy and strategic. These words are used so often that the ability to distinguish them is threatened with extinction. Strategy is the way in which a company or organisation shapes its relation to its environment. The strategy has three dimensions.

In the first place the way in which the company/organisation wishes to position itself in relation to clients and suppliers. This can be done by identifying oneself as supplier of a distinguishing, unique product or as the supplier of a standard 'product', competing in price.

In the second place there is a choice of scope that management strives after. With scope one can think of spreading products/services, in a geographical sense and to an extent of vertical integration. These two dimensions, position and scope, together are referred to as market strategy.

Once this has been set the next question to ask is how to execute this: alone, through acquisition, merger, joint venture, or strategic alliance. This is a third dimension.

From the above description it can be concluded that the following innovations are not of a strategic nature: organisation structure, management development policy, production process, etc. Changes in these areas are indeed necessary to enable strategic innovation, very important as such, but not strategic.

Within these three dimensions it is clear that companies are being innovative, often with different approaches within the same branch.

Positioning

In the past several European car manufactures successfully pursued a strategy of unique products, eg. think of companies in Sweden and Germany. As a result of competition from Japan in these market segments turnover came under pressure. Having to admit that from the

point of view of the client the product became less unique in the course of time was a difficult task for management to face. One of the answers to this is sought in the lowering of the costs. Through liberalising in the airline business it also is becoming more and more necessary to lower prices. With this in mind several airline companies have been forced to lower their prices as well as eliminating first class.

Whether it is legitimate to state from the above that the 'unique' strategy does not have a future is difficult to say as yet. The present gloomy economic situation has a lot to do with it, but this may change in the future. A different matter is whether a product can be made even more unique than before: once every supplier can offer 'zero defect' or, for example, steel doors in the doors of cars it is simply not possible to obtain greater technical uniqueness on this point. In the dimension of positioning there is a clear challenge as far as strategic innovation goes.

Scope

For some time diversification has been an important dimension of a strategy. Just think of Ansoff's product/market matrix. In the course of time opinions on diversification have been very diverse, in both practice and theory. In the sixties many companies diversified, partly because they believed there was a larger market for new products than would be possible with existing products. Success was believed to be attainable only in new markets. What to do in case of a decline in growth was a problem to be dealt with at some time in the future.

Later portfolio management was applied to straighten out the explosive growth of portfolio activities. After that companies reversed to their core business. How to decide on a company's core business is a problem as yet unsolved. Within Philips the division Lighting was at first considered a core activity, but after some time it was not, whereas now it is again core business.

In the last few years one may discern a reference to a 'resource based' vision on the company concerning product diversification. In this context Hamel and Prahalad speak of 'core competencies'. The idea behind this notion is that by combining the unique competencies of a company it is possible to create new products (compare Schumpeter) or to expand its activities. These competencies are not easy to imitate by competitors and therefore give a company a sustainable advantage. The management's view of the future of a company has a great influence on the 'strategic architecture', and the number and type of steps needed to be able to survive in the future. In this context some examples are given of companies where this way of thinking has led to success. They do not give practical hints on how to develop this kind of architecture.

Strategic innovation in the area of product diversification could lie in the field of expansion or decrease of product groups.

As far as geographical spread goes there is a certain amount of strategic innovation. Many Western companies are at this moment operating on the Asian market, due to the prediction made that in the coming decades unlimited possibilities for growth will occur. This reason for internalisation may or may not go together with the reason behind globalisation, whereby a company synchronises its activities in several countries in order to gain an advantage over competitors. Consequently through globalisation a cost advantage can be realised in the development and bringing onto the market of a product. Thus it is cheaper to market one brand worldwide rather than five regional brands. Not every product is suitable for a highly uniform market approach. A product such as beer which is available all over Europe must be advertised in a different way in each country. Whereas an Irishman drinks his beer in a pub in the evening, a Belgian has a pint in the course of the day and a Greek would mostly drink his beer with lunch in a restaurant. The limitations of globalisation can be made clear with many more examples. The advantages in lower costs may be offset against possible loss of flexibility. In this way English researchers discovered that local manufacturers of dishwashers, etc., in France and England were generating far more profit that the large internationally operating competitors.

In some other cases a company may be compelled to restrict geographical operating scope. For example after the Alcazar operation was called off SAS decided they would no longer fly to certain American destinations and would restrict their flights to other destinations. A number of European air routes were also disposed of.

Vertical integration

In the field of **vertical integration** there are many diverse movements. At present a trend can be discerned to dispose of non-core activities, so called 'outsourcing'. A possible danger could lie in disposing of too many activities, in some cases leading to the company being a mere intermediary. The indisputable cost advantages arising from contracting out activities must be weighed against a weaker negotiating position in the long term. Take for example the American television industry. In the course of time an industry that was 100% in American hands is now almost 100% in the hands of foreign companies.

On the other hand a company such as IBM is trying to add value to its activities by extending more service, offering more software and additionally by transferring in-company knowledge to third parties through seminars.

Considerable strategic innovation can be observed which is not always successful, moreover, in the area of diversification. It is of the utmost importance to bear in mind long-term perspectives.

Execution mode

Strategic innovation can be detected by the way in which companies enforce their market strategy. Several possibilities can be recognised. The first consideration must be whether the strategy can be enforced independently or whether acquisitions and mergers are necessary. In this way no problems concerning authority will emerge. These problems will be present with joint ventures, whereby a new legal entity is founded, and also with strategic alliances where the basis of co-operation consists of an agreement.

The influencing factor within these forms of execution are, amongst others, the speed needed to enforce the market strategy, the total amount of costs and the degree of risk that a management is prepared to accept. In some cases legislation in a country also plays an important part. Until recently it was not possible for a foreign company to have a 100% subsidiary in India; also a foreign airline company cannot have a controlling interest in a company in the USA.

Severing the existing strategic execution mode is an important decision and in itself strategic innovation. Within Unilever the main principle was that in the case of collaboration with another company Unilever would take a controlling interest. Recent initiatives show that Unilever no longer applies this fully: a minority share was taken in Mora snacks, and recently the joint venture with Pepsi Cola was announced to bring Lipton Ice Tea on the market. Within a year a worldwide distribution had been set up for this product, because of the worldwide name Lipton had built up in the market, combined with the worldwide bottling and distribution capacity of Pepsi Cola. A major problem concerning the latter two forms of co-operation can be that the aims of each partner may grow apart over the years. Consequently a certain form of instability is intrinsic to this form of co-operation. A sound use of alliances can stabilise the strategic position as can be seen from several Japanese companies.

A well thought out execution strategy can give a company the opportunity to execute more strategic innovations in the dimension of positioning and differentiation.

3. How much innovation is desirable?
From part of the literature on management an image emerges that there is no limit to the amount of innovations desirable. Other sources of literature show that an unrestricted drive for innovation does not always lead to good results.

From research by the profit impact of market strategies (PIMS) it appears that above a certain level innovations lead to a lower return on investment. The reason for this is that the initial costs cannot be recovered completely.

One of the lessons to be learned from the bestseller 'In Search of Excellence' (Peters and Waterman, 1982) is that a company must stick to the business it is best at; the unvoiced presumption being that there must be a future for the business it is good at. Hamel and Prahalad put forward that a number of Japanese companies owe their success partly to the fact that they have 'recycled' technologies and used them in other applications. New shoes are bought but the old ones are kept in case they can still be used for something else.

Withdrawing from certain sectors can cause the loss of new growth potential. In the USA General Electric's decision to withdraw from the market, now called 'consumer electronic market' meant in the long term that they completely missed out on the growth in that sector (a.o. high definition television and multi-media). Most likely the portfolio choice made then, would have been a different one if they had looked further into the future.

In conclusion it can be stated that when taking decisions on strategic innovations the balance between past and present must be studied very carefully.

4. How much innovation is possible?
A Dutch proverb says there is nothing more fickle than a human being.

As companies are a gathering of human beings that should also count for companies. Yet in practice it appears that this is not true. There are clearly boundaries as to the possibility of implementing innovations. The possibility for innovation depends on the view on strategy and the results of a company. Opposed to the traditional view on strategy as a fit between opportunities/threats and strong/weak points Hamel and Prahalad have the view on strategy as a 'stretch'. Successful companies did not always match the 'fit' criterion. Companies such as CNN, Honda and Sony had tremendous ambitions but very few resources (eg. money).

With these companies the strategy of 'stretch' works well. Companies such as IBM and General Motors with plenty of resources but with little ambition were a lot less successful. Additionally, many of the successful companies were able to profit from the resources of other companies by entering into strategic alliances instead of wanting to do everything alone.

Pressure caused by external conditions can facilitate the decisions for management to decide on major changes, even though these changes will not be easy to make. Dutch examples of this are Philips and KLM. In these situations a well chosen use of language can arouse and even intensify a sense of urgency.

5. Who is to initiate innovation?

From the deliberations on strategic innovation it is apparent that innovation can incorporate both new activities and dismantling of the old ones. The long-term danger of this form of organic growth can be that eventually the assortment of activities emerging has very little or insufficient coherence. In this way SHV, a Dutch company, developed from a coal company into a company which also includes shipping and technical illustrations. Each small step was easy to comprehend. The final palette of activities could be brought back 'top-down' to its original core business: trade. The decision to terminate existing activities cannot really be made by the separate operating companies.

Frequently top management is also seen to initiate the starting up of essentially new activities, drastic repositioning, and mergers and takeovers.

6. The importance of language

In the field of strategic management a lot of modernisation of vocabulary is taking place; this may cause confusion to the readers of works in this field. Take for example the differences between the older terms such as 'distinctive competence' and 'strengths' on the one hand and 'core competencies' on the other. The difference in concept is very often much smaller than the difference in language. From a scientific point of view this development is not very desirable. Nevertheless, the linguistic innovation very often has a stimulating effect on the point of view in companies, thereby creating one of the prerequisites for strategic innovation. Seen from a point of view of practicality this is an important contribution. Inside companies it is of great importance to use the language and language concept with great care. Describing clearly what is meant by each concept will prevent unnecessary discussions, misunderstandings and even mistakes. The language used should be attuned to the receiver. Notions such as ROI (Return on Investment), EPS (Earnings Per Share) and shareholder value are not necessarily very inspiring to people on the shopfloor and they are the ones who will have to execute the innovations. A well thought out and well formulated mission statement can be very elucidating for workers at the lower levels.

References

Ansoff, H I (1965) *Corporate Strategy*, McGraw Hill, New York.

Buzzell, R D & Gale, B T (1987) *The Pims Principles*, Free Press, New York.

Hamel, G & Prahalad, C K (1993) 'Strategy as Stretch and Leverage', *Harvard Business Review*, March-April.

Peters, T J & Waterman Jr, R H (1982) *In Search of Excellence*, Harper Row.

Prahalad, C K & Hamel, G (1990) 'The Core Competence of the Corporation', *Harvard Business Review*, May-June.

Autobiographical note

Professor Dr Jan Eppink holds an extraordinary professorship in strategy and environment at the Faculty of Economic Sciences and Econometrics, Vrije Universiteit, Amsterdam, Netherlands. He took his PhD in 1978 with his dissertation entitled 'Managing the unforeseen: a study of flexibility'. He is also the co-author of five books and a great number of published articles. Jan Eppink is an associate of Felix & Co Strategic Management Consultants in Amsterdam and Budapest. He is a director of the Japan Strategic Management Society.

Note: this article is being published simultaneously in the Journal of the Japan Strategic Management Society, thanks to the consideration of its editor Professor Gen-Ichi Nakamura.

Life cycle engineering

RESOURCE 2.2 ◁
Graham McCue,
*Management
Services*, February
1994, Institute of
Management
Services, 20–23

In the dim and distant past methods and techniques such as method study, critical examination, process charts, critical path analysis, and work measurement were basic tools of the trade for the management services practitioner. Whilst still used in some organisations, more 'modern' methods such as total quality management and quality management systems in management services, and structured methods, such as SSADM in computing seem to have gained prominence. These are used as replacements for the basic tools or even as panaceas for management problems.

Don't get me wrong, it's not that I'm against the modern methods. It's just that experience has taught me that many organisations adopt them without having a firm foundation. They are building on sand – what they need first is solid rock.

Enter life cycle Engineering (LCE) – some old favourites recycled to provide a more effective set of integrated methods and tools to enable organisations to make dramatic improvements. It's a case of an old dog doing old tricks in a new way!

Originally developed as an integrated solution to many of the problems that exist in IT departments, the problems LCE addresses are general to all organisations rather than specific to the IT department. Thus they can be applied to any type of organisation. As most of the methods will be familiar to the management services practitioner there is the great benefit that you can put them into practice very quickly, and probably use existing documentation to speed the process.

The way LCE evolved means that it is flexible and versatile enough to cope with modifications and additions. It provides basic methods and tools to which more sophisticated methods, tools and techniques can be added. Be careful though, simply getting together the best collection of methods, tools and techniques can create trouble with integration.

The original philosophy was to 'Keep It Simple, Stupid' (the way I refer to myself when I begin to get too clever), so LCE uses simple, readily available technology. This includes common business software packages such as a word processor, spreadsheet, database and project planning. As I am lazy at heart, I prefer to get machines to do as much work as possible, and to do a number of things at once in such a way as to enable me to do other things with the minimum of effort. This led to the use of project planning software to do much of the dreary number crunching, and the development of diagrams and documentation that can be extended or transformed for other purposes with the minimum of effort, as shown in figure 1 – transforming diagrams.

LCE objectives

The basic objective of the approach is to 'engineer' each of the lifecycles in an organisation, hence life cycle engineering, hyphenated to distinguish it from the general term used in IT.

The integrated nature of the methods and tools enable the organisation to:

1   ensure full information is available and accessible
2   identify and eliminate unnecessary work
3   identify and improve the use of all resources
4   improve planning and control
5   incorporate quality improvement methods at the appropriate levels
6   integrate other approaches such as TQM, SQC and BPR
7   minimise the duration, cost and resources required to satisfy the needs of your customers
8   raise productivity levels
9   reduce time and effort spent on documentation
10 reduce overheads in general
11 track progress more accurately
12 empower the whole workforce
    ... and there's more, too much to list in a short article.

Organisation objectives

LCE is targeted towards the objectives of

the organisation, for regardless of whether an organisation is profit-making, a charity, or a government department it exists to provide products or services to customers. Therefore the whole organisation must be geared to this prime objective. Anything that occurs within the organisation that does not contribute directly or indirectly to the objective should be eliminated, or at least put under very close scrutiny!

As well as this prime objective, there are legal and other obligations that an organisation must meet. There are taxes to pay, returns to make to government and perhaps shareholders to be kept informed.

Each has an objective met by a set of related processes. The set of processes which meets an objective is a life cycle, the minimum unit addressed by LCE. If you wish to 'pilot' LCE, do it with a whole life cycle!

life cycles and processes
life cycles and processes are not the same thing.

A **process** is a supplier/customer relationship within the organisation. That is, a supplier provides a customer with a product, service or information, the customer adds value (hopefully!), and becomes the supplier of the result to another customer.

A **life cycle** is a set of processes that meet a specific objective and is a customer/supplier/customer relationship that may be external or internal. It begins with a customer request, the supplier fulfils the request and the customer accepts the result, for example by payment. A life cycle includes all the work wholly and solely performed because of a request from a customer.

An **external life cycle** is the set of processes required to meet the needs of an external customer, anyone who can request or demand a product, service, information or money from an organisation. This includes requests for information about products and services, orders, complaints, support, and legitimate demands for information from other organisations. Some of these may be implicit, for example VAT returns should be made at regular intervals without the dreaded VAT Man reminding you.

Internal life cycles are all initiated from within the organisation, with some involving external participants, for example recruitment or purchases, otherwise the basic principles are the same as external life cycles.

Owners and devolved authority
The way organisations are structured can have a serious detrimental impact if the structure is allowed to interfere with

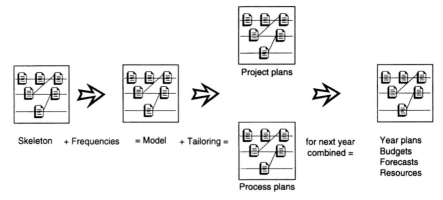

Figure 1: *By using project planning software it is quite easy to transform a Skeleton into a generic Model by applying task frequencies, then tailoring the Model to create a process or project Plan.*

Combining planned projects and processes, with generic models or other anticipated but so far unplanned work, a Year Plan which also gives data for budgets and other forecasts is produced.

attempts at improvement. The scope of improvement must concentrate on improving a complete life cycle, not on the 'efficient running' of a single part of the organisation.

Solving a problem in one area can create problems in others. Someone must take overall responsibility and authority for each process and part of a process to control changes. Therefore each life cycle should have an 'owner' who has prime responsibility and authority for overall improvement.

The owners cannot do all of the improvement work themselves. It would take too long and cost too much. Besides, two heads are better than one, and a dozen are even better when properly utilised. Authority and responsibility should be delegated to owners of sub-processes as they know their problems and have the greatest incentive to solve them. Any solutions they propose are more likely to be acceptable than those imposed from an external group. This can also help to ensure that everyone in the organisation is involved in improving the processes within their own work area and between areas. The methods used are simple enough so that staff of all levels can learn them with a few hours of training, but of course they must be given the time and opportunity to make improvements.

Owners at the various levels cannot be left totally on their own, so external support in the form of 'consultancy' must be provided, preferably by trained and experienced management staff.

It was a deliberate policy from the start that LCE should enable the staff to define their organisation in a simple, standard manner readily understood across all functions. This makes it easier for them to understand the global impact of change, helps with changes outside their own area, and aids cross-training.

life cycle diagrams and documentation show employees where they fit into each life cycle, who their suppliers and customers are, and with whom they need to communicate within their life cycle. The diagrams also provide an index as each task identified on the diagram has a data sheet

and process description that contain or cross-refer to all the information required to perform the task.

LCE components

LCE uses method study, decomposition, critical examination, process model, frequency analysis, CPA/PERT and other methods. Slightly modified, these provide the integrated set of basic methods, tools and techniques.

The basic improvement process is a modified and iterative version of method study, but the scope is predefined as preferably the whole organisation, a life cycle at the very least.

Each life cycle is decomposed down to tasks, a piece of work performed by one person, though others may be involved. For example, interviewing is a task performed by one person with one or more other people participating.

Data is recorded on diagrams created using project planning software, on data sheets that hold key data and cross references to other information, and process descriptions that describe the task in detail. The data gathered can be used at many levels for numerous purposes and there is minimal, flexible documentation.

Process

The process used by LCE is based on that used in method study.

SELECT the life cycle(s)

RECORD the existing system on data sheets and skeleton diagrams

EXAMINE the life cycle critically from the top down using critical examination

DEVELOP the new life cycle and for example, incorporate SPC or BS5750 requirements. Use a 'process model' such as that provided in LCE to validate life cycles and processes

INSTALL the new life cycles and processes. As those doing the work have developed these, implementation should be a matter of doing what they have planned!

MAINTAIN the life cycle. Use more sophisticated methods and techniques if you wish.

Any additional life cycles or processes

identified later should be defined using this process.

It is useful to keep a copy of the existing system for comparison with the improved process. If you and the staff of your organisation have very, very strong constitutions, a very large wall, and planning software that can cope with it, consider creating a full skeleton diagram of your whole organisation. This could be an extremely traumatic experience!

life cycle documentation

A set of simple diagrams and forms are used to record the information relating to a particular life cycle, component or task consisting of:

1 skeleton diagrams show a single occurrence of each process or task
2 data sheets; contain the key data and cross-references to other data
3 process descriptions; of course, contain descriptions of processes.

Diagrams

A skeleton diagram shows a single occurrence of each life cycle, process, activity and task, and a data sheet is produced for each.

You can use any method to produce diagrams, but using a project planning package makes life easier. Not only does this provide a simple, commonly understood and standard form of diagram, but it also provides the means of calculating figures and transforming skeletons into models and plans as described below. Think how much time and effort goes into producing diagrams, and then having to calculate the duration, man-hours and cost, assign resources, and so on. What if there's a change, or you want to compare different proposed solutions? This is handled much more easily via software designed for the job.

The software will also identify the tasks that occur on the critical path, and if there is a specific need to reduce the duration, it is these tasks on which you should concentrate.

Data sheets

These contain the key data and cross

references to other information relating to the item it describes. It thus provides a central point of reference and helps to identify missing and duplicated information. Additional data items can be added later if the use of documentation expands. If you use a database system, make sure it can cope with such modifications.

As there is a data sheet for each life cycle, component and task this provides a simple means of finding the data required for a particular element. For example when performing a planned task, the reference on the plan points directly to the associated data sheet that contains or cross-refers to all information needed to perform the task.

Key data

This is the information necessary to uniquely identify – the component, the resources needed, and the position in the life cycle, plus estimates to calculate the duration, man-hours and cost. Actual data replaces estimates as it becomes available.

For example, the following key data items would appear on a task data sheet:

1 Reference
2 Title
3 Objective
4 Owner
5 Participant role
6 Participant man-hours
7 Participant cost per hour
8 Preceding task(s)
9 Succeeding task(s)
   and the following are calculated from these by the planning software:
10 Task cost and duration
11 Total man-hours, total cost and total duration.

Process descriptions

These are simple step by step descriptions of the process or task. Keep each step as clear and concise as possible, perhaps using structured English for tasks, and listing the component titles at higher levels.

Process model

There are certain things that must be present to make it more likely that a specific process or task will achieve the desired objective. For example, having information such as a clearly defined process with start, completion and success criteria, and details of how to evaluate the result achieved with the desired result will help to improve quality and productivity. Testing each process will also help to identify any weaknesses.

The framework

The skeleton diagrams, data sheets and process descriptions provide a full, detailed description of the existing and new life cycles that describe the whole organisation. This gives a framework for the integration of more sophisticated techniques used either as extensions to the basic methods of LCE or to replace them completely. The philosophy of LCE is to use the best method or tool for improvement that is simple to use and integrates into the overall process, but improved methods and tools become available almost daily, so LCE caters for this.

Productivity and quality improvement

Productivity and quality improvement go hand in hand. Each has an impact on the other. Let's be honest, who would propose a quicker, cheaper method that did not produce the level of quality needed, and who would propose quality improvement techniques that increased the price or delivery of a product or service beyond what was acceptable to the customer?

In many organisations critical examination (CE) is either not used at all ('What's that?'), underused or misused, yet it can give tremendous benefits if oriented towards the objective. Those of you who are familiar with business process re-engineering may have observed that many of the 'basic principles' of BPR can also be achieved with CE.

At this point any specific requirements such as those of BS5750 or SPC can be built into the life cycle, component or task. The greatest impediment to achieving quality is a poor process, so LCE provides a process model. This is a simple guide that enables assessment to be made of the completeness and likelihood of the process achieving the declared objective.

Using the diagrams and documentation

There are many ways of using the diagrams and documentation either to improve current practices, or to enable things to be done that are currently impossible, or would consume too many resources. A few of these are outlined below. Your imagination is the limiting factor.

Models

These are skeleton diagrams of life cycles or processes to which a generic number of frequencies have been applied, to more readily reflect the real world. Models provide simple building blocks for assessing proposed changes to the organisation, templates for process or project plans, and can be used in creating a year planner, budgets and forecasts.

Plans

These are models to which specific frequencies have been applied and can be of various sizes. Project plans produced in the computer department will be able to provide the answer to the question 'How long is a project?'. (The answer of course is the sum of the duration of all tasks along the project critical path.)

A combination of models and plans used in planning software can create planners that also provide budget and forecast data. All that is needed are the numbers of each and any specific start or completion dates, and a few hours to combine them in the planning software.

Evaluating change

Proposed changes or totally new life cycles can be modelled to assess their impact, and to provide forecasts of duration, cost, man-hours and resource requirements. Such an evaluation early on in an improvement project could avoid very expensive mistakes.

Skills analysis

There are three steps to this:
1   identify the skills required for each role. This information is identified from the process descriptions
2   produce a 'master list' of all skills used in the organisation. Ask each person to

identify the skills they have and their level of competence

3 match the two, asking staff to add any other skills they have.

Training

In many cases it is quicker and cheaper to train staff in-house in the specific skills they need, perhaps by self-study and tutorials. All the information necessary to do each task should be documented by the time the new system is installed, including those members of staff who have the necessary skills and can act as tutors.

Waste and pollution

Along with recording all the resources used on the planning software, if your organisation is ecologically minded it can also list and produce figures for the waste products and any pollutants produced. Entered as resources used, most planning software will very generously produce totals. Proposed changes to life cycles or processes can then be assessed as to their impact on these items.

Transferring life cycles

life cycles that achieve the same objective can be compared to see which is the most effective. Any group of organisations such as hospitals or local authorities could co-operate to their mutual advantage. Perhaps hospitals could compare their life cycles for the same medical problem, or local authorities theirs for the council tax and then adopt the most effective, leading to

gains with minimum effort. As each life cycle is a 'self-contained' unit, replacing one with another should be relatively straightforward.

Conclusion

There should be very little in the methods and tools used in LCE to surprise the management services professional, except perhaps that there is so little that is new! The important difference is the way the whole works together providing increasing synergy and potential for improvement in wider areas. As the old song goes 'It ain't what you do, it's the way that you do it, that's what gets results'.

The author: Graham McCue

Having spent twelve years in the army, in 1974 Graham attended a course in Work Study at Oxford Polytechnic. From 1975 to 1979 he worked for London Transport and became interested in computers as tools to improve productivity, leaving to attend a Business Systems Analysis course. In the period from 1979 until this year Graham has held various roles in computing initially in Systems Analysis, Design, Product Design, with the last seven years in Quality Assurance.

About eight years ago Graham became fascinated by the inability of the computer industry to solve problems that he knew Management Services techniques could solve. The original idea of how to improve productivity has grown over the years into what he briefly describes in this article.

> RESOURCE 2.3

Delphi technique

A subject is selected which requires a technological breakthrough to enable advances to be made. The involvement and co-operation of a number of leading thinkers and researchers is required. There is a need to design a special questionnaire which will explore the boundaries of knowledge and stimulate projective thought.

Typical questions could be:

- What is likely to be the 'ultimate' in this subject?
- What advance towards this can be made in 1 year, 2 years etc.?
- What is urgently needed by the market?
- What new materials are now available?
- How are computers being used with this subject? etc.

When the responses have been collated, the data is then circulated to all who have contributed so that further reflective responses can surface. Unusual or dissenting views can be explored further using the collected wisdom and insight of group participants. Obviously contributors can use data in their own organisational research programmes. Advocates of the Delphi technique believe that R and D is helped and speeded up by it.

Hazard and operability study

RESOURCE 2.4 ◁

This is used to identify possible deviations from performance, their likely effect, the cost of rectifying them and how they could be prevented through improved design. Problems with a product or service can be categorised in various ways, for example:

- the commercial cost of a breakdown in a major communications network
- the safety risk caused by a spillage at a nuclear plant
- the political cost of a failed military operation.

Hazard and operability study methodology involves:

- isolation of all the key factors and functions

- identification of all possible areas of risk
- construction of situational models
- examination of the extent of possible damage
- classifying deviations: primary and secondary
- definition of all possible scenarios
- designing action plans and procedures.

To handle the large quantity of data produced during this kind of study, a computerised approach is often used. For relatively simple situations a paper and pencil method will suffice. A matrix will need to be prepared so that all the relational aspects of the data can be considered.

Full details of the system	Deviations from standard which can occur	Causes of the deviation	Effects
Operating conditions			
Quantities			
Demand levels			
Quality issues			
Staffing			
Operational time/week			
Costs			
Speeds			
Queuing			
etc.			

▷ RESOURCE 2.5

Morphological analysis

Morphological analysis is a method used to list logically all the combinations of variables which can be thought of in a given situation. This can either be done manually if the number of combinations is not excessive, or by computer. Many combinations will contain incompatible features and therefore cannot be seriously considered for development. In the midst of all the data produced may be something which will prove a real money-spinner if eventually launched. Analytical thinking plays a part by identifying the dimensions and variables. Creative thought sees the potential in certain combinations, and judicial thinking is involved in later evaluation.

Below is a simple example about the manufacture and marketing of paint, drawn up in a matrix format.

There are 48 possible combinations here. A tube of non-drip paint applied with a spreader would seem very novel to a customer, but there is nothing new involved – assuming the quality of the finish is good!

DIMENSIONS	VARIABLES			
CONTAINER	tin	jar	tube	aerosol
CONSISTENCY	non-drip	standard	one-coat	
APPLICATION	brush	roller	spray	spreader

▷ RESOURCE 3.1

John J Lucey FMS, Management Services, January 1990, Institute of Management Services, pp 16–24

Developing and introducing new consumer products

The following paper is an abridged version of the Institute's 1988 Gold Medal Award winning paper. This award is made to the individual who, in the opinion of the adjudicating panel, submits the best manuscript dealing with one of the Institute's areas of professional concern.

Background

The company manufactures and retails pharmaceuticals, toiletries and cosmetics. In the financial year 1988/89, sales turnover was £2,697 million and profit was £267 million (9.9 per cent). Other interesting facts are as follows:

- Staff – 70,775 (UK 64,004)
- 22 manufacturing units (13 overseas)
- 1,341 retail outlets (162 overseas)
- We manufacture most of our own brand goods
- New products are developed in-house

- Our factories produce 4,073 different products
- Each year approximately 1,800 new products are launched
- Factory output is 336 million units per year.

The company is organised into four divisions, namely:

- –Pharmaceutical
- –Retail
- –Property
- –Central.

The retail sector is extremely competitive, especially products which are price sensitive such as family toiletries.

Statement of the Problem

Over the last five years the life cycle of products has been steadily reducing. At the same time the general quality of products and packs has improved.

The process of developing, producing and marketing products has got more complex and difficult to control. As the life cycles reduce there is a growing pressure to reduce the overall time for new product introduction in order to obtain a competitive advantage.

Increased development activity adds to the cost of introducing new products. The total cost of supporting this activity runs into several million pounds.

Consequently, it was decided to examine the whole procedure to see if it could be improved.

Objective

The objective was to examine the present company procedures and systems for the introduction of new products. To examine critically these procedures and systems, and to propose modifications which will ensure:

a   marketing opportunities are exploited to the full
b   lead times are reduced to a minimum
c   realistic launch dates are specified and achieved
d   project cost and unit cost are kept to a minimum.

Terms of reference

The terms of reference were defined as:

● To determine and record the current systems for launching new products from marketing concept to achievement of stock in warehouse
● To critically examine and evaluate:
   a   the role and responsibility of the various functions involved in the introduction of new products
   b   how the overall project co-ordination and control is undertaken
   c   the consultation process within functional groups and across functional interfaces
   d   the timescale for product formulation, and its subsequent QC testing for market approval
   e   the timescale for packaging developments and its subsequent QC testing for marketing approval
   f   the approval and requisitioning of tooling and other capital items
   g   the procedure for the creation and approval of artwork and label wording
   h   the method and timescale for authority to order materials and their price
   i   the method and accuracy of product cost estimates
   j   the project cost to the company of introducing the new product, including the 'write-offs' of old stock
● To examine the procedures and systems used by other comparable companies in the introduction of their new products
● To develop new systems and procedures, or modifications to existing systems and procedures, in order to achieve the project objectives
● To recommend methods of implementation.

Methodology

By its nature, the project was complex and extended over a long period. It was, however, envisaged to be undertaken in four distinct phases:

Phase Description Estimated Timescale

Phase	Description	Estimated Timescale
1	Situation analysis	6 months
2	Examination of external systems and case studies of internal launches	6 months
3	Critical examination and development of revised procedures	4 months
4	Implementation	3 months

A project steering committee was formed to advise on matters of policy and to offer general guidance. The steering committee included members drawn from marketing, consumer products development, production, purchasing, quality control and printing, together with a chairman and two other members with no departmental loyalties and the author as project leader.

Definition of a new product

For analysis purposes, a new product was defined as 'A product which is introduced by a Production Sales Plan Docket '

(PSPD), but excluding PSPDs for bought-in items and specials.

Plus Christmas gift boxes (XGBs) which are classed as a new product, although they do not have a PSPD. The above definition was approved by the project steering committee.

New product categories

There is a great difference in the work involved in what has been defined as a new product. On the one hand we could have a special offer, and on the other hand, a brand new formulation. For these reasons, the following categories were selected and approved by the steering committee:

    a Special offers
    b Redress/reformulation
    c Range additions
    d Totally new products
    e Miscellaneous, testers, outworks.

Situation analysis

The situation analysis was undertaken by interviewing the staff involved, producing draft procedure descriptions and flow diagrams and then a final check by cross referring information.

Volume of new product introductions

An analysis of the PSPDs issued for the ten and a half months monitoring period is detailed in figure 1. The PSPDs were further analysed by the merchandise controller and the analysis is detailed in figure 2.

Product life cycles

It is noticeable that the product life cycles have become shorter in recent years. Using statistics available on the *average* product turnover rate, the product life has been calculated in figure 3.

The present procedures

The project is most complex and phase 1 involved much more time determining the present procedures than was planned.

No procedural manual existed, consequently flow charts of procedures had to be produced for every function and activity. In total 26 flow charts were produced covering 11 functions and 18 different departments. Often flow charts had to be substantially revised because they

Factory Category	A6	D1	D6	D10	D95	Sterile	Total	%
A Special offers	369	9	19	6	2		405	20
B Redress/ reformulation	246	10	23	40	66	3	388	20
C Range additions	26	7	5	11	10		59	3
D Totally new products	303	48	57	110	18	44	580	29
E Miscellaneous	422	–	–	1	8	9	440	22
XGB	51	22	37	–	–	–	110	6
Totals	1,417	96	141	168	104	56	1,982	100

Figure 1 *Note: In total, 2,363 PSPDs were generated during the 10.5 month period which was monitored. After analysis 491 were omitted, 485 because they were bought in and 6 because they were specials. In addition 110 gift boxes were produced in-house, making a total of 1,982 products.*

were found to be incorrect when cross referenced to other flow charts.

Findings

From discussion with the participating functions and critical examination of the present procedures, a number of activities were subjectively criticised and problems raised. With considerable co-operation and assistance from the departments involved, team members carried out investigations and monitoring exercises. As a result, ten 'areas of concern' were highlighted for in-depth investigation. The ten 'areas of

Factory Merchandise Controller	Number of PSPDs	D1	D6	D10	D95	A6	Sterile
50 Home & Garden	51	3	6	33	8	1	–
60 O G Medical	20	–	5	6	3	6	–
61 O G Cos. & Toil.	1,050	33	37	25	1	954	–
65 Pham. Marketing	15	–	–	1	1	–	13
66 Contract Marketing	185	35	17	68	6	59	–
68 Crooks	63	–	3	5	23	32	–
70 Export	421	3	16	23	62	314	3
72 Optrex	39	–	–	–	–	–	39
74 Foods	13	–	5	7	–	–	1
75 Prod Contracts	15	–	15	–	–	–	–
Total PSPD's	1,872	74	104	168	104	1,366	56

Figure 2 *Bought-in [485], Specials [6] and Gift Boxes [110] are not included*
Note: At the time of this analysis, the present Business Centre structure was not in existence.

Factory	Live Inventory	New Products	Product Turnover %	Product Life (Year)
D1	228	96	42	2.5
D6	456	141	31	3
D10	573	168	29	3
D95	750	104	14	7
A6	2,674	1,417	53	2
Other	–	56	–	–
Total	4,681	1,982	42	2.5

Figure 3: *Average Product Life and Turnover*

concern ' are:

- Cost of new product introduction
- New product lead times
- Production of wording and artwork
- Accuracy of 'estimated pack costs '
- New product planning and control
- Quality control release and testing
- Procurement of product tooling
- Procurement of change parts
- Stock write off
- Comparison with other companies.

Each 'area of concern ' is discussed and the agreed recommendations or actions taken are detailed immediately after each sub-section.

Cost of new product introduction

The total cost of supporting new product introduction for the financial year was calculated. In undertaking the calculation every care was taken to exclude the costs associated with pharmaceutical marketing and consumer products marketing.

The items included in the cost calculation are as follows:

1 Consumer products development (CPD)
2 Design/consultants
3 Stock/component write off (estimated)
4 Quality control
5 Production
6 Purchasing
7 Marketing
8 Printing
9 Tooling and change parts
10 Pharmaceutical formulation.

The costs were regarded as conservative as they did not include advertising, promotion or merchandising. Items 1–4 above were obtained from the accountant responsible for each area. Items 5-10 are small by comparison and were estimated by the team members. It was clear in discussion with other companies that our expenditure was significantly more than theirs. Although it was not possible to make a direct comparison because they do not undertake much formulation development it was felt our costs were proportionately higher.

One of our competitors estimated a cost of £0.5 million per annum for their new product introduction and that included the in-house artwork studio.

Every product is supported by a profitability statement to ensure it is profitable. The statement takes account of demand during the product life, promotional expenses and merchandising costs.

Although a statement of profitability is included in some of our high sales lines, it is not as comprehensive as the analysis referred to above. The best of our competitors marketing staff seemed to have an excellent grasp of how new products were introduced, the timescale involved and where the costs were incurred. The system they used was supported by a new product introduction manual.

Production of wording and artwork

The systems for the generation and approval of wording, artwork and proofing were examined and recorded in a number of charts. At present the approval of artwork is nearly always a critical activity and the most significant cause of failure to meet launch dates. This is not the case with our two best competitors.

Failure can generally be attributed to one or more of the following reasons:

- the approval procedures are lengthy and complicated
- initial pack wording is not enough and final pack wording is not available on time
- designs are not available on time
- designers do not appreciate the constraints of packaging production techniques and the materials to be printed
- artwork is not produced on time.

To overcome the problems with the provision and approval of pack wording the present procedures need to be completely revised. Some streamlining has already taken place, especially in the Quality Control area and Legal Department. To further improve the situation, it is recommended that the first draft wording be produced at the same time as the New Line Specification is generated. Furthermore, wording should only be circulated once for comments with each person knowing exactly what it is they are supposed to be checking. The approval procedures will then cease to be a critical activity and will allow more time for the production and approval of artwork.

The cost of design consultants which includes the production of artworks was the second highest new product cost. The estimate was based on information provided by the Production Accountant.

The design costs do not include consultancy work and design of promotional displays. It was impossible to identify the exact proportion that was attributable to the production of artwork as invoices received did not detail design work and artwork separately. An estimate based on a sample of artworks put the artwork costs at £600,000.

One of our competitors only place design work on outside agencies; they prepare their own artwork in an in-house studio. As we have an in-house design facility, a study was undertaken to establish the feasibility of producing artwork ourselves. Our estimates indicated that our cost would be one tenth of the cost of a design agency. On this basis, the potential saving is approximately £0.5 million.

It was therefore recommended that we should commence artwork production and a presentation was made to the Design Policy Group. The recommendation was accepted in principle and work has commenced on the production of artwork. Obviously some resistance was to be expected from design agencies, but this should be overcome if we have the desire to implement this cost-saving idea.

New Product Lead Times

At the outset of the project, Marketing expressed concern at the length of time to develop new products either completely or partially, ie a new product or packaging redesign.

It was agreed to take 50 Cosmetic and Toiletry products and check the lead time from Development Brief to Stock in Warehouse.

In visits to other companies it was ascertained that our lead times were in general a little faster than theirs. One of the main differences was the degree of forward planning. In general our competitors worked on a longer planning horizon and Marketing were forced to commit themselves sooner. The marketing sections of our competitors were very conscious of the planned lead times and on approximately 80 per cent of occasions they briefed in new products on schedule.

It is felt that on balance our lead times are acceptable and rush launches can be 'walked through the system '. It would be very useful to issue marketing with a set of lead time guidelines for specific categories of new products so they are able to present the development brief in sufficient time to meet the target launch date without 'walking it through the system '.

Consumer Products Development have been asked to produce a comprehensive set of lead times for the various product groups. Once established, they will be incorporated into a new product introduction manual; the production of which has already commenced.

Accuracy of 'Estimated pack Costs '

The 'estimated pack cost ' is produced in CPD, and often forms the basis of deciding if the product proceeds to launch. Marketing expressed concern at the accuracy of these costs, as they had experienced situations where the computerised standard costs were in excess of the 'estimated pack cost ', as a result, the gross margin was adversely affected.

To check this statement, a 12 per cent sample of products was analysed. The results are summarised in figure 4.

The comparison indicates that of the sample, 33 per cent of the standard costs exceeded the 'estimated pack costs ' and this was clearly too high an error rate. However, if a tolerance of +/- five per cent was allowed in the 'estimated pack cost ', then only 15 per cent of these would have been above.

A second, more detailed analysis was carried out on an additional 51 colour cosmetic lines to identify the reasons for such cost variation. The CPD estimate was compared with the standard cost and it was found that ten standard costs and one CPD estimate contained errors. When these were corrected, 12 standard costs differed from the estimated costs by more than +/– ten per cent. (Only two of these were increases over the estimate.) The reasons for the differences were investigated and found to be:

6 increased packing speed
4 changes in packing material order quantities
2 increases in bulk material, packaging material and labour overheads

Accepting that the time delay between compilation of the estimated cost and standard costs will inevitably lead to some variation, it was agreed that variances exceeding ten per cent were not acceptable.

The following recommendations formulated:

a A cost estimate indicating the feasibility of meeting the target cost should be prepared by CPD within six weeks of the issue of the New Line Specification
b An estimated cost should be provided to Marketing/buyers by CPD as soon as feasible. Provisos should be given if necessary, especially for demand changes on component parts.
c CPD will monitor this cost as development proceeds and notify Marketing/buyers if it moves more than +/– ten per cent
d A copy of the initial standard costs should be provided to CPD to compare with the estimate. Variation of greater than ten per cent would be investigated.

After undertaking this analysis, it was decided to undertake a similar exercise for Christmas gift boxes (XGBs) as marketing felt the error rate may be similar. A sample of 39 of the XGBs was undertaken and the results are summarised in figure 5.

The accuracy of the XGB standard cost was found to be acceptable, but Marketing felt that they should receive the cost estimates earlier. CPD agreed to make every effort to do this but it must be emphasised that a high proportion of XGBs are unique and often designs are late in being approved which in turn delays the production of the 'estimated pack costs'

New product development planning and control

During the project, two significant changes occurred which we believe provided for better overall project control:

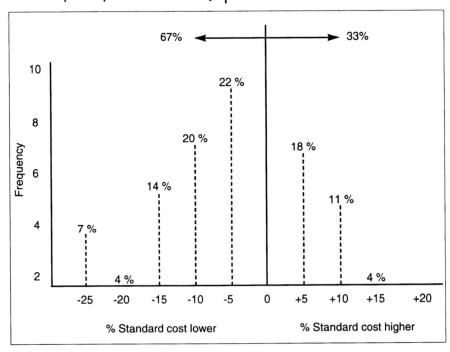

Figure 4: *Comparison of estimated pack cost to standard cost*

- Within CPD a project management structure was introduced which gave senior managers responsibility for the formulation, packaging and planning/co-ordination of the product developments for which they are responsible.
- The structure of the marketing group was changed as part of the retail re-organisation and this allows the buyers to spend more time on new product development.

Notwithstanding these changes, it was clear from our discussion with competitor companies that they achieved their new product introduction targets almost without fail and appeared to do this smoothly and efficiently. Whilst we do, in general meet most launch dates the nature of our introductions lead to a less than healthy degree of acrimony between functions as well as undermining the established procedures and systems.

Although there were significant structural differences in their organisations when compared to ourselves (ie. formulation work done overseas), we did form the following impressions:

- Their marketing staff were more aware of the timescale for new product development
- The proportion of rushed/ last minute projects was much less
- There were fewer and smaller formal meetings, but closer working relationships between participating functions
- There was a more disciplined approach to meeting deadlines
- Last minute or midstream changes in product development were subject to detailed scrutiny and justification
- Responsibility for meeting deadlines and launch targets rested most heavily on the marketing personnel. They did not have dedicated planners.

Discussions were subsequently initiated between some of the team members in CPD to determine ways of improving the efficiency and effectiveness of planning and control. It was recommended that:

– Specialist and dedicated project co-ordinations/planners should be retained and remain under the control of development managers in CPD

– Greater emphasis be placed on longer

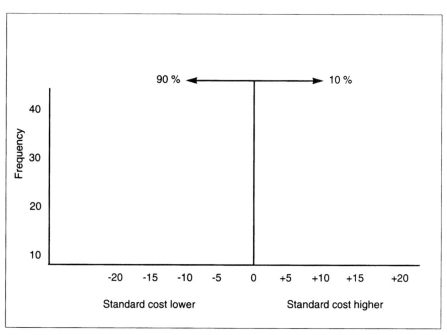

Figure 5: *Comparison of estimated pack cost to standard cost for XGBs*

term planning. Whilst recognising the dynamic nature of our business, major developments should be defined four years from launch. Smaller developments can be agreed on a shorter lead time but all development proposals should ideally be defined not less than two years from launch. Work briefed in on a shorter lead time should not exceed 20 per cent of the total workload

– All marketing managers/buyers must be aware of new product development lead times in order to formulate their plans accordingly. A manual for the introduction of new products should be produced. This should be updated routinely by CPD and used as a regular part of the induction of marketing/buying and development staff.

– The use of information technology to increase the efficiency of information gathering and dissemination should be extended

– Closer liaison should be established between CPD, planners/co-ordinators and marketing/buying staff. Formally programmed meetings should take place, in addition to the monthly progress meetings, between the planners and brand managers. There should be an increased commitment from Marketing in the achievement of early dates in the development programme. Recent changes in the retail marketing structure and the creation of the supply

function should assist in this endeavour.

Quality control release and testing

The involvement of quality control was recorded on a number of charts. During the project some of the release and testing procedures had been internally reviewed by quality control, and as a result, they had been significantly rationalised.

Duplication between quality control and CPD with regard to testing has almost been eliminated and is reviewed regularly. During a visit to a competitor, it was established that they varied the testing time of their products and they did not use the blanket times graduated in months.

It was felt that the testing times of various categories of products should be reviewed to ensure they were not being rounded up to the next month category, ie. ten weeks becomes three months. Once established, the review could be circulated for information and included in the NPI manual.

Procurement of product tooling

The procedure for the selection and ordering of product is the responsibility of the Purchasing Development Section. This section was specifically established to improve the sourcing and purchase of new materials, and tooling associated with new product introduction. When critically

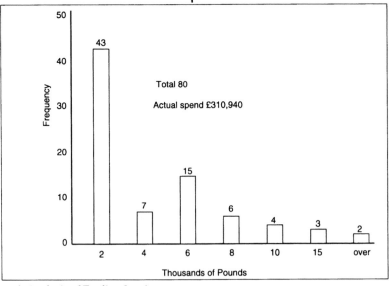

Figure 6: *Analysis of Tooling Invoices*

examined it was found to be extremely long winded and involved frequent referrals to committees for approval of relatively small sums of money.

An analysis of tooling invoices for a typical year is detailed in figure 6.

The majority of tooling invoices are under £2,000 and the recorded procedures are too bureaucratic for such a small sum. As a result, the whole procedure was reviewed and a revised and much simplified procedure proposed. This proposal procedure has now been approved by industrial division board.

Procurement of machine change parts

The procedure for the procurement of product change parts was again recorded on a flow chart. A sample of change part estimates covering the pharmaceutical factories was taken and is summarised in figure 7.

The majority of change part estimates are for less than £4,000 and examination of the present procedures revealed the following:

  –Estimate approval takes longer as the cost increases
  –Lead time for delivery generally increases as cost increase.
  –The time taken for approval varied

from factory to factory.

By comparison one of our competitors allowed change parts to be approved by the department manager. Once the new product had been approved as it was almost academic, ie. the product could not be produced without the change parts.

Changes to the procedure were proposed, however, the steering committee felt that the existing systems were operating in a satisfactory manner providing the personnel involved operated them correctly. No further action was therefore taken.

Stock write off

The total annual stock write off for the pharmaceutical factories has consistently been very high. It has proved difficult to estimate the exact proportion that is due to the introduction of new products, but it is thought to be approximately two thirds.

Stock write off can cover all categories of product from a component to the finished item. Due to differing policies and confidentiality, it was almost impossible to compare our stock write off to other companies. However, one competitor used a comprehensive formal system which they claimed reduced stock write offs to an acceptable level. We estimate that this was approximately a quarter of our write off.

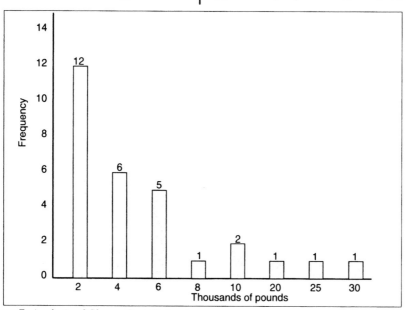

Figure 7: *Analysis of Change Part Estimates*

Our component write offs are charged to the factory and there is some difficulty in attributing accountability for write offs as it is a joint responsibility between the factory and marketing. If the cost of the write offs were changed to the appropriate marketing groups it is felt they would manage the 'run out and run in ' more closely, since failure to do so would result in financial 'pain '.

The system for altering marketing to potential write offs needs to be improved. It is clearly the responsibility of the factory inventory controller to alert the supply manager to any potential overstocks as soon as possible. There must be close liaison between these areas to control and minimise write off. It is the responsibility of the supply manager to ensure maximum notice of discontinuation is given and that forecasts of run out are correct.

A form for advising the inventory controller of discontinuations has been devised.

For larger run outs, such as relaunches, it is proposed that regular meetings are set up to control write off.

The author: John Lucey

John Lucey is Pharmaceutical Industrial Engineering Manager with the Boots Co Plc. Following an engineering apprenticeship he entered work study in 1986 with Worthington-Simpson of Newark. After a short spell with British Leyland as a work study section leader, John joined British MARC in 1974 as Chief Work Study Engineer. During his eight years with this company John undertook further study obtaining his DMS and MSc in Industrial Management at Loughborough University, and rising through several posts to Industrial Engineering Manager. In 1984 John joined The Boots Co to organise and direct the Industrial Engineering function within the pharmaceutical factories group.

With the Institute John is a member of Council of Management and chairman of publications and publicity. A member of the Membership Services committee, he is also very active in the East Midlands Region and on the Boards of the Managers and Pharmaceutical specialist groups.

▷ RESOURCE 3.2

Apple, JA, 1977, *Plant layout and Materials Handling*, John Wiley, New York

Travel charting and frequency travel charts

The frequency of journeys between work areas within a facility is logged onto a flow matrix. A 'five-bar gate' system can be used, but a final total figure is recorded in each square. Entries above the diagonal are known as forward progress entries. Entries below the diagonal are known as backtracking entries. Forward progress is desirable, backtracking is not.

To From	A	B	C	D	Total
A		2	1	3	6
B	2		0	2	4
C	1	1		1	3
D	4	2	0		6
Total	7	5	1	6	19

Present situation

The facility is laid out with four work areas in a straight-line sequence A B C D. The journeys logged can relate to materials, staff or a mixture of both, over a defined time period.

Here is the matrix for one hour of activity:

The system measure (torque) is derived as follows.

Forward progress (above the diagonal):

1 (square above the diagonal) × 3 (sum of entries in those squares)

2 (squares above the diagonal) × 3 (sum of entries in those squares)

3 (squares above the diagonal) × 3 (sum of entries in those squares)

i.e. 1 × 3 = 3

2 × 3 = 6

$3 \times 3 = \dfrac{9}{18}$

Backtracking (below the diagonal) use the same principle:

i.e. 1 × 3 = 3

2 × 3 = 6

$3 \times 4 = \dfrac{12}{21}$

Giving a total torque of 18 + 21 = 39. The layout will be improved, assuming that this one-hour sample was a true reflection of the travel between departments, if the work areas are laid out in the following order: A D B C.

Draw a new matrix with this revised sequence and calculate the new torque yourself to check this.

Solution: Forward progress 12

Backtracking 16

Total 28

The matrix can be adjusted to include quantities, distances, journey times and costs. The main problem that arises with a large layout is that you do not know when the optimum has been reached.

Ergonomics of layout planning

RESOURCE 3.3 ◁

The word 'ergonomics' was coined from the Greek words 'ergon' meaning 'work' and 'nomos' meaning 'natural laws' In the USA, the term 'human factors engineering' is often used.

Ergonomics aims to design facilities, equipment, technical systems and work methods to improve human health, safety, comfort, satisfaction and performance. It is a multidisciplinary activity which gathers data over a period of time from many research, scientific, medical, psychological, sociological and operations management sources, and applies it accordingly in the design of facilities and the work processes within them.

A full study of ergonomics is beyond the scope of this unit and the student is directed to specific texts, several of which are listed under Recommended Reading. To show the relevance, however, of the subject to facilities design, the following outline is provided.

Environmental factors

When providing a facility and designing the work system, a whole range of environmental issues can be addressed from an ergonomic perspective. Failure to undertake this often results in personnel, health, safety, quality and performance problems once the facility is operational.

- **noise and vibration**
  - measurement techniques
  - types of noise
  - acceptable levels
  - designing out noise
  - baffling
  - ear protection
  - very high/very low frequency sound
  - zoning noisy and quiet work
  - detrimental effects of noise
- **illumination**
  - measurement techniques
  - optimal lighting levels
  - shadows and reflective
  - surface glare
  - quality inspection
  - video display units (VDUs)
  - colour coding
  - emergency services colours
  - colour blindness
  - magnification
  - eye protection

- **atmospheric conditions**
  - measurement techniques
  - heating levels
  - coldness
  - special clothing
  - humidity
  - hot or cold processes
  - ventilation
  - fumes and dust
- **protective clothing**
  - masks
  - suits
  - gloves
  - boots

Physiological factors
  - anthropometrical data (body dimensional) data
  - biomechanical data, e.g. energy expenditure
  - posture
  - seat design
  - work surface design and dimensions
  - design of the work method

  - lifting
  - older workers

Information transfer
  - visual and aural intake
  - response times
  - accurate performance
  - information displays (screens, notices, dials, etc.)
  - systems controls, touch
  - person-machine interaction
  - codes

Equipment design
  - reach
  - grip
  - safety
  - maintenance
  - adjustability
  - size
  - controls

Organisational factors
  - group working
  - supervisory structure
  - quality checking system
  - shift working

▷ **RESOURCE 4.1**

Crandall, RE, CPIM, CIRM, *APICS – The Performance Advantage*, American Production and Inventory Control Society, Vancouver, vol 5, no 4, pp. 30–35, April 1995

Inventory – asset *or* liability?

Accounting calls inventory an asset. However, some production and operations management (POM) authorities call inventory a liability, or at least not an asset (Sharma, 1993). Is one right and the other wrong, or are they talking about different things? This article describes these apparent differences and explains how the positions between accounting and POM should be reconciled if a company is to manage its inventory effectively. It addresses the specific questions of:

- Why is inventory called an asset by accounting and never a liability?
- When is inventory considered an asset by POM? When is it a liability?
- What is excess inventory? What are the causes of excess inventory?
- How can excess inventory be disposed of? How can it be prevented?

- What changes in management practices will be needed? Managers who understand both the accounting and operations viewpoint of inventory will do a better job of inventory management for their company.

Background

Accounting views an asset as something a company owns, and a liability as something a company owes; therefore inventory will always be considered as an asset by accounting. For POM purposes, an asset is something that has greater value than its cost, and is able to generate income for the company.

If inventory were always an asset, in both the accounting and POM sense, there would be no difference in viewpoints. This ideal situation exists when finished goods inventory is ready for selling and moves quickly through the distribution chain to the customer. Agreement also exists when the work-in-process inventory is moving steadily through the manufacturing process without undue delays, such as in a Just-in-Time environment. Finally, both parties believe that a raw materials inventory that is compatible with the needs of manufacturing is also an asset. In essence, inventory is an asset when it includes the right quantities of the right goods at the right place at the right time.

Conversely, for POM, a liability is something that has greater potential cost than value, or its presence prevents the sale of other products, thereby causing it to generate a loss of income for the company. When and how can inventory become a liability in the POM sense? A simple answer is when a company has excess inventory at any point along the value chain from raw materials to customer shipment. Rosenfield (1993) defines excess inventory as existing when 'the potential value of excess stock, less the expected storage costs, does not match the salvage value'. If excess inventory is viewed as a liability, there is a need to determine which inventory is excess and what can be done about it. Often a company doesn't recognise that it has excess inventory because the management system (unusually a part of the accounting system) does not adequately identify where and how much excess inventory exists.

Causes of excess inventory

How does a company end up with excess inventory? What, or who, produces it? The following examples are representative, but not exhaustive, of the causes of excess inventory.

- Marketing – Marketing may want to have inventory available for a fast response to the customer, or simply to have product on hand for sale. To do this, they must forecast demand for a variety of items and, no matter how diligent they are and methodologically sound their forecast method, the resultant forecasts are never perfect. Consequently, some finished goods inventory does not move as expected

and eventually becomes unnecessary, or excess. Another possibility is that new products replace existing products, making obsolete the inventory of the replaced products. With the increasing emphasis on customer service and shorter lead times, it will be difficult for marketing to avoid generating excess inventories. Marketing decisions generally affect finished goods inventories.

- Production – Production may want to avoid unfavourable labour variances or to improve labour efficiencies and machine utilisations. This can be done by producing at a level capacity load that also avoids fluctuations in the work force; however, it also produces excess inventories at times. Excess inventories also result when the manufacturing process produces good, but out-of-spec, products that can be sold only if a customer is found who can use them. The temptation is to keep and value these products even with no known customer. Finally, some processes require starting a quantity of parts higher than the order quantity to allow for process defects and assure having enough good units to ship. This often results in an excess of units that may not be shippable but are good units. Again, the inclination is to hold these units in expectation that a repeat order will make them shippable; often, however, they end up as slow-moving, or excess, inventory. Production decisions can affect both work-in-process and finished goods inventory.

- Purchasing – Purchasing may want to buy a larger quantity to get a price discount; this can easily result in excess inventory at the raw materials or purchased parts stage. While this approach may look good in the short term, with favourable purchase price variances, it can generate excess inventories that will be costly in the long term.

- Production planning – Production planning may want to utilise available capacity in the shop. To do so, they schedule the production of standard products that are in constant demand. Eventually, some of these standard products become non-standard, and excess inventory results. Another possible scenario is that a customer requests a manufacturer to produce and hold a certain amount of inventory, at any stage in the process, for that customer's exclusive use. While this situation implies that the manufacturer will not end up holding this special inventory, sometimes they do. Decisions by production planning can affect inventory at any stage of completion: raw materials, work-in-process, or finished goods.

Why is excess inventory created?

Sometimes, the performance measures used in a company cause the build-up of inventory to be attractive. For example, most companies use income, or costs, as a measure of performance, especially for production managers, purchasing agents and marketing managers. These groups tend to focus on the income statement rather than the balance sheet. If the level of inventory does not change, there is no effect on income. An increase in the level of inventory often increases income because it reduces the unfavourable labour and overhead variances that occur when there are erratic or less-than-ideal capacity levels of production. Conversely, a reduction in inventory often causes a reduction in income by introducing variable workloads and unused capacity, causing unfavourable labour and overhead variances.

While the increase in inventories generates income, it decreases available cash. A reduction in inventories has the reverse effect – a positive cash flow. This presents a conflict in that managers in most companies emphasise income as a measure of performance over cash flow. However, the ultimate measure of a company's value is its cash flow - a position that accounting understands but does not always communicate to the rest of the organisation.

Another cause of excess inventories is the mistaken idea that having inventory on hand is always desirable. Most people view assets as something good, and liabilities as

something bad. A better way is to view inventory as stored costs that will eventually be charged to the income statement. Inventory build-up, then, is a way of postponing the reporting of costs until those costs are, in theory, matched against the sales to which they belong.

The Accounting Review Board Ruling 43 says that: 'In accounting for the goods in the inventory at any point of time, the major objective is the matching of appropriate costs against revenues in order that there may be a proper determination of the realised income.'

The methods used to value inventory are limited in helping us to deal with excess inventories.

How is inventory valued?

Two questions need to be addressed in deciding how to value inventory: (1) Is the individual unit of inventory correctly valued, or has excess cost been assigned to each unit; and (2) Does the inventory contain excess units that should have less than full value? The latter question involves evaluating the probability that the unit will be sold and when it will be sold.

These questions require a way to assign an initial value to the unit, and some way to revalue the units as the units remain in inventory unsold.

Initial valuation

Accounting provides two ways of valuing inventory: cost or market value, whichever is lower. The lower value purports to provide a conservative value for the company and its reported income. While conservatism is the objective, it may not be the result. As pointed out below, full absorption costing is the least conservative way of valuing inventory of the methods described, yet it is the only one generally accepted by accounting practice.

Market value – Market value is not a practical way to value inventory, in most cases. It not only requires a way to determine the market value of inventory but also a way of adjusting the value of inventory as the market value fluctuates. Trying to develop a dynamic (adjusted through time) estimate of this factor is beyond the capability of most accounting departments. As a result, most companies do not attempt to use market value of inventory as an on-going valuation method.

Cost value – One of the key decisions in valuing inventory is to decide which costs should be stored. These costs include direct materials, direct labour, and fixed and variable overhead expenses. Historically, accounting practice required that all of the above elements be assigned to the product and stored in inventory until the product is sold. In recent years, several alternative viewpoints have been proposed: activity-based costing and theory of constraints (TOC).

● Activity-based costing (ABC). This supports the traditional approach of assigning all overhead costs to the product and storing them in inventory; however, it questions the methods of allocating the overhead expenses to the products. This approach allocates the overhead expenses differently, and goes beyond cost allocation to emphasise a closer analysis of overhead to eliminate the non-value-added portion as unnecessary.

● Direct costing. Many management accountants like this costing method for use in planning, analysis and control; however, financial accountants have never accepted it as a method for valuing inventory. It advocates the assignment of fixed overhead expenses to the period in which they were incurred, and not to be stored in inventory as a product cost. This means that inventory has a lower cost value, and therefore less impact on the income statement. It also more clearly identifies overhead elements, offering greater opportunities to reduce them.

● Theory of constraints (TOC). As with direct costing, this approach advocates that all overhead should be a period expense. They go further to say that even direct labour is more fixed than variable in today's manufacturing environments and should be a period expense. This means that only direct material purchase cost would be stored as costs in inventory, resulting in even lower inventory values than for direct costs. TOC also promotes the idea that only product that is sold (throughput) should be

recognised as inventory (8).

Note: Although valuing inventory at the cost of materials may initially appear to be a very conservative valuation, it may not be. As manufacturers move more toward being final assemblers and increase their purchases of subassemblies or fabricated parts, the direct materials portion increases to a point where it represents 60 to 70 per cent of the cost of sales. However, accounting practices can be misleading. Material costs to a final assembler are material, labour and overhead to a subassembler; material costs to a subassembler are material, labour and overhead to a fabricator; and material costs to a fabricator are material, labour and overhead to a materials processor. Figure 1 shows how the cumulative effect of this sequence could reduce the direct material content to a very low portion if one considers only the materials cost of the materials processor. The most conservative way to value inventory is at the scrap value of the raw materials used.

Each of the above positions differs from the traditional method of full absorption costing that assigns the maximum amount of cost to the product. The traditional approach stores the greatest amount of costs to be 'matched' against subsequent revenue; the more recently proposed approaches store less for future release against revenue and, as a result, cause less distortion of the income statement during inventory build-up and reduction. Even more important, the three approaches listed above actively promote the analysis of overhead costs and the elimination of costs that are unnecessary. The full absorption method disguises and discourages careful analysis; it is a financial accounting tool, not a management accounting tool.

The current thinking of many managers, including some accountants, is to store less costs in inventory and to reduce the impact of inventory changes on the income statement.

Revaluation of inventory

Most companies use full absorption costing to value inventory. This does not present a problem if inventories are low and goods are moving smoothly through the manufacturing and distribution process. In this situation, the overhead costs are not stored in inventory very long and do not seriously affect the income statement.

However, when inventories build up and become excess to the needs of the business (when the probability that they will be sold at a price higher than their accumulated cost is low), they become liabilities and the inventory valuation should reflect this through some re-evaluation process. Inventories that do not sell promptly fall into this category. However, most companies do not discriminate among inventories when assigning an initial value; they assume that all product will be sold, no matter why it was created.

Auditors attempt to assess such factors as age, potential obsolescence, damage and other degradation of inventory in assigning an overall reduction in the inventory value. However, they usually do this only during the annual audit and seldom do it in a way that would be of benefit to inventory managers in identifying the causes of excess inventory that could lead to preventing or reducing the build-up of excess inventory.

Changes required

To reduce existing excess inventory and prevent its recurrence, a company requires changes in attitudes, objectives, performance measures, operating methods and accounting practices. It also requires the integration of various functions within the organisation.

Changes in attitudes

Managers need to change their thinking about the desirability of having inventory versus the desirability of not having inventory. Table 1 contains a comparison of the reasons for having inventory (the traditional perspective) and the reasons for not having inventory (the contemporary perspective).

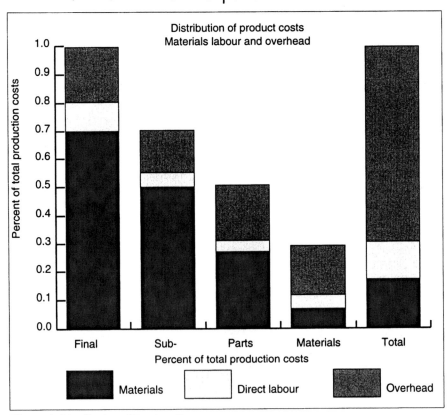

Figure 1. *Distribution of Product Costs*

These changes in attitude come from the realisation that today's competitive environment requires attention to customer service, product flexibility and product quality, as well as product cost.

Changes in objectives

Transition from the traditional way of thinking to the contemporary requires a combination of rethinking strategic objectives and changes in the performance measurement system. Part of this change process involves establishing global objectives that can be translated into local objectives for each organisational function, such as marketing, production, materials management and accounting. As previously mentioned, the choice of inventory level and product mix may present conflicts among functions and requires a holistic approach to reach a common objective.

Changes in measurement

It is necessary for the local (functional) performance measures to be closely related to the general financial performance measures, such as income and return on investment. As previously mentioned, building inventory is a way to show improved performance in income, which is used directly, or in some related form, as a measure of performance for functional areas such as marketing, production and purchasing. If other performance measures were used, such as customer service levels, the practice of building inventories, especially the less-saleable inventories, would probably decrease.

Changes in operating practices

Marketing, production and purchasing have to effect the needed changes to eliminate excess inventories and minimise the build-up of future excess inventories. To do this, they need help from the accounting function in identifying and measuring the status and causes of the excess inventories.

● Marketing – Disposing of excess inventory usually falls to sales and marketing. This is not a welcome task and often has a lower priority than new product or key account programs; however, it must be done. Marketing should be among the most enthusiastic supporters of programs to prevent excess inventory. They can help by

Function	Reasons to increase	Reasons to decrease
Marketing **Finished goods**	Increase sales through immediate delivery Reduce lead time to customers	Change mix to have saleable items available Make cash available for other programs
Production **Work-in-process**	Fill in low load periods to level production Increase labour efficiency and machine utilisation	Reduce congestion on shop floor Reduce lead times to provide faster service
Purchasing **Raw materials**	Obtain quantity (volume) discounts Reduce number of purchase orders required	Shift emphasis from cost to quality and delivery Reduce number of vendors to be dealt with
Production planning	Reduce the number of late shipments to customers Ship more from stock to meet shorter due dates Reduce number of production orders	Keep production capacity open for customer orders Shorten due dates by wait times in the process Increase flexibility to respond to customers
Accounting	Reduce overhead volume variances Increase working capital	Reduce physical inventory task Reduce cash requirements

Table 1. *Incentives to increase/decrease inventory*

working more closely with customers to obtain better forecasts of customer demand; communicate with engineering and production about introductions of new products and phase-outs of discontinued products; participate in the reduction of production and delivery lead times to reduce the need for finished goods inventories; and become a closely integrated link in the company's planning and control system.

- Production – Several current movements in production and inventory management include a focus on reducing the level of inventories. Just-in-Time includes a major emphasis on reducing the causes of inventory to reduce the absolute level of inventory. Materials requirements planning (MRP), when properly applied, will reduce excess and slow-moving inventory. Total quality management (TQM) attempts, among other things, to reduce the level of defects. Lower defects result in less uncertainty and fewer overruns on production orders.

Changes in accounting

Accounting can help to identify, reduce and prevent excess inventory; however, they must change some of their practices to make accounting information more useful to production/operations managers. These changes include how to value inventory, how to revalue inventory over time, how to reduce build-up of excess inventory through proper financial performance measures, and how income and cash flow must both be considered in planning inventory.

Initial valuation – The initial valuation of inventory should separate the planned and readily resaleable product in inventory from the unplanned product with uncertain resaleablity. This process should be dynamic, in that the status of certain products will evolve as they move through the product life cycle. To show the extremes of this method, a regularly sold, standard product could be valued with full absorption costs, as done currently; at the other extreme, inventory of non-standard product generated as the result of a production overrun, could be valued at the scrap value of the material.

A factor to be considered in the initial valuation is the probability that the unit will be sold. In the standard unit described above, the assumption is that the probability of sale is near 100 per cent and the unit can be assigned full cost value. In the overrun unit, the probability of sale as a completed unit is near zero, and the unit value is only the revenue generated when sold as scrap. The values for these extreme groups of products are logical; however, how about units of inventory that fall between the end groups? How does a company value them?

When the probability of sale is less than 100 per cent, one approach is to value the units at some cost less than full absorption cost, such as the direct cost or the purchased material cost. This is a way of reducing the average cost of the units in inventory and allowing some costs to flow through as period expenses during the production period. However, it is an expedient method of devaluing, and does not address the probability of sale.

Another approach is to value the units at full absorption cost and then group them in a category of '25 per cent probability of sale', '50 per cent probability of sale', etc. This forces an evaluation of the potential saleability of the product, but it requires extensive additional attention and record keeping; however, it reflects the reality of the situation. In addition, it offers a way to assign responsibility to the source of the excess inventory, thereby suggesting a way to prevent reoccurrences.

Revaluation of inventory – The total inventory should be classified by major product lines, and by method of initial valuation. These adjustments could be handled in an 'Allowance for Inventory Revaluation', in much the same way as an 'Allowance for Uncollectable Accounts Receivable'.

While this method requires judgement, this judgement can be systematically applied, and the process will identify areas of concern or potential liability to the company. Adjustments in inventory value are not unheard of. Retail stores do it through the markdown procedure. This reduces the income when the product is sold, and the cost is matched with the sale. Wholesale companies, because of their narrow margins, sometimes revalue their inventories higher when notified of price increases by their suppliers. This has the effect of increasing income at the time of purchase, not at the time of sale, presumably because the inventory has increased in value.

Integration of functions

Identification , disposal and prevention of excess inventories requires a co-ordinated effort by all functions of a business, particularly marketing, operations and accounting. This co-ordinated effort starts with the strategic planning process and carries through to the day-to-day operations.

If all parties concerned were more aware of the effect of inventory changes on both income and cash flow, better decisions could be made about the best levels of inventory and the most desirable product mix. This requires better communications among the operating groups and accounting during the business planning process and recognition of the responsibilities of the marketing and production groups in the cash management program.

Inventory is not an asset to a company if it is excess inventory. The sooner production/operations management and accounting recognise this and adjust their performance measures and operating practices, the sooner companies will be motivated to identify and reduce, or better still, to prevent excess inventory.

References
Farmer, James R, 'Re-engineering, achieving productivity success', *APICS – The Performance Advantage*, March, 1993, pp. 38–42.

Gaither, Norman, *Production and Operations Management*, (Fourth Edition), The Dryden Press, Chicago, 1990.

Jenkins, Carolyn, 'Accurate Forecasting Reduces Inventory', *APICS-The Performance Advantage*, September, 1992, pp. 37–39.

Lee, Hau L, and Corey Billington, 'Managing Supply Chain Inventory: Pitfalls and Opportunities', *Sloan Management Review*, Spring, 1992, pp. 65–73.

Schaeffer, Randall, 'A New View of Inventory Management', *APICS – The Performance Advantage*, January, 1993, pp. 21–24.

Umble, M. Michael and M. L. Srikanth, *Synchronous Manufacturing*, South Western Publishing Co., Cincinnati, 1990, p. 29.

Vollman, Thomas E, William L. Berry and D. Clay Whybark, *Integrated Production and Inventory Management*, Business One Irwin, Homewood, Illinois, 1993.

The author: Richard E Crandall, CPIM, CIRM
Richard E. Crandall is an associate professor in the College of Business at Appalachian State University, Boone, N C. He is past president of the Foothills Chapter of APICS, a registered engineer and a certified public accountant.

RESOURCE 5.1

What to look for when purchasing a network planning package

- a suitable size relative to the number of activities likely to be encountered in typical projects.
- ability to handle both activity-on-arrow (AOA) and activity-on-node (AON) types of network.
- ability to identify activities on the critical path and its duration.
- choice of time units: minutes, hours, days, weeks, months.
- built-in calendar which takes account of leap years, and in which proposed non-working days can be easily entered.
- user-friendly in terms of learning and use, with a clear manual.
- menu-driven with easy editing facility.
- easy to rectify wrong data entry.
- ability to calculate three types of float (slack): total, free and independent.
- ability to handle both projected and crash costs.
- ability to produce a range of management reports: e.g. tabular analysis of float, schedules based on a Gantt chart format, resource cost analysis, labour histogram levelling etc.

- ability to draw the network diagram on a suitable printer including as much mathematical data as possible.
- extent to which the whole or part of the network be seen on the VDU: is scrolling required?
- ability to compare planned progress to actual achievement.
- enables exploration of managerial options using a ' what if?' approach.
- presents information to non-specialists in an attractive and easily understandable format.
- ability to handle the three time estimates used to determine the weighted average activity time when using PERT.
- ability to interface with a spreadsheet for financial work.
- reasonable cost relative to the facilities provided.
- windows which permit different functions in screen sections.

Example of a PC package: Pertmaster Advanced (Abtex Software Ltd, Campus Road, Listerhills Science Park, Bradford BD7 1HR).

RESOURCE 6.1

The Economist, 14 January 1995, pp. 65–66,

The straining of quality

American companies are discovering what happens when total quality meets total choas. Has life lost a little of its quality for American firms? W Edwards Deming, the American who set off the total quality revolution, is dead. Joseph Juran, the co-founder of the quality movement, gave his farewell lecture tour last year. The American Quality Foundation has been disbanded. And, tellingly, applications for the Baldrige award, America's prestigious prize for quality, have slumped (see chart below). In 1994 only 71 firms vied for a Baldrige, a fall of a third in three years.

Optimists believe that waning interest in the Baldrige award is evidence of American firms' new-found self-confidence in the quality of their quality – after all, why bother to take part if you know you're the tops? Indeed, a recent study by Boston University, Tokyo's Waseda University and INSEAD, a European business school, concluded that American companies had caught up with and overtaken their Japanese competitors in terms of quality.

Perhaps. But the Baldrige's decline is more a reflection of corporate America's increasing tussle with total quality management (TQM). Even the 1980's most ardent adherents to quality are finding that TQM does not readily blend with wave after wave of restructuring and re-engineering. And the challenge of developing products and bringing them to market ever more swiftly – especially in industries where prices are tumbling, such as computers – adds to the strain on TQM. So far, America is bearing the brunt of this quality chaos. But Japan and Western Europe, increasingly obsessed with fads such as re-engineering, could soon be in its throes.

In their hearts, American managers want to believe that TQM amounts to a viable way of cutting costs. They would dearly love to emulate Richard Buetow, director of quality at Motorola. He reckons that, thanks to fanatical devotion to quality, the chips-to-cellphones maker has saved a staggering $6.5 billion in manufacturing costs since 1987 (the year before it won a Baldrige). But, outside Motorola, most managers still believe that cutting jobs cuts costs faster. According to Challenger, Gray & Christmas, a Chicago consultancy, 2.6m American workers have been sacked since early 1990.

The snag is that downsizing undermines a cornerstone of TQM: employee motivation. To achieve perfect quality, said Deming, companies must 'drive out fear, so that everyone may work effectively'. Yet downsizing fosters fear, as Xerox, the world's biggest photocopier maker (and a Baldrige winner in 1989), has discovered. Hector Motroni, head of quality at Xerox, says the firm has been through '11 years of wrenching change' since it adopted TQM in 1983. And although Mr Motroni credits total quality with reinvigorating the firm, he concedes that job cuts and the loss of management layers – Xerox is in the process of cutting its workforce by another 12%, to 85,000 – has damaged motivation and made it harder to sell the TQM message.

To overcome this, the firm encourages individual workers (instead of, say, departments) to focus on the needs of customers. All employees are given responsibility for quality. This, hopes Mr Motroni, will give workers a goal; it should also help bypass broken lines of communication. Dick LeVitt, director of corporate quality at Hewlett-Packard,

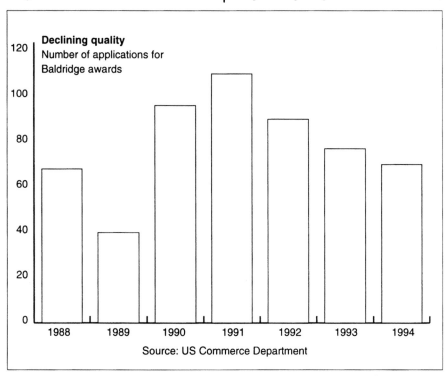

Declining quality
Number of applications for Baldridge awards

Source: US Commerce Department

agrees that such 'empowerment' is essential in firms facing chaotic change: 'You have to connect employees with the consequences of their work.' One recent study suggests that the effect of making that connection can be dramatic. It found that TQM programmes which delegate responsibility for quality to individual shopfloor workers tend to be twice as likely to succeed as those which rely on 'top down' management (thought the fad for teams brings problems too). With slimmer resources, companies are also discovering that they must focus their total quality efforts on what customers actually want. 'In the 1980s we pushed quality too much for its own sake,' says Mr LeVitt. So did Florida Power & Light (FP&L), an electrical utility which by the late 1980s boasted an 85-strong quality department and 1,900 quality teams – none of which seemed to bring about a significant improvement in its services. FP&L eventually scrapped most of its quality bureaucracy, and its service improved. Hewlett-Packard now treats TQM like any other investment: if a particular total quality initiative doesn't show a quick return in terms of higher sales, lower costs or happier customers, it is redesigned or scrapped.

IBM, which has seen its workforce fall by half since 1986 (and this week underwent its latest management shake-up) is taking a similar tack. Big Blue no longer has formal, stand-alone TQM programmes; responsibility for quality has been pushed down to the factory floor; and it is trying to infuse every part of its corporate activities with the notion of quality. IBM's most ambitious goal, however, is to reconcile its massive re-engineering programme with its quality goals. And this, thinks Jim Patell of California's Stanford Business School, is where firms often trip up.

The dilemma facing managers is that whereas total quality management emphasises continuous, step-by-step improvement, re-engineering relies on a radical, once-and-for-all scrapping of existing business processes. The tension between the two, says Mr Patell, can end up sabotaging a company's total quality programme. Wilson Lowery, head of quality and re-engineering at IBM, says his company is now carefully monitoring its re-engineering programme to ensure, at the very least, that each bit of it improves, rather than worsens, quality. But this does not address the differing velocities of the two strategies. 'We've a long way to go,' says Mr Lowery

Quality timed
Even if their total quality schemes survive downsizing and re-engineering, many firms find themselves facing another challenge: speed. Until recently, Xerox used to put dedicated teams together to implement total quality practices for new products, a process that could take up to six months. Now, Xerox rotates teams of engineers and managers from existing products to new products, in an attempt to learn from its past total quality errors and break out of 'functional silos'. This is tougher than it sounds, says Mr Motroni, because some TQM knowledge is invariably lost when teams are transferred.

Hewlett-Packard is taking a different approach to solving shaky quality in rapidly introduced products. Most glitches, says Mr LeVitt, arise during the transition from one product to its successor. In the past, Hewlett-Packard undertook what it calls 'hard roll' product changeovers, in which production of the Mark I version of a product was replaced by the Mark II in one fell swoop. The result: a big initial dip in quality which had to be fixed before the new version could be put in the shops.

Hewlett-Packard is now experimenting with 'soft' product changeovers. Once the specification of, say, a Mark II version is complete, the new features are incorporated, one by one, into selected production-runs of the Mark I. The Mark II is officially launched – and the new features made visible to customers – only when this gradual roll-over has been finished successfully. As a result, says Mr LeVitt, the time taken to hit total quality targets in new products is being slashed. And the new technique may also help the firm avoid the sort of gaffe - involving defective paper-rollers in 1.5m printers – it made public on January 9th.

As their product life cycles collapse and

price competition hots up, many firms are finding that the only way to maintain quality is to make their products simpler to manufacture. IBM's range of mass-market PCs are now built using fewer than 20 interchangeable modules; three years ago they were built from custom components. At Hewlett-Packard, 'design for re-use' – designing components for use not only in several products but also over several generations of those products – helps to improve quality while cutting costs. A drawback of this, concedes IBM's Mr Lowery, is that it can reduce customer choice - and satisfaction. But if TQM is to keep up with today's chaotic markets, firms must cut complexity.

Few companies are likely to give up the quality struggle, if only because - despite all the obstacles– TQM does seem to cut costs in the long run. And big cost savings, says Motorola's Mr Buetow, are the main reason why his firm will remain obsessive about TQM even beyond the point of perfection. Callers may not care if their Motorola carphone will work for a claimed 40-50 years before failing. But Motorola can at least rest easy that it should never have to dial up a costly recall.

Getting the numbers right

RESOURCE 6.2 ◁
European Quality,
Sept./Oct. 1995, vol.
5, no 5, pp. 28–32,
European Quality
Publications Limited

Being right first time is the start in the challenges facing BT Operator Services Directorate, the UK's leading telephone number information and operator services provider. Its rigorous deployment of total quality principles, flexible staffing policies and willingness to put itself to the test help it to meet one of the stiffest service quality workloads in Europe.

Company overview

BT Operator Services was formed in October 1990 following a major company re-organisation of its parent, BT. It was joined by International Operator Services in April 1991 to provide a fully integrated structure for Great Britain. Part of BT's Personal Communications Division, the organisation provides: national and international telephone number directory information services (including telex and fax numbers); a bulk number list service; special assistance and billing services; call connect services for international travellers; wholesale services for other licensed operators such as cable TV companies; free emergency services assistance; a free blind deaf and disabled persons' directory assistance service; an electronic database of telephone numbers for remote access by customers; and international directory services for 136,000 BT employees.

The organisation delivers these services through 44 national and three international directory assistance centres, and 20 national and five international operator assistance centres. Its workforce currently numbers 8,900 and consists of both BT employees and some 3,500 agency workers.

BT Operator Services is a volume business. The organisation handles over 700 million calls every year – including some 540 million directory enquiries (people looking for someone's phone number in the UK or overseas) with the remainder being requests for operator assistance (such as help with placing a call). The organisation's potential customer base is huge – 'any person with access to a telephone', according to its 1995 European Quality Award application document. In its home market in the UK, this includes more than 20 million customers of its parent company, telecommunications giant BT, together with the customers of other UK licensed telephone operators, overseas telecommunications companies and administrations.

While BT Operator Services does not yet have a single major competitor across its entire range of products and services (see company overview), Mercury Communications provides directory information for its own customers and for some cable television companies. In addition, a growing number of organisations provide number information for niche markets.

Four million new personal customers came onto the BT network over the past ten years to take the total over the 20 million mark, while the number of business customers has risen by 2.4 million in the same period to a total of over six million connections. The number of providers is on the increase, too, largely in the form of cable TV companies offering telephone services as part of their overall package. All of which adds to the volume of business for BT Operator Services, which offers information on behalf of many licensed telephone operators in addition to its parent.

Trevor Boon, quality programme manager, describes the directory assistance operation as a 'straightforward number information business'. But the sheer scale of the operation means that it is no simple task to meet quality targets of speed and accuracy of response demanded by both BT and the UK's telephone regulatory authorities. 'The biggest challenge is keeping the database up to date,' Mr Boon explains. 'Every night there are roughly 40,000 changes in the form of people stopping service or changing number and new ones signing up. The number of ex-directory (unlisted) customers is also a major factor in our being able to meet customer requirements – this can be a significant percentage of our residential customers in some areas.'

Having the right number available is certainly the key to the business, but that is just where the complex service quality challenges start. One key issue hinges on the fact that most callers to directory assistance would rather not have made the call. They are really interested in the phone call that follows the one to directory assistance. 'People only talk to us because they want to make the next call,' Mr Boon explains. 'They want what the transaction with us enables them to do. But if they do not get through, they will blame us, even if the number is unlisted. That is the price of being a front-end business.'

Costs and quality

The word 'transaction' is a key one for BT Operator Services. While around 80% of the calls to BT operator assistance remain free - such calls to the emergency services as well as directory assistance and special services for blind, deaf and disabled people – the decision to change for the directory assistance service as part of the tariff rebalancing strategy ushered in a series of new business challenges. BT Operator Services was formed in October 1990 following a major reorganisation of its BT parent, whose chairman, Sir Iain Vallance believes that 'change, for a large organisation like BT, has to be really big if it is to be successful. 'Incrementalism gets you nowhere.'

Six months after its formation, BT Operator Services began a fundamental change after it was allowed by the regulatory authorities to charge for directory assistance. The cost centre organisation was transformed overnight into a profit centre which had to pay its way. And the costs of the business were significant – the paybill alone in 1991 was a pure overhead of around £300 million.

By the early 1990s, keen cost control was a key objective in the BT organisation as a whole which had started its massive culture change programme and began implementing total quality management (TQM) practices in the mid 1980s. Faced with an entirely new commercial challenge, controlling costs in a quality way was the key objective, says Mr Boon, who points out that there were some very definite advantages to having access to BT corporate quality programmes. 'We have been able to pick the corporate programmes up and tailor them for our own use. There has been a very definite quality drive from the Chairman, which has affected the whole organisation.'

'When the business was established, the new Director of Operator Services, Charles Williams, firmly believed in quality. He really led from the top and he would have done this in order to keep the cost down to the business – whether the service was directly or indirectly chargeable. I don't think our quality drive was a question of having a price on the service, it was a function of the business we are in and was a means of getting better at it.'

An interesting twist to BT Operator Services' competitive position is that the numbers they provide to people will not necessarily lead to a call on the BT network. In providing directory and operator assistance for cable telephone operators, BT Operator Services is, in some instances, an enabling mechanism for its competitors. A further complication involves keeping up-to-date with changes to other licensed operators' databases. Perhaps because BT is the dominant telecommunications company in the UK and partly because of its historic background as a state owned monopoly, people tend to assume that they will appear on BT's database if they have a phone, even if their service is provided by another operator. The relationship with competitors is further complicated because many of the UK's cable television and telephone services are owned by North American telecoms companies who have formidable expertise in providing telephone services, but who also supply some equipment to BT.

Keeping it simple

Meeting the demands of heightened competition and increased volume demands could be expensive, which is why the organising principles of the BT Operator Services TQM approach play an essential strategic role in the business. BT Operator Services cuts through the complexity of its position by connecting with the dominant service quality and business imperatives in order to provide excellent customer service cost-effectively.

Following the lead set by BT's corporate values, expressed in 23 simple words ('we put our customers first' we are professional; we respect each other; we work as one team; we are committed to continuous improvement'), BT Operator Services has a clearly defined mission, vision and goals. Its mission is 'to help our customers make calls worldwide' and its vision is 'to continuously lead the world through world class people'. While these are admirably straightforward, the real key to the approach is expressed in the goals which represent the measurable components

of the vision: 'all our customers say we are exciting to do business with', 'all our people are empowered to serve their customers' and 'achieve zero waste'.

The organisation works systematically and energetically towards each of these goals. Its quality council – which consists of the director and his directly reporting managers and is responsible for the mission, vision and goals – drives the total quality programme by directing action aimed at delivering results under nine holistic critical success factors (CSFs). The CSFs are: understanding our customers' needs; business planning; total quality implementation; customer first leadership; access; customer information systems; committed people; competent people; and managing suppliers. Each quality council member owns and develops one or more of the 'strategic programmes' that address each CSF.

Key change programmes (KCPs) play a pivotal role. These programmes are specifically designed to deliver a measurable benefit in terms of time, cost and quality. KCPs already completed include 'Quality Management System Implementation,' which focused on providing people with clearly defined roles and responsibilities, procedures, standards and processes. In late 1993, it led to Operator Services becoming the first nationally organised part of BT to achieve ISO 9001 registration. The 'Leadership Programme & Involving Everyone' KCP involved all managers during 1993 and emphasised the role of the manager as a role model who lives the BT values, and was extended to all employees during 1994. More recent change programmes are focusing on total quality management implementation and process management implementation.

Clarity of direction is further strengthened by BT Operator Services' practice of making quality an integral part of the business planning process. Each year the company produces a five year business plan together with a quality plan and budget (QPB), which since 1993 has been structured around the European model for business excellence. The QPB addresses the improvement and resource requirements for the next budget year and is reviewed monthly. KCP improvement activity forms part of this process and is reviewed quarterly to check progress against key measures such as agreed customer perception. Each budget holder is personally accountable for expenditure against the QPB. External measures are important too. Benchmarking plays a key role, with North American and some Scandinavian telecoms companies as key targets. The search for benchmark partners within the telecoms industry is getting harder as competition intensifies, so BT Operator Services has now extended its programme to include other call handlers such as mail order operations, transportation companies and providers of package delivery services.

Strength in flexibility

Maintaining high quality performance in a highly flexible workforce is one of BT Operator Services' key challenges. The business makes extensive use of agency workers and its most productive centre is staffed entirely by part-timers. Far from jeopardising the quality of service provided, this flexibility serves the business well in a number of ways. Lower direct costs is one obvious benefit – as the agency workers are not directly employed by BT, the cost to the business is minimised. The decision to move to agency workers was taken early and, though it has contributed to the release and redeployment of some 20,000 people since 1991 in voluntary programmes under BT's extensive corporate downsizing efforts, it has not led to any reduction in the overall quality of service. Some workers who left under the voluntary release have even returned as agency employees, a situation which pleases BT Operator Services because it can be doubly sure of their abilities.

The effective use of sophisticated technology plays its part in ensuring consistency of service, but because the workers are provided by companies who qualify for inclusion as key suppliers on the BT Operator Services Supplier Index their quality is assured. The nature of the job of a telephone operator points to a further quality and business benefit of flexible working arrangements. 'It is a pretty relentless task being a directory enquiries operator – a very good one can clear 600 calls in a standard day,' Mr Boon explains. 'Part-timers usually do fewer hours so they are a lot fresher at the end of the shift.'

Variations in the volume of traffic are a further reason for maintaining a bank of high quality workers on call. Demand for international numbers peaks during the summer tourist season, for example, and BT Operator Services has found that foreign students are particularly happy and well-equipped to meet this seasonal need. Getting the balance right between agency workers and a core of full-time people is important, but many of the headaches are minimised by BT's policy of not discriminating between agency employees and its own. All employees participate in team briefings and refresher training and have full use of all BT facilities. Indeed, surveys undertaken under the people satisfaction criterion of the European model for business excellence produce consistently higher results from agency employees than from BT's own people – although Mr Boon points out that satisfaction ratings were 87 and 91% respectively.

Measuring satisfaction

There is a close connection between employee satisfaction and customer satisfaction at BT Operator Services which speaks volumes about the depth of its total quality culture. This link is maintained by presenting monthly customer satisfaction results and longer term trends in a form that shows how individual directory assistance centres have performed in the eyes of their customers. The information is gleaned from an extensive BT corporate exercise involving 6,000 to 7,000 customer interviews each month.

The results feed into a scheme for recognising success. Centres have to achieve certain scores in terms of speed of answer, customer satisfaction and a range of other measures in order to get the quarterly award for best centre. The winning centre is given a certificate from the director of operator services and money to hold team events. In recent times one centre team went on a trip to Spain, others give the money to charity. But there is no doubt that it is a prize worth winning and it has led to healthy, quality-based competition between centres. The recognition model, based of the European model for business excellence, has had a very positive effect on people satisfaction and is currently being refined to take more account of performance in terms of the 'enablers' as well as pure 'results'.

As front-line service providers, the operators themselves not only directly influence the customer satisfaction, they are actively involved in complaint logging and resolution. Operators are encouraged to take ownership of problems and do all they can to ensure that customers have their problem solved by the first recipient. This key empowerment issue is reinforced by training operators to be fully aware of the range of options they have available in helping customers reach a satisfactory conclusion to their call. The cost implications on both ends of the line are given careful consideration: there is only so much help a caller wants when he is paying for the call. Some customer service measures are more complex than they seem. Speed of answer, for example, is not a one-way improvement street. The number of customers who complain that their call is being answered too quickly, thereby throwing them off their guard and resulting in a longer handling time, is closely monitored.

One major cause of customer dissatisfaction was easier to predict: price. But thanks to the efficiencies delivered through its total quality programmes, BT Operator Services was happy to respond by introducing a 45% price cut on the inland directory assistance service in 1994. Mr Boon points out that the move was particularly satisfying because it allowed BT Operator Services both to share the benefits of its total quality programme with customers and send a serious message to existing and potential competitors. He is hopeful that the focus group exercises aimed at empowering all employees to work together to identify and eliminate the root causes of customer dissatisfaction will have a similarly beneficial competitive impact.

Doing it faster
Eliminating dissatisfaction is one thing, but satisfaction of itself seems too neutral a word to associate with the BT approach to change (even though BT Operator Services won the 1994 BT Award for Quality in Customer Satisfaction). BT Operator Services' goal of becoming 'exciting' to do business with was deliberately stated as such to convey a challenging and extraordinary target.

According to Mr Boon, this impatience for change will be carried forward into the next phases of the total quality programme. 'At the end of our total quality management implementation key change programme, we said we should have done it faster. We should have done it in two years and not three. We are a more resilient organisation than we thought at first,' he says. 'Do it faster, that's the lesson. Perhaps people underestimate how enthusiastic and adaptable their people are. It is actually harder to keep the momentum rolling over three years than it is over two. We are just going round into relaunch and we are going to do it in two years this time. No doubt we'll get to the end and say we should have done it in one.'

Critical examination guide sheet

Description of activity   Date

_____ Analyst

Key Operation/Inspection No   [   ]

Primary questions		Secondary questions	
Present facts	Reasons why	Alternatives	Selection for development

Completed critical examination guide sheet

Description of activity	Date		
Key operation/inspection No ☐	Analyst		
Primary questions		**Secondary questions**	
Present Facts	**Reasons why**	**Alternatives**	**Selection for development**
WHAT is achieved? Consider the element in isolation (bear in mind the subject of the chart)	**WHY?** Reasons given may not be valid. True reasons must be uncovered	**What ELSE could be achieved?** The answer to this section is never 'nothing'. Three main alternatives which must alway be considered are: (a) Non-achievement (b) Avoid the necessity for the achievement (c) Part achievement Each of these can also be expanded	**What should be achieved?** Helpful to divide into short and long term Under long can go suggestions for future research, customer education etc The aim is elimination or if this is not practicable, modification. The economics of the situation must be borne in mind throughout
HOW is it achieved? Information should be tabulated as simply as possible under these main headings with all relevant details (a) Materials employed (b) Equipment employed (c) Operator's method (d) Posture (e) Safety (f) Protective clothing (g) Working conditions	**WHY THAT WAY ?** Reasons should be investigated for each of the tabulated items under each heading	**How ELSE could be achieved?** Consider all conceivable alternatives for each main heading	**When SHOULD it be achieved?** Each heading should be considered first in isolation and selection made of the most appropriate items, bearing in mind the economics. The selected items should then be knitted together to produce the best, safest and cheapest method
WHEN is it achieved? (a) What are the previous and subsequent significant activities and what are the time factors involved? (b) What is the frequency?	**WHY THEN?** What determines (a) The sequence (b) The frequency	**When ELSE could it be achieved?** All conceivable alternatives should be considered	**When SHOULD it be achieved?** Bear in mind the economics
WHERE is it achieved? Once the fundamental questions have been cleared at the selection stage, only the detailed position within the factory, plant or area is required WHERE appropriate give reference to location and distance from previous and subsequent activity Note: remember the three dimensions	**WHY THERE?** What governs the location today and what were the original reasons?	**Where ELSE could it be achieved?** All conceivable alternatives should be considered	**Where SHOULD it be achieved?** Answer may be in relation to some other activity. Consider limitations and cost of building design and services (steam, air) etc
WHO achieves it? (a) Number of operators (b) Grade, eg unskilled male (c) Employment, eg day worker (d) Designation or name (e) Wage scale and incentive scheme if appropriate	**WHY THAT PERSON?** Reason for each heading?	**Who ELSE could achieve it?** All conceivable alternatives should be considered	**Who SHOULD achieve it?** It may not be possible to select the individual without Work Measurement and recommendations as to wage scale and incentives will usually be made at the development stage

Critical examination sheet (completed for a specific activity)

Description of activity

Date

Pack goods into carton

Analyst

Key operation/Inspection No

Primary questions		Secondary questions	
Present facts	Reasons why	Alternatives	Selection for development
Where is it achieved?	**Why there?**	**Where else?**	
At each workbench (size 2m x 3m)	*Logical locations *Traditional *Tools nearby *Rooms to work	*At the scales *In another department *At another site	
Work conditions are good	*Visible to supervisor		
Near windows			
Who achieves it?	**Why this Person?**	**Who else?**	
3 Male packers Job evaluation Grade 3 £/hour.40 hour/week	*Always been a packers job	*Labourer *Warehousemen *Female packers *Handicapped workers	
	*Packers have the skills, strength and experience		
Training needs – 2 weeks			
How is it achieved? Packer stands at workbench	**Why that Way?** *Easy to do *Cheap *Minimal training *Efficient	**How Else?** *Use a handling device *Other packing materials need different methods	
Grasps wrapped goods with both hands Places goods into carton and releases	*Traditional *Standing is best	*Put corrugated paper liner in first	

Development stage sheet

Critical examination key	What should be done	How should it be done	Where should it be done	When should it be done	Who should do it
1					
2					
3					
4					
5					

Proposal	Advantages	Disadvantages	Adopted?
What should be done			
How should it be done			
Where should it be done			
When should it be done			
Who should do it			

Work specification sheet

Department

Job

Location

Date

Method of working

In broad outline, the method of working is as follows:

Workplace layout

A detailed plan is attached.

Materials

Plant

Tools and equipment

Servicing

Number of service operators =

The duties of the service operator(s) are:

Continues...

Measurement of output
The measurement of output is the responsibility of:
The method of measurement is as follows:

Quality considerations

Rejected production
(a) Payment:
(b) Disposal:

Work recording
A specimen work sheet is attached

Working conditions
Lighting:
Floor:
Atmospheric:
Other conditions:

Grade of operatives

Standard minute values
A list of values is attached

▷ RESOURCE 7.6

Method change form

```
To:        _____

From:      _____      Dept  _____

Job:       _____

Nature of change:
           _____

                                         Signed  _____

                                         Date    _____
```

▷ RESOURCE 8.1

Burgan, JW, *APICS –
The Performance
Advantage*, APICS,
November 1993, vol
3, no 11, pp. 25–29

JIT and MRP II could make beautiful music together

Making the right choice by implementing JIT changes on top of a well-founded MRP II planning system can be the right decision.

Many manufacturing companies are aware of the potential benefits of migrating to a Just-in-Time (JIT) environment. Usually they have already spent years and hundreds of thousands of dollars implementing MRP II systems. Most people are under the impression that the two, JIT and MRP II, are diametrically opposed systems and to go to JIT would require scrapping their MRP II system. There are also those companies without formal planning systems that want to go straight to JIT. Both of these situations are a result of many misconceptions which have delayed the adoption of many of the JIT principles and processes. The strong MRP II planning environment is what will make a JIT execution environment work.

It is imperative that a company has a well-tuned planning system to assure that materials are available for the 'pull scheduling' system that JIT provides. Companies with little or no planning constants tend to overcompensate by making more product earlier than necessary, thus over-building inventories. MRP II planning systems address over-compensation by making sure that only the right materials and resources are available at the proper time. JIT espouses reduced lot sizes and lead times while making parts and products only to satisfy real demands instead of economic order quantities (EOQ) rules. Both MRP II and JIT have the same message. MRP II embodies 'pull planning'; making the product just before it is needed.

When JIT is implemented, it becomes critical that the master schedule be as stable as possible (that is, firm) for the next planning period. In order that this happens, the MRP II system must be functioning well with the supporting procedures and processes in place. JIT will have an effect on all areas of the manufacturing planning and control system (Figure 1). The 'back end' is changed most radically, in particular with the way the manufacturing and purchase orders are released to the plant floor. Scheduling will be very dynamic, pulling the orders, while the push planning

is applied to assure the materials are available. I am assuming a basic understanding of MRP II concepts in the following discussions.

Execution is the building of what the customer requests (pull) as they need it.

MRP II and JIT
Primary Objective:

Planning ━━━━━━━▶ MRP
Mid & long range parts ordering
Inventory planning
Capacity planning

Execution ━━━━━━▶JIT
Monthly/weekly production
rates setting
Daily parts pull into manufacturing
Execution is the building of what the customer requests (pull) as they need it.

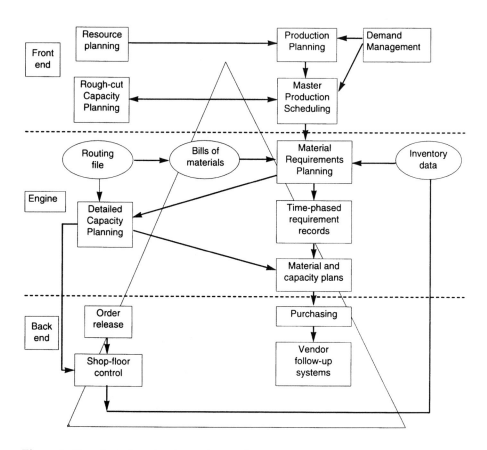

Figure 1. *Manufacturing planning and control systems*

Just-in-Time element

It is important at this point to define what is meant by JIT and discuss its basic features.

JIT attempts to minimise all waste in manufacturing. This does not mean only in the area of inventory and scrap. Waste is anything that does not add value, and value is anything that increases usefulness and reduces cost. All areas of the business are examined to eliminate any unnecessary expenditure of time and energy. Errors are investigated to determine their cause and reduce any recurrence. It not only tries for zero inventories, but zero transactions and zero disturbances.

Some of the key features found in a JIT environment depend on a stable master schedule that balances loads and capacity. The operations must be linked and balanced, providing a smooth and timely movement from operation to operation. These operations are usually set up so they can be visually controlled by the operators and are usually executed without paperwork or complex overhead support.

Master scheduling should plan the monthly 'production rate' in lieu of discrete batch orders. The weekly/daily rates should be scheduled based on these rates. Typically, the work-in-progress inventory is reduced. Inventory is considered a waste and, as it is gradually reduced, problems are uncovered and corrected. For purchased materials, the ties to the vendors are developed to a partnership level and the delivered goods increase in quality and arrive more frequently. Product design should be determined by the customer's definition of quality, therefore trending toward more customisation of products.

Success hinges on change

In an environment where many different product mixes are produced in any given month, reduction in the set-up time will be key. Typically, lot sizes spread the cost of expensive setups across many parts. If you can reduce the set-up times, it follows that the lot sizes can be reduced accordingly. Reductions can be accomplished by separating setups into internal and external. In 1985 Shigeo Shingo estimated that set-up can be reduced 30 to 50 per cent merely by doing this. Internal setups are those that must be done when the equipment is not operating and external setups can be accomplished while the equipment is operating. External setups could then be accomplished while overlapping the previous operation. The internal set-up processes should be analysed and set-up methodologies put in place for consistency. Changing the layout from functional to cellular also has the effect of reducing setups since the cells are typically laid out based on group technologies. This may not be feasible throughout the entire plant but may be possible for certain component lines or operations. Replacement of older equipment with newer technology will usually have the added benefit of much reduced set-up times. Other methods for reducing set-up times are:

- Colour coding
- Standard die heights
- Locator pins
- Quick disconnects
- Duplicate tooling for smaller tools
- People involvement
- Many small incremental improvements
- Tool and die maker involvement from the beginning.

Shrinking the lot size will allow much more flexibility in the planning of what is built, how many are built and when they are built.

Continuous improvement

Another required change is a 'continuous improvement' program for higher quality or total quality management (TQM). It must be implemented from the product design, through the process design and continue through the supplier of purchased parts. Statistical process control (SPC) focuses on the operation's critical processes. It attempts to stabilise each process by spotting trends with the goal of improving the quality of the yield. Operators must be responsible for the quality of their output and have the authority to stop production when necessary. Total productive maintenance (TPM) focuses on the maintenance of both the equipment and process, again with the goal of the highest quality output. Foolproof operations are an attempt to eliminate poor quality by examining the operations for areas where mistakes are likely and making it difficult to make that mistake again by either changing the process or providing checkpoints to catch the error before it happens. A 'fishbone' analysis should be used to determine the cause and effect of production quality problems. Preventive and predictive maintenance should be used to maintain the equipment and tools. Finally, using operator knowledge and close observation of equipment, the operator can sense potential failures. The costs of defects will be reduced as these programs are introduced, because the defects are caught before or as they occur. Continual improvement means making thousands of smaller incremental improvements and not necessarily large steps forward (Figure 2).

The U-cell layout
The cellular manufacturing layout, or U-cell layout, causes many additional physical changes in addition to set-up time reductions. Group technology should be used to identify parts made with similar processes, thus determining the most effective layouts. Because the machines are laid out based on the routing, the distances are obviously shorter from operation to operation, thus requiring much less handling and resulting in less damage. Since the U-cell may take the raw materials through many levels of the bill of material, there is the added benefit of fewer manufacturing orders released to produce a component. If you previously released an order for each level and returned the product to the stores area between each release, you now reduce all that travel and material handling. The workers in the U-cell layout must be capable of running several machines as well as providing basic maintenance to those machines. They can see and react to problems more quickly and provide help to each other when necessary. This flexibility must be nurtured and training must be provided to make this a

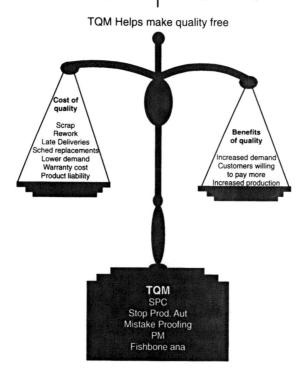

Figure 2. *Total quality management helps make quality free*

reality. The operations within the U-cell should have some flexibility built in to provide for volume fluctuations. This 'band width' flexibility is especially critical at potential bottleneck stations (Figure 3). The use of value added efficiency (VAE) to measure manufacturing efficiency is key at this point. Since VAE is operations time divided by manufacturing lead time, you will get a more accurate picture of the percentage of time each part is being processed. As the VAE percentage is increased, significant lead time reductions are occurring, thus responding to customer demands much more quickly. The planning for the loads on each line should be as level as possible and balanced to reduce the fluctuations as much as possible. This should be accomplished by freezing the master schedule for that period.

How does JIT affect MRP II?

Using Figure 1 as a guide and the base knowledge of JIT just described, letís look at how a company can move toward a JIT operation and the effects this would have on the manufacturing planning and control system.

Looking first at the 'front end', let's address the demand management area. Since a company will be making some of each product daily via a more stable, level production rate, the lead times for products will be reduced. This, in turn, will reduce the on-hand finished goods inventories. As the inventories shrink the company will slowly shift from a make-to-stock to an assemble-to-order or make-to-order company. The company will become much more responsive to customer wants and needs by supplying the right product at the right time without carrying the associated inventories. Forecasting of product families or groups will be more critical with less emphasis on forecasting individual items. It will be very important for the production plan and the master production schedule to be checked against the resources to assure level loading. The master production schedule must be rate-based and be firm for the following month or period so that weekly and daily production rates can be determined. This will result in smooth shop operations with the minor variances in volumes being handled by the use of band widths within the cells.

Looking at the 'engine', the main impact there will be in the MRP and CRP

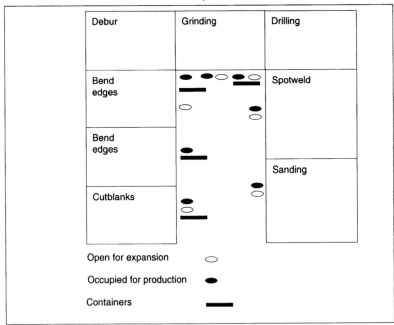

Figure 3. *Sample volume 'band width' for fabrication process*

areas. Because of the redesign of the manufacturing process, either with the U-cell or actual redesign of the product, there will be far fewer component product numbers for the system and people to deal with. Reducing the number of parts also reduces the number of levels of the bill of material for that part. This drastically reduces the time and complexity of the MRP runs. Many companies have reduced MRP planning by as much as 75 per cent. Since the daily rates of the equipment would be known, as long as the production rates are within this limit, it would not be necessary to make any CRP runs. There will be significantly fewer manufacturing orders to release and, therefore, much less movement of materials into and out of stores.

Looking at the 'back end' you will see the more significant changes. Because of the reduced cycle time, orders move through the plant more quickly. Tracking from operation to operation becomes unnecessary and a waste of time, as the order will probably be completed before anyone gets a chance to look at the information on the order status. This eliminates the need for a complex shop-floor control system. It may become necessary only to track the order's entry and exit from the system. When the finished product is received back into stock, you backflush the component inventories to update their balances. Logistics transactions reduced or eliminated are ordering, execution, confirmation of materials moving from location to location, shipping, receiving and expediting. There will no longer be a need to create this detailed work-in-process accounting system, and the high volume of transactions associated with it will no longer be slowing down the system. This type of system requires a great amount of data integrity. This simplistic approach is the result of well designed products, manufacturing cells and systems. With the higher quality being produced, the products will flow through the process smoothly and quickly, again reducing the need for detail records and overhead staff.

Vendors must adopt JIT as well

Once JIT is working effectively in-house, a lot of the same principles can be extended to vendors. Relationships with vendors must be based on trust, with quality as the main objective. Based on the vendor's capabilities you may be able to take advantage of the supplier's competencies and actually include him in the product design effort. In other situations, you may have to increase the technical support you provide the vendor if the design is complex and beyond his capabilities. A prerequisite to this is the ability to provide a reasonably certain, fairly stable production schedule. Good planning in the MPS precedes excellence in execution, both internal and with vendors. Good communication will become critical, as will a vendor certification program. Electronic kanbans can be created through an EDI system, which will allow the sharing of schedules and forecasts. It will take time for the vendor to provide the quality and timeliness required, just as it will internally. Flexibility and learning together will be important while doing business. As quality improves, the number of inspections of incoming components can be reduced or eliminated. The increased frequency of deliveries will also help the vendors determine when and where they are producing poor quality. A natural result of this process will be a pruning of vendors and much more contact with those remaining, in some cases involving the line workers themselves. Using standard size kanbans and delivery to the line eliminates additional paperwork and checking. Partnerships should be developed, nurtured and kept as simple as possible.

Throughout this process, mutual respect is key between all organisations, employees, customers, vendors and shippers. A major team effort will be required that involves flexibility and authority being given to each member and using everyone's mind and ideas, not just their hands and backs.

Case history example

A recent situation starts to bring many of these concepts home. The company is a make-to-stock manufacturer of trailers, and an MRP II user with a great amount of control over its inventory and manufacturing orders. One would think that this situation would make the company very competitive. Unfortunately, today's environment requires more than a good planning system. Shorter cycle times in a make-to-order environment are becoming the norm.

This client makes 28 models of trailers to which can be added certain features and options. The firm makes 96 per cent of its components from the raw material level. This results in a tremendous number of orders being released to produce the 3,000 components needed for the final assembly stage. All components are kept in a storage area almost as large as the manufacturing area itself.

A tremendous amount of time is wasted in the picking and movement of materials to and from stores and the operations. There are two final assembly lines allowing each model to be built once a month. It takes the pickers three days to pick the components for final assembly. The equipment on the floor is functionally organised causing a tremendous amount of movement between functional areas or back and forth to the stockroom. Materials, labour and orders are all tracked manually on paper with updates from four to 24 hours late entering the system.

To move this Class A MRP II user towards a JIT environment, we suggested the following changes:

- Change many of the operations to U-cell layouts where feasible, thus minimising handling, movements and overall cycle time
- Change the bills of materials to reflect the cell layout, therefore reducing the number of levels in the bill and its overall complexity
- Cross train the highly specialised workers to be able to perform more operations and work different equipment. Also change the incentive system to support these changes
- Use the finished goods inventory as a base to fill orders and as individual trailers are sold, release an order to the plant to replace those trailers, thus pulling through the plant orders to replace only what is being purchased
- Implement a data collection system to track orders, materials and labour. Since orders would be moving through the plant much quicker, the inventory and orders need to be updated on a more timely basis.

This company is indicative of many companies. They are looking to stay competitive by utilising and combining the best support systems and processes available. Implementing these JIT changes on top of a well founded MRP II planning system will truly be 'pulling it all together'.

References

1 Thomas Vollmann et al., *Manufacturing Planning and Control Systems*, Richard D. Irwin, Inc. , 1988.
2 Ellis, S and B. Conlon, 'JIT points the way to gains in quality, cost and lead time', *APICS – The Performance Advantage*, August 1992.
3 Mirsky, M., 'The Missing Link', *APICS – The Performance Advantage*, September 1992.
4 Anderson, C., 'The IBM Austin CFM Story', IBM, Austin, Texas.
5 Bowman, J., 'Just-in-Time and MRP II: A Winning Combination', APICS – *The Performance Advantage*, October 1992.
6 *Production and Inventory Management Journal*, Volume 33, Number 3, American Production and Inventory Control Society, 1992.

Credit: Figure 1 from *Manufacturing, Planning and Control Systems*, Thomas Vollmann et al., Richard D Irwin Inc., 1988.

The author: John W Burgan
John W Burgan, CPIM, has over 20 years' experience working with manufacturers and is currently affiliated with Skill Dynamics/IBM in Marietta, Ga.

Manufacturing technology survey

RESOURCE 9.1 ◁

The Economist, 5
March 1994,
pp. 19–21

In the modern world, everyone can know the time exactly and carry it with them anywhere. In the pre-industrial world, only precise observation of the heavens could provide accuracy, and time was encased in all-but immovable clocks. The difference was both brought about and necessitated by industrialisation. Greenwich mean time was taken from London to the provinces by clocks on steam engines, the better to synchronise the rhythms of the nation's work. Time's unmeasured flow became controlled, paid for, subdivided. Factory whistles punctuated it, Frederick Taylor and his stopwatches measured it exactly, punching the clock gave it value.

At present, the industrial obsession with time is focused on two issues; time to market, and being just-in-time. Time to market depends largely on design; just-in-time depends largely on working practices. In a company convinced of the value of being just-in-time, orders trigger production, rather than triggering a trip to a warehouse that is being continuously filled by the production process. It is a large part of what is meant by 'leanness' in manufacturing, and much in favour. It has not, to date, had much to do with technology: it has been about management and the design of work.

The idea is to avoid tying up capital in work in progress. If the production system is thought of as a machine, work in progress corresponds to the tolerances between the parts. It is tolerance in time and money, not space: the inventory between two parts of the process represents the degree of uncertainty over the time they take, and over the speed at which the whole system may have to work. Computer-controlled machining and CAD have allowed engineers to make pieces with tolerances finer than ever before as a matter of routine. Can analogous technologies do the same for time tolerances?

According to 12 Technologies, formerly known as Intellection, they can. The Dallas-based company starts from an analysis of the weakness of the just-in-time approach. In this, the message to up the pace or slow it down travels upstream from the customer through to the component supplier like a tidal bore running up a river. If the process is simple, that is easy enough. However, if the process is complicated and many-branched – that is, flexible enough to turn out many different products – things get trickier. There are more likely to be bottlenecks in the process that distort its speed. And if the changes in the market are extremely quick, quicker than the time it takes for information to travel step by step up the manufacturing stream, then the system loses stability like a pendulum swung beyond its accustomed range.

12's solution looks simple; it is a program that plans the path of work through a manufacturing plant, saying what parts will be needed where and which machines will do what. Such programs have been around for a long time– there is a large installed base of software dealing with material resource planning (MRP). But Rhythm, 12's product, is smarter and better at details. An object-oriented approach allows it to solve scheduling problems by looking at the starting condition and the desired outcome, and bringing the two together. Traditional programs are more idealised, starting with assumptions such as an infinite supply of components and slowly running through long loops of calculations before coming to an answer.

The result is that Rhythm can produce schedules in minutes, not days. Work can be planned by the hour rather than the week. That means the tolerances are tighter; if the system gives good results by the hour, there is no need to keep a week's worth of production around. Another advantage of Rhythm is that it can be used to schedule things machine by machine. It, and better software like it which will surely follow, can take a floor full of machines so that they become 'virtual cells', linking machines far apart into the sort of tight-knit unit seen in an FMS. They will not quite match an FMS in throughput, perhaps; but they can be refigured quickly and easily. Factory layout moves from the material world into the world of information.

Rhythm's speed allows it to reroute work more or less on the fly. Earl Mott, who has put Rhythm into the heart of Black & Decker's manufacturing division, enthuses about its ability to answer hypothetical questions. It can tell you what is gained and lost by giving an order high priority. And according to Sanjiv Sidhu, president of 12, it can do this for a whole company, not just for a factory. It can tell you whether shipping parts over from the Singapore plant is an easier way to fulfil an urgent order than building them on the spot. It allows you to commit to a delivery date with a high degree of confidence. Delivering on time is a problem for a lot of companies. Many do not even meet the date that the customer really wants. Improving that performance would provide a competitive edge. Mr Sidhu notes that many of his company's customers are firms that were quick to tackle quality, a crucial issue of the 1980s. They now see timeliness taking its place as the ground for competition. Quality is no longer a stake to be raised. It is the ante necessary to enter the game. Time is where the stakes are being laid.

With Rhythm, a company can go beyond simply having a flexible facility; it can know just how flexible the system is through simulations, and it can know what making use of that flexibility to prefer one job over another will cost. Remember Dr Upton's notion of a factory as a marketplace, where machines bid for parts, and the work ends up efficiently allocated. Rhythm provides similar capabilities; but rather than setting up a surrogate market, it allows the scheduler to let the real market into the factory, and set priorities accordingly.

There are other technologies that can offer similar insights into how factories actually work– a whole new category of software that can be seen as fitting between traditional MRP and what actually happens, called manufacturing execution software, is forecast to grow by 20% a year through the 1990s by Frost & Sullivan, a consultancy. And there are technologies to allow computers to know what is really going on. Computers work on the idea that what should be happening is happening. Once something goes wrong, this approach can amplify the problem and widen the divide between idea and reality. Stand upstream of a robot on a production line and push the pieces it is working on out of kilter; it is fun if you enjoy watching futility. Now factories are turning towards barcodes and other sorts of labelling to keep track of reality. If the software and the people running it are flexible enough to cope with the data, this does a lot of good.

To see such technologies working together, look at Motorola's Fusion production facility. Fusion is the company's name for a family of pagers, designed to be easily customised, and the processes of design, manufacture and marketing that surround it. A customer phones in a requirement – a pager, say, of a particular size and colour (it matches his tie) that plays a particular tune. The Fusion computer system turns the specifications into a set of parts, and nips into a virtual manufacturing world to preassemble them and make sure they add up to a product. Then it releases the design as a series of routing instructions to the manufacturing facility. As the piece goes through the facility, it is continuously tracked. Nothing is made until it is ordered; mass production in lots of one.

The advantages go beyond single facilities, though. Hewlett-Packard has realised that, like many companies, it is not yet delivering to its customers at the speed they would like. A company-wide object-oriented database, showing exactly where everything is, is part of the solution; so are changes in management and in attitude. Their new technology is part of a general corporate re-engineering; the changes involved make sense only in the context of one another.

The tools turn in

Such re-engineering is all the rage, and technology is a good tool for it. What sort of companies might eventually emerge from the makeovers that the new tools will offer?

One of the most influential visions of future manufacturing in the past few years goes by the name of 'agile manufacturing'. It is outlined in the '21st century manufacturing enterprise strategy', produced by Lehigh University's Iacocca Institute for America's defence department. Agile manufacturing requires companies to have more than just the fast, lean and pro-active virtues of the 1980s. Like 'new men' they have to be butch but caring, ever responsive to the needs of others. They also have to co-operate. Agility resides in the provision of a product, rather than in any single company. The visionaries like to talk of virtual enterprises, ad hoc coalitions put together around a promising new idea. An idea is born, a design made, a design verified, parts built, a product assembled, marketed, shipped: a need is fulfilled. Each step could be done by someone different; the last step is the product of the whole.

There are various preconditions for success in such a venture. One is clear communication. Here the new standard for product data, STEP, will undoubtedly be useful, especially since it can carry quite a lot of data about the product on top of its geometrical form. Standards have their drawbacks; they always lag the leading technologies. The history-based approach of Parametric's CAD software, for example, which allows the far-flung repercussions of changes to be felt, cannot be communicated through STEP: when a model is moved through the STEP standard, it loses this aspect of its history. But interoperability will, in the end, matter more than pure performance, and assuring that systems in different companies work together will definitely require standards.

The precondition that matters most, though, is predictability. The essence of agility is sensitivity to time. The different companies involved have to know their capabilities exactly, and the time they take exactly. This is what new factory management technologies make possible.

When a virtual enterprise is assembling itself, it has to know precisely the dimensions of its parts, not in breadth, length and depth, but in terms of such things as process time and quality. At present, few companies can accurately measure themselves in many of these dimensions.

There are hints of these virtual worlds already to be seen. The American military is encouraging them, as it encouraged NC machining. A programme called CALS will require every new piece of equipment to come with a form of electronic product model, and in so doing begin to tie the supply chain into a sort of virtual enterprise. And there are less technologically advanced models available elsewhere. One is found south of Beretta's home in Gardone: the fabric mills of Prato. In the 18th century, the old guilds were unified into vertically integrated mills. In the 1970s the mills subdivided themselves back into small units. They now provide a marketplace of capacity co-ordinated by a few brokers and served by a united retailing operation. The industry, once moribund, is now flourishing.

Dr Upton and his colleague Ramchandran Jaikumar have pointed out that there is a growing potential for this to happen elsewhere, in the other industries. Manufacturing plants that can work from CAD files are spreading. The size of many manufacturers is shrinking. With a modern multi-purpose CNC tool, a man in a garage can bid for work that would have needed a job shop in the past. Versatile scheduling can give a few such machines great capabilities. The information networks needed to join such places together are almost in place, offering high data-rates to any user in an industrial country that needs them. And the software for good product modelling is being written. Without product models, such schemes are doomed.

It may be that another great change is on the way. Once parts became interchangeable, people soon followed suit. Now the factories themselves may go the same way. The parts will evolve, their histories guiding and limiting them. The new whole, the new machines of production, remains to be invented.

▷ RESOURCE 9.2
Blaser, J, and
Westbrook, B, *APICS
– The Performance
Advantage*, January
1995, vol 5, No. 1,
pp. 43–48

The Supply Chain Revolution

Is your company its own worst enemy?
Many of the methods used to move and sell consumer products are inefficient, ineffective and out-of touch with today's increasingly value-driven markets. In the future, brand franchises won't be enough to sustain companies that don't significantly reduce their costs and, with their trading partners, reduce the inventory in their joint supply chains. Manufacturers, wholesalers, retailers and supply chain service providers must reinvent their business relationships or embark on what we call 'the supply chain revolution'. They must attack current methods of buying, selling and distributing products to remove layers of excess inventory and costs from the system.

Supply chain revolutions
Successful efforts in supply chain integration by industry leaders like Motorola and Wal-Mart have inspired many companies to re-examine their operations. Applying improvement methodologies like re-engineering and total quality, many companies have come to a conclusion that the cartoon character Pogo once summed up nicely: 'We have met the enemy and he is us!'

Corporations may be their own worst enemy, but too many remedies focus inward only. They create well-manicured, operationally efficient departments when what many corporations really need, if they are to thrive in today's marketplace, are social skills. Many companies may look good in short-term financial performance, but the way they interact with their peers – suppliers, buyers and consumers – has a greater impact on their long-term profits and competitiveness.

Manufacturers need to reflect on practices that affect their performance and ask themselves: Do current strategies increase sales or merely rearrange steady demand into peaks and troughs? Do operations complement the legitimate role of channel members, or distort the economics of distribution and merchandise assortment? In short, do we reward or punish low-cost operators? Are we reinforcing our brand image or creating a climate for the entry of private labels?

Financial renovation
The total system cost of supply chain activity devours a lion's share of corporate profits, but few firms ever realise their life bread is at stake. The reason: individual customer, function and product costs that nibble away at corporate profits lie buried between line items. Few corporate accounting systems accumulate or properly allocate these costs. (Figure 1) Order processing, transportation, warehousing, inventory control, packaging and related support activities, typically reported under selling and administrative expense on the income statement, have traditionally received the most scrutiny by senior executives. Unfortunately, these costs are usually only reviewed as individual functions and few executives dig deeper, analysing service costs incurred at the customer, product or even channel level. New activity-based costing approaches relate these fragmented facts into meaningful, manageable performance measures.

Likewise, a more sophisticated, holistic read of the income statement can reveal the impact purchasing, materials requirements planning, production scheduling and control have upon the cost of goods sold. (Figure 2) Balance sheets, the linchpin of long-term corporate success and failure, should be inspected in a new light as well. Supply chain assets and liabilities associated with inventories, property, plant and equipment act as counter-levers, having a direct impact on cash flow and return on investment. In a perfect world, finished product would be delivered to customers immediately upon manufacture at a rate exactly matching demand.

That's why much of package consumer goods manufacturer's technological development in the past decade has been aimed at linking manufacturing systems to actual retailer demand (eg. POS data). Entire industries are now banding together to drive excessive costs associated with distribution, handling, transportation and inventory out of the system by electronically linking these functions. Following the example set by quick response in the apparel industry and automotive Just-in-Time (JIT) programs, the grocery industry has undertaken a supply chain rationalisation effort entitled efficient customer response (ECR), which will save the industry an estimated 11 per cent of its total system cost or $30 billion dollars.

The total supply chain

Senior executives must be concerned with how products are sourced, manufactured, bought, sold, moved and merchandised. Ultimately, they must ensure that customers are satisfied. In short, they must integrate what we refer to as the total supply chain. This means creating organisational and process links and seamless information between marketing, sales, purchasing, finance, manufacturing, distribution and transportation as well as externally to customers, suppliers, carriers and retailers

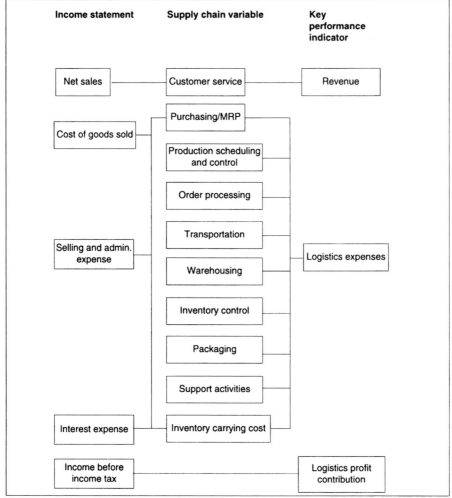

Figure 1: *Few corporate accounting systems accumulate or properly allocate the total system costs of supply chain activity.*

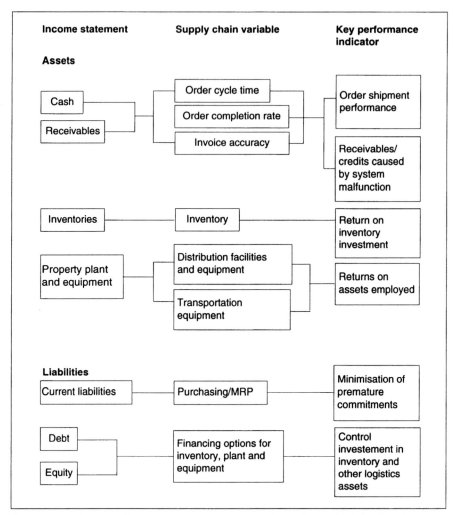

Figure 2: *By the mid-1970s, two overlapping layers of distribution had developed.*

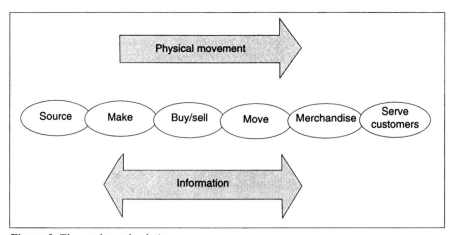

Figure 3: *The total supply chain*

(Figure 3). More importantly, it means aligning corporate strategies, working to achieve common goals and physically redesigning the movement of goods to maximise channel value and lower net landed cost.

Many consumer goods manufacturers have already realised the potential savings in capital-binding assets such as transportation, distribution and warehousing by optimising and re-optimising these functions. In these companies, it is no longer the physical links in the supply chain that cause inefficiency; it is the buying/selling behaviour that confounds the system. Where once economies of scale predominated and quantity buys dictated a reduction in acquisition cost, recent fine-tuning of distribution functions has taught us that quantities tailored to the unique characteristics of the product and channel are most efficient. Price structures should reflect this reality.

Rumblings of a revolution

While these objectives may seem simple, executives today have inherited an industrial infrastructure that, at best, inhibits and, at worst, runs counter to these ideals. Further, it is imperative to understand the history and dynamics of this system before effective change can be made.

1945–1975: Physical distribution in support of marketing-driven trends

Beginning around 1945, distribution systems in the United States were being built to support marketing-driven trends initiated by larger consumer products companies like General Mills, Proctor & Gamble and Nabisco. Mass production had been refined by wartime retooling and, for the first time in history, consumers were able to purchase products of consistently good quality at affordable prices. Manufacturers maintained profitable margins and protected distribution channels by adjusting bracket prices to match production-based economies of scale.

Meanwhile, wholesalers and retailers made money by buying on volume: if they ordered a carload of product, they got the best price. It was a simple system that was slow and erratic, but it worked. Manufacturers typically produced all of their products in large, full-line plants and when wholesalers and retailers placed an order, the product was shipped directly to their warehouse and later delivered to individual stores. To sustain growth, a multitude of new products was released on the market and consumer product manufacturers began to maintain many, many product-specific plants to support demand. Retailers became assortment-based, luring customers by offering as many brands of as many products as they could carry. This plethora of product lines began to clog plants and warehouses. Getting product to stores became a problem and, ultimately, manufacturers, wholesalers, chain stores and independents all built additional distribution centres and warehouses to support geographic markets. Consequently, two overlapping layers of distribution developed: one to collect manufactured product and the other to receive and breakdown volume shipments to stores (Figure 4).

1975–1992: Trade promotions/SKU explosion create a hostile environment

Not surprisingly, product proliferation began to splinter markets and manufacturers' sales in old channels and categories began to stabilise. In response, manufacturers devised trade promotions and couponing to incite for all those new SKUs, creating hostility between manufacturers and retailers along the way. While manufacturer promotions stimulated sales, they created a systemic problem as more than 80 per cent of all goods were purchased on deal and about 40 per cent were either pushed into forward buys or diverted. Encouraged by rising inflation, retailers and wholesalers also began holding great tubs of inventory to enhance profits as prices rose. Despite their high gross margin, traditional retailers actually received lower returns on their investments due to higher supply chain costs, which opened the door for more economic-based retail formats – everyday low price (EDLP) and club stores.

Club and EDLP stores fundamentally and irrevocably redefined the way

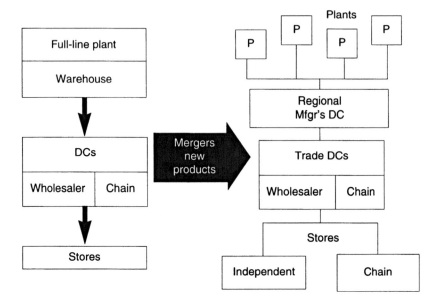

Figure 4: *by the mid-1970s, two overlapping layers of distribution had developed.*

manufacturers and retailers interacted by issuing a single demand: dead net pricing and no promotions. By carrying a limited number of SKUs in club packs delivered directly to the store on pallets, club stores lowered the cost of operations by streamlining and pushing the cost of distribution back onto the manufacturer (Figure 5). They gained an estimated 26 per cent price advantage over independent and chain stores and commandeered 25 per cent market shares in important categories. Similarly, by only accepting rock bottom pricing and eliminating the cost of handling promotions and forward deals, EDLP formats were able to consistently offer prices at 15 per cent to 25 per cent below competing trade channels.

Market dynamics continue to shift power from manufacturer to retailer. The independent stores that used to pepper the cityscape have been boarded up. More and more deep discount and EDLP players have entered the retail scene, resulting in dwindling effectiveness of trade promotions and causing more production and distribution inefficiencies than their incremental profits justify. Meanwhile, consumer goods manufacturers have been left laden with supply chain infrastructures that were designed to efficiently operate in a paradigm that no longer exists.

Bottoms up approach

Like an age-old paradox, the answer to consumer goods manufacturers' current dilemma lies in the problem that they have not adapted their supply chains to meet changing consumer values and the channels that support them. Clearly, the 1945-era method is no longer appropriate. Today, Wal-Mart wants Procter & Gamble to worry about whether or not they have enough *Tide* in their stores to support demand and club stores don't care if they're out of a specific brand of ketchup because they sell only what they buy on deal.

Consumer goods manufacturers need to throw out the old business philosophy and ask, 'What do the *consumers* want in each of the channels we sell to?' and then create individual supply chain infrastructures to support their needs. The sum of all the channel-specific studies can then be melded into an effective strategy. To illustrate this point, Figure 6 compares merchandising and pricing strategies by channel, which can aid the design of consumer goods manufacturers' supply chains to support those systems.

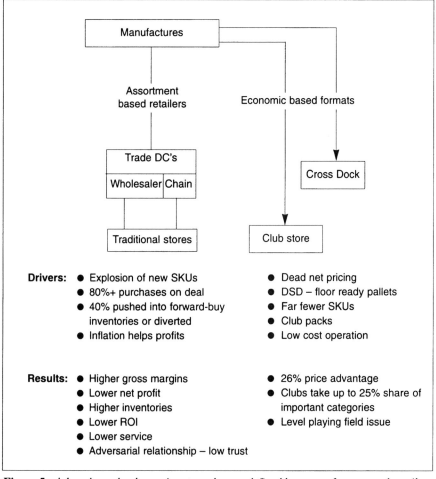

Figure 5: *club and everday-low-price stores have redefined how manufactures and retailers interact.*

The chart assumes that the baseline price for a hypothetical product is $1 and that it is available through all of the trade channels listed in the left-hand column. Likewise, each trade channel differentiates itself by providing a mix of three classic merchandising maxims: value, assortment and convenience, which consumers weigh when deciding where to shop. The relative price point column provides a comparison of the markup or discount associated with the purchase of the baseline product in each channel. Integrating all of this information, a consumer goods manufacturer can deduce that, for example, grocery chains and mass merchants are fairly symmetrical, offering prices around the $1 baseline while swaying shoppers with great assortment and

convenience. Meanwhile, EDLP players who have realised the benefits of streamlined supply chains pass those savings on to the consumer in the form of 15 per cent to 25 per cent price reductions. Chain drug stores, on the other hand, offer great convenience, extremely broad assortment, but not much value.

Conversely, deep discount drug stores take a similar strategy to the club players, offering only what they buy on deal, providing a great price to the consumer. Finally, as their name suggests, convenience In the process of 'unbundling' their prices, manufacturers need to consider the following:

● Order quantities: evaluating the cost of manufacturing based on whether order

Trade channel	Relative price point	Merchandising strategy		
		Value	Assortment	Convenience
C-store	$1.60			✓
Independent grocer	$1.80	✓	✓	✓
Chain drug	$1.25		✓	✓
Grocery chain	$0.95 – $1.25	✓	✓	✓
Promotional/Mass Merch.	$0.80 – $1.10	✓	✓	✓
EDLP Mass merchant	$0.85	✓	✓	✓
Deep discount drug	$0.80 – $0.85	✓		
Club store	$0.75	✓		

Figure 6: *a comparision of merchandising and pricing strategies by channel, assuming the baseline price for a hypothetical product of $1.00*

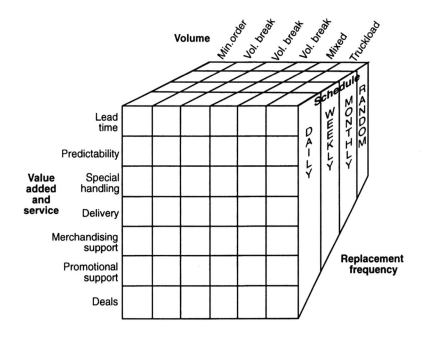

Figure 7: *Cost elements needed to provide customizable, yet supportable prices.*

quantities match the production cycle, are compatible with production schedules, or disturb the cycle because they are completely random

- Order flow: assigning system costs to orders based on their saturation of pipeline flow, consistency (ie. continuous replenishment),or randomness

- Product packaging: charging more for orders that require special pallet construction, multi-packs and displays, special labelling, or sizing. Merchandising support: accruing the time and labour involved in helping customers with planograms, resets, in-store merchandising and displays.
- Promotion support: de-loading the trade

of excess inventory and uncoupling advertising.

- Deals and allowances: coming clean with the impact of off-invoice pricing, slotting allowances, seasonal promotions and introductory offers have upon pricing consistency.

The conceptual database shown in this 'cube' (Figure 7) presents the array of cost elements needed to provide highly customised, yet supportable prices.

A continuing dialog

Because value-driven market trends could outpace a company's ability to deploy new methods of buying, selling, moving and retailing consumer products, now is the time to explore new operating principles. Senior executives must begin investigating the potential of unbundling costs and creating individual supply chains for their organisations. For those that do, the concepts introduced here will be useful in traversing the current supply chain revolution.

Authors: Jim Blaser and Bruce Westbrook
Jim Blaser and Bruce Westbrook are partners in Coopers & Lybrand Consulting's SysteCon Division, which is devoted to helping clients improve their management of material flows from source point to final consumer.

The kindergarten that will change the world

RESOURCE 9.3 ◁

The Economist
4 March, 1995
pp. 81–82

Toyota's Japanese plants may be fighting a losing battle against the rising yen, but its new manufacturing techniques – this time based around workers as much as machines – will change the car industry yet again.

The first thing you notice is the silence. There is neither the hiss of swooping robots nor the anvil chorus that greets you at every other modern car factory from Wolfsburg to Detroit. Indeed, there are no robots to be seen – no machines heaving engines, banging rivets or clamping doors. Then there is the light: the factory is as bright as a kindergarten, with vividly painted walls. One worker, sitting on a suspended swing-like chair, grabs a dashboard suspended from another hook, lowers it into a vehicle and secures it with a few quiet clicks.

The world 's first post-modern car factory is making a new four-wheel-drive vehicle called the RAV4 at Toyota City, a manufacturing centre south-west of Tokyo that makes as many cars as the whole French motor industry. The rest of Toyota is watching the RAV4 line, and the rest of the world's car industry is watching Toyota –

for 25 years the international benchmark against which every other company measures itself. The company's legendary Toyota Production System (TPS) was the basis of the lean-production revolution (everything from just-in-time delivery through total quality management to continuous improvement). The TPS was dubbed 'the machine that changed the world Now, under pressure not only from rivals who have copied its techniques but also from the high yen (which has risen by 64% against the dollar since its low point in 1990), Toyota is pushing ahead again – towards a system which, rather than replacing workers with machines, tries more clearly than ever to restrict the machines to doing only those things that make life easier for the workers.

The RAV4 workers at Toyota City still work around a conventional assembly chain, with car bodies coming along on an overhead conveyor. But the line is sub-divided into five parts with buffer zones in between to make the work less stressful; three or four cars at a time enter a given sub-section of the line. Further cars can come in only when the workers there are ready for them. Workers stand on their own little rubber conveyor belts that follow the car they are working on as it moves through their area. The only other signs of automation are simple rolling devices to move engines and gearboxes in position, so that they can be fitted in without stopping the line.

No one is sweating, yet 428 finished cars roll off the line every day. Toyota does not give out precise productivity figures, but the man-hours per vehicle could be as low as ten – over twice as efficient as conventional American assembly plants. The production rate of 9,000 cars a month is more than four times the break-even point, which is so low because investment has been minimal. Rather than being a greenfield site, the plant is a revamped 36-year-old factory. Compared with a normal assembly line, automation has been cut back by 66%.

To switch from machines to people looks a strange strategy – particularly given Japan's astronomical labour costs. Barely two years ago, Toyota, alongside other Japanese car makers, was opening huge new car plants on Japans southern island, Kyushu, that were the last word in automation. But the promised economies proved to be false ones. Toyota, for instance, found that although automation reduced the number of line workers at its new factory, the number of maintenance personnel rose dramatically. Since they alone really understood the robots, there was little scope for *kaizen*, or continuous improvement. On the new, less automated RAV4 line, the number of defects has fallen to barely 12% of its previous level, and productivity has risen by one-fifth.

The RAV4 is not only built in a novel way; it was designed in one too. It took barely 43 months to get the off-road vehicle from design to production. Designers, engineers, manufacturing and purchasing people all worked as a team. Toyota has copied 'value engineering techniques from American manufacturers such as Chrysler and Ford: these minimise the number of parts in a new model. Nearly half the parts in the RAV4 were already knocking around

in other Toyota models.

The aim now is to have each new Toyota model 70% built from parts common to its predecessor. Simplifying parts such as cooling-system pipes, indicators and bumper assemblies has cut costs of those parts by 20–30%. 'Across the whole company value engineering has saved Toyota ¥ 50 billion ($500m) so far. Hiroshi Okuda, an executive vice-president in charge of purchasing, says he is looking for savings of 15% from suppliers over the next two years alone. Part of this can be achieved by getting the suppliers more closely involved in the design and engineering of whole sub-assemblies of cars, rather than just supplying parts to order.

Coming your way soon

Toyota has already shaved ¥ 220 billion off its annual production costs since it started to overhaul itself nearly two years ago in an effort to live with the strong yen. In its half-year results to the end of December, its operating profit - ie. before allowing for either tax or interest income - rose from a paltry ¥ 9.3 billion (on sales of nearly ¥ 4 trillion) to ¥ 87 billion (on sales just 2.1% higher). Of the profit rise, some ¥ 20 billion is through factory improvements such as those on the RAV4 line at Toyota City.

However, there is a limit to how much Toyota can cut. Its president, Tatsuro Toyoda, denies that the firm's aim is to make itself competitive at ¥ 80 to the dollar. 'That level would be unthinkable, he says. Similarly, Mr Okuda concedes that Toyotas future cost-cutting is unlikely to wring us out as many savings as that over the past two years. Toyota 's operating profit is only 2.1% of sales, a far cry from the 8% margin the Japanese company enjoyed in its glory days. 'The aim now is to move back to a more modest level of 4% next year.

What American and European competitors have to fear is not just today 's improvements in performance in Japan, where the high yen will constrain Toyota's competitiveness; it is tomorrows efficiency transferred to the companys car factories in Kentucky or Derbyshire. Ominously from Detroits point of view, Mikio Kitano, the manager who has presided over the RAV4 line has been promoted to run Toyota's factory in Kentucky.

At present, Toyota makes about 4m vehicles a year in its home base, and around 1.2m abroad, mostly in America. Within five years, says Mr Toyoda, the company will be making 6m cars a year - with all the growth coming offshore. Toyota either owns or has stakes in three factories in Europe, six in North America, three in Latin America and 14 around Asia and Australasia. Outside North America and Europe, these operations mostly just assemble imported car kits. But new plants are being started up in Australia and Turkey, and expansion is planned for Taiwan and Thailand.

In the past, vehicles made overseas have mostly just been sold in that country. ' But we are moving to a different, more global pattern now, ' Mr Toyoda explains, 'where we make cars and parts abroad to serve a whole region. The companys chief concern is Europe, where, like other Japanese companies, Toyota has seen its sales fall even as the market has recovered in the past 15 months.

There has been a debate within the company over whether to increase production at its loss-making Derbyshire factory in Britain; and whether to expand production of its Carina-E model or add the Corolla, a cheaper volume car, as a second model. The Corolla seems to have been chosen: on March 16th, Toyota will make its long-delayed announcement about moving to the second phase of its British investment. But, according to Mr Okuda, it could be up to two years before the cars roll off the line.

One reason why Toyota has decided to flag the expansion now, so far ahead of it coming into production, is that it wants to send a clear signal that it is committed to selling more in the European market. With Japanese factories in Europe set to increase production towards 1M vehicles a year, Toyotas managers fret about renewed trade friction. They would rather the argument is over before they go into full production.

'Now that the machine that changed the world is speeding up again, perhaps Toyota managers are right to fear that increased revolutions inevitably mean more friction.

GLOSSARY

ABC analysis

Also known as Pareto analysis or the '80/20 rule'. This is a classification which attempts to distinguish the 'vital few from the trivial many'. In inventory management ranking is done on the basis of annual value (units x price) or on unit value. A, B, and C are categories of importance in that order. Once defined, different rules or controls are adopted for each category. It is also applicable in many other areas of management.

Aggregate plan

The highest-level operations plan. Is derived from the marketing, finance and business plans. Uses as inputs the sales forecast and inventory targets. The aggregate planning process involves trading off the costs of inventory, normal time, overtime, hiring, layoff, rate changes, etc. Can also be synonymous with the *production plan*.

Agile manufacturing

Term coined by the Iacocca Institute to indicate a longer-term aim of being able to manufacture largely to customer specification with minimal lead time. Incorporates ideas from JIT, mass customisation, supply chain logistics, but applies to all functions within an enterprise and along the supply chain.

Andon board

Overhead problem display board used by Toyota to indicate location and type of problem.

Attribute control chart

An SPC chart for the control of discrete units that can take on only integer or yes/no values. Examples are percentage charts and *c* charts. See also *SPC*

Backward scheduling

A process for determining scheduled start dates. The calculation process begins with the completion date, and works backwards to determine start dates for each activity.

Baldridge

An American total quality award.

Basic times

Work study measurement for carrying out an element or work that takes into account the standard time for the job and the relaxation allowance.

Bill of materials (BOM)

'A listing of all the subassemblies, intermediates, parts, and raw materials that go into a parent assembly showing the quantity of each required to make an assembly' (*APICS Dictionary*).

Broadcast

Used in car assembly plants to ensure that various assembly lines synchronise exactly; for example, that the right car gets the right engine.

Buffer

A quantity of inventory awaiting further processing, usually held in front of a workcentre to allow for disruption at previous workcentres. The term is sometimes used for safety stock.

Capacity

'The capability of a worker, machine, work centre, plant, or organisation to produce output per time period.' *(APICS Dictionary)*

Capability index

A measure which compares the spread of the specification limits to the spread of the control limits. Values greater than 1 are increasingly acceptable. Values less than 1 are unacceptable.

Capacity Requirements Planning (CRP)

The activity of evaluating and establishing the capacity required to execute the material requirements plan. CRP translates the output of materials requirements planning (MRP) (expressed in planned and released orders) into hours of work required by workcentres in future time periods.

Cause and effect diagram

A fishbone-shaped diagram used for brainstorming. Also known as the Ishikawa diagram.

Cell

Cells may be organised according to group technology principles, where the aim is to make a family of parts that share common manufacturing processes. The cell comprises a group of unlike machines that are able to make a complete part. They are located close together and are often arranged in a U shape. A cell may also be used in a service environment.

Changeover time

Time taken from the last product of one batch to the first good product of the next batch. Comprises set-up time and adjust time.

Closed Loop Manufacturing (or Closed Loop MRP)

A set of interacting modules, including *MPS, RCCP, MRP, CRP*, and production activity control. The term 'closed loop' implies that, as the level of detail increases through the planning process, and through time, it may become necessary to revise higher-level or earlier plans.

Control

The activity which measures deviations from planned performance and provides information upon which corrective action can be taken, if required, to alter future performance or the original plan.

Control chart

A chart that may be used for statistical process control (SPC), but generally any chart used for quality control.

Control limit

A limit closely corresponding to the natural variation or spread of a process.

Cost of quality (CoQ)

A management or accounting procedure for tracking the costs of poor quality and the costs of prevention and inspection.

Cross docking

Distribution procedure whereby goods are moved and sorted between two trucks without going into storage.

Cycle counting

An inventory audit technique whereby inventory is counted in regular cycles according to importance, rather than once per year. Ideally, a few different items are counted every day.

Dependent demand

Demand, usually for component items, that can be related to the demand for a final product. This type of demand should be calculated, not forecast.

Design of experiments (DoE)

A statistical procedure for identifying the most sensitive characteristics that affect product quality.

Due date

The date on which customers expect delivery, or production is expected to be complete, or material is due for delivery.

Economic order quantity (EOQ)

A fixed order quantity of inventory that reflects the optimal balance between ordering costs and holding costs.

Electronic Data Interchange (EDI)

Inter-computer communication protocol enabling direct transfer of data. There are several standard systems, for example EDIFACT and Tradanet.

European Quality Award (EQA)

The European Quality Award for total quality management organisied by the European Foundation for Quality Management (EFQM).

External set-up time

Time taken to change a machine over from one batch to another, which can be done whilst the old batch is still being produced. Preparation time.

Feedback

This is the process which uses information about past performance to affect the future. See also *positive feedback* and *neagtive feedback.*

Finite scheduling

Schedule preparation that takes into account the available capacity, and that attempts to complete the schedule preparation without exceeding available capacity.

Five whys

Toyota-originated procedure whereby 'why?' is asked successively, typically five times, so as to get to the 'root cause' of the problem.

Forward scheduling

A process for determining scheduled start dates. The calculation process begins with the start date of the first operation and works forwards to determine start dates for each activity.

Gantt chart

A chart which shows graphically the times taken, or due to be take, on various processes.

Gross requirements

The total of independent and dependent demand for a component or product prior to the netting of on-hand inventory and scheduled receipts. (Adapted from *APICS Dictionary*.)

Homeostasis

See *Steady state, dynamic equilbrum*

Independent demand

'Demand for an item that is unrelated to demand for other items' (*APICS Dictionary*).

Internal set-up time

Time taken to change a machine over from batch to batch when the machine is actually stopped, as distinct from *external set-up time.*

Infinite scheduling

Schedule preparation that takes no account of the available capacity. The MRP process assumes infinite capacity.

Ishikawa diagram

See *Cause and effect diagram.*

Jidoka

Japanese for a system to stop the process or line if a fault is detected. May be manual (line stop) or automatic (pokayoke).

Just-in-Time (JIT)

'A philosophy of manufacturing based on planned elimination of all waste and continuous improvement of productivity. It encompasses the successful execution of all manufacturing activities required to produce a final product, from design engineering to delivery and including all stages of conversion from raw material onward. The primary elements ... are to have only the required inventory when needed; to improve quality to zero defects, to reduce lead times by reducing set-up times, queue lengths, and lot sizes; to incrementally revise the operations themselves; and to accomplish these things at minimum cost. In the broad sense it applies to all forms of manufacturing, job shop and process as well as repetitive. Synonym: short-cycle manufacturing, stockless production, zero inventories.' (*APICS Dictionary*).

Kaizen

Japanese word associated with continuous improvement. A management philosophy developed by Imai.

Kanban

A signalling system to authorise the making of the next batch or unit on the previous process, or the delivery of parts. Can take many forms, for example: cards, squares, lights, ping-pong balls, faxban, EDI-ban, or even voice.

Lean manufacturing

A term made famous by the book '*The Machine that Changed the World*' by Womack *et al*, 1990. A new term for JIT manufacturing in the broad context, to distinguish it from the narrow, scheduling view, of JIT.

Lead time

Supply lead time is the time required from placing an order to receiving it. Manufacturing lead time is the time required to make a complete product. In materials requirements planning (MRP), lead time is the time required to complete a stage of manufacturing once all the required parts are on hand.

Line balancing

The balancing of work on an assembly line with the aim of equalising the time taken by each operator or process. The upper limit of time is governed by the required production rate.

Linearity

Production at a constant rate, usually measured daily.

Line stop

Originated at Toyota: the ability of an operator to pull a cord if a problem is encountered which, if not alleviated within a short time, will have the effect of stopping the assembly line. Usually connected to *Andon board*. See also *Jidoka*.

Load

'The amount of planned work scheduled and actual work released for a facility, workcentre, or operation for a specific span of time. Usually expressed in terms of standard hours of work...' *(APICS Dictionary)*.

Logistics

In Britain, used to indicate the resources (people, vehicles, warehouses, plans, etc.) used in distribution and supply. In Germany, the term includes manufacturing as well. Increasingly this latter meaning is being adopted.

Manufacturing resource planning (MRPII)

An integrated computer package for manufacturing planning and control comprising production planning, master production scheduling, material requirements planning, capacity requirements planning, and production activity control. The output from these is linked with finance and accounting, and usually has simulation capabilities. MRPII is an extension of closed loop manufacturing.

Master production schedule (MPS)

The schedule of products that it is anticipated will be made, or services that will be offered. It should be compatible with the production plan. In services, the MPS may be expressed in terms of a timetable or a booking list. In manufacturing, the MPS may be the basis for the final assembly schedule.

Mass customisation

Term coined by Joseph Pine to indicate the combination of the economics of mass production with customer-specified variety. An outgrowth of JIT and time-based competitiveness. See also *Agile manufacturing*.

Material requirements planning (MRP)

A technique for calculating the requirements for, and timing of, components and assemblies that will be required to make an end product. MRP is also the name given to computer packages which carry out this calculation process, and which include bill of material records, on-hand inventory records, as well as features such as firm planned orders and pegging.

Mixed model scheduling

A production schedule which makes a variety of products in short repeating sequences rather than in batches of similar products.

Negative feedback

Negative feedback is essential for control. It acts as a damper on fluctuations and stimulates managerial control towards achieving a standard or planned level of performance. When negative feedback loops are strongly in evidence, the system approaches towards stability.

Net requirements

In MRP, net requirements in each period are calculated from gross requirements less scheduled receipts and on-hand inventory.

Network sourcing

A co-operation between suppliers and manufacturers incorporating partnership principles and JIT delivery.

Pareto analysis

A procedure for identifying the 'vital few'. See also *ABC analysis*.

Planned order release

The required quantity of parts that must be released to begin a stage of manufacture on a particular date in order to complete the product according to the MPS requirement.

Pokayoke

A Japanese term for a failsafing or a foolproofing device, used for defect prevention.

Positive feedback

Positive feedback loops cause growth. They reinforce the direction in which the system is moving. When planned in a system such loops can be powerful stimuli, for example, repeated advertising in ways which have generated business causes growth in the firm. When it is unplanned, positive feedback can have destructive tendencies which feed on themselves. The resultant inertia, chaos or compounded problems can ruin a business.

Production plan

See *Aggregate plan*.

Process

A transformation of material (as in a manufacturing process), or of information (as in a business process). A step or stage.

Procurement

A function including planning, supplier evaluation and selection, purchasing, inventory control, and incoming inspection.

Processing time

The time taken to produce a product or component on a particular machine.

Quality circles

Staff are organised into groups that meet regularly to identify and solve problems. Targets are set within the group. They originated in Japan in 1962. They are common in Japanese companies, and although they have been tried in the West, in the different context, they are not as successful.

Reorder point (ROP)

In inventory management, that level of inventory which, when reached, triggers a replenishment order in sufficient time for it to be delivered without running out, provided that average demand is maintained.

Rough Cut Capacity Plan (RCCP)

The activity which evaluates the capacity implications of the MPS. Normally applies to only the more critical machines or workcentres.

Safety stock (SS)

Inventory held against uncertainty, usually in demand.

Scheduled receipt

A quantity of inventory that is due to be delivered as a result of an order that has already been placed.

Service level

A measure of the percentage of demand that is routinely satisfied by an inventory holding.

SERVQUAL

A service quality measurement system developed by Parasuraman *et al*, and associated with the five dimensions of service quality.

Set-up

Time taken to change a machine from producing one batch to another, but excluding adjustment. See also *Internal set-up time*, *External set-up time* and *Changeover time*.

Sequencing

The activity to determine the order in which jobs are to be undertaken on a machine or process.

Seven wastes

A list devised by Taiichi Ohno of the seven types of waste found in all operations-based organisations.

Seven tools

Seven basic tools for quality and problem measurement and improvement.

Six Sigma

A term first used by Motorola to indicate a target level of process capability, equivalent to 3.4 defects per million parts.

Specification limit

The acceptable range of variation of a product's dimension or performance, as specified by the designer or engineer.

Standard deviation

A measure of spread in a statistical distribution.

Standard time

This is the time that it actually takes to do a job and an 'allowance' as the operator cannot work at exactly the same pace throughout the working day. It is a measure used in work study. Standard time can be measured in minutes (SMs) or hours (SHrs).

Statistical Process Control (SPC)

A family of quality control procedures, aimed at prevention.

Steady state, dynamic equilibrium

As an open system interacts with its environment it copes with changes forced upon it. The condition which results is steady state, or dynamic equilibrium. The words describe a system which whilst remaining essentially the same, is continually changing in response to its environment.

Simultaneous engineering

The process of bringing a prototype product to the stage of production whereby the functions involved work in parallel as a team rather than in sequence.

Single-source supplier

A supplier totally responsible for the supply of a particular component.

Sole source supplier

A supplier who is the only one able to supply a component, due to technology, patent, or skill.

Tolerance limit

See *Specification limit*.

Total productive (preventive) maintenance (TPM)

Maintenance activities aimed at prevention and improvement, making use of the workforce, not just maintenance specialists.

Variable control chart

A control chart for a characteristic or dimension that can take on non-integer values. An x bar and r chart.

Value analysis/engineering

A disciplined but creative team-based procedure aimed at reducing cost for the same product functionality, or at improved functionality at the same cost.

Waste

Any activity that does not add value for the customer.

World-class manufacturing

Synonym for broad Just-in-Time JIT, lean manufacturing. Used by Schonberger (1982).